D0574696

Youth Aggression and Violence

A Psychological Approach

THOMAS G. MOELLER
Mary Washington College

LEA LAWRENCE ERLBAUM ASSOCIATES, PUBLISHERS
2001   Mahwah, New Jersey   London

Copyright © 2001 by Lawrence Erlbaum Associates, Inc.

All rights reserved. No part of this book may be reproduced in any form,
by photostat, microfilm, retrieval system, or any other means,
without prior written permission of the publisher.

Lawrence Erlbaum Associates, Inc., Publishers
10 Industrial Avenue
Mahwah, NJ 07430

Cover design by Kathryn Houghtaling Lacey

LIBRARY OF CONGRESS CATALOGING-IN-PUBLICATION DATA
Moeller, Thomas G.
    Youth aggression and violence : a psychological approach / Thomas G. Moeller
        p.   cm.
    Includes bibliographical references and indexes.
    ISBN 0–8058–3713–2 (cloth : alk. paper)—ISBN 0–8058–3714–0 (pbk. : alk. paper)
    1. Aggressiveness in youth. 2. Aggressiveness in adolescence. 3. Violence in
adolescence. I. Title.
BF724.3.A34 M64 2001
155.4'18232—dc21   00–0068145

Books published by Lawrence Erlbaum Associates are printed on acid-free paper,
and their bindings are chosen for strength and durability.

Printed in the United States of America
10   9   8   7   6   5   4   3   2   1

To my parents, Raymond Johnson Dietz Moeller
and Agnes Marie Berger Moeller

Contents

Preface

The idea for this book first came to me in the mid-1990s while I was developing an undergraduate psychology course on youth aggression and violence. As a developmental psychologist, I was familiar with theory and research on moral development and aggression in "normal" children. At the same time, I also knew that research in developmental psychopathology had produced a large body of information on clinical manifestations of youthful antisocial behavior and violence. However, I could find no one book that integrated these two bodies of information. This book attempts to fill that void and draws on research from the fields of sociology, criminology, and history as well.

Two major goals guided me in writing. The first was to provide readers with information based on methodologically sound empirical research. Because I also wanted readers to understand the continuity of research, I have mentioned many older "classical" studies along with more recent ones. In addition, I have acknowledged the global nature of youth violence by including studies conducted by researchers from around the world.

The second goal was to help make the subject of youth aggression "come alive" for the reader. To this end, I have described carefully considered qualitative and descriptive research along with quantitative work, and have provided numerous "real life" examples of youthful aggression and violence. And finally, I have included some brief case studies as well as quotations from aggressive youngsters themselves.

ACKNOWLEDGMENTS

A summer faculty development grant and a semester's sabbatical leave provided me with an initial block of time with which to begin this project in earnest. My thanks to Mary Washington College for this opportunity and to my department chairperson, Steve Hampton, for his assistance in this regard. I would also like to thank the staff of the Simpson Library for their help; in particular, Carla Bailey attended to my interlibrary loan requests with professionalism, efficiency, and good cheer. In addition, I would like to thank my colleague, Roy Smith, for sharing information with me regarding the genetics and biology of behavior.

A number of others also contributed to the writing of this book. Martha Heuser, Dave MacEwen, and the personnel at Mary Washington College's Design Services Office produced the figures for me. Brianne Patchell read the entire manuscript and provided excellent feedback from a student's point of view. Jean Bennett, our departmental administrative assistant, aided my effort in numerous ways large and small. Anonymous reviewers for Lawrence Erlbaum Associates offered helpful suggestions, and my editor, Susan Milmoe, provided sound advice and constant encouragement. Finally, I owe an inestimable debt of gratitude to my wife, Providence Moeller, who supported me continually throughout the two years I spent writing this book.

A NOTE ON LANGUAGE

Wherever possible, the plural form of nouns and pronouns has been used to produce gender-neutral language. When sense requires the use of the singular, the form "he" or "she" has been used to avoid the distraction inherent in forms such as "he/she." Because aggression is predominantly a male problem, the male pronoun has been used when the context makes its use appropriate.

CHAPTER I

Introduction

In Richmond, California, prosecutors charged a 6-year old boy with attempted murder in the beating of a 1-month-old baby. Police said the boy, along with 8-year-old twins, sneaked into the baby's house, allegedly to steal a tricycle. In the process, police said, the 6-year-old knocked the baby out of his crib and then beat and kicked the baby in the head. Although the baby survived, doctors believed the baby suffered permanent brain damage ("Their baby," 1996).

In rural Goochland County, Virginia, police said that two 7-year-old boys used a brick to break a window of a neighbor's house, then smeared the contents of the refrigerator throughout the house, broke china and crystal, poured detergent on the carpet, pulled insulation loose from under the house, dumped rocks into the gas tank of a jet ski, and spread crème de menthe over walls, furniture, and an antique grand piano. The damage was so extensive that family members had to find other housing during the more than 2 days that it took to clean up the mess ("7-year-old vandals," 1995).

In Philadelphia, third graders wrote letters threatening a newspaper editor, allegedly because the editor refused to publish a photograph of their teacher. "I will kill you," wrote one child. Another wrote: "You ugly rat and four eyed geeks . . . I'm going rip all your hair off, put it in your mouth and take your clothes and put them over your head and beat you up, you rat." The principal of the school defended the children, saying that they were "only defending the honor of their teacher" ("Third-graders give," 1992).

In suburban St. Louis, Missouri, a 12-year-old basketball player allegedly used a metal chair to break the ankle of the game's referee, who lay unconscious and bleeding on the gym floor as the result of a punch thrown by the young player's coach. The youngster apparently did not think that the official had been punished enough for one of his calls. As a result of the incident, the referee lost two teeth, received 25 stitches, spent 5 days in a hospital, convalesced for 2 months with a cast on his leg, spent 1 month in rehabilitation, and had extensive oral surgery (Lhotka, 1994).

In Spotsylvania County, Virginia, two 16-year-old males were arrested for a robbery in which a 26-year-old female convenience clerk was shot in the stomach with a sawed-off shotgun. Sixteen years earlier, the clerk had watched in horror as her own mother was fatally stabbed 27 times by a male acquaintance (Epps & Bailey, 1998).

YOUTH AGGRESSION AND VIOLENCE: AN OVERVIEW

Why do such incidents as these occur? What motivates youths to act in such a manner? And what are they thinking about and feeling when they behave like this? In this book, we seek to answer these and other questions concerning youthful aggression and violence.

As I use it, the term *youths* includes children as well as adolescents. It is similar to the legal concept of a *juvenile,* which refers to someone who has not yet attained the age of legal adulthood, which in most of the United States is 18 (Snyder & Sickmund, 1999). Thus, although reports of youth violence sometimes refer to persons 18 and older, attention in this book is focused on persons under 18.

In a broad sense, *aggression* refers to an action that harms an object or person. However, some behaviors that harm are unintentional, and so many psychologists argue that to be aggressive, an act must include an intention to do harm. In this book, I follow Bartol's (1995) definition of aggression as "behavior perpetrated or attempted with the intention of harming another individual physically or psychologically (as opposed to socially) or to destroy an object" (p. 184). As we will see, aggression can be either verbal or physical and can vary from mild to severe.

Although often used interchangeably with aggression, the term *violence* connotes more "serious and extreme" forms of aggression (Tolan & Guerra, 1994, p. 2). The most extreme type of violence is called *criminal violence,* defined by the U.S. government as consisting of nonnegligent criminal homicide, forcible rape, robbery, and aggravated assault (Federal Bureau of Investigation [FBI], 1998). Definitions of these terms are provided in Box 1.1.

As we will see, some aggression is expected and normal (Tolan & Guerra, 1994). In other cases, however, aggression is clearly inappropriate and abnormal. Throughout the book I use the term *hyperaggressive* to describe youngsters whose aggression is clearly beyond the normal range expected for their chronological age, gender, and other relevant personal characteristics. Thus, hyperaggressive youths are those whose aggression is noticeably more frequent, of greater intensity, and of longer duration than that of normal children. As a rule of thumb, these children are in the upper 5% to 10% of their peers with respect to aggressiveness.

Aggression and violence are types of *antisocial* behavior, which is defined as any action that violates accepted moral, ethical, or legal standards. Although the emphasis throughout this book will be on aggression and violence, some research focuses only on the broader category of antisocial behavior. Moreover, hyperaggressive youths often engage in other antisocial behaviors such as lying, theft, and drug abuse. Consequently, at various points throughout the book, I discuss information regarding antisocial youths as well as material that pertains strictly to hyperaggressive youngsters.

BOX 1.1

DEFINITIONS OF TYPES OF CRIMINAL VIOLENCE

Murder: the intentional killing of one person by another with "malice afore-thought" (Bartol, 1995, p. 215).

Nonnegligent Manslaughter: the killing of another, but without premeditation (Bartol, 1995).

Nonnegligent Criminal Homicide: includes both murder and nonnegligent manslaughter (Bartol, 1995).

Forcible Rape: "the carnal knowledge of a female forcibly and against her will" (FBI, 1998, p. 25).

Robbery: the taking or attempted taking of anything of value from a person by force or threat of force (Bartol, 1995).

Aggravated assault: the attempt to inflict bodily injury on someone with the intention to do serious bodily harm, usually with a weapon (Bartol, 1995).

In contrast to antisocial behavior, *prosocial* behavior includes activities such as helping, being altruistic, cooperating, and the like. In general, hyperaggressive children typically exhibit a great deal of antisocial behavior and relatively little genuine prosocial behavior.

The Extent of Aggression and Violence Among Youth

The incidents already described vividly illustrate the popular view that youthful aggression and violence are running rampant in American society. Newspapers routinely report acts of violence occurring in homes, in neighborhoods, and at school. The nightly television news regularly chronicles yet another example of youthful mayhem. Public opinion polls consistently rate crime and violence as among the major concerns facing the country today. Interviews with parents, teachers, social workers, therapists, and people on the street all lament the growing propensity toward violence seen among our young people. Anecdotal reports indicate that youth violence has become more prevalent, that children are becoming violent at younger and younger ages, and that more violence now involves the use of weapons (especially firearms) than in the past. In response, cities develop delinquency-prevention plans; state legislatures scramble to reform a juvenile justice system that many believe is too lenient on youngsters who commit violent crimes; and Congress, besieged to "do something," enacts new laws that it hopes will stem the tide of youth violence. Clearly, the public perceives youth violence to be a major problem. But what about the facts? Do they bear out public concern, or is the public's concern in fact overblown?

At one level, the extent of youthful aggression and violence is difficult to determine. Virtually all children are aggressive at some point in their lives, and aggression can be considered to be "normative" at certain stages of development. Furthermore, much youthful aggression consists of low-level aggressive behaviors such as being impolite, engaging in horseplay, making minor threats, writing graffiti, violating minor rules, and using inappropriate language (Goldstein & Conoley, 1997). Although these types of behaviors might be annoying, researchers have typically not attempted to keep records of the extent of this kind of aggression. Thus, although both the public and researchers might suspect that this type of youthful aggression has increased over the years, little hard data exist with which to corroborate this viewpoint.

We are, however, in a better position to determine the historic ebb and flow of violent juvenile crimes. For one thing, law enforcement agencies have kept track of such crimes for a number of years. In addition, researchers have also independently obtained information regarding juvenile delinquency and crime. Before examining the results of this research, however, let us first consider the methods researchers use to garner data regarding this issue.

Information on youth crime derives from three major types of sources. The first, generally referred to as *victimization studies,* consists of interviews with a representative sample of whichever group is being studied. For example, in the *National Crime Victimization Survey* (NCVS), the United States Bureau of the Census contacts a nationally representative sample of households and asks respondents to describe the personal crimes they have experienced (Snyder & Sickmund, 1999). This type of study is generally considered to produce the most accurate information about the extent to which persons over the age of 12 have been victimized. In order to obtain information about juveniles who commit violent acts, researchers often use a second approach, the self-report study. In a self-report study, researchers use interviews or questionnaires to obtain information directly from offenders or potential offenders. Finally, researchers obtain some of their information from official police and court records. Each year, for example, the FBI summarizes much of this information in a volume called *Crime in the United States,* more popularly known as the FBI Uniform Crime Reports (UCR; FBI, 1985–1999).

Each of these methods has its advantages and limitations. Because victimization studies involve representative sampling, they tend to give a better overall picture of violence than do self-report studies (whose samples might not be representative), or official statistics (which might either under- or overreport certain types of crimes). Also, because both victimization and self-report studies are generally anonymous, respondents are more likely to tell the truth than when their identities are known. Self-report studies are also a better index of the extent of juvenile delinquency than are official statistics, because not all crimes are reported to officials, and those that are might not be put on the official record. But official records have certain advantages over the other two methods.

For example, because virtually all murders come to the attention of law enforcement agencies, official records serve as the most accurate source of information on homicides. In addition, self-report data are susceptible to distortion, either intentional or unintentional. Thus, self-report data must be treated cautiously.

Now that we know something about how data on youth crime and victimization are collected, let's examine the magnitude of violent offenses committed by juveniles and the extent to which the incidence of these crimes has changed in the past 20 years.

In their historical study of juvenile crime in Europe and in the United States, Michael Rutter and colleagues concluded that "it seems likely that juvenile crime has risen in most industrialized nations over the last five decades" (Rutter, Giller, & Hagell, 1998, p. 77). And as indicated in Fig. 1.1, official crime statistics indicate that violent juvenile crime in the United States has generally been increasing since the mid-1960s.

However, the most dramatic increase in youthful violent crime appeared to occur from the mid-1980s to the mid-1990s. For example, crime report data show that although adolescent arrest rates for both murder and violent crimes remained fairly stable between 1971 and 1984, they both began to increase dramatically in 1985 (Fig. 1.1). Because the NCVS data depicted in Fig. 1.2 show the same trend, it is likely that this increase was a real phenomenon and not merely due to the methodological limitations of official records.

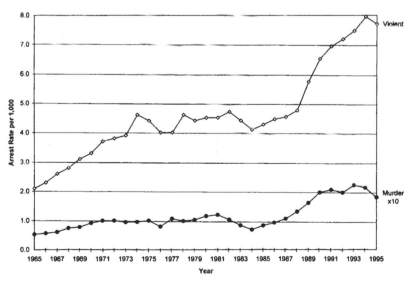

FIG. 1.1.   Arrest rates for youths ages 13 to 17 per 1,000 population, FBI index crimes of violence. From p. 40 of "The Epidemic in Youth Violence," by P. J. Cook and J. H. Laub, 1998, in M. Tonry & M. H. Moore (Eds.), *Youth Violence: Crime and Justice* (Vol. 24, pp. 27–64). Copyright 1998 by the University of Chicago Press. Reprinted with permission.

FIG. 1.2.   Serious violent crime victimizations by juveniles per 100,000 persons ages 10–17. Serious violent crime includes rape and other sexual assaults, robbery, and aggravated assault. From p. 62 of *Juvenile Offenders and Victims: 1999 National Report*, by H. N. Snyder and M. Sickmund, 1999, Washington, DC: Office of Juvenile Justice and Delinquency Prevention. Reprinted with permission of the National Center for Juvenile Justice.

The increased violence in the early 1990s was accompanied by a comparable increase in the use of weapons by juveniles. A study by the Justice Department showed that juveniles accounted for 23% of all weapons crime arrests in 1993, compared with 16% in 1974. And juvenile arrests for crimes with weapons increased from 30,000 in 1985 to more than 61,000 in 1993 ("Offenses on the rise," 1995).

Fortunately, both official statistics and victimization studies indicate that violent crimes committed by juveniles peaked in 1993 and then decreased in the last half of the decade. For example, UCR data show that the juvenile murder arrest rate decreased by almost 50% from 1993 to 1998, while the overall juvenile violent crime rate decreased by 30% (Snyder, 1999). A similar analysis of NCVS data indicates that between 1993 and 1997, robberies by juveniles decreased by 37%, aggravated assaults by 30%, and violent sexual assaults by 45% (Snyder & Sickmund, 1999). In addition, according to one recent study, the proportion of male high school students who reported carrying a weapon to school at least 1 day within a month of the study declined from 14% in 1993 to 9% in 1996 (National Center for Education Statistics, 1998).

In summary, youth violence apparently began to increase in the United States in the 1960s, remained relatively stable from the early 1970s to the mid-1980s, then rose dramatically until 1993. Since then, the most extreme type of violence seems to be on the decline. Nevertheless, we have little hard data on low-level youthful aggression; the rate of violent juvenile crimes is still high relative to the earlier part of the 20th century; and a series of school shootings and bombings in the late 1990s suggests that youth violence continues to remain a central issue for the United States as we enter the new millennium.

Factors Related to Youth Violence

Now that we are familiar with some of the statistics on youth violence, let's look at some factors related to this phenomenon.

Gender and Youth Violence. Males exhibit more physical aggression than females; furthermore, the most extremely aggressive children also tend to be boys (Beal, 1994; Eme, 1979). Indeed, the 1991 NCVS found that 88% of juvenile crimes were committed by males (Snyder & Sickmund, 1995). In addition, more than 90% of all juvenile murderers are male (Snyder & Sickmund, 1999). It is thus clear that youthful physical aggression and violence is perpetrated primarily by males. At the same time, however, the proportion of juvenile females arrested for violent crimes increased steadily and substantially from 1965 to 1995; indeed, between 1990 and 1994, the violence arrest rate for females increased 48%, compared to only 23% for males (Cook & Laub, 1998).

Race and Youth Violence. Victimization studies indicate that approximately 50% of juvenile offenders are White, 40% are Black, and 10% come from other races (Snyder & Sickmund, 1995). In addition, homicide statistics show that although 47% of juvenile murderers are White, homicide rates are six times higher for Black youths than for Whites (Snyder & Sickmund, 1995). Moreover, between 1984 and 1991, the homicide rate for young White males increased by about 65% whereas that for young Blacks went up 210% (Snyder & Sickmund, 1995).

The racial profile of violent crime victims varies with the race of the offender. In 95% of the cases in which a White juvenile commits a violent crime, the victim is White; in 3%, the victim is Black. Black offenders have a more racially mixed victim profile: In 37% of the cases in which the offender is Black, the victim is also Black; however, in 57% of such cases, the victim is White (Snyder & Sickmund, 1995).

Time of Day and Youth Violence. The emphasis that many communities have placed on nighttime curfews for juveniles leads to the impression that most acts

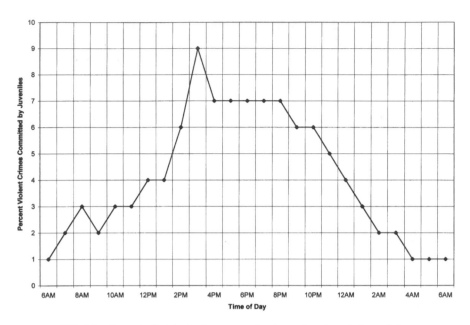

FIG. 1.3.   Percent of violent crimes committed as a function of time of day.
Data are from 12 states. From p. 64 of *Juvenile Offenders and Victims: 1999 National
Report*, by H. N. Snyder and M. Sickmund, 1999, Washington, DC: Office of Juvenile Justice and Delinquency Prevention. Reprinted with permission of the National Center for Juvenile Justice.

of youthful aggression and violence occur late at night or in the early morning.
Although it is true that some youth violence does occur at these times, most
such behavior takes place during the daytime and evening hours. Indeed, as
shown in Fig. 1.3, serious weekday violent crime committed by juveniles actually peaks at the close of the school day, and one in five violent crimes committed by juveniles on schools days occurs between the hours of 3 p.m. and 7 p.m.
(Snyder & Sickmund, 1999). The fact that youngsters get into more trouble in
the afternoon and early evening than late at night suggests that preventive measures should concentrate on these periods and not on late-night curfews and
programs such as "midnight basketball."

"Chronic Offenders" and Youth Violence.   A variety of studies have found that
as many as 90% of U.S. adolescents report having committed at least one delinquent act by the age of 18 (Snyder & Sickmund, 1995). Nevertheless, these studies also find that the large majority of violent crimes are committed by only 5%
to 10% of the male population, a group known as *chronic offenders* (Snyder &
Sickmund, 1995, p. 50).

HOW SOCIAL SCIENTISTS STUDY YOUTH VIOLENCE

Because we all try to understand youth violence at some level, we all "study" this topic, at least informally. In this connection, much of our informal "knowledge" comes from *anecdotal evidence* such as our own experiences and what we see and read in the mass media. However, because anecdotal evidence suffers from a number of problems limiting its effectiveness, social science researchers have developed more systematic ways of studying youth aggression. We now examine some of these methods.

The Sociological and Psychological Perspectives

Youth violence can be studied from a number of viewpoints, two of which are the sociological and psychological. Broadly speaking, *sociology* is the study of groups and social systems and of how they affect behavior. From the sociological perspective, the "real" factors controlling behavior are those emanating from groups and social systems. Hence, from this perspective, youth violence can best be understood in terms of these social factors. For example, sociologists, noting that most youthful aggression is committed by juveniles acting in groups, might seek to understand how group processes contribute to youth violence.

Although psychologists do not dismiss social factors, they emphasize instead the various psychological processes that occur within the individual person. Those who take a psychological perspective point out that many people belong to the same set of groups and experience the same set of social factors, yet behave differently. Moreover, even when sociological variables (such as sex and gender) do affect behavior, they do so only by first affecting the individual's psychological processes. Thus, the psychologists hold that although sociological factors may be important in youth violence, an ultimate understanding of youngsters' aggression requires a knowledge of the psychological processes involved.

This book is written from a psychological perspective. The emphasis throughout is on youths' psychological processes and on the effect that the environment has on these processes, as well as on how youths' psychological makeup affects their reaction to environmental events.

Research

Researchers study problems such as youth violence by developing hypotheses and then by attempting to test these hypotheses by collecting information in a systematic fashion, a process referred to as the *empirical method*. In some cases, as when researchers spend a great deal of time talking with gang members, the information or data that they collect might be qualitative in nature. In other cases, however, researchers not only collect qualitative information, but they also attach numbers to this information, hence producing what is known as *quantitative data.*

Whatever the nature of the information, we must have confidence that it is accurate and that anyone else who collects the same data under the same circumstances would obtain the same results. The extent to which such repeated observations yield the same results is called the *reliability* of the study (Miller, 1998). Reliability is important because it helps to guarantee that the researchers actually do observe what they report they observe.

A second important characteristic of good research is *internal validity,* the extent to which a study allows us to pinpoint the cause of a particular behavior and to rule out other possible explanations (Rosnow & Rosenthal, 1996). For example, one hypothesis we consider in a later chapter is that viewing violence on television causes children to act aggressively. Studies with strong internal validity permit a clear answer to this question, whereas those with weak internal validity do not.

The major determinant of internal validity is the extent to which the researcher is able to control the relevant variables in the study. The more control researchers have over variables that can cause a behavior, the better they can rule out those variables as potential causes and pinpoint a specific variable as the "true" cause.

Finally, we want to be able to accurately generalize the results of a research study to settings other than the one in a particular study and to people other than the participants in the study. Studies that allow us to do this are said to be high in *external validity* (Rosnow & Rosenthal, 1996). For example, if research is conducted in a laboratory setting using a group of Australian children, we would like to generalize those results to the everyday lives of children in Australia and, if possible, to those in other parts of the world as well.

Two major factors contribute to external validity. First, the more similar the setting of the study to the child's everyday environment, the higher the external validity with respect to setting. Similarly, the more similar the participants in the study are to other children to whom we would like to generalize the results, the higher the external validity with respect to persons. In technical terms, the more *representative* the sample, the better the external validity with respect to person.

The characteristics of reliability, internal validity, and external validity are important to consider in interpreting research, and we critically consider them repeatedly throughout the book. Ideally, we would like all research studies to be highly reliable and valid. In many cases, the reliability of research will be acceptable; however, as we will see, many studies are weak in one or both types of validity.

Methods of Collecting Data

Psychologists and other social scientists use a number of methods in collecting data, including record searches, self-reports, surveys, interviews, questionnaires, and behavioral observations. Another commonly used method is the *behavioral checklist*. In this technique, informants are given a series of statements about themselves or someone else and are required to indicate on the form how accurately the statement describes the target person. For example, a mother might be given a list of behaviors and asked to tell how accurately each behavior describes that of her child.

One example of a behavioral checklist that has been used extensively in the study of aggressive children is the *Child Behavior Checklist* (CBCL; Achenbach, 1991), which can be completed by parents, teachers, or youngsters over the age of 10. This instrument yields scores on two general or "broadband" scales labeled *internalizing* and *externalizing*. The internalizing scale measures behaviors that indicate the child is experiencing unpleasant emotions such as anxiety, fear, and depression. The externalizing scale measures behaviors that violate moral and ethical norms, such as lying and aggression. This scale contains two subscales, called *delinquency* and *aggression*. In general, the delinquency subscale measures nonaggressive antisocial behavior such as lying and stealing, whereas the aggression subscale measures more overt aggressive behaviors.

Methods of Analyzing and Interpreting Data

The methods just discussed describe how researchers collect data. However, each of these techniques is used within the context of a more general method, which the researcher uses to analyze and interpret the data that have been collected. The major methods of data analysis used in the study of youth aggression are described in Box 1.2. Although a detailed discussion of methodology is beyond our scope, keep in mind the following points as you read the remainder of this book.

• Qualitative methods often provide context and depth that other types of designs cannot, and for that reason they can give us a good experiential understanding of the topic under study. But because so many potentially causative variables cannot be controlled in these methods, their internal validity is weak.

• The experimental method is important because, if done well, it permits us to infer a cause-and-effect relationship between the independent and dependent variable. For this reason, experiments generally have high internal validity. Because the experiment is often conducted in an artificial and highly controlled laboratory setting, its external validity regarding setting is likely to be low.

• Because quasiexperimental designs and correlational studies do not control for possible pre-existing differences among participants, these designs do not permit inferences regarding causality. Hence, their internal validity is low.

• Whenever two variables are correlated, it is logically possible that one variable causes the other. However, it is also possible that both are caused by some

---

BOX 1.2

METHODS OF ANALYZING AND INTERPRETING DATA

Qualitative Methods

Nature

These are methods in which the information gathered by the researcher consists of qualitative observations rather than quantitative statistical data.

Types

Individual Case Study: an in-depth investigation of a single person.

Observational Methods: the researcher spends a great deal of time with a group of individuals and then writes about that experience. These methods include *participant–observer research* (in which the researcher actually becomes part of the group which he or she is observing), *ethnographic research* (in which the investigator describes some aspect of one or more subcultures), and *clinical research* (in which a mental health professional describes one or more disturbed youngsters with whom he or she is working).

(Box continues)

---

other third variable or that the combination of both variables acts to affect each of them individually. Thus, correlations do not imply causation.

Summary. Social science researchers study youthful aggression using both qualitative and quantitative designs, each of which has its own advantages and limitations. Qualitative designs are most useful for giving us an experiential understanding of youth violence. Quantitative experimental designs can demonstrate cause-and-effect relationships; however, their results might not be generalizable outside the laboratory setting. Finally, quantitative associational designs can demonstrate relationships among variables but are limited in their ability to demonstrate causality.

Methods of Summarizing Research Findings

Social scientists not only conduct and publish original research studies, but they often write reports and even books summarizing what is known about topics such as youth violence. In some cases the writer's summary will be a qualitative *review,* in which the author subjectively analyzes or interprets the research results.

More recently, researchers have developed a quantitative method of drawing conclusions about a body of research studies. This technique, called *meta-*

BOX 1.2 (Continued)

Quantitative Methods

Nature

In these methods, researchers use quantitative or statistical approaches in their research.

Types

The Experimental Method (sometimes referred to as the *true experiment*): the researcher manipulates an independent variable to determine its effect on a dependent variable, while at the same time holding constant the value of any other variable which could potentially affect the dependent variable.

Associational Methods: methods that show some type of an association (or relationship, or link) between two variables. They include the following:

The Quasiexperimental Method: participants are categorized into groups based on some pre-existing condition, then the groups are compared on some type of dependent variable.

The Correlational Method: a correlation coefficient is computed that shows the direction and magnitude of the relationship between two variables.

Multiple Regression Analysis: a technique that tells how two or more "predictor" variables relate to a single "criterion" variable.

Path Analysis: the use of regression analysis to test for causal relationships within a theoretical model. Results are often expressed graphically.

Structural Equation Modeling: the use of regression models in an attempt to specify causal relationships involving theoretical "latent variables," which are derived from more observable "measurement variables."

---

analysis, is a statistical procedure used to compare the results of a large number of studies, each of which has tested a specific research hypothesis (Rosnow & Rosenthal, 1996). In conducting a meta-analysis, the researcher computes what is known as the *effect size* (d), an estimate of how strongly the hypothesis has been supported. A positive effect size indicates that the experimental treatment is more effective than the control condition, whereas a negative effect size indicates the opposite. Effect sizes of .20 or less are considered small; those of .50 are considered to be medium; and those of .80 or more are considered to be large.

We will encounter a number of meta-analyses in our examination of youth aggression. This type of method is useful in that it provides a more "objective" evaluation of the results of a body of research studies than does the traditional review. On the other hand, however, this technique does not allow for the fact that studies might differ in quality and that higher quality studies may be more informative than studies of lower quality. Thus, meta-analyses should not be used as the sole basis on which to make a decision about the viability of an hypothesis under study.

AGGRESSION AND MORAL DEVELOPMENT

As children grow older, development occurs in the processes by which they begin to understand, internalize, and act in accord with moral and ethical values. This set of processes, called *moral development,* encompasses prosocial behaviors as well as antisocial behaviors such as aggression and violence. Because some understanding of these processes is necessary in order to understand the development of aggression, I turn to a brief examination of children's moral development.

Prenatal Development and Birth

Psychological development begins at conception and continues until death. At the time of conception, the offspring acquires the full complement of genes that will serve as the building blocks of the child's future development (Papalia, Olds, & Feldman, 1999). As we see in chapter 4, evidence indicates that at least some portion of youths' aggressive behavior has a genetic basis.

We know that factors such as poor maternal nutrition and certain types of prenatal environmental factors called *teratogens* can have a negative impact on the developing offspring during pregnancy (Papalia et al., 1999). Examples of teratogens include maternal illnesses, environmental toxins ingested by the mother (e.g., nicotine, alcohol, cocaine, and other drugs), and maternal exposure to radiation. These factors are especially important during the second half of pregnancy when the fetus' brain is undergoing the most rapid development and is hence the most vulnerable (Papalia et al., 1999).

The birth process itself can also be dangerous to the infant. In particular, situations that diminish or eliminate oxygen flow to the baby's brain (a condition called *anoxia*) can cause potentially serious neurological deficits (Papalia et al., 1999). As we will see, some research has linked medical complications during pregnancy and birth to children's subsequent aggression.

Temperamental Factors

Much of the theorizing and research regarding the effects of innate biological factors on moral development has focused on the concept of *temperament,* defined as "constitutionally based individual differences in emotional, motor, and attentional reactivity and self-regulation" (Rothbart & Bates, 1998, p. 109).

BOX 1.3

THE SIX DIMENSIONS OF TEMPERAMENT

1. The rapidity with which the child adapts to new situations (fearful distress).
2. Irritability and fussiness (irritable distress).
3. The extent to which the child exhibits positive emotions such as smiling and laughing (positive affect).
4. Activity level.
5. The child's attention span and persistence while engaged in a task (attention span/persistence).
6. The regularity of the child's sleeping and eating cycles (rhythmicity).

Source: Rothbart & Bates (1998, p. 111).

Although the pioneering researchers, Stella Chess, Alexander Thomas, and Herbert Birch described nine aspects of basic temperament (Chess & Thomas, 1986; Chess, Thomas, & Birch, 1965; Thomas & Chess, 1977), subsequent factor analytic studies suggest that the list can be shortened to six dimensions (see Box 1.3).

Thomas and Chess (1977) found that they could classify 65% of their subjects into one of three temperamental types:

• The *easy* type included 40% of the subjects. Babies in this type are characterized by having predictable eating and sleeping cycles; by possessing a generally positive mood and by giving generally positive reactions to new situations; and by adapting quickly to new situations.

• Another 10% were classified as having a *difficult* temperament. Babies in this category show unpredictable eating and sleeping cycles and negative reactions to new situations; they adapt very slowly to new situations; and they commonly exhibit a negative emotional mood. Chess and Thomas (1986) found that children with difficult temperaments were more at risk for developing behavior problems than children with other temperamental types.

• Finally, the remaining 15% fell into the category of the *slow-to-warm-up* temperament. Infants with this type of temperament show predictable eating and sleeping cycles, and they initially react warily to new situations but will eventually adapt if allowed to explore at their own pace.

In a related conception of temperament, Kagan and colleagues distinguish between *inhibited* and *uninhibited* children (Kagan, 1998). According to Kagan (1998), "Inhibited children react to many different types of unfamiliarity with an initial avoidance, distress, or subdued affect" (Kagan, 1998, p. 212). Uninhibited

children, on the other hand, are characterized by "a sociable, affectively sponta-
neous reaction to unfamiliar people, situations, and events" (Kagan, 1998, p. 212).

Development in Infancy

During the first year of life, the baby is essentially an amoral being whose behavior initially seems to be largely determined by the subcortical areas of the
brain, and whose ability to control primitive emotions and impulses develops
slowly over the course of the first year. However, one precursor to later prosocial behavior might be a sort of emotional contagion effect in which babies as
young as 6 months of age will start to cry when they hear another baby cry
(Hay, Nash, & Pedersen, 1981).

Psychoanalytic theorist Erik Erikson (1950) thought that the most important
psychological task of infancy was the development of *basic trust,* whereby the
infant begins to see other humans as helpful and benign. More recent theory
and research have emphasized the importance of *attachment,* which begins
around the age of 6 or 7 months and is defined as "an affectional tie that one
person or animal forms between himself and another specific one" (Ainsworth
& Bell, 1970, p. 50). In terms of positive emotions, attachment is indicated when
the baby selectively follows another person (either by crawling or walking or
with his eyes), or when the baby smiles or coos selectively to one person but not
to others. In terms of negative emotions, attachment is indicated when the baby
cries at the departure of the other (*separation anxiety*) or when the baby cries at
the sight of a stranger (*stranger anxiety*). By promoting physical contact with the
caregiver, attachment allows the child to experience comfort in the face of
stress induced either from within (e.g., tiredness) or from without (e.g., fear-
provoking environmental stimuli) (Rutter, 1997).

In the laboratory, attachment is assessed through a procedure called the
Strange Situation Test (Ainsworth, Blehar, Waters, & Wall, 1978). Based on these
tests, researchers generally describe four major types of attachment (Ainsworth
et al., 1978; Main & Solomon, 1986, 1990).

- *Secure attachment* is found in approximately 65% of infants (van IJzendoorn
& Kroonenberg, 1988). These infants actively explore while with the mother,
are visibly upset when the mother departs, greet the mother warmly when the
mother returns, and enjoy physical contact with the mother.

- *Insecure/avoidant attachment* accounts for about 20% of 1-year-olds (van
IJzendoorn & Kroonenberg, 1988). These infants have little interest in exploration when the mother is present, they show little distress when she leaves, and
they often avoid contact when she returns. They often show little or no distress
when strangers appear, and often avoid the strangers as they do their mothers.

- *Insecure/ambivalent attachment* is found in about 10% to 15% of 1-year-olds
(van IJzendoorn & Kroonenberg, 1988). These infants appear anxious and show

little exploration when the mother is present, yet they are extremely distressed when she leaves. However, when she returns, they are ambivalent, crying when she comes in, but resisting when she picks them up and tries to console them. In addition, they show anger and often reject toys offered by the mother. These babies are quite wary of strangers, even when their mother is present.

• *Insecure/disorganized attachment* occurs in a small proportion of babies, predominately those from high-risk families (Lyons-Ruth, 1996). According to Main and Solomon (1986), infants in this group lack coherent coping mechanisms to deal with a brief separation from and reunion with their mothers. Although the particular type of separation-induced response seems to vary from child to child, these children typically exhibit apprehension, helplessness, signs of depression, and prolonged motoric freezing (Lyons-Ruth, 1996). Their behavior upon reunion shows undirected movements, apprehension, confusion, and indications of depression (Main & Solomon, 1986).

Recent research supports the idea that the child's attachment status might be an important aspect in moral development.

Development in Toddlerhood

Certain precursors of antisocial behaviors begin to emerge around the end of the first year. For example, Holmberg (1980) found that 1-year-olds often took objects from each other and interfered in each others' activities. Prosocial-like behaviors also emerge around the same time. At 11 months, for example, babies have been observed to cry and look distressed when they see another child fall and begin to cry (Hoffman, 1979). By the age of 1 year, infants often "share" an interesting experience by pointing, and sometimes offer their toys to other children (Hay, Caplan, Castle, & Stimson, 1991; Leung & Rheingold, 1981). Rheingold (1982) reported that some 18-month-olds attempt to help with household chores. And during the second year, toddlers begin to help, sympathize with, and try to comfort another person in distress, and this behavior increases dramatically between the ages of 18 and 24 months (Zahn-Waxler, Radke-Yarrow, Wagner, & Chapman, 1992).

Development During Early Childhood

Numerous occurrences related to moral development happen during the years from 3 to 7, especially early in this period.

Empathy. Although *empathy,* the ability to accurately feel another person's emotion, has its precursors in the first 2 years of life, a major advance occurs in early childhood. Due to the cognitive advances of this period, children are now able to separate the personal distress they feel at the plight of another from the sympathetic concern they feel for the other person (LaFreniere, 2000). There is evidence that empathy marked with sympathetic concern is likely to lead to prosocial behaviors, whereas empathy accompanied by personal distress might lead to avoidance and antisocial behaviors (LaFreniere, 2000).

Conscience.   According to Freud, the *superego* consists of the *ego ideal* (the child's moral standards or values that have been internalized from the parents) and the *conscience* (the "internalized parent" that punishes the child through guilt for violating moral standards but rewards the child through pride for following them; Eisenberg, 1986). More recently, Kochanska and colleagues (Kochanska, 1991) proposed that internalized conscience consists of two processes: (1.) the ability to experience emotional distress following or preceding an anticipated wrongdoing (the *affective* aspect, or *guilt*); and (2.) the ability to inhibit one's impulse to engage in a forbidden activity (the *self-regulation, behavioral inhibition,* or *self-control* aspect).

1. *Guilt.*   In terms of the affective aspect of conscience, children younger than 2 often react with generalized arousal to others' distress. At around age 2, children begin to show distress when a standard is violated or cannot be met. Two-year-olds also start to demonstrate both specific negative emotions to their own transgressions as well as the beginnings of self-regulation. In the third year, children begin to exhibit a variety of emotional responses to mishaps they have caused, as well as behavioral attempts to repair the damage they have done (Kochanska, 1993; Zahn-Waxler, Radke-Yarrow, & King, 1979).

From a theoretical point of view, Bybee and colleagues delineated two different types of guilt that they call *predispositional guilt* and *chronic guilt* (Bybee & Quiles, 1998). Predispositional guilt refers to a negative emotional response to "specific, circumscribed, and eliciting situations," whereas chronic guilt is considered an "ongoing condition of guiltiness, regret, and remorse unattached to an immediate precipitating event" (Bybee & Quiles, 1998, p. 272). As we will see, predispositional guilt seems to enhance prosocial responding, whereas chronic guilt is associated with antisocial behavior.

According to Baumeister (1998), predispositional guilt "originates as an emotional response to hurting someone with whom one has a positive social bond" (p. 129). As the child grows older and begins to move outside the family, Baumeister argues that guilt involving close personal relationships gives way to guilt involving "communal" relationships, defined as "norms that people should care about each other's welfare, independent of material self-interest" (Baumeister, 1998, p. 130). In other words, norms relating to loved ones should generalize to others. Over the past 20 years, some mental health professionals have given guilt a bad name. As a result, many parents and educators today seem to have abandoned the idea that children should be held to clear moral behavioral standards (see Damon, 1995, for a discussion of the deleterious effects of "child-

---

BOX 1.4

JANE ADDAMS AND GUILT

An example of the power of guilt comes from the life of Jane Addams, a 19th-century American woman most famous for the founding of Hull House, a settlement house for immigrants in Chicago. Addams recorded that, as a child, she would lie in bed after she told a lie, racked by guilt. Finally, she would go and confess to her father, whose reply was: "If he had a little girl who told lies, he felt very glad that she felt too bad to go to sleep afterwards" (Tims, 1961, p. 19).

Note the predispositional quality of Addams' guilt: It was directed toward a specific behavior and it motivated confession and an attempt at reparation. Given how Addams turned out, perhaps more parents ought to take the attitude toward morality espoused by her father. In Baumeister's (1998) words, "It is plausible that the high rates of crime and other antisocial behaviors that currently plague the United States would be much lower if many individuals had been brought up with a stronger sense of guilt and a weaker sense of personal superiority and entitlement (i.e., self-esteem)" (p. 137).

---

centered" parenting and education). However, recent theorizing and research paints a different view of guilt, specifically, predispositional guilt. As Bybee and Quiles (1998) stated: "Guilt is good . . . By providing punishment from within, punishment from without becomes less necessary. When guilt is absent, aggression, acting out, and even sociopathy may ensue" (p. 287). Or, as Baumeister (1998) puts it, "parents should perhaps stop feeling so, well, guilty about inducing guilt in their children" (p. 127). An example of one father who apparently agreed with Baumeister is described in Box 1.4.

2. *Self-Regulation.* Defined as the ability to inhibit behavioral tendencies in the face of temptation and in the absence of external surveillance, *self-regulation* also begins to develop during the preschool years. In one study, Vaughn and colleagues asked 18- to 30-month-old children to do three things while the experimenter was out of the room: Refrain from touching a toy telephone; not eat raisins hidden under a cup; and not open a gift (Vaughn, Kopp, & Krakow, 1984). Although 18-month-olds showed little inhibition, this ability increased dramatically for the 24-month-olds, and even more for the 30-month-olds. Thus, even 2½-year-olds are able to delay gratification for short periods of time when called on to do so. In general, the development of inhibitory control seems to parallel the increasing maturation of the frontal cortex during the ages of 2 to 5, as well as the development of language and representational thought (or *inner speech;* Luria, 1961; Vygotsky, 1962).

The existence of self-regulation at an early age is a good prognostic sign. For example, Silverman and Ragusa (1992) found that ability to delay gratification at age 2 was positively related to other measures of self-control at the age of 4. Similarly, Olson and Hoza (1993) found a significant negative correlation between the ability to delay gratification in preschool and children's conduct problems in kindergarten. The authors concluded that "one specific measure of impulsivity, delay ability, emerged as the most important developmental correlate of stable conduct problems in young boys" (p. 65).

The ability to delay gratification during the preschool years seems to affect behavior even as long as 10 years later. Mischel, Shoda, and Peake (1988) studied 15-year-olds who had originally served as subjects in delay-of-gratification experiments at a mean age of 4½. As rated by their parents, children's ability to resist temptation and delay gratification in preschool was significantly related to descriptions of them 10 years later as academically competent ($r = .27$), socially competent ($r = .39$), and able to cope with frustration and resist temptation ($r = .39$). In discussing these results, Mischel and his colleagues drew the following conclusion: "The impressive correlates of self-imposed delay obtained with the present paradigm for both sexes and spanning many years suggests that such delay assesses a stable and seemingly basic cognitive and social competence that may have extensive implications for the individual's cognitive and social coping and adaptation" (p. 695).

Development During Middle Childhood

During the early school years, children move through the *5 to 7 shift* (Fischer & Lazerson, 1984; White, 1970), a time of dramatic physical and psychological change that makes the 8-year-old a very different type of person from the 4-year-old. Brain development seems to underlie this period: Many of the rapid changes of the previous 5 years are now complete or nearly so, and children's brain waves now begin to look like those of adults. In addition, many cognitive changes occur as well: Both attention and recall memory improve; children begin to better understand their own mental processes as well as those of others; children's ability to take on the perspective of others increases; and children can now use words, thoughts, and images as aids in the learning process (Fischer & Lazerson, 1984).

Consistent with these changes, children's prosocial behavior increases. Grade school children are more likely to help others than are younger children, perhaps because they have developed the skills needed to provide such help (Ladd, Lange, & Stremmel, 1983). Furthermore, prosocial behaviors such as sharing and helping also become more common as children develop from the ages of 5 to 14 (Green & Schneider, 1974).

Development During Adolescence

Starting somewhere around the age of 12, children begin to experience a group of physical and psychological changes that are collectively called *puberty* and that mark the beginning of *adolescence* (Papalia et al., 1999).

Characteristics. Adolescence contains a number of characteristics that are related to an understanding of youthful aggression and violence.

• Physiological and cognitive changes combine to cause the adolescent to question his or her parents in particular and much of adult authority in general (Conger & Galambos, 1997). Adolescents often seem to "chomp at the bit" to develop their own identity and to "do their own thing" (Erikson, 1950; Papalia et al., 1999). At the same time, their cognitive capacity allows them to see their parents as more human and less omniscient, and hence to criticize and rebel against their parents and society at large (Papalia et al., 1999).

• The peer group becomes an important aspect of the adolescent's life, and finding a peer group with whom the adolescent feels comfortable becomes an important goal (Papalia et al., 1999).

• Adolescents' increased strength and sexual urges often lead them to behave in ways not totally compatible with the desires of the larger society (Papalia et al., 1999).

• Adolescents often experience the twin processes of the *imaginary audience* and the *personal fable.* The concept of the imaginary audience refers to adolescents' beliefs that, like actors on a stage, they are the center of other peoples' attention. The term personal fable refers to a process that makes adolescents believe that they are invincible and cannot be hurt or killed (Papalia et al., 1999).

Antisocial Behavior. Self-report studies indicate that antisocial behavior is the norm in adolescence. Indeed, a number of studies have repeatedly shown that 80% to 90% of adolescents report having engaged in some type of delinquent behavior before the age of 18 (Snyder & Sickmund, 1995). Aggression is also common at this time: In one study, for example, 30% of males and 10% of females had reported committing at least three violent offenses within the year prior to their 18th birthday (Snyder & Sickmund, 1995).

Methods of Studying Development

Because psychological development involves the study of changes over time, researchers have developed methodologies specifically designed for this task.

The Longitudinal Method. The major type of design researchers use to study such developmental changes is called the *longitudinal* method (Miller, 1998). In this design, researchers select a group of children and then study them at least twice in their lives. *Short-term* developmental studies are more common in infancy and early childhood and might cover a span of weeks or months. *Long-term* studies, on the other hand, might span years or even decades. Throughout our examination of youth violence we will encounter numerous long-term longitudinal studies, some of them beginning in early childhood and continuing on into adulthood.

In addition to being short term or long term, longitudinal studies can also be either *prospective* or *retrospective* (Wicks-Nelson & Israel, 2000). In prospective studies (sometimes also called *follow-up* studies), the research begins when the children are young and continues as they grow older. In retrospective (*follow-back*) studies, the researcher begins with a group of adults and then studies what the members of the group were like when they were younger.

Panel Studies.   A special type of longitudinal design is called the *cross-lagged panel design* (or *panel study;* Rosnow & Rosenthal, 1996). This type of study consists of a longitudinal design in which correlations are compared at two different times in order to provide more definitive information regarding causation (Rosnow & Rosenthal, 1996). For example, suppose we are interested in the question of whether watching violence on television causes children to act aggressively. Using a panel design, we would measure both television viewing and aggressiveness at two different times, and then compute the various correlations. If television viewing at time one is correlated more strongly with aggressiveness at time two than aggressiveness at time one is correlated with television viewing at time two, this result would support the hypothesis that television viewing causes aggressiveness.

Despite the fact that panel designs provide interesting data, statisticians have pointed out some logical limitations associated with these designs. Hence, as is the case with other associational designs we have examined, these designs should not be used to infer causality (Rosnow & Rosenthal, 1996).

SUMMARY AND PREVIEW

This is a book about why youngsters under the age of 18 develop behaviors intended to hurt others, and why some become especially hyperaggressive and violent. The focus throughout will be on factors that affect youthful aggression and on the psychological processes by which aggressive youths respond to these factors.

Aggression can range from "low-level" acts such as being impolite, violating minor rules, and generally being noisy and disruptive to acts of "criminal violence" such as murder, homicide, rape, aggravated assault, and robbery. Whether or not low-level aggression is as prevalent as commonly assumed is difficult to determine. Criminal violence, on the other hand, increased dramatically from the mid-1980s to the mid-1990s, but has been decreasing since that time.

In order to understand research on youthful aggression, we must understand some of the methods social scientists use to study this phenomenon. These include both qualitative as well as quantitative designs. The type of quantitative research known as the experimental method can, if done well, yield information regarding the causes of youth violence. Associational methods, however, yield information regarding relationships, but not causation. Reliability, internal validity, and external validity are three characteristics against which research studies are judged. One method of summarizing research results is the meta-analysis, a technique that yields a quantitative estimate of the effect size or extent to which the research supports a particular hypothesis.

Because aggression changes as children grow older, youth violence must be understood from a developmental perspective. Children enter the world with certain temperamental qualities that seem to predispose them to certain types of behaviors. Two of the most important processes involved in moral development are attachment (which occurs around the age of 6 months) and the development of conscience (which occurs in the third year). Although middle childhood is generally a time of increased prosocial behavior, antisocial behaviors become normative in adolescence.

Our discussion of youthful aggression and violence leads us down a number of paths. First, we examine the development of both "normal" and "abnormal" forms of aggression (chaps. 2 and 3). Next, we consider genetic, biological, familial, and social-cultural factors that contribute to youthful aggression (chaps. 4 through 7). Third, we examine aggressive youngsters' psychological characteristics and behavior, paying special attention to juvenile homicide and violence in the schools (chaps. 8 through 11). Fourth, we review the nature and effects of intervention and prevention measures used with hyperaggressive youths (chap. 12). And finally, I attempt to summarize what we know about youthful aggression and to point out the limitations of our current knowledge (chap. 13).

CHAPTER 2

Overview of Aggression

Having considered moral development generally in the previous chapter, we now turn specifically to aggression. In this chapter, we consider the nature of aggression, discuss a number of theoretical ideas about aggression, and then examine the development of the "normal" forms of aggression typically found in the vast majority of children.

NATURE AND TYPES OF AGGRESSION

As we saw in chapter 1, aggression refers to behaviors intended to harm another person physically or psychologically or to damage, destroy, or take that person's property (Bartol, 1995). This definition of aggression has a number of implications:

• Aggression is *behavior,* by which we mean that it consists of overt action that can be observed by others. In contrast, *anger* is an emotion; that is, a subjective state of feeling that can be directly experienced only by the person who is angry. We will explore the potential relationship between aggression and anger later in this chapter.

• Aggression involves a hostile intent. Nonaggressive acts might also inflict damage, but they lack such an intent. For example, if a child impulsively turns around and his elbow strikes another child in the face, that action would not be considered aggressive if the child did not intend to do harm.

• Aggression can be intended to do psychological as well as physical harm. Thus, a child who threatens another or who says mean things with the intention of hurting another's feelings would be committing aggression.

• Aggression can be directed at either a person or at an object (including an animal). For example, the child who maliciously harms a pet or who destroys the property of another child would be guilty of aggression.

This definition of aggression causes problems for psychologists, primarily because of the difficulty in determining the intent of the child. If one child hits another, that action is an overt behavior, and most observers will be able to agree whether the hitting actually occurred or not. However, only the child knows for sure what his intent was; thus, intent is some mental state of the child that is not overt and hence not directly observable to others. Having to decide whether intent to harm is present reduces the reliability of the observation and thus produces the risk of error, both in psychological studies and in "real life" as well. We have all heard a child protest, "I didn't mean it," and sometimes it's hard to determine whether that statement is true or not.

Types of Aggression. Historically, psychologists have delineated two major types of aggression, *physical aggression* and *verbal aggression*. Physical aggression includes activities in which actual physical harm is intentionally done to a person, animal, or object. Examples of physical aggression include hitting, kicking, stabbing, shooting, pushing and shoving, throwing objects, breaking windows, defacing property, and setting fires, to name a few. Verbal aggression, on the other hand, involves the use of words to harm another. Verbal aggression can involve behaviors such as making threats or writing threatening notes or letters, calling names, spreading gossip, and teasing.

More recently, researchers have begun to examine a third type of aggression called *relational aggression,* defined as "behaviors that harm others through damage (or the threat of damage) to relationships or feelings of acceptance, friendship, or group inclusion" (Crick et al., 1999, p. 77). This type of aggression is similar to but distinct from both *indirect aggression* (in which the target is not confronted directly) and *social aggression* (in which the target is another's self-esteem or social status, but not necessarily another's social relationships; Crick et al., 1999).

Aggression can also be *hostile, instrumental,* or *reactive.* Hostile aggression has the primary goal of doing harm to the victim or of making the victim suffer, whereas instrumental aggression involves the use of force in order to obtain some nonaggressive goal (such as when one child beats up another child in order to take some money). Reactive aggression refers to an angry aggressive act in response to some precipitating environmental event or behavior. Instrumental aggression is sometimes referred to as *unprovoked aggression,* whereas reactive aggression is also called *provoked aggression* (Bartol, 1995; Dodge, Coie, Pettit, & Price, 1990; Olweus, 1986).

THEORIES OF AGGRESSION

A variety of psychological theories have been developed in an attempt to explain why children become aggressive. We now examine some of these theoretical explanations.

Genetic and Biological Theories of Aggression

A number of theories have postulated that aggression is due to either genetic or biological factors. Genetic theories argue that aggressiveness (or at least the basis for aggressiveness) is transmitted by means of genetic inheritance from one generation to the next. Biological theories attempt to specify the biological processes and mechanisms by which genetic factors and innate characteristics get translated into actual aggressiveness. We examine these issues in more detail in chapter 4.

Freud's Theory

Freud, too, held that aggression is rooted in biology. According to him, humans are born with a drive (called the *Thanatos*) that seeks the cessation of life (see Feshbach, 1970, for a discussion). Although the Thanatos might be directed toward the self (thus resulting in self-injury or even death), it can also be discharged toward others (thus resulting in aggression). Freud also believed that the strength of the Thanatos builds up gradually and that, when its strength hits a certain level (or threshold), it demands to be discharged. One way of discharging the Thanatos is through the defense mechanism of *sublimation,* a process by which unacceptable drives are channeled into socially acceptable alternatives. Thus, for example, children might sublimate their aggressiveness drive by using that "psychic energy" to play sports, rather than by engaging in direct aggressive behavior (Thomas, 1992).

Displacement.   Another Freudian process involved in aggression is the defense mechanism of *displacement.* When applied to frustration, this process is sometimes called the "kick the cat" phenomenon. The idea is that when a child is frustrated, he often cannot retaliate against the person causing the frustration, for a number of possible reasons. For example, if the person causing the frustration is the father, the child might fear physical or psychological retaliation if he should attack the parent. Because the child cannot attack the parent directly, he chooses a "safe" target, yet one which might also symbolize the father (Feshbach, 1970). In such a case, the child might unconsciously "choose" to kick the cat (i.e., displace his aggression onto the cat), because the cat probably won't retaliate and might in some way symbolize the father. Thus, in Freudian theory, the object of a child's aggression might not be the "true" object at all, but might instead only be a symbolic substitute for the true object of the child's aggression.

Catharsis.   Freud also introduced the idea of *catharsis* into the discussion on aggression (Feshbach, 1970). According to Freud, if the strength of the aggressive drive begins to build up, something must be done to release the energy associated with the drive before it becomes too intense and overt aggression is discharged in its entire fury (Renfrew, 1997). According to the *cathartic hypothesis,* the pressure associated with the aggressive drive is reduced by any aggressive act, including displaced aggressive responses as well as fantasy modes of aggression such as watching violence on television (Feshbach, 1970; Renfrew, 1997).

This view might be thought of as the "pressure cooker" theory of anger, because it is seen as analogous to what happens in a pressure cooker. As you might know, a pressure cooker is a type of pot used to cook various types of meats and vegetables. Water is placed over the contents in the pot, and then a lid seals the pot tight. When the water is heated, steam builds up. Normally, a small valve on the lid of the pressure cooker allows a little steam to escape in a gradual fashion, and everything works fine. However, if something clogs the escape valve, too much steam builds up and the top eventually blows off the cooker.

According to the cathartic hypothesis, this is what happens with the aggressive drive. If the drive can be released a little at a time (e.g., through sublimation), then everything works fine. But if too much of the drive builds up, the child will figuratively "blow his top," and an aggressive outburst will occur. Catharsis is a process designed to promote the "draining off" of aggressive energy. It consists of letting the child express his anger, often in an indirect or symbolic fashion. For example, the child might be told to go hit a punching bag or throw darts at a target when he is angry.

Because the cathartic hypothesis states that such activity will help the child learn to control his aggressive behavior, it is important to determine how well empirical evidence supports this idea. One classic study on this hypothesis was conducted on children by Mallick and McCandless (1966). In this research, two groups of children were frustrated. Subsequently, one group (the "catharsis group") was allowed to play aggressively, whereas a second group (the "noncatharsis group") was given no chance to drain off their aggressiveness. Later, children in both groups were allowed to aggress toward the source of their frustration. In this case, children in the catharsis group were no less likely to aggress toward the source of their frustration than were children in the noncatharsis group, thus casting doubt on the validity of the cathartic hypothesis.

Subsequent tests of this hypothesis have been conducted with both children and adults. In general, the results of such research not only support the original Mallick and McCandless (1966) results, but often also indicate that participants who are allowed to "vent their anger" subsequently become even more aggressive than those not given this opportunity (Tavris, 1982). Venting one's anger seems to have the effect of allowing the person to practice aggressiveness, thus becoming more likely to exhibit aggression in the future.

Behavioristic/Social-Learning Theory

Behavioristic/social-learning theory emphasizes the learning of aggression within a social context. These theorists argue that aggression can be learned, maintained, and unlearned through the processes of observational learning and classical and operant conditioning. In general, aggression tends to be learned through the first two processes and strengthened and maintained through the latter.

Observational Learning. One of the best-articulated social-learning theories is that of Albert Bandura (1977, 1989), who argues that observational
learning represents one process by which aggression can be learned. Bandura
and colleagues (Bandura, Ross, & Ross, 1961) were the first to conduct true
experiments on the hypothesis that children learn aggression by viewing an
aggressive model. In their famous Bobo Doll study, one group of preschool
children first saw a live adult model deliver a series of distinctive verbal and
physical aggressive behaviors toward a large inflatable "Bobo" doll; children
in a second group observed a model who acted nonaggressively; and children
in a control group did not see any model. Following this phase of the study,
the children were then frustrated by having their play interrupted for a brief
period. Afterward, their aggressive behavior in a "free play" situation was observed. Children who saw the aggressive model subsequently exhibited many
of the same distinctive aggressive responses to the doll they had observed,
whereas those in the other two groups were generally less aggressive and did
not show the distinctive aggressive responses performed by the model. This
research suggested that the children had learned their aggressiveness through
observational learning.

In another experiment, Bandura, Ross, and Ross (1963) compared the effects
of a live aggressive adult model, a filmed aggressive adult model, and a filmed
aggressive cartoon character model. In general, the aggressive model on film
produced the most aggression in these children, thus suggesting the possibility
that children might learn violence by exposure to films and television.

In still another study, Bandura (1965) attempted to determine whether seeing the model's behavior reinforced or punished would affect children's tendency to imitate the aggressive responses they had witnessed. In this case, one
group of children saw the model being rewarded for aggression, a second group
saw the model being punished, and the third group saw the model receive no
consequences for aggression. Children in the "model-rewarded" and "no-conse-
quences" groups subsequently showed more imitation of aggression than those
in the "model-punished" group. However, when Bandura offered the children
monetary incentives for demonstrating all the distinctive aggressive responses
which the model had made, children in all three groups performed at the same
high level.

The results of this study point out the important distinction between learning and performance. All the children had learned aggression through observing the model. Initially, however, only the children in the first two groups performed the learned response, indicating that observing a model being punished
reduces the child's subsequent *performance* of aggression. However, seeing the
model being punished did not stop these children from *learning* aggression.
Consequently, when the payoff for performing the aggressive responses was
great enough, even the children in the "model-punished" condition could perform what they had learned. Thus, children might well learn aggression through

observational learning, but they might need some extrinsic reinforcement or punishment in order to actually perform or inhibit the learned behavior.

Classical Conditioning. Another way aggression can be learned is through classical conditioning. According to this theory, if a stimulus for an aggressive response repeatedly occurs at the same time and in the same place as some initially neutral environmental stimulus, that aggressive response will eventually begin to occur in the presence of the initially neutral stimulus. In Pavlov's terms, the environmental stimulus becomes the conditioned stimulus for the conditioned response of aggression. For example, if a provocation causes a child to get into fights with other players during ice-hockey games, the stimulus cues of the hockey game should eventually result in the child fighting in that context even in the absence of any other provocation.

Research with animals indicates that it is possible to classically condition aggression, at least under certain circumstances. In one study, for example, Hutchinson, Renfew, and Young (1971) presented either an auditory or a visual stimulus just prior to shocking the tails of squirrel monkeys (a procedure that evoked biting among the monkeys). They found that the monkeys would subsequently respond to both the auditory and visual stimuli with biting; thus, biting had become learned to these conditioned stimuli. Unfortunately for scientists (but fortunately for children), such laboratory experiments with humans are unethical; hence, we really can't say whether aggression can also be classically conditioned in children as well as in monkeys.

Operant Conditioning. As with any other response, it is reasonable to hypoth esize that aggressive responses that are reinforced will be strengthened and maintained. This can happen in one of two ways. First, the aggressive response might produce some positive payoff, in which case the aggression is strengthened through *positive reinforcement*. Alternatively, the aggressive response can either terminate an unpleasant situation (escape learning) or cause it to be avoided all together (avoidance learning), in which case the response is strengthened through *negative reinforcement*. Note that negative reinforcement is *not* punishment, and that in both positive and negative reinforcement, the aggressive response that is reinforced becomes stronger as a result.

Research shows that children can learn aggression through both positive and negative reinforcement. For example, Cowan and Walters (1963) taught children to hit a Bobo doll by reinforcing them with marbles (positive reinforcement); and Patterson, Littman, and Bricker (1967) showed that initially passive preschool children would learn to fight off attackers if their aggression allowed them to avoid future attacks (negative reinforcement). In another study (Lovaas, 1961), children were reinforced for either making aggressive statements or nonaggressive statements as they played with toys. Not only did children who were reinforced for aggression make more aggressive statements than those who were not, but, in a subsequent session, the children who were reinforced for aggression were more likely to choose to play with an aggressive toy than were the children reinforced for nonaggression. It is as if reinforcing the child for one type of aggression teaches the child to perform other types of aggression as well.

Stimulus Discrimination.   Aggressive responses are always made within some environmental context, and hence these responses can come under the control of the stimulus cues associated with that context. For example, if a rat's biting response is reinforced in a Skinner box when a green light is turned on but not when a red light is present, the rat will eventually learn to make the response only in the presence of the green light. This procedure by which a response comes to be controlled by specific environmental stimuli is called *stimulus discrimination*. In one demonstration of this principle with animals, Reynolds, Catania, and Skinner (1963) taught pigeons to attack when a colored light was present, but not when a white light was present.

Stimulus discrimination occurs in children as well. In one classic study, Sears and colleagues (Sears, Whiting, Nowlis, & Sears, 1953) found that preschool children who were severely punished for aggressive behavior at home were more likely to show aggression during "permissive doll play" at school than were children who were not punished severely at home. The learning theory explanation is that these children had learned to discriminate when aggression would pay off and when it would not. They had learned, in other words, that aggression within the context of the home would be punished; hence, their aggression in that setting decreased. However, in a school context where punishment for aggression was unlikely, their aggressive behavior became manifest.

The process of stimulus discrimination is related to the theory of "opportunities for crime" (Rutter et al., 1998). According to this view, whether a child behaves antisocially will depend both on the characteristics of the child as well as the extent to which the external environment is conducive to this type of behavior. For example, aggression is more likely to occur in areas of a school that are unsupervised than in those areas that are well supervised. In learning theory terms, the environmental stimulus context serves as a discriminative stimulus for either prosocial or antisocial behavior.

Stimulus Generalization.   Not only do animals and children learn to make aggressive responses in specific stimulus contexts, but they also learn to transfer these responses to other contexts that are similar to the original ones. The process by which a response learned to one stimulus also comes to be made in the presence of a similar stimulus is called *stimulus generalization*. For example, a rat trained to be aggressive in the presence of a green light will also show similar aggressiveness to a blue–green light. The aggressiveness response has thus been generalized to a new context.

Similar situations occur with children. For example, a child who learns to fight on the playground of a school might well generalize his fighting to the inside of the school as well, because both contexts have some similarities. Likewise, the suppression of aggression in one context might also generalize to another context.

Note the similarity between the behaviorists' concept of stimulus generalization and Freud's concept of displacement. In both cases, aggression moves from one context to the other, and in both cases, there exists some postulated similarity between the original context and the new context.

Differential Association and Reinforcement Theory

One variant of behavioristic/social-learning theory emanating from a sociological context is *differential association/reinforcement theory*, originally proposed by Sutherland (1939) and revised by Akers (1985). Sutherland's main idea was that people become criminals when the number of messages they hear that favor criminality outweigh the number of messages they hear that oppose criminality. Because this ratio typically occurs because the child tends to associate with individuals who espouse antisocial ideas, this part of the theory is referred to as "differential association" (Sutherland & Cressy, 1974).

Akers expanded this idea to incorporate the concept of reinforcement. He argued that deviant behavior occurs primarily as a result of the amount of social reinforcement the person receives for deviant acts, typically from peers. The group develops its own normative definitions about which behaviors are right or wrong, and then members of the group reinforce each other accordingly. In addition, members of the group begin to normalize or justify behavior that violates societal norms (e.g., "It's not so bad," "She deserved it," "Everybody's doing it"). The more the child's peer group justifies aggressive and antisocial behavior, the more they reinforce each other for it, and the more they engage in it (Akers, 1985).

The Frustration–Aggression Hypothesis

Probably the best-known hypothesis regarding children's aggression is the famous *frustration–aggression hypothesis* advanced by John Dollard and his colleagues more than a half century ago (Dollard, Doob, Miller, Mowrer, & Sears, 1939). These researchers defined frustration as a situation in which some goal-directed behavior is blocked or otherwise thwarted. For example, frustration occurs when a child who has a goal of riding a bike or playing with a doll is told to stop while in the middle of the activity. These researchers argued that "aggressive behavior always presupposes the existence of frustration and . . . the existence of frustration always leads to some form of aggression" (Dollard et al., 1939, p. 1).

Some research suggests that the closer to a goal frustration occurs, the more arousal it produces. In one study, Haner and Brown (1955) told children they could win a prize if they could place one marble in each of 36 holes of a game-board before any of the marbles dropped out. However, if any of the marbles dropped out, a buzzer would sound and the child would have to press a lever and would not win the prize. As you might have guessed, the marbles were rigged to fall out at certain times. In some cases, the marbles would fall out after the child had placed only a few marbles in the holes; in other cases, the marbles would fall out just as the child was about to place the last marble in the final hole. The researchers found that children who were frustrated closer to the goal pushed harder on the lever than those who were frustrated farther away from the goal, thus suggesting a greater degree of frustration (and hence arousal) as the child gets closer to a goal.

"Common sense" explanations of aggression are often versions of the frus-tration–aggression hypothesis. For example, in 1994, a youth who was 13 at the time of the crime was convicted of killing a 4-year-old boy. Friends described the killer as a meek child who apparently took all that he could from bigger kids, then "snapped" and took out his aggression on the little boy (Nordheimer, 1994). In other words, frustration had built up to such a level in the youngster that it eventually produced overt but displaced aggression.

Because a number of explanations incorporate some version of the frus-tration–aggression hypothesis, we would like to know the extent to which em-pirical evidence supports this position. According to Renfrew (1997), research with animals provides some positive support. For example, many studies have demonstrated that, at least in animals, frustration often produces a directed retaliatory response: The animal clearly orients to the source of frustration, approaches it, and attacks it (Renfrew, 1997). Furthermore, the removal of rein-forcement often also produces aggression. However, other evidence is not so supportive. For example, work on animals suggests that the most immediate effect of frustration might be to increase arousal level generally, rather than to promote aggression specifically (Renfrew, 1997).

Child psychologists have also tested the theory empirically. In one classic study, researchers first allowed a group of preschool children to play with a set of attractive toys (Barker, Dembo, & Lewin, 1941). After the children had played with the toys, the researchers then lowered a screen between the children and the toys, cutting off the children's access to the attractive toys and leaving them only some less attractive toys with which to play. In observing the children's re-action to this frustrating situation, the researchers found that although some children did display aggression (e.g., by hitting the experimenter or the screen), their major reaction was *regression;* that is, the children's play behavior became less mature and constructive than it had been previously. These results thus indicated that although frustration might indeed result in aggression, such is not always the case.

Other research with children has also failed to support the inevitability of the frustration–aggression link. For example, the amount of childhood frustration is not a good predictor of the child's later level of aggression, and frustration sometimes motivates children to work harder at a task (Durkin, 1995). Thus, the initial frustration–aggression hypothesis as originally stated is probably not correct. Nevertheless, some link between the two does seem to exist.

Berkowitz's Revisions.   These problems with the original version of the frustration–aggression hypothesis led Leonard Berkowitz to develop a revised version of the theory (Berkowitz, 1965, 1974). According to Berkowitz's revision, overt aggressive behavior involves an interaction between environmental frustration, certain psychological characteristics of the individual, and specific cues for aggression that occur in the environment. For Berkowitz, frustration directly produces the emotional response of anger. Anger, in turn, combines with the child's existing aggressive habits to generate a motivational *"readiness* for aggressive acts" (Berkowitz, 1965, p. 308; emphasis in original). If this readiness to aggress is extremely high (above a certain threshold), then overt aggression will occur. However, if the readiness to aggress is below the cutoff threshold, then aggression will occur only if the immediate situation includes specific cues for aggression (see Fig. 2.1).

Berkowitz's theory is interesting for a number of reasons. First, by postulating that frustration produces anger rather than aggression, it can potentially explain why frustration does not necessarily result in aggression. In addition, note the similarity between Berkowitz's theory and the finding from animal research that frustration seems to produce emotional arousal rather than behavioral aggression. Berkowitz's theory also takes into account both the child's current propensity for aggressiveness (based, no doubt, on his past experience)

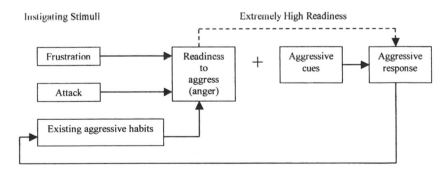

FIG. 2.1.   Berkowitz's theory relating frustration and anger to aggression, as adapted from Berkowitz (1994). From *Social and Personality Development, 3rd Edition,* by D. R. Shaffer, 1994, p. 332. Copyright 1994 by Wadsworth, a division of Thomson Learning (Fax 800–730–2215). Reprinted with permission.

as well as frustration. Thus, frustration can affect children differentially, depending on their current predisposition toward aggression. The theory also incorporates the importance of specific environmental cues or stimuli. It can thus potentially explain why one child might get violent when a gun is available, but might not if the gun were absent.

Berkowitz later revised this theory to make it more cognitive in nature (Berkowitz, 1989). In this revision, he argued that frustration and negative environmental events can produce a variety of negative emotions, including not only anger but also sadness and depression. The child then applies a cognitive appraisal to the event, and if the child believes that someone has intentionally tried to hurt him, the child is apt to become aggressive. On the other hand, if the cognitive appraisal indicates that the hurt was unintentional, then the child is more likely to inhibit his aggressiveness. Thus, this version of Berkowitz's theory incorporates a cognitive attributional process that was lacking in his previous scheme.

Cognitive Theory

Cognitive theory emphasizes the role that thinking and information processing play in the development and maintenance of aggression. One such theory comes from the work of Kenneth Dodge and associates (Dodge, 1980, 1986; Dodge & Frame, 1982), who apply an attributional analysis to aggression.

Attribution Theory.   *Attribution theory* emphasizes children's self-explanations for their own behavior and the behavior of others. In his version of this theory, Dodge assumes that when children experience a potentially aggression-provoking event, they go through the following sequence of cognitive processes: First, they attempt to *decode* the event (i.e., to gather information about the event from the environment). Next, they *interpret* the event. In this phase, children take the decoded information, consider it in light of their goals and past experience, and try to make sense of it. Third, children then perform a *response search:* They seek out possible responses they can make in this situation. In the next *response decision* phase, children evaluate the adequacy of each potential response, then select the one they view as optimal. Finally, they *encode* the response; that is, they make the observable response they had selected.

One important aspect of Dodge's theory is his concept of *hostile attributional bias.* According to this view, unusually aggressive children tend to do two things: First, they overattribute hostile intentions to others, especially in situations that are ambiguous; and second, they view such "hostile" people as belligerents who deserve to be dealt with in a forceful manner (Shaffer, 1994).

In one test of this theory, Dodge (1980) studied aggressive and nonaggressive elementary and middle school boys. Each boy worked on a puzzle in one room while a peer worked on a similar puzzle in a second room. During a break in the

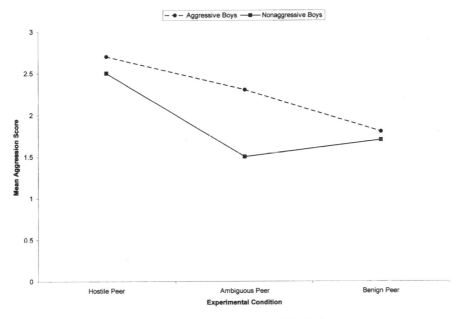

FIG. 2.2. Boys' aggressive behavior as a function of level of aggressiveness and perceived intent. From "Social Cognition and Children's Aggressive Behavior," by K. A. Dodge, 1980, *Child Development, 51*, p. 166. Adapted with permission.

work, the participant heard the voice of another child over an intercom. Although the children were led to believe that the voice was that of the other child who was working on the puzzle, in reality it was not. One-third of the children heard the voice express a "hostile intent" ("Gee, he's got a lot done—I'll mess it up"); one third heard the voice express a "helpful intent" ("I'll help him—oh no, I didn't mean to drop it"); and the other third heard the voice express an "ambiguous statement" ("Gee, he's got a lot done"). The researchers then measured the amount of aggression exhibited by each participant as indicated, for example, by the child messing up the other child's puzzle or expressing verbal hostility toward the other child. Results indicated no difference between the aggressive and nonaggressive boys except in the "ambiguous" condition, where the aggressive boys showed much more hostility than the nonaggressive boys (see Fig. 2.2). Thus, the results of this research are consistent with Dodge's theory.

Subsequent research has also tended to support the basic idea of hostile attributional bias. For example, highly aggressive girls seem to have the same kind of hostile attributional bias as highly aggressive boys (Dodge, Murphy, & Buchsbaum, 1984). In addition, the tendency toward exhibiting such a bias seems to increase when highly aggressive children feel threatened, as opposed to when they feel relaxed (Dodge & Somberg, 1987). Moreover, because nonaggressive children are more likely to retaliate when an aggressor has a reputation for aggression (Dodge & Frame, 1982), the aggressive child's hostile attribution bias might eventually become an accurate assessment of the situation. Thus, a vicious cycle seems to develop: First, the aggressive child exhibits a hostile attribution and thus attacks other children even when the others lack a hostile intent. Eventually, the other children begin retaliating, which only magnifies the aggressive child's paranoia, making him even more likely to retaliate and thus to provoke an attack. Finally, the aggressive child begins to feel threatened from all sides, thus becoming even more likely to overinterpret the hostility of others.

Dodge's theory is interesting because it specifies a number of processes that could be involved in aggressiveness. The decoding phase is important because children who lack good cognitive and social–perceptual abilities are likely to miss important cues. The interpretive phase sounds very much like Berkowitz's idea that the child applies a cognitive appraisal to a frustrating situation. The response selection process is important, because if the child only has one response available (e.g., hitting), then the conclusion is foreordained. For this reason, it is important that children learn a wide variety of prosocial responses that can be used in potentially aggressive situations. Similarly, in order to inhibit aggression, the child must decide that aggression does not pay. He must know that aggression will have negative consequences and that prosocial behavior will have positive consequences. Furthermore, he must have learned that prosocial behaviors can be used to get what he wants. This theory thus provides both guidelines for teaching children how to act prosocially, as well as a blueprint for intervening in the lives of children who have already developed a high degree of aggression.

Maintenance of Aggressive Behavior.   Cognitive theory also discusses the issue of why aggressive is maintained once it is learned. Shaffer (1994), following the lead of Bandura, described four reasons why aggression might persist:

- *Aggressive children expect that their aggressive behavior will pay off for them.* They believe that aggression is easy for them, and that it will yield tangible payoffs and terminate others' noxious behavior. In the process, they also believe that aggression will increase their self-esteem.

- *Aggressive children attach much value to their ability to dominate and control others, and they find that their aggressive behavior enhances this goal.*

- *Aggressive children's antisocial behavior is often socially sanctioned by their peers.* As we will see, aggressive children often socialize with other aggressive children and thus reinforce each others' aggressiveness.

- *Aggression may be intrinsically reinforcing for these children.* Because their value system might consider aggression to be a positive value, aggressive youngsters might exhibit a sense of pride in their ability to hurt others.

Social Control and Self-Control Theory

Travis Hirschi and his colleagues have developed two influential theories of delinquency, one emphasizing *social control,* the other *self-control* (M. R. Gottfredson & Hirschi, 1990; Hirschi, 1969). We examine each of these in turn.

Social Control. Social control theory assumes that children and adolescents have a natural tendency to commit antisocial behaviors and that this tendency must be controlled by society (hence the name "social control"; Shoemaker, 1996). Hirschi (1969) argued that this unruly tendency is kept in check by emotional bonds and attachments that have been developed between the child and society. More specifically, Hirschi postulates that the social bond consists of four components: Attachment, commitment, involvement, and belief.

Attachment refers to the emotional bond the child feels toward other persons and groups. To some extent, Hirschi's use of the concept of attachment is similar to that of psychologists, in that both describe an emotional bond between the child and someone else. Child psychologists, however, stress the importance of the initial attachment to the caregiver, but have rather neglected the child's attachment to other individuals and groups. Hirschi, on the other hand, emphasizes the child's attachments to groups (such as the family, school, and peers) more than to individuals. Children who develop strong attachments to individuals and groups that uphold conventional values are more likely to hold those values than are children who lack such attachments.

A second aspect of the social bond is *commitment,* a measure of the extent to which the benefits of conformity to social conventions outweigh the benefits of conforming to antisocial values. If working hard and adhering to conventional morality pays off both materially and psychologically, then the child will continue to uphold societal standards. Conversely, if antisocial behaviors such as aggression, cheating, stealing, and lying pay off more than prosocial behaviors, the child will act antisocially. This aspect of Hirschi's theory sounds a lot like reinforcement theory.

Involvement, the third aspect of the social bond, refers to the extent that the child participates in activities sanctioned by the larger society. This would include, for example, the extent to which children participate in school activities, community service activities, community recreational activities, et cetera. The assumption is that the more children participate in such societal activities, the more they become invested in the values their society holds.

The final aspect of the social bond consists of the *beliefs* that children hold. This aspect involves the acceptance of the community's value system. However, if the community lacks such a shared value system, children will develop their values from other sources. Thus, any factors that weaken such shared values also make antisocial behavior more likely.

Social control theory places a great deal of emphasis on the emotional relationship between the child and others as well as on the set of values the child holds. It concurs with attachment theory that the development of emotional bonds between the child and others is a crucial component of moral development, but it expands attachment theory by arguing that the importance of attachment lies in the fact that an attached child is more likely to internalize the values of the parent and society than is a nonattached child. Another interesting aspect is its assumption that involvement in "conventional" activities will strengthen the social bond. Today, this aspect of control theory is probably best seen in the increasing tendency of school systems to impose some kind of a community service requirement on students. (The potential negative aspect of such a requirement, however, is that if students are coerced into such activities, they might attribute their service behavior to external constraints and not to internal desires.)

Self-Control. More recently, Hirschi and Gottfredson (1994) developed a *self-control* theory of delinquency. According to this formulation, criminal acts occur because the individual is insensitive to and hence ignores the long-term negative consequences of antisocial behavior, while at the same time being unusually sensitive to the immediate pleasures the antisocial act produces. In their view, the problem is that individuals who habitually commit antisocial acts do so because of a lack of self-control, defined as the ability to avoid antisocial acts whose long-term consequences exceed their momentary pleasure. Thus, for example, the young child who cheats on a test manifests a lack of self-control because he is unable to resist an act that is immediately satisfying but will have long-term negative consequences.

Hirschi and Gottfredson see self-control as a personality trait that begins to develop in childhood and becomes more stable as the child reaches adolescence and adulthood. Children who develop self-control can inhibit their antisocial tendencies, but those who lack this trait will focus only on the present, and not on any long-term consequences, no matter how strong the long-term consequences might be.

Self-control theory relates to the self-regulation processes, which we examined in connection with children's moral development. In both cases, the ability to self-regulate and to value long-term consequences over short-term gains are seen as important elements in the development of prosocial behavior. Indeed, self-control theory's emphasis on the long-term importance of self-regulation is supported by the results of the Mischel et al. (1988) study in which delay of gratification at age 4 was related to positive effects 10 years later.

DEVELOPMENT OF AGGRESSION IN "NORMAL" CHILDREN

The development of aggression, as well as the ability to control it, is part of children's normal development. Before we consider "abnormal" forms of aggression, let's look at how aggression develops in "normal" children.

Infancy and Toddlerhood

Because aggression as we define it involves intent, and because young infants are cognitively incapable of *intending* harm, young infants cannot show aggression. Instead, a more primitive emotional response of anger appears to emerge somewhere between 2 and 7 months (Stenberg, Campos, & Emde, 1983). Initially, this emotion seems to be rather diffuse, but becomes more focused as the infant moves into the second half of the first year (Izard, Hembree, Dougherty, & Spizzirri, 1983). During this time, anger seems to be instigated by problems in routine physical activities such as bathing, feeding, and being put to bed (Goodenough, 1931).

As we have seen, more obvious aggressive behaviors begin to emerge around the end of the first year. Initially, instrumental aggression seems to predominate, as indicated by Holmberg's (1980) finding that 1-year-olds often take objects from each other.

During the second year, much aggression among toddlers is related to toy play (Caplan, Vespo, Pederson, & Hay, 1991). In addition, toileting and being refused permission to do something also characterize a substantial number of anger-provoking situations (Goodenough, 1931). Observational studies suggest that anger occurs on average between 5% and 10% of the time during toddlerhood (Radke-Yarrow & Kochanska, 1990).

Early Childhood

In a classic study, Dawe (1934) trained observers to record information about the quarrels of 2- to 5-year-old children during free-play time in a nursery school. Most disagreements produced motor responses such as pushing or shoving, and most were short-lived, averaging only 24 seconds. Boys quarreled more than girls, intrasex quarrels were more common than intersex disputes, and intersex quarrels were settled more often by negotiation than were intrasex disputes. Retaliative acts increased over this age, even though the number of quarrels decreased.

Siblings become a source of aggression during the preschool years, with up to 45% of interactions between older and younger siblings producing conflict (Abramovich, Corter, & Lando, 1979). In general, older siblings instigate the conflicts by threatening or taking objects from the younger child, who in turn might learn aggression through imitation.

A number of studies have revealed high rates of temper tantrums and peer fighting among 3-year-olds, and this age seems to be the high-water mark of physical aggression among preschoolers (Coie & Dodge, 1998). Indeed, parental concerns regarding behavior problems peak at this time (S. Jenkins, Bax, & Hart, 1980).

Goodenough (1931) found that temper tantrums peaked around the age of 3½, and that by the age of 4, aggressive behaviors became more focused as the children retaliated physically by hitting and kicking other children who had frustrated or attacked them. Goodenough also reported that the children in her sample showed more aggressive episodes on days when they were ill than when they were healthy.

Hartup (1974) found that beginning around age 4, direct physical aggression began to decrease, whereas verbal aggression (such as name-calling and teasing) became more common. In addition, relational aggression also becomes evident between the ages of 3 to 5 (Crick et al., 1999).

The emergence of many of the processes that we discussed in connection with moral development seems to account for the gradual decline of physical aggression between the ages of 3 and 5. During this time, children develop more self-regulation and the control of antisocial behaviors moves from the external to the internal. In addition, the development of language enables the child to use verbal aggression as well as or in addition to physical aggression.

Middle Childhood

After the preschool years, aggression tends to be elicited primarily by perceived threats and by attacks against one's ego or sense of self (Hartup, 1974). At this time, children's aggression tends to be more intentional, hostile, and reactive than instrumental. Children are now better able to differentiate intentional from unintentional harm and are less likely to retaliate against unintentional harm. In addition, aggression becomes progressively more verbal and symbolic, in part because children's increased verbal abilities permit more verbal expressions of anger than was the case in the preschool period (Hartup, 1974). Because of cognitive advances and the increased saliency of social relationships, relational aggression becomes more pominant during middle childhood (Crick et al., 1999).

How stable is aggression in "normal" children? In order to determine the answer to this question, Kohn (1977) conducted a 5-year longitudinal study ending when the children were in the fourth grade. On the one hand, angry–defiant aggression over this period was fairly stable, with aggressiveness in preschool correlating 0.36 with aggressiveness in the fourth grade. On the other hand, 59% of the preschoolers who had scored highest on aggression were no longer considered disturbed in fourth grade, and 14% of the high-scoring preschool children were now considered among the best-adjusted fourth graders. Moreover, about 15% of children who were considered well adjusted in preschool were rated in the fourth grade as either extremely aggressive or extremely apathetic. Thus, although there is some stability of aggression in the early elementary years, extreme change can occur as well. The task is to determine whether we can find reliable ways to decide which specific aggressive preschool children will remain aggressive, and which will change.

Some hints regarding an answer to this question come from the work of S.B. Campbell (1991) and Egeland, Kalkoske, Gottesman, and Erickson (1990). Campbell (1991) found that when aggressiveness and noncompliance in kindergarten children were accompanied by hyperactivity and inattentiveness, the aggression was more likely to persist into the school years. The presence of stress in the family and a negative and conflictful relationship between the mother and child also predicted stability of aggression. In a similar vein, Egeland et al. (1990) found that aggression was more likely to persist over the first three grades of school if the mother was diagnosed as having depression. Thus, increased stability of aggression seems to be related to both characteristics of the child (hyperactivity and inattention) and to characteristics of the home situation (stress, maternal depression, and poor mother–child relationships).

Middle and High School Years

In an attempt to get a picture of aggression in the late elementary and early adolescent years, Cairns and colleagues (R. B. Cairns, B. D. Cairns, Neckerman, Ferguson, & Gariépy, 1989) conducted a longitudinal study of children from Grade 4 through Grade 9 (ages 10 through 15). They found that although boys continued to show aggression through direct attacks and confrontations, girls' physical aggression decreased while their verbal and indirect aggression increased. For example, girls would attack other girls by ostracizing them or by spreading tales about them. Interestingly, the researchers also found that the proportion of highly aggressive boys decreased during this period, a finding consistent with the data reported in chapter 1 that a large proportion of violent juvenile crime is actually committed by a very small proportion of youths.

Adolescence presents a two-edged sword. Aggression shows a general decline during this period (Loeber, 1982). At the same time, however, the overall level of antisocial and delinquent behavior increases, at least temporarily (D. R. Moore & Arthur, 1989). More importantly, self-reported serious violent offenses rise dramatically beginning around age 12 and peak at age 17 (Coie & Dodge, 1998).

Sex Differences

Research indicates that males exhibit more physical aggression than do females and that this difference manifests itself "beginning in the toddler period when children first become capable of hostile intentions" (Beal, 1994, p. 187). Indeed, precursors to this difference occur as early as 6 months, when males are more likely than females to grab toys held by same-age peers (Hay, Nash, & Pedersen, 1983). However, it is not until the preschool years that this difference becomes striking (Coie & Dodge, 1998).

Within the United States, this sex difference in physical aggression holds across socioeconomic status (Beal, 1994; Coie & Dodge, 1998). In addition, it is also manifest in a variety of regions around the world, including Mexico, Britian, Switzerland, Ethiopia, Kenya, India, the Philippines, and Okinawa (Coie & Dodge, 1998).

Both teacher and peer reports indicate that preschool girls show more relational aggression and less physical aggression than do boys (Crick et al., 1999). In addition, this sex difference appears to hold, albeit it less strongly, during middle childhood as well. Finally, as suggested by the results of the Cairns et al. study just described, adolescent females also seem to engage in more relational aggression than do males (Crick et al., 1999).

Although males show more physical aggression than females, the difference between the total amount of aggression exhibited by males and females narrows considerably in middle childhood when both physical and relational aggression are taken into account (Crick et al., 1999). Interestingly, physically aggressive females and relationally aggressive males show more psychological maladjustment than do relationally aggressive females and physically aggressive males (Crick et al., 1999).

Researchers have suggested a number of possible reasons for observed sex differences in aggression:

- Innate differences in behaviors, such as impulsivity, might mediate early sex differences in conflict and aggression (Coie & Dodge, 1998).
- Because males have an innately higher level of pain tolerance, they might persist longer than females in instrumentally aggressive behaviors that result in conflict with their peers (Coie & Dodge, 1998).
- Relatedly, young females might withdraw relatively quickly from competition for objects, hence negatively reinforcing boys' instrumental aggression (Coie & Dodge, 1998).
- Parental perception of male infants as stronger and more hardy than females might lead to self-fulfilling prophecies in behavioral outcomes (Coie & Dodge, 1998).
- Females' more advanced verbal development might help them to inhibit physical aggression and to employ verbal aggression instead (Crick et al., 1999).
- The generally rougher, hierarchical, and more competitive nature of young boys' play groups might also reinforce boys' physical aggression (Beal, 1994).

- Because girls' play groups generally involve cooperation and verbal social interaction and relationship building, frustration in such situations might make girls more prone to relational aggression (Beal, 1994; Crick et al., 1999).

This discussion of sex differences in aggression has been necessarily brief. However, the question of the relationship between aggression and gender is a complicated one that we continue to examine in various contexts throughout the remainder of this volume.

SUMMARY

Aggression is defined as overt behavior designed to do damage to another person or to that person's property. The three major types of aggression are physical, verbal, and relational aggression. In addition, aggression can be hostile (designed to cause suffering), instrumental (used as a means of obtaining something else), or reactive (an act committed in response to another act).

A multitude of theories have been developed to explain aggression. Freud emphasized the importance of biologically based drives and processes such as sublimation, displacement, and catharsis. Despite its popularity, the cathartic hypothesis has received little support from empirical research.

According to behavioristic/social-learning theory, aggression can be learned through the processes of classical conditioning and observational learning and maintained through both positive and negative reinforcement (including escape and avoidance learning). Perhaps the most famous theory of aggression is the frustration–aggression hypothesis. Although frustration-based explanations of aggression are popular, research indicates that frustration often produces general arousal or regression rather than aggression. For this reason, theorists such as Berkowitz have postulated an indirect path from frustration to aggression.

Much current theorizing on children's aggression focuses on the role of cognitions, especially the child's social information processing. Recent research indicates that hyperaggressive children might have a hostile attributional bias that leads to aggression. Other theorists argue that aggression is maintained because aggressive children expect that their aggressive behavior will pay off and because they attach much value to their ability to dominate and control others.

Some theorists believe that children have a natural propensity toward aggression that must be controlled either from without or from within. Social control theory argues that aggression is controlled by emotional bonds built up between the child and society. Self-control theory, on the other hand, hypothesizes that aggressive children are driven by short-term gains and hence unable to delay immediate gratification.

Research has delineated the developmental course of aggression in childhood and adolescence. Initially, the infant reacts to frustrating situations with intense negative emotional behavior that becomes more focused as the baby grows older. During toddlerhood and the preschool years, children begin to develop full-fledged aggression and to use motor activity (such as biting, hitting, and kicking) to express this aggression toward others. In particular, children's aggression at this time is often physical and instrumental, designed to get the child something tangible such as a toy.

As children move into the elementary school years, aggression becomes more reactive, intentional, retaliatory, and symbolic (Hartup, 1974). In addition, aggression becomes more verbal and hostile. Finally, relational aggression is quite common among 9- to 12-year-olds.

Two major sex differences in aggression have emerged. First, by the early preschool years, males are more physically aggressive, whereas females are more verbally aggressive. And secondly, females tend to be more relationally aggressive than males.

Overall, aggression declines as youngsters learn new methods of meeting their needs. Thus, by the time youths begin to enter puberty, a myriad of developmental forces have combined to reduce aggressiveness and to help them control this aspect of their behavior. As we shall see, however, these controlling factors sometimes fail to do the job and the juvenile, instead of exhibiting less aggression, begins to show even more. I discuss this issue in the next chapter.

CHAPTER 3

Abnormal Manifestations
of Youthful Aggression

In the previous chapter, we considered how aggression develops and becomes controlled in the case of "normal" children. In this chapter, we now turn to a discussion of "abnormal" manifestations of youthful aggression.

"NORMAL" AND "ABNORMAL" FORMS OF AGGRESSION

If children and adolescents—especially males—often act aggressively in the process of growing up, how do we distinguish such normal aggression from the type of aggression and violence we consider to be excessive or abnormal? Although there is no single answer to this question, the following guidelines can be helpful:

• *Abnormally aggressive behavior deviates qualitatively from "normal" forms of aggression.* For example, we have seen that getting into physical and verbal spats is quite common among preschool and early elementary school children. But the acts of setting fires and torturing animals (particularly pets) are qualitatively different from such normal displays of aggression, and as such would probably be considered abnormal.

• *Abnormal aggression differs quantitatively from normal aggression in terms of its frequency, intensity, or duration.* For example, a certain number of temper tantrums are normal for preschool children, but when a 3-year-old throws one tantrum after another, that would probably be considered abnormal. Likewise, small children often hit each other in the course of play. However, if one child's hitting were clearly more intense than that of other children, that aggression would again be considered abnormal. Finally, as Dawe (1934) discovered, most spats involving preschool children last less than 1 minute. Thus, if a preschooler's aggression typically last much longer than this (e.g., 5 minutes), this too would be considered abnormal.

• *Abnormal aggression deviates significantly from that which is "normal" for children of the same developmental level and gender.* As we have seen, some forms of aggression are normal at some ages but not at other ages. For example, diffuse temper tantrums are normal for young preschool children but not for elementary school children. Similarly, because physical aggression is more common in males than in females, the same level of physical aggression in a 7-year-old girl would probably be of more concern than it would in a 7-year-old boy.

Hyperaggressive Functioning

In addition to the question of how abnormal aggressive behavior differs from normal aggression, we might also want to know whether a child's aggression indicates that the child is functioning in a psychologically abnormal fashion. The following guidelines can help us answer this question:

• *In hyperaggressive children, the number of* different *aggressive behaviors deviates significantly from the norm.* For some children, aggression might be limited just to hitting with the hands. Other children, however, might engage in a wide variety of aggressive behaviors, including hitting with the hand, biting, shoving, hitting with weapons, starting fires, and using knives. Clearly, the greater the number of different aggressive behaviors, the more concerned we would be.

• *Hyperaggressive children's aggression tends to significantly interfere with other aspects of their development.* For example, a child might be so aggressive in school that it affects his school performance. Or, a child might be so aggressive that the other children shun and ostracize him. In both cases, the child's aggressiveness interferes with important developmental processes such as school learning and social interaction.

• *The behavior of hyperaggressive children significantly interferes with the behavior or property of others.* Most of the inconvenience, harm, and property damage related to children's aggression are minor and episodic. However, sometimes they are not. For example, the child who is continually aggressive in school might also negatively affect the ability of other children to learn. Or, the child who burns down a building will cause considerable damage to someone else.

The Nature of Psychological Disorders

Do hyperaggressive children have a psychological disorder, or are they (as some of my students ask) just "bad kids"? In order to deal with this questions, we first consider the question of what constitutes a "real" or "true" psychological disorder.

In most cases, it is relatively simple to determine if a child has a real physical disorder such as strep throat or pneumonia. Both cases involve certain external symptoms such as an elevated temperature, coughing, or a red throat. However, if the external symptoms leave the issue in doubt, the underlying tissue can be examined to determine the presence of the disease-causing agent.

Such is seldom the case for psychological disorders, because there is no underlying tissue to examine except in rare circumstances where the disorder involves physical abnormalities within the brain or nervous system. Thus, the question arises: How do we know if a psychological disorder is real (true) or not?

The very pragmatic answer to this question is that a psychological disorder is one which is defined as such in *The Diagnostic and Statistical Manual of Mental Disorders*. This book, commonly referred to as the *DSM*, contains the official list of psychological disorders as determined by experts in psychiatry and abnormal psychology. At various intervals, these experts divide into committees, which in turn recommend which psychological disorders to include in the *DSM*. The *DSM* is currently in its fourth edition, and hence is commonly referred to as the *DSM-IV* (American Psychiatric Association [APA], 1994). In the *DSM*, each disorder is defined by a listing of behaviorally defined symptoms or what I call *definitional criteria*. Those disorders included constitute the official mental disorders accepted by the psychological and psychiatric communities. Those that are not included are not considered official disorders.

Some authorities might argue that a psychological disorder could be considered real if it is contained in the *DSM*. However, just defining something as a disorder does not necessarily make it one. After all, in the process of changing from one edition of the *DSM* to another, names and definitions of disorders are sometimes modified. Indeed, entire disorders sometimes come into and go out of existence from one edition to the next. For example, *homosexuality* used to be considered a disorder in earlier versions of the *DSM*, but not anymore. It is thus apparent that in order to be considered real, a psychological disorder needs something more than a place in the *DSM*. In this case, I argue that something more turns out to be specific aspects of the psychometric qualities of *reliability* and *validity* that I discussed briefly in chapter 1.

As applied to psychological disorders, "reliability refers to the consistency of results obtained from using a diagnostic instrument" (Wenar, 1994, p. 75). In other words, reliability is the quality that allows multiple mental health practitioners to agree that a particular child has a particular disorder. Reliability thus helps ensure that whatever is being diagnosed is being diagnosed consistently from one child to the next.

The second important characteristic that a psychological disorder must have to be considered real is the type of validity known as *construct validity*, defined as the extent of the relationship between an hypothesized psychological disorder "and other variables that should be related to it theoretically" (Wenar, 1994, p. 75).

Waldman and colleagues described two major aspects of construct validity (Waldman, Lilienfeld, & Lahey, 1995). The first, *structural validation*, refers to the extent to which the disorder's actual internal structure parallels the disorder's hypothesized internal structure. For example, if it is hypothesized that a psychological disorder consists of two interrelated dimensions and if empirical research indicates that the disorder actually does possess those two interrelated dimensions, then that disorder possesses structural validation. In general, studies of structural validation involve the use of a number of statistical techniques such as *internal consistency analysis, factor analysis,* and *cluster analysis* (Waldman et al., 1995).

A second major aspect of construct validity is *external validation.* This aspect refers to the extent that the category provides additional information above and beyond the information provided by the definitional criteria themselves. For example, knowing that a child has a disorder should give us more knowledge about the child than simply the fact that he or she meets the definitional criteria for that disorder. If this is actually the case, then that disorder possesses external validation.

Wicks-Nelson and Israel (2000) indicated a number of specific types of information important for good external validation:

- *Information regarding the cause (or etiology) of the disorder.*
- *Information regarding the course of the disorder in the absence of treatment.*
- *Information regarding appropriate types of therapy for this disorder.*
- *Information about the prognosis (or likely outcome) of the disorder with therapy.*
- *Information regarding "correlates" of the disorder.* Unlike *definitional criteria,* which are the behavioral symptoms the child must have in order to be diagnosed with a particular psychological disorder, *correlates* are behaviors and characteristics that often accompany the disorder but are not part of the diagnosis. To the extent that a diagnosis of a disorder also enables us to predict accurately which other characteristics and behaviors the child will have, to that extent the disorder has external validation.

The *external validation* aspect of construct validity, then, refers to the extent that knowing the child's diagnosis enables one to know other psychologically relevant things about the child as well. Note that external validation "saves" the diagnosis from being a purely descriptive label. Without such validation, the diagnosis would be nothing more than a shorthand label for the behaviors that define the disorder. However, a diagnosis with good external validation is much more than a label, because it provides information over and above that supplied by the label itself.

PSYCHOLOGICAL DISORDERS
RELATED TO YOUTHFUL AGGRESSION

As indicated in the previous section, the question of whether hyperaggressive children have a real psychological disorder boils down to the question of whether certain relevant psychological disorders possess reliability and construct validity. In a very real sense, much of the remainder of this book constitutes an attempt to deal with this issue. I begin this task by discussing a number of psychological disorders related to youthful aggression and violence.

Oppositional Defiant Disorder

Oppositional defiant disorder (ODD) involves a "recurrent pattern of defiant, disobedient, and hostile behavior which is manifested toward authority figures" and which causes the child "significant impairment" in everyday functioning (APA, 1994, p. 91). As seen in Box 3.1, children with this disorder are often noncompliant and lose their temper easily. This pattern of behavior must last for 6 months or longer before the child can be diagnosed as having ODD. This dis-

---

BOX 3.1

DEFINITIONAL CRITERIA FOR OPPOSITIONAL DEFIANT DISORDER

A. A pattern of negativistic, hostile, and defiant behavior lasting at least 6 months, during which four (or more) of the following are present:

1. Often loses temper
2. often argues with adults
3. often actively defies or refuses to comply with adults' requests or rules
4. often deliberately annoys people
5. often blames others for his or her mistakes or misbehavior
6. is often touchy or easily annoyed by others
7. is often angry and resentful
8. is often spiteful or vindictive.

   Note: Consider a criterion met only if the behavior occurs more frequently than is typically observed in individuals of comparable age and developmental level.

B. The disturbance in behavior causes clinically significant impairment in social, academic, or occupational functioning.

C. The behaviors do not occur exclusively during the course of a Psychotic or Mood Disorder.

D. Criteria are not met for Conduct Disorder, and, if the individual is age 18 years or older, criteria are not met for Antisocial Personality Disorder.

Source: APA (1994, pp. 93–94). Reprinted with permission from the *Diagnostic and Statistical Manual of Mental Disorders,* Fourth Edition. Copyright © 1994 American Psychiatric Association.

order usually develops over a period of years and typically manifests itself before the age of 8. It occurs in from 2% to 16% of the population, and is more prevalent among males prior to puberty (APA, 1994).

As you can see, many of the definitional criteria for ODD involve anger, aggression, or related behaviors. For example, "losing temper" could well involve aggressive verbal behaviors such as yelling, making threats, and name-calling, as well as aggressive physical behaviors such as hitting, biting, and kicking. "Annoying others" could also involve aggressive behaviors such as interrupting, name-calling, teasing, poking, stealing things, or hitting. Finally, "spiteful" and "resentful" behaviors could also involve aggressive components, especially the intent to harm either physically or psychologically.

Conduct Disorder

Whereas ODD relates primarily to the refusal of the child to obey commands from authority figures, the term *conduct disorder* (CD) is more directly related to childhood aggression and violence (see Box 3.2). Defined as "a repetitive and persistent pattern of behavior in which the basic rights of others or major age-appropriate societal norms or rules are violated" (APA, 1994, p. 85), CD involves aggression to people and animals, the destruction of property, deceitfulness or theft, and serious violation of rules. Three or more of the specific behaviors must have occurred within the past year in order for the diagnosis to be made. In general, the diagnosis is typically made for youths under the age of 18. Conduct disorder is estimated to occur in from 6% to 16% of males under 18, and from 2% to 9% of females under 18 (APA, 1994). It is interesting to note that although the characteristic of "little empathy and little concern for the feelings, wishes, and well-being of others" is considered a correlate of CD, it is not one of the definitional criteria (APA, 1994).

Subtypes.   A number of researchers have suggested various subtypes of CD. For example, children with the *aggressive* subtype tend to engage in fighting, property destruction, and cruelty to animals or persons. On the other hand, children considered as having the *delinquent* subtype are more likely to engage in theft, running away, lying, setting fires, and truancy (Achenbach, 1993; Kazdin, 1995).

Earlier versions of the *DSM* recognized the distinction between *undersocialized* and *socialized* types of CD (APA, 1980, 1987). The undersocialized type refers to youths who are not able to form social relationships and who tend to commit antisocial acts by themselves, whereas the socialized type refers to youngsters who do maintain social relationships and tend to commit antisocial acts with others (Frick, 1998). In general, undersocialized juveniles tend to be aggressive, whereas socialized youths tend to be delinquent.

Another distinction involves the *overt* versus *covert* type of CD (Kazdin, 1995). Overt types of CD include behaviors that are observable or confrontative in

---

BOX 3.2

DEFINITIONAL CRITERIA FOR CONDUCT DISORDER

A. A repetitive and persistent pattern of behavior in which the basic rights of others or major age-appropriate societal norms or rules are violated, as manifested by the presence of three (or more) of the following criteria in the past 12 months, with at least one criterion present in the past 6 months.

Aggression to people and animals

1. Often bullies, threatens, or intimidates others
2. often initiates physical fights
3. has used a weapon that can cause serious physical harm to others (e.g., a bat, brick, broken bottle, knife, gun)
4. has been physically cruel to people
5. has been physically cruel to animals
6. has stolen while confronting a victim (e g , mugging, purse snatching, extortion, armed robbery)
7. has forced someone into sexual activity.

Destruction of property

8. Has deliberately engaged in fire setting with intention of causing serious damage
9. has deliberately destroyed others' property (other than by fire setting).

Deceitfulness or theft

10. Has broken into someone else's house, building, or car
11. often lies to obtain goods or favors or to avoid obligations (i.e., "con" others)
12. has stolen items of nontrivial value without confronting a victim (e.g., shoplifting, but without breaking and entering; forgery).

Serious violations of rules

13. Often stays out at night despite parental prohibitions, beginning before age 13 years
14. has run away from home overnight at least twice while living in parental or parental surrogate home (or once without returning for a lengthy period)
15. is often truant from school, beginning before age 13 years.

B. The disturbance in behavior causes clinically significant impairment in social, academic, or occupational functioning.

C. If the individual is age 18 years or older, criteria are not met for Antisocial Personality Disorder.

Source: APA (1994, pp. 90–91). Reprinted with permission from the *Diagnostic and Statistical Manual of Mental Disorders,* Fourth Edition. Copyright © 1994 American Psychiatric Association.

nature, such as fighting, arguing, and throwing temper tantrums (Kazdin, 1995). Covert problems, on the other hand, are more concealed and involve behaviors such as stealing, lying, setting fires, and being truant (Kazdin, 1995). Support for the construct validity of this distinction comes from studies that find the behaviors defining these two subtypes tend to cluster together (Loeber & Schmaling, 1985a). In addition, overt CD children tend to experience family conflict and to be irritable, negative, and resentful, whereas covert children tend come from homes lower in family cohesion and to be less social, more anxious, and more suspicious of others (Kazdin, 1992). The overt type of CD thus seems more related to hyperaggression than does the covert type.

More recently, Frick and his colleagues have proposed the distinction between the *callous–unemotional* and *impulsive/conduct-problem* types of CD (Frick, O'Brien, Wootton, & McBurnett, 1994). Callous–unemotional youngsters show a willingness to use others for their own gain as well as a lack of empathy and guilt. Impulsive/conduct-problem youths exhibit impulsivity, lack of self-regulation, and an inability to tolerate frustration or delay gratification (Frick et al., 1994).

Age of Onset. CD can either begin in childhood or adolescence. Whereas the *childhood onset type* starts by the age of 10 and is fully manifest by puberty, the *adolescent-onset type* is diagnosed only when the criteria become evident after the age of 10. Childhood-onset CD is found predominantly in males and is characterized by hyperactivity, aggression, poor verbal skills, poor school achievement, and poor interpersonal relationships. Because this type of CD is more likely to persist into adulthood, this group of children is referred to as having the *childhood life-course-persistent* type of CD (Moffitt, 1993).

As you might suspect, CD seems more prevalent among adolescents (where it involves approximately 7% of the population) than among children (where it occurs in about 4% of children; Kazdin, 1995). Males predominate less in the adolescent-onset variety of CD, which involves less aggressiveness and fewer school problems. In addition, adolescent-onset youths tend to have better social skills and to be more involved with their peers and more heavily influenced by delinquent companions (Maughan & Rutter, 1998). In part, these differences might reflect the sex differences already mentioned. Because adolescent-onset CD is often of limited duration, Moffitt and colleagues refer to this type of antisocial behavior as *adolescence-limited* CD (Moffitt, 1993).

Comorbidity. The terms *comorbidity* or *co-occurrence* refer to the tendency for one disorder to be accompanied by the presence of another disorder, and the extent of comorbidity is referred to as the *comorbidity rate* (Wicks-Nelson & Israel, 2000). Research demonstrates that the comorbidity rate between CD and ODD is quite high; in one study, for example, from 84% to 96% of children with CD also met the criteria for ODD (Hinshaw, Lahey, & Hart, 1993). But most children diagnosed as ODD do not progress to CD: 50% maintain their ODD diagnosis, 25% eventually cease to display ODD problems, and only 25% receive a subsequent diagnosis of CD (Hinshaw et al., 1993). It appears that most oppositional children do not become conduct disordered, but that most children who develop CD are also oppositional.

The results of the Hinshaw et al. (1993) study might lead one to wonder whether CD and ODD are in fact the same disorder. In one study, Frick and colleagues examined the question of whether ODD was simply a less severe form of CD (Frick et al., 1991). The results indicated that the participants could be classified into one group of children with predominantly ODD symptoms and a second group with a combination of both ODD and CD symptoms. This research thus indicates that ODD is separate from CD and can be found without CD being present; it also suggests that ODD often accompanies CD.

If ODD and CD are in fact two separate disorders, what specific factors distinguish them from each other? To study this question, Frick and colleagues analyzed descriptive data from parents and teachers by use of the technique of factor analysis (Frick et al., 1991). Essentially, this procedure yields separate and identifiable "clumps" of behaviors. The behaviors in each clump tend to correlate highly with each other, but not with behaviors in other clumps. These clumps are called *factors,* and each factor is given a name indicating what seems to be its essential nature.

Frick et al. (1991) found two such factors in their study, which they called *ODD/aggression* and *CD/delinquency.* In general, the ODD/aggression factor corresponded to the *DSM-IV* definitional criteria for ODD, and the CD/delinquency factor corresponded to the *DSM-IV* definition of CD. Nevertheless, there were some differences. First, four common behaviors occurred in both factors: Lies, blames others, bullies, and fights. Thus, these behaviors seem to be common to both ODD and CD. Second, the common factors included two aspects of aggression, bullies and fights, thus suggesting that ODD involves aggression toward peers in addition to defiance of authority. Third, the CD/delinquency factor included behaviors associated with stealing, whereas the ODD/aggression factor did not, thus suggesting that ODD/aggression is more concerned with aggression toward persons, whereas CD/delinquency is more concerned with aggression toward property.

Attention-Deficit/Hyperactivity Disorder

Attention-deficit/hyperactivity disorder (ADHD) refers to a "persistent pattern of inattention and/or hyperactivity–impulsivity that is more frequent and severe than is typically observed in individuals at a comparable level of development" (APA, 1994, p. 78). This disorder involves three major symptoms: attentional problems, impulsivity, and motor hyperactivity. In addition, the symptoms must have been present before age 7, some impairment must occur in at least two settings (e.g., both at home and at school), and the symptoms must interfere with some other aspect of the child's development. This disorder, which occurs in 3% to 5% of elementary school children, is more prevalent among males than females by a ratio between 4:1 and 9:1 (APA, 1994).

ADHD children are not necessarily aggressive. However, the core symptom of impulsivity suggests a lack of behavioral inhibition that might also be found in aggression. In addition, the core symptom of "interrupts or intrudes on others" can also involve aggression. Furthermore, researcher and theoretician Russell Barkley (1997) argued that "ADHD involves delays in the development of inhibition and self-regulation" (p. viii), two processes that, as we have seen, are intimately linked with moral development and aggression.

It is clear that ADHD is closely related to the problem of hyperaggressiveness in children and adolescents. Indeed, it is estimated that as many as 65% of ADHD children are comorbid for ODD (Barkley, Anastopoulos, Guevremont, & Fletcher, 1992), while as many as 30% are comorbid for CD (Barkley, 1990). Thus, many children diagnosed with ADHD also have one or more other disorders related to increased levels of aggressive behavior.

Are ADHD and CD the same disorder? In one relevant study, Schachar and Wachsmuth (1991) compared ADHD and CD children in terms of the amount of psychosocial adversity and family dysfunction the children experienced. The ADHD-alone group was associated with prolonged child–parent separations, but not with parent–child dysfunctions. The CD-alone group was associated with high levels of both adversity and child–parent dysfunction. Finally, the combined ADHD–CD group was associated with moderate adversity and dysfunctional parent–child relationships. Since the ADHD-alone and CD-alone groups manifested distinct sets of correlates, this study supports the construct validity of the two disorders. In addition, it also suggests that CD is more directly related to dysfunctional parent–child interaction than is ADHD.

Research indicates that children with a dual diagnosis of ADHD and CD have a particularly poor prognosis. For example, in one study of incarcerated 16-year-olds, juveniles in a combined ADHD–CD group had more arrests and were arrested at an earlier age than were those in a CD-only group (Forehand, Wierson, Frame, Kempton, & Armistead, 1991). Because the average age at first arrest for the ADHD-CD group was 11.64 years, and because Tolan (1987) found that committing a first offense before the age of 12 is the best predictor of future delinquency, the prognosis for children having both ADHD and CD seems especially poor.

The combination of early aggression and hyperactivity is also related to problems in adulthood. For example, Magnusson and colleagues (Andersson, Magnusson, & Wennberg, 1997) obtained teacher ratings on hyperactivity and aggressiveness for 540 13-year-old males. Twelve years later, the researchers found that of the subjects who were rated as unusually hyperactive and aggressive at age 13, 28% developed alcoholism and criminality before the age of 25, compared with 3% of the "normal" boys.

In a follow-back study, Vitelli (1996) studied the relationship between adult criminality and childhood CD and ADHD. Based on the results of record searches and self-reports of 100 adult maximum security inmates, Vitelli found that 63% of the inmates met the *DSM-IV* criteria for CD. However, although significant comorbidity was found between CD and ADHD for this sample, CD was the only significant predictor of adult criminality. Thus, ADHD by itself does not seem to be a potent predictor of adult criminality.

In summing up the research on differences between ADHD and CD children, Wenar (1994) suggested that ADHD children have more cognitive deficits, more achievement deficits, more off-task behavior, and a more prominent organic etiology. On the other hand, CD children have more antisocial parents, more family hostility, come from a lower socioeconomic status, have more social skills, and have a worse prognosis. Finally, as we have seen, children comorbid for both disorders have the worst of both worlds: lower academic attainment, more school expulsions, more antisocial behavior, more substance abuse, a poorer occupational adjustment, more parental hostility, and more parental delinquency.

Other Psychological Disorders

ODD, CD, and ADHD are considered to be "disruptive behavior disorders" (APA, 1994) and are most closely associated with youthful aggression and violence. I now examine some other disorders related to juvenile antisocial behavior.

Depression. The *DSM-IV* contains categories for two types of depression: *major depressive disorder* (also called *depression*) and *bipolor disorder* (also called *manic-depressive disorder*; APA, 1994). Depressed children exhibit signs of intense and pervasive unhappiness, a lack of interest or pleasure in activities, feelings of worthlessness or guilt, and changes in physical activities such as eating, sleeping, and motor activity. These children are constantly "down" and may be suicidal. Children with bipolar disorder also show the aforementioned symptoms. However, for these children, such depressive episodes tend to alternate with "manic" episodes in which the child shows an unusual amount of optimism, activity, and energy. Although neither of these disorders involves aggression as a defining characteristic, we will see that many aggressive children also exhibit depressive symptoms of one type or another.

Posttraumatic Stress Disorder. Children who experience *posttraumatic stress disorder* (PTSD) have undergone an extremely traumatic event that they subsequently re-experience in an emotionally negative fashion (APA, 1994). Among the symptoms of PTSD are anger and irritability, and we will see that young-sters living in dangerous neighborhoods are especially at risk for this disorder.

Intermittent Explosive Disorder.   *Intermittent explosive disorder* (IED) is char-acterized by "discrete episodes of failure to resist aggressive impulses resulting in serious assaults or destruction of property" (APA, 1994, p. 609). The *DSM-IV* considers this to be a disorder of late adolescence or early adulthood and directs that it be diagnosed only if other potential disorders of aggression have been ruled out.

Juvenile Delinquency

ADHD, ODD, CD, depression, bipolar disorder, PTSD, and IED are all psycho-logical or psychiatric concepts that refer to mental or psychological disorders. On the other hand, *juvenile delinquency* is not a psychological term but rather a *legal* concept, which refers to a situation in which a court finds that a juvenile has committed an illegal act (Shoemaker, 1996). There are typically two types of acts that are illegal for juveniles, *index crimes* and *status offenses.* An index crime is an act that is illegal no matter what the age of the perpetrator. For example, murder and theft are both index crimes, because they are illegal no matter whether the person committing the act is 12 or 112. Status offenses, on the other hand, are acts that are illegal only for a juvenile (typically defined as some-one beneath the age of 18). Examples of status crimes might include being tru-ant and running away (Wicks-Nelson & Israel, 2000).

Studies based on participants' reports of their own behavior indicate that as many as 80% to 90% of youths engage in behavior that is technically illegal (Moore & Arthur, 1989). Some of these delinquent acts include aggression, but many of them do not. In general, given the apparently widespread tendency of adolescents to violate some aspect of the law, a certain amount of delinquency must be considered statistically normal at this stage in life. However, serious and/or frequent episodes of delinquency are cause for concern, and it is this persistent and serious delinquency that seems most related to the hyperaggres-siveness with which we are concerned.

Antisocial Personality Disorder

One psychological disorder of adulthood that is closely related to youthful aggression and violence is that of *antisocial personality disorder* (APD). This dis-order involves a "pervasive pattern of disregard for, and violation of, the rights of others" (APA, 1994, p. 645). Behavioral patterns associated with APD in-clude such acts as assault, destroying property, harassing others, stealing, il-legal activity whether or not detected, driving while intoxicated, and related activities (APA, 1994). In order to be diagnosed with APD, the individual must be over the age of 18 and must have shown symptoms of CD since at least the age of 15.

APD is related to the concept of *psychopathy.* In his classic work, Cleckley (1976) described *psychopaths* as superficially charming and often intelligent people who are selfish, unable to give love or affection, and who have no internalized moral or ethical standards. These individuals experience no guilt at violating ethical norms. Psychopaths might or might not engage in criminal careers and might or might not commit violent acts. Although many individuals diagnosed with APD might also be considered psychopaths, APD refers to a set of behaviors, whereas psychopathy refers to a set of personality characteristics.

Related to the term psychopath is the term *sociopath.* Although these two terms are often used interchangeably, there is a technical difference: The sociopath is an *"habitual* criminal offender who fails to learn from experience" (Bartol, 1995, p. 58, emphasis in original), whereas the psychopath does not necessarily engage in criminal activity.

HYPERAGGRESSIVE CHILDREN: A QUALITATIVE OVERVIEW

Although we have already seen the list of the behaviors needed for children to be classified as having one of the disruptive behavior disorders, such clinical lists often do not provide an experiential understanding of these children. In order to get a better idea of what it's like to live with a hyperaggressive child, we turn to a picture of these children drawn largely through the qualitative research of Carolyn Webster-Stratton and colleagues (Webster-Stratton & Herbert, 1994; Webster-Stratton & Spitzer, 1996).

Aggressive Behavior

Parents of hyperaggressive children portray their offspring as being tyrants who are prone to fits of physical aggression. Parents are often the targets of their child's aggression, and parents report feeling victimized, insecure, and of always having to be "on guard" against their child (Webster-Stratton & Herbert, 1994). In one case, a child threw his booster seat at his mother, hitting her in the jaw. In another case, a child "flew into a rage" and threw a fork at his mother, hitting her in the face and causing her to bleed (Webster-Stratton & Herbert, 1994). These children also use verbal aggression, as in the case of the child who told her father she wished he was dead (Webster-Stratton & Spitzer, 1996).

In addition, these children also exhibit aggression toward other members of the family, including pets. In one case, a child split his sister's lip, knocked her out by hitting her over the head with a brass pitcher, and put plastic bags over her head. Another child was once caught holding the head of the family's cat in the toilet with the lid shut (Webster-Stratton & Herbert, 1994). Finally, these children often destroy property and household objects. In one case, the parents reported that their aggressive child was literally destroying their new house (Webster-Stratton & Herbert, 1994).

Hyperaggressive children also behave violently toward children outside the family. One parent described how her son would seem to "seek out" other children to hurt them. She reported that when they went to the zoo, she found her son taking handfuls of sand and throwing them at little children in strollers (Webster-Stratton & Herbert, 1994). In some cases, this aggression is sexual in nature. In general, their aggressive behavior causes these children to be rejected by their peers and by their peers' parents. Thus, hyperaggressive children often lack "normal" friends; moreover, their parents are often shunned by other parents who don't want their own children associating with them (Webster-Stratton & Herbert, 1994). Parents also report that their hyperaggressive children are noncompliant and defiant. These children are described as stubborn and as enjoying the power that their tantrums and threats of tantrums get them. Parents routinely describe huge arguments with their children that often end with screaming and yelling. When parents do get their hyperaggressive children to comply, it is often only after they have expended a great deal of energy in the process (Webster-Stratton & Spitzer, 1996).

Other Behavioral Problems

Hyperaggressive children also exhibit other behavioral problems in addition to aggression and noncompliance. Sleeping and eating are especially troublesome. These children often battle parents about bedtime and sometimes seem to have little need for sleep. Similarly, fights over eating and meals are also common (Webster-Stratton & Herbert, 1994). In addition, changes in routines and transitions from one activity to another often provoke antisocial outbursts. These children are also prone to fears, especially at night. In one case, a father reported that his son lay awake in his bed for hours due to anxieties (Webster-Stratton & Herbert, 1994). Finally, many parents describe their hyperaggressive children as highly active, loud, overexcited, "wound up," and out of control from an early age. One mother reported that her son began at the age of 15 months to run around and destroy things and had continued to do so ever since. A father reported that his son often ran through the house screaming in a "fit of hyper-activity" (Webster-Stratton & Herbert, 1994, p. 50).

Positive Qualities

And yet, these children also have positive qualities as well. Many parents describe their children as sensitive to the moods of others, as having unique cognitive abilities, and as being developmentally advanced (Webster-Stratton & Herbert, 1994). These good qualities often lead parents to view their hyperaggressive children as having *Jekyll and Hyde personalities* (Webster-Stratton & Spitzer, 1996, p. 20). Thus, these children can sometimes be sweet and charming and good natured, but then their "other side" emerges and the child turns defiant, angry, and aggressive (Webster-Stratton & Spitzer, 1996).

Effects on the Family

All of this has a strong negative effect on the family. Life with conduct-disordered children introduces stressors into the family system that often produce negative effects on the parents' marital relationship and on other members of the family. Parents (especially mothers, who typically are the primary caregivers for these children) often feel beleaguered and exhausted. Because the father commonly spends less time at home, he often has a better relationship with the child and may think that the mother is overreacting. Mothers and fathers can get into arguments over appropriate disciplinary techniques, can blame each other, and can become resentful of each other (Webster-Stratton & Spitzer, 1996).

Siblings and other members of the family can also be affected (Webster-Stratton & Spitzer, 1996). Not only are siblings directly affected, but they might experience indirect effects as well. For example, siblings might resent the parents for spending so much time with the aggressive child while ignoring them. In addition, parents might also place unreasonable expectations and responsibilities on the siblings (Webster-Stratton & Spitzer, 1996). Furthermore, the child's aggressive behavior might affect the relationship between the parents and other members of their family (e.g., grandparents, aunts, and uncles). Finally, the child's behavior not only affects the nuclear and extended family, but also the relationship between the family and other members of the community as well (Webster-Stratton & Spitzer, 1996). In Webster-Stratton's words, the child's aggression ends up having a "ripple effect" across the entire community (Webster-Stratton & Herbert, 1994, p. 50).

THE DEVELOPMENT OF ANTISOCIAL BEHAVIOR

We now turn to the question of the extent to which antisocial children will continue to manifest various externalizing problems in adolescence and adulthood. I begin with a consideration of two classic studies, one conducted in the inner city of St. Louis, the other in a semi-rural county in New York State.

The St. Louis Study

Lee Robins' study of White youths who grew up in St. Louis in the 1920s was designed to determine the childhood predictors of adult sociopathy (Robins, 1966). In this research, more than 500 subjects who had been seen as children in a guidance clinic during the 1920s were compared with 100 normal control subjects who had lived in the same neighborhood but who had not been referred for professional help. Childhood characteristics were determined on the basis of records made available to the researchers, who then determined adult characteristics through interviews with the participants.

Major Findings.   The major findings of this monumental work can be summarized as follows:

• *Children (especially boys) who were referred for antisocial behavior were more likely than other children to be diagnosed in adolescence and adulthood as delinquents, sociopaths, and criminals.*

Children who tended to develop sociopathic personalities as adults were primarily boys who had been referred to the clinic for a variety of antisocial behaviors, including (most prominently) theft, incorrigibility, running away, truancy, associating with bad companions, sexual activities, staying out late, discipline problems in school, aggressiveness, impulsivity, lack of guilt, and lying without cause.

Of all the subjects referred for antisocial behavior as children, more than a quarter (28%) were later diagnosed as sociopaths in adulthood, compared with only 2% of control children and only 4% of clinic children who received other psychiatric diagnoses as children.

Robins also found that 66% of the boys and 50% of the girls who were referred to the clinic for antisocial behavior later became officially adjudicated delinquents. In addition, 71% of the males and 40% of the females who were referred to the clinic for antisocial behavior were arrested as adults for nontraffic offenses. Indeed, arrests for murder, rape, and prostitution came *only* from persons in this group. By the time of last follow-up (at about age 44), 12% of the adult sociopaths "had given up their antisocial behavior, and an additional 27% had reduced it markedly" (Robins, 1966, p. 296). However, the remaining 61% were still very antisocial.

• *Children who were referred for antisocial behavior manifested a wide variety of nonsociopathic problems as adults.*

Of the clinic sample referred for antisocial behavior as children, only 16% were free of psychological disturbances as adults. On the other hand, 30% of the clinic sample who had other diagnoses as children were free of adult disturbance, as were 52% of the control children. Fourteen percent of the antisocial children exhibited neuroses as adults, 11% were diagnosed as psychotic, and 8% exhibited alcoholism or drug addiction. In addition, the antisocial children also exhibited a variety of other problems, including poor work histories, financial problems, marital difficulties, serious injuries, and premature death. It is thus clear that children whose aggressive and antisocial behavior is bad enough to warrant referral in the early years are at great risk for a variety of psychological problems as adults (Robins, 1966).

- *The problem behaviors of children diagnosed as sociopaths dated back, on the average, to the age of 7.*

Although the average age of referral was 14, the onset of the symptoms dated back to the beginning of school. These symptoms included aggressiveness toward parents and teachers and offenses against businesses and strangers.

- *The best single childhood predictor of later sociopathic personality was the sheer amount of childhood antisocial behavior.*

Adult sociopathic behavior could be equally well predicted by any of the following: (a) the number of different symptoms; (b) the number of episodes; and (c) the seriousness of the behavior. In particular, children with six or more different antisocial symptoms were much more likely to be diagnosed as sociopaths than other children.

- *Another major predictor of later sociopathic personality was a father who was extremely antisocial, whether or not the father lived in the home.*

Most of the children who became sociopaths had fathers who were either sociopathic or alcoholic. As a result, a large number of these children came from what Robins called "impoverished" and "broken" homes (Robins, 1966, p. 296). The father's antisocial behavior was related not only to adult sociopathy in children who were unusually antisocial, but also in children who were minimally antisocial. Furthermore, this association held up even when the father was absent due to desertion or divorce. On one hand, this finding could support a genetic theory of sociopathic personality. On the other hand, it is also compatible with an environmental explanation as well. For example, children of such fathers might live in areas where they are exposed to other antisocial children; they might receive less discipline from their mothers; they might be more likely to experience contact with the law; and the mother might also have antisocial tendencies.

- *Males and females differed in their adult outcomes.*

Robins found three major sex differences in the study. First, although boys' antisocial behaviors tended to involve theft and aggression, girls were most often referred for sexual activities, and their difficulties began somewhat later than for boys. Second, adult sociopathy occurred almost exclusively for males. And third, whereas antisocial behavior among Robins' adult men involved aggressiveness and property crimes, problems for psychopathic women tended to be confined to sexual and family areas; for example, 85% of Robins' adult female sociopaths married men with serious behavior problems.

Variables Not Related to Sociopathy.   Robins' study is almost as interesting for what it found was unrelated to adult sociopathy as for what it found was related.

- *Parental rejection (as measured by the parent treating the child in a cold manner and being strict with the child), did not predict sociopathy.*

As a matter of fact, Robins found that, "The child of the cold, stern parent had a particularly *low* rate of this disease" (Robins, 1966 p. 179, emphasis in original).

• *Living in poverty did not predict sociopathy.*

Robins' results indicated that the crucial variables in a child's future success or failure were the presence of an antisocial father and the child's own level of aggressiveness, and *not* whether the child lived in poverty.

• *Stigmatizing or labeling the child did not cause the child's subsequent sociopathic behavior.*

According to the *stigmatization* (or *labeling*) *hypothesis,* children develop later antisocial behaviors as a result of being stigmatized as being bad at an earlier age. The idea is that a child so stigmatized will first develop the identity of an antisocial child and then later behave in accord with that identity. If this hypothesis were true, then in Robins' study, *all* the children who had been referred to the clinic should have been equally sociopathic. However, it was primarily the antisocial children, and especially those antisocial children with serious symptoms, who became sociopathic adults. Thus, this finding is inconsistent with the stigmatization hypothesis.

• *Antisocial symptoms did* not *serve as a defense against anxiety.*

In other words, this study did not support the hypothesis that antisocial behaviors occur because the child is unconsciously anxious and "acts out" this anxiety through antisocial behavior.

• *"Bad company" did not cause the child to act antisocially.*

Parents and other adults often believe that the typical pattern is for an otherwise "good child" to fall into the company of other bad children and thus turn into a "bad child." Robins' findings suggest, however, that rather than the good child "falling" into bad company, it is the antisocial child who actively seeks out others who are also antisocial.

Summary.   Children in the Robins' (1966) study were raised in an urban area in the 1920s and 1930s, and many things have changed since then. For example, the ensuing 70 years have witnessed marked changes in the composition of families and in societal attitudes. Furthermore, our expectations for girls are now very different than they were then, and in many respects we now see females acting more similarly to males than was the case previously. Furthermore, diagnostic categories have changed markedly, and it is likely that many of the children in Robins' study would receive different diagnoses today than they did in the 1960s.

For all of these reasons, we must be skeptical about the results of Robins' study, and, in particular, about whether they would continue to hold today. Nevertheless, as we will see throughout the rest of the book, Robins' research has demonstrated a great deal of "holding power," and many of her major conclusions are still consistent with what we know today.

The Columbia County Longitudinal Study

This prospective research began in 1960 when Leonard Eron and Rowell Hues-mann and colleagues intensively studied all 875 third graders in New York state's Columbia County (Eron, 1987; Huesmann, Eron, Lefkowitz, & Walder, 1984; Lefkowitz, Eron, Walder, & Huesmann, 1977). At this time, the modal age of the children was 8. In about 75% of the cases, mothers and fathers were also interviewed. As measured primarily by peer ratings, "aggression" in this study included a combination of physical and verbal aggression as well as noncompliance, stealing, and lying.

First Phase. Two major findings when the children were 8 concerned the relationship between parents' behavior and the child's aggression:

* *The less nurturant and accepting the parents were at home, the more aggressive the child was at school. In addition, the more the child was punished for aggression at home, the more aggressive he was at school.*

These results seem consistent with social learning theory, the frustration–aggression hypothesis, and the displacement of the aggression hypothesis. By punishing the child, the parents became models for the learning of aggressive behavior. By being nonnurturant, the parents presumably frustrated the child a great deal, thus producing additional aggression. However, because the child could not display aggression at home for fear of punishment, the child then displaced his learned aggression to the school setting.

* *For children who identified strongly with their fathers, punishment for aggression at home was associated with a* low *amount of aggression at school. Furthermore, the less the child identified with either or both parents, the more aggressive he was at school.*

The child's emotional relationship with his or her parents (especially with the father) seemed to interact with physical punishment in affecting the learning and/or performance of aggression. This result resembles Robins' (1966) finding that children of cold and stern parents had a particularly *low* rate of adult sociopathy.

Second Phase. In 1971, the researchers reinterviewed 427 of the original subjects, whose modal age was now 19. The major results from this phase are as follows:

* *Both boys and girls who were rated as aggressive by their peers at age 8 tended to be also rated as aggressive at age 19. Moreover, these aggressive children rated themselves as more aggressive at age 19, rated others as more aggressive, and were more likely to see the world as an aggressive place. Finally, the aggressive 8-year-olds were three times more likely to have had police contacts than were nonaggressive 8-year-olds.*

Overall, despite the differences between the two studies, these results are remarkably consistent with those of Robins (1966).

• *Motor similarity of the child to the parents (in terms of behaviors such as eating, walking, and talking) were "potent" predictors of teen-age aggressiveness, regardless of the child's sex.*

This result suggests two possible interpretations. First, the child's motor and moral behaviors might have been inherited from his or her parent. Alternatively, the child might have learned a variety of behaviors from the parents, including aggression.

• *Internalized moral standards and guilt at age 8 predicted prosocial behavior at age 19, independent of social class.*

These findings are consistent with our discussion in chapter 1 on the importance of the early development of predispositional guilt and self-regulation. In Eron's (1987) words: "It seems that what the youngsters were learning at age 8 and what stayed with them over 10 years were attitudes, standards, and norms for behavior and problem-solving styles" (p. 439).

• *"One of the best predictors of how aggressive a young man would be at age 19 was the violence of the television programs he preferred when he was 8 years old" (Eron, 1987, p. 438).*

We deal with this finding in more detail when we discuss the role of television violence.

Third Phase.   In 1981, the researchers again interviewed approximately 295 of the original subjects in person and received completed questionnaires from 114. The modal age at this follow-up was 30. In addition, the researchers obtained data about these subjects and 223 other subjects from the New York State Division of Criminal Justice Service and other state agencies. They also interviewed spouses of 165 subjects, and 82 of the subjects' own children, whose average age was 8. As in the St. Louis Study, the results of this phase indicated the relative stability of hyperaggressive behavior:

• *Aggressive behavior at age 8 predicted aggression and antisocial behavior at age 30.*

In Eron's (1987) words: "Aggression manifested during interactions with peers in the early elementary school grades predicted criminal behavior, number of moving traffic violations, convictions for driving while intoxicated, aggressiveness toward spouses, and how severely the subjects punished their own children" (p. 439). Based on these data, Eron estimated that the stability of aggressive behavior from age 8 to age 30 is .50 for men and .35 for women.

• *Popularity and aggressive avoidance at age 8 predicted prosocial behavior (e.g., educational and occupational attainment, social success, good mental health) at age 30. On the other hand, aggression at age 8 predicted social failure, psychopathology, aggression, and low educational and occupational success at age 30, even when social class was held constant.*

These results are thus consistent with those of the St. Louis study in showing that childhood aggressiveness does not merely predict adulthood aggressiveness, but rather a whole host of problems involving aggression, interpersonal problems, overall psychological well-being, and occupational and social success.

• *Aggressive-children-turned-parents also had aggressive children of their own.*

Interestingly, the offspring's aggression was more strongly related to their parents' aggression at age 8 than to their parents' aggression as adults. It is thus clear that aggression is transmitted across generations.

• *"The more frequently youngsters watched TV at age 8, the more serious were the crimes for which they were convicted at age 30" (Eron, 1987, p. 440).*

Note that this relationship is between television viewing in general, and not just the viewing of violent television programs. We return to this issue in more detail in chapter 6.

Interpretation.   Eron (1987) argued that "aggression and prosocial behavior represent opposite kinds of interpersonal problem-solving strategies that are learned early in life. If a child learns one mode well, he or she does not tend to learn the other well" (p. 440). The results of this study are thus consistent with the idea that the learning of moral behaviors, emotions, and attitudes in childhood is crucial to the development of prosocial behavior in adulthood. As Eron (1987) put it: "To behave appropriately, but not aggressively, when contingencies are remote, the child must have internalized a model or script of such behaviors (a program that he or she can follow). In other words, the child must learn the prosocial behaviors we mentioned earlier" (p. 440).

Other Research

In addition to the two studies just discussed, numerous other research has considered the relationship between children's antisocial behavior and subsequent hyperaggressiveness.

Age of Onset.   The St. Louis and Columbia County studies suggested that unusual aggressiveness by the age of 8 predicts subsequent adult problems. More recent research suggests that adult aggressiveness might be reliably predicted at an even earlier age. For example, Caspi, Moffitt, Newman, and Silva (1996) found that both males and females who were undercontrolled (impulsive, restless, and distractible) at age 3 were more likely than comparison groups at age 21 to meet the diagnostic criteria for APD, to have been convicted more than once for a violent crime, and to have attempted suicide. The authors caution that the effect size was small; nevertheless, the study does suggest some stability over 18 years. In addition, these results are also consistent with those of Mischel et al. (1988) showing the positive effects of delay of gratification from age 4 to age 14.

Stability of Fighting.   As we have seen, hyperaggressive is generally fairly stable from the early elementary school years onward. However, approximately 50% of such children eventually desist from their aggression (Maughan & Rutter, 1998). Furthermore, we also know that a substantial portion of adolescents develop CD without major signs of aggression in childhood (Kazdin, 1995). In an attempt to delineate the pattern of onset and desistence of fighting, Tremblay and colleagues (Haapasalo & Tremblay, 1994) studied this phenomenon among French-speaking Canadian boys from the ages of 6 to 14.

Based on teacher reports at ages 6, 10, 11, and 12, these researchers classified 47% of the children as *fighters,* divided into the following four mutually exclusive groups:

- *Stable high fighters* (8.4% of the total sample), who were already high fighters in kindergarten and who continued in this behavior throughout the study.
- *High fighters with late onset* (9.1%), who did not start fighting until at least the age of 10.
- *Variable high fighters* (17.1%), who showed intermittent patterns of fighting.
- *Desisting high fighters* (12.4%), who were high fighters in kindergarten but who later stopped fighting.

As shown in Table 3.1, stable high fighters were more than seven times as likely to become adjudicated delinquents by the age of 14 than were nonfighters. Moreover, even desisting high fighters were more than four times more

TABLE 3.1
Proportion of Delinquent Boys
From Ages 10 to 14 From Each Fighter Group

Fighter Group	n	% Delinquent
Stable high fighters	71	19.7
High fighters with late onset	84	13.1
Desisting high fighters	108	11.1
Variable high fighters	142	12.0
Nonfighters	467	2.6
Total	872	7.6

Source: Adapted from "Physically Aggressive Boys from Ages 6 to 12: Family Background, Parenting Behavior, and Prediction of Delinquency," by J. Haapasalo and R. E. Tremblay, 1994, *Journal of Consulting and Clinical Psychology, 62,* p. 1049. Copyright © 1994 by the American Psychological Association. Adapted with permission.

likely to become delinquent than were nonfighters. Clearly, high fighting at any period from ages 6 to 12 puts boys at risk for later delinquent behavior.

Developmental Pathways. Rolf Loeber and his colleagues (Loeber & Hay, 1994; Loeber & Stouthamer-Loeber, 1998) proposed three *developmental pathways* that youths travel in their antisocial behavior:

• The *overt pathway* was most strictly followed by the youngest boys in Loeber's study. This pathway begins with minor aggression (such as bullying and annoying others), moves on to physical fighting (including gang fighting), and culminates with violent acts (such as rape and strong-arm attack).

• The *covert pathway* begins with minor covert behavior, such as shoplifting and frequent lying. It then moves to property damage (vandalism and fire setting). Finally, it culminates in moderate to serious delinquency (such as fraud, burglary, and serious theft).

• The *authority conflict pathway* first involves stubborn behavior, which then moves into defiance and disobedience, and finally into authority avoidance (characterized by behaviors such as truancy, staying out late, and running away).

Loeber's concept of developmental pathways suggests that some individuals will follow one of these paths, a second group will follow a second path, and a third group will follow the third path. Furthermore, the "paths" amount to sequences of behavior that should follow in chronological order. Loeber suggests that young children begin at the first stage, whereas adolescents might begin at the middle stage. Finally, Loeber also indicates that some children might follow both the overt and covert pathway, thus ending up as adults who commit both interpersonal violence as well as property offenses.

Partial support for Loeber's theory comes from a recent study, which found two "developmental trajectories" for French-Canadian boys studied from the ages of 6 to 17 (Nagin & Tremblay, 1999). Holding hyperactivity and physical aggression constant, oppositional 6-year-olds showed a path leading to adolescent theft but not to more serious delinquency. However, physically aggressive boys exhibited a trajectory leading to more serious and violent delinquency.

Persistence. Serious antisocial behavior is quite persistent. For example, Lahey and colleagues (Lahey et al., 1995) conducted a 4-year prospective study of boys referred for disruptive behavior disorders. Only about 50% of the boys originally diagnosed with CD in Year 1 still met the criteria for CD 1 year later. However, 88% met the criteria at least once during the next 3 years, and for most boys, the symptoms remained relatively high overall. Improvement was not related to whether the boys were receiving treatment for their disorder; indeed, the only boys who clearly improved were those with above-average verbal IQs and without a parent who had APD.

Prognosis. Kazdin (1995) summarized the outlook for conduct-disordered children. As youngsters and adults, these individuals show:

- *Problems with physical health,* including higher rates of hospitalization and higher mortality rates.
- *Greater psychiatric impairment,* including antisocial personality disorder and drug and alcohol abuse.
- *A higher rate of adult criminal behavior,* including more serious crimes and longer jail terms.
- *Lower educational attainment,* including more dropping out of school and lower final attainment for those who stay in school.
- *Poor occupational adjustment,* including lower wages, more frequent bouts of unemployment, and more time on welfare.
- *More marital problems,* including higher rates of divorce.
- *Less social participation,* including less participation with family, friends, and neighbors.

Development in Females

We have seen that girls tend to exhibit less physical aggression than boys and are less likely to exhibit the more serious type of childhood-onset conduct disorder. However, although the prevalence of CD is less for females than for males, girls with CD appear to be at greater risk for more serious outcomes than are males (Loeber & Stouthamer-Loeber, 1998). This conclusion is consistent with the *gender paradox effect,* which holds for a variety of psychological disorders and reflects the fact that in disorders with an unequal sex ratio, members of the sex with the lower prevalence rate tend to be more seriously affected than comparable members of the other sex (Loeber & Stouthamer-Loeber, 1998). Thus, for example, females who qualify for a diagnosis of CD are two to three times more likely to develop a personality disorder than are similar males (Loeber & Stouthamer-Loeber, 1998). However, whether this effect reflects real differences or is simply an artifact of the diagnostic process remains to be determined (Loeber & Stouthamer-Loeber, 1998).

Some research suggests that the antecedents of later antisocial behavior might be different for females than for males. For example, in one prospective study begun when the children were in Grades 3 through 6, Roff and Wirt (1984) found that the predictors of subsequent antisocial behavior differed significantly for males as compared with females. For males, childhood aggressiveness–rebelliousness and nonaggressive antisocial behavior served as direct predictors of both juvenile delinquency and adult criminality, whereas social class and family factors showed no such direct link. For females, adult criminality was so rare that predictors for this behavior could not be assessed. As for subsequent delinquency, the best predictor for females was degree of family disturbance, with no direct path between early aggressiveness and later delinquency. It thus appears that family factors might be more related to subsequent antisocial behaviors in females than in males and that the path to later antisocial and violent behavior might be different for females than for males.

For females, adolescence brings with it a sharp increase in both psychopathology in general and the prevalence of antisocial and aggressive behavior in particular (Loeber & Stouthamer-Loeber, 1998). Some research suggests that biological factors might play a role in this process. For example, one study conducted in Sweden found that early maturing females exhibited more norm-breaking behavior than on time or later maturing females (Stattin & Magnusson, 1990). Other research, however, suggests that pubertal status might exert its effect only in combination with certain psychosocial variables. For example, Caspi, Lynam, Moffitt, and Silva (1993) found that early maturing girls who attended mixed-sex schools were more at risk for later delinquency than were females who attended all girls schools. In another study, early maturing girls who had a history of childhood behavior problems showed more such problems in adolescence than early maturing girls without such a history (Caspi & Moffitt, 1991). It is possible that, in mixed settings, early maturing females who are prone to antisocial behavior might have more opportunities to both seek out and be sought by older males, who might themselves engage in antisocial behavior. This differential affiliation might, in turn, "accentuate" these girls' antisocial tendencies. Such a dynamic would be consistent with Robins' (1966) finding that sociopathic females tended to marry males with serious behavior problems.

Whatever the dynamics, it is clear that the presence of CD among adolescent females is a poor prognostic sign. In a study conducted solely on females, CD at age 15 predicted APD, substance dependence, illegal behavior, dependence on multiple welfare sources, early home-leaving, multiple cohabitation partners, and physical partner violence at age 21 (Bardone, Moffitt, Caspi, & Dickson, 1996). These results thus suggest a poor prognosis for young females diagnosed as having CD.

SUMMARY

As we have seen, much research has delineated the picture of the development of hyperaggressiveness over the lifespan. We conclude with an overview of development in this area.

Childhood

The developmental course of the disruptive behaviors disorders goes something like this. First, some children who exhibit early signs of inattention, impulsivity and/or hyperactivity will be diagnosed with ADHD in either their preschool or early elementary years. At some point, perhaps as many as 30% of these children will also be diagnosed with CD. In addition, they will also retain their ADHD symptoms. These children will have an especially poor prognosis in both adolescence and adulthood.

Another group of children whose major difficulties seem to involve non-compliance, defiance, and anger/aggressiveness will be diagnosed with ODD in their preschool or early elementary school years. Again, a significant portion of these children will eventually also be diagnosed with CD. Interestingly, however, most children diagnosed as ODD *do not* become CD (Hinshaw et al., 1993).

Conduct disordered children who receive their diagnosis before the age of 10 constitute the childhood-onset type. Some of these might have had a prior diagnosis of either ADHD or ODD. Because this group of children tends to exhibit rather serious offenses, and because their offenses tend to be more persistent (APA, 1994), the prognosis for this group in the absence of treatment is not good. A substantial number of these children will end up being involved with both the juvenile and adult justice systems, especially if they have a dual diagnosis of ADHD and CD.

Adolescence

Another group of children seem to have few problems of antisocial behavior during childhood but develop clinical symptoms after the age of 10, which result in their being diagnosed as having adolescent-onset CD. Because their behaviors are less serious and persistent than is the case for child-onset CD, their prognosis is better (McGee, Feehan, Williams, & Anderson, 1992; Moffitt, 1993). Nevertheless, some of the youths in this group might also become officially adjudicated delinquents.

We have already seen that delinquent behaviors are common in adolescence. However, it is estimated that approximately 50% of teenagers who come into contact with the legal system never do so again. The problem of serious youth violence thus seems to lie with a small group of juveniles who end up being responsible for the majority of juvenile crime, especially repeat and serious crimes (Wolfgang, Figlio, & Sellin, 1972).

Adulthood

Children who are diagnosed with CD before the age of 15 are at risk to continue their antisocial behavior and receive a diagnosis of APD sometime in their adult lives. Some of these children-turned-adults and some juvenile delinquents will continue with their antisocial behavior as adults, thus putting them at risk for a variety of adult problems, including incarceration, substance abuse, work problems, marital problems, medical problems, and difficulties in interpersonal relationships. But more than 50% who were aggressive as children or adolescents now settle down and become nonaggressive, law-abiding citizens (Moffitt, Caspi, Dickson, Silva, & Stanton, 1996).

Most of the research indicates that individuals pass through different stages of increasingly antisocial behaviors, but only a relatively few pass through all the stages. Children who begin early tend to persist the longest in their antisocial activities. Less serious acts precede more serious acts, but many children and adolescents stop somewhere along the process (Nagin & Tremblay, 1999). Unfortunately, some do not, and these youths are the focus of much of the rest of this book.

CHAPTER 4

The Child's Contribution: Genetic, Biological, and Temperamental Factors

Perhaps no question in developmental psychology has created more controversy than that of whether psychological traits and behaviors are caused by the child's "natural" endowment or whether they are caused by the environmental experiences the child has in the course of his or her life. Referred to as the *nature–nurture controversy,* this issue has been as powerfully debated by those concerned with youthful aggression as by other developmental psychologists. In the context of youth violence, the extreme form of the nature–nurture controversy boils down to the question of whether a child's aggression is caused by the child's innate biological disposition, or whether it is caused by environmental factors such as the child's early experiences, family life, economic conditions, school experiences, and choice of friends.

In reality, because neither nature nor nurture can operate in the absence of the other, all behavior (including aggression) is actually caused by the joint contributions of both. Exactly how this process works is not completely understood. However, one possibility is that a child's innate characteristics predispose him to aggression, but that actual aggressive behavior occurs only when a predisposed child is exposed to an environment that facilitates such behavior. This theory is commonly called the *diathesis–stress* or *vulnerability–stress* model (Wicks-Nelson & Israel, 2000).

In later chapters, we discuss numerous environmental factors that might affect children's aggression. In this chapter, however, we examine the role that children's own biological and psychological characteristics play in the development of their aggressive behavior.

GENETIC FACTORS

A number of theories have postulated that aggression is due to the genes the person inherits. In addition, empirical research indicates that animals can be bred for aggression, thus suggesting the importance of genetically inherited characteristics (Renfrew, 1997). For example, Lagerspetz (1979) interbred mice over 19 generations, a procedure that ultimately produced one "*hyper*aggressive" genetic strain of animals and another "*hypo*aggressive" strain. By that time, the "biting level" of the hyperaggressive mice had risen to the 52% level, whereas that of the hypoaggressive mice had fallen to the 5% level. Moreover, compared to their nonaggressive peers, the hyperaggressive mice had more of the neurotransmitter norepinephrine in their brain stems and less serotonin in their forebrains. Interestingly, however, these differences were able to be reduced in just one generation of cross-breeding the two extreme strains of mice together.

A child's genetic endowment is set at conception when the sperm fertilizes the ovum, a process that normally results in a single-cell organism with 46 pairs of chromosomes. Each chromosome, in turn, consists of a strand of the DNA molecule, with a specific section of DNA constituting a gene. Throughout the 9 months of prenatal development, the child's DNA sends out instructions by which certain biochemical components are used to "build" the physical body (including the brain) of the developing offspring. It is important to understand that during the prenatal period, the developing organism always interacts with biochemical components produced by the mother. The mother's nutritional level, whether she smokes, whether she takes drugs, any diseases she may have, any exposure to radiation she may undergo—all of these factors and others contribute to how the DNA "instructions" get carried out. This is especially important when it comes to the development of the brain and the central nervous systems, because prenatal problems in the development of these structures are likely to result in psychological problems after birth (Papalia et al., 1999).

The specific set of genes the child acquires at contraception is called the child's *genotype*. However, the newborn's *phenotype* (the physical and behavioral manifestation of the genotype) is a result of the combination of the child's genetic endowment plus the prenatal environment to which the developing organism has been exposed. The term *genetic* thus refers to the child's genotype at conception, whereas the term *innate* refers to the totality of the child's characteristics at birth.

At the moment of birth, the child's innate set of physical and psychological characteristics begins to be influenced by the child's environment, a process that continues throughout life. Because this is the case, and because children do not exhibit aggressive behavior until at least 1 year after birth, how can psychologists determine the role that genetics might play in children's aggression? In order to answer this question, we turn to a subfield of psychology called *behavior genetics* (Plomin, DeFries, McClearn, & Rutter, 1997).

Behavior Genetics

Behavior genetics is an area of scientific inquiry devoted to the study of the effects of genetics on behavior. As part of this work, behavior geneticists have developed a number of research methodologies that allow them to determine the extent to which certain behaviors and behavioral traits are influenced by genetics, the environment, or some combination of both.

One such methodology is the *twin study*, in which *monozygotic* (or *identical*) twins are compared with *dizygotic* (or *fraternal*) twins. Because monozygotic twins develop from the same fertilized ovum, they have exactly the same DNA and hence the same genes. Dizygotic twins, on the other hand, arise from two separate fertilized ova; hence, they are no more genetically similar than if they were biological siblings. Thus, if monozygotic twins are more similar with respect to a certain psychological trait than are dizygotic twins, that similarity supports the hypothesis that the trait is influenced by genetics (Plomin et al., 1997).

Various measures may be used to determine the similarity between twin pairs on any particular trait. In some cases, researchers determine the extent to which both members of a twin pair have the same trait or psychological disorder, a measure called the *concordance rate*. A pairwise concordance rate of 1.00 (or 100%) indicates that in 100% of the cases studied, both members of the twin pair possess the same trait or disorder (Plomin et al., 1997). Another measure is the correlation coefficient for identical and nonidentical twins. For example, the correlation for IQ scores for identical twin pairs might be .70, compared with a correlation of .53 for fraternal twin pairs. In general, the higher the concordance rate for identical twins compared with fraternal twins, or the greater the correlation for identical twin pairs compared with fraternal twin pairs, the greater the genetic contribution to that trait or disorder (Plomin et al., 1997).

A second methodology is that of the *adoption study*. In this design, researchers study siblings who are separated at birth and raised in different environments. The role of genetics in a trait is implicated if the trait of an adoptive child is more similar to that of the child's biological parents and siblings than to that of the adoptive parents and siblings (Papalia et al., 1999).

Psychologists have also combined these two methods into a *twins raised apart* design. In this method, the researcher studies sets of identical and fraternal twins who are separated at an early age and raised in very different environments. (I want to emphasize that psychologists do not actually separate the children at birth, but only study those children who were separated for some other reason.) If, in such a case, identical twins are still more similar with respect to a trait than are fraternal twins, then this method provides strong evidence that the trait has a genetic basis.

One method that is not very helpful in untangling the relative contributions of genetics and environment is the *family study* design. In this method, investigators study the extent to which traits are "passed down" from generation to generation in the same family. For example, investigators may study violent men and their sons to determine whether violent fathers have sons who are also violent. The problem with this method is that any violence that is "passed down" from one generation to the next could be due either to genetic inheritance or to environmental influences the child experiences while growing up. For example, if a violent man fathers a child who becomes violent, the son's violence may be due to the genes he inherited from his father, but it could also be due to the son's experience of growing up in a violent home. Unfortunately, the family study method does not permit a clear determination of which of these two possibilities is most likely (Papalia et al., 1999).

The statistic that is most commonly used to indicate the relative influence of genetics on behavior is called *heritability* (h^2), defined as the proportion of variance in a group of scores that is accounted for by genetic differences (Plomin et al., 1997). Thus, if we have a group of scores representing children's aggressive behavior, heritability tells us what proportion of the variance in that group of scores is due to the genetic differences among the members of the group. For example, if h^2 for a group of scores is .40, then 40% of the variance of those scores is accounted for by genetic factors within the group.

When interpreting the heritability measure, we need to keep a number of things in mind. First, each heritability score is an estimate from a specific sample and can vary depending on a number of factors. Second, heritability cannot automatically be generalized from one distinct population of children to another. And third, heritability allows us to estimate the extent to which genetic factors contribute to a trait in a large group, however, it does not tell us what proportion of a trait is due to genetics for an individual child (Plomin et al., 1997). For example, many studies suggest that the heritability of IQ is approximately .50 for Caucasian children as a group (Plomin et al., 1997). However, we cannot say that 50% of an individual child's IQ is due to genetics. Similarly, the heritability estimate cannot tell us how much of an individual child's aggression is due to genetics and how much is due to the environment (Plomin et al., 1997).

In addition to estimating the effects of heredity, behavior geneticists often estimate the effects of two aspects of the environment, called the *shared* (or *common*) environment and the *unshared* (or *unique*) environment (Plomin et al., 1997). The shared environment represents all those experiences siblings have in common, whereas the unshared environment refers to experiences unique to each member of the family. The measures c^2 and e^2 estimate the proportion of variance due to the shared and unshared environment, respectively.

The environment may affect the child's genetic makeup in a number of ways. First, it is possible that a genotype may be expressed phenotypically under some environmental conditions but not under others, a situation referred to as a *genotype–environment interaction* (Papalia et al., 1999; Rutter et al., 1998). In addition, environmental conditions may serve to strengthen or amplify existing genetic predispositions, a situation referred to as a *genotype–environment correlation* (Papalia et al., 1999; Rutter et al., 1998). Researchers have identified three types of such correlations:

- *Passive genotype–environmental correlations,* in which a parent provides the child with the genetic basis for a trait as well as an environment conducive to the expression of that trait.

- *Evocative genotype–environmental correlations,* in which the child's behavior evokes a response from the environment that strengthens the genetically based trait;

- *Active genotype–environmental correlations,* in which a child actively seeks out activities and environments consistent with the nature of his or her genetically based trait.

With this background in mind, we now examine the relationship between genetics and externalizing behavior.

Research on Adults

Studies using both the twin and adoption methodologies suggest that there is some genetic component involved in adult antisocial behavior and criminality (Kazdin, 1995; Lytton, 1990; Raine, 1993). For example, across 13 studies using the twin-study methodology, Raine (1993) found an average concordance rate of 51.5% for monozygotic twins and 20.6% for dizygotic twins. More recent twin studies have shown significant heritability for both motor aggression and symptoms of antisocial personality disorder (Coccaro, Bergeman, Kavoussi, & Seroczynski, 1997; Lyons et al., 1995). Adoption studies also suggest that genetic factors may play a role in adult crime (Blackburn, 1993; Kazdin, 1995; Lytton, 1990; Raine, 1993). Interestingly, however, research relating genetics to different types of crime has found more evidence for a genetics effect on property crime than on violent crimes (Raine, 1993).

Research on Juveniles

Prior to the 1990s, the major research regarding the effects of genetics on juveniles' antisocial behavior consisted of adoption studies reported by Cadoret and colleagues (as integrated in Cadoret, Cain, & Crowe, 1983) and twin studies conducted by Rowe (1983) and by Ghodsian-Carpey and Baker (1987). Since 1990, a number of additional adoption and twin studies have been reported (see Table 4.1). Participants in these latter studies span the ages between 3 and adulthood and come from a number of countries. Data on youngsters' behavior have generally been supplied by the parents, but teachers, trained observers, and the participants themselves have also been used as informational sources. In terms of dependent measures, many of these studies have employed some combination of the externalizing, aggressive, and delinquent scales of Achenbach's (1991) Child Behavior Checklist (CBCL; see Table 4.1). Other research has utilized youngsters' self-reports of antisocial behaviors (Cadoret et al., 1983; Rowe,

TABLE 4.1

Selected Recent Studies on the Heritability of Juveniles' Externalizing Behavior

Author	Type	Nationality	Ages & Sexes	Rater	Behavior
Schmitz et al., 1995	T	United States	3, M/F	M	CBCL (A,E)
			8, M/F	M	CBCL (A,D,E)
Leve et al., 1998	T	United States	6–11, M/F	P, O	CBCL (E)
					Coded
					Observations
Gjone et al., 1996	T	Norwegian	5–15, M/F	P	CBCL (A, E, D)
Deater-Deckard & Plomin, 1999	A/S	United States	7–12, M/F	P	CBCL (A,D)
Eley et al., 1999	T	Swedish	7–9, M/F	P	CBCL (A, D)
		British	8–16, M/F	P	CBCL (A, D)
Hewitt et al., 1992	T	United States	8–11, M/F	M, F	CBCL (E)
Eaves et al., 1997	T	United States	8–16, M/F	S,P,T	Conduct disorder symptoms
Simonoff et al., 1998	T	United States	8–16, M	S, M	4 subtypes of conduct disorder
Van den Oord, Boomsma, & Verhulst, 1994	A	Dutch	12, M/F	P	CBCL (A, D, E)
Rowe, 1983	T	United States	13–18, M/F	S	4 measures of general delinquency (including aggression)
Cadoret et al., 1983	A	United States	Adolescent, M/F	S	General antisocial and delinquent behaviors
Lyons et al., 1995	T	United States	Adult, M	S	Symptoms of conduct disorder
Slutske et al., 1997	T	Australian	Adult, M/F	S	Symptoms of conduct disorder

Notes. Type of study: T = twin study; A = adoption study; A/S = adoption study with siblings. Ages are given in years. Sexes: M = male; F = female. Rater: M = mother; F = father; P = parent; S = self-report; O = trained observer; T = teacher. Behavior: CBCL–A = Child Behavior Checklist Aggression subscale; CBCL–D = Child Behavior Checklist Delinquency subscale; CBCL–E = Child Behavior Checklist Externalizing scale.

1983) or questionnaires designed to detect the presence of conduct-disordered behavior (Simonoff, Pickles, Meyer, Silberg, & Maes, 1998). Adult studies have classified respondents as conduct disordered based on participants' retrospective reports about their behavior as juveniles (Lyons et al., 1995; Slutske et al., 1997).

Effects of Genetics.   Virtually all of the available research indicates a significant genetic component in children's externalizing behavior. For example, in his study of self-reported delinquency, Rowe (1983) found that a model that excluded a genetics factor did not fit the data, and Leve, Winebarger, Fagot, Reid, and Goldsmith (1998) found that genetic factors accounted for the majority of the variance in parent-reported externalizing behavior. The median heritability estimate from the studies listed in Table 4.2 is .40, suggesting that slightly less than half of the variability in youths' externalizing behavior can be attributed to genetics.

Despite the relative strength of these findings, they must be interpreted with some caution. In the first place, most of the data come solely from parental reports, typically from the mother. However, results from studies utilizing more than one informational source indicate that heritability estimates can vary considerably from rater to rater (Deater-Deckard & Plomin, 1999; Eaves et al., 1997; Ghodsian-Carpey & Baker, 1987; Simonoff et al., 1998), thus calling into question the reliability of data obtained from a single source such as a parent.

A second limitation of these studies involves external validity. Samples collected from outside the United States have involved primarily British and Northern European youngsters, and some of the samples from U.S. studies have included an overrepresentation of Caucasian children and an underrepresentation of children from other racial and ethnic groups (Schmitz, Fulker, & Mrazek, 1995; Simonoff et al., 1998). Moreover, most of this research has been conducted using "normal," nonclinical samples, rather than youngsters who would be considered extremely aggressive. Thus, the extent to which these findings can be generalized to highly aggressive U.S. children other than Caucasians of northern European descent remains unclear.

We have seen that externalizing behavior that dates from the early elementary school years tends to be more aggressive, more serious, and more persistent than that which begins in adolescence, which in turn tends to involve time-limited and nonaggressive acts committed in the company of others. Because of its early onset and persistent nature, we might suspect that child-onset externalizing behavior is more heritable than adolescent-onset delinquency, which might be more environmentally driven and peer-induced. If such is the case, heritability estimates for measures of aggressive behavior should be higher than those for nonaggressive delinquency or generalized externalizing behaviors.

The available research generally supports this hypothesis, but with some reservations. For example, among their 3-year-olds, Schmitz et al. (1995) found

TABLE 4.2
Results of Selected Recent Studies on the Heritability
of Juveniles' Externalizing Behavior

Author	Age & Sex	Rater	Behavior	h^2	c^2	e^2
Schmitz et al., 1995	3, M/F	M	CBCL–A	.52	.16	.32
			CBCL–E	.34	.32	.34
	8, M/F	M	CBCL–A	.55	.19	.26
			CBCL–D	.79	.00	.21
			CBCL–E	.57	.22	.21
Gjone et al., 1996	5–15, M/F	P	CBCL–E	.83	.06	---
Deater-Deckard & Plomin, 1999	7–12, M/F	P	CBCL–A	.24	.27	.49
			CBCL–D	.36	.22	.42
		T	CBCL–A	.49	.00	.51
			CBCL–D	.17	.13	.70
Eley et al., 1999	7–9, M/F	P	CBCL–A, Model 1	.70	.07	.23
			CBCL–D, Model 1	.47	.29	.24
	8–16, M/F	P	CBCL–A, Model 1	.69	.04	.27
			CBCL–D, Model 1	.37	.34	.29
Hewitt et al., 1992	8–11, M/F	M, F	CBCL–E	.40	.59	.01
Eaves et al., 1997	8–16, M/F	S	CD Questionnaire	.24	.52	.24
	8–16, M/F	M	CD Questionnaire	.61	.25	.14
	8–16, M/F	F	CD Questionnaire	.36	.26	.38
	8–16, M/F	T	CD Questionnaire	.53	.47	.00
Simonoff et al., 1998	8–16, M	S	Theft/Vandalism	.25	.07	.68
			Status Violations	.17	.13	.70
			Defiant Behavior	.29	.06	.65
			Physical Aggression	.31	.02	.67
	8–16, M	M	Theft/Vandalism	.47	.19	.34
			Status Violations	.24	.60	.16
			Defiant Behavior	.13	.61	.26
			Physical Aggression	.57	.18	.25
Van den Oord et al., 1994	12, M/F	P	CBCL–A	.70	---	---
			CBCL–D	.39	---	---
			CBCL–E	.65	.17	---

Notes. Ages are given in years. Sexes: M = male; F = female. Rater: M = mother; F = father; P = parent; S = self-report; O = trained observer; T = teacher. Behavior: CBCL–A = Child Behavior Checklist Aggression subscale; CBCL–D = Child Behavior Checklist Delinquency subscale; CBCL–E = Child Behavior Checklist Externalizing scale. h^2 = heritability; c^2 = shared environmental effect; e^2 = unshared environmental effect.

Dashes indicate unavailable data.

higher heritability for aggression than for externalizing behavior in general. Similarly, in their middle-school sample, Deater-Deckard and Plomin (1999) found higher heritability for teacher-rated aggression than for teacher-rated delinquency. In addition, in their study of British and Swedish twins ages 8 to 16, Eley, Lichtenstein, and Stevenson (1999) found that for both nationalities, genetic factors exerted a far greater influence over aggressive antisocial behavior than over nonaggressive antisocial behavior. Finally, Simonoff et al. (1998) found that maternal ratings produced higher heritability estimates for aggressive forms of conduct disorder than for nonaggressive forms. However, Schmitz et al. (1995) failed to find an aggression-externalizing difference among their 8-year-olds, and Deater-Deckard and Plomin (1999) found that maternal ratings produced a notably higher heritability estimate for delinquency than for aggression (see Table 4.2). Clearly, additional research is needed in order to clarify these discrepancies.

Role of the Environment.   Although these studies indicate that genes play a part in children's aggression, they also consistently implicate the role of the environment as well. For instance, Rowe (1983) found that only models incorporating an environmental variable fit his data, and Cadoret et al. (1983) found that the best fit for their data involved a genetics–environment interaction. It is thus clear that environmental as well as genetic factors contribute to youthful aggressive behavior. What is less clear, however, is the relative influence of youngsters' common shared environment compared with their unique unshared experiences, an important issue for understanding the environmental basis of children's antisocial and aggressive behavior.

Overall, most of the evidence indicates that the unshared environment is relatively more influential than the shared environment (see Table 4.2). Interestingly, the influence of the shared environment seems to decrease as aggression becomes more serious (Gjone, Stevenson, Sundet, & Eilertsen, 1996) and as individuals move from adolescence to adulthood (Lyons et al., 1995). Moreover, the relative importance of the unshared environment seems to be greater for aggressive behaviors than for nonaggressive antisocial behaviors (Deater-Deckard & Plomin, 1999; Schmitz et al., 1995; Simonoff et al., 1998). These findings thus suggest that family factors may be relatively less influential in affecting individuals' aggressive antisocial behaviors than in influencing their nonaggressive antisocial behaviors, especially as children move into adulthood and leave the home.

Some research suggests that as children grow older, genetic factors become more prominent and children begin to find their own *genetic niche,* thus resulting in increased heritability estimates from early childhood to adulthood (Papalia et al, 1999; Plomin et al., 1997). Support for this hypothesis comes from studies conducted on both children (Schmitz et al., 1995) and adults (Lyons et al., 1995). For example, Lyons et al. (1995) found that genetics explained six times more variance in adult antisocial behaviors than in similar behaviors in juveniles. Additional research will be needed to examine this question more closely.

Summary

Available research indicates that much of the variability of youngsters' externalizing behavior is due to genetics and that aggressive behavior might be more heritable than general externalizing behavior (Mason & Frick, 1994). However, because of problems associated with rater reliability and external validity, the exact magnitude of the genetic effect remains unclear. Moreover, although genetics might predispose children toward aggressive behavior, it is likely that a certain level of environmental risk must also be present in order to produce overt behavioral aggression. It also appears that unshared environmental experiences exert a greater effect on youths' externalizing behavior than do common shared environmental experiences. Because this question is related to the relative role of family and nonfamily factors in the determination of youthful antisocial and aggressive behaviors (Harris, 1998), additional research on this question should prove highly important.

BIOLOGICAL FACTORS

In addition to the possibility that they might be predisposed toward violence due to their genetic endowment, children might also be biologically predisposed toward aggressive behavior either innately or as a result of early environmental experiences.

Activation-Inhibition Theory

Biological theories attempt to specify the biological processes and mechanisms by which genetic factors and innate characteristics get translated into actual aggressiveness. One such theory has been proposed by Gray (1976, 1987) and extended by a number of other researchers (Fowles, 1988; Newman, 1997; Newman & Wallace, 1993; Quay, 1993). Gray's model contains two major processes called the *Behavioral Activation System* (BAS) and the *Behavioral Inhibition System* (BIS).

The BAS is a reward-seeking system that activates behavior in response to cues associated with positive reinforcement. BAS activity inhibits BIS activity and is also implicated in *active avoidance* behavior, in which making a response allows the child to avoid an unpleasant stimulus. Emotionally, the BAS seems to involve pleasure. At a biological level, BAS activity is hypothetically associated with increased dopamine activity and heart rate acceleration (Newman, 1997; Raine, 1993).

The BIS inhibits reward-motivated behavior in response to cues that indicate that the response will be followed by punishment, nonreward, or frustration. In this connection, BIS activity helps the child to learn from punishment. In addition, the BIS is implicated in *passive avoidance,* in which the inhibition of a response allows the child to avoid an unpleasant stimulus. BIS activity also interrupts ongoing or anticipated motor activity and directs attention to relevant stimuli. Emotionally, BIS activity is associated with fear or anxiety. Biologically, BIS activity is hypothetically related to increased levels of serotonin and norepinephrine and to increased skin conductance (Newman, 1997).

Applied to aggression, Gray's theory suggests that children with an overactive BAS might be more motivated to seek immediate rewards, even when aggression and violence are needed to attain these rewards. On the other hand, children with an underactive BIS might be less sensitive to punishment and hence less likely to "learn from experience." Furthermore, because of their deficit in passive avoidance learning, these children would be more likely to act impulsively, thus being less able to inhibit any aggressive response tendencies they might experience (Newman, 1997). Compared with nonaggressive children, instrumentally hyperaggressive youths might be expected to exhibit a strong BAS but a normal BIS, whereas reactively hyperaggressive youngsters might exhibit a normal BAS but a weak BIS. Children who manifest both types of hyperaggressive behavior might exhibit both an overactive BAS as well as an underactive BIS.

Neurological Abnormalities

A number of findings indicate that neurological abnormalities are common among violent youth. For example, Lewis et al. (1988) compared incarcerated juvenile murderers with violent and nonviolent incarcerated adolescents. Results indicated that 58% of the murderers and 62% of the violent juveniles showed major neurological impairment. However, only 6% of the nonviolent incarcerated juveniles exhibited similar difficulties. The authors suggested that violent juvenile offenders are more neurologically impaired than their nonviolent counterparts. Similar findings have also been reported by Zagar, Arbit, Sylvies, Busch, and Hughes (1990).

With respect to antisocial behavior in general and aggressive behavior in particular, much recent work has focused on the *limbic system* and the *frontal cortex.* The limbic system, an important site of impulses involving anger and aggression, includes the subcortical structures of the hypothalamus and the amygdala, but also involves projections into the *prefrontal cortex,* that part of the frontal cortex located directly behind the forehead (Niehoff, 1999). One function of the cortex is to inhibit impulses arising from the limbic system (Lahey, Hart, Pliszka, Applegate, & McBurnett, 1993). Cortical damage or dysfunction to this part of the cortex might be expected to reduce the ability of the cortex to inhibit these impulses, thus allowing them to be expressed in overt aggressive and angry behavior.

The cortex might also affect aggression in other ways. In most adults, the left hemisphere is specialized for language use, and language is thought to play a role in the planning, organization, control, and inhibition of behavior (Luria, 1961). In addition, the frontal cortex seems to regulate thinking, planning, and decision making (Barkley, 1997). Finally, Gray (1976, 1987) hypothesized that the frontal cortex plays an important role in the BIS. Deficiencies in the frontal and prefrontal cortices might therefore negatively affect planning and self-regulation and thus result in relatively uninhibited and aggressive behavior (Moffitt, 1997).

In a test of this hypothesis, Yeudall, Fromm-Auch, and Davies (1982) reported the results of the Halstead–Reitan neuropsychological test battery on 99 chronic juvenile offenders. Compared to nondelinquent controls, the offenders showed significantly more neuropsychological dysfunction, apparently in the left hemisphere and frontal cortex. Similarly, Krynicki (1978) found that assaultive and organically impaired adolescents were distinguished from less assaultive delinquents on tests suggesting left hemispheric dysfunction.

More recent research on antisocial adults implicates the prefrontal cortex more specifically. In one study of adult killers, those who killed impulsively were found to have lower glucose functioning in the prefrontal cortex than control subjects or murderers who killed in a premeditated and planned fashion (Raine et al., 1998). The prefrontal cortex was also studied in a follow-up study of two children known to have suffered prefrontal cortical damage before the age of 16 months (S. W. Anderson, Bechara, H. Damasio, Tranel, & A. R. Damasio, 1999). As adults, these two individuals exhibited classic psychopathic behaviors reminiscent of the subjects in the St. Louis study.

Neurotransmitters

Because behavior is mediated by the brain, and brain activity involves biochemical processes, a great deal of research has sought to determine the relationship between certain types of neurochemicals and children's aggressive and antisocial behavior.

Serotonin. Serotonin is a neurotransmitter found in the limbic system and seems to serve primarily as an inhibitor of emotional behavior and sympathetic nervous system activity (Lahey et al., 1993). As such, serotonin is also believed to be positively related to BIS activity. Furthermore, serotonin has been found to modulate aggressive behavior in every species of mammal in which it has been studied, and drugs that increase serotonin levels also reduce aggression across a wide variety of lower animals (Lahey et al., 1993). In view of these considerations, Raine (1993) hypothesized that the serotonin level among antisocial and aggressive children should be relatively low.

Since it is not possible to directly measure children's levels of brain serotonin, research into this hypothesis typically uses the following measures. First, cerebrospinal fluid drawn from the child produces a metabolite called *5-hydroxy-indoleacetic acid* (CSF 5-HIAA), which is positively correlated with the amount of serotonin in the frontal cortex (Lahey et al., 1993). Second, blood samples can be analyzed for whole-blood serotonin. However, blood serotonin and brain serotonin are generally inversely related to each other; moreover, because much serotonin in the blood originates in the digestive system, the exact interpretation of blood serotonin levels remains unclear (Lahey et al., 1993). Third, urine samples also yield an estimate of serotonin; however, most of the serotonin in such samples comes from peripheral sources rather than from the brain, thus making interpretation of the results somewhat problematic (Lahey et al., 1993; Raine, 1993).

Most of the relevant research regarding serotonin and aggression has used the CSF 5-HIAA measure. Among adults, low levels of CSF 5-HIAA are associated with psychopathy, aggressive behavior, and recidivism among violent offenders (Lahey et al., 1993). One study on children with conduct disorder, oppositional defiant disorder, and attention-deficit/hyperactivity disorder also found that these children exhibited significantly lower concentrations of CSF 5-HIAA than matched controls with a diagnosis of obsessive-compulsive disorder (Kruesi et al., 1990). In addition, among the full sample of children, CSF 5-HIAA was positively correlated ($r = .39$) with parent-rated social competence. Furthermore, in a 2-year follow-up, initial CSF 5-HIAA level significantly predicted severity of physical aggression, even after partialing out the effects of age and the children's initial level of aggression (Kruesi et al., 1992).

These results are consistent with Raine's (1993) meta-analysis of studies conducted prior to 1990, which found a significant negative relationship between CSF 5-HIAA and violence against persons for both adults and children ($d = -.89$). It thus appears that the relationship between CSF 5-HIAA is stable over time and that it is significantly lower for aggressive children and adults than for their nonaggressive peers (Lahey et al., 1993).

Norepinephrine.   Another neurotransmitter studied for its relationship with children's aggression is *norepinephrine,* found in the limbic system and sympathetic nervous system and hypothesized to relate positively to BIS activity. As with serotonin, estimates of norepinephrine can be obtained from the cerebrospinal fluid (CSF), from the blood, or from urine (Raine, 1993). In addition, level of norepinephrine can also be estimated from *dopamine-beta-hydroxylase* (DBH), an enzyme that converts dopamine into norepinephrine (Lahey et al., 1993).

Raine's (1993) meta-analysis suggested a negative relationship between measures of both central and peripheral norepinephrine and aggression in human adults, and research with children generally supports this finding. For example, one study of children and adolescents that used a CSF measure of norepinephrine found a negative correlation ($r = -.37$) between norepinephrine and aggression in a clinic-referred sample (Kruesi et al., 1990). In addition, Olweus (1987) and Magnusson (1988) found negative correlations (ranging from −.34 to −.44) between norepinephrine and peer ratings of aggressiveness in adolescents. Similarly, Rogeness and colleagues (Rogeness, Javors, Maas, & Macedo, 1990) reported lower levels of DBH in boys classified with an undersocialized–aggressive conduct disorder, but not in boys with other types of CD or with other diagnoses. It thus appears that compared to their nonaggressive peers, aggressive boys have relatively low levels of norepinephrine.

Hormones

A number of studies have investigated the relationship between certain hormones and youths' aggressive behavior.

Testosterone.   Because diagnosed conduct disorder is four times more prevalent in males than in females, researchers have studied the role that male sex hormones (especially *testosterone*) might play in aggression. In one study, Olweus (1986) found that male adolescents showed elevated testosterone levels to "provoked" but not to "unprovoked" aggression, and Olweus, Mattesson, Schalling, and Low (1988) reported a direct causal path from testosterone levels in Grade 6 to provoked aggression in Grade 9, but an indirect path (mediated by low frustration tolerance) for unprovoked aggression. More recently, Brooks and Reddon (1996), in a sample of adolescents aged 15 to 17, found that violent offenders showed significantly higher levels of testosterone than either nonviolent offenders or sex offenders. However, Brain and Susman (1997) noted that studies with younger children do not show a relationship between testosterone and aggression, suggesting that the elevated levels found in adolescents may be a consequence, rather than a cause, of aggressive behavior. Thus, although these data are provocative, additional research is needed in order to determine the validity of these findings and any possible cause-and-effect relationships that might exist.

Cortisol.   Taken together, the *hypothalamus,* the *pituitary gland,* and the *adrenal gland* are referred to as the *HPA axis* and are involved in autonomic nervous system functioning, especially that associated with sympathetic activity and cortical arousal (Lahey et al., 1993). *Cortisol,* a hormone secreted by the adrenal cortex, can be measured from blood, urine, or saliva and has been used frequently as an index of HPA functioning and arousal, with high levels of cortisol indicating hyperarousal and low levels indicating hypoarousal (Brain & Susman, 1997).

Aggressive conduct-disordered boys have been found to possess significantly lower levels of salivary cortisol than nonaggressive controls (McBurnett, Swanson, Pfiffner, & Harris, 1991; Vanyukov et al., 1993). In addition, negative correlations were found in the McBurnett et al. (1991) sample between cortisol concentrations and the number of aggressive symptoms ($r = -.41$), the number of peer nominations for being the "meanest" ($r = -.39$), and the number of peer nominations as the child who "fights most" ($r = -.40$). The results of these studies thus suggest that hyperaggressive youngsters may be *hypoaroused* compared with their nonaggressive peers.

Psychophysiological Measures

Psychophysiology is the study of the relationships between environmental events, psychological conditions, and physiological states and processes (Raine, 1993). Dependent variables typically include physiological measures such as *heart rate, skin conductance,* and *brain waves.* Research then attempts to relate these measures to various types of hypothesized psychological processes.

   Heart Rate.   Heart rate is theoretically important because low resting heart rate is considered a measure of low central nervous system arousal. If highly aggressive children are hypoaroused, we would expect them to exhibit significantly lower heart rate levels than nonaggressive children.

   Raine (1993) summarized the results of 14 studies that examined the *resting heart rate level* (HRL) of antisocial children. Individuals in these studies ranged in age from 7 to 25 (Raine, 1993). Participants included children and adolescents of both sexes from both the United States and Europe. A wide range of antisocial behavior was measured, including legal criminality, juvenile delinquency, diagnosed conduct disorders, teacher ratings of antisocial behavior, and self-reported antisocial behavior. In addition, HRL was also measured in various ways. Twelve of the studies involved children drawn from the normal population. In sum, the studies were extensive, methodologically sound, and involved various definitions of both antisocial behavior and HRL. All 14 studies found significantly lower resting HRL in antisocial groups compared with normal control groups. This effect was found for females as well as for males. Interestingly, HRL tended to be lowest for those who were especially aggressive or violent.

   More recent data confirm and extend these findings. In a longitudinal study begun when the participants were 3 years old, Raine and colleagues examined heart rate and externalizing behavior in more than 1,700 children from the island of Mauritius, a small country in the Indian Ocean between Africa and India (Raine, Venables, & Mednick, 1997). Heart rate measured at age 3 was used to predict behavior at age 11, at which time the results of a parental checklist were used to classify children as either "high" or "low" on aggression, nonaggressive antisocial behavior, and total antisocial behavior. The investigators controlled a large number of possible confounds, including height, weight, motor activity levels, physical development, health, muscle tone, temperament, family discord, socioeconomic status, and the presence of hyperactivity. As seen in Fig. 4.1, children rated as highly aggressive at age 11 had significantly lower heart rates at age 3 than did low-aggressive children. However, such was not the

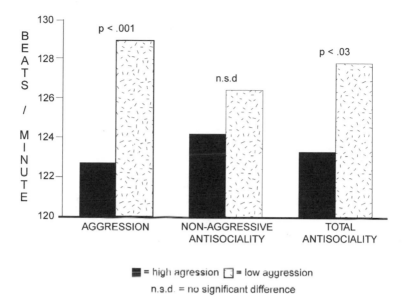

FIG. 4.1. Resting heart rate at age 3 as a function of type of antisocial behavior at age 11. From "Low resting heart rate at age 3 years predisposes to aggression at age 11 years: Evidence from the Mauritius Child Health Project," by A. Raine, P. H. Venables, and S. A. Mednick, 1997, *Journal of the American Academy of Child and Adolescent Psychiatry, 36*, p. 1460. Copyright 1997 by Williams & Wilkins. Reprinted with permission.

case for nonaggressive antisocial behavior, thus suggesting that the relationship is specific to aggression and not to antisocial behavior in general. None of the potentially confounding variables affected these findings.

Skin Conductance. One major measure of skin conductance is the *resting skin conductance response* (RSCR), which is measured during some type of rest period. Like heart rate, RSCR has also been used as an indication of arousal (Lahey et al., 1993; Raine, 1993).

Research assessing the RSCR in antisocial youths has produced mixed results (Lahey et al., 1993; Raine, 1997). For example, although both Venables (1989) and McBurnett et al. (1991) found lower skin conductance levels for conduct-disordered children, other researchers have failed to find significant differences between the RSCL of conduct-disordered children and that of normal controls (e.g., Garralda, Connell, & Taylor, 1991; Schmidt, Solant, & Bridger, 1985). On balance, however, the research suggests that low skin conductance might characterize severe and persistent forms of conduct disorder (Lahey et al., 1993).

A second measure of skin conductance is the *skin conductance recovery rate* (SCRR), an indication of how quickly the SCR goes back to its resting level once it has reached its peak following the introduction of a stimulus. Mednick (1977) argued that SCRR is a measure of how long it takes anxiety to dissipate once it has been aroused. He hypothesizes that children who experience a brief SCRR will learn to inhibit their responses better once anxiety is aroused than children who experience a slow dissipation of the SCRR (and hence, presumably, a slow dissipation of anxiety).

To understand this hypothesis, consider a situation in which a child begins to think about performing a forbidden activity. As the child thinks about the forbidden activity, anxiety is aroused (a SCR is made). If the child then inhibits the forbidden response, anxiety will decrease, resulting in negative reinforcement. Mednick hypothesizes that children whose anxiety dissipates faster will receive more reinforcement for inhibiting the forbidden response than children whose anxiety dissipates more slowly. Hence, they will learn to inhibit forbidden responses more quickly than children whose anxiety dissipates at a slower rate. Thus, Mednick's analysis implies that children who do not inhibit forbidden responses (i.e., antisocial children) should show a longer SCRR than children who do inhibit forbidden responses.

As for empirical results, Loeb and Mednick (1977) found in a prospective study that slow SCRR among their adolescent subjects predicted criminal behavior 5 to 14 years later. In another prospective study, Venables (1989) found that slow SCRR at age 3 predicted fighting at age 9.

Brain-Wave Activity.   Brain-wave measurements reflect the electrical activity of the brain (Raine, 1993). Overall brain activity is measured by the *electroencephalogram* (EEG). Unfortunately, EEG research on aggression is fraught with methodological difficulties and has produced conflicting results, thus rendering its usefulness questionable (Raine, 1993). However, another type of brain-wave measurement called the *event-related potential* (ERP) has produced more promising outcomes.

An ERP is a brain wave produced in response to a specific stimulus (Lahey et al., 1993). One particular type of ERP is called the *P300 wave* because it peaks approximately 300 ms after stimulus onset. In a sample of nonreferred 15-year-old English boys, Raine and Venables (1987) found that boys diagnosed as "undersocialized–psychopathic" showed significantly larger P300 waves than did other boys. Relatedly, Raine, Venables, and Williams (1990) found that 15-year-old boys who had developed a criminal record by the age of 24 showed larger P300 waves than did normal controls. Similar results have also been found for psychopathic adult prisoners (Lahey et al., 1993). These findings are interesting due to the fact that larger P300 waves have been linked theoretically to risk taking and stimulation seeking (Raine, 1993). If confirmed, these findings would provide support for the hypothesis that hyperaggressive children are "bored" with conventional activity and abnormally attracted to risky and thrilling behaviors.

Minor Physical Anomalies

Minor physical anomalies (MPAs) involve relatively minor physical deviations from the norm, including distinctive features such as a curved fifth finger, gaps between the first and second toe, unusual ear placement, and a single transverse palmar crease. Because these deviations typically go unnoticed (even by those who have them), any effects related to MPAs probably do not arise from the reactions to them by either the child or by others in the child's environment (Raine, 1993). And, because the presence of these deviations seems to be linked more closely to environmental prenatal teratogens than to genetic factors, some researchers hypothesize that prenatal teratogens cause both MPAs and alterations in the central nervous system. These neurological changes are in turn hypothesized to result in an innate biological predisposition to aggressive behavior (Raine, 1993).

Research indicates elevated levels of MPAs among aggressive and impulsive preschool boys as well as among elementary school boys diagnosed with conduct disorders (Halverson & Victor, 1976; Paulus & Martin, 1986). In addition, Mednick and Kandel (1988) conducted a study in which an experienced pediatrician assessed the presence of MPAs among 129 12-year-old boys. In a follow-up 9 years later, it was found that childhood MPAs were correlated with subsequent violent offenses, but not with property crimes. Interestingly, however, this relationship held only for youths coming from unstable and nonintact homes but not for those coming from stable homes.

Prenatal, Perinatal, and Early Postnatal Problems

Complications during pregnancy (*prenatal complications*) and those surrounding the birth process itself (*perinatal complications*) have long been hypothesized to play a role in the development of children's behavior problems. In addition, early *postnatal health problems and accidents* have also been implicated in later aggressive behavior.

In a long-term prospective study on Danish boys, Raine and colleagues (Raine, Brennan, B. Mednick, & S. A. Mednick, 1996) found that complications during pregnancy and birth predicted violent crime in late adolescence. Participants were divided into three clusters, depending on their early risk factors: The "biosocial" group (characterized by neonatal neurological problems, slow motor development in infancy, maternal rejection, family conflict, family instability, and parental criminality); the "obstetric" group (characterized by complications during pregnancy and birth, prematurity, and slow motor development during infancy); and the "poverty" group (characterized by multiple social, economic, educational, employment, and living status problems). At the average age of 19, both the biosocial and obstetric groups showed significantly higher levels of violent crime than the poverty group. The results of this study support those of an earlier longitudinal study conducted by Lambert (1988), who found that the combination of prenatal problems, perinatal complications, early postnatal accidents and illness, and the child's early temperament predicted both aggressive and nonaggressive types of conduct disorder in adolescence.

In a related 34-year longitudinal study also conducted in Denmark, Raine and colleagues studied the relationship among socioeconomic status, birth complications, early rejection by the mother, and violent behavior at the average age of 18 (Raine, Brennan, & S. A. Mednick, 1994). Birth complications included events such as the use of forceps, breech delivery, umbilical cord prolapse, and long duration of the birth process. Maternal rejection was indicated by the mother's not wanting the pregnancy, by an attempt at an abortion, and/or by the child's being placed for care into a full-time public institution for at least 4 months during the first year.

As indicated in Figure 4.2, violent crimes (as opposed to nonviolent ones) were more likely to be committed by males who experienced both birth complications and early maternal rejection. Even so, however, only 9% of the members of the this group had committed violent crimes by the age of 18. Interestingly, socioeconomic status itself did not affect the results. A follow-up study when participants were in their mid-30s showed that these results continued to hold for more serious forms of violence (such as murder, rape, assault,

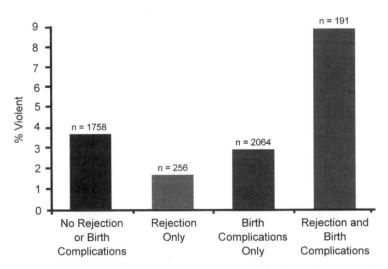

FIG. 4.2.   Criminal violence at age 18 as a function of birth complications and maternal rejection at age 1. From "Birth complications combined with early maternal rejection at age 1 year predispose to violent crime at age 18 years," by A. Raine, P. Brennan, and S. A. Mednick, 1994, *Archives of General Psychiatry, 51*, p. 986. Copyright 1994 by the American Medical Association. Reprinted with permission.

and domestic violence) but not for lesser forms (such as threats and weapons violations; Raine, Brennan, & S. A. Mednick, 1997). These findings are also consistent with those of an earlier study by Cohen, Velez, Brook, and Smith (1989).

In sum, these studies indicate that prenatal and perinatal problems as well as early postnatal health may play a role in the development of aggression. However, exactly what this role may be, and how these factors may lead to later aggression, remain to be elucidated. Moreover, the research indicates that these biological variables may have an effect only when they are combined with other environmental adversities such as negative parental reactions toward the pregnancy and the young child (Farrington, 1998). Additional research is needed to clarify these issues.

Summary and Conclusion

A variety of research suggests that chronically aggressive children and adolescents may differ biologically from less aggressive children. More specifically, these youths tend to show more evidence of brain damage and dysfunction (especially related to the left frontal cortex and precortex), lower levels of the neurotransmitters serotonin and norepinephrine, lower levels of cortisol, a lower resting heart rate, a lower level of resting skin conductance, and longer skin conductance recovery rates. Furthermore, these youths also tend to have more minor physical anomalies and to have experienced more birth complications than their nonaggressive peers.

At a theoretical level, Gray's theory implies that reactive hyperaggression might be related to a weak BIS, whereas instrumental hyperaggression might be related to an overactive BAS. Evidence regarding cortical functioning, neurotransmitter levels, and psychophysiological responses provide some support for the hypothesized link between BIS activity and aggression. However, whether these findings relate specifically to the reactive type of aggression is unclear. Furthermore, virtually no evidence has been found that links hypothesized BAS activity to instrumental aggression.

Perhaps the strongest conclusion we can draw from this body of research is that hyperaggressive youngsters appear to live in a state of chronic central nervous system underarousal. Consistent with our discussion regarding the BIS, it is possible that low arousal might indicate an impaired sense of fear or anxiety, which in turn might make it more difficult for the hyperaggressive youth to learn from punishment (Raine, 1997). This interpretation is consistent with SCRR studies suggesting that anxiety dissipates less quickly in aggressive children than in nonaggressive children. Alternatively, low arousal might also signify a lack of stimulation, which might be felt as an aversive state of boredom (Raine, 1997). In turn, this boredom might motivate aggressive children to become "stimulation seekers" or "thrill seekers," an interpretation consistent with findings based on the P300 wave. Finally, it is also possible that low arousal might signal a child who is both fearless and a thrill seeker. Future research is needed to clarify these possibilities.

CHILD EFFECTS

One theory on child development holds that "bad parents make bad children." Applied to children's aggression, this constitutes what one might call the *parental effects* or *Father Flanagan theory*, named after the founder of Boys Town, who allegedly said, "There are no bad boys, only bad parents." According to this view, any child subjected to "bad parenting" would develop hyperaggressive behavior. A second theory is the *child effects theory*, which holds that children's inherent characteristics cause both their own antisocial behavior as well as negative reactions from others. This view holds that a "bad" child will develop hyperaggressiveness even if given "good" parenting.

As you may have noticed, the parental-effects and child-effects theories are really versions of the more general "nurture" and "nature" viewpoints described at the beginning of this chapter. In chapter 5 we discuss the parental-effects model in more detail. In this section, we concentrate on the child's contribution to the development of his or her aggressive behavior.

Theoretical Overview

Although both the parental-effects and child-effects viewpoints are no doubt oversimplified notions of reality, much of the biological evidence just reviewed suggests that some children may be biologically predisposed toward antisocial behavior and aggression, either because of their genetic makeup or because of their prenatal or early postnatal environmental experiences. This evidence suggests that children make their own contribution to the development of their aggressive behavior (Bell, 1968; Lytton, 1990).

One theorist who has proposed a version of the child-effects position is psychologist Stanton Samenow. Essentially, Samenow (1989) argued that there are some children who, for reasons not yet clear, are simply bad. These children engage in antisocial behavior, not because of poor parenting, socioeconomic disadvantage, peer rejection, or poor academic performance. Rather, they do what they do because they make the choices to do so.

Other psychologists espouse a more deterministically based view of the child-effects model. Primary among these is Hugh Lytton (1990), who has reviewed a great deal of evidence regarding child-effects on aggressive behavior and who concludes that "the child's tendencies predominate over parental characteristics in this domain" (p. 693). More recently, Harris (1998) also argued in favor of a child-effects position.

Data Supporting the Child-Effects Model

In general, the child-effects model is supported by research that shows the stability of aggression from an earlier to a later age; or shows that some previous characteristic of the child is related to subsequent aggression; or shows that the child's characteristics affect another person and that this effect in turn exacerbates the child's own aggression.

Effects From Infancy. One type of child-effects research examines the relationship between the characteristics of very young children and behaviors or traits these children exhibit in later life. These studies are important because results that show a strong link between the child's early and later characteristics support the hypothesis that the later characteristics derive from the earlier ones and not from intervening environmental experiences. On the other hand, results showing a lack of continuity would support the hypothesis that later behaviors arise in large part because of the environment to which the child is exposed during development.

A number of investigators have studied the relationship between infant characteristics and later aggressive behavior. Some of these studies involve the concept of *temperament*, which we discussed in chapter 1. For example, in one prospective study, the researchers assessed more than 100 normal infants during the first year of life (Bates, Maslin, & Frankel, 1985). Degree of *difficultness* (composed of items involving the infant's perceived moodiness, fussiness, crying, and degree of emotional intensity) predicted problem behavior at ages 2 and 3 and conduct disorder at ages 5, 8, and 10.

In research that corroborated and extended these results, Olweus' (1980) longitudinal study found both direct and indirect paths between a difficult-type temperament (highly active, strong willed, and impulsive) in infancy and later aggressiveness in middle childhood. The indirect path was mediated through maternal behavior: Mothers of these boys became more tolerant of the boys' aggressiveness, and this situation in turn led to an increase in aggressiveness. Olweus (1980) concluded that a boy with an active and impulsive temperament might simply "exhaust his mother, resulting in her becoming more permissive of aggression in the boy" (p. 658).

Further evidence for the long-term effects of temperament comes from Werner and Smith's (1982) 20-year prospective study of children born during 1955 on the Hawaiian island of Kauai. One of the major predictors of subsequent learning and/or behavior problems in this study was the mother's perception of her baby as being temperamentally overactive, as having sleeping and eating difficulties, as being nonresponsive to the mother's attempt at emotional closeness, and as not wanting to be cuddled. The mothers reportedly grew frustrated by what they perceived to be their baby's rebuff at their attempts to develop emotional closeness. By the second year, "caregiver and child appeared caught in a vicious cycle of increasing frustration, characterized by parental behavior that was perceived as 'careless,' 'erratic,' 'indifferent,' 'ambivalent,' or 'overprotective' by psychologists during the 20-month examination" (Werner & Smith, 1982, p. 33). This parental behavior, in turn, was related to later behavioral problems in the children.

In these types of studies, it is not clear whether the operative variable in this study was the child's temperament per se, or merely the parents' perception of the child's temperament (Shaw & Winslow, 1997). Methodologically, it thus becomes important that child characteristics be assessed by someone other than those whose interactions with the child can affect the child's subsequent behavior. In this connection, the research showing a link between minor physical anomalies and aggression is especially important, because, as we have seen, MPAs are objectively defined and the effects are not likely due to the reactions of the possessor or of others (Raine, 1993).

Effects From the Preschool Period.   Other research has examined the role of temperament dating from the preschool period. In the longitudinal study of Mauritian children previously described, Raine and colleagues (Scerbo, Raine, Venables, & Mednick, 1995) found that children rated as extremely uninhibited at age 3 were significantly likely to remain uninhibited at age 11. In addition, and consistent with our earlier discussion, uninhibited children at ages 3 and 8 had significantly lower heart rates than inhibited children, and children who remained stably uninhibited between 3 and 8 were twice as likely to have both lower heart rates and lower skin conductance measured at age 3. These differences could not be attributed to physical variables such as the subjects' height and weight (Raine, 1997).

In related research, children's "not easy" temperament during the preschool period predicted aggression at ages 10 to 16 and delinquency at ages 15 to 21 (Loeber, Stouthamer-Loeber, & Green, 1987). This relationship held even when parents' child-rearing practices had been controlled statistically through the use of partial correlations. Thus, the results of this study also provide strong support for the child-effects model.

As we have seen, a variety of research indicates that aggression and antisocial conduct problems are fairly stable in both the short and long term, even when the problem is noticed as early as age 2. In one study, Shaw et al. (1995) found that noncompliance at 18 months predicted aggression at 24 months, which in turn predicted externalizing problems at 36 months. In another study, Campbell and Ewing (1990) conducted a prospective study on a group of 3-year-olds who had been referred because their parents were having trouble managing the children's tantrums, noncompliance, and overactivity. Six years later, two-thirds of these children still had externalizing problems that were severe enough to warrant a DSM diagnosis of ADHD, CD, or ODD.

By age 4, children's hyperaggressive behavior elicits negative responses from peers. Olson (1992) found that 4- and 5-year-old boys who were identified as

socially aggressive at the beginning of a school year tended to show similar behaviors at the end of the year. As the year progressed, these children's aggressive
behaviors elicited more and more counteraggression from their peers, leading
Olson (1992) to conclude that "these findings were consistent with the hypothesis that disliked children initially behave in ways which 'invite' peer rejection"
(p. 346).

Effects From the Elementary School Years. We have already examined research
showing that hyperaggressiveness is relatively stable from age 8 through adulthood (e.g, Huesmann et al., 1984; Robins, 1966; Roff & Wirt, 1984). Other studies also support a child-effects model. For example, West and Farrington (1973)
conducted a 9-year prospective study on 411 children first seen at the age of 8.
They found that "troublesomeness" (assessed at ages 8 and 10 by teacher and
peer ratings) was a potent predictor of delinquency at age 17 and remained so
even when environmental factors such as parental criminality, large family size,
and poor parental supervision had been statistically taken into account. However, when the child's early troublesomeness was taken into account, those
parental characteristics were eliminated as significant predictors of delinquency
at age 17.

The child-effects hypothesis is also supported by an experiment conducted
by K. E. Anderson, Lytton, and Romney (1986), who studied one group of 6- to
12-year-old conduct-disordered boys and their mothers as well as a contrast
group of "normal" boys and their mothers. In one aspect of the study, each
mother interacted with one conduct-disordered boy and one normal child (neither of whom was her son). If conduct disorder is due to parental effects, then
one would expect mothers of conduct-disordered boys to show "bad parenting"
to both types of boys, whereas parents of normal boys would be expected to
show "good parenting" toward both groups. If conduct disorder is due to the
child's own constitutional makeup, then one would expect to find no differences
between "conduct-disordered" and "normal" mothers.

The results of this study were clear: The two groups of mothers did not differ from each other in how they related to the boys in terms of positive behaviors shown toward the boys, negative behaviors shown toward the boys, or
in terms of commands given to the boys. Furthermore, mothers of conduct-
disordered boys were no more likely to be negative toward conduct-disordered
boys than were mothers of normal boys. However, in what might be considered
to be an example of an evocative genotype–environment correlation, both
groups of mothers directed significantly more negative responses and commands to conduct-disordered boys than to normal boys.

Conclusions

A large body of empirical data supports the child-effects hypothesis that characteristics of the child are important determinants of his or her aggressive behav-

ior. In this connection, research strongly indicates that past aggression is the best predictor of future aggression and that young children who are unusually aggressive will likely develop into older children, adolescents, and adults who are also unusually aggressive (e.g., Campbell & Ewing, 1990; Robins, 1966). Other research on temperament, genetics, and biological processes also supports the child-effects position (Lytton, 1990).

SUMMARY

Psychologists have debated for decades the extent to which children's behavior is due to genetic and innate characteristics or to their subsequent environmental experiences. A large and growing body of evidence now indicates that a substantial part of children's hyperaggressiveness is due to internal biological and psychological processes which, if not innate, emerge within the first few years of life. In particular, a number of studies have shown a positive relationship between difficult and uninhibited temperaments in infancy and early childhood and subsequent aggression, delinquency and violence in childhood, adolescence, and adulthood. Furthermore, other characteristics of the child such as minor physical anomalies, unique brain waves, and early neurological impairment are also related to later aggression. Moreover, this relationship appears to be stronger for more violent types of aggression than for less violent types. It now seems highly likely that some children are born with a predisposition to develop hyperaggression and violence, and recent research indicates that these predispositions might have a genetic basis.

Because of a variety of methodological problems, research examining the biological correlates of youthful aggression must be interpreted with caution. In general, however, these studies indicate that hyperaggressivness is associated with neurological impairment, lower levels of certain neurotransmitters and hormones, lower resting heart rate and skin conductance levels, and a larger P300 brain wave. Taken together, these results suggest that hyperaggressive youngsters might experience cortical underarousal and a weak inhibitory system, which in turn might lead to fearlessness, thrill-seeking behavior, and problems in learning from punishment.

Some research indicates that complications before and during birth might affect later aggression. For example, minor physical anomalies, which are linked to prenatal adversity (Raine, 1993), have been shown to be correlated with children's conduct disorders and violent offending in adulthood (Halverson & Victor, 1976; Mednick & Kandel, 1988). Furthermore, birth complications have also been found to predict childhood conduct disorders (P. C. Cohen et al., 1989). But such prenatal and perinatal complications might have their effect only when they interact with other variables such as maternal rejection and stressful family circumstances. Thus, although aggression might have an innate substrate, environmental factors might also be important in determining whether and to what extent this predisposition develops into actual aggressive behavior.

CHAPTER 5

Family Factors

Violent parents tend to have violent children (Eron, 1987; Robins, 1966). This relationship holds for female offspring as well as for males (e.g., Robins, West, & Herjanic, 1975) and is independent of socioeconomic status (Farrington, 1978), neighborhood (S. Glueck & E. T. Glueck, 1968), and intelligence (Farrington, 1978; S. Glueck & E. T. Glueck, 1968). It is thus clear that violence is transmitted intergenerationally.

One possible explanation for this fact is that such intergenerational transmission has a genetic basis (Frick, 1994; Robins, 1966). An alternative view is that violent parents tend to have violent children because of family environments that are similar for both generations (F. E. Gardner, 1992; Hetherington & Martin, 1986; Patterson, DeBaryshe, & Ramsey, 1989). In this chapter, we consider some of the ways in which variables associated with the child's family might play a role in the development of antisocial and hyperaggressive behavior.

PARENTAL CHARACTERISTICS

Two major parental risk factors tend to characterize hyperaggressive children: First, such children tend to be born to mothers under the age of 18; and second, the parents of these children tend to show high rates of certain types of psychopathology.

Teenage Mothers

A variety of studies indicates that males born to unmarried teenage mothers are at high risk for antisocial and aggressive behavior (see Rutter et al., 1998, for a review). Part of this risk appears to be related to characteristics of the woman herself. For example, many of these mothers leave school early and exhibit delinquent behavior (Rutter et al., 1998). As we have seen, delinquent females tend to mate with antisocial males, and any offspring of such a union might be innately predisposed toward antisocial behavior. In addition, teenage mothers often experience a great deal of conflict with their mates, often resulting in the dissolution of the relationship (Rutter et al., 1998). Furthermore, these women also experience a myriad of other risk factors such as low socioeconomic status and lack of emotional support. Combined with single parenthood, these factors can have a negative effect on the mother's parenting skills and hence increase the likelihood that the child will develop antisocial behavior (Rutter et al., 1998).

Parental Psychopathology

Parents of hyperaggressive children tend to show high rates of three types of psychopathology: antisocial behavior, alcoholism, and depression (Biederman, Munir, & Knee, 1987; Frick, 1998; Webster-Stratton & Hammond, 1988).

Parental antisocial behavior and criminality are potent predictors of future antisocial behavior, delinquency, and adult criminality (Gardner, 1992; S. Glueck & E. T. Glueck, 1950; Lahey et al., 1988; Raine, 1993; Robins, 1966). For example, in Farrington's (1989) longitudinal study, parental criminality was the only variable measured at ages 8 to 10 that predicted later adolescent aggression and delinquency. Nevertheless, parental criminality accounts for only about 10% of the variance in the behavior of antisocial children (Farrington & Hawkins, 1991).

Parental alcoholism has also been associated with children's hyperaggression. For example, Frick et al. (1992) found that both oppositional defiant disorder (ODD) and conduct disorder (CD) were significantly associated with parental alcoholism and antisocial personality disorder (mostly in biological fathers). However, other research suggests that paternal criminality is the major predictive factor in sons' future antisocial behavior and that parental alcoholism may be significant only because it is confounded with paternal criminality (McCord, 1991).

Although some researchers have reported an association between externalizing disorders and depression in parents (Griest, Forehand, Wells, & McMahon, 1980; Webster-Stratton, 1988), others have not (Frick et al., 1992). Furthermore, unlike parental antisocial behavior, which seems to be related rather specifically to children's externalizing behavior, parental depression seems to be linked to a wide range of childhood psychopathology, including but not limited to externalizing behavior and conduct disorder (Downey & Coyne, 1990; Frick, 1998). The research thus seems to support the conclusion that "depression does not appear to be necessary or sufficient to produce child behavior problems" (Kendziora & O'Leary, 1993, p. 188).

ATTACHMENT

In chapter 1, we examined the theoretical role that *attachment* plays in children's moral development. As you recall, researchers have delineated four major types of attachment: *secure, insecure/avoidant, insecure/ambivalent,* and *insecure/disorganized.* If attachment is important in the development of children's prosocial behavior, then problems in attachment might also affect children's antisocial and aggressive behavior as well.

Attachment Processes

Theoretical Issues.   According to contemporary researchers, the attachment process is activated when the child experiences stress. In such a situation, secure attachment allows infants to reinstate a sense of security by achieving close physical proximity with a familiar caregiver (Lyons-Ruth, 1996). However, inse-cure/disorganized infants in particular apparently lack a "consistent strategy for organizing responses to the need for comfort and security when under stress" (Lyons-Ruth, 1996, p. 67). As these children move into the preschool years, this disorganized and helpless pattern of responding theoretically gives way to behaviors designed to control or coerce the parent, thus resulting in con-flict, oppositionalism, and aggression (Lyons-Ruth, 1996).

Many researchers view secure attachment as developing from parental be-haviors that are sensitive and responsive to the child's emotional state (e.g., Carlson, 1998; Fonagy et al., 1997). Insecure attachment, on the other hand, arises theoretically from parental behaviors that are erratic, intrusive, and/or inconsistent with the child's needs (Carlson, 1998; Fonagy et al., 1997). Because the caregiver does not respond positively to the child's typical proximity seeking behaviors, the child comes to believe that others are uncaring and consequently begins to imitate this type of callous behavior (Goldberg, 1997). Such infants might develop a kind of cognitive script by which they learn that "you cannot count on or trust others" (Goldberg, 1997, p. 174). Finally, these infants might also engage in oppositional and/or aggressive behavior toward the caregiver in order to "help them maintain their attachments to their otherwise unresponsive parents" (Greenberg, DeKlyen, Speltz, & Endriga, 1997, p. 201).

Research.   Despite the theoretical importance of this topic, relatively few controlled empirical studies have been conducted on the relationship between attachment and aggression, and the results have been mixed: Although some studies have found that insecure attachment is related to subsequent aggres-sion, others have failed to find such a relationship (see Lyons-Ruth, 1996, for a review).

One major set of findings on this topic comes from the Minnesota High Risk Study conducted in the early 1980s (Erickson, Sroufe, & Egeland, 1985). In this prospective study, the researchers related infant attachment status to social be-havior at the age of 4. They found that insecurely attached children tended to be more impulsive and aggressive than securely attached children. A subsequent follow-up study found that avoidant attachment in infancy continued to predict aggression for first- to third-grade boys, but not for girls (Cohn, 1990; Renken, Egeland, Marvinney, Mangelsdorf, & Sroufe, 1989; Turner, 1991).

Research on the relationship between insecure/disorganized attachment and aggression has also produced mixed results. In one study, Lyons-Ruth, Alpern, and Repacholi (1993) found that insecure/disorganized attachment at 18 months predicted hostile aggression toward peers among low-income kindergarten children. In another study, Lyons-Ruth, Easterbrooks, and Cibelli (1997) found that clinical levels of externalizing behavior among 7-year-olds were predicted by the interaction of insecure/disorganized attachment in infancy and low mental development scores obtained at 18 months. However, in a prospective longitudinal study spanning the time between infancy and age 19, Carlson (1998) found that although insecure/disorganized attachment predicted pre-school behavior problems among a group of at-risk children, it was unrelated to teacher-reported externalizing behavior measured five times between first grade and high school.

Results implicating attachment difficulties in children's subsequent antisocial behavior have been found most often among economically and socially at-risk families. As many as 80% of infants in such families have been observed to exhibit insecure/disorganized attachment (Lyons-Ruth, 1996). As Rutter (1997) pointed out, environments that put children at risk regarding attachment might also cause other problems as well. Given this potential confounding, attachment might or might not play a causal role in related psychopathological behavior.

In many studies, attachment status seems to affect aggression through an interaction with other variables such as gender (Cohn, 1990; Renken et al., 1989; Speltz, Greenberg, & DeKlyen, 1990; Turner, 1991), maternal depression (Lyons-Ruth et al., 1993), the mother's hostile, intrusive behavior toward the child (Lyons-Ruth et al., 1993), lack of a partner living with the mother (Renken et al., 1989), and the child's intelligence (Lyons-Ruth et al., 1997). Attachment is also related to the child's temperament, with difficult children tending to be less securely attached than easy children (Hetherington & Martin, 1986). Exactly which variables interact with attachment, and how the process works, remains to be elucidated.

Much remains to be learned regarding the relationship between attachment and children's hyperaggressive behavior. For example, insecure/avoidant, insecure/ambivalent, and insecure/disorganized types have all been linked with aggression (Renken et al., 1989), but the question of which type of insecure attachment might lead to aggression has not been resolved. In addition, most of the findings to date have involved subclinical levels of aggression and children under the age of 8, with little data relating infant attachment status to later hyperaggressive behavior of the type found among CD children and adolescents.

In view of the fact that most children with insecure forms of attachment do not manifest externalizing psychopathology, and that many children with secure forms do show behavioral problems, it is not likely that attachment deficiencies are direct causes of children's hyperaggressive behavior (Fonagy et al., 1997). As one group of researchers put it, although attachment might be an important risk factor, it is "neither a necessary nor sufficient cause for later externalizing problems" (Greenberg et al., 1997, p. 199).

"Attachment Disorder": A New Disorder?

Despite the lack of supporting research, some writers have popularized the notion that lack of attachment causes subsequent antisocial and aggressive behavior. According to this view, when the baby's needs become too strong, the baby will respond with a *rage reaction,* a behavior designed to motivate the caregiver to meet the baby's needs (Magid & McKelvey, 1987, chap. 5). If the baby's needs are consistently met, the baby will develop trust and attachment toward the attentive caregiver. However, failure to meet the baby's needs produces a lack of trust and an inability on the part of the baby to bond with other humans. As a result, the child fails to develop a conscience (Magid & McKelvey, 1987) and instead manifests a set of antisocial symptoms which are said to comprise *attachment disorder* (Levy & Orlans, 1998).

According to Levy and Orlans (1998) "attachment disorder" is defined by six categories of symptoms, each of which consists of a number of specific behavioral symptoms. These six categories are the *behavioral* (which includes 20 separate specific symptoms); the *cognitive* (5 symptoms); the *affective* (5 symptoms); the *social* (10 symptoms); the *physical* (6 symptoms); and the *moral/spiritual* (4 symptoms). Some examples of these symptoms are listed in Box 5.1. Unlike the case with the *DSM-IV,* Levy and Orlans (1998) gave no guidelines as to how many symptoms from each category should be present in order for a diagnosis to be made.

Evaluation.   Although the concept of attachment disorder has intuitive appeal, there are a number of reasons to question its use:

• As we saw in chapter 3, a psychological disorder is "true" or "real" to the extent to which it can be demonstrated to have both reliability and construct validity. In terms of reliability, many of the alleged symptoms of attachment disorder are vague and lack behavioral definitions. For example, how does one determine whether a child is "not affectionate on parents' terms"? Or, how does one know if a child lacks "meaning and purpose"? The lack of clear behavioral definitions limits the reliability of the category of attachment disorder. As for validity, I have been unable to find any published empirical research regarding the construct validity of attachment disorder.

• Many variables that might cause later aggressiveness are often confounded in the cases of children who exhibit attachment disorder. For example, many of the children cited as having attachment disorder are either foster children or children who have been adopted (Levy & Orlans, 1998). These children might have been sent to foster homes or given up for adoption precisely because they

BOX 5.1

SOME SYMPTOMS OF "ATTACHMENT DISORDER"

Category	Symptom
Behavioral	Lack of impulse control
	Destruction of property
	Aggression toward others
	Stealing
	Lying
	Hoarding
	Cruelty to animals
	Enuresis and Encopresis
	Oppositional
	Hyperactivity
	Persistent nonsense questions and incessant chatter
	Poor hygiene
Cognitive	Lack of cause-and-effect thinking
	Learning disorders
	Language disorders
Affective	Not affectionate on parents' terms
	Intense displays of anger
	Frequently sad, depressed, or helpless
Social	Superficially engaging and charming
	Lack of eye contact for closeness
	Lack of stable peer relationships
	Cannot tolerate limits and external control
	Victimizes others
	Victimized by others
Physical	Poor hygiene
	Chronic body tension
	Accident prone
Moral / Spiritual	Lack of meaning and purpose
	Lack of faith, compassion, and other spiritual values
	Identification with evil and the dark side of life

Note: From *Attachment, Trauma, and Healing* (pp. 93–105) by T. M. Levy and M. Orlans, 1995, Washington, DC: CWLA Press.

have a history of risk factors (e.g., psychopathological parent, prenatal difficulties, abuse, etc.), which have been implicated in the genesis of hyperaggressiveness. Thus, any aggressiveness exhibited by these children might be due to these other factors and not to a lack of attachment per se.

• Some of the symptoms of this alleged disorder (e.g., oppositional, aggression, stealing, lying, and destruction of property) are also found as definitional criteria for ODD or CD, whereas others (e.g., hyperactivity, unstable peer relationships, and problems in self-control) seem to be correlates of these disorders. It thus appears that many of the children who are said to have attachment disorder could easily be classified as having ODD or CD, thus calling into question the validity of another similar syndrome.

In summary, the use of the concept of attachment disorder seems completely unwarranted. Rather than continuing to make use of a such a questionable concept, educators and mental health professionals would be better off using traditional diagnostic categories, which at least have the benefit of a body of empirical knowledge to support them.

PARENT-CHILD INTERACTIONS

We now turn to an examination of the manner in which parent–child interactions might be related to children's aggressive behavior.

Theoretical Considerations

Baumrind's Theory. Maccoby and Martin (1983) proposed that parents' child-rearing behaviors can be classified according to two major dimensions. The *warm-responsive versus cold-rejecting* dimension emphasizes the emotional relationship between parent and child (Hetherington & Martin, 1986). The second dimension, called *demanding-strict versus undemanding-lax,* refers to the extent to which parents set behavioral expectations for their children and demand that children meet these expectations. In her work, Diana Baumrind (1967, 1971) has applied these two dimensions to specify four major types of parenting styles: *authoritarian* (cold–demanding), *authoritative* (warm–demanding), *neglectful* (cold–lax), and *permissive* (warm–lax).

Research by Baumrind and others (see Maccoby & Martin, 1983) indicated that authoritative parents are most likely to produce children who have high internal standards of morality and who tend to maintain these standards in their behavior. But neglectful and permissive parents seem to have children who are the least self-controlled and the most aggressive (Maccoby & Martin, 1983). Based on these considerations, Baumrind's theory would predict that aspects of authoritative parenting should be positively associated with children's prosocial behavior, whereas aspects of the other three types should be found among antisocial and aggressive children.

Patterson's Theory. Another important theory in this area has been the *coercion theory* proposed by Gerald Patterson and his colleagues (Patterson, 1982; Patterson et al., 1989; Patterson, Reid, & Dishion, 1992).

According to this theory, children's hyperaggression develops from a multitude of daily behavioral exchanges within the family. In some cases, the exchange begins with a parental request or command. The child then refuses to comply, either actively (e.g., by arguing) or passively (by continuing what he is doing). In response, the parent might initially nag or natter the child. When the child still refuses, the behaviors of both parent and child are likely to escalate into yelling or other unpleasant emotional exchanges (such as the child hitting the parent, or vice versa). Ultimately, however, the parent backs down and the child's noncompliance and aggressiveness are thus negatively reinforced by the termination of the parent's demands. In Patterson's terms, the child learns a pattern of *coercive behavior.* Relatedly, the parent's withdrawal from the situation is also negatively reinforced by the termination of the child's aggression. Thus, both child and parent behaviors are reinforced: The child becomes more likely to refuse to comply in the future and to aggress when pressed to do so, and the parent becomes less likely to try to force the child to comply.

Another situation arises when the child makes a demand (such as wanting to watch television) or when the child actively aggresses (as when one preschool child takes a toy from another). In such cases, the child's demandingness or aggression might be positively reinforced: For example, if the parent allows the child to watch television, or if the child is allowed to play with the purloined toy, those behaviors become more likely in the future. Furthermore, the parent's behaviors are negatively reinforced, because giving in to the child or allowing the child to play with the toy allows the parent to avoid a possible confrontation with the child.

In sum, Patterson hypothesizes that when conflicts with their child arise, parents of aggressive children typically respond ineffectually. As a result, the child learns a set of coercive behaviors and the parent learns child management behaviors that are effective in the short term (because they terminate the child's aggression) but ineffective in the long run (because they perpetuate the child's antisocial behavior).

This reciprocal parent–child behavior pattern is learned gradually. Over time, these unpleasant cycles of behavior become more intense (often involving physical aggression) and more ingrained within the family of aggressive children. Hence, "the child eventually learns to control other family members through coercive means" (Patterson et al., 1989, p. 330). At the same time, the child's parents fail to reinforce prosocial behaviors. Thus, children in these families develop a prepotent set of antisocial behaviors but fail to develop important prosocial behaviors (Patterson et al., 1989).

On the basis of his past research, Patterson hypothesizes a number of specific child management problems faced by parents of highly aggressive children. First, these parents classify more behaviors as deviant than do parents of "normal" children, and they fail to ignore relatively minor instances of inappropriate behavior. Second, they tend to nag their child for inappropriate behavior but fail to act appropriately to back up their commands. Third, when these parents do punish their children, the punishment often increases the coercive behavior (a phenomenon known as *punishment acceleration*). And fourth, these parents often do not know where their children are, with whom they are associating, what they are doing, or when they will come home (Patterson et al., 1992).

Summary.   Both Baumrind and Patterson have developed provocative theories regarding the manner in which parent–child interactions might contribute to the development of children's antisocial and hyperaggressive behaviors. We now examine this issue in more detail.

Parent–Child Affective Relationships

A good deal of research supports the hypothesis that families of hyperaggressive children are characterized by a low level of emotional warmth and a high level of mutual hostility (Bandura & Walters, 1959; Cernkovich & Giordano, 1987; K. J. Conger & R. D. Conger, 1994; S. Glueck & E. T. Glueck, 1950; Hanson, Henggeler, Haefele, & Rodick, 1984; Loeber & Dishion, 1984; Seydlitz & Jenkins, 1998). Moreover, in structured laboratory situations, families of delinquents display less warmth and more hostility toward each other than is the case for families of nondelinquents (Hetherington, Stouwie, & Ridberg, 1971). However, emotional hostility between parents and children is positively associated with antisocial and aggressive behavior, whereas an emotionally warm relationship seems to protect children against externalizing behaviors (McCord, 1983; Rothbaum & Weisz, 1994).

Parental Commands

As described previously, research on the relationship between ODD and CD suggests that these two disorders are closely linked (Hinshaw et al., 1993). If this is so, then any family factors that contribute to the development of ODD might also be important for the understanding of CD.

Rex Forehand and his colleagues have found that parents of ODD children differ from parents of control children in the types of commands they issue and in how they follow through with commands (Forehand, King, Peed, & Yoder, 1975; Forehand & McMahon, 1981). Forehand distinguishes two types of commands, *alpha* commands and *beta* commands. Alpha commands are direct and require a motor response. Beta commands, on the other hand, are vague, or are such that the child has a difficult time complying with them. Parents of problem children tend to give beta commands rather than alpha commands. In addition, they issue a greater number of commands and they present commands in a nagging, angry, or humiliating manner. Thus, parents of ODD children differ from "normal" parents in both the quality and quantity of commands they give, and this difference is in turn related to the child's noncompliant behavior (Lobitz & Johnson, 1975).

Parental Modeling

The hypothesis that children learn antisocial and aggressive behavior through observational learning has received some empirical support. For example, Simons, Whitbeck, Conger, and Chyi-In (1991), studying four hypotheses regarding the intergenerational transmission of aggression, found strong support for the modeling hypothesis for both mothers and fathers. This hypothesis is also consistent with the fact that children who are physically abused are at risk for elevated levels of aggressive behavior.

On the other hand, other findings cause some complications for a pure modeling explanation. For example, Truscott (1992) found that violence among juvenile delinquents was associated with the child experiencing violence in the home, but not with simply witnessing it. Thus, it took more than simply observing a violent model to turn these boys into violent juveniles. In a similar vein, Eron (1987) found that children who identified with their parents did not show a high level of aggression, even under high levels of physical punishment. Because modeling theory predicts that learning will more often occur when the child identifies with the model, this finding poses a problem for observational learning theory. Therefore, although there is good theoretical reason to suspect observational learning as an important process in the development of chronic aggressiveness, the relatively sparse amount of available research is not totally consistent with this hypothesis.

Reinforcement of Coercive Behaviors

As just mentioned, Patterson's theory holds that aggressive children and their parents become embroiled in a coercive chain of behavior in which the child's aggression is negatively reinforced by the parents. In testing this hypothesis with CD preschool children and their mothers, F. E. Gardner (1989) found that the CD mothers were eight times more likely to capitulate to their children's demands than were the normal mothers, especially when the behavioral sequence began with a command from the mother as opposed to a demand from the child. In addition, there was also some evidence that CD mothers were more likely to positively reinforce children's demands than were mothers of normal children. A more recent observational study reported similar results (Snyder & Patterson, 1995), thus lending further support to the coercion hypothesis. However, even in these at-risk families, less than 20% of the interactions involve some sort of conflict (F. E. Gardner, 1987).

Tolerance of Antisocial Behavior

A number of studies have shown that *lax parental discipline* (i.e., parental failure to insist that children behave prosocially and to impose appropriate negative consequences when children behave antisocially) is also positively related to children's aggression. For example, Hoge, Andrews, and Leschied (1994) found that low parental supervision, lack of discipline, and inconsistent discipline significantly predicted serious crime (including violent activities) for a large group of convicted male and female adolescent offenders between the ages of 12 and 17. Other research indicates that fathers of both aggressive and hyperactive aggressive children allow their children more free rein in their behavior than do fathers of less aggressive children (W. McCord, J. McCord, & Howard, 1961; Stormont-Spurgin & Zentall, 1996). Finally, Laybourn (1986) found that lax discipline and low behavioral standards were positively associated with delinquency.

Physical Punishment

Parental use of *harsh physical punishment* is positively correlated with youngsters' antisocial and delinquent behavior (Snyder & Patterson, 1987). For example, Farrington (1989) found that harsh physical discipline measured at age 8 and an authoritarian discipline style measured at age 10 predicted violent criminal offending at age 32. Similarly, McCord (1991) found that fathers' physical punishment predicted their offsprings' adult criminality even when paternal criminality was controlled. Other studies, however, have raised questions regarding the existence of a direct link between harsh physical punishment and aggression (Eron, 1987; Robins, 1966).

Recent research provides a more complex picture regarding the relationship between punishment and youngsters' externalizing behaviors (Coie & Dodge, 1998). First, some studies indicate that the affective relationship between parent and child might mediate the effects of harsh parental punishment (Eron, 1987; Deater-Deckard & Dodge, 1997). Second, it is possible that parents might initially use harsh physical punishment primarily in response to the child's already existing aggressive behavior, and that in turn this type of punishment might then cause the child's existing antisocial behavior to become even worse (Cohen & Brook, 1995; Kandel & Wu, 1995). Third, some research on this topic might have confounded parental punishment with parent–child conflict. For example, one study found that high levels of parentally reported punishment toward high-risk 9-year-olds were associated with low levels of externalizing behavior 15 months later (Wasserman, Miller, Pinner, & Jaramillo, 1996). The authors concluded that "once the conflictual aspect of parent–child interaction is taken into account, greater discipline, *harsh or otherwise,* reduces conduct problems" (Wasserman et al., 1996, p. 1234, emphasis added). Finally, some research suggests that severe punishment is likely to increase antisocial behavior only during the transitional period from childhood to adolescence (Cohen & Brook, 1995). Taken together, these findings thus suggest a rather complex relationship between physical punishment and aggression.

Consistency of Consequences

Some researchers have argued that "the *consistency* of parental behavior is more important than the methods parents use for enforcing their demands" (W. Mc-Cord & J. McCord, 1959, p. 78, emphasis in the original). Unfortunately, many of the studies regarding this issue have confounded consistency with one or more other variables. For example, in their meta-analysis, Loeber and Stouthamer-Loeber (1986) found it necessary to consider consistency along with strictness, because so few studies had focused solely on consistency. Nevertheless, the studies that have been conducted on this issue suggest that inconsistent discipline is indeed related to children's hyperaggressiveness (S. Glueck & E. T. Glueck, 1950; W. McCord & J. McCord, 1959; Moore & Arthur, 1989).

Parental Supervision and Monitoring

Parents' failure to supervise and monitor their children's behavior is one of the best predictors of children's later aggressiveness and delinquency (Blumstein, Cohen, Roth, & Visher, 1986; Loeber & Stouthamer-Loeber, 1986). This *parental supervision and monitoring* variable has been shown to be important in a methodologically diverse group of studies (Loeber & Schmaling, 1985b; West & Farrington, 1973); to hold both in the United States and abroad (Haapasalo & Tremblay, 1994; Laybourn, 1986; Patterson & Dishion, 1985); and to occur in studies in which delinquency has been measured by self-report as well as by official records (West & Farrington, 1973; Wilson, 1980). This variable has also been linked to children's physical aggressiveness both at home and at school (Loeber & Dishion, 1984) and has been shown to predict conduct disorder, delinquency, and adult criminality (Farrington, 1979; McCord, 1979). In addition, parental supervision is related to the seriousness of adult crime, as well as recidivism in adulthood (Snyder & Patterson, 1987). Finally, Patterson and Yoerger (1993) indicated that this variable might be a better predictor in cases where antisocial behavior begins before the age of 14 than when its onset is later.

A variety of studies suggest that parental monitoring may be especially important for at-risk youths such as brothers of older delinquents, those living in single-parent homes, or those living in neighborhoods perceived to be unsafe (Cernkovich & Giordano, 1987; Laybourn, 1986; Pettit, Bates, Dodge, & Meece, 1999; Wasserman et al., 1996). Other research indicates at least three reasons why this should be the case. First, unmonitored youths have more unsupervised time during which they can engage in delinquent acts (Patterson & Dishion, 1985). Second, unmonitored youths not only have more time on their hands, but they use this time to interact with antisocial peers, thus increasing the likelihood of subsequent delinquent behaviors (Patterson & Dishion, 1985). And third, parental monitoring enhances youngsters' ability to resist peer pressure to perform delinquent acts (Fridrich & Flannery, 1995).

Parental Involvement

The extent to which parents and children become involved with each other and engage in leisure activities together has been closely linked to youngsters' moral behavior (Canter, 1982; Hirschi, 1969). Indeed, Farrington and Hawkins (1991) reported that low *parental involvement* with boys in leisure activities at age 11 was the best predictor of both early onset of criminal offending (by the age of 13) and the persistence of offending from ages 21 to 32. Moreover, this variable was an even better predictor of adult offending than was self-reported delinquency at age 18.

Raine (1993) pointed out that parental involvement may be so powerful because "it manages to encapsulate a wide number of other familial variables" (p. 261). For example, when children and parents spend leisure time together, it is likely that the child has become attached to the parent, that the parent nurtures and accepts the child, and that the parent monitors the child's activities. In addition, identification with the parent also predisposes the child to choose peers whose values are congruent with those of the parents, thus increasing the likelihood of continuing prosocial behavior. A lack of leisure time involvement might indicate a host of other family related problems, such as a lack of attachment, nurturance, and identification; a harsh parental discipline style; and a generally conflictful family situation.

Summary

The bulk of the research discussed supports both Baumrind's and Patterson's theories. More specifically, children's aggression is reduced by authoritative parenting practices that emphasize a positive affective relationship between parents and children combined with parental monitoring and supervision, limit-setting, and consistently applied and appropriate negative consequences when limits are transgressed. At the same time, antisocial and aggressive behavior is more likely when parents model such behavior, when they are overly harsh and punitive, when they fail to issue commands effectively, and when they reinforce coercive behavior, either positively or negatively.

CHILD ABUSE AND NEGLECT

Child abuse and neglect has been widely linked to youthful antisocial and aggressive behavior (see Widom, 1997, for a review). In this connection, researchers have delineated four categories of child maltreatment.

- *Physical abuse* is defined as any act that results in nonaccidental injury to the child committed by someone caring for a child (Wenar, 1994). Injuries due to physical abuse might result from either commissions or omissions and might be minor or serious.
- *Sexual abuse* involves a situation in which an adult engages in any sexual act with a child, including incest, sexual molestation, unwanted touching and kissing, or intercourse (Wenar, 1994; Widom, 1997).
- *Emotional abuse* (also called *psychological abuse*) has been defined as involving "acts of rejection; coercive, punitive, and erratic discipline; denigration; unrealistic behavioral expectations; chaotic family environment; and refusal to provide help to an emotionally disturbed child" (Wolfe & St. Pierre, 1989, p. 378). Some authorities believe that emotional abuse is an inherent part of all forms of child maltreatment (Wolfe & St. Pierre, 1989).
- *Child neglect* involves any situation in which a caregiver fails to provide the child with necessities such as food, shelter, health care, supervision, and education (Wenar, 1994; Widom, 1997).

Most instances of child maltreatment involve either neglect or physical abuse resulting in minor injuries (Wolfe & St. Pierre, 1989). For example, in 1996, approximately 52% of reported cases involved neglect and 24% involved physical abuse, with most of the physical abuse involving minor injuries such as cuts, welts, and bruises. About 12% of reported cases involved sexual abuse, whereas the remainder involved either emotional abuse or medical neglect (U.S. Bureau of the Census, 1998; Wicks-Nelson & Israel, 2000).

Most child abuse occurs within the family and, as a general rule, maltreated children are more likely to experience a variety of environmental stressors and to grow up in families on public assistance and headed by single mothers (Wicks-Nelson & Israel, 2000; Wolfe & St. Pierre, 1989). However, children experiencing neglect tend to grow up in lower socioeconomic conditions than do those who are abused (Wolock & Horowitz, 1984). Finally, neglect and various types of abuse might also be found in the same family (Lewis, 1994).

Child Maltreatment and Youthful Aggression

Much of the research regarding the possible relationship between child maltreatment and children's contemporaneous and subsequent aggression is fraught with methodological difficulties (Schwartz, Rendon, & Hsieh, 1994; Widom, 1989c, 1997). Because of these problems, this body of research must be interpreted with caution.

In general, the bulk of the research suggests that child abuse and neglect affects children's development "in a circuitous and unpredictable manner that shows little patterning of symptoms" (Wolfe & St. Pierre, 1989, p. 394). These symptoms include not only aggression and noncompliance, but also poor peer relationships, insecure attachment, impaired moral development, indications of anxiety and insecurity, speech and language difficulties, impaired social cognition, and poor academic achievement (Azar, Ferraro, & Breton, 1998; Wolfe & St. Pierre, 1989).

Although many studies have confounded the various types of maltreatment, physical abuse appears most clearly related to youngsters' aggressive and antisocial behavior (Coie & Dodge, 1998). For example, physically abused infants and toddlers have been found to physically assault caregivers and peers more than do comparison children (George & Main, 1979), and physically abused 3-to-5-year-olds engage in more aggressive behavior than sexually abused or neglected children or matched nonabused controls (Fagot, Hagan, Youngblade, & Potter, 1989; Hoffman-Plotkin & Twentyman, 1984). However, some studies with preschool children have failed to find differences between physically abused children and normal controls (e.g., Rohrbeck & Twentyman, 1986).

Other studies suggest that older abused children are also more aggressive than their nonabused peers. For example, Reidy (1977) found that abused 6- and 7-year-olds showed more aggression in fantasy and free play than did neglected and normal comparison children. In another study examining 8- to 12-year-old Israeli children, physically abused children showed more self-reported externalizing problems than a matched control group (Sternberg et al., 1993).

Finally, evidence also indicates that abused adolescents show elevated levels of aggression compared with nonabused peers. For example, McCord (1983) found that 22% of abused boys and 23% of neglected boys were subsequently convicted for serious juvenile crimes, compared with 11% of matched-control boys. Other studies have shown that abuse is prevalent among extremely violent adolescents (Lewis et al., 1988; Truscott, 1992). However, one study found that child maltreatment was related to adolescent status offenses but not to property crimes or crimes of violence (Zingraff, Leiter, Myers, & Johnsen, 1993), thus suggesting that such delinquent behaviors are an attempt to escape the maltreatment rather than an indication of an aggressive personality (Schwartz et al., 1994). This hypothesis is supported by data showing that "the antisocial impact from parental abuse, neglect and rejection is largely reflected in juvenile delinquency" rather than in adult criminality (McCord, 1983, p. 268).

The "Cycle of Violence" Hypothesis

It is popularly believed that "violence begets violence" and that experiencing abuse as a child causes violent behavior in adulthood (Widom, 1989c), but research on this *cycle of violence* hypothesis has produced mixed results. Widom's (1989a) longitudinal study comparing a large sample of substantiated cases of physical and sexual abuse and neglect with those of a matched control group with no history of abuse seemed to provide evidence in support of this hypothesis. When records of these two groups were compared when the victims were in their mid-twenties, abused and neglected subjects had a higher rate of having an adult criminal record than did nonabused subjects. Furthermore, abused subjects had higher rates of arrest for violent offenses than did control subjects.

Thus far, Widom's results seem consistent with the cycle of violence hypothesis. However, other considerations cast doubt on this interpretation. For one thing, only 29% of the abused and neglected children in Widom's study had criminal records (Widom, 1989a), thus indicating that more than two thirds of such children do not become adult criminals. In addition, Raine's (1993) analysis indicates that Widom's results were due primarily to the data from the Black males in her sample and did not hold for females and Whites. Furthermore, another analysis of Widom's data showed that children who experienced only neglect as children were almost as likely to become violent adults as were children who experienced only physical abuse (Widom, 1989b). Finally, Widom's (1989b) data also showed that children who experienced a combination of both physical abuse and neglect were less likely to become violent adults than were control subjects.

Subsequent studies on this issue have not produced entirely consistent results. Using retrospective reports of exposure to interparental violence obtained at age 18, Fergusson and Horwood (1998) found that even after adjustment for potentially confounding factors, exposure to paternal-initiated violence was associated with an increased risk for adolescent conduct disorder and property crime. Similarly, both Weiler and Widom (1996) and Koivisto and Haapasalo (1996) found that childhood abuse and neglect predicted subsequent psychopathy in adulthood. However, one prospective study found that although abused/ neglected females were at significantly higher risk for arrests for violent crimes in adulthood, males were at risk for arrest for nonviolent crimes (Widom & White, 1997). Thus, although there does seem to be an elevated level of violence among adults who were abused and neglected as children, the exact relationship between childhood maltreatment and adult violence remains to be elucidated.

Potential Mediating Processes

Recent research has begun to delineate the psychological processes that might mediate the relationship between abuse and neglect and aggression. For example, some studies suggest that maltreatment might cause young children to focus on their personal distress, hence interfering with these youngsters' ability to empathize with others. Support for this hypothesis comes from studies showing that nonabused preschool children react to peers with interest and/or concern, whereas abused children react by displays of anger and physical aggression (Klimes-Dougan & Kistner, 1990; Main & George, 1985).

Lewis (1994) pointed out that physical maltreatment of animals tends to produce a hypervigilant type of behavior that has also been found among some abused children. Furthermore, Lewis also indicates that the symptoms most characteristic of the violent youngsters she studied are paranoid ideation and misperception, both of which are reminiscent of the hypervigilance found in some abused children. In a similar vein, Dodge and colleagues found that physical abuse in kindergarten predicted a number of social information-processing problems among third and fourth graders. These problems, which included hypervigilance to hostile cues, hostile attributional biases, and aggressive problem-solving strategies, contributed to as much as half of the relationship between early physical abuse and subsequent aggressive behavior (Coie & Dodge, 1998; Weiss, Dodge, Bates, & Pettit, 1992).

Finally, consistent with our discussion on the biological correlates of aggression, Lewis (1994) suggested the possibility that chronic exposure to abuse might contribute to children's aggression by reducing their level of serotonin while increasing their level of testosterone.

Conclusions

A vast amount of research has established a relationship between various forms of child maltreatment and children's contemporaneous and subsequent aggression. At the same time, however, severe methodological flaws limit the interpretation of much of this literature (Schwartz et al., 1994). In addition, Widom (1997) noted that no more than a third of abused children become delinquent, and that no more than a quarter of delinquents have been abused. Furthermore, abuse seems to produce a diffuse pattern of symptoms that, in any one child, does not necessarily include aggression or other externalizing disorders (Azar et al., 1998; Wolfe & St. Pierre, 1989). Thus, although child maltreatment may play an important role in the etiological mix affecting youthful aggression, its exact role in the causation of children's hyperaggressiveness remains to be clarified (Schwartz et al., 1994).

FAMILY COMPOSITION

Because of the vast changes in family structure in the United States over the past 40 years, family composition is a potentially important variable for understanding youth violence. We now turn to an examination of this issue.

Research

Intact Families. The majority of available research indicates that children living with both biological parents (i.e., those living in *intact families*) are less likely to exhibit aggressive and antisocial behavior than are those living in other types of homes (*nonintact families;* Amato & Keith, 1991; Angel & Angel, 1993; Borkhuis & Patalano, 1997; Haurin, 1992; Kalter, Riemer, Brickman, & Woo Chen, 1985; Kellam, Ensminger, & Turner, 1977; Shaw, Winslow, & Flanagan, 1999; Tremblay, Mâsse, Pagani, & Vitaro, 1996; Vaden-Kiernan, Ialongo, Pearson, & Kellam, 1995; Webster-Stratton, 1989; Wells & Rankin, 1991). However, some studies have not found less aggression and antisocial behavior among children raised in intact families (Ellison, 1983; Enos & Handal, 1986; Hess & Camara, 1979; F. I. Nye, 1957; Zimmerman, Salem, & Maton, 1995), especially in cases where marital conflict is high (Amato & Keith, 1991; Cummings & Davies, 1994; Emery, 1982; Grych & Fincham, 1990; Peterson & Zill, 1986).

Parental Death. Children from single-parent homes due to the death of a parent are at minimal risk for future antisocial or aggressive behavior problems (Hetherington, Bridges, & Insabella, 1998; Robins, 1979; Rutter, 1982; Wadsworth, 1979; West & Farrington, 1973).

Single-Parent Homes. Most research indicates that children in single-parent, mother-alone homes show elevated levels of externalizing problems (Angel & Angel, 1993; Blum, Boyle, & Offord, 1988; Conseur, Rivara, Barnoski, & Emanuel, 1997; Dodge, Pettit, & Bates, 1994; Dornbusch et al., 1985; Duncan, Brooks-Gunn, & Klebanov, 1994; Ensminger, Kellam, & Rubin, 1983; Kellam et al., 1977; Shaw et al., 1999; Webster-Stratton, 1989). This finding is especially true for boys and holds even after controlling for socioeconomic status (Hetherington et al., 1998).

Effects of Divorce. In general, children who live in homes that have been disrupted by divorce are more likely to exhibit antisocial and aggressive behavior than are children who live in intact families (Amato & Keith, 1991; Demo & Acock, 1988; Duncan et al., 1994; Hetherington et al., 1998; Wells & Rankin, 1991). In this connection, Hetherington et al. (1998) concluded that youngsters from divorced or remarried families are twice as likely as those from intact families to exhibit externalizing behaviors (including CD), to become involved with delinquent activities and substance abuse, and to associate with antisocial peers. Interestingly, in the Amato and Keith (1991) meta-analysis, the effect of divorce on externalizing behavior was no different for boys than for girls.

"Step-" or "Blended" Families. Although evidence regarding the relationship between living in a *step-family* (or *blended family*) and children's aggression is mixed, it appears that having a stepfather in the house might put children (and especially boys) at some additional risk for antisocial and aggressive behavior (Amato & Keith, 1991; Dornbusch et al., 1985; Ganong & Coleman, 1993; Kellam et al., 1977; McCord, 1982).

Explanations

Although children living in intact homes seem to be at less risk for antisocial and aggressive behaviors than are children living in other family arrangements, this relationship appears to be modest and may be due to confounded factors rather than to family composition itself. We now examine some of the most promising explanations for this situation.

Parental Characteristics. The first explanation suggests that the relationship between family composition and children's aggression is spurious because both factors are caused by parental personality and behavioral characteristics. More specifically, this position holds that antisocial and aggressive parents (especially fathers) are both more likely to have aggressive-prone children and to experience marital difficulties (Harris, 1998). This perspective is supported by findings that antisocial males are more likely to have antisocial sons and to get divorced (Lahey et al., 1988), and that, compared with parents who do not get divorced, parents whose marriages will be disrupted are irritable and nonauthoritative as much as 8 to 12 years prior to the divorce (Amato & Booth, 1996). The fact that divorce is heritable (Jockin, McGue, & Lykken, 1996) suggests that parental characteristics associated with aggressive offspring might be heritable as well.

Marital Discord and Conflict. A popular hypothesis states that the discord and conflict surrounding an unhappy marriage might be the best explanation for the externalizing problems exhibited by children living in disrupted family situations (e.g., Amato & Keith, 1991; Cummings & Davies, 1994; Grych & Fincham, 1990).

A variety of mechanisms have been postulated to account for this relationship. First, children might learn from observing their parents' fights that anger and aggression are the preferred methods for getting one's way and solving conflicts (Camara & Resnick, 1989). Second, children might exhibit either externalizing or internalizing behaviors in order to gain the attention of parents who are preoccupied with their own conflicts (Camara & Resnick, 1989) or in order to consciously diffuse their parents' anger toward each other (Cummings & Davies, 1994). Third, studies indicate that children respond to background anger with signs of physiological changes associated with aggression; therefore, children exposed to high levels of marital conflict might thus exhibit higher levels of overt aggression (Cummings & Davies, 1994). Fourth, parental conflict might reduce the effectiveness of parental child-rearing practices (e.g., through more lax discipline and less monitoring), thus promoting more aggression (Fincham, Grych, & Osborne, 1994). Finally, parental conflict might reduce the ability of parents to respond to their children in an emotionally warm manner, thus threatening the children's sense of security and promoting acting-out behavior (Fincham et al., 1994).

A fairly substantial body of evidence supports this *marital conflict* hypothesis. For example, children from high-conflict intact families exhibit more externalizing behavior and delinquency than do those from low-conflict intact families (Amato & Keith, 1991; Peterson & Zill, 1986). Furthermore, delinquents are as likely to come from intact, conflictful homes as from nonintact homes (Browning, 1960; Nye, 1957). Moreover, once divorce has occurred, children who continue to live in situations featuring high conflict between parents show more aggression and acting-out behavior than do those living in low-conflict situations (Hetherington, Cox, & Cox, 1982). Finally, adolescents' antisocial behavior is more strongly related to marital conflict than to family structure (Peterson & Zill, 1986)

Although overt marital conflict seems to be related to children's aggression, general marital unhappiness or stress is not (Grych & Fincham, 1990; Hetherington et al., 1982; Patterson et al., 1992). Indeed, recent research indicates that the type of conflict that promotes externalizing behavior in children is that which is intense, which is unresolved or poorly resolved, which involves child-related content, and which involves mutual aggression between spouses (Cummings & Davies, 1994; Fincham et al., 1994; Jouriles, Murphy, & O'Leary, 1989).

Why do some children show increased aggression to marital conflict, whereas others do not? Cummings and Davies (1994) suggested that children's temperament might mediate this relationship. Relatedly, Grych and Fincham (1990) hypothesized that individual differences in children's cognitive appraisal processes could account for diverse reactions to conflict. For example, children predisposed toward hostile attributions might show even more such attributions (and hence more aggressive behavior) after exposure to marital conflict than would children predisposed to self-blame. In sum, personality differences between children could mediate the effect of marital conflict on aggression.

Children's antisocial behavior might also affect their parents' marital stability. Comparing children's adjustment before their parents' divorce, Block, Block, and Gjerde (1988) found that sons whose parents subsequently divorced tended to be "impulsive and undercontrolled" relative to boys in families that would remain intact (p. 204). Moreover, they also found that fathers who would later experience divorce expressed more anger and conflict with their sons than did fathers whose marriages remained intact. It is thus possible that these boys might not only respond negatively to parental conflict, but might even play some role in the instigation of the conflict. Alternatively, it is also possible that paternal characteristics might be responsible both for the high level of conflict and for the subsequent divorce (Harris, 1998; Lahey et al., 1988).

In sum, there is fairly strong evidence that marital conflict, especially when it is overt, intense, and poorly resolved, might mediate the effects that divorce has on children's subsequent aggression and antisocial behavior. At the same time, however, the nature and effects of marital conflict might be affected by characteristics of both the parents and children.

Family Attachment.   The *family attachment* hypothesis suggests that the effect of intact homes in protecting against antisocial behavior might be related to the emotional cohesiveness of the family (Sokol-Katz, Dunham, & Zimmerman, 1997). According to this view, members living in intact homes might experience a stronger emotional attachment to the family unit than those living in nonintact homes. In turn, this strong positive attachment might promote the development of the prosocial behaviors parents are attempting to foster, hence helping to protect these children from antisocial and aggressive behaviors.

In one test of this hypothesis, Sokol-Katz et al. (1997) conducted a 3-year prospective study of more than 1,100 male and female middle-school students, 75% of whom were either Black or Hispanic. For self-reported "serious delinquency" (including gang fights, using force to take valuables, breaking and entering, auto theft), the researchers found that coming from an intact home directly predicted a sense of "family attachment" (a positive affective relationship toward the family), which in turn directly protected the youngster from serious delinquency (see Fig. 5.1). In addition, family attachment also had an indirect effect on serious delinquency through its effect on the importance of believing in the law. The implication of this study is that adolescents from intact homes are more likely to have positive feelings toward their families, and that this relationship toward their family helps to shield them from serious delinquency both directly and indirectly.

Summary.   In general, children living in nonintact homes are more likely to exhibit antisocial and aggressive behavior than are those living with biological parents in intact homes. Variables that seem most likely to account for these findings include parental personality characteristics, marital conflict, and family attachment. Although children who grow up without both biological parents can and do develop into prosocial youths and adults, evidence suggests that these children (and their custodial parent) face a much more difficult time than do children growing up in intact homes. As Peterson and Zill (1986) put it, "We must not lose sight of the fact that among all the statuses considered, children

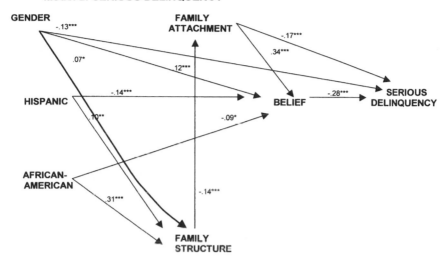

FIG. 5.1. Relationship between family structure, family attachment, and serious delinquency. *Note:* p < .001 = ***, p < .01 = **, p < .05 = *. From "Family Structure Versus Parental Attachment in Controlling Adolescent Deviant Behavior: A Social Control Model," by J. Sokol-Katz, R. Dunham, and R. Zimmerman, 1997, *Adolescence, 32*, p. 207. Copyright 1997 by Libra Publishers. Reprinted with permission.

are clearly better off living in intact families with low to moderate levels of conflict" (p. 307). Fortunately, as these authors also point out, "The majority of children enjoy just such a situation" (Peterson & Zill, 1986, p. 307).

ENVIRONMENTAL STRESSORS

A number of studies indicate a positive relationship between certain stressors experienced by a family and the offsprings' antisocial and hyperaggressive behaviors. These stressors include large family size, poverty, underemployment and unemployment, social isolation and lack of social support, living on welfare, poor housing, highly stressful life events (e.g., death of a relative), and daily hassles (Gardner, 1992; Hawkins, Catalano, & Miller, 1992; Kazdin, 1995; Moore & Arthur, 1989; Webster-Stratton, 1990). We now examine two of these stressors in more detail.

Large Family Size

A number of studies indicate that being reared in families with four or more children is a significant risk factor for antisocial behavior (Rutter et al., 1998).

In their analysis, Rutter et al. (1998) offer three possible explanations for this finding:

- This effect might be due to the tendency for antisocial individuals to have larger families than "normal" individuals. One study, for example, showed that controlling for parental criminality greatly reduced the influence of family size on children's aggression, whereas controlling for family size did not reduce the influence of parental criminality (Rowe & Farrington, 1997).
- Having a large family might put additional stress on parents, thereby reducing the effectiveness of their parenting behaviors (Rutter et al., 1998).
- This effect might arise because younger males in the family learn antisocial behavior from older delinquent brothers. This hypothesis is supported by findings that the phenomenon is associated with the number of brothers in a family but not with the number of sisters (Offord, 1982).

Finally, of course, it is possible that all three mechanisms might be functioning simultaneously.

Family Poverty

Most of the stressors just described are associated with family poverty and low socioeconomic status (SES), which in turn have been linked with a variety of behavior problems, including nonclinical levels of externalizing behaviors in preschool and school-age children (Dodge et al., 1994; Duncan et al., 1994), childhood and adolescent conduct disorder (Kazdin, 1995), adolescent externalizing behavior and delinquency (Conger, Ge, Elder, Lorenz, & Simons, 1994; West, 1982), and adult criminality (Kolvin, Miller, Fleeting, & Kolvin, 1988).

Poverty as Causative Agent. Despite these linkages, however, the role of poverty as a causative agent in youthful problem behavior is not clear. For example, in their prospective study of children born in Kauai, Werner and Smith concluded that "*poverty alone* was not a sufficient condition for the development of maladaption" (Werner & Smith, 1982, p. 31, emphasis in original). Instead, they found that poverty was problematic only when it interacted with other variables. "In *both* poor and middle-class homes," they wrote, "infants with 'difficult' temperaments who interacted with distressed caretakers in a disorganized, unstable family, had a greater chance of developing serious and persistent learning and behavior problems than infants perceived as rewarding by their caretakers and who grew up in stable, supportive homes" (Werner & Smith, 1982, p. 32, emphasis in original). Similarly, in their study of Danish youths, Raine and colleagues found that children at risk due to poverty had lower levels of violent crime than those at risk due to either biosocial or obstetric problems. These researchers concluded that their finding "challenges the traditional stereotype of poverty and crime going hand in hand and instead suggests that such associated stigmatizaion of all poor, underserved populations, although not intentional, is unjustified" (Raine et al., 1996, pp. 548–549).

Poverty and Other Variables.   Because family poverty is confounded with a host of other risk factors, the exact nature of the relationship between poverty and youthful aggression is difficult to determine. In order to deal with this problem, many recent studies have utilized techniques that permit the researcher to examine the effects of poverty while at the same time statistically controlling for other variables. With other possible causative variables thus controlled, poverty sometimes exerts an effect, but sometimes does not. For example, Duncan et al. (1994) found that family economic status predicted the externalizing behavior of preterm 5-year-olds even after controlling for variables such as gender, ethnicity, and family composition. Similarly, Dodge et al. (1994) found that racial differences were fully accounted for by a family's economic status. On the other hand, Renken et al. (1989) found that significant correlations between children's aggression and their socioeconomic status disappeared when the authors controlled for the children's early attachment security and negative affect, as well as for the mother's hostility toward the child.

These latter results are consistent with findings indicating that even when poverty does have an effect, so do other variables. For example, Duncan et al (1994) found that "persistent, never-married female headship as well as a change in family structure that ends up in a female headship situation continues to exert an influence even after we adjust for differences in family income" (p. 313). Similarly, Dodge et al. (1994) also found that single-parent status predicted children's problem behavior even after controlling for the family's SES. Thus, although poverty might affect children's externalizing behavior, other variables are important as well.

Indirect Effects of Poverty.   Some research indicates that poverty directly or indirectly affects parenting behavior, which in turn affects youthful antisocial behavior. In one study, for example, Sampson and Laub (1994) reanalyzed data from Sheldon and Eleanor Glueck's classic study on serious and chronic juvenile delinquents (S. Glueck & E. T. Glueck, 1950). In their research, the Gluecks had studied 500 White 10- to 17-year-old male delinquents and 500 matched nondelinquents raised during the Great Depression in the same slum environments of central Boston. Consistent with the hypothesis that poverty acts as a stressor that diminishes effective parenting, Sampson and Laub found that family poverty negatively affected delinquency through its effect on "informal social control" within the family (see Fig. 5.2). In addition, however, they found that the "child antisocial" factor, a variable measuring a combination of the child's difficult temperament and early antisocial behavior, also affected subsequent delinquency through its effect on parenting.

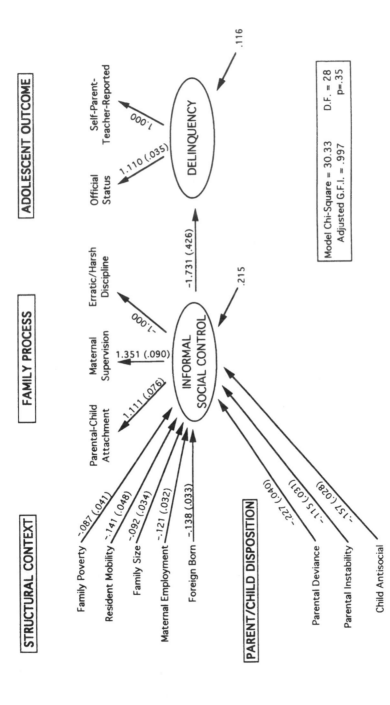

FIG. 5.2. Model relating structural context, parent/child disposition, informal social control, and delinquency. *Note:* All parameter estimates are significant at p < .05. From "Urban Poverty and the Family Context of Delinquency: A New Look at Structure and Process in a Classic Study," 1994, by R. J. Sampson and J. H. Laub, *Child Development, 65,* p. 537. Copyright 1994 by the University of Michigan Press. Reprinted with permission.

Other family-process variables that have been found to relate to family poverty are harshness of discipline, the extent to which the child is exposed to violence, the amount of social support received by the mother, the extent to which the mother positively values aggression, the mother's warmth toward the child, maternal depression, maternal lack of optimism, and father irritability (Brody et al., 1994; Conger et al., 1994; Skinner, Elder, & Conger, 1992).

Other research indicates that family poverty exerts an indirect effect through the neighborhood in which the child lives. For example, Duncan et al. (1994) found that living in economically deprived neighborhoods "modestly" affected the externalizing behavior of preschool children even after other variables had been controlled. Similarly, Simons et al. (1996) found that for a group of young adolescent males living in the rural midwest, community disadvantage indirectly increased the probability of conduct problems by disrupting parenting and increasing affiliation with deviant peers.

SEX DIFFERENCES

Although much of the research on the relationship between family factors and youthful aggression has failed to find sex differences, some variables do seem to differentially affect males and females. We now turn to a brief examination of some of these findings.

• *Parental rejection and marital conflict seem to be better predictors of subsequent antisocial behavior for females, whereas lack of parental supervision and monitoring seem to be better predictors for males* (Loper, 1999).

As we have seen, preschool girls tend to engage in fine motor play and relationship-building activities, whereas young boys tend to play more roughly and to be more competitive (Beal, 1994). As time goes by, a positive emotional relationship between parent and child might become more important for girls than for boys, and hence perceived emotional rejection by parents might be more likely to motivate antisocial behavior in females. Males tend to be more physically aggressive and might be more likely to roam farther from home than females (Loper, 1999). Hence, close monitoring and supervision might be more important in restraining aggression for males than for females.

• *Boys exhibit more externalizing behavior in nonintact homes when the mother is the custodial parent than when the father is the custodial parent* (Hetherington et al., 1998; Rothbaum & Weisz, 1994).

Some studies suggest that fathers might be more important for boys than for girls (e.g., Clarke-Stewart & Hayward, 1996; Werner & Smith, 1982). Given boys' propensity for noncompliance and aggression, it is possible that mothers might be less adroit than fathers in dealing with boys' coercive behavior. The presence of the father in the home might help to mitigate this situation. However, in the absence of the father and under other stressors associated with single parenting, mothers' difficulty in this area might be compounded (Rothbaum & Weisz, 1994), thus leading to an increase in boys' coercive behavior. In addition, single mothers might be less effective in supervising and monitoring their sons' behavior, thus also contributing to boys' antisocial behavior.

• *Abused and neglected females are more likely to exhibit subsequent delinquency and violence than are abused males* (Loper, 1999; Rivera & Widom, 1990).

Girls are twice as likely to be sexually abused as boys, and adolescent females are more likely to be physically abused than are adolescent males (Azar et al., 1998). In view of the fact that much abuse is perpetrated within the home, it is likely that such maltreatment weakens the important emotional relationship between girls and their parents, thus making antisocial behavior more likely. In addition, a history of abuse might motivate the girl to run away from home, a situation that can lead to prostitution, drug abuse, and association with antisocial males (Loper, 1999), all of which increase the risk of subsequent antisocial and aggressive behavior.

SUMMARY

Perhaps the major conclusion to be drawn from our consideration of family related variables is that no single factor seems to be the crucial variable in causing children's hyperaggressive behavior. What seems to be important is the extent to which children are exposed to a number of different family risk factors, rather than whether they experience any single variable in isolation.

In this connection, Michael Rutter and his colleagues have identified a set of *family adversity factors* they found to be consistently related to children's conduct disorder (Rutter, 1978; Rutter, Tizard, & Whitmore, 1970; Rutter et al., 1975). Not surprisingly, these factors include parental criminality, maternal mental illness, parental unemployment or underemployment, poor housing, and marital discord. Rutter and his colleagues found that the more of these factors present in the child's life, the more the child was at risk for CD. Thus, for example, the greater prevalence of CD in London compared with the Isle of Wight was attributed to the presence of more family adversity factors in the city than on the island.

In light of this understanding, it is not surprising that many of the variables we have examined in this chapter seem to produce their effects only when combined with other variables. For example, the child's attachment status might be important only when it interacts with other risk factors such as poverty and maternal psychopathology (Lyons-Ruth et al., 1997). Unfortunately, families of hyperaggressive children seldom experience just one isolated risk factor. Instead, these families seem to experience a number of such variables concurrently. For example, paternal criminality is often accompanied by other variables such as low SES, maternal mental illness, marital discord, low parental involvement and supervision, harsh physical punishment and physical abuse, and low parent–child affective relations—all of which have been implicated in the development of children's antisocial and hyperaggressive behavior. In the sense that youngsters often experience numerous risk factors at once, children's aggressive behavior is said to be *overdetermined*.

Although this chapter has emphasized the "effects" of the family on the development of the child's hyperaggression, the story is probably more complicated. As we have seen, it is entirely possible that many of the effects attributed to family related variables might actually be due wholly or in part to parental and child personality characteristics, which may have either a genetic or innate basis. For example, the findings regarding the role of parental psychopathology suggest the possibility of a passive genotype environment correlation in which an antisocial father passes down to his offspring both an antisocial genotype as well as an "antisocial" family environment.

Harris (1998) argued that a child's long-term personality is determined primarily by heredity and peer interaction and only secondarily by parents. Consistent with this view, we have already seen that innate factors and nonshared environmental effects seem to be more closely related to youthful aggression than are the shared environmental factors which primarily involve experiences within the family. And yet, we have also seen that developing a positive parent–child affective relationship can help steer the child to parent-approved peers; that developing an attachment to the family can promote important pro-law attitudes; and that supervising and monitoring young adolescents can help keep them away from the disruptive influence of antisocial peers. Although parents' behaviors might not "cause" their children's hyperaggression behavior, their behaviors are nevertheless an important part of the complex mix that goes into determining the child's ultimate outcome.

CHAPTER 6

Television and Media Violence

In the late 1980s, Tipper Gore, wife of Senator Al Gore, led a crusade against sexually explicit and violent music lyrics and music videos (Gore, 1990) which she believed were harmful to American youth. In the mid-1990s, Vice President Al Gore led another crusade, this one in favor of requiring television set manufacturers to install so-called V chips ("V" for Violence) in all new television sets (Baker, 1997). According to Mr. Gore, the effects of TV violence on the aggression levels of American youth were so great that these devices, which would allow parents to block out violent television shows, were necessary in order to protect children from the harmful effects of such programs.

These two incidents illustrate the concern that many Americans have over the possible deleterious effects violence in the mass media might have on the aggressive behavior of our children and adolescents. Indeed, in many circles, mass-media portrayal of violence is considered the major cause of youth violence in the United States

TV VIOLENCE AND AGGRESSION: AN OVERVIEW

Perhaps no topic involving youth violence has been discussed more than whether watching violence on television causes children to act aggressively (the *television causes aggression hypothesis*). The fact that this issue has practical as well as theoretical implications was illustrated dramatically in the 1977 case of Ronald Zamora, a 15-year-old Florida youth who was accused of murdering his 82-year-old next-door neighbor (Ayres, 1977; "Did TV," 1977). Zamora and an accomplice were in the act of robbing the neighbor's house while she was out. However, when she returned unexpectedly and surprised the youths, Zamora killed her with a gun the boys had found in the house. At trial, Zamora's lawyer argued that the youngster was insane due to "subliminal television intoxication" ("Did TV," 1977, p. 87). According to the lawyer, the countless hours Zamora had spent watching cops-and-robbers shows such as *Kojak* and *Baretta* had "brainwashed" him into living in a "television fantasy world," which left him incapable of realizing that he was committing cold-blooded murder. Zamora, the lawyer contended, was "just acting out a television script" ("Did TV," 1977,

p. 87). The jury, however, apparently did not agree with this argument and convicted Zamora of murder.

Since the Zamora trial, psychologists and nonpsychologists alike have debated the extent to which watching violence on television affects children's aggression. One reason for concern involves the amount of violent programming on American television. For example, researchers estimate that 32 violent acts per hour occur in children's television programming and that the average U.S. child will have viewed 8,000 murders and 100,000 violent acts on television by the time he or she completes elementary school (Donnerstein, Slaby, & Eron, 1994; Lamson, 1995).

Preliminary Issues

Before examining the research that relates television violence to youthful aggression, we first discuss some important preliminary issues.

Possible Relationships. The possible relationships between television violence and children's aggression are multiple and potentially complex. First, there might be no relationship at all. Second, there might be a correlational relationship (presumably positive in nature) between the extent to which children watch violent television shows and their actual aggressive behavior. If such an association does exist, then other possibilities also loom. For example, watching violence on television might cause aggressive behavior. However, it is also possible that having an aggressive personality might cause children to watch violence on television (a situation you recognize as a *child-effects* position). It is also possible that both watching violence on television and being aggressive might be caused by some third variable (e.g., neglectful parenting). Finally, watching violence on television might not cause aggressive behavior per se but might do so in interaction with one or more other variables. For example, violent television programs might not have an adverse effect on most children, but might be deleterious for certain vulnerable children.

Definitional and Methodological Issues. We must also keep in mind definitional and methodological issues as we examine the research on this topic. With respect to definitions, we would like to know how researchers define "television violence." Do they consider a Bugs Bunny cartoon to be equally as violent as a scene from a slasher movie? Relatedly, how do the researchers operationally measure the concept of *television violence?* Similar questions could also be asked about how the researchers define and measure children's aggression. For example, does the definition encompass both verbal and physical aggression, or just one of those types? And do the data come from actual observations by methodologically "blind" observers, or do they emanate solely from reports by the children or others (such as parents)?

Finally, as discussed in chapter 1, we must also be mindful of other method-ological issues such as questions of internal and external validity. With respect to internal validity, we need to ask questions about experimental control and potentially confounding variables. With respect to external validity, we need to determine the extent to which the results can be confidently generalized to a large population and to real-world settings.

With these issues in mind, let us turn to a discussion of the available research evidence on this question, most of which was conducted prior to the 1990s.

TELEVISION VIOLENCE AND AGGRESSION: IS THERE AN ASSOCIATION?

We first examine the question of whether and to what extent there exists a sta-tistical association between watching violence on TV and children's aggressive behavior.

Associational Studies

Correlational Studies.   Friedrich-Cofer and Huston (1986) stated that numer-ous correlational studies involving thousands of subjects have consistently yielded correlations ranging from .10 to .35 between violent television viewing and aggression. For example, a survey of more than 2,200 teenagers from 13 high schools in Maryland found that the violence of the subjects' four favorite television programs correlated .11 with the subjects' aggressiveness and .16 with subjects' more serious aggressive deviancy (McIntyre & Teevan, 1972). Similarly, McLeod, Atkin, and Chaffee (1972a, 1972b) reported correlations be-tween television violence viewing and aggression of .32 for seventh- and tenth-grade boys and of .30 for girls of the same ages. In view of these and other results, we can conclude that there is a positive correlation between viewing violence on television and youngsters' aggressive behavior (Freedman, 1984).

Quasiexperimental Studies: The Belson Study.   In addition to correlational studies, quasiexperimental designs can also provide evidence that television vio-lence viewing is associated with aggressiveness. For example, Belson (1978) studied the relationship between television violence and aggressiveness in a probability sample of more than 1,500 London males between the ages of 12 and 17. On the basis of interviews in which the teenagers were extensively ques-tioned about their past history and current behavior, Belson tested 25 major hypotheses, each in both a "forward" as well as a "reverse" form. In general, the forward form of each hypothesis postulated that high exposure to violent television had an effect on some other variable, whereas the reverse form postulated that the other variable affected boys' viewing of television violence. For example, the major forward hypothesis was that "High exposure to violence on television increases the degree to which boys commit acts of violence" (Belson, 1978, p. 366). The reverse form of this hypothesis was that "Violent boys, just because they are violent (by disposition), seek out violent television programmes to a greater degree than do boys who are not violent (by disposition)" (Belson, 1978, p. 385).

When Belson tested the forward form of his major hypothesis in this manner, he found that boys in the high-exposure group exhibited significantly more aggression than those in the low-exposure group. Furthermore, this finding occurred for more serious acts of violence as well as for less serious ones. Primarily on this basis, Belson concluded that "high exposure to television violence increases the degree to which boys engage in serious violence" (Belson, 1978, p. 15).

Panel Studies: The Cross-National Studies.   A third group of associational studies include longitudinal cross-lagged panel designs and multiple-regression studies. One example of a panel design involves the Columbia County study discussed in chapter 3 (Eron, Huesmann, Lefkowitz, & Walder, 1972). These researchers reported a correlation of .31 between boys' maternally reported preference for violent television at age 8 and peer ratings of aggressiveness at age 19. Furthermore, frequency of television viewing at age 8 was correlated with seriousness of criminal behavior at age 30 (Eron, 1987).

Perhaps the most ambitious research of this type involves the six-country cross-national studies, which involved children in the United States (Eron & Huesmann, 1986; Huesmann & Eron, 1986), Finland (Lagerspetz & Viemerö, 1986), The Netherlands (Wiegman, Kuttschreuter, & Baarda 1986), Poland (Fraczek, 1986), Israel (Bachrach, 1986), and Australia (Sheehan, 1986). The Israeli study included two separate samples, one from a small city and the second from two *kibbutzim* (cooperative communities in which the children are typically reared apart from their parents in "children's houses"). Although I discuss them together, The Netherlands' data (Wiegman et al., 1986) were published separately from those of the other countries (Huesmann & Eron, 1986).

In general, the design and the variables studied were similar across countries. Two initial cohort groups were selected in each country (one from the first grade and one from the third grade, except in The Netherlands, where the cohort groups were second graders and fourth graders). Each cohort group was then followed for 3 years, during which numerous variables relating to television viewing and aggression were assessed. Children were asked to name their favorite television program and how much they watched it. After judges rated the amount of violence in each favorite program, this number was then multiplied by the amount of time watched to yield an overall "television violence-viewing" score. Aggression was measured by ratings from peers.

The major results of these studies are presented in Table 6.1. Data were not reported by cohort and grade for Israel, and 13 of the possible 64 correlations were also not reported. As can be seen, 50% of the possible correlations ($n = 16$) were significant for males and 41% ($n = 13$) for females. In addition, there were also variations by sex, with the association being stronger for males in Finland and for younger girls but for older boys in The Netherlands.

In an attempt to go beyond simple correlations, the investigators also employed multiple regression analyses to determine the extent to which violent TV-viewing in the first two years of the study predicted aggressiveness in the

TABLE 6.1

Correlations Between Television Violence Viewing
and Peer-Nominated Aggression

Group	United States[a]	Finland[b]	The Netherlands[c]	Poland[d]	Israel City[e]	Israel Kibbutz[e]	Australia[f]
Boys							
Cohort 1							
1st Grade	.16*	.03		.30*			---
2nd Grade	.20*	.27*	.08	.17			---
3rd Grade	.15	.09	.12	---			---
4th Grade			.19*				
Cohort 2							
3rd Grade	.24**	.04		.26*			.18
4th Grade	.18*	.38***	.27**	.18			.33**
5th Grade	.29*	.28*	.37***	---			.21
6th Grade			.17*				
Total					.45**	---	
Girls							
Cohort 1							
1st Grade	.22**	.14		---			---
2nd Grade	.25*	.02	.27**	.18			.22
3rd Grade	.28***	.33**	.40***	---			---
4th Grade			.25*				
Cohort 2							
3rd Grade	.13	.05		.24			.24*
4th Grade	.26***	−.16	.10	.13			---
5th Grade	.29***	.04	.30**	.28*			---
6th Grade			.18				
Total					.48**	---	

Note. Dashes indicate that the data were not reported. [a]Huesmann & Eron, 1986, p. 55. [b]Lagerspetz & Viemerö, 1986, p. 97. [c]Wiegman et al., 1986, p. 64. [d]Fraczek, 1986, p. 139. [e]Bachrach, 1986, p. 224 (data not reported by cohort or grade). [f]Sheehan, 1986, p. 180.
*$p < .05$, **$p < .01$, ***$p < .001$

TABLE 6.2
Standardized Regression Coefficients Predicting Year 3 Aggression
From Overall TV Violence Viewing in Years 1 and 2

Country	Males	Females
USA[a]	.08	.14**
Finland[b]	.21***	.05
The Netherlands[c]	.07	.10
Poland[d]	.15*	.12
Israel City[e]	.29*	.52**
Israel Kibbutz[f]	---	---
Australia[g]	---	---

Note. Dashes indicate that the data were not reported. [a]Huesmann & Eron, 1986, p. 61. [b]Lager-spetz & Viemerö, 1986, p. 111; datum for boys calculated from the "product of TV violence viewing and identification with aggressive TV characters" in the first and second waves. [c]Wiegman et al., 1986, p. 65. [d]Fraczek, 1986, p. 150; data calculated from "preference for violent TV" in the first two waves. [e]Bachrach, 1986, p. 227; the dependent variable consisted of an adjusted aggression score, "the ratio of peer-nominated aggression to peer-nominated aggression avoidance plus 1" (p. 223). [f]Bachrach, 1986, p. 227; data not reported. [g]Sheehan, 1986, p. 187; data not reported.
$*p < .05, **p < .01, ***p < .001$

third year. The results of these analyses are presented in Table 6.2. Unfortunately, these data did not all reflect the same aggression variable, nor were they all calculated from the standard measure of overall television violence viewing, thus making comparisons between countries difficult. For example, although the Finnish investigators used "average television violence viewing" (Lagerspetz & Viemerö, 1986, p. 97) in calculating their correlations and in calculating the multiple-regression coefficient for girls, they used the "product of TV violence viewing and identification with aggressive TV characters" (Lagerspetz & Viemerö, 1986, p. 111) in calculating regression coefficient for the boys. Furthermore, four of the possible 14 coefficients were not reported.

Five the 12 regression coefficients reached significance. We thus see a pattern of some significant results, but also some inconsistency as well as puzzling sex differences, with the regression analysis being significant only for females in the United States but only for males in Finland and Poland. Furthermore, the coefficients were significant for both sexes in the Israeli city, but for neither sex in the kibbutzim.

In summary, the results of the cross-national studies indicated that there is some relationship between viewing violence on television and aggression, but that this relationship is also moderate and erratic. Furthermore, the multiple regression data suggest that whatever the relationship is, it is not causal in nature. As Wiegman et al. (1986) put it, "There would seem to be very little empirical support, on the whole, among the results from the countries involved, for the proposition that the viewing of violence could cause aggression" (p. 127).

Meta-Analyses

Another way to determine the extent of the relationship between viewing violence on television and children's aggression is through the technique of the *meta-analysis* described in chapter 1. As you recall, the major statistic employed in a meta-analysis is that of the effect size (*d*), with effect sizes of .20 or less considered small; .50, medium; and .80, large. With these considerations in mind, we turn to a discussion of four major meta-analyses conducted on this topic (Hearold, 1986; Hogben, 1998; Paik & Comstock, 1994; Wood, Wong, & Chachere, 1991).

Hearold's Study.   Hearold (1986) studied the relationship between violent television viewing and measures of both prosocial and general antisocial behavior (see Table 6.3). Her sample involved both children and adults and included 131 laboratory studies, 33 field studies, and 66 panel studies. Of these 230 studies, 170 had been published in professional journals.

Overall, Hearold (1986) found an average effect size of .30 for antisocial behavior compared with neutral behavior, an effect that is significant and considered moderate. However, when only "high quality" studies were used and when only actual television programs were used, the effect size dropped to .20. Moreover, the effect size for studies with the highest level of external validity was .23. The effect size was .34 for laboratory studies and .32 for survey studies, but dropped to under .10 for field experiments. Interestingly, college students were affected more (*d* = .36) than children (*d* = .28).

Table 6.3 lists the specific antisocial and prosocial effect sizes. These data show that television had its greatest "antisocial" effect on nonviolent and nonaggressive activities (such as a reduction in family discussions, role stereotyping, and less socialization). The effect size for physical aggression was .31, and that for verbal aggression was .05. In addition, the nightly news on television had a greater effect size on antisocial behavior (*d* = .67) than did crime shows and detective programs (*d* = .25). Perhaps most interesting of all, however, the effect size of prosocial television viewing on prosocial behavior was .63, twice the size of the effect for antisocial behavior.

The Wood et al. Study.   Wood et al. (1991) examined 23 studies in which the dependent variable consisted of aggressive behavior among children and adolescents in some naturally occurring social interaction, such as free play on the playground. When the researchers counted the number of significant results in the studies, they found that in 16 studies, aggression was greater for groups exposed to television violence than for appropriate control groups. This result "approached" (*p* < .10) but did not reach significance, probably because in the other 7 studies, subjects in the control group actually showed significantly more aggression than those in the violent-television group.

TABLE 6.3
Effect-Sizes for Types of Antisocial and Prosocial Behaviors

Type of Behavior	Average Effect Size*
Antisocial Behaviors	
Family discussion reduced	2.33
Role stereotyping	.90
Less socialization	.75
Rule breaking	.56
Hurt (rather than help)	.47
Materialism	.40
Perception of world as violent	.40
Playing with aggressive toys	.37
Passivity	.36
Physical aggression	.31
Verbal and physical aggression	.31
Perception of self as powerless	.31
Willingness to use violence/perceived as effective	.27
Pathological behavior: nightmares, wets bed, louder	.26
Negative attitude toward own culture	.17
Unlawful behavior	.13
Increased worry about the future	.11
Use of drugs	.09
Verbal aggression	.05
Prosocial behaviors	
Self-control	.98
Altruism	.83
Buy books	.81
Mixture of socially desirable behaviors	.78
Safety, health, and conservation activism	.69
Positive attitude toward work	.57
Antistereotyping; acceptance of others	.57
Respect for the law	.23
Play without aggression	.21
Socially active/communicative	.17
Creative, imaginative play	.02
Cooperation	.00

*Reported effect-sizes are based on the comparison of antisocial treatment versus other for antisocial behavior and prosocial treatment versus other for prosocial behavior.

Note. Table adapted from "A synthesis of 1043 effects of television on social behavior" by S. Hearold, 1986, *Public Communication and Behavior,* Vol. 1, p. 106, edited by G. Comstock. Copyright © 1986 by Academic Press. All rights of reproduction in any form reserved.

In a further analysis, the authors conducted effect-size tests for 12 studies whose data permitted such calculation. The result of this weighted analysis showed a significant increase in aggression following exposure to media violence, with an effect size of .27. The authors stated that although their effect-size was small to moderate, it was nevertheless noteworthy because the dependent measures occurred in unconstrained social situations and not in a more highly controlled laboratory study.

The Paik and Comstock (1994) Study. This study analyzed 217 studies conducted between 1957 and 1990, 101 of which were included in Hearold's meta-analysis. Dependent variables ranged from aggression against toys to self-reported criminal behavior. The researchers found a significant overall effect size of $d = .65$, with a slightly greater effect for males than for females. Other effect sizes were .87 for laboratory studies; .62 for field studies; .39 for time-series studies; and .38 for surveys. The effect size was slightly higher for verbal aggression ($d = .55$) than for noncriminal physical violence against a person ($d = .49$). The results held for individuals of all ages but were greater for preschool children and college students than for older children, adolescents, and adults. The effect size was greater for cartoons than for other forms of violence, and greater for programs involving erotica alone and those combining erotica and violence than for those involving violence alone.

Hogben's Study. In a more recent meta-analysis, Hogben (1998) examined 56 correlational and field studies, 40 of which involved children as participants. He found an average effect size for television violence of $d = .21$ across all studies. Interestingly, however, for both the United States and total samples, "the mean effect size stops increasing circa 1980" (p. 239), and the correlation between effect size and date of study was actually negative from 1980 onward ($r = -.02$). Effect sizes were greater for children than for adults, and programs involving "implausible settings" (such as cartoons or science fiction) were more strongly related to behavioral aggression than were those involving "plausible settings."

Summary. Three of these four meta-analyses are consistent in showing a generally a "small" to "moderate" relationship between viewing violence on television and children's antisocial and aggressive behavior (Hearold, 1986; Hogben, 1998; Wood et al., 1991). The fourth study reported an overall effect size in the "medium" range, some two to three times the effect size of the other studies (Paik & Comstock, 1994). In general, television violence seems to have more of an effect on young children and on college students than on older children and adolescents (Hearold, 1986; Paik & Comstock, 1994). Cartoons (Hearold, 1986; Hogben, 1998; Paik & Comstock, 1994), violence in news programs (Hearold, 1986), and violent erotica (Paik & Comstock, 1994) seem to have the greatest effect. Interestingly, prosocial programs had a much greater effect on prosocial behavior than violent programs had on antisocial behavior (Hearold, 1986), and the mean effect size for violent programs stopped increasing around 1980 (Hogben, 1998).

Magnitude of the Association

The bulk of the research indicates that there is a modest but fairly consistent relationship between children's aggression and the viewing of violence on television. One way to determine the "importance" of a correlation is through use of the *coefficient of determination*. This statistic, computed by squaring the correlation coefficient, tells how much of the variance in a distribution of scores is accounted for by knowing the nature of the relationship between the two correlated variables (Agresti & Finlay, 1997). As we have seen, correlations between television violence viewing and aggression typically range from .10 to .30, but rarely exceed .35. Based on this information and applying the coefficient of determination, we can conclude that the relationship between television violence viewing and aggression accounts for somewhere between 1% and 10% of the variance in children's aggressive behavior (Paik & Comstock, 1994).

Another way of determining the magnitude of the association is through the use of effect sizes, which in the four meta-analyses just described were .30, .27, .65, and .21. To put these data into perspective, it is perhaps worth noting that the average effect size of 1 year of elementary school on reading is 1.00 (Hearold, 1986); the effect of psychotherapy on improved psychological functioning is .85 (Hearold, 1986); the effect of parental supervision on children's aggression is .83 (Loeber & Stouthamer-Loeber, 1986); and the effect of cerebrospinal serotonin on violence against persons is −.89 (Raine, 1993). Finally, the effect size for the influence of climate (number of hot days) on the incidence of violent crime is 1.21 (Wood et al., 1991).

Conclusion

Numerous correlational, quasiexperimental, and panel studies have demonstrated a positive relationship between children's viewing of violence on television and their current and subsequent aggressive behavior. This relationship appears to be small to moderate and accounts for between 1% and 10% of the variability in children's aggressive behavior.

DOES VIEWING VIOLENCE ON TV CAUSE AGGRESSION?

Although virtually all researchers agree that there is a relationship between violent television viewing and aggression (Van Evra, 1998), there is less agreement about whether watching violence on television causes children to act aggressively. On one hand, many researchers and textbook authors subscribe to this hypothesis (e.g., Coie & Dodge, 1998; Huesmann, Moise, & Podolski, 1997; Papalia et al., 1999). On the other hand, others argue that the causal role of television on aggression has been exaggerated (e.g., Freedman, 1984, 1986; Durkin, 1995; Renfrew, 1997). We now examine this issue in more detail.

Critique of Associational Studies

Although associational studies have yielded significant positive correlations between television violence viewing and children's aggression, the results of these studies cannot be used to demonstrate causality. For one thing, associational designs are always susceptible to the "third variable" problem, which limits their internal validity (see chapter 1). In addition, the results of some associational studies actually fail to support the "television causes violence" hypothesis. For example, Belson (1978) not only found support for many of his "forward" hypotheses, but for many of his "reverse" hypotheses as well, thus suggesting that causality could be operating in either direction. In addition, although Belson (1978) found that high exposure to TV violence was associated with greater aggressiveness, his results showed that such exposure did not increase: the degree to which the boys thought about violence; the degree to which the boys would have liked to commit the kinds of violence shown on television; boys' willingness to commit the kinds of violence which they saw on television; boys' "callousness" toward real-life violence; the degree to which the boys saw violence as a basic part of human nature; or the degree to which boys accepted violence as a way of life. Nor did such exposure reduce the extent to which boys showed consideration for others or their respect for authority. In other words, high exposure to violence on TV did not affect the major psychological processes that Belson thought would explain the relationship between television violence viewing and aggression.

Laboratory and Field Studies

In order to consider the issue of causality more directly, we turn to the results of laboratory experiments and field studies.

The Bobo Doll Experiments.   The prototypic laboratory study comes from the work of Bandura and his colleagues we discussed in chapter 2 (Bandura et al., 1961, 1963). In general, these studies showed that children who were briefly frustrated after viewing aggressive film models subsequently tended to exhibit some of the same distinctive behaviors as the models, thus apparently supporting the hypothesis that televised violence causes aggressive behavior in children through the process of observational learning.

Despite these results, however, these studies have been criticized on a number of grounds (e.g., Durkin, 1995; Freedman, 1984, 1986).

- The "aggressive" behavior of a child hitting a Bobo doll in a laboratory might be qualitatively very different from actual physical aggression in real life (Durkin, 1995). Indeed, Durkin argued that the children in these studies seem to be enjoying themselves and that their behavior looks more like "rough and tumble" play than aggression.

- These studies might have *demand characteristics* (Freedman, 1986) or *sponsor effects* (Felson, 1996); that is, the action of the model and the setup of the study might lead the children to believe that they should act aggressively. As Durkin (1995) puts it: "Where else in life does a 5-year-old find a powerful adult actually showing you how to knock hell out of a dummy and then giving you the opportunity to try it out yourself?" (p. 406).

- The "aggression" in these studies is rather unrealistic: Unlike real children when they are hurt, Bobo feels no pain; he just keeps smiling and bounces back when hit (Durkin, 1995).

These criticisms thus raise questions about the validity of the Bobo doll studies.

Other Laboratory Experiments.   Numerous other laboratory experiments on this topic have been conducted using both adult and child subjects. For example, in an early study, Liebert and Baron (1972) investigated young children's willingness to hurt another child following exposure to either violent or nonviolent television programs. After viewing the videotape, children were allowed to either help or hurt another child by pressing a button on a control panel. Later, these children were also observed in a free-play situation in which aggression was defined as either playing with toy weapons or assaulting a doll. Subjects who had seen the violent video pressed the "hurt" button for a longer period than did those who had seen the neutral videotape. In the free-play situation, younger boys who watched the violent videotape showed more aggression than their age mates who had seen the neutral videotape; however, this effect did not hold for either girls or older boys.

Although some additional studies have provided support for the "television causes violence" hypothesis, other results have been mixed. For example, Hapkiewicz and Roden (1971) found no effects for violent cartoons on children's physical aggression, but boys who saw the violent cartoon were less likely to share their toys than those in a control group. Similarly, Leifer and Roberts (1972) found that, in one study, children were more likely to choose a violent solution to a problem after they had viewed a violent film than were children who viewed a nonviolent film. In a second study, however, this difference did not occur. Thus, although laboratory experiments have provided some support for the television causes violence hypothesis, inconsistent results have occurred as well.

138 6. TELEVISION AND MEDIA VIOLENCE

Field Studies: Experiments. Some field studies involve true experiments in which an independent variable is manipulated and subjects are randomly assigned to conditions. Others, however, involve "naturalistic" experiments in which the "independent variable" occurs naturally and in which random assignment does not take place.

True field experiments have been conducted with young children in preschool settings, with boys and young adolescents in residential settings, and with incarcerated male delinquents. Because these studies take place in real-life settings, and because most involve the use of real television programs, their external validity should be enhanced over that of the laboratory studies considered earlier.

By and large, these studies provide some modest support for the hypothesis that television violence viewing causes aggression. For example, Friedrich and Stein (1973) manipulated the content of the television programs preschool children were allowed to watch. They found that the type of program (violent, neutral, or nonviolent) had no overall effect on the children's aggressive behavior. However, when children were divided into those who were initially high in aggression and those who were initially low in aggression, the highly aggressive children who saw the violent films declined less in overall aggressiveness than the highly aggressive children who saw the other types of programs.

Other studies, however, have provided more obvious support for the television causes violence hypothesis. Chief among these are studies reported by Leyens and colleagues (Leyens, Parke, Camino, & Berkowitz, 1975; Parke, Berkowitz, Leyens, West, & Sebastian, 1977) in which some groups of institutionalized delinquent adolescents in the United States and Belgium were shown violent movies, whereas other groups were shown nonviolent movies. In both countries, subsequent aggressiveness was higher for the groups viewing the violent films. In the Belgian study, however, this effect occurred primarily for the group that was initially high in aggressiveness.

As was the case with laboratory and correlational studies, however, inconsistent results have been found in field experiments as well. For example, Feshbach and R. Singer (1971) randomly assigned boys in seven residential schools to watch either violent or nonviolent television programs for 6 weeks. In 3 of the 7 schools, boys who watched only the nonviolent programs showed significantly more aggression than those who watched the violent programs. Similar but nonsignificant results occurred in 3 of the remaining 4 schools.

Another study that featured inconsistent results was conducted by Josephson (1987), who allowed 400 second- and third-grade boys to play floor hockey after viewing either a violent or nonviolent television clip. Following exposure to the violent clip, boys who were initially high in aggressiveness showed an increase in aggression; however, boys who were initially low in aggression showed a subsequent decrease in aggression.

Naturalistic Experiments: The "Notel" Study. Some of the most interesting research in this area involves studies in which television viewing is "manipulated"

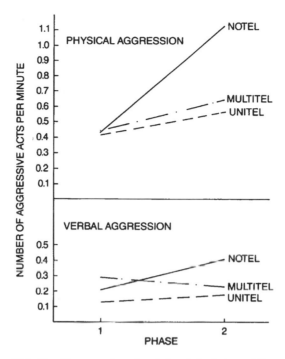

FIG. 6.1. Mean number of verbal and physical aggressive acts per minute by towns, sex, and phase for the longitudinal sample in the "Notel" study. From "Television and aggressive behavior" by T. A. Joy, M. M. Kimball, & M. L. Zabrack, 1986, *The Impact of Television: A Natural Experiment Involving Three Towns* (p. 320), edited by T. M. Williams. Copyright © 1986 by Academic Press. All rights of reproduction in any form reserved.

by evolving cultural situations. One of the most famous is a study by Tanis Mac-Beth Williams and colleagues (Joy, Kimball, & Zabrack, 1986) in which the researchers examined the level of elementary school children's aggression in a Canadian town (called Notel) both before and after the introduction of television service to the area. The aggressiveness of children in Notel was compared with that of children in two other Canadian towns, Unitel and Multitel. At the time of the study, Unitel received only the government-owned Canadian Broadcasting Channel, whereas Multitel received both the Canadian channel as well as the three commercial U.S. networks. Prior to the introduction of television, levels of both verbal and physical aggression were statistically the same in all three towns. However, levels of aggression increased significantly in Notel after the introduction of television, becoming even higher than for Unitel and Multitel. This effect held for both physical and verbal aggression and for both boys and girls, and was unrelated to the children's initial level of aggression (see Fig. 6.1).

Joy et al.'s (1986) Notel study is sometimes cited as support for the television causes violence hypothesis (e.g., Van Evra, 1998). However, a number of aspects of this study mitigate against that interpretation:

• Although the children were asked about how much they watched television, the researchers did not collect information regarding the extent to which children watched violent television shows; thus, the effect could have been due to watching television in general, as opposed to watching violence on television in particular.

• At the time of the study, Canadian television (which was the only programming available to the Notel children) carried virtually no cartoons (which meta-analyses have found to be especially violent) and only two police detective shows were shown per week; moreover, Canadian programming in general is much less violent than that seen on television in the United States (Renfrew, 1997). These facts thus call into question the hypothesis that exposure to violent TV caused the observed increases in aggressiveness in this study.

• Rather than being due to television watching itself, the effects could have been due to one or more factors that might have been confounded with television viewing. For example, perhaps parents supervised their children less after the introduction of television than they had previously; if so, the increased aggressiveness might have been due to this lack of supervision, rather than to television viewing per se.

• If viewing TV causes an increase in violence, why did children in Unitel and Multitel not show a significant increase in either physical or verbal aggression while they were being exposed to television violence over the course of the study? In particular, if American television is more violent than Canadian television, why at least did the children in Multitel not exhibit such an increase?

• Finally, if watching violence on television causes children to become physically aggressive, then the children of Notel should have been less physically aggressive than the children of Unitel and Multitel prior to the introduction of TV. However, as seen in Fig. 6.1, children in all three towns exhibited statistically equivalent amounts of physical aggression before television came to Notel, thus suggesting that television viewing did not cause increased physical aggression among children in Unitel and Multitel.

Intervention Studies

Another method of determining causation is to initiate an intervention aimed at the hypothesized cause of a behavior. Interventions that reduce both the hypothesized cause and the hypothesized effect provide strong support for a causal relationship between the two variables.

Huesmann and colleagues undertook two such interventions in connection with the cross-national studies (Huesmann, Eron, Klein, Brice, & Fischer, 1983).

When a first intervention produced no significant effects 3 months after training, a second intervention was initiated with many of the same children who had participated in the first intervention. In the second intervention, children in the experimental group were taught that watching television was not desirable and that they should not imitate violent television programs. Compared with control group participants, children in the experimental group showed more negative attitudes toward television and less of an increase in peer-rated aggression 4 months after training than they had before training. However, the intervention did not reduce the amount of television violence viewing in either of the two groups, thus failing to support the hypothesis that viewing violence on television was causally related to the children's aggressive behavior.

Summary

A vast body of laboratory research has been conducted on the television causes aggression hypothesis, and many of these studies report results supporting the hypothesis. Nevertheless, many inconsistencies exist and significant questions still remain regarding both the internal and external validity of these studies, thus raising questions about the effects of television violence on children's everyday lives. In the words of two distinguished researchers: "Indeed, if imitation of violence was as potent as is suggested by specific laboratory experiments one could argue that the sheer amount of violence presented on television alone ought to drive millions of people into the streets in daily rampages. Clearly this has not occurred . . ." (J. L. Singer & D. G. Singer, 1981, p. 101).

MEDIATING VARIABLES

Given that there is little evidence "for a simple, unidirectional causal sequence in which viewing of television violence clearly leads to aggressive behavior" (Van Evra, 1998, p. 59), we now turn to an examination of some variables that might mediate this relationship.

Child Characteristics

Although watching violence on television might cause aggression, causality might also flow in the opposite direction. Thus, according to the *selective exposure* hypothesis, children with a biological or psychological predisposition toward aggressive behavior might find violent television shows more interesting (and hence choose to watch more of them) than children with a low predisposition toward aggression (Freedman, 1984, 1986; Zillmann & Bryant, 1985). Note that this possibility is consistent with the concept of an active genotype environmental correlation discussed in chapter 4.

A substantial body of research supports the selective exposure hypothesis. For example, Belson (1978) found that boys who were violent by disposition tended to seek out and watch more violence on television and more television in general than boys who were not violent by disposition. In addition, a 10-year research program of children diagnosed as "emotionally disturbed" found that although these children viewed relatively large amounts of violence on television and preferred violent characters, they were no more likely to behave aggressively following exposure to violent television content than to nonviolent content (Gadow & Sprafkin, 1993). Another study examined television viewing and aggression among child and adult sibling dyads in Northern Ireland (Lynn, Hampson, & Agahi, 1989). More aggressive siblings tended to enjoy watching television violence more than less aggressive ones, but there was no evidence that intrapair behavioral differences were caused by viewing violence on television.

A second possibility is that some aspect of the child's personality might interact with violence on television to produce the child's aggressive behavior. Thus, children who are predisposed toward aggression or who are somehow more "vulnerable" might react aggressively to violence on TV, whereas other children might not. (Note that this hypothesis is consistent with the concept of the genotype environment interaction model discussed in chapter 4.) In addition, initially aggressive children who watch a lot of television violence would be expected to show a subsequent increase in aggression compared with either initially aggressive children who do not watch a lot of television violence or initially nonaggressive children who do watch a lot of violence on television.

Three field studies described earlier provide support for these hypotheses. Recall that although Friedrich and Stein (1973) found no overall effect for type of program on children's aggression, children initially high in aggressiveness who viewed the violent films declined less in overall aggressiveness than the highly aggressive children who saw the other types of programs. In the Leyens et al. (1975) study, aggression following the viewing of the violent films occurred primarily for the group that was initially high in aggressiveness. And in the Josephson (1987) study, only those boys who were initially high in aggressiveness showed increased aggression after viewing the violent video. Furthermore, boys who were initially low in aggressiveness showed a decrease in aggression following the violent film clip. It thus appears that children's existing personality characteristics affect their response to television violence.

It is, of course, possible that both selective exposure and genotype environment interaction could be working simultaneously. According to this view, young children who are predisposed toward aggression find violent television shows interesting and hence watch them a lot. In addition, watching these shows also exacerbates any aggressive tendencies these children might have. In this sense, initially aggressive children might be at a "double risk" for the effects of television violence.

Heavy TV Viewing

Another possible explanation for the association between television violence viewing and children's aggressive behavior is that some "third variable" might cause both television violence viewing and aggressive behavior. One major candidate for such a variable is heavy television viewing. Perhaps children who watch a lot of violence on television also watch a lot of television generally, and it is this heavy viewing (rather than viewing violence in particular) that leads to increased aggression in these children. Of course, any effect of heavy television viewing could be due to the possibility that a large amount of the child's overall television diet might consist of violent programs (J. L. Singer & D. G. Singer, 1986). However, Belson (1978) found that not only did exposure to violence on television increase serious acts of aggression, but so did exposure to television generally and to nonviolent shows as well.

Support for this possibility comes from a variety of sources. For example, in the Columbia County study, seriousness of criminal behavior at age 30 was correlated with the overall frequency of TV viewing at age 8 (Eron, 1987). Similarly, in the cross-national studies, "regularity of TV viewing" was significantly correlated with average aggression for both boys and girls in the United States (Huesmann & Eron, 1986), for older children of both sexes in Australia (Sheehan, 1986), for city boys in Israel (Bachrach, 1986), and for both sexes in The Netherlands (Wiegman et al., 1986). Moreover, Wiegman et al.'s (1986) analysis of the Dutch study indicates that there was "just as much support for the hypothesis that simply a lot of television viewing leads to an increase in aggressive behavior" (pp. 128–129) as for the hypothesis that viewing violence is responsible for such aggression. Finally, J. L. Singer (1992) found that children initially low in aggression but high in overall television viewing more than doubled their levels of overt unwarranted aggressive behavior over 1 year's time. It is thus at least plausible that the observed correlations between television violence viewing and aggression are due to children watching a heavy diet of television generally, rather than to their watching violent television shows specifically.

Heavy television viewing in general might increase children's aggression in a number of ways. First, heavy television viewing might cause viewers to overestimate the threat of violence in the real world, thus creating a hostile attribution bias and thereby making aggression more likely (Pingree & Hawkins, 1981). A second possibility is that heavy television viewing might be associated with "fast paced" material, which could increase children's arousal and hence make aggression more likely (J. L. Singer & D. G. Singer, 1986). And third, heavy television viewing might promote aggression by limiting the viewer's personal interaction with others and emphasizing the importance of materialistic wealth, which can be attained more immediately by antisocial means than through prolonged prosocial behavior (Hagedorn, 1998).

Parenting Practices

Viewing of violence on television or heavy viewing of television generally might also be confounded with parenting practices that are conducive to increased aggression (Wiegman et al. 1986). For example, in their study of preschool children, J. L. Singer and D. G. Singer (1981) found that highly aggressive children who watched a lot of television tended to receive more spankings and less praise than other children. Moreover, the home lives of these children were somewhat more disorganized and they were allowed to stay up later at night and sleep later in the day than children in other groups. In addition, these children were less likely to have a regular bedtime routine; less likely to have stories told to them at bedtime; less likely to have a kind of calming-down period before going to bed; and less likely to be taken to parks, picnics, museums, or other cultural activities, but more likely to be taken to movies. In general, then, these children seemed to be growing up in homes characterized by rather lax discipline and a lack of emotional intimacy, both of which are highly associated with the development of hyperaggressive children (see chap. 5).

Research suggests that any negative effects of television viewing can to some extent be attenuated if parents watch and discuss television shows with their children, a process called *parental mediation*. Effective mediation involves "discussion," as opposed to "prescription" (J. L. Singer, 1992). Mediation is also more effective when parents present moral judgments and explanations about issues presented on television (Desmond, J. L. Singer, & D. G. Singer, 1990). Finally, mediation is most effective when parents employ an inductive disciplinary style (Korzenny, Greenberg, & Atkin, 1979).

Children who watch a lot of television might have parents who are less involved in their children's television watching and are hence less effective mediators. J. L. Singer and D. G. Singer (1981) found that families of heavy TV viewers tended to have few books and that the parents tended to exercise less control over their children's viewing habits. Similarly, Holman and Braithwaite (1982) found that children who watched a lot of television tended to have parents who were less likely to express concern over the possible negative effects of television viewing. These parents were also less likely to perceive the need to control their children's use of television. It is thus likely that parents of children who watch a lot of television are less effective mediators than parents of children who watch less television.

J. L. Singer and colleagues (J. L. Singer, D. G. Singer, Desmond, Hirsch, & Nicol, 1988) showed that the level of parental mediation interacts with amount of television viewing and children's level of aggressiveness (see Fig. 6.2). Preschool children who watch little television have relatively low amounts of aggression, and parental mediation has little effect on their overall aggressiveness. Children who watch a lot of television, but who have parents who are effective mediators, show less aggression than children who watch a lot of television

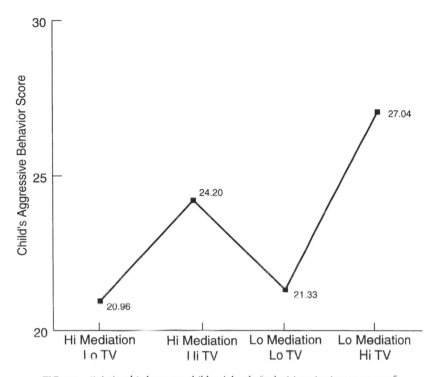

FIG. 6.2. Relationship between children's level of television viewing, amount of parental mediation, and children's aggressiveness scores. *Source:* Singer et al. (1988, Figure 1, p. 343). Reprinted from *Journal of Applied Developmental Psychology*, Vol. 9, by Singer, J. L., Singer, D. G., Desmond, R., Hirsch, B., & Nicol, A., "Family mediation and children's cognition, aggression, and comprehension of television: A longitudinal study," pp. 329–347, copyright © 1988, with permission from Elsevier Science.

whose parents do little mediation. Thus, if parents of children who watch a lot of television tend to engage in little parental mediation, we would expect these children to exhibit more aggression than other children.

IQ and Socioeconomic Status

IQ and socioeconomic status (SES) might also play roles in mediating the relationship between television violence viewing and aggressive behavior. We have already seen that hyperaggressive boys tend to have somewhat lower IQs than nonaggressive children, and in the Dutch cross-national study, IQ was more strongly related to aggression for boys than was television viewing (Wiegman et al., 1986). Research on SES finds that children from lower SES groups tend to watch both more television in general and more violent television in particular than do other children (Huesmann et al., 1997), and that they also show more approval and enjoyment of violence on television than do other children (Van der Voort, 1986). In addition one study also found that SES was negatively and more strongly correlated with aggression than was television violence viewing (Milavsky, Kessler, Stipp, & Rubins, 1982).

Conclusions

The relationship between children's viewing of television violence and their level of aggression might be causal in nature. However, it is also likely that the observed effects are caused by other variables that have been confounded with television violence viewing. In particular, it is possible that aggressive children simply like to watch violent television more than do nonaggressive children. Relatedly, it might be that viewing violence on television exerts its major effect on children who are already predisposed toward violence in some form or another. In addition, the observed effect might be due to the child's overall heavy diet of television viewing and not to watching violent television per se. Finally, all of these variables might interact with parents' child-rearing techniques and the extent to which they are involved with and mediate their children's use of television.

The introduction of the V-chip might indeed help some parents do a better job of monitoring the content of their children's television viewing, but this technology is not likely to affect the viewing habits of children whose parents have little involvement with their children's television-watching behavior. What these children need are parents who limit their children's television viewing, who help their children make sense out of what they do see, and, most of all, who spend time with their children in the everyday social activities of talking, playing, and doing things together.

UNDERLYING PSYCHOLOGICAL PROCESSES

Thus far, we have considered the issue of whether viewing television violence causes children to become more aggressive. A second issue, however, involves the question of how such an effect might occur. In other words, what are the possible psychological processes or mechanisms that could explain such an effect? We now consider this question in more detail.

Theoretical Explanations

Theoreticians and researchers have suggested the following processes by which viewing violence on TV might increase children's subsequent aggression:

- *Observational Learning.* As suggested by the original Bandura et al. (1961) study, children might learn aggressive responses through observing an aggressive model.
- *Cognitive Priming.* Viewing violence might provide children with *cognitive scripts* for violence (Huesmann & Eron, 1986; Eron & Huesmann, 1987) or a *cognitive network of memories* related to aggressive behavior (Berkowitz, 1984). When the child encounters a stimulus or situation in real life that involves some aspect of the script or memory, the aggressive behavior is more likely to "run off" automatically.
- *Disinhibition.* Viewing repeated acts of violence might have a motivational or disinhibiting effect whereby aggressive tendencies become actualized into performance (Bandura, 1965).
- *Normalization.* Frequent viewing of violence might normalize aggression by suggesting that it is socially approved.
- *Desensitization.* According to this view, children who view a lot of violence are likely to become emotionally desensitized and therefore not as likely to show negative emotions to real-life aggression (Gunter & McAleer, 1997).
- *Arousal.* Watching violence might produce increased levels of arousal, which in turn might be interpreted as anger, thus leading to actual aggressive behavior (Berkowitz, 1965).

Empirical Research

The six processes just discussed can be grouped into three classes of explanations: the *learning* explanation, the *motivational* explanation, and the *emotional* explanation. We now examine each of these in turn.

Learning. The observational learning and cognitive priming viewpoints emphasize that the child learns something new (responses, associations, scripts) by watching violence on television. This viewpoint argues that the effect of viewing a specific type of violence on television should be to perform that specific type of violence in the real world.

A number of studies support the learning approaches. For example, many of the early laboratory studies (e.g., Bandura et al., 1961, 1963) were designed specifically to show that children could learn aggression through observational learning. In addition, experiments in which children learned unusual or distinctive aggressive responses have provided especially strong support for this viewpoint. For example, in Josephson's (1987) study, boys were shown either a violent film (in which a walkie-talkie was used) or a nonviolent film. Following the film, the boys were interviewed by someone holding either a walkie-talkie or a microphone. In accord with the cognitive priming hypothesis, it was predicted that aggression would be highest for boys who saw the violent film and the walkie-talkie afterward. This hypothesis was confirmed for children who were considered initially aggressive, thus providing some support for the learning-process view.

Motivation. The disinhibition and normalization positions argue that viewing violence teaches the child that it is permissible to actualize aggressive tendencies into overt behavior. The disinhibition position assumes that *"such violent urges as are present in boys* are rendered much more likely to 'spill out'" (Belson, 1978, p. 523, emphasis in original), whereas the normalization view does not assume the existence of such tendencies. Both views argue that viewing violence on television should affect the child's more general antisocial behavior, rather than a specific aggressive response.

The motivational processes hypothesis has been supported by a variety of evidence. Hearold (1986) found that television violence viewing affected non-aggressive antisocial behaviors as well as aggressive behaviors, and Friedrich and Stein (1973) found that exposure to television violence affected not only aggression, but also tolerance for minor delays, task persistence, and obedience in school. These results, along with those of Hearold's meta-analysis, suggest that media exposure affects a wide range of antisocial behaviors, not just aggression. As such, these results seem to be most consistent with either the disinhibition or normalization hypotheses. That is, the effect might be to reduce the child's general moral inhibitions and/or suggest that antisocial behavior in general might be a socially approved option.

Other research also supports the motivational view. For example, because demand characteristics and sponsor effects imply that aggression is acceptable, these variables might exert their effects through the normalization process (Felson, 1996). Josephson's (1987) study also supports a motivational viewpoint in that his initially aggressive children might have already developed cognitive scripts or associations for aggression that were then disinhibited by exposure to media violence.

Emotions. In the cases of both desensitization and arousal, viewing violence on television should change the child's emotional reactions to violence, either by "dulling" them (desensitization) or by "revving them up" (arousal). Furthermore, both processes could presumably also lead to disinhibition, either because the child's emotional system is too dulled to respond to violence (desensitization) or so excited that antisocial impulses cannot be restrained (arousal).

Drabman and Thomas (1974) attempted to determine whether exposure to television violence reduces children's tolerance of real-life aggression. One group of third- and fourth-graders was shown a Hopalong Cassidy western depicting gun battles, shootings, and fist fights, whereas a second group was shown no film at all. All children then saw a simulated altercation between two younger children which ended in physical aggression. The group that saw the western film took significantly more time to notify an adult about the apparent fight than the group that saw no film. The authors offered both a normalization and a desensitization explanation for their results. Unfortunately, the fact that this study lacked a nonviolent-film control group calls into question its internal validity and makes its interpretation problematic.

We have already seen that frustration might increase arousal, and it appears that frustration might also mediate the relationship between television violence and children's aggression. Thus, Hearold (1986) found that in studies when no subjects were frustrated, the effect size was .28; when all the subjects were frustrated, the effect size increased to .68; and when only the treatment group was frustrated, the effect size increased to .98. However, Josephson (1987) found that viewing television violence can also produce aggression without the presence of frustration.

Josephson's (1987) study suggests that violence-produced arousal can either increase or inhibit the child's aggression. More specifically, arousal might reduce the inhibitions of initially aggressive children, thus increasing aggression. But Josephson (1987) also suggested that such arousal might produce anticipatory guilt in initially nonaggressive children, thus reducing their aggressive behavior. This view suggests that the important element is not whether children are exposed to television violence, but rather the extent to which they possess affectively negative associations to aggression-induced arousal (or to aggression per se).

Conclusions

This body of research suggests a number of possible conclusions. First, the existence of sponsor effects indicates that exposure to violent television might normalize violence by implying that it is socially approved. If TV violence becomes normalized, viewers would still need to possess aggressive response tendencies in order for these tendencies to be actualized into overt behavior. If such tendencies are already available, then the normalization process might disinhibit these tendencies, especially under extreme arousal. If the child lacks such tendencies, then repeated viewing of violence on television might provide the child with aggressive associations, cognitive scripts, or both. Of course, these processes could also work together. Thus, for example, continued viewing of television violence by children with already existing aggressive scripts might initially both normalize and disinhibit antisocial behavior. Continued viewing of TV violence could also help such a child develop new and "better" aggressive scripts, thus resulting in a *bidirectional effect* which would exacerbate the child's already-existing aggression.

OTHER MEDIA

Most of the research on the relationship between media violence and youthful aggression has involved television. We now turn to an overview of what is known regarding other media.

Research Results

Comics and Newspapers.   Although of less concern today, comics and newspapers have also been studied for their impact on youth violence. For example, Belson (1978) found evidence that exposure to violent comics increased boys' moderate and serious forms of violence, whereas exposure to newspapers increased only less serious forms of violence. In both cases, however, there was some evidence that the results could have been due to the boys' own aggressive predilection for violent material.

Music and Music Videos.   Much of the criticism of popular music has centered on *heavy metal* and *rap.* Heavy metal has been described by one critic as "a kind of loud, driving rock and roll made most often by young white males" (DeBecker, 1997, p. 36). Its topics often include sex, violence, death, satanism, and alienation. DeBecker argued that this type of music is dangerous because it "exploits the feelings of isolation and despair that are common among adolescents" (DeBecker, 1997, p. 36). Rap, considered primarily the music of young Black urban males, features themes similar to those in heavy metal (DeBecker, 1997). Within this genre, the police are often the target of violent fantasies, women are often viewed as sex objects and objects of rage, and racism and sexism are viewed as acceptable norms of behavior (DeBecker, 1997; Gore, 1990).

Rap has been associated with at least one homicide committed by a juvenile (Testa, 1998). Unfortunately, much of the sparse experimental research on this topic has focused on the effects of rap music videos on older teenagers and adults, thus limiting our understanding of how this genre might affect children and younger adolescents. In one of the few relevant experiments, J. D. Johnson, Jackson, and Gatto (1995) studied three groups of African-American males between the ages of 11 and 26. One group saw a music video featuring violent rap; a second group saw a video featuring nonviolent rap; and a third group saw no music video. Compared with participants in the other two groups, those in the violent rap group expressed a greater acceptance of the use of violence and reported a higher probability that they would also engage in violence. Interestingly, when a group of juvenile offenders were asked about their views on rap music, most believed that such music was a reflection of their lives rather than a cause of their behavior (Gardstrom, 1999).

Films.   Like television, movies have also been seen as a cause of youth violence (Levy, 1999). Critics argue that films are becoming increasingly violent, a
situation that one expert has traced to the "shift in attitude" about film violence
embodied in the 1967 movie *Bonnie and Clyde* (Hoberman, 1998).

A number of anecdotal reports have surfaced relating specific films to specific acts of youth violence. For example, the movies *The Basketball Diaries* (in
which two teenagers "cut a carnage swath through the Southwest") and *Natural
Born Killers* (in which a youngster daydreams of killing a teacher and fellow
students) were said to have been favorites of some of the youngsters involved
in the U.S. school shootings of 1998 and 1999 (Corliss, 1999). In addition, the
"slasher" films *Scream* and *Scream 2* were implicated in an 1998 incident in which
a 16-year-old California male and his 14-year-old cousin killed the older youth's
mother by stabbing her 45 times with four knives and a screwdriver (Deutsch,
1999).

Most of the empirical research relevant to films has been conducted within
the context of the debate about television; hence, little is known about how
violent movies per se might affect youngsters' aggressive behavior. However,
Hearold (1986) did examine this question and found an effect-size for "mixed
movies" of .40. Likewise, Belson (1978) found a positive effect of viewing violent films on boys' aggressive behavior; however, he also found some support
for a selective exposure effect as well. Thus, although it is possible that films
have inspired the behavior of some violent youngsters, it is hard to know
whether these youths' viewing of violent movies was the cause or merely the
reflection of their aggressive tendencies.

Videocassette Recorders and Portable Recording Equipment.   The wide availability of the videocassette recorder (VCR) has important implications for understanding youth violence (Huesmann et al., 1997). In the first place, VCRs
enable youngsters to record violent television programs, thus saving them for
future viewing. At the same time, this equipment also allows youths to repeatedly replay violent television programs and commercial films, a practice that
has apparently been the case with some young killers (Popyk, 1998). In addition,
the existence of VCRs makes it harder for parents to exert supervision over their
children's television viewing, especially if the child has a VCR in his or her bedroom. And finally, the availability of portable video cameras enables youngsters
to make violent videos as well as to view them. Unfortunately, little if any empirical research has been done on this topic (Huesmann et al., 1997).

Video Games.   Video games have also been criticized for their violent content. For example, one such game was allegedly the favorite of the young killers
in the Columbine High School shooting of 1999 (C. A. Anderson & Dill, 2000).
In their review of the topic, Anderson and Dill (2000) cited four experiments
indicating that video game viewing increases youthful aggression (Cooper &

Mackie, 1986; Irwin & Gross, 1995; Schutte, Malouff, Post-Gorden, & Rodasta, 1988; Silvern & Williamson, 1987) and two other studies showing no effect (Graybill, Strawniak, Hunter, & O'Leary, 1987; Winkel, Novak, & Hopson, 1987). These researchers concluded that "there is little experimental evidence that the violent content of video games can increase aggression in the immediate situation" (Anderson & Dill, 2000, p. 775). Another review also concluded that there was no direct relationship between video game playing and children's psychopathology (Emes, 1997), whereas a recent empirical study on the matter found that children who preferred violent video games were more aggressive than children who did not, thus suggesting the possibility of a selective exposure effect (Wiegman & van Schie, 1998).

Computers and the Internet.   The wide availability of home computers and ready access to the Internet could potentially affect youth violence in a number of ways. One possibility is that youngsters can become acquainted with anti-social individuals through electronic mail (email) or "chat rooms." Such was the case with a 15-year-old New Jersey boy who had a history of psychological problems and who subsequently killed a young boy after being victimized by an adult pedophile whom he met on the Internet (Curran, 1999). Another possibility is that youngsters can order violent materials that they find on the Internet. For example, one of the youths involved in a 1998 school shooting allegedly tried to order books on bomb making from a publisher's Internet site (Dietz, Neville, & Mortenson, 1998). Violent materials can also be downloaded from the Internet. In this connection, Van Evra (1998) described a "virtual" doll which can be downloaded and electronically stuck with pins, stabbed, or burned, and which emits a series of screams each time it is hurt. Finally, youngsters can also make their own violent websites, as was apparently the case with one of the perpetrators of the Columbine High School massacre (Anderson & Dill, 2000). Unfortunately, despite such anecdotal evidence, little controlled research has been conducted on the relationship between computer use and youth violence.

Related Issues

The advent since 1980 of what Van Evra (1998) calls the "new technologies" raises important questions regarding the effect of the media on youth violence. For one thing, youths today are exposed to violent materials from a wide variety of media sources that are potentially more powerful and interactive than was the case prior to the 1980s. Thus, rather than simply examining the effects of each medium separately, we must also consider the interactive and cumulative effects of numerous combined media. Unfortunately, we know little about this issue.

A related question involves the short-term versus long-term effects of media violence (Van Evra, 1998). Most of the studies reviewed in this chapter involved short-term effects, and the long-term cumulative effects of viewing multiple sources of media violence are unknown (Van Evra, 1998).

American children are exposed to a great deal of media violence in the form of music videos, films, video games, and the Internet. Although existing research does suggest a link between these forms of media and youthful aggression, the association might be due to selective exposure rather than to the causative role of media violence. Clearly, much more research needs to be done to clarify the relationship between media violence and youthful aggression.

SUMMARY AND CONCLUSIONS

Most of the research on the possible relationship between media violence and youthful aggression has focused on television. Associational studies indicate that there is a positive relationship between viewing violence on TV and children's aggression, and that this relationship accounts for between 1% and 10% of the variance in youngsters' aggressive behavior. Meta-analyses indicate that the effect of television violence on children's aggression is in the small to medium range.

Despite this relationship, it is likely that viewing violence on television does not directly cause children's aggression. Instead, whatever effects television violence might have on children's aggression are likely mediated by the child's own characteristics as well as those of the child's parents and the family in which the child is raised.

In accord with the selective exposure hypothesis, it is likely that children who are predisposed toward aggression simply enjoy watching violence on television (and perhaps a lot of television in general). In addition, however, as initially aggressive children watch these shows, their view of violence as "normal" may be affirmed, they may learn additional aggressive scripts, and the ensuing arousal may reduce any existing inhibitions regarding aggression they might possess. As a result, their level of behavioral aggression may increase.

This type of outcome is even more likely if an initially aggressive child lives in a family environment that tends to exacerbate the negative effects of television viewing. Unfortunately, it is probably those children who are most at risk for violence who also experience family situations that are the least likely to reduce the potentially negative effects of television viewing.

Processes involved with watching violence on television might also affect children who are not initially violent, especially if these children watch a lot of television and live in families where parental involvement is minimal and child rearing techniques ineffective. More specifically, as these children watch television shows (including violent ones), they might become more inclined to view violence as socially acceptable, they might learn new aggressive scripts and behaviors, and their inhibitions toward aggression might become reduced. Thus, even an initially nonaggressive child might become aggressive if left without supervision to watch a heavy diet of television for long periods of time.

However, it is also possible that viewing violence on television might have little or no negative effect on children. In particular, if parents exert a reasonable amount of control over their children's television watching; if they watch television with their children and engage in effective mediation in the process; if they have a positive emotional relationship with the child; and if they engage in the kinds of authoritative parenting techniques discussed in chapter 5, it is less likely that viewing violence on television will produce an aggressive child. In fact, as suggested by Josephson's (1987) study, it is possible that children initially low in aggression might even become less aggressive by watching violence on television.

We know relatively little about the effects of other media such as music videos, video games, VCRs, computers, and the Internet. However, the advent of these technologies means that children are likely to be exposed to violent content in a wide variety of media, not just through network television shows. Unfortunately, we know little about the cumulative or long-term effects of such exposure.

Critics have asked whether violence in the mass media causes youthful aggression. Given the popularity of such forms of entertainment, perhaps the more interesting question is not whether the mass media cause youthful violence, but why children find violence so appealing in the first place (J. H. Goldstein, 1998).

CHAPTER 7

Social and Cultural Factors

Youth violence cannot be understood apart from the social and cultural contexts in which it occurs. In terms of the larger culture, the United States is considered by many to be an unusually violent society. Indeed, in his historical analysis, Courtwright (1996) stated that, "Violence and disorder constitute the primal problem of American history" (p. 1). As a reflection of this problem, when international comparisons are made for homicide rates for 15- to 24-year-old males, the overall rate for the United States is between 35 and 40 deaths per 100,000 population, compared with under 5 deaths per 100,000 population for all the other major developed countries (Christoffel, 1997).

Children learn not only from the larger culture, but from their specific subculture as well. For some children, that subculture might consist of a mostly White, middle-class, suburban neighborhood. Other children might live within ethnic neighborhoods in the inner city. Still others might inhabit rural areas such as those in the south or northeast. In some cases, subcultures might reinforce the messages from the larger culture; whereas in other cases, subcultural norms might be very discrepant from those of the larger culture.

We now turn to an examination of some of the social and cultural factors related to youth violence.

COMMUNITIES AND NEIGHBORHOODS

Children grow up not only in a family, but also in a community and a *neighborhood* as well. For our purposes, a *community* is the larger geopolitical area where the child lives, whereas the *neighborhood* is a smaller psychosocial area where the child spends most of his or her everyday life.

We like to think of neighborhoods as idyllic places where youngsters can experience a carefree childhood. Unfortunately, this ideal is a myth for many children, especially those growing up in urban areas. As one researcher put it, "The notion of neighborhood as a nurturing setting where older members watch out for and over neighborhood youth and where networks of 'local knowledge' and intergenerational intimacy weave sturdy systems of support for young people and their developing identities, is far from the reality that contemporary inner-city youth experience" (McLaughlin, 1993, p. 54). We now examine some aspects of neighborhoods that have been shown to affect youngster's antisocial and aggressive behavior.

Subcultural Norms

The behavioral expectations a culture transmits to its members are called the *norms* of the culture (Wicks-Nelson & Israel, 2000). In many respects, the norms of the larger American culture seem to promote youthful aggression. For example, our legal system emphasizes the rights of the individual, thus promoting a "rugged individualism" over collective well-being. In addition, our economic system champions capitalism, thus promoting competition over cooperation. And many psychologists exalt the centrality of the *self*, thus encouraging an egotistic self-absorption at the expense of the good of others.

In addition to learning antisocial norms from the broader culture, a child may also be exposed to subcultural norms that promote violence. We now consider this issue in more detail.

The "Code of the Streets."   Although the problem of youth violence is found throughout the country, it is especially acute in our inner cities. And, in order to help understand the problems faced by urban youth, we turn to the ethnographic research of Elijah Anderson (1994, 1997, 1998), who has described the conflict between two types of inner-city families, the *decent families* and the *street families*.

Decent families are generally working poor and tend to be better off financially than street families. They tend to accept the values of the larger mainstream culture more fully and they attempt to instill these norms into their children. They value hard work and self-reliance, have a certain amount of faith in the larger society, and harbor hopes for their children. Many of them attend church and are involved in their children's schooling. They tend to be strict in their child-rearing practices and encourage their children to be morally good and to obey authority. They are polite and considerate and attempt to instill these virtues in their children. The overwhelming number of families in the inner cities reflect this orientation.

Street families, on the other hand, are in a more desperate financial situation and less likely to accept and promote the values of the larger society. In many cases, the parents in street families tend to be single mothers who may be drug addicts, who lead disorganized lives, and who may be abused by men. They often show little consideration for others and teach their children the same lesson. Although street women may love their children, many fail to deal with the demands of parenthood and find it difficult to reconcile their behavior with the needs of their children. They often socialize their children by yelling at them and by trying to "whup the devil" out of them. These children often grow up with little supervision and are said to "come up hard" (Anderson, 1994, p. 83). In some cases, a street-oriented mother may leave her children unattended, sometimes for days at a time, sometimes permanently.

Street children are socialized according to the *code of the streets* (the *Code*), a set of informal rules governing interpersonal public behavior. At the heart of the Code is the concept of *respect,* which is "loosely defined as being treated 'right' or granted the deference one deserves" (Anderson, 1994, p. 82). Among street people, respect is a precious commodity that is hard-won, easily lost, and therefore jealously guarded. Respect is also viewed as a fixed commodity, so that the ability to retain one's own respect is related to one's ability to put the other person down (Anderson, 1994).

Respect is maintained in a number of ways, including one's clothing and one's demeanor. Jackets, sneakers, gold jewelry, and even women determine the respect one is accorded. The willingness to possess things that might require defending is also an element in this process. One's bearing must also send the unmistakable message that one is capable of violence and can take care of oneself.

Central to the Code is *dissing* (disrespecting) someone and *being dissed* by someone. One shows "nerve" by dissing someone; by taking their possession or their woman, by "getting in someone's face," or even by pulling a trigger. Once a person feels dissed, the Code requires retaliation or revenge. "If somebody messes with you, you got to pay them back" is the central message of the Code (Anderson, 1994, p. 86). Thus, if someone disses you by looking at you the wrong way, you are justified in retaliating against him. Or if a mugging victim disses the mugger by trying to resist, the mugger is justified in killing the victim. "Too bad, but it's his fault. He should have known better," is the attitude (Anderson, 1994, p. 89).

Sometimes, retaliation comes through defending oneself verbally. Mostly, though, retaliation requires physical aggression that, of course, produces the risk of counterretaliation, and even death. And yet, for many street people, a violent death is preferable to being dissed. According to Anderson (1994), "Not to be afraid to die is by implication to have few compunctions about taking another's life" (p. 92).

Many children, especially street children, get socialized into the Code at an early age. They hang out with other kids and are allowed to "rip and run" by their parents. They internalize the Code by observing the behavior of others, and they pool the knowledge of the Code they have gleaned individually. They learn that "might makes right" (Anderson, 1994, p. 83), and many parents actually impose sanctions if the child is not aggressive enough. "I didn't raise no punks!" said one parent. "Get back out there and whup his ass" (Anderson, 1994, p. 86).

By the time they are teens, most inner-city youths have either internalized the Code or at least learned how to behave according to it. Even the children of decent families must deal with the Code: If they don't accept it, they must live by it to a certain extent in order to survive. Thus, although the neighborhood might be populated by more decent families than street families, the prevailing culture is often the street culture.

Cool Pose.   Anderson's concept of the code of streets is similar to the *cool pose,* which Majors and Billson (1992) found among Black teenagers in Boston. According to these researchers, cool pose is a "ritualized form of masculinity that entails behavioral scripts, physical posturing, impression management, and carefully crafted performances that deliver a single critical message: pride, strength, and control" (p. 4). It is meant to show that these young men are in control, despite their status in the larger American culture. Unfortunately, it also makes it difficult for a male to avert a physical confrontation or to respond affectionately to a girlfriend.

Summary.   The code of the streets and cool pose share a number of similarities. Both are based on a version of honor and of what constitutes appropriate masculinity. Both also involve the importance of being respected and the necessity of responding when such respect is not given. Finally, both sanction strong physical retaliation for perceived threats to honor.

Community Disadvantage

One of a neighborhood's key elements is its degree of either *social organization* or *social disorganization* (Sampson, 1995). Social organization refers to the extent to which a neighborhood marshals its resources to help its inhabitants meet their needs in a prosocial fashion, whereas social disorganization occurs when social organization breaks down (Sampson, 1995). Closely related to social organization is *social control,* the extent to which a group regulates its members through common principles (Sampson, Raudenbush, & Earls, 1997). Sampson et al. (1997) differentiate the "formal" social control imposed by legal authorities from the "informal" social control exerted by members of the neighborhood itself. One aspect of informal social control is *collective efficacy,* the "willingness of local residents to intervene for the common good" (Sampson et al., 1997, p. 919). Examples of this type of informal social control include adult supervision of youngsters' leisure time activities, adult intervention in street-corner congregation, and adult willingness to challenge youths who seem to "be up to no good" (Sampson, 1995, p. 199).

When it comes to youthful antisocial behavior and hyperaggression, neighborhoods do make a difference. For example, Peeples and Loeber (1994) compared a large group of White eighth graders with a similar group of African-American youths. Overall, the African Americans showed more serious delinquency than the Whites. However, when the African-American youngsters who did not live in "underclass" neighborhoods were compared with the Whites, the two groups did not differ with respect to the amount of serious delinquency they exhibited. These results held even when family composition and family economic status were controlled, suggesting that neighborhood characteristics were relatively more important than certain family variables.

In general, youthful antisocial behavior and delinquency are associated with neighborhoods characterized by a variety of conditions such as physical deterioration, poor housing and dense rates of habitation, high rates of families on welfare, high rates of mobility, high rates of unemployment or underemployment, and low levels of educational achievement (Sampson, 1995; C. R. Shaw & McKay, 1970; Simons et al., 1996). Collectively, these conditions are often referred to as *community disadvantage* (Simons et al., 1996). Research indicates a number of reasons why community disadvantage tends to encourage youthful antisocial behavior:

• Neighborhood deterioration can act as a magnet that attracts antisocial youths and gangs, in part because such deterioration suggests that social control is weak (Sampson, 1995; Seydlitz & Jenkins, 1998).

• The influx of antisocial youths can enhance the value of the code of the streets (E. Anderson, 1994) and reduce the ability of the decent people to resist.

• High rates of community unemployment are associated with Black male joblessness, which increases the prevalence of Black female-headed households (Sampson, 1987). Such family disruption, in turn, "substantially increases the rates of Black murder and robbery, especially by juveniles" (Sampson, 1987, p. 348).

• Community disadvantage has been shown to reduce the collective efficacy of a neighborhood (Sampson et al., 1997).

• Community disadvantage also indirectly affects youthful antisocial behavior by its negative effects on parenting. Indeed, a variety of studies indicate that one of the major effects of community disadvantage is its indirect and negative effect on parental supervision (e.g., Simons et al., 1996; Sampson & Laub, 1994).

• A major aspect of social organization is a neighborhood's ability to control youth groups. By reducing collective efficacy, community disadvantage also reduces the ability of the neighborhood to monitor and control antisocial youths (Sampson, 1995; Sampson et al., 1997). In light of the fact that community disadvantage also reduces parental supervision, the inability of the neighborhood to effectively assume this function further exacerbates a bad situation. For example, one study found that adolescents reporting a high amount of unsupervised peer contact were at greatest risk for behavior problems when they resided in comparatively unsafe neighborhoods and experienced lower levels of parental monitoring (Pettit, Bates, Dodge, & Meece, 1999).

Clearly, neighborhoods play a role in youngsters' antisocial and aggressive behaviors. And yet, family and child characteristics also mediate this effect. For example, Simcha-Fagan & Schwartz (1986) found that community effects accounted for as much as 80% of between-community variance in aggregated measures of delinquency. However, when individual levels of delinquency were examined, community factors accounted for no more than 4% of variance. Relatedly, other research has found that child characteristics (such as hyperactivity and previous antisocial behavior) account for variance over and above that accounted for by community characteristics (Peeples & Loeber, 1994; Sampson & Laub, 1994; Pettit et al., 1999). Thus, youthful antisocial behavior depends on a variety of community, family, and child characteristics, all of which interact to produce their combined effect.

Neighborhood Violence

In addition to their indirect effects, neighborhoods can also have more direct effects on children. Unfortunately for too many youngsters, especially those in the inner cities, neighborhoods have become a source of violence rather than of safety (E. J. Jenkins & Bell, 1997). Not only do adolescents and children in these areas experience high rates of violent crime victimization, but more of this violent crime is now occurring in public than was previously the case (Bureau of Justice Statistics, 1994; E. J. Jenkins & Bell, 1997). Thus, many young people between the ages of 12 and 19 have either been victimized by a violent crime or have witnessed a violent crime being committed (E. J. Jenkins & Bell, 1997).

E. J. Jenkins and Bell (1997) summarized the research on the extent to which children and adolescents actually witness acts of violence. Studies indicate that from 30% to 60% of inner-city youths between the ages of 6 and 18 have witnessed a shooting; between 15% and 45% have seen a stabbing; and between 10% and 40% have witnessed a killing (E. J. Jenkins & Bell, 1994; Osofsky, Wewers, Hann, & Fick, 1993; Richters & Martinez, 1993a). In general, older youth witness more such violence than do young children. Unfortunately, these data only tell part of the story, because youths in these areas witness many more "less violent" acts, such as muggings, beatings, drug deals, and rapes (E. J. Jenkins & Bell, 1997).

In many cases, these young people are personally close to the victims of the crimes they witness. Thus, in the E. J. Jenkins and Bell (1994) study of inner-city high school youths, 70% of those witnessing a shooting or stabbing reported that the victim was a friend or family member. Not only that, but in many cases, the perpetrators of the violent acts are also known to the youngsters (Richters & Martinez, 1993a).

Except for sexual assault, boys are more likely to be victims of violent crimes than are girls (E. J. Jenkins & Bell, 1997). Boys are also more likely to witness violence outside the home, whereas girls are more likely to witness violence within the home (E. J. Jenkins & Bell, 1997). And children from homes without a mother are more likely to witness violence than children whose mothers reside within the home (Schubiner, Scott, & Tzelepis, 1993).

Posttraumatic Stress Disorder. Witnessing such traumatic events can affect children and adolescents in a number of ways, most notably through the emergence of *posttraumatic stress disorder* (PTSD), described briefly in chapter 3. The classic study of children's PTSD involves Terr's description of the incident in which 26 children were kidnapped from a school bus and held hostage in darkened vans and a tractor-trailer truck for 27 hours before being rescued (Terr, 1979, 1983). Terr found that all the children showed symptomatic behavior, with 73% exhibiting moderately severe to severe reactions. Four years later, many children still had symptoms, and all still experienced event-related fears (Terr, 1983).

It is clear that children who witness shootings can develop PTSD. For example, one study of 8- to 10-year-old school children who had experienced a sniper attack found that 74% of the most severely exposed children still reported moderate to severe PTSD symptoms 14 months after the attack (Nader, Pynoos, Fairbanks, & Frederick, 1990). In addition, some community surveys have found that between a quarter and a half of youths living in high violent crime areas meet criteria for PTSD (Fitzpatrick & Boldizar, 1993; Horowitz & Weine, 1994).

Unfortunately, not only does the presence of PTSD increase the level of personal distress among its victims, but it also increases the community's general level of violence as well. For example, aggression and antisocial behavior are two prominent behavioral symptoms of PTSD, especially among adolescents (E. J. Jenkins & Bell, 1997). Furthermore, survey data indicate that victimization and witnessing violence are the strongest predictors of self-reported involvement in fights and weapon-carrying behavior (Durant, Cadenhead, Pendergrast, Slavens, & Linder, 1994). In addition, CD and other disruptive behavior disorders also sometimes accompany the diagnosis of PTSD (E. J. Jenkins & Bell, 1997). As is the case in other situations, community violence tends to feed on itself and create still more violence.

Apart from its direct effects, community violence also has indirect effects on children. For example, Osofsky et al. (1993) reported that mothers of inner city children often teach their children to "sit in their homes or watch television with their heads below the window sills in order to avoid random bullets" (pp. 43–44). Children who are thus confined to an apartment lose the ability to go outside and interact with their peers, an important aspect of children's development. Furthermore, sitting inside and watching television is hardly conducive to good social and emotional development. Not only that, but lack of exercise can also negatively affect physical development as well.

James Garbarino and colleagues (Garbarino & Kostelny, 1997) have compared U.S. inner cities to *war zones*. In both refugee camps and public housing projects, there is a proliferation of weapons and heavily armed young people.

In both cases, the "mainstream" may exert a presence during the day, but gangs control the area at night. In both cases, women experience abnormal stress and depression and men play only marginal roles in the day-to-day life of the family. In both cases, children are neglected and have diminished prospects for the future. There is, however, one difference: "In war zones, there is hope of peace, repatriation, and the renewal of community life. In the case of community violence in America, the war never ends, peace never comes" (Garbarino & Kostelny, 1997, pp. 39–40).

Perhaps the best antidote to PTSD symptomatology lies in the home. Pynoos (1993), for example, found that the prognosis is much better for a child with PTSD if the parent appears appropriately calm and effective in the face of danger than if the parent is not available, not accessible, or is overwhelmed by the danger. In addition, Richters and Martinez (1993b) found that the prognosis for children living in violent environments was affected by the safety and stability of the children's homes, and not by the level of community violence per se. Once again, the importance of the child's home life becomes evident. When that life is filled with violence, children tend to become violent. But when it is filled with love and understanding, children can thrive, even in spite of the larger community.

DRUGS

R. Jessor and S. L. Jessor (1977) have shown that "problem behaviors" tend to cluster in individuals, and other research indicates that youthful aggression and substance abuse are closely related (Leukefeld et al., 1998). We examine this relationship in more detail.

Historical Considerations

Much of the increase in youth violence which began in the mid-1980s has been attributed to drugs, especially to *crack cocaine* (Blumstein, 1995). Although cocaine had played a prominent role in the drug culture of the 1970s, two conditions combined during the mid-1980s to allow this drug to exert an even more powerful effect on youth violence. First, drug smugglers brought so much cocaine into the United States that the price for a pure gram in a one-ounce transaction decreased from $120 at the beginning of the decade to just $50 in 1988 (Blumstein, 1995; Courtwright, 1996). And second, the process of turning powdered cocaine into chunks of crack cocaine that could be smoked reduced the price still further, so that crack could be sold in small vials for $5 or less, thus bringing it within reach of the poor (Courtwright, 1996). The advent of the crack trade thus provided a lucrative opportunity for gangs of adolescents and young adults, particularly for minority youths in urban areas such as Los Angeles, New York, Washington, DC, and Miami (Blumstein, 1995).

Researchers have cited a number of reasons why the rise of the crack market may have also produced an increase in youth violence. First, because crack is inhaled rather than snorted, it provides a quick route to the brain, thus producing a more powerful rush and disrupting synaptic transmissions more than does powdered cocaine (Courtwright, 1996). Second, because it is both cheaper and produces a shorter "high" than does the powdered version, crack tends to be used more frequently than powdered cocaine (Palermo, 1994). Third, the more frequent use of cocaine is associated with brain changes which increase the likelihood of aggressive, impulsive, and paranoid behavior (Dackis & Gold, 1988; Miller, Gold, & Mahler, 1991; Spitz & Rosegan, 1987). Thus, many young users, already predisposed to violence, became even more violent. Fourth, the illegal nature of the trade itself spawns violence, such as when a customer refuses to pay, or when a dealer lower on the chain holds out money from one higher on the chain (Courtwright, 1996). And fifth, as with the alcohol-running gangs of the 1920s, crack dealers fight to maintain and even expand their territory. These considerations, in turn, lead drug dealers to arm themselves, for they understand that "guns and ruthlessness are the prerequisites for surviving in the world of drug dealing" (Courtwright, 1996, p. 258).

In Al Capone's time, drug trafficking was adult work. However, with the advent of the crack market and the concomitant increase in the availability and use of guns, more juveniles became involved in the selling of drugs, especially in the inner cities. In part, this occurred because teenagers will work more cheaply than adults; also, they will do less jail time if caught. Finally, the advantage in strength held by an adult is offset by the advantage of a teenager who carries a gun. For all these reasons, more and more adolescents became caught up in drug trafficking during the late 1980s and early 1990s (Blumstein, 1995; Courtwright, 1996).

Aside from its effect on drug trafficking, the crack epidemic also had other negative side effects related to youth violence. First, even though crack may have been cheaper than powdered cocaine, it wasn't free. Furthermore, because it is so addictive, users will go to great lengths to procure it. So, in order to support their habit, many users turned to crime. When a young aggression-prone crack addict with a gun attempts to rob someone, violence is likely. Sometimes the perpetrator is still under the influence of an earlier high and engages in senseless and gratuitous violence; sometimes the victim resists, triggering the addict's paranoia and impulsivity; and sometimes the offender hurts or kills the victim to keep the victim from identifying him. The latter was apparently the case, for example, with then-81-year-old civil rights pioneer Rosa Parks, who was beaten and robbed of $53 by a crack addict in her Detroit home in September of 1994 (Reynolds, 1994).

"Crack" Mothers and Babies

The crack epidemic was not limited to males. Indeed, by the end of the 1980s, a substantial portion of inner-city crack addicts were females (Courtwright, 1996). In addition to using drugs, many of these young women were also very sexually active. Research indicates that some babies born to cocaine-using women are literally "born addicts." Unfortunately, prenatal exposure to cocaine is associated with a number of adverse neurobehavioral outcomes, including attentional problems, which in turn predict subsequent violence (Mayes, Granger, Frank, Schottenfeld, & Bornstein, 1993). However, it should be noted that crack may not be the only culprit involved in this process. In many cases, cocaine-abusing mothers also abuse other drugs and lack medical care during pregnancy, thus making it difficult to determine whether cocaine use is itself the cause of the child's birth problems (Hawley & Disney, 1992).

Aside from any neurological damage that might have occurred from maternal cocaine use, "crack" babies often grow up in extremely unfavorable circumstances. Approximately ⅔of cocaine-abusing mothers are unmarried, and their children often have little contact with their fathers (Hawley & Disney, 1992). In addition, some addicted mothers abandon their baby ("Crack-addicted mother," 1999; Prothrow-Stith & Weissman, 1991; Revkin, 1989). In some cases, relatives or friends are available to care for the abandoned infant, but often they are not.

Even when the mother does raise the child, her addiction is often so great that her major concern centers on how to maintain her drug habit. In such situations, emotional abuse and neglect are common (Lawton, 1992). Many such mothers have told researchers that a craving for cocaine has become the central motivator in their lives, overpowering their desire to care for their child. In the words of one mother:

> You know, it was just like, damn, I done had a baby. "Go fix this bottle." "Okay, I'll fix it in a minute; let me get this other hit," you know? "Your baby wet!" "Oh damn, I got to get this baby some diapers. I got ten dollars. Well, I just buy me a rock and I try to get him some diapers later on, ask some girl if I can borrow a couple of diapers" (Lawton, 1992, p. 44).

Sometimes, the neglect demonstrated by these mothers is fatal to the baby, as in the case of the 1-month-old daughter of a cocaine-addicted mother in Virginia who died from malnutrition ("Crack-addicted mother," 1999).

The prognosis for such infants is poor. Follow-up studies suggest that many of them show elevated levels on various problem scales of the Child Behavior Checklist (Hawley & Disney, 1992). In addition, we have already seen that infants who have a combination of both neonatal neurological problems and early maternal rejection are at much greater risk for violence at age 18 than are other children (Raine et al., 1996). All too frequently, babies born to cocaine-abusing mothers fit this profile.

Other Drugs

Crack is not the only drug associated with youthful antisocial behavior and violence. For example, in their study of high school students in Rochester, New York, Thornberry and colleagues found that 91% of chronic offenders used alcohol and 76% used marijuana (Thornberry, Bjerregaard, & Miles, 1993). Similarly, in their research on 58 Black and 53 White incarcerated 16-year-olds, Neighbors, Kempton, and Forehand (1992) found that 96% of those with a diagnosis of alcohol and/or marijuana abuse had also had a diagnosis of conduct disorder (CD), while 93% of those with polysubstance abuse also had a diagnosis of CD. It thus appears that the abuse of alcohol, marijuana, and other drugs is associated with youth violence. On the other hand, in view of the fact that 62% of nonabusers in the Neighbors et al. (1992) study were also diagnosed with CD, it is clear that there is no simple relationship between juveniles' drug use and their violence.

Youth Drug Abuse and Violence

Given the strong association between adolescent drug abuse and juvenile aggression, it is not surprising that many of the variables found to predict youthful hyperaggression have also been found to predict drug abuse. For example, in a sample of advantaged middle-class White children, the parents of adolescent abusers tended to abuse drugs themselves. In addition, the parents provided less structure, made fewer maturity demands, and were more frequently absent from the home than were parents of nonabusers (Baumrind, 1991). Similarly, in a 25-year longitudinal study of inner-city Black children, birth complications, early temperamental characteristics, negative mother–child interactions at 8 months, loss of a parent and unfavorable family environment in the first year, and cognitive problems and indices of family adversity at age 7 all combined to predict adult substance abuse at the age of 25 (Friedman, Bransfield, Tomko, & Katz, 1991). These studies indicate that a variety of medical complications, poor parent–child relationships, adverse family situations, parental drug abuse, poor parenting skills, and cognitive problems predict later adolescent and adult drug abuse.

Child Characteristics. Does drug abuse cause aggression, or is adolescent drug use merely another manifestation of a child's existing aggressive personality? Some research supports the latter hypothesis. For example, when Dobkin, Tremblay, Mâsse, and Vitaro (1995) followed a group of disadvantaged Canadian boys from kindergarten through age 13, they found that oppositional behavior, fighting, and hyperactivity in kindergarten predicted similar behaviors at age 10, and that these behaviors in turn directly predicted substance abuse prior to the age of 13 (see Fig. 7.1).

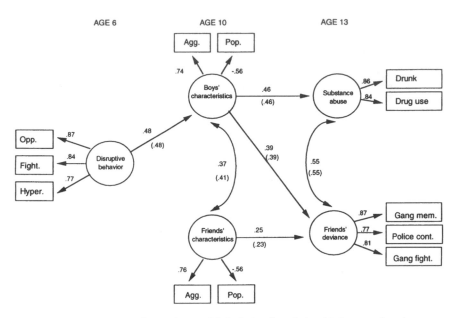

FIG. 7.1. Structural equation model depicting the relationship between boys' characteristics at ages 6 and 10 and their substance abuse at age 13. From "Individual and Peer Characteristics in Predicting Boys' Early Onset of Substance Abuse: A Seven-Year Longitudinal Survey," by P. L. Dobkin, R. E. Tremblay, L. C. Mâsse, & F. Vitaro, 1995, *Child Development, 66*, p. 1209. Copyright 1995 by the Society for Research in Child Development. Reprinted with permission.

Some psychologists argue that peer influence is a major causative factor in adolescent substance abuse (Leukefeld et al., 1998). In testing this hypothesis, however, Dobkin et al. (1995) found that although boys' personality characteristics at age 10 directly predicted their substance abuse at age 13, friends' characteristics at age 10 had no direct effect on boys' subsequent substance abuse (Fig. 7.1). It thus appears that early onset substance abuse is more related to youths' own personality characteristics than to the influence of their friends. By age 13, however, boys' substance abuse and friends' deviance were strongly correlated, thus suggesting a reciprocal interaction effect between the two.

Synergistic Effects. There is also evidence that adolescent drug use has a synergistic effect on youth violence. In one study of New Zealand adolescents, Fergusson, Lynskey, and Horwood (1996) found that a number of variables predicted both adolescent violence and drug abuse. These included the familiar list of low socioeconomic status, family adversity, a family history of alcohol and/ or drug abuse, a history of childhood conduct problems, and the child's association with delinquent peers. However, over and above these variables, the youngster's tendency to abuse alcohol also predicted violent crimes but not property crimes. One explanation for this finding is that when violence-prone youngsters who are under the influence of alcohol get into conflict situations, the pharmacological and/or psychological effects of alcohol may reduce the youths' inhibitions, thus making impulsive and aggressive behavior more likely.

Summary. The relationship between adolescent antisocial behavior and drug use is nicely illustrated by the following summary of a study conducted on upwardly mobile Mexican-American teenagers:

> Based on the findings, violent delinquency among Mexican-American youth develops in the following way. First, the children develop low impulse control and low tolerance for frustration in the context of the family, in which parental rejection, lack of supervision, physical abuse, and other forms of family stress are experienced. Second, the youth adopts values that are in conflict with those that are consistent with productive behavior in "middle class" society. Third, young people experiment with tobacco use, identifying themselves as marginal. In association with peers, they continue to experiment with other gateway and stepping stone drugs, particularly marijuana. In the peer group, drug use is supported, while other deviant behaviors including violence are tolerated. Fourth, family controls are either too little, too late, or none at all. Violent youth tend to be inadequately constrained by family attitudes and supervision. Fifth, physical abuse and family violence make a minor but direct contribution to violent delinquency. Sixth, drug use affects violence pharmacologically, systemically, or economically. (Watts & Wright, 1990, pp. 153–154)

GUNS

The rash of school killings in the United States in the late 1990s underscored what some authorities have described as the "firearm epidemic" of injuries and deaths to American children (Christoffel, 1997, p. 43). The beginning of this "epidemic" can be traced to the mid-1980s, when, as seen in Fig. 7.2, the proportion of gun-related homicides committed by juveniles began to increase dramatically (Blumstein, 1995; H. N. Snyder & Sickmund, 1999). As indicated in Fig. 7.3, this increase in firearms-related deaths was also accompanied by an increase in the number of juveniles arrested for weapons use, most of which involved firearms (H. N. Snyder & Sickmund, 1999).

Fortunately, juveniles' illegal use of guns seems to be declining. For example, the use of firearms by juvenile killers has been decreasing since 1994 (Fig. 7.2). In addition, as we saw in chapter 1, the number of students bringing weapons into schools decreased from 1993 to 1996 (National Center for Education Statistics, 1998). Finally, juvenile arrests for weapons violations decreased from 47,369 in 1993 to 32,232 in 1998, thus suggesting a substantial decline in youths' firearms involvement over that period (Federal Bureau of Investigation [FBI], 1994, 1999).

Historic Overview

For most of our country's history, youths did not generally use guns to kill other people. Indeed, until the 1960s, guns received little mention in discussions regarding adolescent gangs (Fagan & Wilkinson, 1998). By the mid-1980s, however, inner-city youth gangs had turned increasingly to the distribution of illegal drugs, especially crack, and according to some authorities, this activity in turn spawned an increase in youthful gun use (Blumstein, 1995). In Courtwright's (1996) words, "Before the crack revolution a typical street gang had perhaps one good gun stashed away somewhere out of sight and not easily accessible. After crack more and more members, whether they were dealing or not, went about armed with their own high-powered, rapid-fire weapons" (p. 259).

Some researchers argue that involvement with the crack trade increased the rate of gun possession because ruthlessness was necessary for survival in this type of atmosphere and because the use of guns exemplified such ruthlessness (Blumstein, 1995). In addition, guns were also inexpensive and easily available on the black market. In one survey, for example, 74% of adolescents who re-

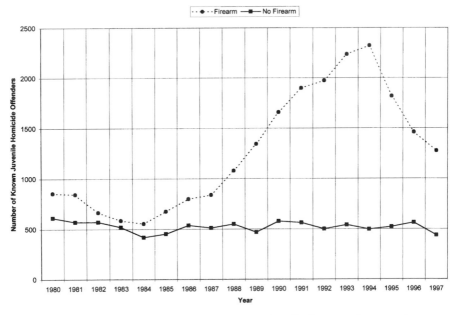

FIG. 7.2. Number of known juvenile homicide offenders as a function of firearms use. From *Juvenile Offenders and Victims: 1999 National Report* (p. 54), by H. N. Snyder and M. Sickmund, 1999, Washington, DC: Office of Juvenile Justice and Delinquency Prevention. Reprinted with permission of the National Center for Juvenile Justice.

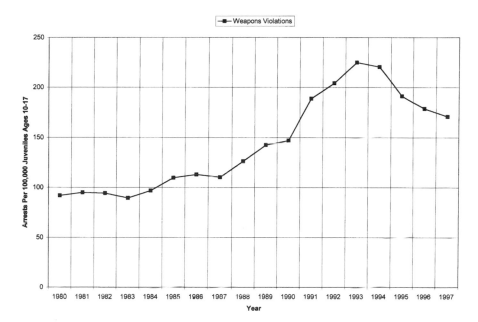

FIG. 7.3. Arrests for weapons violations per 100,000 juveniles ages 10–17. From *Juvenile Offenders and Victims: 1999 National Report* (p 135), by I I. N. Snyder and M Sickmund, 1999, Washington, DC: Office of Juvenile Justice and Delinquency Prevention. Reprinted with permission of the National Center for Juvenile Justice

sponded to the question reported that they got their gun "from the streets," whereas 20% got it from home, and less than 1% got it from a store (McNabb, Farley, Powell, Rolka, & Horan, 1996).

Gun design contributed to both the spread and the effects of juvenile firearms use. Because newer guns were compact and more easily concealed, they were carried more often (Courtwright, 1996). Furthermore, unlike older handguns, automatic or semiautomatic handguns could be used to spray victims, thus rendering marksmanship as superfluous (Courtwright, 1996). Firearm technology also increased the workload for trauma surgeons. The use of automatic weapons meant that victims were often hit by more than one bullet, and the newer and "deformable" Black Talon bullet exploded within the body, thus shredding the tissue in its path rather than passing cleanly through the body (Courtwright, 1996; Fagan & Wilkinson, 1997).

Researchers disagree over the role general gun availability plays in violent crime. For example, Kleck (1991) cited considerable data indicating that gun availability does not influence the overall volume of violent crime, thus suggesting that aggression-prone youths will engage in violence whether or not they have a gun. However, although gun availability might not affect the amount of juvenile violence, it probably does affect the type of violence. For example, as

Cook and Moore (1995) pointed out, there are "few drive-by knifings, or people killed accidentally by stray fists" (p. 273). In addition, gun use seems to have increased the lethality of violence. In the words of Cook and Moore (1995): "The fact that the United States is such a violent country does not have much to do with guns; the fact that our violent crimes are so deadly has much to do with guns" (p. 278).

Data on Youth Gun Possession and Use

Guns primarily kill adolescents rather than children. Of the 2,691 youths age 19 and under who were murdered in 1998, 1,666 (62%) were killed by firearms. Of these, 3% were 4 years old or younger, 4.5% were between the ages of 5 and 12, 21% were 13 to 16, and 71.5% were ages 17 to 19 (Federal Bureau of Investigation, 1985–1999). In absolute terms, 121 children below the age of 13 and 473 below the age of 17 were murdered by firearms in 1998, compared with 1,193 between the ages of 17 and 19 (Federal Bureau of Investigation, 1999). Thus, more than 90% of juveniles murdered by guns in 1998 were adolescents, not young children. Furthermore, nearly 75% of these victims were over the age of 16.

Although recent high-profile school shootings have occurred in rural and suburban areas, the increase in juvenile homicides due to guns occurred primarily in the inner cities. Thus, in the early 1990s, the homicide rate due to firearms for 15- to 19-year-olds was almost seven times higher in the core metropolitan areas than in other areas of the country (O'Donnell, 1995).

In the 1997 National Longitudinal Survey of Youth, 9% of males and 2% of females between the ages of 12 and 16 reported carrying a gun within the previous year (Snyder & Sickmund, 1999). Gun possession is higher among certain minority males and youths living in the inner cities. For example, Sheley & Wright (1995) found that 30% of a sample of violence-prone, inner-city high school males reported ever having owned a gun, and McNabb et al. (1996) found that 29% of a group of community youths in south New Orleans reported carrying a gun. In the New Orleans study, however, only about ⅓ of the gun-carrying adolescents were African Americans (McNabb et al., 1996).

Most guns possessed by inner-city youths are not automatic or semiautomatic rifles. Instead, Sheley & Wright (1995) found that both juvenile inmates and high school students were most likely to own revolvers, followed by automatic or semiautomatic handguns. Few owned assault weapons.

Gun Possession as Protection

A number of authorities argue that young people in the inner cities carry guns primarily to protect themselves (Christoffel, 1997; Fagan & Wilkinson, 1997; McNabb et al., 1996; Sheley & Wright, 1995). For example, Sheley and Wright (1995) pointed out that youths in their sample tended to carry guns only when they thought guns would be needed for self-protection. These researchers concluded that "the desire for protection and the need to arm oneself against enemies were the primary reasons" for obtaining guns, easily outpacing other possible motives such as status, respect, or the need to prove one's manhood (Sheley & Wright, 1995, pp. 67).

Although many youths believe that carrying guns affords them protection, the reality is that gun carrying leads to increased violence. For example, Durant, Getts, Cadenhead, and Woods (1995) found a strong correlation between adolescent fighting behaviors and weapons carrying and suggested that weapons carrying placed their subjects at a higher risk for more violent behaviors. These researchers concluded that the more aggressive adolescents are "more likely to carry illegal weapons" as well as "more likely to engage in violent behaviors because they are armed with a weapon" (Durant et al., 1995, p. 379). Thus, as with other aspects of youth violence, the relationship between juveniles' personality and their gun use is probably interactive.

Legal Versus Illegal Guns. Some research suggests that the problem with guns does not appear to involve youngsters' possession of legal guns (typically rifles used for sport) as much as it does their possession of illegal guns (typically hand guns used for protection). In fact, the "U.S. Department of Justice [DOJ] reports that the rates of delinquency and drug use among male youth who own legal firearms is less than among youth who do not own firearms, both of which are substantially lower than the rates of delinquency and drug use among male adolescents who possess illegal guns" (Durant et al., 1995, p. 380). The DOJ report attributes this difference to differential socialization of gun ownership. According to this view, youngsters who own legal firearms are more likely to receive gun training and safety lessons within the context of the family, whereas those who own illegal firearms are more likely to receive their education regarding guns on the street.

This hypothesis is consistent with the research of Hardy and colleagues (Hardy, Armstrong, Martin, & Strawn, 1996), who reported on factors involving children's use of guns. In this study, pairs of 5-year-old children were allowed to play 10 minutes in a room that included a variety of toys along with two toy guns and two real guns. Following the play session, one member from each pair and that member's parent were given a gun safety presentation. Children were then allowed a second play session.

Results showed that play with a gun (real or toy) in the first session was the most significant predictor of aggression in the second session. In addition, the most significant predictor of overall gun use (both real and toy) was playing with the parent's gun at home (Hardy et al., 1996). Interestingly, it was the children who played with their parents' gun without permission who were most likely to play with a gun in the laboratory; on the other hand, children whose parents allowed them to handle a gun in an educational context at home were less likely to play with guns in the laboratory (M. S. Hardy, personal communication, April 8, 1996). This and other research thus suggests that the problem might not be guns per se, but rather a host of other factors that affect the way in which young people come to be socialized into gun activity (Lizotte, Tesoriero, Thornberry, & Krohn, 1994).

The Psychology of Gun Possession and Use

Which Juveniles Possess Guns?   Juveniles who possess and carry guns illegally tend to be those who are at odds with the law. For example, in the Sheley & Wright (1995) study comparing incarcerated juveniles with inner-city high school students, 86% of the inmates had owned a gun sometime in their lives, compared with 30% of the students. Furthermore, 83% of the prisoners had possessed a gun just prior to confinement, whereas only 22% of at-risk students possessed a gun at the time of the survey (Sheley & Wright, 1995). As for actually carrying guns, 55% of the inmates reported doing so all of the time or most of the time prior to incarceration, while only 12% of the student respondents did so all or most of the time (Sheley & Wright, 1995).

A number of other studies have also found illegal weapons carrying to be correlated with serious crime (e.g., Brounstein, Hatry, Altschuler, & Blair, 1990; Callahan & Rivara, 1992; Durant et al., 1994; Sheley, McGee, & Wright, 1992). For example, Webster, Gainer, and Champion (1993) surveyed 295 students in two junior high schools in Washington, DC. The prevalence of ever carrying a gun among males was 23% in one school and 40% in the other. However, the chances of carrying a gun were 7.7 times higher for males with a history of arrests than for males with a history of no arrests. Furthermore, having been arrested was the single best predictor of carrying a gun for males. Other significant predictors were aggressive behavior patterns (e.g., getting into fights), believing that shooting someone is justifiable under certain circumstances, and perceiving that one's peers accept violence.

Even among nonincarcerated youths, young people who carry guns tend to be already predisposed to violence. For example, in one study, youths who exhibited conduct problems in school were more likely than other teenagers to carry guns, even in regions where hunting is common (Callahan & Rivara, 1992). In another study, 78% of young gun owners in Seattle were members of a gang, involved in drug sales, or had a history of school suspension, assaultive behavior, or both (Callahan & Rivara, 1992). Juveniles who carry guns are thus not simply a representative sample of youth as a whole.

Personality Characteristics of Juvenile Gun Possessors.   We have already seen that the rate of gun possession by young males in the central cities is relatively high. However, somewhere between two thirds and three quarters of such youths do not carry firearms, and we might wonder why this difference exists.

Research by Webster et al. (1993), Brounstein et al. (1990), Callahan and Rivara (1992), and Sheley et al. (1992) suggested that nonpossessors tend to be less antisocial and more conventional than possessors. Conversely, the latter seem to be more antisocial, more aggressive, and less conventional. In this connection, Webster et al. (1993) drew the following conclusion: "Our findings are not consistent with the image of otherwise law-abiding youths carrying guns solely for protection. . . . As was the case in other recent studies . . . gun carrying could more realistically be explained as a part of an extremely aggressive, rather than defensive, system of thought and behavior" (p. 1607).

Fagan and Wilkinson (1998) posited that the crisis of youth gun violence involves the confluence of three forces. First, the presence of guns promotes a "contagion of fear," which leads more and more young people to arm themselves for protection, thus fueling the process even more. Second, guns become "salient symbols of power and status, and strategic means of gaining status, domination, or material goods" (Fagan & Wilkinson, 1998, p. 175). And third, based on the youths' exposure to and internalization of the code of the streets, identities associated with violence become more prevalent in socially isolated neighborhoods, thus reinforcing the importance of physical violence and devaluing identities based on prosocial behavior.

In their analysis of gun use, Sheley and Wright (1995) cited two interrelated reasons for the increased use of firearms by inner-city youth. First, consistent with our earlier discussion regarding delay of gratification and Hirschi and Gottfredson's (1994) concept of self-control, Sheley and Wright (1995) suggested that guns give these youngsters an immediate sense of power and a mechanism by which desires can be gratified immediately. Second, Sheley and Wright postulate that gun use also relates to these youths' moral values:

> Three-quarters of our juvenile inmates have fired a gun at someone. Most did *not* do so because they were high on drugs or because they were strung out and needed more drugs; most did so because they live in a moral universe that ascribes no particular value to a human life, that counsels no hesitancy in pulling the trigger, that promotes immediate gratification for the very simple reason that tomorrow may never come. (Sheley & Wright, 1995, p. 156)

This conclusion is consistent with that of Gardner and Resnik (1996), who argue that many young perpetrators of violence "regard violence and participate in it with no sense of a moral dimension, no remorse, and no compassion for their victims" (p. 167).

Summary

Gun-related violence perpetrated by juveniles was relatively rare through the 1960s, escalated dramatically in the mid-1980s, and apparently reached its peak in the mid-1990s.

Most of the research we have reviewed is consistent with the view that although a relatively large minority of inner-city youths carry and use guns, these juveniles are probably not a representative sample of urban youth as a whole. Instead, for the most part, gun-carrying youngsters have a history of antisocial behavior. Motivationally, they appear driven by the need to dominate and intimidate others, and guns fulfill those needs. In addition, guns also help fulfill these youngsters' need for an identity and immediate self-gratification. Furthermore, these youngsters may believe that carrying a gun is necessary for self-protection, an act that in fact makes subsequent violence only more likely.

PROTECTIVE FACTORS

Throughout this book, we have examined the question of why children become hyperaggressive. In the process, we have discussed a number of variables that might cause or be associated with youth violence. As we have seen, these variables are sometimes called *risk factors*, because children experiencing them are more likely to become hyperaggressive than those who do not. Thus, children who experience more risk factors are more likely to become hyperaggressive than those who do not.

Another question we might ask, however, is why some children do not become hyperaggressive, especially if they do experience a number of risk factors. When we ask this question, we are looking for *protective factors*, those variables that might help children avoid hyperaggressive behavior. Let us examine this issue in more detail.

The Kauai Longitudinal Study

We begin by considering the Kauai Longitudinal Study described in earlier chapters (Werner & Smith, 1982). As you recall, Werner and Smith conducted a prospective study of a number of children born on the island of Kauai in 1955. For our purposes, we consider the substudy of a group of 72 boys and girls, all of whom were raised in chronic poverty and who experienced a significant number of risk factors during infancy. Despite this background, all these children were doing well at the age of 18 in all aspects of their lives. According to Werner and Smith, these youngsters manifested *resilience,* the capacity to cope effectively with both internal vulnerabilities as well as with externally induced stressors (Werner & Smith, 1982).

In trying to determine what could account for this resiliency, the researchers came to a number of conclusions.

• Among the factors that seemed to contribute to the children's resilience, about ½ occurred prior to age 2, another ⅓ occurred between the ages of 2 and

10, and the remaining ⅓ occurred in adolescence. Infancy is clearly a crucial period for the development of future behavior problems.

• Specific factors changed depending on the child's age and sex.

• Predictors of resilience in the first year consisted of certain environmental characteristics as well as the mother's perception of her baby. Resilience occurred for babies who were perceived by mothers as active, easy to deal with, and cuddly; and who experienced a good mother–child relationship coupled with a large amount of maternal attention and a lack of prolonged separation from the mother.

• Significant predictors in the second year included the child's physical health and his or her own competent behavior (a positive, agreeable, and outgoing social orientation; good intelligence; and autonomous and independent behavior).

• Childhood predictors included the composition and coherence in the household, the mother's employment status, and the presence of stressors. The presence of many siblings decreased resilience, whereas an extra adult in the home made it more likely. The presence of the father improved boys' resilience, but impeded that of girls. The mother's full-time, long-term employment improved resilience, but chronic family discord and stressful life events reduced it.

• Adolescent determinants of resilience included the adolescent's perception of a positive emotional relation with the family (especially with the father), and the cumulative number of stressful life events that occurred in adolescence.

Other Research

The Kauai Study involved academic and behavioral problems in general. Other studies focusing more specifically on externalizing behaviors have arrived at similar conclusions. For example, Kolvin and colleagues also examined possible protective factors among high-risk children (I. Kolvin, F. J. W. Miller, Fleeting, & P. A. Kolvin, 1989). They found that during the preschool period, children who had good parental care, positive social circumstances (e.g., good socioeconomic status) and few adverse physical problems seemed to be protected from developing later delinquency. In the preadolescent period, the important factors seemed to be good parental supervision, absence of developmental delays, relatively good intelligence and academic achievement, an easy temperament, and positive interpersonal and social relations.

In general, protective factors seem to be the opposite of risk factors. Based on our discussion in previous chapters and on other research (S.B. Campbell, 1991; Kazdin, 1995; Kolvin et al., 1989), these protective factors include the following:

• *Characteristics of the Child:* Good attention, "easy" temperament, good physical health, good intelligence, and academic success.

- *Prenatal and Perinatal Factors:* Good prenatal care; few or no prenatal or perinatal medical complications.
- *Parental Factors:* Parents older than 21; lack of parental antisocial behavior and psychopathology; moderate to high levels of parental education.
- *Intrafamilial Factors:* A generous amount of parental attention in the first year of life; lack of prolonged separation from the mother; high parental love and involvement; presence of parental monitoring and supervision, especially in adolescence; intact and harmonious families; good parental child rearing skills; small family size; lack of family poverty.
- *Extrafamilial Factors:* Few external stressors; prosocial peer groups; a safe neighborhood; a low rate of adult unemployment and the presence of collective efficacy in the neighborhood.

In addition, some studies also suggest that parent or child religiosity also functions as a protective factor. Let us examine this possibility in more detail.

Religiosity

Religiosity, defined broadly as the extent to which people say that religion is important to them, may be unique in that it is one of the few protective factors that is not merely the opposite of a risk factor. Furthermore, religion seems to be important to a large proportion of U.S. youths. For example, one large-sample study found that 55% to 60% of American adolescents say that religion is "very" or "pretty" important to them (M. J. Donohue & Benson, 1995). Moreover, religion seems to be related to youngsters' moral behavior. Thus, Benson, Williams, and Johnson (1987) found consistently positive correlations between religiosity and adolescent altruism and helping behaviors, with correlations typically ranging between .15 and .25. In addition, religion has a consistent negative correlation of approximately −.20 with substance abuse (Benson et al., 1987). Furthermore, Tittle and Welch (1983) found that 90% of the studies they reviewed reported significant negative relationships between religion and delinquency. (Recall that in the cross-national studies on the effect of television violence, about 50% of the correlations were significant.) In sum, there seems to be a consistent but modest relationship between religiosity and adolescents' moral behavior.

Some recent research suggests that parent or adolescent religiosity may affect moral development indirectly through other processes. For example, a study of 9- to 12-year-old African-American children living in intact homes found that parents' religiosity indirectly affected the child's self-regulation, which was positively related to a measure of prosocial behavior and negatively related to externalizing problems (Brody, Stoneman, & Flor, 1996). Similar results have also been reported for younger Black children living in single-parent homes (Brody & Flor, 1998). Relatedly, another study of more than 1,000 high school students found that adolescents' involvement in religion directly predicted the extent of their conventional beliefs, which in turn directly predicted amount of delinquency (Benda & Whiteside, 1995).

Relatively little research has been conducted on the relationship of religion and youthful aggression and violence. In general, existing data indicate a modest negative relationship between these two factors. Although more research certainly needs to be done on this topic, current findings suggest that involving at-risk youth in religion may be beneficial in helping to prevent youth violence.

SUMMARY AND CONCLUSIONS

Youth violence is affected not only by the child's family, but by broader cultural and subcultural factors as well. In many respects, the norms of the larger American culture seem to promote youthful aggression. In addition, the communities and neighborhoods in which children live exert profound effects as well.

A large part of today's youth violence can be traced to a confluence of forces that have led a "critical mass" of poorly functioning people (especially males) to congregate in certain parts of inner cities that some researchers have referred to as "war zones." These disadvantaged urban areas are often physically run down; housing is poor; police and fire protection are often lacking; emergency and routine medical care are often difficult to obtain; schools are of poor quality; youth gangs are prevalent; and guns and illegal drugs are easily accessible. As unemployment and underemployment increase, female-headed, single-parent families become more prevalent, a situation that not only leaves children without fathers in the home, but that also increases the stress on mothers and hence negatively affects their parenting behaviors. In addition, social control and social organization break down; the neighborhood loses its sense of "collective efficacy"; and social disorganization becomes prevalent. And, as this happens, the neighborhood becomes less attractive to the "decent people" and begins to attract more disaffected inhabitants who adhere to and promote the "code of the streets," the major tenet of which is the importance of winning respect, even at the cost of a physical confrontation.

As they grow up witnessing violence and the deaths of neighborhood acquaintances, as they become socialized into the code of the streets, as they become more cognizant of real or perceived racism and social inequality, and as they see and hear violence celebrated in the media, many inner-city youngsters are likely to become alienated from conventional society and to develop an identity and attitudes favoring the domination of others through physical aggression, including the use of guns. Because they perceive their lifespan as limited in the face of such violence, these youngsters may develop a predisposition for short-term self-gratification, without either the skills or the motivation necessary to inhibit immediate impulses and desires in the service of long-term gain.

Although environmental factors can promote youth violence, they can also help protect against its development. In general, such protective factors are the opposite of risk factors. In addition, some evidence indicates that religiosity also functions as a protective factor as well.

Becoming Hyperaggressive

As we have seen, whether a child actually develops hyperaggressive behaviors seems to depend on a complex mix of biological, familial, and extrafamilial factors. Children are most likely to become antisocial when they experience multiple environmental risk factors combined with minimal protective factors. But genetic or biological variables factors can also play a role: In some cases, these variables might need to combine with a pathogenic environment in order cause actual hyperaggressive behavior (Raine et al., 1994). In other cases, however, it appears that biological factors might cause antisocial behavior even in the presence of a benign environment (S. W. Anderson et al., 1999). Finally, the child's aggression might best be conceptualized as illustrating one of the types of genotype-environment correlations discussed in chapter 4. Thus, for example, antisocial parents often fail to exert appropriate supervision over their at-risk sons (a passive correlation); the aggressive behavior of antisocially predisposed preschool children often evokes retaliatory behavior from peers (an evocative correlation); and aggressively predisposed children often choose to watch violent television programs (an active correlation). In each of these situations, the child's existing predispositions toward aggression and antisocial behavior are strengthened or amplified by his or her interaction with the environment.

Now that we have considered some of the determinants of children's hyperaggression, we next examine the behavior of hyperaggressive children themselves.

CHAPTER 8

Psychological Processes in Hyperaggressive Youths

Bopete is a fourteen-year-old Blood from the Jungle, in Baldwin Hills . . . Sidewinder is also fourteen, a member of one of the largest Crip sets. He is here for participating in a drive-by shooting in which another Crip was killed . . .

I notice that Sidewinder is squinting his eyes as he peers at something across the ground and it occurs to me that he probably needs glasses. His attention is brought back as Bopete begins to talk. "When I get really angry it's like I don't care about nobody. I just want to get my anger out. Fight somebody, do something to get it off my mind . . . At home—on the outs—when I get mad I leave the house, and I don't come back for a while. I go somewhere and get in some trouble. Like, the first thing I look for is my gun. Then I go out and just hold it in my hand—I don't pull it out of my pocket or nothin', I just hold it . . ,

"I might not shoot at 'em. Maybe I just aim their way. But when I'm mad I'm liable to shoot at anybody." He laughs softly. "Just for the fun of it."

— Bing, 1991, pp. 47; 56–57, emphasis in original

What goes through the minds of hyperaggressive youths? What motivates them to fight and kill? And what emotions do they experience in the process? In this chapter, we examine some potential answers to these questions.

A QUALITATIVE OVERVIEW

We begin by considering two studies that employed the clinical research methodology described in chapter 1. This research provides a qualitative descriptive picture of hyperaggressive children, which we will integrate with results of studies utilizing more typical quantitative methodologies.

Redl and Wineman's Pioneer House Study

We turn first to Fritz Redl and David Wineman's (1951) description of the experiences they had in running a group home for wayward children. The facility, called Pioneer House, was home to ten 8- to 11-year-old boys over the course of about 18 months. The behavioral pattern that characterized the Pioneers included "destructiveness, hyperaggression, stealing, running away from home, truancy from school, temper tantrums and lying, sassiness toward adults, and most of the rough and tumble language and behavior that goes into the pattern of a 'toughy' in the making" (Redl & Wineman, 1951, p. 46). However, because Pioneer House was a true house in a residential neighborhood, and the children attended a local school, the boys were not so disturbed that they could not function in that environment. Most of the children had at least one parent with whom they were living at the time of referral, but their home life was characterized by divorce and desertion, the children had often been shuttled between various foster homes, and the boys typically lacked sustained positive relations with adults.

The authors concentrated on two aspects of children's functioning, their *ego* and their *conscience*. In the authors' words, "It is the ego's job to size up the world around us, in its physical or social aspects, and to give danger signals if any one of our desires is too seriously in conflict with the 'reality outside'" (Redl & Wineman, 1951, p. 63). To do this, the ego must be accurately aware of the content of its own id and conscience, it must be able to select from a variety of available behaviors, and it must be able to "choose" the appropriate behavior. The conscience is the child's "moral compass." To be effective, it must contain a set of socially approved values. In addition, it must also experience emotionally charged guilt after the commission of a morally offensive deed, as well as anticipatory guilt (moral anxiety) prior to the commission of such a deed. Furthermore, the affective component must also be strong enough to lead to confession, reparation, and to the inhibition of the malevolent deed.

Disturbances in Ego Functioning.   Redl and Wineman (1951) discovered that the egos of the boys at Pioneer House contained crucial deficiencies in the three functions of *resistance to temptation, delay of gratification,* and *tolerance of frustration.* Even minor temptations would elicit antisocial behavior in these boys. For example, the sight of money sticking out of the pocket of a coat or of a football lying on a chair would be enough to ensure that theft would occur. Nor were the boys able to wait for gratification for even short intervals. On one occasion, for example, a child pounded and kicked on a door and called a counselor a name when the counselor was briefly delayed in opening the door. And even brief frustrations produced immediate antisocial behaviors. For example, boys riding in a station wagon cursed and threw things at a counselor who was driving when the counselor stopped the car at a red light.

Redl and Wineman discussed the effects of *excitement* on the boys at Pioneer House. The authors compared the boys' reaction to excitement to a kind of "toxic inebriation," which induces the children to "break out into stages of impulsive wildness which surpass anything that we usually would expect" of them

(Redl & Wineman, 1951, p. 89). Because excitement can result in an almost total loss of control, even mild forms needed to be monitored for their potentially "intoxicating" effect.

The Pioneers also exhibited another process the authors called *sublimation deafness* (Redl & Wineman, 1951). "Normal" children develop an understanding of the function of items; for example, of the fact that chairs are used to sit on. The Pioneers, however, were "deaf" to such conventional uses, but instead would succumb to the temptation to use such objects as part of their aggressive behavior. For example, one child first began throwing pieces of an erector set into an empty fireplace, then escalated to throwing the pieces at another child. Noting that many objects bought for the children's use thus got destroyed, the authors drew the following conclusion: "The general theory which still prevails and holds that disturbed children will become well if only they are surrounded by worthwhile recreational tools and opportunities, and that their impulsivity will easily yield to sublimated order, if only such a pattern is put within their reach, is invalid" (Redl & Wineman, 1951, p. 93).

Conscience not only involves feelings of guilt after an act has been committed, but also the ability to inhibit the behavior associated with the guilt (Baumeister, 1998). Because this last aspect involves executing a behavioral "choice," Redl and Wineman (1951) considered it to be an ego function, one they found lacking in the boys at Pioneer House.

In addition to these deficiencies, the Pioneers also exhibited a number of problems in cognition and learning. These included impairments in *memory*, in their *sense of time*, and in their *cause-and-effect thinking*, as well as deficiencies in *social cognition* (i.e., the child's ability to think accurately regarding other people) and *perspective taking*.

Although in many respects the egos of the boys at Pioneer House might have seemed deficient, they were overly effective when it came to defending impulse gratification. Indeed, the authors use the term *delinquent ego* to refer to "the ego's effort to secure guilt-free and anxiety-free enjoyment of delinquent impulsivity" (Redl & Wineman, 1951, p. 144). Thus, the egos of these children had developed a "constant and well-planned barrage of counter-techniques" against attempts at changing the child's antisocial behavior" (Redl & Wineman, 1951, p. 144). These include repressing one's own intent, insisting that

> "He did it first"; that "Everybody does such things anyway"; that "Somebody else did that same thing to me before"; that "He had it coming"; that "I had to do it, or I would have lost face"; that "He is a no good so-and-so himself"; that "They are all against me"; or that "I couldn't have gotten it any other way." (Redl & Wineman, 1951, pp. 147–154)

Not content with developing such *alibi tricks*, the delinquent ego also employs some other strategies in the quest for "guiltless enjoyment of delinquent gratifications" (Redl & Wineman, 1951, p. 156). One of these involves the boys' choice of friends. Being uncomfortable around children with nondelinquent behaviors, these children will "associate *on their own choice* with children who may be expected to support, supplement, or contribute to their own constant search for delinquent enjoyment" (Redl & Wineman, 1951, p. 157, emphasis added). As a consequence, these children also drift into gangs or other mobs where they can solidify their individual delinquent defenses into a "group code," thus forming an antidote against whatever individual prosocial tendencies they have remaining.

Redl and Wineman found that the Pioneers would "provoke" someone else into antisocial behavior, then join in with the excuse that "somebody else did it first." The boys also sought out situations that tempted their antisocial behaviors, then used the defense that they had experienced "temptation beyond endurance" (Redl & Wineman, 1951, p. 159). Another strategy the Pioneers used was to incorporate fantasy into the service of their antisocial tendencies. Thus, seeing a movie about gangsters might induce these children to actually go out and steal. Or, watching an outlaw in a western movie might motivate a child to steal a bicycle and run away.

In summary, Redl and Wineman (1951) argued that these children expended an enormous amount of energy on the job of becoming antisocial. As the authors remarked: "From a variety of then still open possibilities such youngsters managed to pick those skills and careers which would also allow them the enjoyment of secondary gains from delinquent exploits" (Redl & Wineman, 1951, p. 165).

Disturbance in Conscience.   Redl and Wineman (1951) disputed the idea that antisocial children "have no conscience," labeling this ideas as "bunk" (p. 201). Instead, they argued, these children do have consciences, but their consciences are deficient in four major respects.

First, the values they possess are antisocial ones. More specifically, these boys have identified with "*a delinquent neighborhood code*" (Redl & Wineman, 1951, p. 201, emphasis in original), a phenomenon reminiscent of E. Anderson's (1994) idea that urban youngsters subscribe to the "code of the streets."

Second, these boys often lack both guilt and anticipatory guilt. Thus, at one point these authors assert: "The main trouble here with the children we talk about is not that they have too many guilt feelings, but that they have too few" (Redl & Wineman, 1951, p. 105). In the rare instances when their boys did experience guilt, their ego was unable to deal with it. Given the weakness of both their ego and their conscience, these boys were highly unlikely to inhibit their antisocial tendencies.

Third, when these boys did exhibit guilt, it was often inappropriate. For example, one young car thief showed no guilt over his thievery, but his letters to his mother were full of guilt for minor childlike infractions against her rules. Instead of helping these boys change their antisocial behaviors, such bouts of guilt typically induced decreased self-disclosure, increased anger and aggression toward others, a general destructiveness, and an increased resistance to routine conformism.

Finally, these boys lacked attachment and identification in their lives, and were unable to develop identification with prosocial models. For example, these children would find it difficult to identify with a teacher, and hence internalize the values the teacher was trying to teach.

Summary and Conclusion. In summary, the Pioneers showed problems in both ego functioning and in conscience. Furthermore, problems in both aspects interacted to produce a very complicated and chronic set of behavior patterns.

I have spent some time describing Redl and Wineman's work because of the rich descriptive material their study provides. However, we must remain appropriately skeptical about both the internal as well as the external validity of this study. With respect to internal validity, the authors used only clinical observations, with no statistics or controls. With regard to external validity, their conclusions were drawn from an all-male sample of 10 boys whose representativeness is certainly questionable. Nevertheless, the authors' descriptions provide a qualitative insight not available from quantitative research. Furthermore, this material also serves as point of departure from which more recent work can be discussed.

Yochelson and Samenow's Research

Another example of clinical research comes from the work of psychiatrist Samuel Yochelson and clinical psychologist Stanton Samenow (Samenow, 1989; Yochelson & Samenow, 1976). Starting in the 1960s, Yochelson (later joined by Samenow) began collecting an extensive amount of information on 255 male criminals at St. Elizabeths Hospital in Washington, DC. Half these men had been committed as not guilty by reason of insanity, whereas the others were convicted felons. Data collection included 150,000 to 200,000 hours of interviews over 17 years, not only with the inmates but also with their spouses, parents, and children. Since publication of their original three volumes, Samenow has continued to work with antisocial individuals and has applied their ideas to children and adolescents (Samenow, 1989).

Briefly, Samenow (1989) argued that aggressive and antisocial youth hold a deviant set of motives and ideas that stem from what he calls *errors in thinking*. In addition, Samenow appears to take a free-will approach toward antisocial behavior, arguing that these children make choices to behave antisocially and that they are victimizers, not victims.

Nature of the Errors in Thinking. The errors in thinking function for Samenow is much the same as *irrational beliefs* function for Albert Ellis. According to

Ellis and Bernard (1983), irrational beliefs are absolutist and imperative ideas about the world that form the basis for the person's behavioral goals. These beliefs include *shoulds* (the way things should be morally), *musts* (the way reality should be), and *awfulizings* (the emotionally negative consequences if the shoulds and musts are not met).

In a similar fashion, Samenow's errors in thinking constitute a set of beliefs that antisocial and aggressive children hold and that form the motivational basis for their behavior. According to Samenow (1989), the thinking of antisocial children can be characterized as follows:

- They believe they should always get what they want, and they should get it immediately, without any delay.
- They see life as a series of unrelated events in which the goal is immediate gain.
- They see life as a never-ending quest for thrills in which "normal" pro-social activities (school, hobbies, sports, etc.) are "boring" and in which conformity is horrible.
- They believe that everything should come easily, without any work or struggle. They anticipate instant success with minimal effort.
- They cannot abide any rule or person that does not cater to their every whim.
- They believe that others exist only as means to their own immediate self-satisfaction. They therefore reject the help of others who are trying to help them change their ways.
- They believe that their own intentions are pure, and that all that matters is the purity of their intentions, not whether what they say is objectively true or false.
- They employ lies to gain and keep control and keep others in the dark.
- They believe that anything they want is right, and anything anybody does that impedes their desires is wrong.
- They believe that they are not responsible for their faults. Instead, they blame others for all their shortcomings. Blaming others maintains the purity of their intentions.

Although Samenow (1989) did not explicitly cite the origin of these children's thinking errors, he does say where they do not come from. Specifically, these errors do not stem from socioeconomic disadvantage, poor parenting, rejection by peers, or poor academic performance. Instead, Samenow argues, it is child's errors in thinking and freely chosen antisocial behaviors that cause poor academic performance and interpersonal difficulties with both parents and peers.

Conclusion. As was the case with Redl and Wineman's (1951) study, the work of Yochelson and Samenow (1976) must be interpreted with caution. Although their sample was also all male, it was larger and perhaps more representative than Redl and Wineman's, thus suggesting a potentially greater external validity. However, the retrospective nature of their interview raises questions about reliability, and their use of interviews creates possible biases and problems for internal validity. Moreover, Samenow subscribes to a free choice and personal responsibility model that seems unique among researchers in this area. Nevertheless, his work also produces a qualitative picture that helps illuminate the quantitative data of other researchers. Furthermore, as we now see, the picture painted by Samenow is strikingly similar to that presented earlier by Wineman and Redl.

Comparison of Redl and Wineman's and Samenow's Views

Similarities. Although Redl and Wineman's and Samenow's work were conducted at different times and on somewhat different populations, they both drew the following similar conclusions:

- Highly antisocial males are qualitatively different from normal males.
- These youths demand instant gratification and cannot abide efforts to thwart their impulses.
- They see life as essentially a never-ending quest for excitement (Redl and Wineman) or for thrills (Samenow) in which the child is locked into a "here and now" time perspective.
- They fail to put themselves either cognitively or emotionally in the shoes of others.
- They experience profound disturbances in ego and conscience.
- Their goal is to ensure a "guilt-free and anxiety-free enjoyment of delinquent impulsivity" (Redl & Wineman, 1951, p. 144).
- They attempt to rationalize their antisocial behavior, evade responsibility, and blame others.
- They associate with similar children "on their own choice" (Redl & Wineman, 1951, p. 157), thereby garnering additional social support for their antisocial behavior.

Differences. But despite these similarities, there are also some differences between the findings of these two groups of researchers.

- Redl and Wineman (1951) place far more emphasis on an unfortunate early environment than do Yochelson and Samenow (1976). Although the former would acknowledge that their boys made choices, they would also argue that many of the choices were at least related to the early deprivation these boys experienced.

• Redl and Wineman (1951) also seem to put more emphasis on abnormal psychological processes such as memory and time perspective. The impression is that abnormalities in these processes might at least contribute to the problems these children have. This view is interesting in light of recent theory and research that I will describe shortly.

• The two views seem to differ with respect to implications for treatment. Redl and Wineman's (1951) viewpoint seems to argue that treatment should focus on developing positive relations between the child and other adults, on gradually helping to make the child's ego processes more accurate, and on attempting to change the value content and emotional functioning of the child's conscience. Samenow (1989), on the other hand, seems to suggest a more confrontational strategy designed to get the child to see the nature of his thinking errors and to make the choices needed to change his antisocial behavior.

Having considered a qualitative view of the psychological processes of hyperaggressive children, let us now examine what more recent quantitative research studies have to say about these issues.

COGNITIVE AND "EGO" PROCESSES

He is seventeen years old, and he is homeless . . .
    We are in my car because I have to run some errands, and I want to save time, so I have decided to take this kid—Faro—along . . .
    "See them two dudes?" Faro's voice, unaccountably, has dropped to a whisper. I nod my head.
    "I'm gonna look crazy at 'em. You watch what they do . . ."
    The driver, sensing that someone is looking at him, glances over at my car. His eyes connect with Faro's, widen for an instant. Then he breaks the contact, looks down, looks away . . .
    I ask Faro what would have happened if they guy had looked crazy back.
    "Then we woulda got into it . . . Then I woulda killed him." (Bing, 1991, pp. 39–41)

Cognitive or *ego processes* involve functions such as memory, problem solving, and judgment, all of which were involved in Faro's decisions about whether and when to engage in aggression. We now examine how these processes function in antisocial youths.

Intelligence

Research has consistently shown a strong inverse relationship between children's measured IQs and their current and subsequent antisocial behavior, including aggression and violence (Henry & Moffitt, 1997; Kazdin, 1995; Maguin & Loeber, 1996; Stattin & Klackenberg-Larsson, 1993; West & Farrington, 1973; Wiegman et al., 1986; Wilson & Herrnstein, 1985). Much of this research has utilized various versions of the *Wechsler Intelligence Scale for Children* (WISC), a test that yields three major outcomes: a *Verbal IQ* (VIQ), which measures "verbal skills, knowledge of the environment, and social understanding"; a *Performance IQ* (PIQ), which measures "perceptual–motor skills, speed, and nonverbal abstraction"; and a *Full Scale IQ* (FSIQ), which reflects a combination of both VIQ and PIQ (Wicks-Nelson & Israel, 2000, p. 279). All three IQs have a mean of 100 and a standard deviation of 15.

In general, antisocial youths have IQs that are approximately 8 to 10 points below the mean (Wilson & Herrnstein, 1985). Although these youngsters tend to have lower VIQs than PIQs (Henry & Moffitt, 1997), their nonverbal intelligence is also lower than that of "normal" youths (West & Farrington, 1973). Such IQ deficits are not explained by socioeconomic status (SES) or racial differences (Henry & Moffitt, 1997; Kazdin, 1995), nor are they due to the possibility that less-intelligent delinquents get caught more than more-intelligent ones (Moffitt & Silva, 1988).

Not only is low IQ related to youthful antisocial behavior, but childhood IQ also predicts later antisocial behavior as well. For example, West and Farrington (1973) found that low nonverbal IQ at ages 8 to 10 predicted both official and self-reported delinquency in adolescence. Schweinhart, Barnes, and Weikart (1993) found that low IQ at age 4 predicted number of arrests up to age 27. Stattin and Klackenberg-Larsson (1993) found that low IQ at age 3 significantly predicted official offending in males up to the age of 30.

In addition to traditional IQ tests, neuropsychological measures that are correlated with IQ also indicate that aggressive children suffer from *verbal deficits*. This finding emerges as early as age 3 and continues to hold after appropriate controls for variables such as socioeconomic status, race, and academic achievement. Such problems precede the onset of delinquent behavior and are strongest for those children with a history of attention-deficit/hyperactivity disorder (ADHD). Furthermore, adolescents with a history of neuropsychological disorders tend to have levels of physical aggression that remain stable from age 3 to age 15. In addition, the lawbreaking acts of such adolescents tend to be more aggressive than those of other delinquents without a history of neuropsychological deficits. Finally, in one study, boys with preadolescent problem behaviors and neuropsychological deficits accounted for 12% of the sample but for 59% of the sample's convictions by age 18 (Henry & Moffitt, 1997; Moffitt & Henry, 1989; White, Moffitt, Caspi, Jeglum, Needles, & Stouthamer-Loeber, 1994).

Theoretically, there are a number of ways in which low IQ (especially verbal IQ) might be related to antisocial behavior and aggression. First, deficits in verbal abilities might affect the ability to child to engage in self-control and delay of gratification, thus producing an impulsive child who acts before thinking. A second possibility is that low IQ might hinder children's ability to learn appropriate moral cognitions and behaviors. In addition to these rather direct effects, IQ might also affect aggressive behavior more indirectly. For example, children with lower IQs might elicit negative responses from others, which in turn might produce frustration, alienation, and subsequent aggression. Finally, low IQ could also hinder the ability to learn and hence to achieve in school, which in turn could lead to frustration and aggression, especially during adolescence.

Despite these findings, however, we supply a number of caveats regarding this relationship. First, because most of these data are correlational, we cannot automatically conclude that IQ is the causative variable in the relationship. Second, low IQ by itself does not seem responsible for children's aggression. And third, low IQ might only characterize a certain portion of hyperaggressive children. Thus, although IQ might be an important variable in children's aggressive behavior, its role is far from being understood.

Social Information-Processing

A large body of research suggests that much of children's aggression is related to the manner in which they process social information. For example, as we saw earlier, Dodge (1980, 1986) postulated that children go through a four-stage process of *decoding, interpretation, response search,* and *response decision making.* Problems in one or more of these stages can lead children to act aggressively.

Decoding involves gathering information about an event from the environment. Research suggests a number of reasons why aggressive youths might have problems with this process. First, in order to obtain information from the external world, the child must first attend to the stimulus. However, numerous studies have implicated inattentiveness as a major correlate of aggressive and CD children (e.g., Farrington, 1994). In particular, aggressive children and adolescents have been found to attend to fewer relevant interpersonal cues before attempting to interpret others' behavior (Dodge, Pettit, McClaskey, & Brown, 1986; Lochman & Dodge, 1994). Second, the generally lower intellectual and verbal abilities found among aggressive children might also hamper this process. Relatedly, as compared with their nonaggressive peers, aggressive children might also have impaired memories for social interactions (Redl & Wineman, 1951).

Aggressive children show deficits in the interpretation stage of interpersonal interactions. For example, studies on both aggressive males and females indicate that these children possess a *hostile attribution bias,* which leads them to attribute hostile intent to others' behavior even when the intent of that behavior is benign (e.g., Dodge, 1980; Dodge, Price, Bachorowski, & Newman, 1990). Furthermore, this relationship holds for extreme levels of aggression as well as for aggression in "normal" children. Thus, Dodge et al. (1990) found a positive correlation between hostile attributional bias and levels of conduct disorder, reactive aggression, and violent crimes. Finally, research on the effects of media violence suggest that television might reinforce the beliefs of aggressive children that the world is a scary and dangerous place (see chap. 6). For all these reasons, aggressive children seem primed to read hostile motives into the behavior of others, especially when the situation may be somewhat ambiguous in the first place.

Aggressive children also might experience deficiencies in the response search process. Studies show that these children are relatively unable to generate prosocial verbal assertion solutions in response to social problems; instead, they tend to generate more antisocial action-oriented solutions (Lochman, Lampron, & Rabiner, 1989; Rabiner, Lenhart, & Lochman, 1990). In part, this tendency might stem from presumed verbal and memory deficits. In addition, however, it is also possible that these children might never have learned such prosocial problem solving behaviors. Thus, the most prepotent and accessible responses for these children are likely to be aggressive and antisocial in nature.

By the time the aggressive child arrives at the response decision process, the result is almost assured: Having failed to decode relevant social cues, having concluded that the other person was acting out of hostile intent, and having antisocial behaviors at the top of his response hierarchy, it is hardly surprising that the aggressive child selects an aggressive response.

Impulsivity and Impulse-Control

At a conceptual level, the term *impulsivity* refers to the tendency of children to act automatically without taking time to think or being able to stop the behavior in question. As we have seen, impulsivity is a major definitional criterion for ADHD (American Psychiatric Association, 1994). Furthermore, impulsivity, either alone or in combination with other variables, has been shown to be an important factor in children's hyperaggressive behavior. For example, we saw evidence in chapter 4 that aggressive youths might possess a hypoactive Behavioral Inhibition System (BIS). In addition, we have seen that children with "difficult" temperaments (characterized by a high amount of motor activity and impulsivity) are especially at risk for aggressiveness (Olweus, 1980).

Barkley (1997) proposed that the lack of behavioral inhibition plays a key role in ADHD. According to this view, inhibition involves three interrelated processes: (a) stopping an initially prepotent response to an event; (b) stopping an ongoing response or response pattern; and (c) the ability to ignore sources of distraction while engaged in another task which requires self-control (Barkley, 1997). With respect to children's aggression, children with a weak BIS would have difficulty in suppressing an "automatic" aggressive response, in stopping the aggressive response once it begins to occur, and in processing cognitive information in the face of aggression-eliciting environmental stimuli.

Redl and Wineman's (1951) description of the Pioneers as well as qualitative research with gangs both suggest that hyperaggressive youths lack impulse control (Patrick, 1973). In addition, quantitative studies have also documented a relationship between some aspects of behavioral impulse control and hyper-aggressive children. For example, Farrington and colleagues (e.g., Farrington, 1994) delineated a personality characteristic that they refer to as a deficit in hyperactivity/impulsivity/attention (HIA). In their longitudinal studies, they found that the HIA deficit becomes manifest between the ages of 2 and 5 and that it predicts subsequent adolescent delinquency (see Farrington, 1994). Similarly, other research also indicates that early inattentiveness and impulsivity are related to later aggressiveness, conduct disorder, and delinquency (Hinshaw, 1992; Maguin & Loeber, 1996; Törestad & Magnusson, 1996; Tremblay, Boulerice, Arseneault, & Niscale, 1995). Clearly, a great deal of evidence implicates impulsivity and inattentiveness as major factors in aggression and antisocial behavior.

Immediate Gratification and Lack of Self-Control

As we have seen, both Redl and Wineman (1951) and Samenow (1989) describe hyperaggressive youths as demanding immediate gratification, as being unable to tolerate even brief frustrations, and as being unable to resist even mild temptations. This description of hyperaggressive youth is consistent with the view that antisocial youths lack *self-control,* the ability to avoid antisocial acts whose long-term consequences exceed their momentary pleasure (Hirschi & Gottfredson, 1994).

In a related development, Barkley (1997) has argued that ADHD consists primarily of an impairment of "rule-governed, goal-directed, and internally guided and motivated" behavior; in other words, a deficit in self-regulation (Barkley, 1997, p. ix). Briefly, Barkley argues that ADHD children suffer an impairment in their psychological sense of time and that this deficit consequently interferes with self-control and the child's ability to be motivated by long-term consequences. According to Barkley, time functions as a fourth dimension, which exerts a crucial control over behavior. When the child's sense of time is disrupted, his behavior is no longer controlled by "space within time," but rather by "space within the temporal moment" (Barkley, 1997, p. 204). Consequently, without an adequate psychological sense of time, the child's behavior becomes bound down to the present moment.

Although Barkley developed this model for ADHD children, Redl and Wineman's (1951) description of the Pioneers' failure to demonstrate a sense of time is consistent with Barkley's theorizing. It is thus plausible that hyperaggressive children as well as ADHD children lack a psychological sense of time and that this deficit might in turn help explain their apparent need for immediate gratification and their lack of self-control. Unfortunately, little controlled research seems to have been conducted regarding the concept of time-related lack of self-control in hyperaggressive youths.

One study that is related to this question involved data collected from more than 1,500 junior and senior high school males as part of the Richmond Youth Study (Brownfield & Sorenson, 1993). In this investigation, the researchers delineated a latent trait that they labeled as *self-control*. This trait consisted of three cognitive variables (grade point average, score on the Differential Aptitude Verbal Test, and a question on how much schooling the person expected to get) and three measures of "present time orientation" ("live for today and let tomorrow take care of itself"; "it's useless to plan for the future"; and "there is no sense looking ahead"). Multiple regression analysis showed that the self-control trait was strongly related to a measure of official delinquency but not to self-reported delinquency. In another related study, Agnew (1993) found that adolescent delinquents generally apportion less weight to the costs than to the rewards of unlawful acts because costs tend to be perceived as less immediate. Thus, both these studies support the hypothesis that antisocial youths possess a "time-orientation deficit." Nevertheless, more research is clearly needed before a definitive conclusion on this issue can be drawn.

MOTIVATIONAL PROCESSES

> Whoops of joy and laughter erupt when a randomly chosen victim is whacked with a baseball bat from a passing car. All of it, and more, is captured on one of America's scariest home videos.
>
> "Bashing" is what the four chortling teen-agers inside the car call their sport. One of them described it as "human head baseball."
>
> The 20-minute video shows the four feckless teen-agers roaming the bleak, nighttime streets of the suburban San Fernando Valley, alternately finding people or vehicles to bash with a bat or shoot with the high-pressure paint gun.
>
> They laugh, hoot, swear and promise more violence and vandalism as they race past a Taco Bell . . .
>
> A man waiting for a bus is hit with the paint gun, and so are several pedestrians and a homeless woman on the pavement next to her shopping cart of aluminum cans.
>
> On the videotape, the voices run together, but the youths are uniform in their glee at the damage and pain they are causing.
>
> "People think we're crazy," one of them says. "But I just think this is fun."
> (D. Anderson, 1996, p. A4)

What motivates youngsters such as these to engage in antisocial behaviors such as "bashing"? In this section, we examine some possible answers to this question.

Sensation-Seeking

A number of both qualitative and quantitative studies suggest that hyperaggressive youths are motivated at least in part by the twin goals of *sensation-seeking* and *thrill-seeking*. In chapter 4, we saw that such children tend to exhibit various physiological responses indicating a need for additional sources of stimulation in order to compensate for a low level of physiological arousal. From this perspective, the mundane everyday experiences common to most children and adolescents do not provide hyperaggressive youths with a sufficient level of arousal. In Samenow's (1989) terms, these children are "bored" and seek thrills and excitement, often by engaging in behaviors that are physically risky and/or antisocial.

Farley (1990) has delineated what he calls the *Type T Personality*. According to this view, one important dimension of personality involves high risk and thrill and stimulation seeking at one end of a continuum and low risk and thrill and stimulation avoidance at the other end. Persons at the high end of this continuum (Type T personalities) are classified either as *T-plus* (those who take risks and seek thrills in a socially approved fashion) or *T-minus* (those who do so through negative and destructive behaviors). Because Farley postulates that individuals who exhibit extreme antisocial behaviors are likely to have T-minus personalities, his theory would thus predict that hyperaggressive children should also have T-minus personalities.

Anecdotal reports such as the one at the beginning of this section and qualitative studies such as Redl and Wineman's (1951) reports of the Pioneers' "diffuse aggression" described earlier support the idea that hyperaggressive youngsters actively seek thrill-providing behaviors. In addition, some quantitative studies also provide support for this view. For example, Russo and colleagues found that, relative to other clinic-referred boys, CD boys were more likely to seek stimulation from their environments due to boredom (Russo et al., 1991; Russo et al., 1993). Relatedly, Frick et al. (1994) found that boredom, risky behavior, and sensation seeking all characterized CD youth.

Other research on both juveniles and young adults provides additional supporting data. For example, in their study of Australian male and female students aged 12 to 19, Gordon and Caltabiano (1996) found that sensation seeking was positively related to crime in both their urban and rural samples. In a study of middle school students, Wills and colleagues found that problem youths showed elevated levels of risk taking and sensation seeking (Wills & Filer, 1996). Finally, in a study of young Australian undergraduate psychology students, Heaven (1996) found that excitement-seeking was positively and significantly correlated with self-reported violent delinquency.

In summary, available data suggest that sensation and thrill seeking might be major factors motivating the antisocial behavior of hyperaggressive youths.

Antisocial Attitudes

A number of theorists have argued that antisocial attitudes and motives are distinguishing characteristics of hyperaggressive and delinquent youths. For example, Hirschi (1969) considered children's belief in a conventional value system to be a major component of the social bond that leads to prosocial behavior; hence, antisocial beliefs would be expected to weaken the social bond and thus promote antisocial behavior. In a similar vein, Samenow (1989) argued that the thinking errors of aggressive children produce a set of antisocial beliefs and attitudes that in turn motivate these children's aggressive behavior. Finally, both Olweus (1992) and Shaffer (1994) suggested that the antisocial behavior of aggressive children is motivated by their need to dominate and control others.

Results from a number of studies support Hirschi's (1969) hypothesis that antisocial and hyperaggressive youths hold nonconventional value systems. For example, Hoge et al. (1994) examined the attitudes of a large group of convicted male and female adolescent offenders between the ages of 12 and 17. They found that *antisocial attitudes* (e.g., delinquent, unconventional, actively rejecting help, callousness, defiance) significantly predicted serious crimes such as violent activities, breaking and entering, theft over $1,000, and drug trafficking. In a similar vein, Eisenman (1993) found that adolescent felons saw crime as the right thing to do and that they considered people as objects to be manipulated. Finally, Agnew (1984), using data from the national Youth in Transition Study of adolescent boys, found that adolescents with a low work ethic were more likely to become delinquent. Unfortunately, most research on this topic has been done with adolescents and we know little about how these attitudes develop among young children.

Attitudes toward the law seem especially important. In one study of more than 1,000 students of both sexes evenly distributed across Grades 9 through 12, Benda and Whiteside (1995) found that students' prosocial moral beliefs (supporting the importance of being honest and of following the law) were inversely related to a measure of general delinquency, including delinquency against persons. Moreover, path analysis showed that of all the variables studied, beliefs had the largest direct effect on delinquency. In another study of more than 1,500 junior and senior high school males, Brownfield and Sorenson (1993) found a positive correlation between a measure of official delinquency and the extent to which youths believed it is okay to get around the law. Similarly, in a study of mostly Black and Hispanic adolescents of both sexes, Sokol-Katz et al. (1997) found that belief in the importance of upholding the law was directly and negatively related to serious delinquent behaviors such as being involved in gang fights, using force to take valuables, breaking and entering, and stealing automobiles. The fact that these three studies found a relationship between delinquency and attitudes toward the law is interesting in light of the fact that education regarding the law seems to be an effective deterrent to delinquency (D. C. Gottfredson & G. D. Gottfredson, 1992).

Self-Efficacy, Outcomes-Expectancies, and Goals

In his theory, Bandura (1982) argued that behavior is dependent on two processes that he calls *self-efficacy* and *outcome expectancy*. Briefly, self-efficacy refers to the child's belief that he or she is able to produce a specific behavior. Outcome expectancy, on the other hand, refers to the extent to which the child believes that a specific behavior will produce a specific outcome.

In terms of self-efficacy, aggressive children report that it is easier for them to behave aggressively and more difficult to inhibit their aggression than it is to produce prosocial behaviors (Ollendick, 1996; Perry, Perry, & Rasmussen, 1986). Aggressive youths also seem to have higher outcome expectancies for aggression (Perry et al., 1986). Furthermore, aggressive children also endorse more hostile social goals than do nonaggressive children (e.g., aggressive children are more focused on punishing their adversary and less focused on maintaining positive interpersonal relationships; Asarnow & Callan, 1985; Erdley & Asher, 1996). Interestingly, even when they attribute benign intent to ambiguous provocations of their peers, aggressive children still endorse hostile retributory behaviors (Erdley & Asher, 1996), thus suggesting that their antisocial motivations might be more important than their inaccurate social cognitions.

EMOTIONAL PROCESSES

> Five Points, in a seedy South Valley section of Albuquerque, New Mexico, is a convergence of five streets, littered parking lots, and shopping centers half boarded up . . .
>
> A man in his 60s enters one of the lots on his morning exercise walk, heading south. A Buick Riviera recently stolen by its two teen occupants cruises slowly along Five Points Road, also heading south. The car circles the lone figure.
>
> On its fourth drive-by one of the youths jumps from the car, holding a police baton, demands money and clubs the man several times. The flat crack of a pistol shot pierces the air and Eddie Torres, 16, falls back and runs to the car, which screeches away . . .
>
> Nine days after the shooting, while Torres was recuperating in the hospital, police arrested him on charges of aggravated battery with a deadly weapon, armed robbery, and conspiracy to commit armed robbery. Nancy Neary, the assistant district attorney, saw Torres as a classic sociopath. "Empathy is not a concept this kid has within him," she said. "He was totally without remorse. He would kill Mr. Kern or anyone else the same way I'd swat a fly." (Englade & Hillerman, 1995, pp. 22–23, 29)

As we saw in chapter 1, emotions such as empathy and remorse seem to be important aspects of youths' moral behaviors. In this section, we examine the role that such emotions might play in youngsters' hyperaggressive behavior.

Ego Absorption

Both Redl and Wineman (1951) and Samenow (1989) suggested that hyperaggressive youths tend to be focused on themselves and unable to take into consideration the perspectives of others. Although little controlled research seems to have been conducted on this issue, a few pieces of evidence support the view of these two anecdotal studies. As we shall see, Baumeister and colleagues (Baumeister, Bushman, & Campbell, 2000; Baumeister, Smart, & Boden, 1996) argued that aggressive youths are consumed by an "excessive egotism" or inflated sense of self. In support of this position, Frick et al. (1994) found that children showing the "impulsive/conduct-problem" aspect of CD were described as thinking they were more important than others and as bragging about their accomplishments. Additionally, Short and Simeonson (1986) found that aggressive male delinquent adolescents showed more egocentric perspective taking than did nonaggressive delinquents from the same institution. In sum, there is at least some evidence that aggressive youths seem to be self-absorbed and hence less likely to think about how their behavior might affect others.

Empathy

Studies with antisocial children have produced mixed results regarding the relationship between *empathy* and aggressive behavior (Alexsic, 1976; Cohen & Strayer, 1996; Frick et al., 1994; Lee & Prentice, 1988; MacQuiddy, Maise, & Hamilton, 1987). Cohen and Strayer (1996) suggested that these discrepancies might be due at least in part to heterogeneity in measures and target populations. Some empathy scales seem to measure primarily cognitive perspective taking; others seem to measure primarily emotional responding; and still others appear to measure both constructs. Measures that include both components seem to differentiate aggressive and nonaggressive children more than those that include only one. Furthermore, it is possible that deficits in empathy might characterize some types of antisocial youths but not others.

In their own study, Cohen and Strayer (1996) compared both cognitive and emotional indices of empathy in a sample of consisting of roughly equal numbers of 15-year-old males and females diagnosed with CD along with a comparison sample of "normal" non-CD peers. A number of interesting results emerged from this study:

- The CD group exhibited significantly less empathy than the control group on both the cognitive and the affective measures and on both measures combined.
- CD females showed less empathy than normal males.
- Although abstract antisocial attitudes were modestly and negatively correlated with empathy, the results suggested that empathy might be more negatively associated with specific antisocial and aggressive behavioral tendencies than with cognitive attitudes.
- Although the CD group was not generally callous or indifferent, they did show higher levels of personal distress than did the control group. The

authors speculate that high levels of personal distress might lead conduct disordered youth to focus on themselves and might thus interfere with their ability to empathize with others.

In view of these results, Cohen and Strayer (1996) concluded that "lower empathy is associated particularly with greater tendencies toward social maladjustment and aggression in youth" (p. 995).

Guilt

In chapter 1, we discussed the distinction between *predispositional guilt* and *chronic guilt*. In general, research indicates that predispositional guilt is inversely related to antisocial behavior and aggression, whereas chronic guilt is positively related to both internalizing and externalizing disorders (Bybee & Quiles, 1998; Tangney, 1998).

These findings suggest that hyperaggressive children might suffer from a deficit of predispositional guilt and an excess of chronic guilt. Redl and Wineman's (1951) anecdotal report seems consistent with this hypothesis. Specifically, the Pioneers often lacked both guilt and anticipatory guilt, and thus appeared to be deficient in predispositional guilt. At the same time, the Pioneers tended to experience what Redl and Wineman (1951) described as inappropriate forms of guilt that seemed to be chronic in nature. Consistent with Bybee's prediction, when the boys did experience this guilt, its presence increased their anger, aggression, and destructiveness.

Results of controlled research also support the view that hyperaggressive children lack appropriate guilt. For example, in the Columbia County study described earlier (Eron, 1987), children who showed evidence of "guilt" by the age of 8 were less aggressive at age 19 than were children who did not exhibit such guilt. Moreover, because it was measured by confession to some specific act and by indications of internalized standards of conduct, the guilt in this study seems more indicative of predispositional guilt than of chronic guilt. More recently, Bybee and Quiles (1998) summarized some of the additional evidence relating predispositional guilt to externalizing behaviors: Lower predispositional guilt correlates with heightened scores of hostility and aggression in both adults and children; delinquents score lower on predispositional guilt than do matched controls; and for delinquents, assaultive behavior is correlated with a lower proclivity for guilt.

As we saw in chapter 3, a lack of guilt over wrongdoing has been associated with the concept of *psychopathy* (Cleckley, 1976; Hare, 1993). However, since the *DSM* does not include lack of guilt as a criterion for CD (Hare, Hart, & Harpur, 1991), little is known regarding the experience of guilt among CD children. To remedy this situation, Frick and colleagues (Christian, Frick, Hill, Tyler, & Frazer, 1997; Frick et al., 1994) gave a group of clinic-referred youngsters a children's version of the Psychopathy Screening Device. Two separable but correlated factors emerged from the factor analysis: An *impulsivity/conduct-problems* (ICP) factor and a *callous/unemotional* (CU) one. The ICP factor reflected poor impulse control, antisocial behavior, and an inflated sense of self-worth. The CU factor was composed of items indicating a lack of guilt, a lack of concern about others, shallow or absent emotions, superficial charm, and a lack of concern about schoolwork. This dimension was positively correlated with sensation seeking and negatively correlated with anxiety.

In a subsequent study, Christian et al. (1997) examined a small subgroup of CD children who scored high on both the ICP and CU factors. Compared with other CD children, these *psychopathic* CD children exhibited higher IQs, more symptoms of CD and ODD, higher scores on scales measuring delinquency and aggressiveness, more contact with the police, and more parental antisocial personality disorder (Christian et al. 1997). Based on this study, it appears that there exists a subgroup of psychopathic CD children who exhibit a marked lack of guilt, superficial charm, and shallow emotions. This group also appears to show more aggressive behavior than do other CD children, and might also have different neuropsychological correlates and a different etiology. Unfortunately, little more is known about this subtype and more research is clearly warranted.

In conclusion, available research provides tentative support for the hypothesis that at least some portion of hyperaggressive children experience a lack of predispositional guilt coupled with an excess of chronic guilt. However, as we have seen, the research base is small. Moreover, researchers on guilt have used predominantly "normal" samples, whereas researchers on CD and delinquency have generally not distinguished between predispositional and chronic guilt. Much more research clearly needs to be conducted on this issue.

Stress and Coping

Aggression, especially reactive aggression that occurs in response to some specific environmental stimulus, might be conceptualized as a method of coping with stress. Within this context, *stress* is viewed as a cognitive emotional state related to some antecedent stimulus condition (the *stressor*) as well as to some subsequent physiological, emotional, and/or behavioral response. In the case of aggressive youth, stress can produce physiological arousal, emotional anger, and behavioral aggression. Theoretically, the effects of stress are mediated by the child's coping ability. Thus, children who cope well in a stressful situation are less likely to react aggressively than are children who cope poorly.

Wills and Filer (1996) developed a stress–coping model for youthful problem behaviors. Although this model focuses more specifically on substance abuse, it also seems applicable to youthful aggression as well. The model delineates two types of coping, called *active coping* (which includes behavioral coping, cognitive coping, and exercise coping) and *avoidance coping* (which includes general avoidance coping, anger coping, and hopelessness coping).

With respect to substance abuse, Wills and Filer (1996) found that active coping helps reduce the amount of avoidance coping and thus helps the adolescent avoid a trajectory that could lead to trouble. They also found that avoidance coping (especially anger coping) is strongly related to substance abuse. More specifically, in a study of middle school students, these researchers found that a cluster representing problem youth was characterized by extreme elevations of anger, poor self-control, risk taking, impulsiveness, sensation seeking, valuing independence, the presence of negative life events, and tolerance for deviance (Wills & Filer, 1996).

Although these researchers concentrated primarily on problem behaviors involving substance abuse, many of their results parallel what we have seen regarding antisocial and aggressive youth. Both groups seem to be characterized by impulsivity, sensation seeking, risk taking, antisocial attitudes, tolerance for deviance, and poor self-control. In both groups, these individual characteristics seem to lead the youth to associate with like-minded peers, and this association in turn exacerbates the already existing tendency toward antisocial behavior. Of course, given the overlap between CD and substance abuse, this parallel is not surprising.

Wills and Filer's (1996) work on coping appears consistent with the results of the Cohen and Strayer (1996) study described, as well as our discussion on abused children in chapter 5. In the Wills and Filer study, when aggressive adolescents were presented with scenarios designed to elicit empathy, they tended to respond with signs of egocentric distress. As you recall, similar results have also been found for abused youngsters (Klimes-Dougan & Kistner, 1990; Main & George, 1985). We might hypothesize that in their attempt to cope with distress, these youths respond with avoidance coping rather than with active coping. Unfortunately, little seems to be known about how aggressive youngsters actually do in fact cope with stressors. Furthermore, virtually nothing is known about whether subgroups of aggressive children (e.g., reactive vs. instrumental, undersocialized vs. oversocialized) might show different patterns of coping. Many additional questions could also be asked, and it is clear that much research remains to be done in this area.

Helplessness

The fact that some of Wills and Filer's (1996) youths demonstrated helpless coping raises the question of the relationship between *helplessness* and youthful aggression. Some anecdotal evidence indicates that feelings of injustice, helplessness, and hopelessness might characterize some aggressive youths, especially those living in poverty stricken urban areas (Garbarino, 1999). If, in fact, these young people believe that their lives can get no worse, that they have been unjustly treated, and that they have no means of improving their lives through prosocial behaviors, they might perceive aggressive behavior directed either toward themselves or others as not only viable but even attractive.

Psychologically, children who believe that they cannot control their own fate are said to have an *external locus of control*. From an attributional viewpoint, they attribute their behavior and its subsequent outcome to external (situational) rather than to internal (dispositional) factors. If feelings of helplessness are relevant to youthful aggression, we would expect aggressive children to experience a more external locus of control than nonaggressive children. Ollendick's (1996) research is relevant to this issue. In this study, aggressive 9- to 11-year-olds exhibited an external locus of control. In other words, these children believed they had little control over the outcomes of their interactions. Although these results are suggestive, much more work needs to be done to determine how locus of control might affect children's aggressive responding.

Anger

Anger is perhaps the emotion most strongly associated with children's aggressive behavior. Indeed, aggressive children are often described as angry, and a number of psychological interventions have been developed that are designed to help aggressive children cope with their anger. From a theoretical viewpoint, Berkowitz (1965) has postulated that anger results from frustration and that it combines with the child's existing aggressive habits to produce a motivational *readiness to aggress*.

Despite the apparent importance of anger in children's hyperaggressive behavior, the actual empirical research on this topic is rather sparse. Tangney and colleagues recently developed an *Anger Response Inventory* (ARI) with versions for children, adolescents, and adults (Tangney et al., 1996). Using a sample of "normal" youths aged 8 to 20, Tangney, Hill-Barlow, et al. (1996) found a positive correlation between children's aggression and delinquency (as measured by the school version of the Child Behavior Checklist) and their scores on the ARI. More specifically, the ARI responses of the aggressive and delinquent youngsters indicated that these children react to their anger through direct physical and verbal aggression and through displacing their aggression onto other people and objects. Children's scores on the ARI also correlated positively with the "social problems" factor on the Child Behavior Checklist, but did not correlate with the *withdrawal, anxious/depressed,* or *somatic complaints* factors, thus suggesting that children are not externalizing their anger as a defense against anxiety.

In another study, Tangney, Borenstein, and Barlow (1995, as cited by Tangney, Hill-Barlow, et al., 1996) found that scores on the *malicious intentions* subscale of the ARI were positively correlated with the tendency to deal with anger through direct, indirect, or displaced aggression. In addition, Tangney and colleagues (Tangney, Wagner, Hill-Barlow, Marschall, & Gramzow, 1996) showed that shame proneness is also associated with high anger on the ARI. Finally, as we have seen, Wills and Filer (1996) found that defensive coping (including the use of anger) was related to higher levels of substance abuse.

The available evidence thus tentatively suggests that aggressive children experience anger and deal with it through direct or indirect expression, rather than through more constructive means such as talking about the problem with the object of their anger. To my knowledge, however, no comparable research has yet been done on children with disruptive behavior disorders.

Self-Esteem

Low Self-Esteem and Aggression.   Low self-esteem is often seen as a correlate if not a cause of youthful aggression and antisocial behavior. Thus, Heide (1997) stated that "Adolescent homicide offenders typically lack a healthy self-concept" (p. 212). Wiehe (1991) says that one possible reason why children abuse their siblings is "to bolster or increase their low self-esteem" (p. 17), and a recent book on treating CD adolescents includes building self-esteem as a treatment goal (Bernstein, 1996).

At a theoretical level, Kaplan (1975) argued that children with low self-esteem are unable to acquire recognition from others in socially conventional ways such as through academics, sports, or extracurricular activities. In addition, these youths might also possess physical and/or behavioral characteristics that evoke negative responses from others. Anxious, insecure, and frustrated with their ability to gain needed recognition, these children thus turn to antisocial and aggressive behaviors in order to get recognized and to feel better about themselves (Kaplan, 1975).

Some studies support the view that low self-esteem is related to antisocial and aggressive behavior among high school students (Bynner, O'Malley, & Bachman, 1981; Kaplan, 1980). In addition, the fact that the comorbidity rate for depression and CD varies between 16% and 31% indicates that many CD children might also suffer from feelings of worthlessness and low self-esteem (Loeber & Keenan, 1994). Finally, some studies of American preadolescent boys and Australian adolescents have reported a negative relationship between self-esteem and aggressive and delinquent behaviors (Gordon & Caltabiano, 1996; Lochman & Dodge, 1994; St. C. Levy, 1997).

It is unlikely, however, that low self-esteem causes hyperaggression. For one thing, comorbid CD does not seem to abate following remission of depression (Loeber & Keenan, 1994), nor does depression appear to enhance the severity of CD or delinquency (Fischer, Rolf, Hasazi, & Cummings, 1984), thus suggesting that depression does not cause aggression. In addition, Bank (1990, as cited by Patterson et al., 1992) found that when prior antisocial behavior was partialed out, self-esteem measured at age 10 did not make a contribution to antisocial behavior at age 12. Similarly, although Bynner et al. (1981) found that delinquent activity increased self-esteem for some males, they also found that self-esteem played little part in influencing subsequent delinquent behavior. Such results have led Patterson et al. (1992) to conclude that "Low self-esteem means there is a problem, but the problem is not caused by the impaired sense of self-worth" (p. 125).

Other studies also call into question the hypothesized relationship between low self-esteem and aggression. For example, Olweus (1992) found that bullies do not suffer from low self-esteem, and Olweus (1992), Robins (1966), and Tangney, Hill-Barlow, et al. (1996) all found that aggressive youths do not behave antisocially as a defense against anxiety or insecurity. Similarly, Truscott (1992), comparing adolescent males who had been admitted for court assessment with a contrast group of high school students, found that violent adolescents showed neither lower self-esteem nor more internalizing defenses than did control subjects.

Some research suggests that aggression might cause poor self-esteem. For example, aggressiveness does seem to predispose youngsters to depression and suicide, thus suggesting that aggression might cause depression (Loeber & Keenan, 1994). In addition, early externalizing behaviors seem to predict later externalizing and internalizing behaviors; however, early internalizing behaviors do not predict later externalizing behaviors (Fischer et al., 1984). It thus seems more likely that aggression produces internalizing problems than vice versa.

High Self-Esteem and Aggression. A second possibility is that some type of high self-esteem causes aggression. Indeed, Roy Baumeister and colleagues (Baumeister et al., 1996, 2000) argued that what causes violence is not too little self-esteem, but too much. According to this view, aggressors have an overly inflated view of themselves that, when threatened, provokes them to aggression (see Fig. 8.1). Thus, when their *excessive egotism* is threatened by some environmental event, they react with aggression and violence.

Baumeister et al. (1996) discussed a variety of data on both adults and juveniles to support their view. In terms of adults, for example, one study on college students led Raskin, Novacek, and Hogan (1991) to conclude that "in the presence of grandiosity, dominance, and narcissism, people who express higher hostility also report higher self-esteem" (p. 917). With respect to the juvenile literature, Baumeister at al. (1996) cited findings from the S. Glueck and E. T. Glueck (1950) studies indicating that delinquents are self-assertive and socially assertive. Reviewing data on gangs, these researchers also concluded that "Gang members apparently think, talk, and act like people with high self-esteem, and there is little to support the view that they are humble or self-deprecating or even that they are privately full of insecurities or self-doubts" (Baumeister et al., 1996, p. 22).

A recent study on aggressive and nonaggressive second and third graders supports Baumeister et al.'s (1996) position (Hughes, Cavell, & Grossman, 1997). The aggressive children in this study gave themselves inflated self-ratings of personal competence, whereas their nonaggressive peers actually tended to underestimate their true functioning. It is tempting to speculate that this ten-

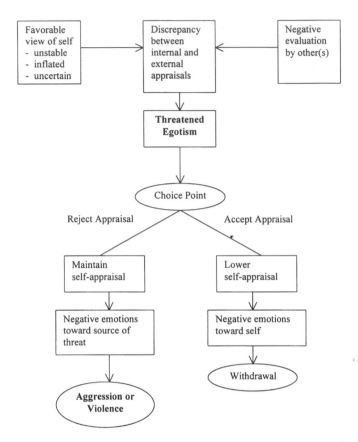

FIG. 8.1.   Hypothesized representation between threatened egotism and violent behavior. From "Relation of Threatened Egotism to Violence and Aggression: The Dark Side of High Self-Esteem," by R. F. Baumeister, L. Smart, and J. M. Boden, 1996, *Psychological Review, 103*, p. 12. Copyright © 1996 by the American Psychological Association. Reprinted with permission.

dency of aggressive children to overinflate their competence might be a developmental precursor of the grandiosity that Raskin, Novacek, and Hogan (1991) noted among their hostile college students.

In conclusion, although it is unlikely that low self-esteem causes aggression, it is possible that chronic antisocial and aggressive behavior might cause low self-esteem and depression. In addition, it is also likely that much aggression is caused by an inflated sense of self-esteem combined with threatened egotism. Additional research is needed to clarify this situation. Meantime, we need to put aside the myth that improving self-esteem is the solution to the problem of youth violence.

SUMMARY AND CONCLUSIONS

As summarized in Box 8.1, the results of both qualitative and quantitative research indicate that a number of cognitive, motivational, and emotional processes might be implicated in the aggressive behavior of antisocial youths. Some of the processes found in these youngsters (such as poor verbal skills, impulsiv-

---

BOX 8.1

COGNITIVE, MOTIVATIONAL, AND EMOTIONAL PROCESSES IMPLICATED IN THE BEHAVIOR OF HYPERAGGRESSIVE YOUTHS

Cognitive Processes

Strong and prepotent set of antisocial and aggressive behavioral tendencies.

Low intelligence (in particular, poor verbal skills, including a poor memory and a poor concept of time).

Defective social information processing (including a hostile attribution bias and problems in decoding, interpretation, response search, and response decision making).

Impulsivity and poor impulse control.

Poor tolerance for frustration, a need for immediate gratification, and poor self-control.

Motivational Processes

Low physiological arousal and a sensation-seeking personality (Type T-minus personality).

Weak social bond and strong antisocial attitudes.

Relatively high self-efficacy for antisocial behaviors, positive outcome-expectancies for antisocial behaviors, and antisocial goals.

Emotional Processes

Strong ego absorption and excessive egotism.

Lack of empathy.

Low predispositional guilt but relatively high chronic guilt.

High levels of anger.

Poor active coping but excessive avoidance coping (including anger coping) in response to stress.

A sense of helplessness and an external locus of control.

In most cases, low anxiety and apparently high but easily threatened self-esteem; in perhaps some cases, high anxiety and low self-esteem.

ity, hypoarousal, and a sensation-seeking personality) might be biologically innate and might contribute to the initial development of the child's set of prepotent aggressive responses. Other process problems, however (such as antisocial
behavioral tendencies, antisocial attitudes, and poor coping skills) might be
learned as a result of children's interaction with their environment. The net
result is that, by the time they reach the middle to late elementary grades, many
hyperaggressive youths possess a set of psychological processes that efficiently
help them maintain their antisocial lifestyle.

Different sets of psychological processes might be associated with different
types of aggressive behavior. For example, in instrumental aggression, the child
uses antisocial behavior to obtain something else, such as money or a possession. In this situation, we might hypothesize that the child's current response
hierarchy and social information processing interact with deviant motivations, a
lack of guilt, poor empathy, and a high self-esteem (see Fig. 8.2). Because aggressive responses are high in the hierarchy, because the child has a high sense of
self-efficacy and outcome expectations for aggressive behavior, and because of
the child's sensation-seeking and antisocial motivation, aggressive behaviors are
selected. This situation is reminiscent of Olweus' (1992) view of bullying as due
to the combination of the child's deviant motivations and habits.

The situation with respect to reactive aggression is schematized in Fig. 8.3.
In this situation, some environmental event provokes an angry and aggressive

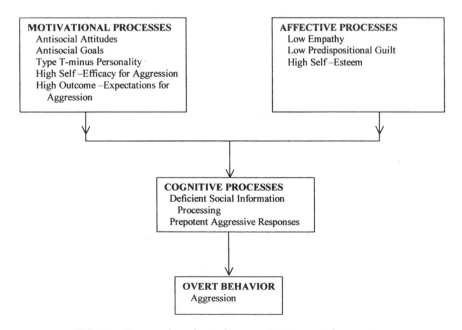

FIG. 8.2.   Processes hypothesized to occur in instrumental aggression.

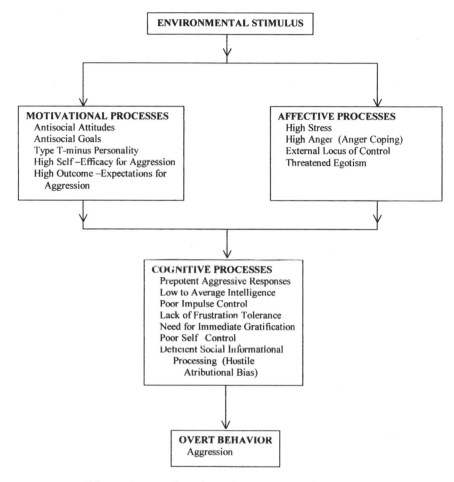

FIG. 8.3.   Processes hypothesized to occur in reactive aggression.

response from the child. In this case, an external stimulus (such as being "dissed" or taunted by another youth) creates a high amount of affective anger, which interacts with impulsivity, poor behavioral control, poor coping skills, and poor social information processing (including a hostile attribution bias), thus producing the aggressive response. This situation is reminiscent of Berkowitz's (1965) view that aggression is due to the interaction of anger and the stimulus situation.

We have seen that hyperaggressive children are a heterogeneous lot, and it is possible that unique sets of psychological processes might be associated with specific subtypes of aggressive children. For example, Box 8.2 describes the processes that hypothetically characterize the callous/unemotional and impulsive/conduct-problem subtypes delineated by Frick and colleagues (Frick et al., 1994).

In addition, the characteristics of these two subtypes might combine into a third subtype which is similar to Christian et al.'s (1997) concept of the *psychopathic* child. Unfortunately, little empirical research has been conducted relating psychological processes to subtypes of aggressive youth, and much more work in this area clearly needs to be done.

The delineation of the processes associated with hyperaggressive youngsters has clinical as well as theoretical implications. For example, the problem of one aggressive youth might lie in a deviant motivational system, whereas that of another aggressive youngster might lie primarily in the affective system. A knowledge of what specific processes underlie the youngster's aggressive behavior would allow the clinician to target relevant processes and avoid targeting irrelevant ones.

Although theoreticians and researchers have delineated a number of psychological processes that seem to be relevant for the understanding of hyperag-

---

BOX 8.2

PROCESSES HYPOTHESIZED TO BE ASSOCIATED WITH THE CALLOUS/UNEMOTIONAL AND IMPULSIVE/CONDUCT-PROBLEM TYPES OF HYPERAGGRESSIVE YOUTHS

Callous/Unemotional

Cognitive Processes

Strong and prepotent set of antisocial and aggressive behavioral tendencies. Normal to above normal intelligence.

Motivational Processes

Low physiological arousal and sensation-seeking personality (Type T-minus personality).

Weak social bonds and strong antisocial attitudes.

Relatively high self-efficacy for antisocial behaviors, positive outcome expectancies for antisocial behaviors, and antisocial goals.

Emotional Processes

Strong ego absorption and excessive egotism.

Lack of empathy.

Low predispositional guilt but relatively high chronic guilt.

Internal locus of control.

Low anxiety and high self-esteem.

(Box continues)

BOX 8.2 (Continued)

Impulsive/Conduct-Problem

Cognitive Processes

Strong and prepotent set of antisocial and aggressive behavioral tendencies.

Low intelligence (in particular, poor verbal skills, including a poor memory and poor concept of time).

Defective social information processing (including a hostile attribution bias and problems in decoding, interpretation, response search, and response decision making).

Impulsivity and poor impulse control.

Poor tolerance for frustration, need for immediate gratification, and poor self-control.

Motivational Processes

Weak social bond and strong antisocial attitudes.

Relatively high self-efficacy for antisocial behaviors, positive outcome expectancies for antisocial behaviors, and antisocial goals.

Emotional Processes

High chronic guilt.

High levels of anger.

Poor active coping but excessive avoidance coping (including anger coping) in response to stress.

A sense of helplessness and an external locus of control.

Low anxiety and apparently high but easily threatened self-esteem.

---

gressive youths, more studies are needed. At the same time, however, existent theoretical and empirical work suggests a number of fruitful avenues that future researchers can take in order to give us a better understanding of the psychological processes that characterize hyperaggressive youngsters.

CHAPTER 9

Aggressive Youths
and Their Peers

Much of the behavior of aggressive children involves social interaction with their peers. In this chapter we examine this interaction, both in terms of how aggressive children affect their peers and how their peers affect them.

PLAY, PEER STATUS, AND FRIENDSHIPS

Play, interaction with other children, and the development of friendships are important parts of childhood. As a result of such social interaction, children not only learn a number of important social skills, but also important lessons that will stay with them for life.

Play and Aggression

Infants begin to interact with peers as early as 6 months of age when they start to smile and vocalize toward other children (Durkin, 1995). As children develop their motor and cognitive competence, they become more interested in others and begin to socialize with their peers through play. During most of the pre-school and elementary school years, children's play is often segregated according to gender, with boys playing with boys and girls playing with girls (Beal, 1994).

One form of behavior that often gets confused with aggression in children (especially in boys) is known as *rough and tumble (R&T) play* (Durkin, 1995). This form of activity, which initially emerges among preschool children but still occurs in adolescence, alarms many adults. As Durkin puts it, "The sight of preschoolers hitting, chasing, and wrestling with each other often distresses parents and many well-intentioned educators" (Durkin, 1995, p. 394). Nevertheless, recent research makes it clear that such R&T behavior is not really aggression. In the first place, R&T behavior is a form of play involving pleasure. As Durkin says, "The participants keep coming back for more, and wear broad smiles over their faces" (Durkin, 1995, p. 394). In addition, R&T play involves cooperation and turn taking, something generally not seen in aggression. Third, R&T play rarely leads to actual aggression or physical injury. And finally, truly aggressive children are typically excluded from R&T play by the other children (J. Goldstein, 1992). Overall, the intent behind R&T is to have fun, not to injure others; and in fact, if someone is hurt during R&T play, play is stopped and apologies made. Thus, R&T is not a form of aggression.

Another form of children's activity that often worries adults is playing with toy guns. Again, many parents and psychologists believe that playing games such as "cowboys," "cops and robbers," and "soldiers" is likely to lead children (especially boys) into violence and aggression. In actuality, very little research has been done on this question. In one of the few available studies, however, Hellendoorn and Harinck (1997) studied the play behavior of 54 Dutch children between the ages of 4 and 7. The researchers furnished the children with two sets of toys (one set of war toys, a second set of neutral toys), and then related the children's play to other variables. The results showed that real object- or person-related aggression was rare and was unrelated to play with the war toys. The researchers did find, however, a great deal of R&T play, which they also regarded as distinct from true aggression. The results of this study, therefore, fail to support the view that playing with aggressive toys produces aggression in children.

Peer Status

Although some childhood play is solitary, children spend increasing amounts of time interacting with their peers. Many psychologists believe that such peer interaction is crucial to the child's psychological development. As one researcher puts it, "Peers do seem to be significant agents of socialization, and the task of becoming *appropriately* sociable with peers is a most important developmental hurdle" (Shaffer, 1994, p. 539, emphasis in original).

Aggression and Rejection.   Research shows that highly aggressive children tend to be rejected by their peers. As early as age 3½, children show greater liking of peers who are friendly, nurturant, and altruistic, and less liking of others who are aggressive, preoccupied with their own distress, or both (Denham, McKinley, Couchoud, & Holt, 1990). Indeed, the most consistent predictor of peer rejection is unprovoked aggression that is intended to dominate and control other children and their possessions (Coie, Dodge, Terry, & Wright, 1991; Dodge et al., 1990).

Rejected aggressive children are the group most at risk for subsequent antisocial behaviors (Asher & Coie, 1990; Kupersmidt & Coie, 1990; Morison & Masten, 1991). For example, one review found that children rejected by peers due to aggression tended to have subsequent school problems and to be involved in crime and delinquency (Parker & Asher, 1987). Similarly, Lochman and Wayland (1994) found that at age 15, boys who were perceived by their classmates as highly aggressive in the fourth grade were more likely than their nonaggressive peers to use marijuana, drugs, and alcohol, and to be involved in interpersonal violence.

Cause or Effect?   Do aggressive children become aggressive because they are rejected, or do they get rejected because of their aggression? Most of the research supports the latter view. For example, when aggressive boys are placed into a new peer group in which the other children are unfamiliar with them, their initial rate of angry reactive and instrumental aggression is twice that of average boys (Dodge et al., 1990). Furthermore, on entering such new groups, the children who are aggressive, pushy, critical of others, and who threaten others end up being rejected by the group (Coie & Kupersmidt, 1983; Dodge et al., 1990; Olson, 1992). In Dodge et al.'s (1990) words, "Boys must carry with them some characteristic (behavioral or otherwise) that leads peers to respond to them consistently across settings" (p. 1305).

Olson's year-long research project on preschool children illustrates this phenomenon (Olson, 1992). At the beginning of the academic year, children who were subsequently rejected by others exhibited a variety of aversive social behaviors, including threats, verbal abuse, grabbing objects from other children, and physical fighting. Initially, these children were not rejected by their classmates. However, as the year progressed, the other classmates began to reject their more aggressive peers. In addition, the other children not only began to react to the rejected children with more aggression of their own, but they even began to initiate aggressive sequences toward these children. Their behavior, in turn, provoked even more retaliatory aggression from the aggressive rejected children. Consistent with the concept of an evocative genotype-environment correlation, both the aggressive rejected children and their peers contributed to the maintenance of the aggressive children's aggression (Olson, 1992).

Effects of a Reputation.   Unfortunately, once aggressive children have been rejected by their peer group, they might have a difficult time being accepted, even if their behavior improves. Hymel (1986) found that when children initially rated by their peers as "popular" engaged in a negative behavior, other children attributed that behavior to some external environmental cause (e.g., "He didn't invite me because he ran out of invitations"). However, when initially rejected children exhibited the same behavior, peers tended to attribute that behavior to the child's personal motives or dispositions (e.g., "He didn't invite me because he's mean"). Furthermore, even when "bad" children performed good deeds, other children attributed these behaviors to the situation, rather than to the child (e.g., "He invited me because his mother made him do it").

It is thus clear that once a child's reputation has been established, other children react not only to the child's behavior, but also to the reputation as well, a fact that is especially unfortunate in view of aggressive children's tendency toward a *hostile attributional bias*. As described in chapter 2, Dodge and Frame (1982) found that such children tend to attribute hostile intentions to other children, especially in ambiguous situations. In addition, however, these researchers also found that nonaggressive children who are attacked under ambiguous circumstances are more likely to retaliate if the instigator has a reputation as an aggressive child (Dodge & Frame, 1982; Sancilio, Plumert, & Hartup, 1989). Thus, the behavior of aggressive children seems to cause them to be rejected by their peers; and, once reputations have been established, their peers then tend to attribute the behavior of aggressive children to these children's internal dispositions rather than to environmental conditions, and to act accordingly.

Unfortunately, attempts at improving the peer status of rejected aggressive children have not fared well (Shaffer, 1994). In one study, for example, Bierman, Miller, and Stabb (1987) found that social skills training improved the status of such children within the training group, but not within their classroom as a whole. In view of our discussion regarding the attributional tendencies of nonaggressive children, this result is not surprising. Apparently, what is needed is a more preventive approach by which the behaviors and social skills of at-risk children can be targeted for improvement *before* such children develop a "bad" reputation among their peers.

Affiliation Patterns

Some psychologists have suggested that hyperaggressive children are lonely and friendless and develop their aggression as a defense against their sense of alienation from others. Although this might be the case for some young people who develop adolescent-onset CD, it is probably not true for children whose hyperaggression begins at an early age. Indeed, as early as the third or fourth grade, aggressive children develop their own "social clusters" and are as likely to have reciprocated "best friendships" as are nonaggressive children (R. B. Cairns, B. D. Cairns, Neckerman, Gest, & Gariépy, 1988; Farmer & Hollowell, 1994). Furthermore, these aggressive social groups are likely to be as central in the school social networks as are nonaggressive groups, and within their group, highly aggressive children are as likely to have a high status as are nonaggressive children in their groups (Farmer & Rodkin, 1996). The difference is that the children with whom aggressive children form friendships and peer groups are aggressive themselves (R. B. Cairns & B. D. Cairns, 1994; Dishion, 1990; Wills & Filer, 1996). As one group of researchers put it:

> The available data now support the conclusion that aggressive and deviant youths have close friends and are members of social groups in both childhood and adolescence. The evidence indicates that these relationships are as numerous and intimate as those of nondeviant youths. But there is a difference in the kinds of persons with whom they affiliate: *Deviant children tend to affiliate with others like themselves,*

and the same holds for nondeviant children. (R. B. Cairns, Cadwallader, Estell, & Neckerman, 1997, p. 197, emphasis added)

Unfortunately, although we know that aggressive youngsters do have friends, we know little about how such children interact with their close friends. In one study, Dishion, Andrews, and Crosby (1995) studied 206 13- and 14-year-old antisocial boys, who were then followed up 1 year later to determine the extent to which the friendships had survived. Results showed that these boys tended to live in the same neighborhood as their friends and to have met their friends in unstructured and unsupervised activities. Friendships were relatively short, seemingly due to the amount of negative and abrasive behavior within the friendship pair. Interestingly, although such negative behavior seemed to undermine the friendship, the boys' positive interpersonal interactions did not solidify it. It was not the lack of positive interactions that soured the relationship, but rather the amount of bossy and coercive interactions. Thus, according to the authors, "antisocial friendships provided another context within which to practice coercion" (Dishion et al., 1995, p. 148). In sum, it does not appear that these boys lacked positive interactive skills, but rather that they engaged in too many negative interactions.

Much of the child's antisocial behavior can be understood in terms of the concept of *limited shopping* (Patterson et al., 1992). Because the young antisocial child is rejected by nondeviant peers, he misses the opportunity to practice the physical and psychological skills that promote prosocial behavior and that can only be learned within the context of the peer group (Harris, 1998; Patterson et al., 1992). Consequently, he begins to fall behind in skills that are status-related for boys of his age, such as playing sports and getting along in groups (Patterson et al., 1992). Each such "missed opportunity" of this type makes it less likely that the antisocial boy will associate with nondeviant peers and more likely that he will associate with antisocial peers. Thus, as a result of such "limited shopping," the antisocial boy spends more and more time in the company of other deviant peers, with increasingly larger portions of his time becoming "opportunities for further deviancy training" (Patterson et al., 1992, p. 118).

PEER GROUPS AND THE TRANSITION TO GANGS

Five boys who allegedly ransacked an old Spotsylvania County store last week left behind an incriminating piece of evidence—a videotape of them in action.

Lt. Mike Timm of the Spotsylvania Sheriff's Office said police found the tape in Orr's Food Mart . . .

The boys, ages 11, 11, 12, 12 and 13, have all been charged with felony vandalism, petty larceny and unauthorized entry . . .

Timm said hundreds of items were damaged, including antiques, porcelain dolls and food products. The aisles were covered with debris, he said. (Epps, 1997, p. C1)

As children move through the elementary school years, peers become more important and peer interaction takes up more of youngsters' time. By the middle elementary school years, most children are immersed in one or more *peer groups* (Shaffer, 1994). Examples of such groups are the "neighborhood gang," the Boy Scouts, the "jocks," or the "antisocial youth gang" (Durkin, 1995; Shaffer, 1994).

Researchers distinguish between two forms of adolescent peer groups, the *clique* and the *crowd*. A clique is a small, intimate group of from two to twelve members whose major function is social interaction. A crowd, on the other hand, is a larger group defined by its reputation and stereotype. Typical crowds in U.S. schools include the "cheerleaders," "jocks," "nerds," and "druggies." Cliques are more important for intimate friendship interactions, whereas crowds provide the adolescent with a sense of identity in the eyes of others (Steinberg, 1996).

As youngsters enter adolescence, they begin to spend more time interacting with their friends and cliques (Papalia et al., 1999). It is not surprising, then, that much adolescent antisocial behavior and aggression (such as the episode described at the beginning of this section) occurs within the context of the group (Zimring, 1998). Indeed, although only about 20% of serious adult crime involves more than one perpetrator, fully 50% of serious juvenile crime is committed within a group context (Snyder & Sickmund, 1999).

Deviant Social Networks

As we have seen, deviant peer social networks and subgroups do not begin suddenly in adolescence but "are alive and well by 10 years of age and before" (R. B. Cairns et al. 1997, p. 197). In one study, for example, Dishion, Patterson, Stoolmiller, and Skinner (1991) found that rejected aggressive preadolescent boys were associating mainly with other hostile, antisocial classmates and were much more likely than nonrejected boys to be involved in antisocial conduct. These boys gathered together to form deviant cliques that devalued prosocial activities and shunned (and were shunned by) more conventional peer cliques. Furthermore, as members of a larger deviant crowd, these groups often promoted antisocial adolescent activities such as sexual misconduct, substance abuse, dropping out of school, and a variety of other delinquent or criminal behaviors (R. B. Cairns, B. D. Cairns, & Neckerman, 1989; Dishion et al., 1991). Given this situation, it is not surprising that at least a certain number of children in these subgroups should be drawn into gangs.

Antisocial groups can affect their members in a number of ways (R. B. Cairns & B. D. Cairns, 1994). First, individuals tend to meld their own actions and attitudes with those around them. Second, social groups are a means by which one can express individual aggression and control. Third, strong reciprocal forces operate on all members of a group toward conformity regarding salient attitudes and behaviors. And fourth, many members of such groups might lack self-regulation, and any self-regulation they do possess might wilt under the peer pressure to engage in antisocial behavior (Zimring, 1998).

Cairns et al. (1997) described two alternative pathways by which adolescents move into involvement with gangs. In one pathway, aggressive groups of children are drawn to deviant gangs of adolescents because of the salient presence of the gangs within the school and community (R. B. Cairns et al., 1997). The gang is socially central and dominant and thus entices deviant subgroups into its arms. In addition, the deterioration of the social community invites gang involvement. In the second pathway, otherwise disaffiliated and ostracized youths (including runaways and homeless youths) more or less "drift" into gang membership. In this situation, the adolescent becomes involved in a cycle of alienation in which one of the only options is the partial security of gang membership. Within the gang, powerful effects of reciprocal influence then lead to high levels of behavioral and attitudinal similarity, regardless of the initial status of the persons involved (R. B. Cairns & B. D. Cairns, 1994).

Differential Association?

The extent to which peers entice an otherwise "good" child into aggressive or antisocial behavior is controversial. At an anecdotal level, many parents defend their child's antisocial behavior on the ground that their offspring is a "good child" who became seduced into antisocial or illegal activity by "bad companions." At a theoretical level, Sutherland's *differential association* theory, Bandura's *social learning* theory, and Akers' *reinforcement* theory all suggest that bad companions can cause a child to develop antisocial behavior.

Although some research on adolescents seems to support the differential association model (Elliott, Huizinga, & Menard, 1989; Hoge et al., 1994; Kandel, 1973; Reiss & Rhodes, 1964), it is possible that these findings reflect the end of the causal chain, rather than the beginning. As suggested by Samenow (1989) and Redl and Wineman (1951), perhaps it is the child's own predilection for aggression that results in his selecting other aggressive children as friends. If such is the case, future delinquency and/or drug abuse might be due to the child's personality rather than to the influence of his peers.

Benda and Whiteside's (1995) study of 1,093 students of both sexes evenly distributed across grades 9 through 12 supports this view. The analysis indicated that the extent of the youths' conventional beliefs directly predicted their differential association with peers, which only indirectly predicted delinquency (see Fig. 9.1). Thus, youths' beliefs about right and wrong affect their choice of peers, and that association in turn strengthens the youths' already existing tendencies in either a prosocial or antisocial direction.

Other research suggests that peer influence in early adolescence might be especially important for "borderline" youngsters. For example, in one study of low-income, French Canadian boys, association with antisocial peers at ages 11

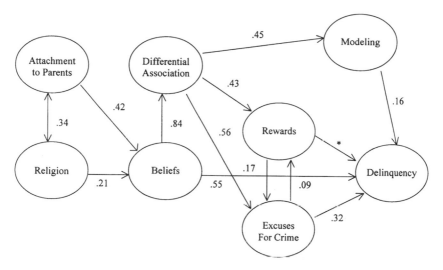

FIG. 9.1. Structural equation model linking adolescents' beliefs and differential associations to delinquency. (Note: Asterisk represents a relationship which is not significant. Shown are standardized coefficients. Paths with two arrows represent correlation relationships; paths with single arrows represent causal relationship.) From "Testing an Integrated Model of Delinquency Using LISREL," by B. B. Benda and L. Whiteside, 1995, *Journal of Social Service Research*, *21*, p. 16. Copyright © The Haworth Press. Reprinted with permission.

and 12 predicted subsequent aggressive behavior for boys who were rated as moderately disruptive in class, but not for boys rated as either nondisruptive or highly disruptive (Vitaro, Tremblay, Kerr, Pagani, & Bukowski, 1997). The highly disruptive boys tended to become delinquent independent of their friends' influence, whereas the nondisruptive boys did not become delinquent. This research suggests that prior personality characteristics mediate peer effects, and that adolescent peers might be more influential in the case of adolescent-onset CD than in the case of childhood-onset CD.

ANTISOCIAL YOUTH GANGS

I tell you somethin'—I don't feel connected to any other kids in this city or in this country or in this world. I only feel comfortable in my 'hood. That's the only thing I'm connected to, that's my family. One big family—that's about it.
— 14-year-old gang member (Bing, 1991, p. 49)

Although gangs are seen as a central force in youths' violent behavior, two major factors make it difficult to come to an understanding of the effects of gangs on youth violence. First, definitional problems abound, both regarding the nature of gangs themselves as well as the meaning of the term *gang-related* (Klein, 1995; Kodluboy, 1997; J. Moore, 1990; Spergel, 1990). And second, gang activity is heterogeneous, not only from city to city, but also from gang type to gang type and within a city itself (Klein, 1995). For these and other reasons, the literature on gangs is filled with much tentative and contradictory information. In this section, I attempt to delineate some of the major findings that seem particularly relevant for a understanding the relationship between gangs and youth violence.

Definition and Nature of Antisocial Youth Gangs

An *antisocial youth gang* is defined as a denotable group of young people whose cohesion "is fostered in large part by their acceptance of or even commitment to delinquent or criminal involvement," who recognize themselves as a distinct group and are so perceived by others in the neighborhood, and whose delinquent behavior has elicited a consistent negative response from either the police or others in the neighborhood (Klein, 1995, p. 218). We must also recognize, however, that there are a wide variety of subtypes of gangs, thus making a single stereotype too simplistic (Moore, 1990; Klein, 1995).

The number of youth gangs in the United States has proliferated rapidly since 1980 (Howell, 1997). During this period, the prevalence of gangs has increased from 286 cities with more than 2,000 gangs and nearly 100,000 members in 1980, to 2,000 jurisdictions with more than 23,000 gangs and more than 650,000 members in 1995 (Howell, 1997). All states, almost all large cities, and 50% of cities and towns with populations under 25,000 reported youth gang problems in 1995 (Howell, 1997).

Most gangs consist of a group of youths from racial minorities, ethnic minorities, or both (Kodluboy, 1997). For the past 20 years or so, U.S. gangs have been primarily Hispanic or African-American; more recently, however, Asian gangs have begun to proliferate (Flannery, Huff, & Manos, 1998). According to Kodluboy (1997), gang members tend to be comprised "mostly of marginal youths within a population already defined by the greater society as marginal" (p. 191). As we have seen, many of these members are antisocial youths who began associating with deviant peers in the early to mid-elementary school years and who subsequently move on to become full-fledged members of an antisocial gang. However, although between 14% and 30% of urban youths join gangs at some point (Howell, 1997), it is clear that most youths from such ethnic or racial groups do not become gang members.

Gangs and Violence

Youth gang members are responsible for a disproportionate amount of violent offenses. Research using gang members' self-reports as the dependent measure finds that although gang members account for at most 30% of the youth population, they are responsible for 68% to 89% of all serious violent adolescent offenses (Howell, 1997). Other studies also support the conclusion that gang members are generally more violent than nonmembers (Snyder & Sickmund, 1999; Spergel, 1990). Furthermore, while in the gang, individual members offend at a higher level than before they join or after they leave. However, even after they leave a gang, their rate of offending remains unusually high, and former gang members are more likely to have serious criminal records and show more recidivism as adults (Howell, 1997; Spergel, 1990).

Gang members show an earlier onset of deviant behavior than do nongang members. For example, Resnick and Blum (1994) found that adolescents who had engaged in nonabusive sexual intercourse before the age of 10 were more likely than other youths to participate in gangs and to have friends who were gang members. Gang members are also more likely to show earlier onset of delinquent behaviors and to affiliate with like-minded antisocial friends (Kodluboy, 1997).

Other areas in which gang members differ from nongang members involve intelligence, self-regulation, and motivation. Some but not all research suggests that gang members tend to have lower IQs than nongang members (Spergel, 1990). This characteristic might be more true of "street fighter" gang members than of members in gangs that engage in more economic pursuits (Farrington, Berkowitz, & West, 1982). Weak self-regulation has also been seen as characteristic of gang members. Indeed, one observer concluded that gang leaders were not the strongest or fittest youths but rather "those with the lowest impulse control" (Patrick, 1973, p. 101). Finally, many male gang members are also seen as being motivated by the need to establish and maintain power (Hagedorn, 1998; Spergel, 1990), precisely the kind of motivation which Olweus (1993) reported as being characteristic of bullies.

Selection or Socialization?   Why are gang members so violent? Thornberry and Krohn (1997) suggested two possible reasons: a *selection effect*, in which the youth's personality characteristics affect peer selection; and a *socialization effect*, in which peer interaction affects the individual's behavior. In their longitudinal study of youths in Rochester, New York, these researchers found evidence for a bidirectional effect between selection and socialization (Thornberry, Lizotte, Krohn, Farnworth, & Jang, 1994). In this connection, it is tempting to speculate that gangs might include both a relatively small core of highly antisocial youths with childhood onset, as well as a larger but less antisocial group with adolescent onset. Because the socialization effect seems to be more characteristic of members who leave the gang after only a short stay (Thornberry, Krohn, Lizotte, & Chard-Wierschem, 1993), it is possible that group processes might be more salient for the adolescent-onset group, whereas bidirectional influences might be more characteristic of the childhood-onset group.

In his research on gangs in Milwaukee, Hagedorn (1998) distinguished between gang members who use instrumental violence (the *new jacks*) and those whose aggression is more reactive in nature (the *homeboys*). According to Hagedorn, the homeboys have more prosocial attitudes and are less committed to violence than are the new jacks, who see violence as a means of obtaining money and hence power.

Has gang-related violence increased over recent years? According to the broader *Los Angeles definition,* any illegal activity involving a gang member is "gang related." However, the more narrow *Chicago definition* requires that an illegal act must include clear gang motivation to be considered "gang-related" (J. Moore, 1990). Moore argues that although violent behavior by individual gang members has increased in recent years, actual gang-related violence has not. However, this view seems to be the minority position, as most researchers suggest that gang-related youth violence has increased over that seen in past decades. For example, the 1950s were the years of intergang "rumbles," in which the weapons of choice were typically bats, bricks, clubs, and chains; however, guns were generally not used and the results were seldom lethal (Goldstein, 1991). Boston street gangs of the 1960s rarely used firearms, and violent acts were relatively rare among Los Angeles Hispanic gangs of the early 1970s (Spergel, 1990). By the mid-1970s, however, gang violence had become more lethal, and the 1980s saw gang violence established at a higher baseline level (Klein & Maxson, 1989).

Spergel (1990) cited estimates that in some cities, gang-related violent crime accounts for as much as ⅓ of all violent crime committed by juveniles. At the same time, however, it should be noted that gang-related violence seems to wax and wane, with a cycle increasing for a period of time and then plateauing (Klein, 1995; J. Moore, 1990; Spergel, 1990). However, as Klein (1995) pointed out, the problem is that the level at which violence plateaus seems to be ever-increasing.

As we saw in chapter 7, much of the increase in youth violence beginning in the mid-1980s has been attributed to gang involvement in the selling of crack cocaine (Blumstein, 1995; Courtwright, 1996). However, the extent to which such violence is related to gang activity per se is controversial. For example, some research suggests that although individual gang members or cliques within gangs might be involved in selling drugs, drug trafficking is typically not an organized gang activity (Howell, 1995). Similarly, one study of Chicago gangs found that gang involvement in homicides was more often related to turf wars than to drug trafficking (Howell, 1995). Hagedorn (1998), however, criticizes this study and presents other data that support a drug–homicide linkage.

Reasons for Joining Gangs

Researchers cite a variety of reasons for why adolescent males join gangs, foremost among which is that gang membership confers a certain status or reputation (*rep*) upon the adolescent (Spergel, 1990). In fact, arrest (especially for murder), imprisonment, and the development of a "bad" image in prison might all be important means of elevating one's status, especially among younger members of the gang (Bing, 1991; Butterfield, 1995; Spergel, 1990). As suggested by the quotation at the beginning of this section, another reason for joining gangs involves emotional support. A number of researchers argue that gangs function like families in many ways and hence might be especially attractive to young males who lack their own functioning family (Spergel, 1990). In the words of one researcher, the gang "is a family with which you can identify" (Jacobs, 1977, p. 153).

A number of family related variables seem important for understanding youths' involvement in gangs. Gang members are often sons or younger brothers of older (or "retired") gang members. Indeed, one study found that the best predictor of gang-related activity was the presence of a gang-member sibling or parent in the home (Spergel & Curry, 1988). Interestingly, family structure might not be an important variable in whether a youngster joins a gang or not; gang and nongang delinquents do not differ on such variables as broken homes and having parents with a criminal history (Spergel, 1990). Instead, extent of parental supervision seems more important, and Reiss (1988) concluded that what leads youngsters into gangs is the territorial concentration of young males who lack at home the firm control they can find in the gang. Even this formulation, however, is probably an oversimplification, because not all male members of the same family will join a gang. In a concession to our collective ignorance, Spergel is forced to conclude that, "Why one brother joins and another does not is not clear" (Spergel, 1990, p. 236).

Females and Gangs

Although most gang members are male, an increasing number of females are participating in gangs (A. Campbell, 1991; Howell, 1995). In general, females appear to comprise anywhere from 20% to 40% of gang membership (Hagedorn, 1998). Some of these women belong to gangs considered to be "auxiliaries" of male gangs, but all-female gangs are extremely diverse in terms of their ethnic composition, structure, range of criminal activity, and relationship to male gangs (Hagedorn, 1998).

Female gang members appear to differ from male members in a number of ways. First, females tend to have a more troubled family life than males and are more likely than males to join gangs as protection against violence in the family and the neighborhood (Flannery et al., 1998; Hagedorn, 1998. Second, female gang members show chronic but less serious delinquency than do male members (Flannery et al., 1998). And third, although many female gang members report that they love to fight, they tend to fight more reactively and to use weapons much less than do males (Hagedorn, 1998). Indeed, some researchers report that the presence of females in a gang tends to reduce the overall amount of violent behavior in the gang (Joe & Chesney-Lind, 1995).

Although females report a variety of reasons for leaving the gang, one reason stands out: motherhood (Hagedorn, 1998). In one study, two thirds of female gang members became teenage mothers, with the vast majority of these being single mothers who considered themselves primarily responsible for their child (Hagedorn, 1998). Hence, most such mothers limit their involvement in gangs and in illegal ventures (Hagedorn, 1998). Unfortunately, the post-gang prognosis for these women is poor: In addition to raising their children without spouses, they are also more likely to be arrested and to become dependent on welfare (Flannery et al., 1998).

BULLYING

> A boy tormented by bullies at one of London's worst schools was cleared yesterday of wounding with intent a fellow pupil who repeatedly threatened him.
>
> A jury took less than an hour to decide that Andrew Grant acted in self-defence when he stabbed Michael Adewusu in the thigh during a confrontation in a history lesson at Dulwich High School for Boys in south-east London.
>
> Grant, who was 14 at the time, said that on the day of the attack Adewusu, 15, had repeatedly picked on him, called him names, and threatened to delete his work from the computer.
>
> He said Adewusu had punched him to the ground and then hit him repeatedly around the head and body. Grant told the jury he produced the knife in a desperate attempt to frighten him off. But, undeterred, Adewusu knocked him to the ground again, and with another pupil kicked and stamped on his head.
>
> Grant said: "I never thought the blows would stop. If I had not stabbed him, he would have carried on hitting and kicking me." (Clough, 1997, p. 3)

As used initially by Heinemann (1973), the term *bullying* meant "mobbing" and referred to a situation in which a large (and sometimes anonymous) group harasses or attacks an individual. As the term evolved, however, it also began to refer to a situation in which a single individual harasses, picks on, pesters, or attacks another (Olweus, 1993). For our purposes, bullying can be defined as a situation in which an individual or group of more powerful individuals intentionally, repeatedly, and over a period of time subjects someone less powerful to negative behaviors such as threats, taunts, teasing, name-calling, or physical injury. In effect, bullying occurs when a more powerful person repeatedly imposes aggression on a less powerful person.

Overview

In large-scale pioneering research conducted in Norway, Dan Olweus (1992, 1993) found that 15% of students in primary or junior high schools were involved in bullying, either as bullies or victims. Of these, 7% were bullies, 9% were victims, and 1% to 2% were both bullies and victims. In the United States,

D. G. Perry, Kusel, and L. C. Perry (1988) found that 10% of U.S. school children between the ages of 9 and 12 could be considered extreme victims of bullying. And in a retrospective report study of middle and high school students in the midwestern United States, Hoover, Oliver, and Hazler (1992) found that 81% of males and 72% of females said they had been bullied at some time during their school years. Other research conducted in Canada, Ireland, England, Sweden, The Netherlands, Spain, Italy, Australia, and Japan all indicate that bullying is common in those countries (Bentley & Li, 1995; Craig & Pepler, 1997; Farrington, 1993; Genta, Menesini, Fonzi, & Costabile, 1996; Olweus, 1993; Stephenson & Smith, 1989). It is thus clear that bullying is an international problem.

Olweus (1993) found that boys were more involved in bullying than were girls, both as perpetrators and victims. Although boys were chiefly bullied by other boys, almost ½ of the girls were also bullied by boys. And although girls were more likely to use verbal and indirect means when they bullied than were boys, harassment using nonphysical means was the major form of bullying among boys as well. Like Olweus (1993), Craig and Pepler (1997) and Genta et al. (1996) also found that boys were more likely to be bullies than girls. However, Hoover et al.'s (1992) results showed that males and females were equally likely to be victims of bullies.

Olweus (1993) also found that bullying was just as prevalent in smaller towns as in larger cities. In addition, most bullying occurred at school, rather than away from school. Interestingly, bullying was not any more frequent in larger schools than in smaller ones; in fact, slightly more bullying occurred in one-room schools than in larger ones.

Although Olweus (1993) found that bullying was most prevalent in the second grade, Hoover et al. (1992) found that in the United States, the amount of bullying increased throughout the elementary years, peaked and remained high in middle school and for the first few years of high school, then declined sharply over the last few years of high school (Fig. 9.2).

During the early elementary school years, bullies seem to be at least as popular as other students (Coie et al., 1991; Pulkkinen & Tremblay, 1992), and sometimes even more so (Dodge, Coie, et al., 1990). In the early grades, bullies are often surrounded by a small group of friends who support them (Cairns et al., 1988). However, their popularity decreases to below average by the ninth grade (Olweus, 1993).

As Olewus found in Norway, bullying in other places seems to involve more physical aggression in the early years but verbal and indirect aggression as children get older (Bentley & Li, 1995; Craig, 1998; Craig & Pepler, 1997; Genta et al., 1996; Hoover et al., 1992). Farrington (1993) and Hoover et al. (1992) provided a picture of the major types of behaviors in which bullies engage. In general, the most prevalent type involves teasing and picking on the victim (Ross, 1996). Next comes practical jokes, followed by acts of physical aggression (such as hitting and kicking) as well as verbal aggression (threatening and extortion).

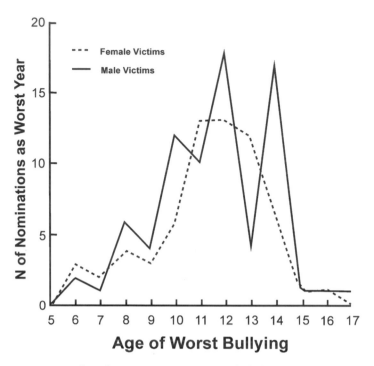

FIG. 9.2. Number of nominations as worst year for bullying by gender. From "Bullying: Perceptions of Adolescent Victims in the Midwestern USA," by J. H. Hoover, R. Oliver, and R. J. Hazler, 1992, *School Psychology International, 13,* p. 10. Copyright 1992 by Sage Publications Ltd. Reprinted with permission.

At a lower level of frequency comes spreading rumors, rejection, and the destruction or theft of the victim's property.

Characteristics of Bullies

Physically, bullies (especially boys) tend to be stronger than other children in general and victims in particular (Olweus, 1993). In addition, bullies also tend to be older than their victims, thus accentuating the difference in physical power (Olweus, 1993). Finally, bullies also show a lack of leadership qualities (Trawick-Smith, 1988).

Olweus (1993) characterized bullies as having a more positive attitude toward violence and the use of violence than children in general, little empathy toward others, a relatively high amount of impulsivity, and a "strong need to dominate others" (Olweus, 1993, p. 34). In a similar vein, Bentley and Li (1995) found that bullies were more likely than other children to report aggression-supporting beliefs. In addition, Perry, Williard, and Perry (1990) found that when aggressive boys contemplate attacks on victims, "they are supremely confident of tangible success" and they are "decidedly unmoved by the prospect of inflicting pain and suffering" (p. 1322). Batsche and Knoff (1994) reported that bullies are pleased with what they do to their victims. These findings are interesting in light of Shaffer's (1994) suggestion that aggression is maintained because aggressive children attach much value to their ability to dominate and control others and because they hold aggressiveness as a positive value.

Self-Esteem. A major issue involving bullies concerns the role that self-esteem might play in motivating their antisocial behavior. Some psychologists argue that bullies are actually anxiety-riddled children who inflict psychological pain on others in order to compensate for their own psychological distress and to enhance their low self-esteem (see Fried & Fried, 1996; Rigby & Cox, 1996; R. Rosenberg & M. Rosenberg, 1978). Olweus' (1993) research, however, contradicts this viewpoint. Using psychological and physiological measures, he found that "bullies had unusually little anxiety and insecurity or were roughly average on such dimensions . . . And they did not suffer from poor self-esteem" (Olweus, 1992, p. 104). These findings regarding Norwegian bullies have been supported by Rigby and Slee's (1993) research on Australian bullies. Moreover, in another study with Australian adolescents, Rigby and Cox (1996) found essentially no correlation between bullying and self-esteem for males, but a small negative correlation ($r = -.17$) for females. The bulk of the research thus suggests that rather than being anxious and insecure persons who taunt others because of their low self-esteem, bullies are children with aggressive behavior patterns who "have a strong need for power and dominance," a "need to subdue others," and who "seem to enjoy being 'in control'" (Olweus, 1993, p. 35).

In summarizing his work on bullies, Olweus (1992) arrived at the following conclusion:

> In my own approach, I stress the view that a good deal of *aggressive behavior,* and in particular bullying, can be seen as *"self-initiated behavior"* with the deliberate aim of inflicting pain and discomfort, of dominating and oppressing others, and of obtaining tangible and prestigious rewards through coercion. In this view, bullying behavior is not primarily seen as a consequence of lack of skills or abilities but rather as *a function of "deviant" motivations and habits.* It is more a question of what the aggressors want to do, and are used to doing, than what they are able to do. (pp. 119–120, emphasis in original)

Characteristics of Victims

Olweus (1993) described two types of victims. *Passive* (or *submissive*) victims are more anxious and insecure than other children, typically weaker physically, have low self-esteem and a feeling of low self-worth, are lonely, lack a single good friend, and have a negative feeling toward violence. In general, these children send signals that they are insecure and will not defend themselves if attacked. The second and smaller *provocative* type consists of victims who are both anxious and aggressive. These children might be especially inattentive or hyperactive, and their behavior often irritates and provokes a large number of their peers. These children thus receive little peer support when attacked by bullies.

Research in the United States generally corroborates the findings of Olweus (Perry et al., 1988). Hoover et al. (1992), however, found a slightly different set of characteristics for male victims as compared with female victims. Male victims described the major reasons for their victimization as "didn't fit in," "physically weak," "short tempered," "who my friends were," and "the clothes I wore." The major female characteristics included "didn't fit in," "facial appearance," "cried/was emotional," "overweight," and "get good grades" (Hoover et al., 1992, p. 11). For both sexes, "didn't fit in" was the leading perceived cause, indicating that bullies pick on children who are different from the majority (Fried & Fried, 1996).

External differences, however, do not tell the whole story. Olweus (1993), for example, found that about three-quarters of nonvictims also had some type of external deviation. It is thus likely that children's physical characteristics interact with their psychological characteristics to produce a "likely victim" profile. For example, Perry et al. (1988) argued that victims have three qualities that make them vulnerable to bullies. First, victims are more likely to reward bullies by giving bullies the things they want. Second, victims are more likely to show outward signs of distress, which in turn might reinforce the bully. And third, victims are less likely to retaliate. Indeed, some psychologists believe that bullies go on a type of "shopping process," by which they carefully observe other children in order to pick out their next victim (Fried & Fried, 1996).

Reactions to Bullying

How do children and adults react to bouts of bullying? In one study of London school children, Mooney, Creeser, and Blatchford (1991) found that approximately 50% of the child-victims retaliated, approximately 40% took no notice, and about 25% told a teacher. When asked why they did not tell a teacher, almost half said it was wrong to tell tales, and another half were afraid that doing so would provoke retaliation from the bully (O'Moore & Hillery, 1991). Interestingly, when Ziegler and Rosenstein-Manner (1991) asked bullies themselves what victims should do, 51% said tell a teacher, 50% said tell a parent, 46% said fight back, 34% said tell a friend, and 21% said talk to the bully.

As for how other children respond to witnessing someone else being bullied, Whitney and Smith (1993) found that, in general, primary school children were more likely to help the victim (54%) than were secondary school children (34%). On the other hand, about one in five from both types of schools said they did nothing and thought it was none of their business. Indeed, a large number of both primary and secondary students thought it was acceptable for them to also participate in the bullying. In fact, Craig and Pepler (1997) found that although peers were involved in 85% of bullying episodes, they only intervened in 11% of episodes.

Unfortunately, adults often fail to take bullying seriously. Olweus' (1993) findings that teachers do relatively little to counteract bullying is supported by research in Canada indicating that adults intervene in only 4% of bullying episodes on the playground (Craig & Pepler, 1997). In the United States, Hoover et al. (1992) found that two-thirds of victims believe that school officials do not responded appropriately to bullying. Thus, although teachers tend to believe that they react appropriately (Farrington, 1993), victims clearly do not think that such is the case.

What about parents? In Olweus' (1993) research, approximately 55% of primary school victims said that someone at home had talked to them about bullying, but only 35% of secondary school victims reported such a discussion. For bullies, the proportion was markedly lower. Olweus (1993) concludes that parents talk with their children about this problem "only to a limited extent" (p. 21).

Consequences of Bullying

Bullying has short- and long-term consequences for the victim, the bully, and for others as well.

For the Victim. In the short term, of course, bullying results in a great deal of emotional pain and turmoil for the victim. For example, victims might find it difficult to concentrate on school work; indeed, approximately ⅓ of the victims studied by Hoover et al. (1992) reported that bullying negatively affected their academic performance. Victims might also be afraid of going to school lest they be victimized (Farrington, 1993). This might be especially true for girls, as Hoover et al. (1992) found that female victims reported being more emotionally troubled by bullying than did male victims.

Bullying is not just a passing phase, and many victims continue to be bullied for years to come (Olweus, 1993). Moreover, the effects of bullying also endure for years. One study found that middle-school children who were bullied in elementary school had more trouble adjusting to middle school, had more academic difficulties, and were more likely to drop out of school than were their peers (Parker & Asher, 1987). Girls who are bullied seem more prone to depression (Kupersmidt & Patterson, 1991), and some evidence suggests that being bullied might negatively affect the sexual adjustment of male victims (Gilmartin, 1987).

The most devastating long-term effect of bullying, however, is suicide. Olweus (1993) cited the case of a 16-year-old male who hanged himself "after being constantly threatened, pushed around and humiliated by three of his classmates" (p. 8). In addition, Fried and Fried (1996) reported a number of instances in which adolescents have committed suicide after a history of being bullied. In one case, a 15-year-old female shot herself to death, leaving a note that said she could no longer endure harassment by three other girls in her school.

For the Bully. For the bully, the short-term consequences are likely to be positive. In the long term, however, bullying is associated with a number of problems. Rigby and Cox (1996) found that bullying at a younger age predicts delinquency in adolescence, and Olweus (1993) found that from 35% to 40% of former bullies had three or more court convictions by the age of 24, compared with 10% of children who were neither bullies nor victims. Similarly, Farrington (1993) reported that bullies in England engaged in more violence after leaving school than did their nonbully peers. Thus, children who bully are clearly at risk for later problems involving aggression and other antisocial behavior.

For Others. Although bullying might seem to affect only the victim, such is not the case. Askew (1989), for example, pointed out that when bullying exists in a school, other children are anxious and vigilant lest they become the next victim. This type of atmosphere inhibits learning and encourages absenteeism (Ross, 1996).

Causes of Bullying

On the basis of his research, Olweus (1993) specified four major factors contributing to the development of bullying: First, negative attitudes of the parents toward the child bully, accompanied by a lack of emotional warmth and involvement; second, a lack of clear limits being set by the parents, accompanied by a permissive and tolerant attitude toward the child's aggression; third, the parents' use of "power-assertive" techniques, accompanied by physical punishment and violent emotional outbursts. In their research comparing provocative victims with nonvictim bullies, Schwartz, Dodge, Pettit, and Bates (1997) found that provocative victims were more likely to experience violence in the home, whereas nonvictim bullies were more likely to simply witness it. The fourth factor is an active and "hot-headed" temperament. In general, Olweus (1993) argued that "too little love and too much 'freedom' in childhood" (p. 39) strongly contribute to the development of bullying.

Another set of factors that contribute to bullying involves the reactions of both adults and children. As we have seen, adults tend to trivialize bullying, and other children often tend to support the bully. The fact that the bully gets what he wants from the victim, that adults typically ignore his behavior, and that other students might either tacitly or openly support the bullying behavior—all these factors tend to reinforce the bully's behavior. As one child put it when asked why someone becomes a bully: "Being a bully is fun" (Fried & Fried, 1996, p. 108). Finally, following multiple instances of being bullied, the victim might come to be perceived as a "fairly worthless" person who almost asks to be beaten up and who deserves what he gets.

Intervention Strategies

We will discuss school-based antibullying programs in chapter 11. In this section, I summarize some of the actions recommended for parents to take when their children report being bullied (Farrington, 1993; Fried & Fried, 1996; Ross, 1996):

- Parents must help the child break the "code of silence," which states that adults should not be told about bullying. Children must know that bullying is not acceptable and that this type of behavior needs to be reported to adults.

- Parents must provide emotional support to their victimized child and must make it clear that the child is not responsible for the bullying.

- Parents can help children devise possible steps to take in self-protection. In particular, they can help children learn appropriate assertiveness skills.

- Although most experts advise against encouraging victims to retaliate physically against bullies, some type of self-defense lessons might be appropriate. Children should be taught that self defense when being physically attacked is an appropriate response.

- Parents should develop written documentation of the bullying incidents in as much detail as possible. In some cases, parents have even "wired" their children to get such documentation (Ross, 1996).

- Parents can confront the bully directly, making sure the bully understands that future bullying will not be tolerated.

- Parents can send a registered letter to both the parents of the bully and to the school (if the incident occurred at school). This letter should document the incident and make it clear that such behavior must stop, and that legal steps will be taken if the bullying persists.

- Parents can also send such documentation to the police, pointing out that assault is a criminal matter.

- If the bully's parents and/or the school react negatively, parents can take legal action (either by requesting police action against the bully or by bringing suit).

In sum, parents of victims need to be willing to take sensitive and decisive steps in order to bring a swift end to the bullying.

JUVENILE SEXUAL OFFENDING

In a wealthy suburb of Detroit, an 18-year-old former high school class president was sentenced to 4½ months in jail for having sex with underage girls ("Former class president," 1998). And in Texas, an 11-year-old boy was convicted of stripping naked a 3-year-old girl and then assaulting her after she followed him and two younger boys to a creek near their homes ("11-year-old convicted," 1998).

Overview

Sexual offenses include rape, fondling, exhibitionism, verbal harassment, and other, noncontact offenses (Becker & Hunter, 1997). Historically, adults (especially adult males) have been seen as responsible for most such sexual offenses. However, available evidence suggests that juveniles might be responsible for as many as 20% of rapes and 30% of child sexual abuse (Brown, Flannagan, & McLeon, 1984; Fehrenbach, Smith, Monastersky, & Deisher, 1986). In addition, one survey found that 58% of adult sex offenders reported that the onset of their deviant sexual behaviors occurred prior to the age of 18 (Abel, Mittelman, & Becker, 1985). Unfortunately, however, the research literature on this topic is quite sparse and relatively little is known about this group of juveniles (Becker & Hunter, 1997).

According to one study, the most common type of juvenile sexual offense is fondling (committed by 59% of an offender sample), followed by rape (23%), and exhibitionism (11%; Fehrenbach et al., 1986). One study of 12- to 15-year-old males incarcerated for sexual offenses found that offenders had committed a median of 69.5 sexual offenses each, with a median of 16.5 victims each (Wieckowski, Hartsoe, Mayer, & Shortz, 1998) It thus appears that for at least some juveniles, sex offending begins early and occurs often.

Young sex offenders tend to come from disorganized and unstable homes in which they experience physical abuse, sexual abuse, or both (Becker & Hunter, 1997; Ford & Linney, 1995). Indeed, a number of studies indicate that abuse is the most common characteristic of these juveniles. Kobayashi, Sales, Becker, Figueredo, and Kaplan (1995) found that sexual aggressiveness among juvenile males was positively related to being physically abused by the father and sexually abused by a male, but negatively related to bonding by the mother. Other research suggests that abused sex offenders experience abuse at an earlier age and for a longer period of time than do abused juveniles who are not offenders (Hunter & Figueredo, 1995, as cited by Becker & Hunter, 1997). It thus seems that the experience of early and continuing sexual abuse is related to higher levels of subsequent sex offending. However, not all juvenile sex offenders have been abused (Becker & Hunter, 1997).

Although pornography has sometimes been linked to sexual offending, the relationship is unclear. For example, in one study of juvenile sex offenders, Becker and Stein (1991) found that 35% of their sample reported using sexually explicit magazines and 26% reported using similar videotapes. However, 9% said they used no explicit sexual material, and no significant relationship was found between the use of sexual materials and the number of victims. In Ford and Linney's (1995) study, 42% of the offender sample reported using sexually explicit magazines, compared with 29% of violent nonsexual offenders. In addition, the offenders typically began exposure between the ages of 5 and 8. Other researchers also reported a link between early exposure to sexually explicit material and subsequent sexual offending, at least in males (Wieckowski et al., 1998; Zgourides, Monto, & Harris, 1997).

Sex Offenders and Aggression

Perhaps not surprisingly, juvenile sex offenders tend to exhibit a number of general antisocial and aggressive tendencies. For example, they are likely to have academic problems and to commit nonsexual delinquent acts (Ford & Linney, 1995). In addition, conduct disorder is the most common diagnosis for juvenile sexual offenders (Kavoussi, Kaplan, & Becker, 1988). Rape, in particular, is related to CD: In one study, 75% of adolescents who had raped were diagnosed as CD, compared with only 38% of those who had molested. Other comorbid conditions include attention-deficit/hyperactivity disorder and depression (Becker & Hunter, 1997).

Researchers have had only limited success in their attempts to differentiate juvenile sex offenders from other groups of antisocial youths. One study found that juvenile sex offenders were more likely to experience parental violence and physical and sexual abuse than were status offenders and violent nonsexual offenders (Ford & Linney, 1995). In another study, CD adolescents scored higher than juvenile sex offenders on socialized aggression, aggressive coping, avoidance coping, and coping by engaging in sexual behavior (Hastings, Anderson, & Hemphill, 1997). Other researchers, however, found no differences between incarcerated sexual offenders and a contrast group of nonoffenders (Jacobs, Kennedy, & Meyer, 1997).

Personality profiles of male sexual offenders suggest a pattern of general aggressiveness. Valliant and Bergeron (1997) found that such offenders were socially isolated, assaultive, and resentful when compared with general offenders. Other research suggests that these youths have a need for interpersonal control (Ford & Linney, 1995) and that they meet this need by using force, threats, or violence in their sexual behavior (Wieckowski et al., 1998). Taken together, these results indicate that male juvenile sexual offending represents an aggressive response more than a sexual one (Jacobs et al., 1997).

Although most juvenile sex offending is perpetrated by males, adolescent females also engage in this behavior, but at a lower rate. Female sex offenders tend to be less aggressive than males and to molest other younger females, often in the context of baby-sitting (Fehrenbach & Monastersky, 1988; Ray & English, 1995). In addition, female offenders appear to experience earlier and more severe abuse than do males (Matthews, Hunter & Vuz, 1997).

Treatment

Despite the fact that many treatment programs exist for adolescent sex offenders, little is known about treatment efficacy. Becker and colleagues developed a multicomponent treatment model designed to get the adolescent to accept responsibility for his or her behavior, and to prevent further victimization and psychosexual problems. The elements of this model include values clarification, cognitive restructuring, empathy training, education in human sexuality, anger management, impulse control training, academic assistance, vocational and independent living skills, and family therapy (Becker & Hunter, 1997).

Becker and Hunter (1997) summarized a number of studies regarding recidivism following treatment. In general, sex offense recidivism for juvenile sex offenders runs between 6% and 12%, with the median around 8%. In one study, however, the recidivism rate for nonsexual offenses was 45%. It thus appears that juveniles who are convicted of sexual offenses are subsequently more likely to commit nonsexual than sexual offenses. Because most of these studies were short term, however, longer term follow-ups are needed.

SIBLING ABUSE

Relatively little is known about sibling abuse and no reliable estimate of its prevalence is available.

Perhaps the most extensive study on sibling abuse has been conducted by Wiehe (1997), who surveyed 150 adult victims of sibling abuse recruited through newspaper ads. Nine in ten respondents were female, 85% were White, and 3% were Black; the average age at the time of responding was 37 years. Most of the abuse came from brothers. Wiehe (1997) acknowledged that this study was merely exploratory and that the sample was not representative. Nevertheless, this descriptive research does constitute a beginning.

Types of Sibling Abuse

Wiehe (1997) described three types of sibling abuse. The most common forms of *physical abuse* included hitting, biting, slapping, shoving, and punching. *Emotional abuse* took the form of name calling, ridicule, degradation, belittling, exacerbating a fear, and destroying personal possessions. Finally, *sexual abuse* (*sibling incest*) included behaviors such as removing clothing, touching and fondling, kissing, performing oral sex, masturbation, and vaginal intercourse.

Four criteria can be used to distinguish between typical sibling squabbles and actual sibling abuse (Wiehe, 1997). First, sibling abuse is often age-inappropriate, as in the case of a 10-year-old who destroys his 3-year-old sister's doll by pulling its hair out strand by strand. Second, sibling abuse occurs when the behavior occurs frequently over a long period of time, especially when it involves a pattern of behavior. Third, sibling abuse involves victimization, often by trickery or deceit (as when a 12-year-old uses a candy bar to bribe his 4-year-old sister to go to his tree house, then sexually abuses her). And fourth, sibling abuse occurs when the purpose of the behavior appears to be humiliation, domination, or self-gratification (as when the perpetrator continues to degrade the victim because of the latter's weight).

Multiple forms of abuse were most common in this sample, with 71% reporting that they had experienced all three types of abuse. More than two-thirds of the sample said that their parents were aware of physical or emotional abuse, but only 18% reported parental awareness of sexual abuse. It thus appears that sexual abuse is the most hidden type of sibling abuse.

Wiehe (1997) stated that there is usually no one single cause of sibling abuse, but that a complex variety of interacting factors might be at work. First and foremost, he views sibling abuse as the result of an abuse of power. And because most abusers are males and most victims are female, he argues that this abuse of power is due to differential socialization and to males' belief that they are entitled to dominate females. However, other factors also play a role. For example, much sibling abuse occurs when the perpetrator is older and placed in charge of the victim, either after school or when the parents are away from the home at night. In many cases, the parents themselves are also involved in an abusive relationship, which the children then imitate. Finally, many parents are overwhelmed by their own stressors, mental illnesses, alcohol or drug abuse, or all three. In general, many of these children grow up in dysfunctional families (Rosenthal & Doherty, 1984).

Parental Behavior

Most victims reported that they told their parents about the abuse, but most also said that their reporting of this abusive behavior had little positive effect and sometimes produced negative results. When parents were told, they often refused to believe that abuse was occurring, ignored or minimized the abuse, sometimes joined the abuse, or sometimes blamed the victim. Occasionally, parents did attempt to intervene, but were ineffective, either because they lacked the skills to stop the abuse, because they inappropriately used violence as a remedy, or because they gave up out of frustration. Wiehe (1997) suggested that parents use the S-A-F-E approach: *Stop* the action (separate the siblings and arrange a cooling-off period if necessary); *Assess* (find out what happened by having each child tell what *he* or *she* did, not what the other one did); *Find* a solution (engage in a problem-solving process and decide on a mutually agreeable solution); and *Evaluate* the results.

Parents can take a number of steps to prevent sibling abuse, chief among which is to really listen to children and to take seriously what the children say (Wiehe, 1997). Another important step that parents can take is to provide quality supervision in their absence. Educating children about sex, becoming sensitive to violence in the home, and encouraging and rewarding positive sibling interactions are additional steps parents can take.

SUMMARY

Children learn many aspects of socialization through their play and their interaction with their peers. Although some play does involve aggression, much of the rough and tumble play of young children (especially boys) does not seem aggressive in nature.

Researchers have consistently found that aggressive children tend to be rejected by their peers, with approximately half of rejected children being aggressive. Aggressive rejected children are at risk fo8r subsequent school problems and antisocial behavior, including delinquency and crime. Research supports the view that these children's aggressive behavior is the cause of their rejection, rather than the result of it. Unfortunately, however, once these children have been labeled by peers as aggressive and rejected, even their good deeds tend to be viewed negatively by other children.

Although aggressive children seem to develop as many reciprocated best friendships as do nonaggressive children, these children's best friends also tend to be aggressive. By the fourth grade, the peer groups of aggressive boys tend to include other aggressive boys. These deviant cliques devalue prosocial behavior and promote various types of antisocial behavior, including aggression. As these boys grow older, the lure of the gang increases, in part because the gang's values match those of the aggressive youth, in part because of the social centrality of the gang, and in part because the alienated young person sees no socially accepted group that will meet his needs. As aggressive youths begin to associate with each other in deviant groups, they mutually reinforce each other's antisocial tendencies.

Since antisocial youth gangs tend to be composed of antisocial youths, it is no surprise that gang members are responsible for a disproportionate share of youth violence. Most research indicates that gang violence has increased over the years, but the extent of gang involvement in drug trafficking remains controversial. Two of males' major motives for joining gangs are to gain a reputation and to belong to a "family." Females are more likely to join gangs as protection against violence. Whatever the motivation for joining, the prognosis for gang members is bleak.

Bullying, especially in school, is a worldwide problem with negative consequences for the bully, the victim, and the larger society. Contrary to much popular opinion, the majority of research indicates that rather than being anxious and lacking self-esteem, bullies have a need to control and dominate others and enjoy behaving violently. As is true for other groups of aggressive children, bullies' problems seem to stem more from their deviant motivations than from a lack of positive social skills. Victims are anxious, insecure, and socially isolated, and they do lack social skills. Bullies seem to "sense" victims' vulnerability and to take measures to exploit it. Unfortunately, the bully's behavior is often reinforced by both adults and other children, many of whom believe that bullying is "none of their business."

Juveniles might be responsible for as many as 20% of rapes and 30% of sexual abuse cases in the United States. Young sex offenders tend to come from disorganized and unstable homes and to experience early and continuing sexual abuse. These youngsters also tend to have academic problems and to exhibit nonsexual antisocial and aggressive behavior. Unfortunately, little is known about effective treatment for this population.

Siblings can abuse each other physically, emotionally, or sexually. In many ways, sibling abuse seems to parallel bullying. Both situations involve an attempt by one child to dominate and intimidate another less-powerful child, and in both cases, adults often fail to take the victim's plight seriously.

CHAPTER 10

Youthful Homicide

Someone was throwing stones: Roger was dropping them, his one hand still on the lever. Below him, Ralph was a shock of hair and Piggy a bag of fat . . .

High overhead, Roger, with a sense of delirious abandonment, leaned all his weight on the lever.

Ralph heard the rock long before he saw it . . .

The rock struck Piggy a glancing blow from chin to knee; the conch exploded into a thousand white fragments and ceased to exist. Piggy, saying nothing, with no time for even a grunt, traveled through the air sideways from the rock, turning over as he went . . . Piggy fell forty feet and landed on his back across that square red rock in the sea. His head opened and stuff came out and turned red. Piggy's arms and legs twitched a bit, like a pig's after it has been killed. Then the sea breathed again in a long, slow sigh, the water boiled white and pink over the rock; and when it went, sucking back again, the body of Piggy was gone.

—Golding (1955, pp. 166–167)

Perhaps nowhere in modern literature have children's homicidal tendencies been bared so shockingly as in William Golding's classic novel *Lord of the Flies,* a symbolic tale of how thin the veneer of civilization is and of how easily that veneer can be punctured. In the book, a group of British school children between the ages of 6 and 12 are marooned on an island after the plane in which they are riding is shot down by enemy fire. Alone with no adults, the boys first vote on a "chief," agree to abide by certain rules, and adopt certain roles and responsibilities. Soon, however, beset by fears and their biological urges, they abandon their responsibilities, paint their faces, and descend into the "jolly good fun" of being savage hunters. When Piggy (the overweight, asthmatic voice of reason) protests, he is violently killed.

In our country, we have recently been bombarded by news stories suggesting that our youths may have descended into their own type of savagery. Headlines such as, "17-Year-Old Sentenced to Life for Hammer Slayings of 5," and "12-Year-Old Who Helped in Search for 5-Year-Old Charged in Her Death" seem commonplace. And just as Golding's rescuers must have wondered how British boys could have descended to such savagery ("After all, we're not savages. We're

English," says one boy early in the novel; Golding, 1955, p. 38), so we wonder how American youths can commit some of the savage murders taking place in our own country.

Statistical Overview

Juvenile homicide consists of murder or nonnegligent manslaughter committed by an individual under the age of 18. As indicated in Fig. 10.1, the number of juvenile arrests for homicide remained relatively stable from 1972 to 1982, reached a low in 1984, then began an upward spiral that peaked in 1993 (Snyder & Sickmund, 1999). And although the number of known homicides by adults increased only 20% between 1984 and 1991, the number of such offenses by juveniles more than doubled over that same period (Snyder & Sickmund, 1995).

The good news, however, is that since 1993, the number of juvenile homicides has again begun to decrease (Fig. 10.1). Moreover, 85% of all counties in the United States recorded no juvenile homicides in 1997 (Snyder & Snyder, 1999); only about 3% of U.S. murders consist of a person under 18 killing another person under 18 (Donohue, Schiraldi, & Zidenberg, 1998); and just 7% of U.S. counties experienced two or more juvenile homicides in 1997 (Snyder &

FIG. 10.1.   Number of murder arrests of juveniles, 1972–1997. From p. 134 of *Juvenile offenders and victims: 1999 national report,* by H. N. Snyder and M. Sickmund, 1999, Washington, DC: Office of Juvenile Justice and Delinquency Prevention. Reprinted with permission of the National Center for Juvenile Justice.

Sickmund, 1999). Nevertheless, the 1997 juvenile homicide rate was still higher than that of 1987, thus supporting the media-induced impression that today, youthful homicide is still a major problem in our society (Sniffen, 1998).

Relation to Victim.   Approximately 14% of murders by juveniles involve family members as victims, whereas 55% involve friends or acquaintances and 31% involve strangers (Snyder & Sickmund, 1999). Thus, two thirds of youth-perpetrated killings involve someone known by the offender. As can be seen in Fig. 10.2, the large increase in murders by juveniles from 1984 to 1993 is accounted for primarily by an increase in the killings of strangers and acquaintances rather than family members.

Sex.   As with other forms of aggression, juvenile homicide is primarily a male problem. More than 90% of juveniles arrested for intentional homicide are males (Snyder & Sickmund, 1999), and between 1984 and 1993 the number of homicides by male juveniles more than doubled, whereas the number by females remained constant (Snyder & Sickmund, 1999). As indicated in Fig. 10.3,

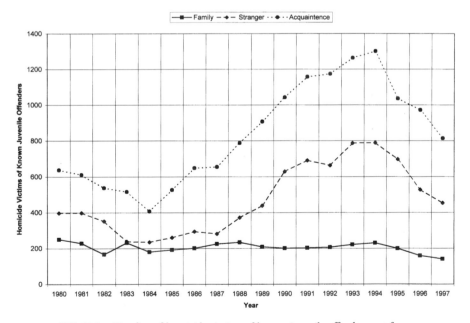

FIG. 10.2.   Number of homicide victims of known juvenile offenders as a function of year and relationship between offender and victim. From p. 56 of *Juvenile offenders and victims: 1999 national report*, by H. N. Snyder and M. Sickmund, 1999, Washington, DC: Office of Juvenile Justice and Delinquency Prevention. Reprinted with permission of the National Center for Juvenile Justice.

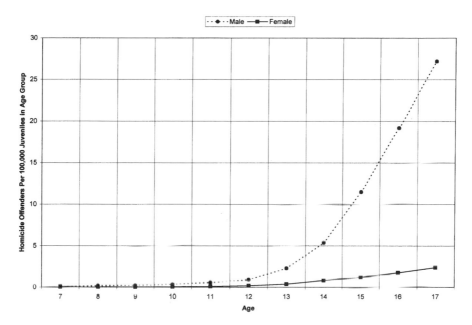

FIG. 10.3. Juvenile homicide offending rate per 100,000 juveniles in each age group as a function of age and sex. From p. 57 of *Juvenile offenders and victims: A national report,* by H. N. Snyder and M. Sickmund, 1995, Washington, DC: Office of Juvenile Justice and Delinquency Prevention. Reprinted with permission of the National Center for Juvenile Justice.

although the homicide rate is slightly higher for males than for females until about age 10, the rates begin to diverge noticeably after that time (Snyder & Sickmund, 1995).

Age. Most killings by juveniles involve adolescent perpetrators as opposed to children. Indeed, more than 85% of known juvenile killers are at least 15 years of age (Snyder & Sickmund, 1999). Not only do adolescents kill at a higher rate than younger children, but the homicide offending rate for 14- to 17-year-olds increased substantially from 1984 to 1993, whereas the rate for younger children remained stable (Snyder & Sickmund, 1999). Thus, juvenile homicide is clearly more of a teenage problem than a childhood one.

Type of Weapon. Between 1980 and 1987, firearms were used in just over 50% of murders committed by juveniles (Snyder & Sickmund, 1999). However, as we saw in chapter 7, the use of firearms in murders committed by juveniles increased dramatically in the late 1980s, so that by 1994, fully 80% of juvenile killings involved a firearm (Snyder & Sickmund, 1999). Fortunately, this trend began to be reversed after 1994, and the sharp decline in homicides since

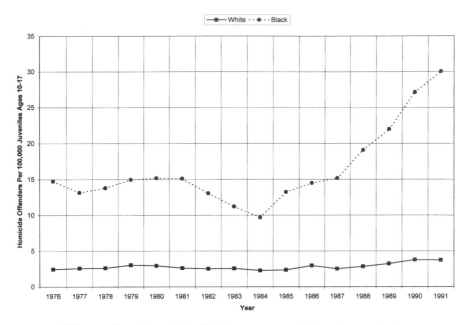

FIG. 10.4.   Juvenile homicide offending rate per 100,000 juveniles ages 10–17 as
a function of year and race. From p. 56 of of *Juvenile offenders and victims: A national report*, by H. N. Snyder and M. Sickmund, 1995, Washington, DC: Office of
Juvenile Justice and Delinquency Prevention. Reprinted with permission of the
National Center for Juvenile Justice.

that time is attributable entirely to a decrease in firearm use (Snyder & Sickmund, 1999).

Race and Ethnicity.   Juvenile homicide is more common among some racial and ethnic groups than others. As indicated in Fig. 10.4, the homicide offending rate has been historically higher for Black juveniles than for Whites and rose sharply for Blacks between the mid-1980s and the early 1990s (Snyder & Sickmund, 1995). Indeed, in his analysis, Cornell (1993) concluded that "the largest increases in juvenile homicide can be found among minority males using handguns to kill acquaintances" (p. 389). Even allowing for discrimination within the justice system, the data indicate that African-American youths commit a vastly disproportionate number of juvenile homicides (C. P. Ewing, 1990a, 1990b). At the same time, however, Black youths were also responsible for the decline in juvenile homicide offending beginning in 1994 (Snyder & Sickmund, 1999).

Most juvenile homicides involve offenders and victims from the same race. Thus, 90% of victims of youthful White killers are White and 76% of victims of Black killers are Black (Snyder & Sickmund, 1999). When we look at victims, we find that 91% of White juvenile victims are killed by Whites and 94% of

Black juvenile victims of homicide are killed by Blacks (Snyder & Sickmund, 1999).

INTRAFAMILIAL AND EXTRAFAMILIAL KILLINGS

Researchers distinguish between *intrafamilial* homicides, in which juveniles kill a family member, and *extrafamilial* homicides, in which they kill acquaintances or strangers (Rowley, C. P. Ewing, & Singer, 1987).

Intrafamilial killings typically differ from extrafamilial killings in a number of ways. First, more than 80% of youth-perpetrated intrafamilial killings are committed by a single individual, whereas only about half of extrafamilial killings involve a single juvenile perpetrator (Rowley et al., 1987). Second, intrafamilial killings are more likely to be sparked by conflict and less likely than extrafamilial killings to occur in connection with a theft (Rowley et al., 1987). And third, when family members are victims, the offender is usually a White male using a gun; however, when friends or acquaintances are killed, the perpetrator is equally likely to be a Black or White male who kills with a gun as the result of an argument or a brawl (Snyder & Sickmund, 1995).

Intrafamilial Killings

Compared with perpetrators of extrafamilial killings, young intrafamilial killers are more likely to have been physically abused, to come from homes where their mothers were physically abused, and to have amnesia for the incident (Corder, Ball, Haizlip, Rollins, & Beaumont, 1976). In addition, these youths are less likely to have a history of hyperaggressive behavior, and many are considered exemplary adolescents (Ewing, 1990a; Mones, 1991).

Parricide.   *Parricide,* the murder of a parent, typically involves non-Hispanic Caucasian families, with *patricide* (the murder of the father) being more common than *matricide* (the murder of a mother; Ewing, 1997). Approximately 2% of homicides in the United States involve parricide (Mones, 1991), and more than 300 parents are killed each year by their child and adult offspring (Heide, 1995). Juveniles kill 15% of mother parricide victims, 25% of father victims, 30% of stepmother victims, and 34% of stepfather victims (Heide, 1995). And, as you might expect, most parricide is committed by sons rather than by daughters (Ewing, 1997).

Patricide commonly appears to be motivated by some type of parental abuse committed toward the child, the mother, and / or other family members (Ewing, 1997; Heide, 1995; Mones, 1991). Repeated physical abuse is often a prime cause of patricide. For example, in 1984, 18-year-old Robert Lee Moody ambushed and killed his father with three blasts from his father's own shotgun (Ewing,

1990a). Although a judge convicted Robert of manslaughter, he also publicly denounced Robert's father as "the scum of the earth" for terrorizing his family for years, raping his two older daughters, forcing his wife into prostitution, molesting his younger daughter, and urging Robert to watch pornographic movies and to take drugs. For Robert, a born-again Christian, the "last straw" apparently occurred when Robert's mother refused to press charges after his father slammed her head into a microwave oven. That day, Robert found the shotgun and killed his father (Ewing, 1990a).

Ewing (1990a, 1990b) concluded that matricide is often motivated more by emotional abuse than by physical abuse, and in their study, Scherl and Mack (1966) argued that this type of murder involves provocation, deprivation, harshness, and severe early restrictiveness by the mother. To support their claim, they cite the case of a 14-year-old who shot his mother while she slept. The mother had repeatedly kicked and slapped the boy, called him names, locked him in his room, forced him to kneel for hours at a time, and exposed her breasts and genitalia to him. Apparently the boy, who had an above-normal IQ and no major psychological disorders, simply could not take the abuse any longer.

Some *family conspiracy* cases might involve one parent tacitly encouraging the child to kill the other parent, such as an incident in which an 8-year-old boy shot and killed his father after his mother often expressed the hope that the father would die (Sargent, 1962). In other instances, the parent encourages the child more directly. In one case, for example, an abused mother gave her 15-year-old son a gun, saying: "I know you're big enough to protect me now." The boy promptly took the gun and killed the father (Ewing, 1990a). In still other situations, the mother explicitly asks the child to kill, as in the case of an 11-year-old girl who shot her stepfather to death after being requested to do so by her mother (Ewing, 1990a).

Youths occasionally kill not only one parent, but both of them, as illustrated by the 1982 case of the Jahnke family of Cheyenne, Wyoming. As Richard Jahnke and his wife returned home one November night from celebrating the 20th anniversary of the day they met, they were both shot to death by 16-year-old Richard, Jr., who had plotted the killing along with his 17-year-old sister Deborah (Ewing, 1990a). Evidence indicated that over the course of 14 years, Jahnke had "repeatedly and brutally beaten and psychologically abused his children and wife" and had sexually abused his daughter (Ewing, 1990a, p. 15).

In some cases, parricides occur not because of abuse, but because parents set limits that the children regard as unreasonable. In New Hampshire, two brothers ages 14 and 17 were accused of shooting their parents to death. Prosecutors said the boys took turns shooting the parents, wrapped up the bodies, hid them in the house, then spent the weekend playing and partying with friends. In the course of the slaying, the younger brother allegedly referred to the killing as "fun," and the older brother reportedly said to his mother, "Die, bitch" ("New Hampshire teen," 1997; Ramer, 1997, p. A4). At his brother's trial, the younger brother said he felt a twinge of regret when his dying father said, "I can't believe my own son did this" (Ramer, 1997, p. A4). Prosecutors said the boys were upset over what they considered to be the parents' strict rules ("New Hampshire teen," 1997; Ramer, 1997).

Fratricide.   The killing of a sibling is called *fratricide.* Sometimes, siblings are killed along with their parents, in which case the motive might be to eliminate a witness or to get revenge on a sibling who is perceived to have received more favorable treatment from the parents. Both motives might have been at work when Bryan Freeman, 15, and his brother David, 16, stabbed and bludgeoned to death their parents and their 11-year-old brother Eric while the three slept in their family home near Allentown, Pennsylvania. The two "skinhead" brothers had a history of aggressive behavior and allegedly hated their Jehovah's Witnesses parents because the parents wouldn't let them do whatever they wanted (Koller, 1995).

When cases of pure fratricide do occur, they tend to involve a variety of factors, including psychopathology, jealously, and depression (C. P. Ewing, 1990b). In some cases, such killings also occur in order to cover up some other illicit act. Thus, for example, one 15-year-old shot his sister to death because of fear that the sister would expose the fact that he had molested her several years earlier (C. P. Ewing, 1990b).

Extrafamilial Killings

We now turn to an examination of killings by juveniles perpetrated outside the family.

Crime-Related Homicides.   Cornell and colleagues (Cornell, 1993; Cornell, Benedek, & Benedek, 1987) proposed a distinction between *crime-related killings,* which occur in the context of another crime, and *conflict-related killings,* which occur as a result of an interpersonal conflict between the killer and his victim.

Many crime-related homicides can be classified as *theft-related* killings, which occur while the juvenile is in the act of committing an illegal act such as robbery, burglary, or larceny. In their study, Rowley et al. (1987) found that 22% of juvenile homicides were theft-related, with 6% of acquaintance homicides and 58% of stranger homicides being incidental to theft. However, only a very minute percentage of juvenile theft incidents result in a killing (C. P. Ewing, 1990b). One such example involves 13-year-old, 240-pound Craig "Iron Man" Price, who killed two women and two girls, ages 8 and 10, while robbing their homes in a Rhode Island town in 1987. The victims were beaten and stabbed repeatedly, one as many as 58 times. At the time of the killings, Price was already on probation for assault and burglary (C. P. Ewing, 1990a).

Many if not most theft-related killings seem to involve unintentional panic reactions in which the perpetrator is surprised while in the act of another crime, or when the victim either forcibly resists or attempts to resist (C. P. Ewing, 1990b). In other instances, juveniles might kill their victims in order to keep from being identified, as is sometimes the case when youngsters rape elderly women, then kill them to escape detection. In still other cases, juveniles might be under the influence of drugs during the crime. Indeed, Cornell et al. (1987) found that 73% of youths who killed in the course of another crime were under the influence of alcohol or other drugs at the time of the killing. Other killings occur in the course of thefts designed to provide money for drugs, or in disputes between youthful drug dealers (C. P. Ewing, 1990b).

When killings are perpetrated by two or more youths in the course of committing another crime, one of the youths often appears to be the "leader," whereas the other seems to be the "follower." In such cases, it appears that an older and/or more violent youth commands psychological control over the others, and that the ensuing violence reduces their inhibitions and leads to a particularly horrific crime (C. P. Ewing, 1990b).

When rape or sexual assault has occurred, sexual motives might come into play (Ewing, 1990a, 1990b). Such undoubtedly is the case when women are first raped and then killed by groups of males (C. P. Ewing, 1990b). In these situations, the decision to rape is sometimes thought out, sometimes impulsive. Whatever the case, the sexual violence escalates and results in murder, often of an horrific nature such as those seen in other multiperpetrator murders. In general, it appears that when two or more youths become involved in killing, they tend to both stimulate and feed off each other, resulting in an especially gruesome type of murder (C. P. Ewing, 1990b).

One example of a sexually related killing involved a 1997 New Jersey case in which 15-year-old Sam Manzie sexually assaulted and strangled to death an 11-year-old boy who disappeared while selling candy door to door as part of a school fund-raising project (Curran, 1999). Manzie, who had a history of psychological problems and had been victimized by an adult pedophile whom he met on the Internet, lured the young victim into his house, tried to have oral sex with him, then strangled him with an electric cord and a necktie. Afterwards, Manzie took a picture of the dead boy's body as a memento of the killing. Manzie later pleaded guilty to murder and was sentenced to 70 years in prison (Curran, 1999; "New Jersey teen," 1998).

Conflict-Related Homicides. Many killings by juveniles occur as a result of an interpersonal conflict between the killer and his victim. As is the case with many abuse-related intrafamilial homicides, some extrafamilial killings seem motivated by a desire to escape from an intolerable situation. In one incident, for example, a 12-year-old Missouri boy, who was constantly teased about his weight, pulled a gun from his gym bag, killed a classmate, then turned the gun on himself (C. P. Ewing, 1990b). In other cases, however, extrafamilial killings seem to involve an attempt to exact revenge rather than to permit escape. For example, a 17-year-old youth killed a Boy Scout leader who had previous abused the youth (Ewing, 1990b). The teenager was apparently upset that the leader had received a jail sentence of only 15 days for the abuse.

Another type of conflict-related homicide occurs when an adult objects to the youth's behavior. In one case, 16-year-old Victor Brancaccio killed an 81-year-old woman who complained about his "foul-mouthed rapping" (Testa, 1998). Brancaccio, who had a history of aggressive behavior and was being treated medically for depression, had gone out for air one evening in his upscale Florida neighborhood after an argument with his mother. Within a block of leaving his home, he ran into the woman, who scolded him for rapping the lyrics of the Dr. Dre song, *Stranded on Death Row* ("Man convicted of killing woman," 1999). In response, Brancaccio dragged the woman into a field, punched and kicked her, bashed in her skull with a toy gun, then jumped on her rib cage, crushing her ribs. The next day, he returned to the body, threw red paint over it, and unsuccessfully tried to burn it (Testa, 1998). Although an appeals court overturned his 1995 conviction, a jury again convicted Brancaccio of murder in January of 1999 ("Man convicted of killing woman," 1999).

"Senseless" Homicides.   In one sense, of course, all killings by juveniles are *senseless homicides*. Some, however, seem somewhat understandable in light of the youth's situation (such as being abused, or panicking when surprised in the act of a crime). But in other cases, such motivation is lacking. Perhaps the least understandable senseless killings are those which Ewing describes as *thrill killings*. According to prosecutors, an example of this type of killing occurred in 1997 when a 17- and an 18-year-old gunned down two pizza delivery men after luring the victims to an abandoned house in a secluded area of New Jersey. According to police, the teens killed for the thrill of finding out what it was like to kill someone. The older teen was subsequently sentenced to death, while the 17-year-old was sentenced to life in prison for the incident ("Man convicted of killing pizza delivery man," 1999; "'Thrill killing,'" 2000).

In a particularly gruesome case of senseless killing, a teenager was sentenced to life in prison for killing a woman who tape-recorded the incident. The middle-aged New Jersey woman, mother of a 6-year-old son, was en route to a college examination when she stopped for a sandwich. After the assailant forced his way into her car at gunpoint, the woman managed to turn on a portable tape-recorder. The tape showed that the woman attempted to understand and befriend her 16-year-old attacker. At one point she said: "You haven't done anything yet. All you have to do is let me go and take my car" (Curran, 1996, p. A6). Instead, the youth smothered her to death and dumped her body in a wooded area near a highway. The youngster was subsequently convicted and sentenced to life in prison (Curran, 1996; "Teen who was taped," 1997).

Other types of senseless killings involve bias against groups such as homeless people, homosexuals, and racial minorities (Ewing, 1990b). Still other senseless killings seem to result from the youth's fascination with the occult or with occult fantasy games (C. P. Ewing, 1990b). According to C. P. Ewing (1990b), "there certainly have been cases in which killings committed by juveniles were at least somehow related to the perpetrator's interest or involvement in fantasy games, including Dungeons and Dragons" (p. 75).

Gang-Related Killings.   Many *gang-related killings* apparently involve drug trafficking (C. P. Ewing, 1990b). In other cases, gang members commit assaults in connection with other illegal activities such as rape and robbery. In addition, gang members often kill each other, either for revenge or to gain control of territory; in fact, some research suggests that gang-related homicides are more often turf related than drug related (Howell, 1995). In one such case, a 17-year-old and several fellow gang members attacked members of a rival gang, killing one of them. The attack occurred after members of the rival gang crossed out graffiti placed there by the perpetrators' gang and replaced it with their own insignia. The members of the perpetrators' gang viewed this action as a symbolic challenge to the perpetrators' gang, which could not go unanswered (C. P. Ewing, 1990b).

C. P. Ewing (1990b) characterized most gang-related killings as "senseless." One example involves a 3-year-old girl killed by Los Angeles gang members after the car in which she was riding made a wrong turn onto a road nicknamed the "Street of Assassins." Prosecutors said the gang members felt that the driver's action "disrespected" them and they thus opened fire, killing the girl and wounding her father and 2-year-old brother. Two adults and a 17-year-old were subsequently convicted in the killing ("L.A. gang members," 1997).

Sometimes, however, gang members' attempts to kill each other go awry, and innocent victims are killed in so-called "drive-by" shootings. An especially notorious such case occurred in 1994 in Chicago. One August night, 14-year-old Shavon Dean was playing outside her house when she was killed by a stray bullet from a gang shooting. The suspect was quickly identified as 4′8″ tall, 11-year-old Robert "Yummy" Sandifer, who received his nickname because of his love of cookies. According to police, Sandifer was a gang member who had shot at members of another gang standing on the street where Shavon lived. Two other nongang teenagers were also wounded in the attack (Cotliar & Fornek, 1994).

Police immediately began a search for Sandifer, concerned that other gang members might find him first and silence him by killing him (Robinson, 1997a). Three days later, the police did find Sandifer, shot to death in a pedestrian tunnel (Cotliar & Fornek, 1994). Two teenage brothers, 14-year-old Derrick and 16-year-old Cragg Hardaway, were arrested for killing Sandifer. Although Cragg said that someone named "Kenny" did the shooting, both brothers were subsequently convicted: Derrick received a sentence of 45 years in prison, while Cragg, the alleged trigger man, got 60 years (Robinson, 1997b).

Cult-Related Killings. In addition to gang-related killings, *cult-related* killings have also been reported. In some instances, the killing appears to be part of a cult ritual. Such was probably the case with Sean Sellers, who together with a fellow teenage devil worshiper, conducted the ritual murder of a convenience store clerk in 1985. The next year, Sean shot and killed his parents as they slept (C. P. Ewing, 1990a). In February, 1999, Sellers became the first person in 40 years to be put to death for a crime committed at age 16 ("Oklahoma man," 1999).

When the killing occurs within a cult context, the involvement seems apparent. However, when members of a cult kill someone, it is often not clear whether membership in the cult played a causative role in the killing, or whether the cult's influence was only incidental to the psychological makeup of the perpetrators.

Peer-Group-Related Killings. Many killings by juveniles occur in the context of a loosely organized peer group. Such was the case for a 15-year-old Pennsylvania girl killed while in the midst of a group of peers she barely knew. The incident occurred after the victim, described as overweight and wanting to "fit in," became involved with a group of teenagers who were planning to run away to Florida. When one of the members of the so-called "runaway gang" suggested that the victim might tell adults of their plans, the group decided to teach the girl a lesson. The victim was first hung by her neck with a rope until unconscious, then killed by being smashed in the head with a rock the size of a basketball. A 16-year-old female was subsequently convicted of the murder and sentenced to life in prison. Five other teenagers were also convicted of lesser crimes in the incident (Coates, 1998; Kinney, 1999; "16-year-old," 1999).

KILLINGS BY PREADOLESCENTS AND FEMALES

Although most juvenile murders are committed by adolescent males, younger children or females also kill. We now examine these two situations.

Preadolescents

Preadolescents rarely commit homicide. Between 1987 and 1996, children under the age of 10 accounted for less than 1% of all juvenile arrests for homicide, and children ages 10 to 12 accounted for less than 1.5% of such arrests (Heide, 1999). In absolute figures, the number of youths under the age of 10 who commit murder each year can be counted on the fingers of two hands (Snyder & Sickmund, 1999).

Preadolescents' Ability to Murder. At what age do youngsters develop a mature understanding of what it means to kill someone else, and at what age can they intentionally act to do so? In order to answer these questions, we first discuss the following related questions:

1. When do children understand the concept of "life"?
2. When do children understand the concept of "death"?
3. When can children begin actually decide to carry out some desire?
4. When do children understand the difference between reality and fantasy?

Jean Piaget concluded that young children were confused about what is alive and what is not (Papalia et al., 1999). Later research, however, indicated that by the age of 4, children generally understand the difference between living things and nonliving things (Gelman, Spelke, & Meck, 1983).

In order to really understand what it means to kill someone, children must not only understand what "life" means, but also what "death" means. Research suggests that most children understand the three components of the *finality, irreversibility,* and *universality* of death by age 9 (Crase & Crase, 1976; Nagy, 1948; Stambrook & Parker, 1987). However, children younger than age 9 seem to have an impaired ability to experience the emotions associated with death (Menig-Peterson & McCabe, 1977–1978).

Interestingly, children's understanding of human death develops before their understanding of animal death (Orbach, Gross, Glaubman, & Berman, 1985). Children who have experienced the death of someone close to them seem to have a stronger attraction to death and a greater repulsion toward life than do other children (Gutierrez, King, & Ghaziuddin, 1996). Some research also suggests that hopeless children are less repulsed by death than are more hopeful children (Cotton & Range, 1993). Finally, suicidal children seem to have less mature concepts of death and to see death as more attractive and less permanent than do nonsuicidal children. However, aggressive children's concepts regarding death have not been investigated (Cuddy-Casey & Orvaschel, 1997).

Another issue concerns the question of whether children can intend to harm or kill someone. To do so requires, in part, that children understand the relationship between their thought and their behavior. Research suggests that, by age 5, children know that their desires lead to their actions, they know that they can create their desires, and they know that they can engage in behaviors they desire (see Siegler, 1998, for a discussion).

We know that young children often play pretend games involving guns and death. At what point, however, do children understand the difference between reality and fantasy, between what really is, and what only seems to be? Research on this topic indicates that by age 5, children have a fairly good idea of the distinction between reality and fantasy. They understand the difference between a real dog and a dog in a dream, between something invisible but real (such as air) and something imaginary, and between pretend and not pretend (see Papalia et al., 1999, for a discussion). It thus appears that by age 5, children typically have at least some understanding of what is real and what is fantasy or make believe (J. H. Flavell, E. R. Flavell, & Green, 1983).

In light of this research, it appears that at least by age 9, most children are cognitively able to understand what it means to kill another person and to intend to carry out that action. At the same time, however, even older juveniles might not meet the legal criteria necessary for full adult culpability (Zimring, 1998).

Intrafamilial Killings.   Many killings by young children involve family members, and the motives and dynamics for intrafamilial murders are often the same for young family members as they are for older members (C. P. Ewing, 1990a). As with older youth, most parricides committed by preteens involve patricide (C. P. Ewing, 1990b). In one striking case, a 3-year-old boy in Detroit shot his father to death as the father was beating the boy's mother. Although the mother described the killing as an accident, the boy reportedly told authorities: "I killed him. Now he's dead. If he would have hit my mother, I would have shot him again" (as quoted in C. P. Ewing, 1990b, p. 25). At first, police did not believe that the boy had perpetrated the crime, but forensics tests confirmed that the boy was the only person present who shot the gun (C. P. Ewing, 1990b).

Interestingly, the most common killing perpetrated by preteens involves fratricide (DeBecker, 1997). In one case in Oregon, a 9-year-old boy allegedly punished his 5-year-old sister for refusing to go to her room by killing her with his father's hunting rifle. The mother testified that she left the boy in charge of his two younger siblings while she took three older children to a dance rehearsal. When the sister refused to go to her room, the boy took an empty rifle from a closet, loaded it with shells that he found in a brother's foot locker, and shot his sister ("Brother accused," 1995).

Petti and Davidman (1981) described a sample of 9 children ages 6 to 11, 7 of whom either tried or succeeded in killing one or more of their siblings. Two of the 9 were living in intact homes, 3 had been abused, and 7 were depressed. Three were characterized as borderline psychotic, but none was frankly psychotic.

Extrafamilial Killings.   As with intrafamilial killings, when preteens kill outside the family, they often kill younger children. In one graphic 1994 case, two boys, ages 10 and 11, were convicted of dropping a 5-year-old to his death from a 14th story window in a Chicago public housing project. The victim's 8-year-old brother fought unsuccessfully to help his sibling. According to police, the killing was in retaliation for the fact that the victim had refused to steal candy for the older boys. Both assailants had criminal records at the time of the arrest, and both said their fathers were in prison ("Boy, 5," 1994).

In some cases, the victims are infants. Adelson (1972) reported five instances in which children under the age of 8 killed infants. All victims died of craniocerebral trauma: Two were dropped on the floor, one was hit with metal toys, another was bitten and struck repeatedly with a shoe, and the last one was hit with the leg of a spinning wheel. Overall, Adelson attributed these killings to the young killers' jealousy, rage, and lack of impulse control, as well as to the relative frailty of the victims' heads.

One bizarre example of this type of killing occurred in a 1998 case in which a 2½-year-old girl killed her 10-month-old brother by drowning him in a bathtub while the mother slept after a night of partying. Testifying for the prosecution, the mother's fiance said that the girl often hit her brother and had previously tried to smother him in his crib. A jury decided that the mother had feloniously neglected her son ("Mom who slept," 1999).

Ewing concluded that easy accessibility of firearms in the home "is indeed a major factor in homicides committed by preteens" (C. P. Ewing, 1990b, p. 98). In general, Ewing argues that acts of killing by younger children are less intentional and more impulsive than are killings by older children. In some cases, these children are emotionally disturbed, but more often they are simply immature and do not comprehend the finality of their act (C. P. Ewing, 1990b).

The Bulger Case.   One of the most publicized killings involving young children took place in Liverpool, England, in February, 1993. Two 10-year-old boys, playing hookey from school, abducted 2-year-old James Bulger from a shopping center, walked with him for 2½ miles to a railway yard, and then beat him to death with bricks and an iron bar (Morrison, 1997).

Both Robert Thompson and Jon Venables lived in a low socioeconomic neighborhood, and both came from troubled families (Morrison, 1997). Both boys had often been truant from school, and when they did attend school, both boys were described as troublesome. The headmistress of their school described Robert as a cunning liar, and another teacher said that Robert lied naturally and made bullets for others to shoot. According to a log that one teacher kept of Jon's behavior, he defied school control, stood on desks, threw chairs, butted his head against the wall, pulled artwork off the wall, slashed himself on purpose with scissors, cut holes in his socks, once hung himself upside down from coat pegs like a bat, and once pinned a child's throat to a desk with a 12-inch ruler before finally being dragged off. Groundings and deprivations had no effect, and the teacher said that on the day before the attack, Jon's behavior was the worst she had seen (Morrison, 1997).

On the day of the killing, Jon allegedly said: "Let's get a kid, I haven't hit one for ages" (Morrison, 1997, p. 45). And Robert allegedly said: "Let's get this kid lost, let's get him lost outside so when he goes into the road he'll get knocked over" (Morrison, 1997, p. 45). Robert and Jon found James standing outside a butcher shop in the shopping center while his mother was inside buying a piece of meat. In less than 2 minutes, James held out his hand to the two older boys, who then led him out of the center and on a 2½-mile walk back to their neighborhood. Before beginning their journey, they first tried to get James to drown in some water; failing this, they dropped him on his head, producing a big bump. On their 2-hour walk, they encountered numerous adults, none of whom intervened (Morrison, 1997).

Arriving back in Robert's neighborhood only 100 yards from a police station, which Robert knew was there, they took James up a bank and through a gap in the fence and into a railway yard. There they smeared blue paint on him, threw bricks at him, and hit him with an iron bar. When James no longer moved, they placed him, apparently still alive, over a train track, where a train would later sever his body in two (Morrison, 1997).

Robert and Jon were subsequently convicted and sentenced to a minimum term of 8 years ("Boys who killed toddler," 2000).

Females Who Kill

As we have seen, girls are much less likely to commit murder than are boys. Because they so rarely murder, little research has been done on youthful female killers.

Intrafamilial Killings. Females are much more likely to participate in intrafamilial killings than in the killing of strangers (Rowley et al., 1987; Snyder & Sickmund, 1995). Interestingly, intrafamilial killings committed by females differ in two major ways from those committed by males. In the first place, girls are more likely to have accomplices than are males. For example, Rowley et al. (1987) found that in 95% of the cases in which intrafamilial homicides were committed by more than one person, the perpetrator related to the victim was a female. Second, although older males are more likely to kill their fathers and younger boys are more apt to kill their siblings, older females are more likely to kill young infants, a process called *infanticide.* In fact, intrafamilial infanticide is "committed almost exclusively by females" (C. P. Ewing, 1990b, p. 107), especially by unwed teenage mothers seeking to conceal their status as a mother.

One such case involved 18-year-old New Jersey high school student Melissa Drexler. On the way to her senior prom, Drexler began having cramps. Arriving at the prom site, she went into a bathroom stall where she delivered a baby, then strangled it to death. Until that time, Drexler had managed to hide her pregnancy, and according to a psychiatric report in the case, acknowledging the baby was something she could not do. Drexler later pleaded guilty to aggravated manslaughter and was sentenced to 15 years in prison ("Woman who threw away," 1998).

Females also sometimes enlist the aid of a boyfriend or older male to kill a parent, often because the parent has been abusive or because the parent objects to the daughter's romantic involvement (C. P. Ewing, 1990b). In addition, females might also kill a parent because they object to a parent's romantic partner ("Kids charged," 1999).

Extrafamilial Killings.   When girls kill outside the family, the victim is likely to be a friend or acquaintance; the situation is more likely to involve interpersonal conflict rather than a crime; the weapon is more likely to be a knife than a firearm; and, as with intrafamilial killings, the girl is also likely to have an accomplice (Loper & Cornell, 1996). In one such type of killing, the victim is a romantic rival. In a 1995 Texas case, for example, a high school senior enticed her boyfriend to help her kill a sophomore girl with whom the boyfriend allegedly had a one-night sexual affair. When David Graham told Diane Zamora about his affair, Zamora became upset and insisted that the two kill 16-year-old Adrianne Jones. According to confessions the two gave 10 months after the killing, Graham lured Jones into his car while Zamora hid in the trunk. After Graham had driven to a secluded spot and had stopped the car, Zamora got out of the trunk and hit Jones over the head with a dumbbell. Graham then shot Jones twice in the head. A few months after the slaying, Graham entered the Air Force Academy and Zamora entered the Naval Academy. The couple was arrested after Zamora told one of her academy classmates about the killing. Both were subsequently convicted of murder (Romano, 1998).

Girls occasionally but rarely kill in the course of perpetrating other crimes. In such situations, however, they almost always have accomplices. Ewing states that although these killings are rare, "they are likely to be among the most heinous of all juvenile killings" (C. P. Ewing, 1990b, p. 109). A famous example of this phenomenon involves the case of Paula Cooper. At the age of 13, Cooper and three other teenage girls robbed the home of an elderly Bible teacher in Indiana. In the course of the robbery, Cooper stabbed the woman 33 times with a foot-long butcher knife. The girls fled with $10 and the victim's car (C. P. Ewing, 1990b).

CHARACTERISTICS OF YOUTHFUL KILLERS

What characterizes youthful killers? Do these youngsters differ in systematic ways from "normal" children who do not have problems with the law, or from youngsters who are antisocial but not violent? And are there differences between violent youths who kill and those who do not? Although these are important questions, they are difficult to answer definitively. For one thing, many of the relevant published studies involve clinical impressions as opposed to measures from well-validated research instruments. In addition, even when controlled research has been undertaken, many of the samples have been unsatisfactory, both in terms of quantity and quality.

Research

Despite these problems, investigators are now beginning to provide answers to important questions. Researchers have examined subgroups of juvenile killers

(Myers, Scott, A. W. Burgess, & A. G. Burgess, 1995) and have compared juvenile killers with other violent juveniles, with nonviolent delinquents, and with nondelinquent control groups (Lewis et al., 1988; Santtila & Haapasalo, 1997; Zagar, Arbit, Hughes, Busell, & Busch, 1989; Zagar et al., 1990). The results of these studies indicate that juvenile killers differ from nonviolent delinquents in the following ways:

• *Youngsters who kill live in a conflict-filled family atmosphere in which they often experience physical violence on the part of the father* (Bailey, 1996; Lewis et al., 1988; Myers et al., 1995; Santtila & Haapasalo, 1997; Zagar et al., 1989, 1990). This finding is especially interesting in light of other research suggesting that hyper-aggressive youths are more likely to experience violence in the home than to simply witness it (Schwartz et al., 1997; Truscott, 1992).

• *These youngsters have neurological dysfunctions (especially seizures), which might hinder learning and impede impulse control* (Lewis et al., 1988; Zagar et al., 1989, 1990). This finding is consistent with evidence of frontal cortex dysfunction among impulsive adult killers (Raine et al., 1998), as well as with a case study in which a homicidal youth was found to have a brain lesion in the right nucleus amygdalae (Martinius & Strunk, 1979).

• *Some adolescent killers might also experience periodic psychotic symptoms (such as auditory or visual hallucinations or paranoid ideation) which might contribute to their behavior* (Lewis et al., 1988). However, few appear to be frankly psychotic at the time of evaluation (Cornell et al., 1987).

• *As children, adolescent murderers develop a set of aggressive responses, which seem to become progressively more violent as they grow older* (Lewis et al., 1988; Myers et al., 1995; Zagar et al., 1989, 1990). However, many of them have no history of prior arrests (Cornell et al., 1987).

• *These youths begin to abuse hard drugs and alcohol at an early age and to join gangs, thus further exacerbating their aggressive tendencies* (Bailey, 1996; Santtila & Haapasalo, 1997; Zagar et al., 1989, 1990).

It should be noted that much of this research was conducted on youthful killers who were spending time in prison for their crimes. As such, it tends to exclude youngsters who may have killed but who were not convicted, or whose psychological state rendered them legally insane. It is likely that this research tends to apply more to chronically aggressive children, rather than to typically nonviolent children who kill because their inhibitions have been overwhelmed by stress.

Although the preceding characteristics seem to differentiate young killers from nonviolent delinquents, researchers have had more difficulty in differentiating juvenile killers from other violent juveniles (Lewis et al., 1988; Santtila & Haapasalo, 1997). Indeed, Lewis and colleagues argued that juvenile killers are very much like other violent youngsters and that "with few exceptions, homicide by juveniles is *not* a single act of uncontrolled violence in an otherwise peaceful childhood" (Lewis et al., 1988, p. 587, emphasis in the original). Other researchers have suggested that juvenile killers are characterized by the so-called *homicidal triad* of enuresis, fire-setting, and cruelty to animals (C. P. Ewing, 1990a). Although some research does support the inclusion of enuresis and cruelty to animals in this group (C. P. Ewing, 1990a; Santtila & Haapasalo, 1997), the empirical basis for this claim remains weak. Perhaps, as some researchers suggest, the only difference between juvenile killers and other violent delinquents is "the luck of the draw" (Lewis et al., 1988, p. 587).

RISK FACTORS

Because juvenile killers appear for the most part to be a subset of hyperaggressive youth in general, many of the factors that have been identified as contributing to the etiology of youthful killers are the same biological, intrapersonal, familial, and social–environmental risk factors that we already discussed in conjunction with children's aggressive behavior in general. In this section, I emphasize some of the factors that seem to be particularly relevant for an understanding of juvenile killers.

Biological Factors

As we have seen, homicidal youths have been found to have neurological dysfunctions, often accompanied by seizures (Lewis et al., 1988; Zagar et al., 1989, 1990).

Intrapersonal Processes

Deindividuation and Diffusion of Responsibility. We have seen that homicides involving more than one juvenile offender tend to involve more violence than those in which the perpetrator acts alone and that the presence of more than one juvenile tends to increase the probability that a homicide will be committed. This type of synergistic effect that youths have on each other in a potential homicide situation was captured in *Lord of the Flies* (Golding, 1955). Initially, the boys acted like proper British lads. Once they started to paint themselves and to begin their descent into savagery, however, their individuality became lost in a kind of group frenzy. The group chant, *"Kill the pig. Cut her throat. Spill her blood"* became a repeated refrain which seemed to have a sort of mesmerizing effect on all involved (Golding, 1955, p. 63, emphasis in original).

From a psychological point, these kinds of behaviors are probably best understood in terms of the concepts of *deindividuation* and *diffusion of responsibility.* Deindividuation refers to the tendency of people within groups to lose their individual identities and to become anonymous members of the groups (Zimbardo, 1969). This process probably occurs most often when youths become involved with large groups, such as cults or gangs. Closely associated with deindividuation is the concept of diffusion of responsibility (Mynatt & Sherman, 1975). When a youth acts alone, there is no one onto whom he can project responsibility for his action. However, when youngsters act in groups, they can each project (or diffuse) their personal responsibility onto the other members of the group, thus in effect denying any personal responsibility. This process might operate in many situations in which two or more youths commit homicides together. This process might also help explain why group homicides (such as the case in which Paula Cooper stabbed an elderly woman 33 times with a one-foot-long butcher knife) are often so heinous.

Thrill-Seeking. Some killings, especially "senseless" ones, might reflect the fact that the adolescent is hypoaroused and finds such behavior "fun." In a review, Heide states that many young killers are "bored" rather than angry, and that for these youths, "robbing and using guns often seemed like fun and a way in which to reduce boredom" (Heide, 1999, p. 48).

Indeed, the word "fun" often occurs in connection with the motives of youthful killers. For example, when a 19-year-male begged his three "friends" to tell him why they were beating him to death with baseball bats, one of them replied: "Because it's fun, Steve" (C. P. Ewing, 1990a, p. 77). Another youthful killer described his antisocial behavior this way: "It was fun. It's like getting away with something. It's like a high, excitement" (Treaster, 1992, p. D6). The 16-year-old female convicted in the hanging and beating death of the 15-year-old girl reportedly said: "It was fun to hang someone" (Kinney, 1999, p. A1). A 17-year old girl, describing how she feels after stabbing someone, said: "I feel good" (Kennedy, 1992, p. D5). And finally, a 14-year-old gang member put it like this: "Anybody can just sit around, just drink, smoke a little Thai. But that ain't fun like shootin' guns and stabbin' people. *That's* fun" (Bing, 1991, p. 49, emphasis in the original).

Nonconventional Attitudes. Many young killers seem to lack attachments to significant others, to the larger society, or to both. It is also clear that many of these young killers are not involved in conventional activities and do not believe in the benefits of conforming to social conventions. Thus, many young killers disdain school and join gangs (Bailey, 1996; Lewis et al., 1988; Myers et al., 1995; Zagar et al., 1989, 1990). As Heide (1997) said, "Many of the young killers whom I evaluated were not involved in conventional and prosocial activities, such as school, sports, or work" (p. 213).

Many young killers also seem to lack the moral values of the larger society, particularly those related to the value of life. Cruelty to animals characterizes the behavior of some young killers (Santtila & Haapasalo, 1997). In addition, many of these youths also seem to believe that human life is unimportant. For example, Treaster (1992) reported that the young killers whom he interviewed "did not seem to care much, one way or the other," about the consequences of their actions (p. A1). And a 17-year-old girl, describing what it is like to stab someone, said "It's like cutting meat. It's like you start in and you want to keep on stabbing them" (Kennedy, 1992, p. D5).

Garbarino (1999) employed the concept of the *moral circle* to explain this type of attitude. According to Garbarino, some aggressive acts lie inside our moral circle of justification and are not morally permitted, whereas others lie outside our moral circle and are hence justified. For example, for many of us, killing a human being lies inside our moral circle and hence is not permitted, whereas killing a worm lies outside our moral circle and is thus morally justified. Garbarino argues that many inner city youths have relatively small moral circles. For example, when one youth "disses" a second youth, that act places the first youth outside the moral circle of the second youth, and hence morally justifies retaliation on the part of the second youth (Garbarino, 1999).

Anger and Hate.   Anecdotally, anger and hate have been linked to killings by juveniles. As we saw in chapter 8, for example, 14-year-old Sidewinder, incarcerated for his part in a drive-by shooting, explained that sometimes he gets so angry that he has to do something to get his anger out, even if it means shooting at somebody. As for hate, we have already seen that some killings by youths seem to be motivated by hatred toward certain groups. Despite these anecdotal reports, however, little systematic research has been conducted on the relationship between these two emotions and juvenile homicide.

Pessimism and Hopelessness.   Some young killers might also exhibit a *pessimistic* cognitive framework and believe that they have no control over their fate (Seligman, 1995). For example, Petti and Davidman (1981) found that a group of nine homicidal 6- to 11-year-olds perceived themselves as more externally controlled than did members of a contrast group. Feeling a lack of self-control, such children might eventually develop symptoms of *learned helplessness* such as passivity, apathy, lethargy, and even clinical depression. Ultimately, they may come to believe that there is no hope.

Some children might develop a sense of hopelessness from growing up in an abusive family situation. They perceive their situation to be so bad that only killing the abuser will alleviate it: No matter what the consequences, nothing could be worse than continuing to experience the abuse. For other youths, hopelessness might be the result of growing up in a poverty stricken environment in which violence is endemic, life-expectancy is short, and escape is perceived to be impossible (Garbarino, 1999).

Research indicates that suicidal and hopeless children seem to perceive death as more attractive than do other children (Cotton & Range, 1993; Cuddy-Casey

& Orvaschel, 1997). It is possible that such is also the case for at least certain types of homicidal children. We might hypothesize that these children, having come to believe that life is hopeless, might find killing another person less repulsive than would normally be the case. In Heide's (1999) words, "many young killers growing up in the 1990s have *little or nothing left to lose*" (p. 49, emphasis in the original).

Arousal, Disinhibition, and Desensitization. The processes of *arousal, disinhibition,* and *desensitization* (discussed in chap. 6) might also play a role in acts of homicide committed by juveniles.

Arousal and disinhibition are closely related. Under high levels of arousal, cognitive processes can be overwhelmed by emotional processes and cortical inhibitions can be weakened by subcortical excitation. In many cases, young killers find themselves in emotionally arousing circumstances. These include situations in which youths are involved in another crime, when they are sexually aroused, or when they are in the company of a group of peers.

Desensitization and disinhibition might also be related. As discussed in other contexts, becoming immersed in violent television shows, songs, video games, or all of these can potentially reduce a youngster's negative emotional reaction to violence, thus leading to disinhibition of already existing violent responses.

Family Factors

The family life of youthful killers is often characterized by conflict, physical and sexual abuse, and alcohol and drug abuse, most often on the part of the father (Heide, 1995, 1999; Lewis et al., 1988; Mones, 1991; Morris, 1985; Zagar et al., 1989, 1990). Indeed, child abuse (especially physical abuse) is probably the best documented antecedent of youthful homicide.

Changes in family structure and child neglect have also been linked to childhood aggression (Heide, 1997, 1999). Heide pointed out that changes in family life in the last 25 years often manifest themselves as a lack of parental supervision and monitoring, conditions that also contribute to youth violence. As Heide (1999) said, "Many of the adolescent homicide offenders I examine are not in school during the day and are out late at night. Their parents do not know where they are, in what activities they are involved, or with whom they are associating" (p. 41).

Another effect associated with the changes in family structure involves the absence of a positive male role model and the relationship between single mothers and their sons. Heide (1997) argued that when fathers are absent, young males are more likely to exaggerate their "masculinity," mostly in manifestations of aggressive behavior. In addition, Heide (1997) also stated that although violent sons may profess to love mothers, they often do not obey them. She quotes one homicidal male as saying about his mother, " 'She give me anything.

She try to tell me what good and what bad for me. But, I just, I didn't listen'"
(Heide, 1997, p. 208).

Although parents are often blamed for their children's homicidal behavior,
many parents of youthful killers have been aware of their child's violent behavior and have tried, unsuccessfully, to do something about it. For example, the
parents of the Freeman brothers had placed their sons in residential treatment
(Bayles, 1995); the parents of school shooter Kip Kinkel had gotten counseling
for him (L. Dodge, 1998); and the parents of Sam Manzie had petitioned the
court to have him committed to a treatment facility (Curran, 1999). In each
case, however, the youth subsequently killed one or more persons, thus illustrating the fact that even when parents try to do the right thing, they are not
always able to stop the violence of their offspring.

Social-Environmental Factors

Homicides by children and adolescents have also been blamed on a number
of social and environmental factors, including poverty, racism, violent neighborhoods, the prevalence of drugs and guns, media violence, and a culture that
encourages violence (Heide, 1997).

Interaction Effects

As with children's aggression in general, it is unlikely that youthful homicide
is caused by a single factor. Many young killers experience multiple risk factors.
At the same time, many of these youngsters typically lack the protective factors
that seem to be important in helping them resist antisocial behavior. In the
words of Lewis et al. (1988):

> Individually, each of the vulnerabilities characteristic of juvenile murderers may
> be present, to a greater or lesser extent, in nonviolent delinquents and even in
> nondelinquents. It is, rather, the combination of serious intrinsic vulnerabilities
> in the context of an abusive or violent environment that is associated with the
> development of aggression. (p. 587)

Thus, although none of the factors just discussed might cause homicidal behavior by itself, their combination can be lethal, both for the youngster and his
victim.

SUBTYPES OF YOUTHFUL KILLERS

Juvenile killers are not a homogeneous group. They come from a variety of
backgrounds, kill for a variety of motives, and use a variety of means. Each is a
unique individual who can only be understood in the context of his or her own

life history. Nevertheless, as an aid to understanding, Cornell (1998) has suggested that these youngsters can profitably be subdivided into three subtypes, which I label the *psychotic* group, the *overstressed* group, and the *aggressive* group.

Psychotic Killers

Psychotic killers are those who experience a full-blown psychosis or a psychotic episode that limits their understanding of reality and leads them to kill without an appreciation of what they are doing. As we have seen, some young killers exhibit psychotic symptoms such as delusions and hallucinations (Lewis et al., 1988). Youngsters with delusions of paranoia might feel that the only way to escape their perceived persecution is through killing; alternatively, psychotic youths might experience auditory hallucinations directing them to kill. In either case, their psychological disturbance might drive them to engage in a homicidal act that they never would have committed in the absence of a psychotic disorder. It is thus possible that at least some juvenile killings might be due to the presence of a psychosis or a psychotic incident.

Most controlled research suggests that few young killers are frankly psychotic. For example, Cornell et al. (1987) found that only 7% of the 72 young killers whom they studied were psychotic at the time of the incident. In a review, Heide (1999) suggested that young killers might experience more mood disorders and brief psychotic episodes than cases of chronic psychosis, which the author concluded are rare among this population.

Overstressed Killers

Some young killers, rather than being psychotic, seem to kill because they are stressed beyond the limits of their frustration tolerance. This group is similar to Megargee's (1966) concept of the *overcontrolled* assaultive offender who aggresses only under extreme stress, but then does so very violently. In general, these youngsters exhibit reactive aggression in situations in which they lose control (Cornell, 1998).

In some cases, these youths might be psychologically normal children who experience an overwhelming amount of stress in their lives. Perhaps the best example of this type of killer is the child who commits parricide after growing up in an abusive home, especially if the abuse also targets the mother and other siblings. In many cases, these children put up with abuse for years. At some point, however, the abuse exceeds a threshold which the child can no longer tolerate, thus precipitating the killing (Darby, Allan, & Kashani, 1998).

In other cases, the child might have certain psychological characteristics, which interact with environmental stressors to precipitate the killing. For example, some children with attention-deficit/hyperactivity disorder (or impulsive tendencies) or who suffer from clinical depression might be unable to control their impulses in the presence of an environmental stressor. Under nonstressful circumstances, such children would never consider killing someone. Under provocation, however, these children might be more likely to kill than children who lack their psychological vulnerabilities.

Intellectually, youths in this group might be slightly below normal to above normal. They might have strong social bonds and an internalized set of appropriate moral values. And yet, although they may feel they have been wronged, they are unable to express their hurt and anger in an appropriate fashion. In some cases, a "final straw" may strip away the last vestige of their frustration tolerance. At least in their present psychological condition, killing becomes the only way out.

This group appears to be similar to Cornell's classification of youths who kill while involved in an intense interpersonal conflict or dispute with someone else (Cornell et al., 1987). Because their actions involve interpersonally generated stress, we would expect these youths to kill either family members or acquaintances, rather than strangers. Motives seem to involve escape, retaliation, or revenge. Research indicates that this group scores relatively high on stressful life events but relatively low on school adjustment problems, substance abuse, and prior criminality (see Heide, 1999, for a summary).

This subtype seems to account for the apparently "good kids" who suddenly "snap" and commit murders that seem to be totally out of character for them. Children who kill bullies probably belong to this group, as might at least some of the youths who have been involved in school killings. However, more research must be done in order to validate the characteristics of this group.

Aggressive Killers

A third subtype of juvenile killer is characterized by a long history of aggressive and antisocial behavior (Lewis et al., 1988; Myers et al., 1995; Zagar et al., 1989, 1990). This group, consisting of perhaps half of all juvenile killers (Cornell, 1998), seems similar to those described as *antisocial* (Cornell, 1998), *undercontrolled* (Megargee, 1966), *nonempathic* (Zenoff & Zients, 1979) or *nihilistic* (Heide, 1999). These youths are motivated by antisocial goals and use instrumental aggression to get what they want (Cornell, 1998).

We might expect these children to have a psychiatric diagnosis of either oppositional defiant disorder or conduct disorder, perhaps in conjunction with ADHD. Appearing to fit the picture of young killers painted by Lewis, Zagar, and other researchers, these youngsters typically come from at-risk homes, have certain physical and neurocognitive deficits, fail in school both academically and socially, use and abuse both legal and illegal drugs, and become involved with gangs. Cognitively, we might expect these youngsters to have normal to below normal IQs as well as a hostile–attributional bias. In terms of personality characteristics, we might hypothesize that these youngsters are "thrill seekers" who have a low level of frustration tolerance and a poor ability to regulate their behavior.

This group is similar to Cornell's category of youths who kill in the course of some other crime (Cornell et al., 1987). Compared with those in the conflict-related group, young crime-related killers exhibit more evidence of psychopathology, show more serious histories of substance abuse and prior delinquent behavior, are more likely to act with others, are more likely to dehumanize others, and are more likely to respond violently when frustrated (Heide, 1999). Heide (1999) characterized these youngsters as becoming animated when describing incidents in which they have intimidated others, have beaten others badly, or have destroyed other living things such as dogs, cats, and lizards. These youngsters most probably kill acquaintances or strangers rather than family members. We would expect these killers to be involved in crime-related and senseless killings, and in gang-related killings.

SCHOOL SHOOTINGS

Between February, 1996, and April 20, 1999, the United States was shocked by six shooting incidents at schools across the country. In all cases, the shooters were students at the school. In the course of these shootings, 25 students, three teachers, and three parents died at the hands of a total of eight young killers, two of whom killed themselves as well. Details of these shootings are described in Box 10.1.

Some commonalities emerged from these six incidents. First, all the killers were White males between the ages of 11 and 18, whereas the majority of victims were female students. Second, all the incidents involved random shootings and more than one death. Third, all occurred in small towns or suburbs rather than in urban areas. And fourth, all the killings were carried out with guns, and in four of the cases, multiple guns were used.

Attempts to understand these shootings face a number of obstacles. First, because virtually no controlled research on this phenomenon has been conducted, most of what we know comes from less reliable and less valid anecdotal reports such as interviews and media accounts. Relatedly, relatively little reliable information regarding the psychology of these youngsters has come from public trials or hearings. Indeed, of the eight killers, only Barry Loukaitis and Luke Woodham had full-fledged trials. Michael Carneal, Mitchell Johnson, and Kip Kinkel pleaded guilty without a trial; a judge found Andrew Golden guilty after quickly rejecting a plea of temporary insanity; and Eric Harris and Dylan Klebold both killed themselves. In view of these methodological problems, any conclusions regarding the psychology of school shooters must be considered tentative and open to revision. However, our current knowledge suggests the following tentative portrait of youthful school shooters.

BOX 10.1

SUMMARY OF U.S. SCHOOL SHOOTINGS, 1996–1999

Moses Lake, Washington

In February, 1996, 14-year-old Barry Loukaitis, dressed in an all-black cowboy outfit, walked into his junior high school mathematics class, pulled out a rifle from under a trenchcoat and opened fire, killing two students and a teacher, wounding another student, and holding the class hostage. Although defense attorneys argued that Loukaitis suffered from a mental illness compounded by an unstable family life and an obsession with violent media, he was later found guilty of three counts of murder ("Washington teen found guilty," 1997).

Pearl, Mississippi

On October 1, 1997, 16-year-old Luke Woodham entered Pearl High School and opened fire with a rifle. Two classmates were killed and seven others were wounded. One of the victims was Woodham's former girlfriend, who had recently broken up with him. Hours before the shooting, Woodham had also stabbed to death his 50-year-old mother. Woodham was later convicted of all three murders and sentenced to life in prison (Edsall, 1997; Hughes, 1998a, 1998b).

West Paducah, Kentucky

Just before classes began at Heath High School in West Paducah, on December 1, 1997, 14-year-old Michael Carneal opened fire on a group of students who were leaving a prayer gathering in the school's lobby. Three students were killed and five were wounded (Bridis, 1997a, 1997b; "Eight students shot," 1997). Carneal subsequently pleaded guilty but mentally ill, thereby receiving a sentence of life in prison without possibility of parole for 25 years (Prichard, 1998).

(Box continues)

Hypothesized Dynamics

Youths who engage in school shootings are typically White males who live in suburban areas or small towns. From their early years, these youngsters seem to have a difficult temperament, to be noncompliant and oppositional, and to exhibit anger and aggression, especially in reaction to frustration. However, although they might also show an interest in violence from an early age, school shooters are typically not considered to be major troublemakers. In some cases, in fact, they might be considered to be "good quiet kids" and hence not candidates for later lethal violence.

As young children, these youths often feel "different" and have trouble "fitting in" with their peers. They might have academic problems, especially in reading.

BOX 10.1 *(Continued)*

Jonesboro, Arkansas

In Jonesboro, on March 24, 1998, 11-year-old Andrew Golden first pulled the fire alarm in Westside Middle School, then ran outside and joined 13-year-old Mitchell Johnson in opening fire on students and staff who were pouring out of the school in response to the alarm. When the shooting was over, four female students and a teacher were dead, and 11 others were wounded. Johnson subsequently pleaded guilty to the shootings and a judge found Golden guilty after rejecting a plea of temporary insanity (Breed, 1998; Lieb, 1998).

Springfield, Oregon

On May 21, 1998, 15-year-old Kipland "Kip" Kinkel parked his car a few blocks from Thurston High School in Springfield. Entering the cafeteria with a rifle and two handguns, Kinkel opened fire, killing two students and wounding about 24 more. The previous evening, Kinkel had shot his parents to death (Barnard, 1998a, 1998b). Kinkel was subsequently sentenced to 112 years in prison after pleading guilty to four counts of murder and 26 counts of attempted murder (Barnard, 1999).

Littleton, Colorado

The most notorious recent case of U.S. school killings occurred in the Denver suburb of Littleton on April 20, 1999. Shortly before noon, 18-year-old Eric Harris and 17-year-old Dylan Klebold began shooting and detonating bombs at Columbine High School, from which they were scheduled to graduate in less than 3 weeks. When the siege was over, 12 students and a teacher had been killed, and both Harris and Klebold had taken their own lives. In the course of securing the school, police found more than 50 bombs scattered in and around the school (Bai, 1999; Thompson, 1999).

They seem to lack the physical or psychological skills that enable most boys to develop their own niche in life, and they often perceive themselves to be friendless and neglected by other children. Furthermore, no matter how hard they try to fit in, nothing seems to work, thus leading them to adopt an external locus of control.

At some point, these youngsters begin to feel rejected by peers and adults. In some cases, their own aggressive tendencies might contribute to this state of affairs. In most cases, however, these youngsters' thought processes probably exaggerate the extent of the perceived rejection. In addition, these boys might also come to believe that they are abject failures and totally unloved, even in the face of evidence to the contrary. Consequently, they come to believe that the world is unfair and they begin to experience anger toward others, especially toward those viewed as their "enemies." Eventually, the frustration they experience in their social relationships combines with their distorted thinking and external locus of control to produce anger, hate, depression, and a sense of hopelessness.

At the same time, these youngsters seem to be attracted to things and people that exemplify the "darker side" of life, including violent entertainment. Thus, they might watch a lot of violence on television or become fascinated with violence in music, in movies, in video games, or on the Internet. As a result of such exposure, they learn new aggressive cognitive scripts, their violent tendencies become normalized, and their inhibitions against overt behavioral aggression are weakened.

In addition, these boys often seek out the company of others who might be similar to them in terms of perceived rejection and interest in violence. Indeed, of the eight young killers just described, four worked in pairs (Golden & Johnson; Harris & Klebold); one became a member of a cult (Woodham); and one was said to associate with antisocial peers (Kinkel). Only Loukaitis and Carneal seemed to have been loners in their endeavor. As a result of this association, the youngsters' antisocial tendencies are vindicated and reinforced, and they thus come to believe that some type of violent revenge against their perceived enemies is justified.

As time goes on, these youngsters become more obsessed with violence, and they begin to acquire guns and bomb-making materials by either legal or illegal means. The more they engage in this type of activity, the more likely they become to use their weapons of destruction.

Initially, these boys plot their revenge in fantasy. In their mind, killing their "enemies" provides them with the sense of control that they lack in their everyday social encounters. In addition, the phenomenon of the imaginary audience (described in chapter 1) leads them to believe that others will admire them for their actions, thus enabling these youngsters to attain the recognition that has eluded them for so long.

In some cases, these youngsters hope that their action will result in their own death. For example, in a statement to police, Woodham said he expected to die at the hands of police (Hughes, 1998a); Kinkel reportedly asked fellow students to kill him as they were subduing him after his shooting spree (Kirk & Boyer, 2000); and Harris and Klebold both killed themselves at the end of their massacre (Bai, 1999).

At some point, these youths might begin to experience depressive symptoms, psychotic symptoms, or both. As we have seen, depression might not only distort thought processes, but might also produce the type of hopelessness and pessimism that seems to characterize some of these youngsters. In addition, it is possible that some of these young killers might also perceive voices that encourage them in their antisocial tendencies. However, the extent to which young school killers are psychotic is difficult to determine.

Eventually, fantasy begins to override the youngster's sense of reality, and the boy takes steps to enact his fantasy into reality. Finally, some event occurs that leads the youngster into an abyss of perceived hopelessness and triggers the incident. At this point, the youth's distorted thought processes, overwhelming desire for revenge, and aroused emotional state all combine to set the lethal plan into motion.

TREATMENT AND PROGNOSIS

The fate of young killers in the United States depends on a variety of factors. Those who are tried as juveniles are typically confined to a juvenile detention facility until they reach the age of majority, usually 18. Those convicted of murder as adults face prison terms or perhaps even execution. Finally, those tried as adults but found not guilty by reason of insanity are typically committed to some type of a mental health facility.

Heide (1999) conducted an 11- to 13-year follow-up study of 59 juveniles committed for murder or attempted murder during the years 1982 and 1983. Although many of these youths had received lengthy sentences, two thirds of them had been released within that 13-year period. Those who had not yet been released had typically received extra time for offenses committed while in prison. As Heide (1999) pointed out, very few juvenile killers are sentenced to life without parole, and even fewer are sentenced to death. In view of the results of this study, it is thus clear that ultimately, most young killers are released back into society.

Treatment

Available evidence indicates that very little psychological treatment or rehabilitation occurs for juveniles incarcerated in adult prisons or in juvenile correctional facilities (Heide, 1999). Although preadolescent killers are often committed to psychiatric hospitals, such is rarely the case for adolescents, who are considered to be antisocial rather than psychologically disturbed. Adolescents are more likely to be hospitalized when they remain homicidal, when they show signs of being psychotic, or when they need intensive medical supervision (Heide, 1999).

Very little is known empirically about how to treat juvenile killers. For one thing, the research is sparse and suffers from methodological flaws (Heide, 1999). Moreover, as we have seen, the population of juvenile killers is heterogeneous; hence, therapeutic techniques that work with some young killers might not work with others, and some killers might be less amenable to therapeutic intervention than are others.

In her clinical work with young killers, Agee (1995) found that these youngsters differ from other violent youths in three ways. First, they typically minimize their homicidal behavior; thus, treatment must help them accept responsibility for their actions. Second, these young killers typically exhibit strong psychological defenses that protect them from feelings such as guilt, sadness, fear, and anger; therefore, therapy must help them identify and process these feelings. And third, they have weak egos; hence, therapy must help them develop personal and academic skills.

Based on Agee's (1995) work, Heide (1999) suggested a set of 12 therapeutic components needed for effective intervention with youthful killers (see Box 10.2). As we will see in subsequent chapters, many of these interventions are used with nonhomicidal aggressive youngsters as well. Unfortunately, the empirical effectiveness of this therapeutic package remains to be proven.

Prognosis

The prognosis for juvenile killers is difficult to determine. For one thing, the records of those processed through the juvenile justice system are often shrouded

---

BOX 10.2

COMPONENTS OF EFFECTIVE INTERVENTION
FOR JUVENILES IN CORRECTIONAL FACILITIES

Assessment

  1. Effective and extensive assessment.[a]

Ego Enhancement

  2. Education and vocational training.[b]
  3. Comprehensive cognitive-behavioral restructuring.[a]
  4. Training in prosocial skills.[a]
  5. Drug and alcohol abuse education and counseling.[a]
  6. Medication when necessary.[a]

Emotional Restructuring

  7. Anger management training.[a]
  8. Empathy training.[a]

Institutional Management

  9. Development of a positive peer culture within the institution.[a]
  10. Providing clear, firm, and consistent discipline.[a]
  11. Providing for the transition between the institution and society (including family therapy when appropriate).[a]
  12. Intensive and extended aftercare.[a]

Source: [a]Agee (1995); [b]Heide (1999).

in secrecy and little is known of the youngster's adult status. In addition, the prognosis might also depend on variables such as age, sex of the offender, and type of killing (e.g., intrafamilial, extrafamilial, crime-related, conflict-related). Finally, very few systematic postrelease studies have been performed on this population.

In a follow-up study of 59 juvenile killers already described, Heide (1999) found that slightly more than half of the 40 released killers had been returned to prison during the period of the study. Of the 21 returnees, 15 had been recommitted to prison for violent crimes, including second-degree murder, manslaughter, robbery, battery, and carrying concealed weapons. Similar results were obtained by Hagan (1997) in his study of homicide offenders who were released from a juvenile correctional facility.

Most of the evidence suggests that the prognosis is relatively good for youngsters who kill family members (Benedek, Cornell, & Staresina, 1989; Corder et al., 1976). In light of the fact that many intrafamilial killings involve otherwise nonviolent youths who kill to escape from an abusive situation, this finding is not surprising. The prognosis is more mixed, however, in the case of extrafamilial killings, and is worse for those involved in "crime-related" killings than for those involved in "conflict-related" killings. For example, in one study, Toupin (1993) found that adolescent killers in the "crime" group committed more postrelease offenses, violent offenses, and serious offenses than did those in the "conflict" group. These findings support the view that youthful killers are a heterogeneous group and suggest that extensive treatment of otherwise nonviolent killers could produce beneficial outcomes.

SUMMARY

Although the juvenile homicide rate increased dramatically from 1984 to 1993, it has since begun to decrease. Most of this increase and decline is attributable to African-American adolescent males using handguns to kill strangers and acquaintances.

Homicides committed by children and adolescents can be divided into the approximately 10% which involve the killing of a family member (intrafamilial killing) and the 90% which involve the killing of an acquaintance or stranger (extrafamilial killing).

Most intrafamilial killings involve patricide and are commonly perpetrated by adolescent males who are motivated to end the father's physical and/or sexual abuse. Matricide might be related more to emotional abuse than to physical or sexual abuse, whereas fratricide often occurs in order to eliminate a witness or to get revenge on a "more favored" family member.

A large number of extrafamilial killings occur while the young perpetrator is committing another crime, such as robbery or rape. In these cases, the killing is often due either to panic or to a desire to eliminate a witness. In some instances, sexual motives also come into play, and in others, the perpetrator is under the influence of drugs. Other extrafamilial killings involve a psychological conflict between the perpetrator and the victim, with revenge often being a major motive. Some extrafamilial killings, however, seem to be senseless.

Many youthful killings occur while the perpetrator is involved with a group of peers. In some cases, the perpetrator might be a member of an organized gang or of a cult; in other cases, the group might be more loosely organized. In any event, killings that involve two or more youths are often especially heinous.

Most youthful killing is perpetrated by adolescent males using guns to kill acquaintances and strangers. Killings by preadolescents tend to involve younger children and often seem to be due to the child's inability to control aggressive impulses, rather than to a thought-out decision. Females are more likely to kill family members (especially infants), are more likely to have accomplices, and are less likely to use a gun.

Although controlled research on youthful killers is relative rare, the studies that have been conducted to date suggest that these youngsters live in a conflictful family situation in which they often experience physical abuse, often have neurological dysfunctions that might hamper learning and impede impulse control, and might experience periodic psychotic symptoms (such as delusions or hallucinations). They develop a set of aggressive behaviors that become worse as they get older, and they often abuse drugs and join gangs at an early age. Many of the factors that have been identified as contributing to the etiology of youthful killers are the same biological, intrapersonal, familial, and social–cultural risk factors we have already discussed in conjunction with children's aggressive behavior in general.

Research suggests that young killers can be divided into a psychotic group, an overstressed group, and an aggressive group. Psychotic killers, although rare, are those whose psychosis limits their understanding of reality and leads them to kill without an appreciation of what they are doing. Overstressed killers aggress only under extreme stress, but then do so very violently. Aggressive killers, who constitute the largest group, are antisocial youths whose violence escalates and results in killing.

The youngsters involved in the rash of school shootings in the United States in the late 1990s did not suddenly become violent overnight. On the contrary, their acts were the culmination of a long-standing psychological process aimed at gaining revenge, recognition, and control.

Most juvenile killers ultimately return to the community. Unfortunately, very little is known about how to treat this group of young people. Follow-up studies indicate that the long-term prognosis is good for intrafamilial killers but worse for youths who kill in conjunction with another crime.

CHAPTER II

School Aggression

The widespread rash of threatened and actual school violence that followed the 1999 Columbine High School massacre provoked a national reexamination of issues involving school safety and youth violence ("Littleton shooting backlash," 1999). We now turn to an examination of this topic.

INTRODUCTION

Youthful aggression and violence in school is a relatively recent phenomenon. Indeed, citing evidence that most teachers in the mid-1950s considered their pupils to be either well behaved or exceptionally well behaved, Arnold Goldstein and colleagues argued that the years prior to 1960 can be called the "pre-escalation period" in American school violence (A. P. Goldstein, Harootunian, & Conoley, 1994, p. 8). Beginning in the 1960s, however, children's behavioral problems began to increase both in and out of school (Damon, 1995; Kilpatrick, 1992). By the year 2000, many school administrators considered physical violence to be a major problem in the schools ("Physical violence," 2000), and a nationwide survey revealed that 75% of parents worried about violence in the schools ("Parents rank violence," 2000).

How Common Is School Violence?

Although school violence has caught the national attention, some researchers argue that this problem has been blown out of proportion by sensationalized media coverage (E. Donohue, Schiraldi, & Zidenberg, 1998). For example, D.C. Anderson's (1998) analysis of six nationwide surveys conducted in the 1990s found only scant evidence of widespread school violence. Furthermore, according to one report, more than 99% of violent deaths of children occur off school grounds, and children have a one-in-a-million chance of being killed in school (E. Donohue et al., 1998). In addition, according to this same report, 90% of principals surveyed in a 1996 study reported no incidents of serious crime in their schools. Finally, approximately 90% of students in a 1993 survey (including those in urban schools) reported that they felt either very safe or somewhat safe at school (E. Donohue et al., 1998).

Even though such data suggest that schools are relatively safe, these might not tell the entire story. For one thing, although the number of violent incidents might not have increased, some researchers argue that school violence has changed qualitatively, especially in terms of the number of guns being brought into the schools (D. C. Anderson, 1998). Other data indicate that the situation is getting worse. For example, a study of 700 city school districts found a significant increase in school violence in nearly 40% of those districts (National League of Cities, 1994). In addition, many surveys have not measured types of behaviors that might be objectionable but not violent. Thus, although little if any data are kept on manners, politeness, and courtesy, anecdotal evidence suggests that many children show few of these "civilizing" behaviors (A. P. Goldstein, Palumbo, Striepling, & Voutsinas, 1995). Another example is language. In a telephone poll of 504 secondary school principals, 89% said they experience profane language and provocative insults toward teachers or other students on a regular basis (Barber, 1997). Thus, although increases in school violence might be difficult to document quantitatively, it does appear that student antisocial behavior and aggression are far too common in the nation's schools.

Gangs and Schools

A recent study showed that slightly more than a quarter of U.S. students believe that gangs are operating in their school (National Center for Education Statistics [NCES], 1998). However, research suggests that for the most part, organized gang violence does not occur within schools. Rather, gang members use school as a place to recruit new members and to plan gang activities, which are then conducted after school is dismissed for the day (A. P. Goldstein & Kodluboy, 1998). Actual gang violence such as shootings typically occurs outside the school, but sometimes such actions can spill over onto the school grounds or affect children coming to or from school (Kodluboy, 1997).

Schools reporting a large gang presence are likely to be in poor urban areas. In these schools, students often report being afraid both at school and on the way to and from school; they are more likely to avoid private areas of the schools such as restrooms; and they are more likely to report being victimized and to say that drugs are easy to obtain (Bastian & Taylor, 1995).

According to Spergel (1990), gang members are found disproportionately among special education students and those attending alternative education sites. Lyon, Henggeler, and Hall (1992) found greater delinquency, greater aggression, and less social maturity among male gang members than among nonmembers. It thus appears that individual gang members may be responsible for much of the violence that occurs in schools.

Correlates of School Violence

Research has delineated some correlates of school violence. As you might expect, geography plays a role: 15% of schools in large cities report serious levels of violence, compared with 6% in suburban areas, and 4% in rural areas (A. P. Goldstein et al., 1994). School size is also a factor, with less violence at smaller, more intimate schools (A. P. Goldstein et al., 1994). Vandalism is most likely to occur in schools characterized by poor upkeep and little evidence of pride in the building's physical appearance (Pablant & Baxter, 1996). Within schools, aggression occurs most frequently in crowded areas such as stairways, hallways, and cafeterias; in areas of potential isolation such as bathrooms and locker rooms; and on the playground (A. P. Goldstein et al., 1994).

TYPES OF STUDENT AGGRESSION

"Low-Level" Aggression

Although we often think of incidents such as shootings and bombings when we think of "school violence," Goldstein and colleagues emphasize the importance which so-called *low-level aggression* has on the emotional climate of the school (A. P. Goldstein, 1999, A. P. Goldstein & Conoley, 1997; A. P. Goldstein et al., 1995). This type of behavior includes not only "minor" aggression (such as verbal "bad mouthing," pushing and shoving, "incivility," and graffiti writing), but also nonaggressive antisocial behaviors (such as theft, tardiness, littering, violating rules, cursing, and being disruptive). Theft, especially, is one of the most common types of antisocial acts performed in school (Snyder & Sickmund, 1999), with 12% of teachers and 11% of students being victimized by thefts each month (G. Miller & Prinz, 1991).

Both A. P. Goldstein (1999) and Toby (1995) viewed low-level aggression as the springboard from which more violent behaviors arise: When students succeed at low-level aggression, they feel emboldened to engage in even more deviant behavior. According to A. P. Goldstein et al. (1995), school staff often must spend so much time and energy dealing with more major acts of aggression that they ignore the less-major forms, thus allowing these "subthreshold" behaviors to continue as the source for more major problems. These authors argue that "aggression at the lower levels facilitates its high-level expression," and they conclude that "'Catch it low, prevent it high'" is a productive intervention strategy" (A. P. Goldstein et al., 1995, p. 20).

Aggression Toward Property: Vandalism and Arson

Interestingly, no federal agency keeps data on school vandalism. However, from data compiled from state agencies, insurance claims, various surveys and anecdotal reports, Goldstein and Conoley (1997) conclude that "school vandalism levels are both absolutely high and still growing" (p. 14), and they estimate that such destruction costs more than $600 million every year. In addition to tangible costs, vandalism can also exert social costs that arise from things such as the unavailability of equipment and the fear students and staff may have as a result of vandalism (A. P. Goldstein & Conoley, 1997). According to A. P. Goldstein et al. (1995), school vandals are likely to be youngsters ages 11 to 16 who are chronically suspended and/or truant. They come from both sexes, all ethnic groups, and from higher as well as lower socioeconomic levels.

In addition to vandalism, schools also face the possibility of arson. In 1994, arson accounted for approximately 57% of all school fires, or about eight such fires per day. In 80% of the cases, the arsonists in these fires are juveniles (R. Jones, 1996).

Threats

In one study, 8% of teachers reported being threatened with injury in the previous year (D. C. Anderson, 1998). In one case, a 17-year-old Virginia student was allowed to return to school in the fall after making a death threat against a teacher the preceding spring ("Student back," 1996). In another episode, a Kentucky high school senior was arrested in 1998 after allegedly threatening to kill his baseball coach for not putting him in the starting lineup (McLaughlin, 1998).

Threats toward other students come in a variety of forms. For example, a 17-year-old Rhode Island student was charged with disorderly conduct after allegedly threatening to kill three female classmates (McLaughlin, 1998). More recently, threats have been made electronically, as in the case of an 18-year-old Florida man who pleaded guilty to threatening a Columbine High School student over the Internet ("Teenager pleads guilty," 2000).

Physical Aggression

Violence Toward Teachers.   One example of how schools have changed in the past 40 years involves student violence toward teachers. In 1955, 18,000 assaults on teachers were reported (A. P. Goldstein et al., 1994); by the early 1990s, this number had increased to 51,000 (D. C. Anderson, 1998; A. P. Goldstein & Kodluboy, 1998). A total of 51% of public school teachers in the United States say they have been verbally abused at some point over the course of their careers; 16% say they have been threatened; and 7% say they have been physically attacked (D. C. Anderson, 1998). And, in the period between 1992 and 1996, U.S. teachers experienced an annual average of approximately 123,000 nonfatal violent crimes (rape or sexual assault, robbery, or aggravated and simple assault; NCES, 1998). In general, middle school teachers experience more violent crime than do either high school or elementary school teachers (NCES, 1998).

Examples of aggression toward teachers abound. In St. Louis, a 51-year-old substitute teacher died, apparently of a heart attack, after being punched in the chest by a 9-year-old boy who refused to do an assignment the substitute had handed out. Witnesses said the teacher was struck several times by the boy and collapsed while trying to escape from the classroom ("Fourth-grader's assault," 1995).

Sometimes, several children conspire against a teacher. In one case, seven Georgia sixth graders plotted for months against their teacher—dumping chemicals in her iced tea, trying to trip her on stairs, and smuggling weapons into school. According to police, the four boys and three girls wanted to kill the teacher because she tried to discipline them ("Police say," 1993).

Children occasionally attack school personnel who are trying to help them. In Florida, a 5-year-old kindergarten girl was arrested for allegedly biting and scratching her 51-year-old school counselor. A school spokeswoman said the girl threw furniture, inflicted at least 27 deep scratches, and bit the female counselor's arm hard enough to cause "significant bleeding" ("5-year-old arrested," 1998).

Teasing and Bullying. As we have seen, teasing and bullying are quite common in schools around the world. Thus, one nationwide study found that 8% of students in Grades 6 through 12 reported being bullied during the 1992–1993 school year (NCES, 1998). And in one Canadian study, bullying occurred approximately once every 7 minutes on the playground and lasted for an average of approximately 38 seconds (Craig & Pepler, 1997).

Sexual Assaults and Rapes. Sexual assaults and rapes typically involve one or more males assaulting a female. In Philadelphia, two teenage boys, ages 13 and 14, were found guilty of raping a mentally disabled 13-year-old girl behind a chalkboard in a noisy classroom supervised by a substitute teacher. Classmates told police the rape occurred as other students jumped rope and chased each other around the room while the substitute teacher was alternately reading and dozing off ("Two teens convicted," 1997). In the 1996–1997 school year, 5% and 8% of schools reported at least one incident of sexual battery and rape, respectively (Snyder & Sickmund, 1999).

Disputes and Fights. Fights and arguments also occur. In 1993, six teenage girls were charged with mob assault after they got into a fight with a 15-year-old girl at a Norfolk, Virginia, high school. The 15-year-old was also charged with slashing four of the other girls with a box cutter ("Teens charged," 1993).

Sometimes, school disputes even end in court. Two fifth-grade girls twice appeared before a judge in Michigan after one of the girls said the other had verbally and physically harassed her for a year. The alleged victim claimed the other girl continually teased her, taunted her, called her names, and pulled her hair. After the victim's mother obtained a personal protection order, the girls got into another fight, prompting the judge to call them back to court and warn the parents that if the problem continued, one of them would be going to jail (Hettena, 1997; "10-year-old girls," 1997).

Possession of Weapons. Weapons' possession at school actually seems to be on the decline (NCES, 1998). According to one nationwide survey, 9% of high school students reported carrying a weapon to school at least once within a month of the study, and 7% of these students said they had been injured or threatened with a weapon at school during the previous year (Snyder & Sickmund, 1999). However, weapons possession is not limited to older youths. In one case, for example, a 5-year-old kindergartner was arrested after bringing a loaded gun to school because he allegedly wanted to kill his teacher for punishing him with a "time out." Police quoted the child as saying he wanted to kill several other pupils in addition to the teacher. Court officials said the boy got the gun from the top of his grandfather's bedroom dresser ("Angry 5-year-old," 1998).

In response to violent incidents and more stringent laws, many schools have developed what is known as a "zero tolerance" policy on the possession of weapons such as guns and knives ("Student arrested," 1999; "Student suspended," 1999). In one Virginia case, a judge reversed a 2-day suspension officials gave to a fourth-grade boy who brought a toy gun to school ("Fourth-grader," 2000).

Kidnappings and Hostage Takings. Kidnappings and hostage takings also occur. In Washington state, a 15-year-old male pulled out a semiautomatic pistol on a school bus, ordered his ex-girlfriend off the bus with him, then took her to his home, where he shot himself in the head as her father tried to break down the door (Ammons, 1998). And in Syracuse, a 14-year-old boy who tried to take a cafeteria full of students hostage fired several shots into the ceiling before being subdued by police. According to a friend, the boy said he was having trouble at home and warned that "I have a surprise for you" ("Teen captured," 1998).

Bomb Threats and Bombings. At least until recently, school bombings were relatively rare. For example, one study found 42 incidents of real and fake bombs in the nation's schools from 1993 to 1995 (School Security Report, 1995). These incidents resulted in 29 explosions, most of which occurred at high schools, with only nine of the incidents occurring at either middle or elementary schools.

More recently, however, the number of bombings and bomb threats appears to have increased. For example, in a 1998 case in West Virginia, two seniors were charged with plotting to bomb their high school graduation ceremony ("Two students charged," 1998). In another case in early April of 1999, three teenagers were arrested on suspicion of having detonated three homemade bombs at a high school in rural Texas ("Three Texas teenagers," 1999). And following the Littleton tragedy, a number of students were arrested for setting off bombs or making bomb threats in a variety of locations in the United States, including Illinois, Louisiana, Nebraska, and Virginia ("Littleton shooting backlash," 1999; "Police arrested student," 1999; "Small bomb," 1999; "Teen admits," 1999). It is unclear whether these bombings and threats are simply a short-term reaction to recent school shootings and bombings, or whether they signify the beginning of a long-term trend.

Shootings and Stabbings. Killings also occur in schools, even though they are relatively rare. For the school years 1992 to 1994, a total of 86 individuals (including 76 students) were killed intentionally either at school or on the way to or from school. For that reporting period, 78% of school-related violent deaths (including suicides) were committed by minority group students, 61% occurred in urban areas, and 87% occurred in high schools (NCES, 1998).

The Columbine shootings seem to have spurred additional shootings both at home and abroad. In the United States, for example, a 15-year-old male was accused of nonfatally shooting six classmates at his school in Georgia ("Judge: Teen," 1999), and a 6-year-old first grader allegedly shot a girl to death in front of their horrified classmates ("First-grade shooting," 2000). Fatal shootings also occurred in Canada ("Teen held," 1999) and in The Netherlands ("School shooting," 1999).

Some school children die from stabbings rather than shootings. For example, in 1993, a high school student was charged with stabbing to death another 16-year-old student at a Hampton, Virginia, high school. Police said that the altercation began inside the school and then moved to the parking lot, where the stabbing occurred ("Student killed," 1993).

POTENTIAL SCHOOL-RELATED CAUSES OF AGGRESSION

The rash of school shootings in the United States in the late 1990s led to questions of why youths behave aggressively and violently in schools. In this section, we examine some potential school-related causes of youthful aggression.

Early Academic Failure and Aggression

One of the best documented facts regarding antisocial and aggressive children and adolescents is that they do not perform well in school (Hawkins & Lishner, 1987; Patterson et al., 1992; Wilson & Herrnstein, 1985). For example, one meta-analysis (Maguin & Loeber, 1996) concluded that 35% of low academically performing children become delinquent, compared with only 20% of high academically performing children (Maguin & Loeber, 1996). Furthermore, this relationship was stronger for more serious and violent offenses than for less serious behaviors.

Do Academic Problems Cause Aggression?   One possibility is that children with poor academic skills become frustrated, lose academic motivation, and as a result eventually adopt antisocial and aggressive behavior. Although this hypothesis has a good deal of intuitive appeal, Hawkins and Lishner's (1987) review concluded that "the relationship between indicators of achievement and ability in early elementary grades and subsequent delinquency is not well established" (p. 182). In one study, for example, Ensminger, Kellam, and Rubin (1983) found that although aggressiveness and shyness in first grade predicted self-reported delinquency in adolescence, first-grade learning problems did not. Other more recent studies have also failed to find a relationship between early academic skills and subsequent behavioral problems (Törestad & Magnusson, 1996; Tremblay et al., 1992).

The research cited above involved general academic skills. Another possibility, however, is that the child's aggression might be due to poor reading skills rather than to general academic problems. Indeed, the Isle of Wight studies (Rutter et al., 1970) suggested that reading difficulties preceded and perhaps contributed to the later onset of CD. However, as is the case for academic achievement generally, there are now a number of reasons to believe that early reading problems do not cause later behavioral problems (Fergusson & Lynskey, 1997; Smart, Sanson, & Prior, 1996).

First, many children who develop subsequent reading problems also show behavioral problems before they have even begun formal academic learning (Jorm, Share, Matthews, & Maclean, 1986; McMichael, 1979). In addition, behavioral problems tend to occur more in poor readers who have low IQs than in poor readers who have normal to above-normal IQs, thus suggesting that the problem might be related to the child's low overall cognitive functioning rather than to reading achievement. And finally, a number of studies have found that reading problems play little if any role in psychiatric problems after middle childhood (Maughan, Gray, & Rutter, 1985; Maughan, Pickles, Hagell, Rutter, & Yule, 1996; McGee, Feehan, Williams, & J. Anderson, 1992; Rutter, Tizard, Yule, Graham, & Whitmore, 1976).

Does Aggression Cause Academic Problems?   An alternative hypothesis is that children's aggressive behavior hinders their academic performance. Indeed, Hawkins and Lishner (1987) cited a number of studies showing a relationship between "student misbehavior in early grades, and both subsequent academic and behavior problems" (p. 182). Many of these studies, however, failed to control potential confounding variables that could account for this relationship (Hinshaw, 1992). Furthermore, some studies have shown a relationship between early internalizing behaviors and subsequent reading problems (e.g., Richman, Stevenson, & Graham, 1982), and others have found that "only *some* children with noteworthy externalizing behavior problems in kindergarten

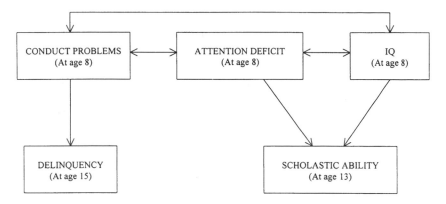

FIG. 11.1. Relationship between early behavior, early IQ, and later delinquency and scholastic ability. Adapted from "Early disruptive behavior, IQ, and later school achievement and delinquent behavior," by D. M. Fergusson and L. J. Horwood, 1995, *Journal of Abnormal Child Psychology, 23,* p. 192. Copyright 1995 by Kluwer Academic / Plenum Publishers. Adapted with permission.

go on to development underachievement" (Hinshaw, 1992, p. 150, emphasis added). It thus unlikely that early aggression is the major cause of later academic failure.

Do Common Antecedents Cause Both Problems? A final hypothesis suggests that both aggression and academic failure might be caused by certain common antecedents, including low intelligence, language deficits, and attentional and neurocognitive problems. This *common antecedents hypothesis* has received generally strong support. For example, in a study of New Zealand children, Fergusson and Horwood (1995) compared measures of children's disruptive conduct, attentional problems, and IQs at age 8 with measures of scholastic ability at age 13 and delinquency at age 15. As can be seen from Fig. 11.1, attentional problems and low IQ at age 8 directly affected scholastic ability at age 13, but only indirectly affected delinquency through their effects on conduct problems at age 8. Moreover, attention exerted the greater impact on conduct problems and IQ the greater impact on scholastic attainment. In addition, once the effects of early conduct problems, attentional problems, and IQ were taken into account, scholastic achievement had no effect on delinquency. Interestingly, variables such as gender and socioeconomic class did not predict future delinquency when the children's early behavior and IQ were taken into account. These results are consistent with other studies that have also implicated early attentional problems as a potential common cause of both reading problems and antisocial behavior (Frick et al., 1991; Hinshaw, 1992; Maguin & Loeber, 1996; Maughan et al., 1996).

Summary. The negative relationship between academic achievement and later antisocial behavior and aggression seems primarily due to a common set of variables that are present by the time children enter school and affect both behavior and academic performance in complicated ways. Of these, attentional problems seem more related to externalizing behaviors, whereas IQ seems to be more related to academic achievement.

Inadequate Schools

Do schools themselves have a role in causing youthful antisocial behavior and aggression? Some evidence suggests that they do. For example, Bachman, O'Malley, and Johnston (1978) found that boys who reported committing a large number of delinquent acts tended to drop out of school before graduation; however, after they left school, their self-reported delinquency rates did not increase. In a similar study, Elliott and Voss (1974) found that the delinquency rates actually decreased for a group of antisocial adolescents after they dropped out of school.

Poor Physical Conditions. One hypothesis holds that poor physical conditions and inadequate facilities and equipment contribute to the development of antisocial behavior within a school. According to this view, children entering such schools receive the message that the community does not care about education. This perception, in turn, decreases these youngsters' academic motivation and their commitment to conventional values (Conger & Galambos, 1997). A number of studies, however, call this contention into question. For example, in their study of British secondary schools, Rutter and colleagues found that differences in academic and behavioral outcomes "were *not* due to such physical factors as the size of the school, the age of the buildings or the space available" (Rutter, Maughan, Mortimore, & Ouston, 1979, p. 178, emphasis in original). Similar results have also been found for U.S. schools (Coleman, Hoffer, & Kilgore, 1982), thus suggesting that poor physical facilities do not cause student aggression.

Opportunity Provision. Goldstein and colleagues point out that aggression always involves characteristics of the person acting within a specific environmental context (A. P. Goldstein, 1999). Although public schools have no direct control over the characteristics of their students, a number of physical and organizational characteristics of the school might function as environmental *opportunity providers* for student aggression. For example, failure to keep the physical characteristics of the school in good repair might suggest that physical damage to the building is socially acceptable, thus functioning as a "releaser cue" for vandalism (A. P. Goldstein, 1999). Other potential opportunity providers include school sites where students are densely packed together (such as hallways), or isolated school areas where students are free from surveillance from adults (such as bathrooms). Reducing the number of such opportunity providers is one strategy schools can use to combat student aggression and violence (A. P. Goldstein et al., 1994).

Tracking. Much of the research on the role of the school has focused on the practice of tracking. For example, in their study of high school students, Polk and Schafer (1972) found that school misconduct and official rates of delinquency were greater for students in nonacademic tracks than for those in college preparatory tracks. In a similar vein, Frease (1973) found that students in the lower tracks became increasingly dissatisfied with and less committed to school and more likely to associate with antisocial peers. Finally, Kelly (1975) found that tracking was the best predictor of delinquency when other factors such as academic achievement, gender, and socioeconomic status were taken into account.

One explanation for the tracking studies is based on Rosenthal's concept of the *Pygmalion Effect*, which states that teacher expectations are subtly conveyed to the students, who then either live "up" or "down" to the expectations in a kind of self-fulfilling prophecy (Rosenthal & Jacobson, 1968). Applied to tracking, this finding suggests that teachers will expect less of students in the lower academic tracks, and that these students in turn will "live down" to the teachers' expectations by derogating academic achievement and developing antisocial values.

However, research on the effects of teacher expectations calls into question this stigmatization explanation. For one thing, it is not clear that teachers typically expect less of disadvantaged children (Doherty & Hier, 1988). In addition, other research suggests that teacher expectations predict student performance more because the expectations are accurate reflections of students' abilities than because they cause student performance (Jussim, 1989).

We have already seen that antisocial peers seem to have a synergistic effect on each other, especially during the middle and high school years. Thus, any negative effects of tracking might arise because this practice provides a means whereby children with antisocial tendencies can socialize with each other. This hypothesis is consistent with a number of studies. For example, Dishion and Andrews (1995) found that at-risk adolescents who received training in a peer-group format with other at-risk children showed more subsequent tobacco use and problem behaviors than did similar adolescents in a no-treatment control group. Apparently, the added interaction between antisocial youths was responsible for this increase. A similar effect could be operating for aggression-prone children who are placed together in lower academic tracks.

However, whether tracking really increases antisocial behavior is debatable. Some studies have failed to control for possible confounding variables such as IQ or preexisting antisocial tendencies (e.g., Kelly, 1975). And when Bachman, O'Malley, & Johnston (1978) did control for such variables, tracking had no effect on the frequency or seriousness of reported delinquency among high school students; moreover, the most powerful predictor of delinquency at the end of high school was level of delinquency at the beginning of high school. Finally, in a multivariate analysis, Farrington and Hawkins (1991) found that neither track placement nor school achievement entered into the equation for predicting persistence into adult offending. The role of tracking in causing antisocial and aggressive behavior thus remains unproven.

Curricular and Pedagogical Deficiencies.   Another hypothesis is that students' antisocial and aggressive behavior is due to an irrelevant and uninspired curriculum combined with teaching techniques that fail to engage students' interest, especially at the secondary level (D. C. Gottfredson & G. D. Gottfredson, 1992). According to this position, students become bored, skip school, and thus begin to engage in antisocial and aggressive behavior (Conger & Galambos, 1997).

One way to determine the relationship between school practices and antisocial behavior is through experimental interventions. Gottfredson and Gottfredson (1992) conducted a number of field studies designed to determine whether changes in school curriculum and pedagogy can increase academic achievement and decrease delinquency. Their most successful intervention has been the *Student Training Through Urban Strategies* (STATUS) project (D. C. Gottfredson & G. D. Gottfredson, 1992). At-risk students in both junior and senior high school were assigned to either a treatment or control condition. Students in the treatment condition attended a special combined English and social studies class which featured a 1-year-long program designed to promote student understanding of society and its system of laws. In addition, the class included active learning, hands-on activities, guest speakers, field trips, and in general a "high interest" curriculum combined with participatory instructional methods.

Overall, the program increased academic achievement and reduced self-reported serious delinquency. The authors attributed the successful outcome to the program's ability to decrease alienation, increase academic success, and increase belief in the law and society. Unfortunately, it is impossible to determine how much of this effect was due to the content of the curriculum itself, how much was due to the innovative pedagogy, and how much was due to the combination of the two.

Adult Indifference and Ignorance.   At least until the spate of school shootings in the late 1990s, many school administrators might not have considered school violence to be a major concern (A. P. Goldstein et al., 1994). Indeed, Wynne and Ryan (1993) made the point that administrators are less likely to perceive problems in schools than are teachers, and that teachers are less likely to do so than are students. Thus, in one survey, three times as many teachers as administrators thought that student behavior had gotten worse over a certain period of time; and in another survey, students were twice as likely as teachers to believe that a serious problem existed in their school (Wynne & Ryan, 1993). In this connection, the first step toward reducing school violence "may be the explicit admission that violent behavior is a problem in the school" (A. P. Goldstein et al., 1994, p. 201).

It also appears that many school administrators and staff members might be ill-informed about student aggression. For example, we have already seen that school staff members often have not taken bullying seriously (Olweus, 1993). In addition, many teachers and administrators have not appreciated the importance of stopping low-level aggression before it escalates into more extreme violence (A. P. Goldstein, 1999). Finally, school personnel have often failed to heed warning signs of future violence. For example, the superintendent of Kip Kinkel's school district was quoted as saying: "If we detained every kid who said they were going to kill someone, we'd have a very large of number of people detained. That's a common thing for kids to say" (Claiborne, 1998, p. A1).

Poor School Ethos. A number of studies have sought to determine the characteristics that distinguish schools with high amounts of antisocial behavior and delinquency from those with low amounts. One of the classic studies in this regard was conducted in twelve British secondary schools by Rutter and colleagues (Rutter et al., 1979). Two major sets of predictors were examined: *intake variables* (the characteristics of students when they entered the schools) and *school process variables* (characteristics of the school itself). Students' in-school antisocial behavior (which included a variety of milder problems, along with violence and fights) was exclusively related to school processes. However, officially recorded delinquency was most strongly related to the school's intake variables, and, to a lesser extent, school processes.

The school process variables which Rutter et al. (1979) found to be related to good school conduct consisted of the following:

- *Good classroom management* on the part of the teacher (well-prepared lessons, a large amount of time on task, prompt transitions from one activity to the next, frequent amount of praise, and dealing with misbehavior early but quietly).
- *Clear schoolwide norms* (high behavioral expectations, positive role-modeling, and positive feedback for good behavior).
- *Consistency of school values* (schoolwide values supported by the entire staff).

The authors concluded that, taken together, these three factors constitute the *ethos* of the school, and that this ethos is important in producing good academic performance as well as good student conduct.

Summary. Students' antisocial behavior is probably more related to the overall ethos of the school than to specific factors such as poor physical facilities,

tracking, or the "relevance" of the curriculum. Student aggression is also promoted by school characteristics that provide opportunities for antisocial behavior and by school personnel's indifference to and lack of training regarding this
issue.

Conclusions

In their review, Hawkins and Lishner (1987) proposed a developmental model
that, with some modifications, seems to do a fairly good job of accounting for
the relationship among schooling, academic performance, and delinquency. As
indicated in Fig. 11.2, children enter school with a set of characteristics that
combine to affect both their academic performance and their moral behavior.
By the first or second grade, children with low IQs, neurocognitive problems,
and a high amount of motor restlessness might also have developed school misconduct. As children move into the later elementary years, externalizing behaviors and academic failure interactively affect each other. Beginning in the late
elementary grades, these characteristics also might interact with school variables (e.g., opportunities for aggression, the school's ethos) to produce poor
academic performance. These factors, in turn, might lead to association with
other "deviant" peers, dropping out, and subsequent delinquency.

PREVENTION PROGRAMS

In this section, we discuss prevention programs aimed at minimizing aggressive
behavior in the schools. As I use it, the term *primary prevention* refers to programs that are delivered to all the students in a school and are designed to keep
aggression from occurring at all. *Secondary prevention,* on the other hand, includes
programs delivered to students who are at high risk for problem behaviors, or
to those who exhibit a problem at a very low level. Before discussing prevention
more specifically, however, we first examine some general programs that have
been developed to target the cognitive, emotional, and behavioral problems
exhibited by aggressive youngsters.

Programs That Target Cognitions, Emotions, and Behaviors

Cognition-Targeted Programs.   Cognitively, aggressive youths might lack appropriate *social interaction skills.* One of the earliest attempts to teach such skills
was developed by Spivak and Shure (1974), whose *Interpersonal Cognitive Problem-
Solving* (ICPS) program for young children uses materials such as drawings, pup-
pets, stories, and role playing (Shure, 1992a, 1992b). Among the skills taught are
understanding cause and effect, identifying feelings, listening and attending, and
creating alternative solutions. In addition, children are taught social–cognitive
skills such as assertiveness and role-taking.

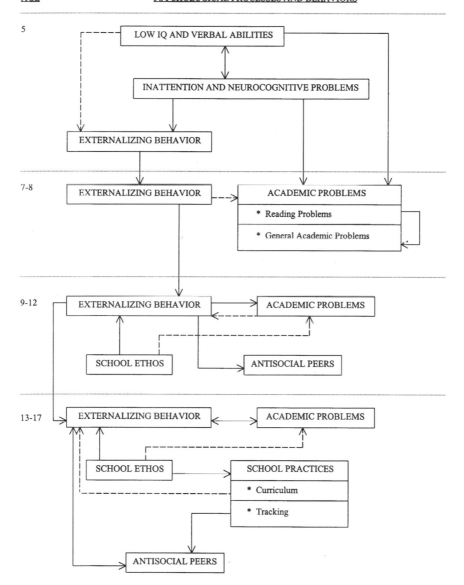

FIG. 11.2. Hypothesized relationships between school-related factors and youths' externalizing behavior in school. Solid lines indicate stronger relationships, whereas broken lines indicate weaker relationships. From *Handbook on Crime and Delinquency Prevention,* by J. D. Hawkins and D. M. Lishner (p. 185). Copyright © 1987. Adapted with permission of Greenwood Publishing Group, Inc., Westport, CT.

Problem-solving programs such as the ICPS typically teach children the following skills: (a) identify the problem, (b) brainstorm solutions, (c) predict the consequences of each solution, (d) evaluate the solutions, (e) select a solution, (f) implement the solution in a concrete fashion, and (g) evaluate the outcome. Both Shure (1992a, 1992b) and Elias and Clabby (1992) developed school-based, problem-solving programs that describe in detail how this approach can be implemented within the complexities of the actual school situation. Research indicates that although the interpersonal problem-solving model has generally demonstrated positive short-term effects, its long-term outcomes are unclear (Keller & Tapasak, 1997).

Emotion-Targeted Programs.   *Anger control training* attempts to teach children how to control angry feelings that can initiate aggressive behaviors (Beland, 1996; A. P. Goldstein et al., 1994; Lochman & Wells, 1996). One such program designed for school use is the *Anger Coping Program* (ACP; Lochman & Wells, 1996). This small-group program is typically targeted for at-risk children in grades 4 through 6, but can be used with younger children as well. Children are taught to identify the emotional and physiological signs that precede anger and to use inhibitory self-directions ("Stop. Think") to control their automatic aggressive responses. Social perspective-taking tasks are also used to help children identify the intentions of others. Finally, a social problem-solving component helps children learn how to make appropriate decisions. A number of rigorous empirical investigations have supported the effectiveness of this program (Lochman & Wells, 1996).

Behavior-Targeted Programs.   As we have seen, aggressive youth often develop antisocial behaviors at the expense of prosocial habits; consequently, a number of programs have been developed to teach children prosocial skills and behavioral habits.

As one example, Goldstein and colleagues have developed the *Skillstreaming* technique for use with both children and adolescents (A. P. Goldstein et al., 1994; A. P. Goldstein & McGinniss, 1997; McGinniss & A. P. Goldstein, 1997). This program teaches children prosocial behaviors that have been broken down into numerous sets of interrelated behavioral skills. For example, the set of "beginning social skills" involves eight specific skills: Listening, starting a conversation, having a conversation, asking a question, saying thank you, introducing yourself, introducing other people, and giving a compliment (A. P. Goldstein et al., 1994).

Children are taught in groups, and each skill is taught through a four-step process:

1. The skill is modeled by the trainer or teacher.
2. The students discuss the skill, after which each student then practices the skill.

3. Following each practice, the student receives feedback from other students and the trainer.

4. As homework, each student is required to perform the skill during the week and to report on the outcome in the next session.

Particular care is taken to have students overlearn the skills and help them develop transfer and maintenance of training (A. P. Goldstein & McGinniss, 1997; McGinniss & A. P. Goldstein, 1997).

According to Keller and Tapasak (1997), evaluation research on Skillstreaming and similar approaches shows positive acquisition of social skills in the short term and modest transfer and maintenance effects; however, the direct effects on students' aggressive behavior are less clear.

Another school-based strategy used to promote prosocial behaviors incorporates the use of behavioral techniques such as reinforcement and various types of punishment (see A. P. Goldstein et al., 1994, for a thorough discussion of the use of behavioral techniques in the school). Depending on the situation, the behavioral program might be developed by the school psychologist, the school counselor, or the teacher, in consultation with the parent and the child. In some cases, the behavioral program at school might be integrated with a similar one at home.

The use of behavioral learning principles can be quite effective in helping to teach prosocial behaviors and eliminate antisocial and aggressive behavior. In fact, A. P. Goldstein et al. (1994) stated that "No other existing means for altering, influencing, or modifying human behavior in appropriate directions rests on a comparably broad and deep empirical foundation" (p. 118). However, the implementation of these procedures within a classroom setting can be difficult. For example, the teacher might not be able to observe or respond to the child immediately when the child performs an appropriate prosocial behavior. Or, the back-up reinforcers that have been chosen might not be powerful enough to affect the child's behavior. For these and other reasons, many teachers find that these behavioral techniques do not automatically produce the desired results.

Primary Prevention Programs

Primary prevention programs attempt to help all children learn prosocial behaviors and eliminate antisocial and aggressive behaviors.

Moral Education Programs. Historically, public schools in the United States have had the dual goals of helping youngsters to learn academically and to develop morally good conduct (Lickona, 1991). Not only were children taught information about the world, but they were also taught everyday moral values such as telling the truth, being polite, working hard, obeying legitimate authority, and being kind and considerate to others (Wynne & Ryan, 1993).

Prior to the 1960s, most moral education in the United States was referred to as *character education* and employed didactic instruction as a means of inculcating specific values such as honesty, truthfulness, and curse-free language (Wynne & Ryan, 1993). By the 1960s, however, character education in the United States had begun to wane, due in part to the secularization of public education and to the decline in the belief of the legitimacy of adult authority (Damon, 1995; Magnet, 1993; Nord, 1995).

The demise of character education was accompanied by the rise of the *moral reasoning* approach pioneered by Lawrence Kohlberg (1975). Kohlberg argued that cognitive reasoning regarding moral issues passes through a sequence of universal stages, culminating in self-chosen, yet universal and abstract ethical principles. In each successive stage, the person develops a more "advanced" state of moral reasoning, with each stage building on and incorporating the other "lower" stages. Although Kohlberg agreed that moral reasoning is not the only determinant of moral behavior, he argued that it is the single most important or influential factor affecting moral behavior (Kohlberg, 1975).

As part of his work on moral development, Kohlberg also developed a method of moral education (Kohlberg, 1975). In this method, the teacher attempts to understand the stage of moral reasoning exhibited by the child, and then tries to help the child begin to reason at the next-higher stage. Techniques used in this process can involve exposing the child to higher level reasoning, suggesting the incompleteness of the child's current level of reasoning, and/or posing questions that cause the child to reconsider her current level of moral reasoning.

Kohlberg's program has attracted its share of critics. For one thing, although character education is criticized for being "indoctrinative," Kohlberg's program seems open to the same criticism because its goal is to move the student to higher levels of thinking where moral issues often have a single "correct" answer (Kohlberg, 1975). Furthermore, although Kohlberg's program emphasizes moral thought as the major determinant of moral behavior, much moral behavior depends on the extent to which behavioral moral habits have been nourished in the child over a period of time (Burton, 1984; Damon, 1995).

Finally, in his summary of the research, Leming (1997) concluded that "only weak associations between moral reasoning and moral behavior have been detected and these associations lack practical significance among school-aged populations" (p. 39). In support of this view, both Gibbs, Arnold, Ahlborn, and Chessman (1984) and Niles (1986) found that although moral reasoning training changed delinquents' moral thinking, it did not change their behavior. One major study has found a change in both moral reasoning and moral behavior among at-risk middle and high school students; however, this study also included additional training in communication and listening skills and an emphasis on empathy (Arbuthnot, 1992; Arbuthnot & Gordon, 1986). It is thus unclear how much of the change in student behavior was due to moral reasoning and how much was due to the program's other components.

During the 1990s, concern with youngsters' antisocial behavior produced a revival of moral education in the United States. Some writers have advocated a revised form of character education (Benninga, 1997; Lickona, 1991; Kilpatrick, 1992; Wynne & Ryan, 1993), whereas others proffer a somewhat modified view of Kohlberg's moral reasoning approach (Arbuthnot & Gordon, 1986; A. Kohn, 1997; Schaps, Battistich, & Solomon, 1997).

Although there are some differences between various proponents of the "new" character education, most agree that schools must explicitly teach a specific set of moral values and behaviors and that this can be done in a nonsectarian manner which respects court decisions and popular concerns regarding the relationship between public education and religion (Lickona, 1991). A general consensus has also emerged that the major values to be taught include respect for oneself and others, responsibility, trustworthiness, caring, fairness, and citizenship (Lickona, 1991).

The "new" moral reasoning approach integrates Kohlberg's approach with other practices designed to tap the child's intrinsic motivation and needs for competence and autonomy (Kohn, 1997; Schaps et al., 1997). Rather than trying to instill values into students, these approaches aim to draw values out of students (Schaps et al., 1997). And whereas character education emphasizes "individualistic" values such as respect and responsibility, the moral-reasoning advocates attempt to create a more "caring community" by emphasizing "social" values such as justice, tolerance, rights of women and homosexuals, the ecology, and a sense of community (Purpel, 1997; Schaps et al., 1997).

Despite the recent increased interest in moral education, little empirical research seems to have been conducted on this topic, especially regarding character education programs. One exception, however, involves a comparison between a character education program (CEP) and a moral reasoning program called the Child Development Project (CDP; Benninga, 1997; Benninga et al., 1991). The study compared one CEP classroom, three CDP classrooms, and three contrast classrooms over a 4-year period during which the children progressed from the second to the fifth grade. Schools were all in middle-class neighborhoods that exhibited a lot of support for education.

In general, both programs seemed to result in prosocial, academically motivated and happy children who liked their school. With respect to moral behavior, the moral reasoning program seemed to produce harmonious and helpful children, whereas the character education program seemed to result in children who were diligent, respectful toward authority, and who had high self-esteem (Benninga, 1997; Benninga et al., 1991). Although more research on various types of moral education programs is clearly warranted, these results indicate that well-developed and well-implemented moral education programs can enhance children's prosocial behavior within the school.

The Good Behavior Game. Kellam's *Good Behavior Game* involves a classroom-based application of the behavioral approach just discussed (Kellam & Rebok,

1992; Kellam, Rebok, Ialongo, & Mayer, 1994). Children within the classroom are divided into teams, each of which consists of an equal number of disruptive children. When the game is in progress, the teacher assigns a checkmark on the chalkboard to each team whenever any of its members engage in a disruptive behavior. At the end of the game period, teams with fewer than a set number of checkmarks win a reward.

At the beginning of the program, the game periods are announced by the teacher, and children on "winning" teams receive tangible rewards at the end of the period. As the year progresses, the teacher begins the game unannounced, and rewards become delayed and less tangible. In addition, teams that "win" the most times during the week receive a special reward on Fridays.

A version of this program was tested among ethnically diverse public schools in the city of Baltimore, Maryland. When the children were in the first grade, researchers randomly assigned children to receive the Good Behavior Game, a mastery learning intervention, or no intervention. After the first year, teachers and peers rated the "game" participants as significantly less aggressive and shy than control subjects, with the largest effects being found for the most aggressive students. In a subsequent follow-up study, "game" boys who were rated as highly aggressive in the first grade were rated as significantly less aggressive in the sixth grade than were comparable boys in either of the other two conditions (Kellam & Rebok, 1992; Kellam et al., 1994).

Second Step.   Beland's *Second Step* program (Beland, 1992, 1996) is an attempt to integrate the cognitive, affective, and behavioral components of violence prevention into one schoolwide curriculum for grades kindergarten through eighth grade. Like Skillstreaming, Beland's program involves learning through observation, practicing the behavior through role-playing, and receiving feedback and reinforcement. The major skills that are taught include empathy, problem solving, social interaction behaviors, and anger management. The program attempts to teach these skills in a manner sensitive to the child's developmental level and that makes the child an active participant in discovering the answers.

Second Step also attempts to deal with a number of problems faced by prevention programs. In order to get adults and children to "buy into" the program, the school staff needs to be committed and children need to believe that the program offers them something they want and need, and so Second Step offers specific guidelines on how these objectives can be accomplished. In addition, the program explicitly teaches for transfer of training and the generalization of learning from the classroom. Third, the program is implemented throughout the school and children receive instruction and supportive feedback at every grade level. Finally, Second Step also recognizes the importance of parental involvement, so the program suggests a number of ways to include parents in the process.

One evaluation of this program found that 6 months after completing training, Second Step children showed a significant reduction in physical aggression in the classroom but not on the playground or in the cafeteria (Grossman et al., 1997). The authors concluded that the program leads to modest reductions in aggression and increases in neutral/prosocial behaviors, with some effects apparently persisting as long as 6 months following the end of training. Unfortunately, due to the ambiguous nature of the dependent measures, the practical implications of this study are unclear (Green & Wintfeld, 1997; Grossman, Koepsell, Rivara, & Neckerman, 1997). Thus, although this program is promising, additional research is needed in order to provide stronger empirical support for its effectiveness.

The Peacemakers Program.   The *Teaching Students to Be Peacemakers* program (D. W. Johnson & R. T. Johnson, 1995, 1996) is based on the belief that conflicts are inevitable and ultimately positive situations that children need to be *taught* to solve. The program is a guided curriculum for Grades 1 through 12 that presents conflict and mediation procedures at increasing levels of sophistication as the children grow older.

The philosophical core of the program is the belief that solutions to disputes among children can either be imposed by adults or solved by the children themselves. Teaching children how to solve conflicts, and at the same time empowering them to do so, should ultimately produce more self-regulated behavior.

The program consists of five components: (a) a cooperative learning environment; (b) an atmosphere in which the nature and desirability of conflict are understood; (c) a program for teaching children how to negotiate conflicts; (d) a peer-mediation program; and (e) frequent follow-up lessons. D. W. Johnson and R. T. Johnson (1996) emphasized that the program needs to be progressively implemented because it "takes years and years to acquire such competence" (p. 323).

The program has been evaluated in more than 12 field studies. In general, the research finds that 75% of students retain an understanding of the major negotiation procedures for at least a year; that negotiation skills of trained students transfer to school sites outside of the classroom and to home; and that principals in Peacemaker schools report a significant reduction in the number of conflicts referred to teachers and administrators (D. W. Johnson & R. T. Johnson, 1996). Additional research by disinterested third parties that focuses on actual behavioral outcomes would help to validate the benefits of this program.

Secondary Prevention Programs

We now examine some secondary prevention programs that are aimed at specifically targeted children rather than at all students indiscriminately.

The Montreal Experimental Project.   One of the most promising aggression-prevention programs is the *Montreal Experimental Project.* This longitudinal program compared three groups of 166 French-speaking Canadian boys with a contrast group of 605 nondisruptive, no-treatment peers (Tremblay, Mâsse et al., 1996; Tremblay et al., 1992). The disruptive boys were further divided into a treatment group, a no-treatment group, and an attention-placebo group. All the children came from a low socioeconomic background and were considered at risk for later academic and behavioral problems.

The program, which began as the boys were entering the second grade and lasted for 2 years, consisted of two major components. The first, a parent-training component, was delivered by trained professionals, each of whom was assigned to a small group of families. This component was based on Patterson's (1982) social-learning model and involved training parents to monitor their children's behavior, to provide positive reinforcement for prosocial behavior, to punish effectively without being abusive, and to manage family crises. The professionals worked with parents biweekly for a 2-year period.

The second component involved another group of professionals teaching social skills to the children. The emphasis during the first year focused on general social skills such as how to make friends, how to help others, and how to invite others into the group. The second year emphasized self-control skills such as how to follow rules, how to react when being teased, and how to deal with anger. In addition, some of the boys were given treatments involving fantasy play and lessons on how to view television critically (Tremblay et al., 1996; Tremblay, Vitaro, et al., 1992).

The boys were assessed annually on a number of measures beginning one year after the end of the intervention. An assessment when the boys were 15 revealed that, compared with the contrast group, the treated boys were less likely to report being a gang member, less likely to get drunk, less likely to report using drugs, and less likely to report being arrested. However, there were no differences between treated and untreated boys in terms of prevalence of sexual intercourse or in terms of being in an age-appropriate classroom (Tremblay et al., 1996). The fact that this secondary treatment program had significant positive effects 6 years after completion is extremely encouraging.

Antibullying Programs.   We have already seen that bullying is a pervasive problem in schools. Although a number of interventions have been developed to counteract this type of behavior (see Ross, 1996), I focus on the program developed by Olweus (1992, 1993), which emphasized the importance of involving the entire school in securing what he considers the right of potential victims *"to be spared oppression and repeated, intentional humiliation, in school as in society at large"* (Olweus, 1993, p. 48, emphasis in original).

Olweus' program attempts to take into account research-based knowledge regarding the nature of the bully, the nature of the victim, and the manner in which the reactions of other children and adults contribute to this problem (Olweus, 1993). In addition, this program, which spans Grades 4 through 7, is based on the following major principles:

- A school environment must be created that is characterized by warmth, positive interest, adult involvement, and firm limits to unacceptable behavior.
- In cases of violations of appropriate norms regarding aggression and bullying, nonhostile sanctions must be applied consistently.
- Adults in the school must do a certain amount of monitoring and surveillance of students' activities, both in and out of the building.
- Adults must act as authority figures, at least in some respects.

The program involves interventions at the level of the school, the class, and the individual child. Details of these interventions are described in Box 11.1.

BOX 11.1

LEVELS OF INTERVENTIONS
IN OLWEUS' ANTIBULLYING PROGRAM

The School Level

In order to be successful, Olweus (1993) argued that antibullying programs must encompass the entire school. His program includes the following components:

- *Adult supervision.* Because most bullying occurs at school, it is important to have adequate supervision while children are at school but out of class. Adult supervisors should carry the attitude, "We don't accept bullying," they should be prepared to intervene sooner rather than later, and they must be prepared to intervene quickly and decisively. In addition, the non-classroom environment should be conducive to prosocial activities.
- *A telephone "hotline."* A specially trained staff member is assigned to take telephone calls from students or parents who wish to anonymously discuss bullying.
- *Parent discussion groups.* The school (or the PTA) can organize small support groups wherein parents can discuss issues regarding bullying.

The Class Level

In addition to the school as a whole, the classroom must also emphasize prosocial interactions as well as the prohibition against bullying.

- *Class rules.* Besides more general behavioral rules, each class should have one or more specific and explicit rule regarding bullying. These can be supplemented through material such as videocassette and fictionalized accounts of bullying. Children should be told that passive participation in bullying is not appropriate and that telling an adult about bullying is not "tattling," but rather something that is expected.
- *Praise for antibullying behavior.* Children should receive praise from teachers for prosocial behavior and behavior that attempts to counteract bullying.

(Box continues)

BOX 11.1 (Continued)

- *Sanctions for bullying.* Classroom teachers should coordinate sanctions against bullying with the school administrators. Sanctions might include "serious talks" with the student, having the child sit in the principal's office or in another class or in a designated "time-out room," or depriving the student of some privilege. These sanctions should be nonviolent but consistently enforced.
- *Class meetings.* Class meetings should be held regularly to discuss issues such as bullying as well as other social issues in the class.
- *Cooperative learning.* This technique can teach children better social interaction and self-responsibility skills.

The Individual Level

Ultimately, issues involving bullying require the interaction of an adult with either the bully, the victim, or both.

- *"Serious talks" with the bully.* The primary aim is not to "understand" the bullying, but to make the bully stop the inappropriate behavior. The message must be, *"We don't accept bullying in our school/class and will see to it that it comes to an end"* (Olweus, 1993, p. 97, emphasis in original). This talk is best done in connection with behavioral consequences and the class meeting.
- *Talks with the victim.* The major point that the teacher must make here is that the school will guarantee the victim protection against harassment.
- *Talks with parents.* It is often appropriate for the school to arrange talks with the parents of both the bully and the victim. The aim of this meeting is to establish communication with the parents and support them in developing influence over their children.

Initial evaluations of Olweus' program were quite promising. Thus, at 8 and 20 months after completion, the program produced as much as a 50% reduction in bullying for both boys and girls, with the decrease being greater at 20 months than at 8 months (Olweus, 1993). In addition, the program seemed to improve the "social climate" of the schools, to reduce the amount of students' overall antisocial behavior, and to decrease the number of new cases of bullying (Olweus, 1993).

However, other evaluations of this and similar programs have produced mixed results. For example, in a 3-year follow-up of Olweus' program, Roland (1989) found that although the number of female victims had decreased slightly, the number of male bullies and victims had increased. In another study, a 1-year follow-up of the class-level component of an antibullying program found positive effects for children ages 10 to 12 but not for young people ages 13 to 16 (Stevens, Van Oost, & de Bourdeaudhuij, 2000). Other research indicates that class-level interventions can be effective with secondary school students (Smith & Sharp, 1994). Given these conflicting results, it is clear that much more research needs to be done to determine the effectiveness of this type of program.

Peer Mediation Programs. In recent years, many schools have adopted *peer mediation programs* in which students trained in negotiation skills (the *mediators*) help other students (the *disputants*) resolve their difficulties through discussion rather than through aggression (Araki, 1990; Bickford, Kormann, & Moeller, 1996; D. W. Johnson & R. T. Johnson, 1994). A cadre of peer mediators is either selected by school personnel or elected by their fellow students. The mediators are then given extensive training in negotiation, mediation, and interpersonal problem-solving techniques under the supervision of someone such as the school counselor, school psychologist, or a specialist in mediation. Two mediators are typically assigned to each dispute (D. W. Johnson & R. T. Johnson, 1994).

Disputes referred to mediation generally include small daily interpersonal spats such as gossip and rumor, dirty looks, jealousy, name-calling, verbal arguments, and threats (Araki, 1990). Physical aggression, threats of physical aggression, and more extreme forms of verbal aggression are generally handled by administrators rather than through mediation.

Anecdotal reports and controlled research generally support the global effectiveness of conflict resolution programs (Gentry & Benenson, 1993; D. W. Johnson & R. T. Johnson, 1994). However, some researchers have raised cautions about these results. For one thing, baseline data are not always available against which to judge the effectiveness of the program. In addition, agreements do not always solve the problems; for example, Bickford et al. (1996) reported that ⅓ of the student pairs who made agreements had further disputes. Finally, Webster (1993) found that most adolescent conflicts did not occur because of a lack of negotiation skills but were due to issues not easily negotiated, such as status, respect, dominance, gangs, and lovers. In sum, although these programs are promising, the effectiveness of peer-mediation has yet to be conclusively demonstrated through high-quality, controlled research and schools should thus not consider these programs to be a panacea for all student problems (Sherman et al., 1997).

Gang Prevention and Intervention Programs. The prevalence of gang activity in and around schools has prompted the development of programs designed to prevent gang-related violence and to intervene effectively when it does occur. A. P. Goldstein and Kodluboy (1998) argued that to be successful, school-based antigang programs must include "in-school safety and control procedures, in-school enrichment procedures, and formal linkages to community-based interventions" (p. 13).

Unfortunately, many available programs have either not been evaluated or have not been found to be effective. For example, even though many schools employ former gang members as motivational speakers to dissuade youth from joining gangs, this approach has not been shown to be effective and might even by counterproductive (Kodluboy & Evinrud, 1993).

Other possible antigang interventions include staff training, a comprehensive school safety plan, dress and behavior codes, and *alternative education,* in which disruptive students are placed in special classes or schools (D. C. Anderson, 1998). Kodluboy (1997), A. P. Goldstein and Kodluboy (1998), and A. P. Goldstein et al. (1995) provided details on staff training and school safety programs. As for dress codes, Kodluboy (1997) described some of the ethical and legal considerations that schools must take into account when considering such measures. Finally, a meta-analysis on alternative schools indicates that although such programs might have a small positive impact on academic achievement, attitude toward school, and self-esteem, they have not been shown to decrease delinquent behavior (Cox, Davidson, & Bynum, 1995).

Other Prevention Programs

In addition to the programs just described, many other school-based violence intervention and prevention programs have been developed (D. C. Anderson, 1998; Brewer, Hawkins, Catalano, & Neckerman, 1995; A. P. Goldstein et al., 1995; Larson, 1994).

Promising Programs.   Two promising programs with some empirical support are the *Seattle Social Development Project* (an experimental primary prevention program for children in the first through fourth grades; Hawkins, Catalano, Morrison, O'Donnell, Abbott, & Day, 1992) and the *Fast Track Program* (a long-term secondary prevention program that is currently being implemented and evaluated in rural Pennsylvania, Seattle, Durham, and Nashville; Bierman, Greenberg, & the Conduct Problems Prevention Research Group, 1996). A third program, *Positive Adolescent Choices Training* (PACT; Hammond & Yung, 1995), was developed specifically for use with African-American youths and includes gender-specific videocassettes in which anger management techniques are demonstrated.

Apparently Ineffective Programs.   Unfortunately, a number of school-based programs that seemed promising for either theoretical or empirical reasons have been shown to be ineffective in preventing or reducing children's aggression. These include suspension, detention, expulsion, the use of security guards, corporal punishment, recreational programs (such as "midnight basketball"), tutoring, mentoring, and any intervention that increases the peer contact of antisocial youth (D. C. Anderson, 1998; Dryfoos, 1990; Goldstein & Kodluboy, 1998; Sherman et al., 1997).

BOX 11.2

SELECTED LIST OF SCHOOL PREVENTION PROGRAMS

	Type of Prevention Program	
Type of School	Primary	Secondary
Elementary	Moral Education Good Behavior Game Second Step Peacemakers	Montreal Experimental Project Peer Mediation
Middle	Moral Education Law-Related Curriculum Second Step Peacemakers	Antibullying Programs Peer Mediation
High School	Law-Related Curriculum Peacemakers	Antibullying Programs Peer Mediation Gang Intervention Programs

Summary

A large number of primary and secondary prevention programs have been developed in an effort to promote students' prosocial behavior and decrease antisocial and aggressive behavior (see Box 11.2). Some of these programs have been rigorously tested and shown to be effective; others have shown promise but need more evaluation; and others appear to be of little value. Additional research should help delineate what clearly works from what does not, and why.

INTERVENTION

Although prevention programs can be successful, it is estimated that from 5% to 10% of school children might need some type of *intervention* program in which a counselor or other staff member works with a troubled student either individually or in a group format.

Warning Signs

Early warning signs, which may indicate the need for individual interventions, are listed in Box 11.3 (Dwyer, Osher, & Warger, 1998). In some cases, these behaviors might not be aggressive in nature but may lead to future aggression if

---

BOX 11.3

**EARLY WARNING SIGNS
OF POTENTIAL FUTURE VIOLENT BEHAVIOR**

- Social withdrawal.
- Extensive feelings of isolation and being alone.
- Excessive feelings of rejection.
- Being a victim of violence.
- Feelings of being picked on and persecuted.
- Low school interest and poor academic performance.
- Expression of violence in writings and drawings.
- Uncontrolled anger.
- Patterns of impulsive and chronic hitting, intimidating, and bullying behaviors.
- History of discipline problems.
- Past history of violent and aggressive behavior.
- Intolerance of differences and prejudicial attitudes.
- Drug and alcohol use.
- Affiliation with gangs.

Source: Dwyer et al. (1998, pp. 8–11).

---

they are not modified. In other cases, the warning signs involve some type of aggression that warrants attention.

In contrast to early warning signs, *imminent warning signs* indicate "that the student is very close to behaving in a way that is potentially dangerous to self and/or others" (Dwyer et al., 1998, p. 11). These signs include:

- *Serious physical fighting with peers or family members.*
- *Severe destruction of property.*
- *Severe rage for seemingly minor reasons.*
- *Detailed threats of lethal violence.*
- *Unauthorized possession of and/or use of firearms and other weapons.*
- *Self-injurious behavior or threats of suicide.*

When imminent danger signs occur, parents should be notified immediately and action should be taken in accord with school board policy (Dwyer et al., 1998).

Schools should have appropriate psychological and support services available for students who are referred for potentially violent behavior. Trained school psychologists, school counselors, or both should be available to handle routine referrals as well as acute crises. In addition, other school personnel should be able to coordinate services with community agencies such as social services, health organizations, and the courts (Dwyer et al., 1998).

Interventions

Intervention with troubled students may take a variety of forms. First, parents should be contacted and should play an active role in any type of intervention (Dwyer et al., 1998). Second, the school psychologist or counselor might provide some short-term, in-school counseling to the student, either as an individual or as a member of a small group. This counseling might employ some combination of techniques that target the child's cognitive, emotional, or behavioral processes. Third, a school-based behavior modification program might be developed to target the child's aggression. Fourth, the school staff might recommend outside professional counseling or therapy for the student, the parents, or both. Fifth, a referral might also be made to other professionals and/or agencies in the community. And sixth, steps might be taken to assess the child's needs for educational interventions such as special education or assignment to an alternative school program.

Interventions with troubled students should emphasize both the safety of all the students as well as helping the troubled student. In cases of clear and imminent danger, safety must be the first concern. In addition, early warning signs should be used as a means of identifying students who may need help and not as a method of stereotyping or punishing children. Finally, the most effective interventions are those that occur early and are sustained, multiple, and coordinated (Dwyer et al., 1998).

CONCLUSIONS

The spate of school shootings and bombings in the late 1990s has focused a great deal of attention on the problem of students' antisocial and aggressive behavior. Research on potential school-based causes of youthful aggression and on programs designed to prevent such behavior suggests a number of points:

• *The ethos of a school is critical in determining the school's academic and behavioral climate.* Nonviolent schools are those that set high academic standards, model and have clear schoolwide expectations for prosocial behavior, and reward prosocial behavior but appropriately sanction antisocial behavior.

• *Good classroom management is also a crucial element in reducing student aggression.* Students are less apt to be aggressive when lessons are well prepared, when transitions from one activity to another are prompt, and when a large proportion of time is spent on task rather than on peripheral matters.

• *Low-level aggression is the precursor of higher levels of aggression and should be dealt with at an early stage.* When students know that low-level aggression will not be tolerated, and when teachers take firm but nonhostile steps to stop such behavior immediately, aggression is reduced.

• *Successful prevention programs target all aspects of children's psychological functioning and involve parents as well as children.*

• *Dealing with antisocial and aggressive behavior in the early grades prevents trouble in the upper grades.* We have seen repeatedly that aggression as early as the first grade predicts later aggression, especially if classroom conditions are conducive to continued antisocial behavior. Conversely, primary and secondary prevention programs also indicate that an "ounce of prevention" in the early years can mitigate aggression in the upper grades.

In summary, although school practices do not necessarily cause youthful antisocial behavior and aggression, schools can do a great deal to eliminate or reduce this type of behavior. Ideally, schools should begin the process of promoting prosocial behavior in kindergarten, for, as Robert Fulgham (1990) reminded us, everything worth knowing can be learned in kindergarten:

> All I really need to know about how to live and what to do and how to be I learned in kindergarten. Wisdom was not at the top of the graduate-school mountain, but there in the sandpile at Sunday School. These are the things I learned:
>> Share everything.
>> Play fair.
>> Don't hit people.
>> Put things back where you found them.
>> Clean up your own mess.
>> Don't take things that aren't yours.
>> Say you're sorry when you hurt somebody. (p. 6)

CHAPTER 12

Intervention and Prevention

As we have seen throughout this book, hyperaggressive behavior tends to manifest itself at a relatively early age and often continues unabated into adulthood. In this chapter, we examine some of the currently available interventions, as well as some of the programs and strategies designed to prevent such behavior in the first place.

COGNITIVE, BEHAVIORAL, AND FAMILY INTERVENTIONS

Numerous psychological interventions have been developed in order to treat antisocial and aggressive children and adolescents. In most cases, these children will have psychiatric diagnoses of oppositional defiant disorder (ODD) or conduct disorder (CD). These diagnoses may sometimes be accompanied by either a comorbid psychological condition such as attention-deficit/hyperactivity disorder (ADHD) or a legal classification of delinquency. Unfortunately, our attempts to eliminate or significantly reduce these children's externalizing behaviors have met with only moderate success. Successful treatment is difficult, and even in the best of programs, as many as half of treated children fail to show continuous long-term benefits (McMahon & Forehand, 1984).

Theoretical Overview

In order to understand the therapies we discuss, we must first examine some of the major theories underlying these approaches.

Cognitive Approaches. Cognitive approaches are based on the hypothesis that children's aggressive behaviors are related to their thought processes, and that changing the latter will change the former. Examples of these types of therapies include social problem-solving training, social-skills training, and attributional retraining (Hudley & Graham, 1993; Kazdin, 1995; Tolan & Guerra, 1994).

Programs designed to improve youths' *social problem-solving skills* seem promising (Kazdin, 1995; Tolan & Guerra, 1994). Through games, academic activities, and stories, youths are taught a structured, step-by-step approach to solving interpersonal problems. Participants are taught to generate alternative solutions, consider the potential consequences, weigh the advantages and disadvantages of each solution, and then decide on the best solution. Therapists model the processes, provide feedback, and reinforce appropriate behavior. Participants then practice the processes within the session before gradually applying their skills in "homework" assigned by the therapist.

Some outcome studies indicate that this approach can significantly reduce youths' externalizing behaviors at home, at school, and in the community, and that therapeutic gains are evident up to a year after treatment (Kazdin, 1995; Kazdin, Bass, Siegel, & Thomas, 1989). For example, in one study of 120 adolescents incarcerated for violent crimes, Guerra and Slaby (1990) found that adolescents who attended a 12-session problem-solving program (*Viewpoints Training Program*) were subsequently rated by staff as less impulsive and aggressive than other adolescents who had been assigned to two control conditions. Disappointingly, however, a 2-year-postrelease study showed no difference between the groups in terms of number of parole violations.

Social skills training emphasizes "the development of discrete behavioral responses to increase prosocial responses in problematic social situations" (Tolan & Guerra, 1994, p. 21). This type of treatment involves the use of discussion, modeling, behavioral rehearsal, and feedback. Perhaps the best-known program of this type is the *Aggression Replacement Training* (ART) program, which integrates anger control and moral reasoning training with social skills training (A. P. Goldstein & Glick, 1994; A. P. Goldstein, Glick, Reiner, Zimmerman, & Coultry, 1986). Research on this and similar programs has provided mixed results (Tolan & Guerra, 1994). In general, these programs seem more effective at reducing violence within relationships than violence that is instrumental or predatory in nature (Tolan & Guerra, 1994).

Attributional retraining is based on the finding that hyperaggressive children exhibit the hostile attributional bias described by Dodge and colleagues (Dodge & Frame, 1982). In one version of this intervention, preadolescent boys completed a 12-lesson treatment designed to reduce their hostile attributions (Hudley & Graham, 1993). Through discussion, role-play and other activities, the children were first taught to search for, interpret, and properly categorize the intentions of others. The second phase was designed to increase the likelihood that the boys would make nonhostile attributions in ambiguous situations. In the third phase, the boys were taught to link their attributions with their behavioral responses.

Hudley and Graham (1993) tested this intervention with a group of both teacher- and peer-nominated aggressive and nonaggressive African-American boys in the fourth to sixth grades. Participants were randomly assigned to an attributional retraining group, an attention training group, or a no-treatment control group. In a subsequent laboratory simulation of ambiguous provocation, aggressive boys in the attributional retraining group were less likely to presume hostile intent by peers, less likely to endorse hostile retaliation, and less likely to engage in verbally hostile behaviors. In addition, only aggressive boys in the attributional-retraining group showed a significant decrease in teacher-rated reactive aggression following training. Thus, the results of this study indicate that attributional retraining may be an effective intervention for youthful aggression. However, more research is needed to determine both the short-term and long-term effectiveness of this approach.

Behavioral Approaches.   The behavioral approach has been among the most widely used therapies with antisocial children (Kazdin, 1995). This approach, commonly used in parent training programs, is based on social learning and operant conditioning theories of aggression and on Patterson's coercion theory of conduct disorder. Parents are taught to increase children's prosocial behaviors through the modeling and reinforcement of appropriate behavior. They are also taught how to reduce children's antisocial behavior through the application of negative consequences (see Box 12.1). It is expected that as the parents learn and apply these skills to their child, the child's antisocial behaviors will decrease (Kazdin, 1995).

BOX 12.1

**BEHAVIORAL TECHNIQUES USED
FOR TREATING AGGRESSIVE YOUTHS**

Increasing Prosocial Behaviors

Modeling. A "model" performs the desired response while the child observes.

Social Reinforcement. The child receives some positive social interaction (e.g., verbal praise, a hug, a pat on the back) contingent on performing the desired response.

Activity Reinforcement. The child is allowed to perform some desired activity (e.g., to play with the parent, watch television, play outside) contingent on performing the desired response.

Shaping. The child is first reinforced for some approximation of the desired response. Once this first approximation has been learned, the child is then reinforced only for a better approximation. This procedure is repeated until the child is making the desired response.

Token Systems. The child receives some type of symbol (a "token") contingent on performing the desired response. These tokens are later traded in for some type of desired "back-up" reinforcement.

(Box continues)

BOX 11.1 (*Continued*)

Decreasing Antisocial Behaviors

Extinction. The reinforcement that was maintaining the undesirable response is withheld or withdrawn. In many cases, the reinforcement is adult attention and extinction consists of ignoring the undesirable response.

Time-Out From Positive Reinforcement ("Time-Out"). The child is removed from all forms of reinforcement whenever he or she performs the undesirable response. In practice, this often results in the child being removed to some quiet part of the house for a matter of minutes.

Response Cost. Something that the child values is taken away contingent on the child performing the undesirable response. Common examples of response cost are "grounding" and paying fines.

Punishment. The child experiences some unpleasant consequence contingent on the performance of the undesirable response. Spanking and scoldings are common examples of punishment.

Family Systems Approaches.   Unlike the other two approaches, which locate psychopathology within the child, *family systems approaches* view the child's antisocial behavior as a symptom of the malfunctioning of the family system (Henggeler & Borduin, 1990). According to this view, the behavior of each member of the family affects all the other members in a circular and interactive manner, thus producing a functioning family system that is different from and irreducible to the individuals who comprise it. In this view, the child's antisocial behavior occurs not because of some cognitive or behavioral deficit within the child, but because that behavior plays a role in maintaining the functioning of the family. For example, the child's aggression within the family might serve to: (a) give some control to an otherwise powerless child; (b) permit the parents to focus their energies on the child and hence not have to deal with their marital conflict; or (c) keep the parents' attention away from the other children, who are then free to do "their own thing" within the family. Because the child's symptomatic behavior serves a function within the family, changing the child's behavior without dealing with the other aspects of family functioning is viewed as futile, because either the child or someone else in the family will become symptomatic again. Thus, the goal of family therapy is to change the functioning of the entire family by treating the entire family together (Henggeler & Borduin, 1990).

The specific techniques employed by family therapists depend on the theoretical orientation of the therapist (Henggeler & Borduin, 1990). Some commonly used techniques are described in Box 12.2. Family therapists use these and a variety of other techniques as a means of changing the functioning of the entire family, thus in principle eliminating the need for the child's symptomatic behavior.

We now turn to a discussion of some of the promising therapies for children's externalizing behavior.

The Parent Training Model

One of the most widely used interventions for children's externalizing behavior is *parent management training* or PMT (Kazdin, 1995). The basic premise of this model is that children's antisocial and aggressive behaviors are inadvertently developed and maintained by ineffective parenting practices. In this model, par-

---

BOX 12.2

SOME FAMILY THERAPY TECHNIQUES

Joining. The process by which the therapist enters and experiences the family's reality, develops rapport with the family, and becomes part of the family's experience.

Enactment. The process of activating a dysfunctional family pattern and then encouraging the family to experience alternative coping strategies. In enactment, the therapist allows or even encourages a dysfunctional pattern to occur. An enactment is an actual occurrence, not a role-play.

Forming Alliances. The process by which the therapist gives emotional support to one or more members of the family. The therapist may form different alliances with different members of the family at different times, and for different reasons.

Strengthening Subsystems. By forming alliances with the various family subsystems (e.g., the parents as a group), the therapist can help strengthen these subsystems. This technique is often used to help parents work together to get control of an oppositional child.

Reframing. The process by which the therapist interprets a behavior from a viewpoint different from that one or more members of the family.

Giving Advice and Directives. The therapist might give the family advice and suggestions. For example, the therapist might give advice about child rearing issues; enlist members of the family to help another member do (or not do) something; help the parent to set up a system of reinforcements and punishments; tell a member of the family to do something in a different way or in a different sequence; or "prescribe the symptom" (i.e., tell a family member to engage in the problem behavior).

Note: Summarized from Barker (1981).

ents meet with a therapist who teaches them behavioral techniques for reducing the child's antisocial behavior and increasing his or her prosocial behavior.

Application to ODD.   Parent training has been used extensively with parents whose children who exhibit ODD. Because there is a close relationship between ODD and CD (Frick et al., 1991; Hinshaw et al., 1993), it appears that the successful treatment of children's oppositional and noncompliant behavior might reduce their angry and aggressive behaviors as well.

One behaviorally based method designed to treat such noncompliant behavior in preschool and younger elementary school children was initially developed by Hanf (1969) and subsequently adapted by a number of other clinicians (e.g., Barkley, 1981; Foote, Eyberg, & Schuhmann, 1998; Forehand & McMahon, 1981). Described by Foote et al. (1998) as *parent–child treatment* (PCT), this model focuses on changing children's antisocial behavior by helping parents to develop better parenting skills. Based on behavior theory as well as the theoretical work of Baumrind (1967), this model assumes that children's behaviors are due to a combination of the affective bond between parents and children as well as to parents' abilities to set and enforce limits in an appropriate manner (Foote et al., 1998). Thus, the purpose of this training is to help parents develop better skills in both these areas.

Most PCT programs consist of eight to ten sessions (Barkley, 1981; Forehand & McMahon, 1981) and involve both the parent and the child. The training format is didactic and interactive in nature. Within each session, the therapist first reviews the homework from the previous week's lesson. Next, the therapist moves on to teaching the lesson for the week, first, by explaining the principles and skills to be taught, and then by role-playing the skills with the parent. Subsequently, the child is brought in and the parent practices the skill with the child. Finally, the therapist assigns homework for the following week (Forehand & McMahon, 1981).

The training is essentially broken down into two major phases, the *Child's Game* and the *Parent's Game* (Forehand & McMahon, 1981). In the Child's Game, the parent is instructed to play with the target child alone for 15 minutes per day in an activity the child chooses. Initially, the parent is taught to simply describe the child's appropriate behavior (e.g., "You're stacking all the blocks"). During this time, the parent may neither give commands nor reprimand the child. The purpose of teaching this skill is to improve the affective relationship between the child and the parent. Once this skill has been learned, the parent is then taught how to provide social reinforcement to the child when the child is playing nicely in the Child's Game. Finally, the parent is shown how to develop a token reinforcement system for use in the home.

The Parent's Game involves both parent and child and is used at the clinic to teach the parent more appropriate child-management skills. Here, the parent structures the game situation and issues commands to the child. Since Forehand

and colleagues found that parents of ODD children typically have trouble giving appropriate commands, the PCT program emphasizes this issue. The therapist first teaches the parent to recognize instances of poor commands (*beta* commands), then trains the parent how to give proper commands (*alpha* commands). Following command training, the therapist then teaches the parent the proper manner of implementing time-out or response-cost procedures if the command is not obeyed (Forehand & McMahon, 1981).

Various adaptations of the PCT model have been tested empirically and have been shown to be highly effective in promoting more positive parent–child interaction as well as reducing children's noncompliance (see Foote et al., 1998, for a review). Moreover, the results generalize to nontargeted behaviors and to the behaviors of nontargeted siblings, and they hold for preschool ADHD children and language-impaired children. Follow-up studies indicate that treatment gains are maintained for at least 1 year (Foote et al., 1998).

Despite these findings, some difficulties still remain. For example, attrition is a problem, with one study finding a drop-out rate of 38% (Eyberg, 1996). In order to reduce attrition, various authorities have suggested modifications such as employing monetary incentives, sending reminder notices, providing transportation and child care, implementing therapy in the home instead of in the office, being more sensitive to cultural variation, and addressing parents' concerns about other problems they are having in their life (Foote et al., 1998).

Another problem involves the fact that the maintenance of treatment gains past 1 year is questionable (Foote et al., 1998). In one study, for example, only 50% of treated children continued to show clinically significant improvement 2 years after the end of the initial intervention (Newcomb, 1995). These results suggest that clinicians should take steps to enhance long-term gains, perhaps by utilizing an overlearning procedure during training and/or by providing regular follow-up "booster" sessions.

Applications to CD. The PMT model has been applied to children's CD as well as to noncompliance. In general, the results parallel those of the PCT model for oppositional behavior: Treatment is effective at reducing antisocial behavior at home and at school and in the community; follow-up studies show that treatment gains are maintained as long as 3 years; nontargeted behaviors and nontargeted siblings also improve; and maternal depression often declines as a result of treatment (see Kazdin, 1995, for a review).

Despite this success, however, PMT still suffers from a number of problems (Kazdin, 1995). In some cases, the parent may either not learn the skills or may fail to apply them at home. Sometimes, even when the parent does apply the skills, the child's behavior may not change or other problem behaviors may emerge. Parents may also show "resistance" (e.g., by complaining that they can't learn the skills, that the skills don't work, that the procedure is too difficult; or by attempting to get the therapist to talk about things other than the day's skill training). Alternatively, parents may fail to attend some sessions or drop out altogether. And although PMT often produces short-term gains, its long-term effectiveness is questionable. PMT is also more effective with younger children than with older children and adolescents. Finally, PMT tends to be less successful for families who are socially isolated, economically disadvantaged, or both in part because of the high attrition rate seen among these families (Dumas & Wahler, 1983; McMahon, Forehand, Griest, & Wells, 1981).

The Collaborative-Integrative Model

Webster-Stratton and colleagues suggested two reasons for the limited value of traditional PMT approaches. First, they argue that therapists' lack of empathy toward parents of CD children may contribute to the problems of resistance and attrition (Webster-Stratton & Herbert, 1994; Webster-Stratton & Spitzer, 1996). And second, they believe that intervention with families of externalizing children must move beyond mere parent training and begin to address the wide variety of problems experienced by these families (Webster-Stratton, 1996). Because they advocate that therapists need to be more collaborative and integrative, I have labeled their method the *collaborative–integrative* (CI) approach.

Nature of the Model.   With respect to collaboration, Webster-Stratton and colleagues suggest that adherence to a "parental skills deficiency" model has led therapists to overemphasize the content of therapy and to underemphasize the importance of the affective relationship between themselves and parents of CD children. In addition, this group also argues that the therapist's role should be to

> understand the parents' perspectives, to clarify issues, to summarize important ideas and themes raised by the parents, to teach and interpret in a way which is culturally sensitive, and finally, to teach and suggest possible alternative approaches or choices when parents request assistance and when misunderstandings occur. (Webster-Stratton & Herbert, 1994, p. 108)

As for integration, the Webster-Stratton group sees traditional parent training as only one of a number of components needed to ensure long-term success. Like other behaviorally oriented therapists, Webster-Stratton teaches parents to strengthen their children's appropriate behavior through the processes of modeling, positive reinforcement, differential attention to appropriate behavior, shaping, and clear limit setting. Similarly, parents are also taught how to reduce inappropriate behaviors through time-out, response-cost, and the use of natural consequences. However, in addition to this 14-session basic program, Webster-Stratton also incorporates a number of other important elements into intervention.

First, in order to deal with the stressors and social isolation typically experienced by parents of CD children, Webster-Stratton developed a 14-session program designed to help parents learn personal self-control, communications, problem-solving skills, and to strengthen their social support system (Webster-Stratton, 1996). Second, a six-session program has been developed to help parents foster their children's school success and to learn how to collaborate better with school personnel (Webster-Stratton, 1996). Finally, a 22-session program has also been developed to teach young children psychological skills such as empathy, problem solving, anger control, positive peer interaction, interpersonal communication, and effective school behaviors (Webster-Stratton, 1996).

Most of Webster-Stratton's interventions have featured group work with parents of ODD and/or CD children ages 3 to 8. She and her colleagues have developed 300 videotape vignettes of parents interacting with their children in both the "right way" and the "wrong way." After viewing a vignette (which typically runs 1 or 2 minutes) the parents and therapists use the episode as the basis for further discussion and elucidation (Webster-Stratton, 1996; Webster-Stratton & Herbert, 1994). Suggestions by group members for how parents in a "wrong way" vignette might have handled the situation help to enhance the parents' analytic abilities and to increase their self-confidence (Webster-Stratton, 1996).

Because one of the goals is to produce cost-effective and replicable treatments, Webster-Stratton has also experimented with a completely self-administered intervention program. In this model, parents take the videotapes home and learn solely from viewing the videotaped vignettes (Webster-Stratton, 1996). In some cases, brief therapist consultations have also been added to this approach (Webster-Stratton, 1996).

Evaluation. Webster-Stratton (1996) recently summarized the evaluations of this approach. In terms of both parental and child behavior, the basic group-led procedure was as effective as individualized, one-to-one parent training; in addition, it was also five times more cost effective (Webster-Stratton, 1996). Although the self-completion program also produced immediate gains, these gains had dissipated 3 years after treatment, whereas those of the group-discussion condition were maintained (Webster-Stratton, 1996). Adding a consultation component to the self-completion program enhanced the value of that program (Webster-Stratton, 1996).

In analyzing these results, Webster-Stratton found that the strongest predictors of poor posttreatment outcomes were single-parent status, marital distress, and negative life-stressors (Webster-Stratton, 1996). In order to improve program effectiveness, Webster-Stratton added the parental social-skills and child-training components just described to the basic program. Compared with the basic program, adding the parental social-skills component improved the parents' marital and parenting skills and children's prosocial behavior (Webster-Stratton, 1996). A subsequent evaluation indicated that combining the parental social-skills component with the child-training module produced the best results, both initially and at a 1-year follow-up (Webster-Stratton & Hammond, 1997). These results thus support the efficacy of Webster-Stratton's approach and also indicate the importance of including a child-training component into the program as well.

The CI model appears to be the state of the art approach for oppositional and aggressive young children. Not only does it integrate PMT with a more empathetic approach to parents, but the use of the group format and video-taped vignettes also makes this approach extremely cost-effective. However, the CI model generally has been limited to relatively young children and its long-term benefits have yet to be proven.

The Family Intervention Model

Although the behavioral and collaborative models have been successful with preschool and early elementary school children, they have been less effective with older children and adolescents (Kazdin, 1995). One reason for this may be that although behavioral programs often involve the child and a parent, none of them routinely involves the entire family. Family members who are not directly involved in the therapy may not be motivated to help the child change his or her antisocial behavior and hence may "sabotage" the therapy, either consciously or unconsciously. For this reason, some clinicians have developed therapies designed for the entire family. One such type of intervention for families of delinquent adolescents is known as *multisystemic therapy* (MST; Henggeler & Borduin, 1990).

In MST, all members of the family participate in the therapy sessions, which occur either in the home or in community settings. The initial assessment involves an attempt to determine strengths and weaknesses within the child, the individual parents, the marriage, the sibling subsystem, the school, and the child and family's peer and social networks (Henggeler & Borduin, 1990). Once the assessment has been completed, the therapist devises a coherent system of interventions that are logically associated with the child's problem behavior and build on the strengths identified in the various systems. These interventions might include typical family systems theory techniques such as joining, reframing, and enactment. In addition, other techniques, including cognitive and behavioral interventions, might also be integrated into treatment. Issues such as the parents' marital adjustment, parent–school relationships, and the child's peer relations are addressed. Individual treatment of the child, the parents, or both may also be included in the therapy (Henggeler & Borduin, 1990). In sum, MST can be viewed as a "package of interventions" that is tailored to the individual needs of the child and the family and used on an "as needed" basis (Kazdin, 1995).

MST has been used extensively with severely antisocial adolescents arrested and/or incarcerated for violent crimes such as manslaughter and aggravated assault, and the outcome data are extremely encouraging (Kazdin, 1995). In one study, for example, 96 youths were assigned randomly to either MST or to a combination of institutional treatment and community probation and parole. The participants had an average of 3.5 prior arrests and 10 weeks of prior incarceration. In addition, 54% of them had at least one arrest for a violent crime. Within 1 year after referral, only 20% of MST youths (compared with 68% of control youths) had been reincarcerated. Two- and 4-year follow-ups showed that these gains had been maintained. Furthermore, the effectiveness of MST was unaffected by demographic characteristics. Finally, the cost per client for MST was estimated at $2,800, compared with $16,000 for 1 year of incarceration (Henggeler, Melton, & Smith, 1992; Henggeler, Melton, Smith, Schoenwald, & Hanley, 1993; Kazdin, 1995; Tate, Reppucci, & Mulvey, 1995). Several other empirical evaluations by Henggeler and colleagues report similar findings (Borduin, 1994; Henggeler & Borduin, 1990).

There are several reasons why MST seems to offer more promise for reducing adolescent violence than any other therapy. First, by bringing therapy to the client, MST promotes a sense of collaboration and thereby minimizes the likelihood of resistance and attrition that seem to plague other therapies. Second, its nature as family therapy helps to integrate the entire family, not just the child or the parent, into the change process. And third, as we have seen, many variables, including the child's characteristics as well as intra- and extra-familial factors, affect children's hyperaggression. The fact that MST targets all of these factors makes success more likely.

Summary

Research on psychological interventions with antisocial and hyperaggressive children leads to the following conclusions:

- In view of the potential long-term nature of ODD and child-onset CD, interventions aimed at these children's behavior should begin early.
- Interventions that target both the child's cognitive and behavioral processes are more likely to be successful than those only aimed at reducing the child's problem behaviors.
- Interventions that target the child's behavior in a number of settings (including school and the peer group) are more likely to produce long-term success than those that do not. This principle implies that the successful therapist will need to take on the added role of a case manager.
- Interventions should generally involve both the child and parent and preferably the entire family (see Henggeler & Borduin, 1990, chap. 2, for a discussion of when individual therapy is indicated).
- "Collaborative" therapies are more likely to be successful than "prescriptive" therapies.

- Therapies set in the community or in the home are more likely to be successful than those in the therapist's office.

- In order to be successful for at-risk families, therapy should target all the stress-producing systems for the family.

- Although early and effective treatment might reduce symptoms in a significant proportion of youth, children's disruptive behavior disorders (especially CD) should be considered chronic and potentially life-long conditions that will likely require preplanned periodic monitoring and retreatment.

In sum, we now know at least some of the things we need to do in order to make therapy with aggressive children more successful. However, the practicality of implementing such "best practices" is daunting. For example, full-time therapists would probably find it very difficult to conduct therapy sessions in community settings or in clients' homes on a regular basis. Furthermore, doing "state of the art" therapy with families of hyperaggressive youths would be extremely time-consuming and expensive. For example, adopting all of the components of Webster-Stratton's (1996) model would require a total of 56 sessions, many of them lasting more than 1 hour. It is highly unlikely that many third-party payers would be willing to pay for that much psychological intervention, much less for the probable follow-up.

OTHER PSYCHOLOGICAL
AND PSYCHIATRIC INTERVENTIONS

In addition to the cognitive, behavioral, and family approaches discussed in the previous section, other psychological and psychiatric intervention techniques have also been used in an effort to decrease youthful hyperaggressive behavior. We turn to an examination of some of these approaches.

Psychodynamic Psychotherapy

The *psychodynamic* approach derives initially from Freudian concepts and "focuses on changing intrapsychic factors that are presumed to underlie violent behavior" (Tolan & Guerra, 1994, p. 15). One especially common version of this type of treatment is called *relationship/insight therapy* (Tate et al., 1995). Within this framework, the goal of the therapist is to develop an emotionally positive relationship with the aggressive youth, while at the same time, providing the youngster with insight into the psychodynamic processes believed to underlie the aggression. In the context of a supportive therapeutic relationship, this insight should then encourage the youth to deal with the problem in a new and psychologically better manner. For example, the therapist might hypothesize that the youth's aggression stems from the unresolved anger the youth experiences toward his father. The therapist then tries to get the youth to understand this dynamic and to take steps to resolve the anger. Once this has been accomplished, the youth should have no more need for his previous antisocial behavior.

Despite the widespread use of this approach with antisocial youths, evidence fails to support its effectiveness (Tate et al., 1995; Tolan & Guerra, 1994). Indeed, Tolan and Guerra (1994) reported that evaluations of this type of therapy for institutionalized violent youths have found minimal effects within the institution and negative effects at postrelease follow-up. Thus, despite its allure, this type of therapy cannot be recommended for aggressive and violent youths.

Group Therapy

Another widely used treatment with aggressive youths is *Guided-Group Interaction* (GGI), which consists of adult-led peer-group discussions aimed at confronting negative behavior and reinforcing positive behavior (G. D. Gottfredson, 1987). However, although this type of therapy is popular, available research indicates that it is not only ineffective, but potentially counterproductive as well (Brewer et al., 1995). In one relevant study, Feldman, Caplinger, and Wodarski (1983) examined the effects of certain types of treatment on youths ages 8 to 17. In some conditions, all members were antisocial youths, whereas in other conditions, membership was composed of both antisocial and non-antisocial "normal" youths. Interestingly, antisocial youths in the mixed groups showed reductions in their antisocial behavior, whereas those in the all-antisocial groups did not (Feldman, 1992). This result mirrors our earlier discussion about the synergistic effects of youths in antisocial peer groups: When antisocial youths are placed together in a homogeneous group, they become even more antisocial. The implication is that any treatment that employs such groups is most likely to fail. On the other hand, integrating a few antisocial youths into a group of predominantly prosocial youth may yield more positive results (Tolan & Guerra, 1994).

"Holding" Therapies

The relative intractability of severe forms of CD has spawned a number of new attempts to treat this disorder. One such therapy that has become popular in recent years is called *holding therapy*, an intervention based on the idea that severely aggressive children suffer from attachment disorder (described in chap. 5). According to one version of holding therapy called *rage reduction therapy* (RRT; Magid & McKelvey, 1987), the key to treating aggressive children is to help these youngsters become "reattached" to their parents or guardians. In order to do so, however, the children must first confront the rage they feel toward the person or persons who failed to meet their needs during infancy. Thus, in

RRT, "the psychopathic patient is encouraged to work through his unbelievable rage and anger while being forced to accept another's total control" (Magid & McKelvey, 1987).

In RRT, the child typically lies on his back, either on a floor or spread across the laps of adults who are sitting on a couch (Magid & McKelvey, 1987). In some cases, the child is rolled up in a rug or some other cloth used as a restraint to keep the child's arms and legs from moving. The child's head typically lies on a pillow cradled by the therapist, who plays the role of the original, nonresponsive parent. A session may last as long as 8 hours. Magid and McKelvey (1987) described what happens next:

> With the child's head lying in his lap, the therapist controls resistant responses and provokes rage reactions by stimulating the patient's rib cage with his fingers. The motion is similar to when one teases and tickles another person. At first the motion tickles the patient but soon it becomes irritating, much as it does when someone is tickling you and won't stop. As the irritation builds, the therapist talks and shouts along with the child, drawing out the rage inside. The anger begins to surface as the patient struggles with giving up controlling behavior. Eventually reasonable behavior starts to emerge, as the child surrenders to the control of the therapist. But this state can only emerge if the therapy is correctly administered.
>
> The previously uncontrollable child is restrained by the body holders so that he cannot get away from the therapist's treatment. They also gently keep the child from hurting himself or others.
>
> Such children hate this control and resist by squirming, raging and generally being resistant. (p. 210)

A major goal of RRT is to teach the child who is the boss. A second goal is to provoke the rage reaction, which occurs partially as a result of the techniques just described. Once these goals have been met, the therapist attempts to promote reattachment by encouraging the child to express love toward the parent or parent substitute (Magid & McKelvey, 1987).

The use of RRT as an intervention for ODD or CD is suspect from both an empirical as well as an ethical perspective. To my knowledge, no systematic controlled study of the effectiveness of RRT on aggressive children has been undertaken. In addition, some of the behaviors of the therapist (e.g., prolonged tickling under the rib cage in order to provoke a reaction) raise ethical concerns and could potentially be considered emotional or physical child abuse if administered by a parent, teacher, or daycare provider. For these reasons, RRT must be viewed cautiously.

A more recent version of holding therapy, called the *holding nurturant process* (HNP), combines a more gentle type of "in arms" holding within a broader *corrective attachment therapy*. Integrated into this therapy are a number of more conventional therapeutic techniques such as teaching the child social skills and teaching parents better means of developing control over the child (Levy & Orlans, 1998). Although the effectiveness of this version of holding therapy has yet to be demonstrated through carefully controlled evaluation, it is more promising than RRT at both the theoretical and ethical level.

Drug Treatment for Hyperaggressive Youths

The possibility that CD has a biological basis suggests that children's hyperaggressive behavior might be treated successfully through the use of various psychoactive drugs. Some drugs used for this purpose include the mood-stabilizer, *lithium carbonate* (sometimes used with children exhibiting organic brain disorders or conduct disorder); the anticonvulsant drug, *carbamazepine* (used for organic brain disorders); beta-blockers, such as *propranolol;* and antihypertensives, such as *clonidine* and *guanfacine* (Johnson, Rasbury, & Siegel, 1997; Kutcher, 1997).

Unfortunately, relatively little research on this topic has been conducted, and many of the findings of published studies fail to support the use of these drugs for this purpose with juveniles. For example, one double blind study on the effects of lithium with CD adolescents concluded that lithium does not appear beneficial for this use (Rifkin et al., 1997). Another study examined the effectiveness of carbamazepine with CD children between the ages of 5 and 12. Not only was carbamazepine not superior to a placebo, but it also produced a number of untoward side effects (Cueva et al., 1996).

In some cases, drugs might be used to treat comorbid disorders such as depression or ADHD. We have already seen that comorbid CD does not seem to abate following remission of depression (Loeber & Keenan, 1994). Similarly, Kazdin (1995) concludes that "no strong evidence exists that stimulant medication can alter the constellation of symptoms (e.g., fighting, stealing) associated with conduct disorder" (pp. 94–95). On the other hand, a recent study of seven children ages 3 to 6 indicates that clonidine may be useful in reducing the aggression seen in preschool children diagnosed as having posttraumatic stress disorder (Harmon & Riggs, 1996).

Some writers have suggested that psychoactive drugs used to treat comorbid conditions of CD might actually enhance children's aggressive tendencies (O'Meara, 1999). Empirical research on this question, however, appears to be lacking.

Community Residential Programs

Severely antisocial and/or aggressive youths who can no longer be maintained in their own homes are sometimes placed in foster homes or in a group home within the community. In this section, we examine the effects of one model of community placement called the *adult-mediated behavioral model (behavioral model)*, which emphasizes "the use of contingency management systems and promotion of positive relationships with mentoring adults" (Chamberlain, 1996, p. 64).

Probably the most researched example of the behavioral model is that of *Achievement Place*, a small-group residential setting whose initial program was developed and implemented in Lawrence, Kansas, and subsequently replicated in other settings (Phillips, Phillips, Fixsen, & Wolf, 1971). Evaluations of this program showed that minor delinquent behavior could be reduced through the use of behavioral techniques used in the homes. However, postrelease gains were sometimes not maintained, and the effects of the program seemed to depend on the quality of the program implementation (see Tolan & Guerra, 1994, for a review).

More recently, Chamberlain and colleagues have developed a community residential program that places a single antisocial youth with a set of specially trained foster parents (Chamberlain, 1996). Each youth in this *treatment foster-care model* (TFC) has an individual treatment plan the foster parents implement using a behavior-contingency point system. Each week, the child and his or her postplacement caregiver (e.g., family) undergo therapy, and the child's behavior in school is carefully monitored. A case manager coordinates all aspects of the youth's plan. Chamberlain (1996) provided some preliminary outcome data, which indicate that the TFC program is a promising alternative to more restrictive institutionalization.

LEGAL INTERVENTIONS

As we have seen, legal minors who commit either an index crime or a status offense are considered to be *juvenile delinquents* (or, more simply, *delinquents*). Prior to the 20th century, the legal system treated juvenile delinquents in essentially the same way as it did adult criminals; in fact, under British law, children in the 18th century were hanged for theft (Wicks-Nelson & Israel, 1997). Today, most juveniles who face legal difficulties are tried as minors within the juvenile justice system, which emphasizes reform over punishment (Googins, 1998). However, the escalation of youth violence beginning in the mid-1980s has fostered calls for treating perpetrators of serious juvenile crimes as adults (e.g., Barr, 1992).

Wolfgang's classic study (Wolfgang et al., 1972) showed that only about ½ of officially adjudicated delinquents commit another offense and that *chronic offenders*, who comprise about 6% of the juvenile population, are responsible for 50% or more of serious crime committed by juveniles. As you may suspect, these chronic offenders tend to show antisocial and hyperaggressive behavior from the elementary school years, they have criminal parents, come from "delinquent" neighborhoods and dysfunctional family situations, have low IQs and attentional problems, and use and abuse drugs at an early age (J. Q. Wilson, 1994). Indeed, Tolan (1987) found that committing a first juvenile offense before the age of 12 was the single best predictor of the number, variety, and seriousness of future offenses.

The challenge faced by the juvenile justice system is to differentially identify these "6-percenters" at an early age and then to provide effective interventions to reduce these young people's antisocial and aggressive behaviors. In this section, we examine some of the interventions that have been developed for youths who come into contact with the legal system.

Institutionalization

The most restrictive sanction a judge can impose on a juvenile involves institutionalization in prison or some type of juvenile correctional center, detention center, training center, reform school, or shock incarceration program (boot camp). The major measure of the effectiveness of such interventions is *recidivism*, the extent to which the youth experiences subsequent contact with the law. There is very little evidence that institutionalization reduces recidivism rates (Mulvey, Arthur, & Reppucci, 1993).

Cadwalader's (1986, 1988) discussion of the innovative reform school he and his colleagues ran on isolated Penikese Island in Massachusetts illustrates some of the problems faced by these types of institutions. Cadwalader's program was based on the belief that delinquents' behavior is due to a lack of opportunity and that the solution was to "put these boys in a self-sufficient community where honesty and cooperation would contribute so visibly to everyone's well-being that our students would adopt these values as their own" (Cadwalader, 1986, p. C3). Unfortunately, an evaluation 5 years after the program began showed that only 16% of their "graduates" had managed to turn themselves around, whereas 84% had "gone on to lives destructive in varying degrees to themselves and society" (Cadwalader, 1986, p. C3).

One type of correctional program that has incurred a great deal of publicity is known informally as the *boot camp* (MacKenzie, 1991). In this program, offenders spend a relatively short amount of time (typically 90 days) in a military style camp before being released into community supervision. The program emphasizes discipline, military drills, and physical training in an attempt to increase the prisoner's sense of responsibility, confidence, self-discipline, self-respect, and respect for authority (MacKenzie, 1991). The effectiveness of this program is questionable. For example, MacKenzie (1991) studied a group of older adolescent and young adult prisoners sentenced to a boot camp program. Almost 20% of the boot camp group dropped out (either voluntarily or involuntarily) before the program ended. Results showed no difference in recidivism of the boot camp graduates compared with one group of similar prisoners who served their sentence and a second group who were given probation with no prison time. Subsequent research on boot camps has produced mixed results (Hagan, 1995; Jones, 1997).

There are a number of possible explanations for the ineffectiveness of institutionalization. According to Cadwalader (1986), the major reason is that years of experiencing a lack of predictable relations between behavior and consequence have taught severely antisocial youths "simply to satisfy the impulse of the moment" (p. C3). When forced to adapt to the structure of a correctional facility, these youngsters are able to do so. However, once back on the street, they are equally malleable to the unpredictable environment that had produced them in the first place.

A number of other factors also contribute to the poor showing of institutions. First, as we have seen repeatedly, when antisocial and aggressive youths are placed together in close proximity over time, they tend to exacerbate each others' antisocial behaviors. Second, many facilities provide little therapy or provide ineffective therapy (Chamberlain & Friman, 1997). For example, Garrett (1985) found that commonly available group therapy programs have no effect on subsequent recidivism rates. Moreover, even though many rehabilitation programs lack a cognitive component, Izzo and Ross (1990) found that the addition of such a component greatly enhanced a program's therapeutic effectiveness. Third, even though family therapy has been found to lower recidivism, youths in correctional institutions are often isolated from their families and receive little or no family therapy (Chamberlain & Friman, 1997; Garrett, 1985). And finally, although close community supervision on release seems to be an important determinant of recidivism, such *aftercare* for most delinquents is sparse and of poor quality (MacKenzie & Brame, 1995).

Other Interventions

In addition to institutionalization and community placement, many other types of interventions have been developed for chronically aggressive youngsters (Borduin & Schaeffer, 1998; Krisberg, Currie, Onek, & Wiebush, 1995; Stanton & Meyer, 1998; Wiebush, Baird, Krisberg, & Onek, 1995). The goal of some of these programs is to provide services while maintaining the delinquent in his or her own home. These types of programs include *probation, intensive probation,* and *diversion* (which involves removing juveniles from the juvenile justice system by providing services through a variety of other community agencies; Stanton & Meyer, 1998). In a more innovative kind of approach called the *wraparound model,* an interdisciplinary team of service providers develops a set of integrated interventions for the target youth and his family (Borduin & Shaeffer, 1998).

One type of diversion program involves the so-called *prisoner-run programs,* perhaps the best-known of which is *Scared Straight,* a program developed in New Jersey in the 1970s. While targeted youths spent a grueling 2-hour session inside a maximum security prison, the prison's convicts gave the youngsters a vivid dose of what prison life was really like. Although the media has portrayed this program as highly successful, a carefully conducted 6-month follow-up of the program showed that youngsters who attended the program actually showed a higher rate of recidivism (41%) than did a control group that did not attend the program (11%; Finckenauer, 1979). Other research is consistent in showing that such prisoner-run programs do not reduce recidivism rates (Stanton & Meyer, 1998).

A popular type of out-of-home placement involves *therapeutic wilderness approaches* such as *VisionQuest* (Krisberg et al., 1995). These programs utilize the challenges presented by a wilderness setting as a means of promoting group cooperation and prosocial behavior. Evaluations of these types of programs have produced mixed results (Borduin, 1994; Krisberg et al., 1995).

One of the best evaluations of delinquency intervention programs was reported by Lipsey (1992). Lipsey found that programs that produced the most positive results were community based and involved behaviorally oriented, skill-oriented, and multimodal treatment methods. Programs consisting of deterrence and "shock" approaches produced negative effects.

PREVENTION

The relative ineffectiveness of interventions for extremely antisocial and aggressive youths underscores the need to prevent children from developing these disorders in the first place. In turn, the ability to stop a psychological disorder from occurring at all depends initially on knowing the factor or factors that cause the disorder. Fortunately, many risk factors related to children's hyperaggressive behavior have been identified and are listed in Box 12.3. Unfortunately, many of these factors may not be amenable to manipulation, thus making prevention

---

BOX 12.3

RISK AND PROTECTIVE FACTORS ASSOCIATED WITH CHILDREN'S HYPERAGGRESSIVE BEHAVIOR

Risk Factors

Prenatal and Perinatal Factors. Prenatal medical complications; perinatal medical complications.

Child-Related Factors. Genetic factors; difficult temperament; low IQ; poor language ability; poor academic performance; poor social–informational processing skills (especially a tendency toward the hostile attributional bias); poor impulse control; immediate gratification and poor self-control; sensation-seeking; antisocial attitudes; ego absorption; lack of empathy and guilt; poor coping strategies; high levels of helplessness and anger.

(Box continues)

BOX 12.3 *(Continued)*

Parent-Related Factors. Adolescent parents (especially mother); antisocial behavior (especially paternal criminality and antisocial personality disorder); psychopathology (especially paternal substance abuse and maternal depression); low levels of education.

Family Factors. Poor parent–child affective relationships (especially parental rejection of the child and lack of attachment and nurturance); low levels of parental involvement; lack of parental monitoring and supervision; parental modeling of antisocial and aggressive behavior; ineffective parental limit setting; parental reinforcement of coercive behaviors; parental tolerance of antisocial behavior; harsh physical punishment; parental inconsistency in discipline; child abuse and neglect; nonintact families; marital discord and conflict; father absence; large family size; family isolation and insularity; family poverty; presence of guns in the home; antisocial siblings; stress-producing life events.

Social and Cultural Factors. Substandard housing; violence and crime in the neighborhood; high rate of adult unemployment and poverty in the neighborhood; poor governmental services; high rates of mobility; antisocial peer groups; a high proportion of low-achieving students in the schools; lack of collective efficacy; a weak bond between the neighborhood's subculture and the larger culture; stress-producing life events; media violence; cultural and subcultural acceptance of violence; and accessibility of weapons (especially guns).

Protective Factors

Prenatal and Perinatal Factors. Good prenatal care; few or no prenatal or medical complications.

Child Factors. Genetic factors; easy temperament; moderate to high IQ; good language ability; good academic performance; good interpersonal skills and positive peer relations; good self-control; prosocial attitudes; empathy and predispositional guilt; good coping strategies; high levels of optimism.

Parental Factors. Parents older than 21 (especially mother); lack of parental antisocial behavior and psychopathology; moderate to high levels of education.

Intrafamilial Factors. Good parent–child affective relationships; high amount of attention in the first year of life; high levels of parental involvement; presence of parental monitoring and supervision; parental modeling of prosocial behavior; effective parental limit setting; parental reinforcement of prosocial behavior; parental consistency in discipline; parental monitoring and mediation of child television viewing; lack of access to firearms; intact and harmonious families; marital stability; family interaction with others; lack of family poverty; family religiosity.

Extrafamilial Factors. Middle to upper class neighborhood; prosocial peer groups; low rate of adult unemployment in the neighborhood; presence of collective efficacy.

more problematic. Furthermore, if the risk factor is merely a correlate and not a cause of aggression, manipulating the risk factor might have no positive effect on the aggression. Nevertheless, at this point, basing prevention programs on known risk and protective factors seems to be the most promising approach we can take.

The Cambridge–Somerville Youth Study

As a point of departure for our discussion on prevention, I first describe one of the earliest attempts to prevent children's antisocial behavior, a program conducted in two suburbs of Boston and hence known as the *Cambridge–Somerville Youth Study*.

In this program, which dates back to the late 1930s, pairs of both "difficult" (high-risk) and matched-control "average" boys between the ages of 5 and 13 were targeted for inclusion in the intervention (McCord, 1978, 1992). One member of each pair was randomly assigned to an intervention group or a control group. The boys averaged 10½ years of age when the program began, and the intervention lasted for an average of 5 years (McCord, 1978). The premise of the program was that the guidance and support from one or more individuals outside the family would serve to divert these boys from antisocial behavior and criminal acts (Allport, 1951). Thus, boys in the intervention group received visits from a counselor twice a month. Many of them also received academic tutoring and medical or psychiatric attention. One-fourth of this group were taken to summer camp and most were put into contact with community groups such as the Boy Scouts and the YMCA. Boys in the control group received no services and participated only through providing information about themselves (McCord, 1978).

An initial evaluation of the program when the youths were adolescents found no differences between the intervention and control groups. However, a 30-year follow-up evaluation produced more interesting results (McCord, 1978). Two thirds of the men in the intervention group stated that the program had been beneficial. These men believed that the program had helped them to become better people, and their questionnaires were sprinkled with positive comments about the program and their counselors. In fact, more than a quarter of these respondents expressed an interest in communicating with their former counselors. Objective data, however, presented another picture. As adults, equal numbers from both the intervention and the control groups had been convicted of at least one crime. However, compared with the control group, men from the intervention group committed more multiple crimes, showed more alcoholism and health problems, died at younger ages, and had less prestigious and satisfying jobs. In sum, not only did this program fail to prevent delinquency and crime, but it also appeared to have a number of negative side-effects as well (McCord, 1978).

The findings of the Cambridge-Somerville Youth Study are disquieting, not only because they replicated other such failures (McCord, 1978), but also because the intensity and breadth of the program stood in stark contrast to the disappointing results. In addition, the participants' subjective positive feelings toward the program and the counselors provided a vivid contrast with the objective data. From a methodological perspective, this study should caution us against the uncritical acceptance of self-report and self-satisfaction data as the basis for outcome evaluations.

McCord (1992) suggested that the failure of the Cambridge–Somerville Youth Study was due to some erroneous assumptions (e.g., that children not loved at home should be given love and that children doing badly in school should be helped to do better). Another possibility is that this particular program began too late in the children's life, and that interventions within the first 5 years of life might have produced better outcomes. We now turn to an examination of this possibility.

Early Childhood Prevention Programs

In his review of prevention studies, Yoshikawa (1994) noted four prevention programs that have produced long-term reductions in youths' antisocial behavior and delinquency. These include the *Syracuse Family Development Research Project* (Lally, Mangione, & Honig, 1988), the *Yale Child Welfare Project* (Seitz, Rosenbaum, & Apfel, 1985), the *Houston Parent–Child Development Center Program* (D. L. Johnson & Walker, 1987), and the *Perry Preschool Project* (Berrueta-Clement, Schweinhart, Barnett, Epstein, & Weikart, 1984).

The Syracuse Project. This program, which began during the woman's pregnancy and continued until the child reached age 5, targeted low-income and poorly educated young mothers. Trained paraprofessionals gave the mothers weekly help with nutrition, health, and other problems before birth, plus child-rearing education after the child was born. In addition, the children received free daycare until the program ended. A matched-control comparison group was chosen when the children reached age 3. A 10-year follow-up showed that only 6% of the treated children (compared with 22% of the control children) had juvenile court records; moreover, control youths showed more serious crime than did intervention youths (Lally et al., 1988).

The Yale Project. This program also targeted low-income women who were experiencing their first pregnancy. During the prenatal period and first 2½ years of the child's life, a social worker visited the home and helped the mother with medical, financial, and support services as well as with occupational counseling. A 10-year follow-up showed that the experimental boys exhibited significantly less teacher-rated aggression and other antisocial behaviors and required less special education than did boys from a matched-control group recruited after the study had begun (Seitz et al., 1985).

The Houston Project. When the child was 1 year of age, low-income Mexican-American families were randomly assigned either to the intervention program or to a control condition. In the intervention condition, paraprofessional home visitors advised the mother about child development and parenting skills and tried to foster good affective relationships between the mother and the child. In addition, parents were given classes on parenting skills and children were provided with educational daycare in the second year. At age 11, treated children were rated by teachers as less aggressive, disruptive, impulsive, and restless than control children (D. L. Johnson & Walker, 1987).

The Perry Preschool. This program provided preschool services to low-income African-American children between the ages of 3 and 5. High-risk preschool children were randomly assigned to either an intervention or a control group. Children in the project were given high quality and academically oriented preschool experiences for 2 years in addition to parent meetings and home visits by the teachers. A 14-year follow-up showed that only 7% of the treated youths were chronic criminal offenders, compared with 17% of control group youths (Berrueta-Clement et al., 1984).

Summary and Conclusions. These programs contained a number of common elements (Yoshikawa, 1994). First, they all began within the first 5 years of life and they all lasted for at least 2 years. Second, they all involved home visits. Third, they all provided some type of educational preschool experience. Fourth, the intervention focused not only on the child but also on other aspects of the mother's life, such as assistance with medical and occupational issues. And fifth, two of the four programs provided assistance to the mother during her pregnancy. Interestingly, two of the four also utilized trained paraprofessionals for the home visits. The results of these programs thus suggest that well-delivered prenatal and early childhood prevention programs can positively affect youths' academic achievement while reducing their subsequent aggression, antisocial behavior, and criminal activity (Yoshikawa, 1994).

Other Prevention Possibilities

Most of the prevention interventions described above have targeted children's behaviors rather directly. Box 12.3 suggests four other possible types of prevention programs.

Programs That Target Parent-Related Factors. In principle, programs that can ameliorate or mitigate parent-related factors associated with hyperaggressive children should help to prevent the development of aggression in offspring. Programs showing promising results include those aimed at helping teenagers delay childbearing, such as the *Dollar A Day* pregnancy prevention program (Brown, Saunders, & Dick, 1999); interventions aimed at parental alcohol and drug abuse (Nye, Zucker, & Fitzgerald, 1999); and those that help to prevent or mitigate major depressive disorder (Seligman, 1998). However, whether these programs can be effective with the parents of children who are at risk for hyper-aggressive behavior remains to be determined. And, even if these programs do prove effective, we will still need to demonstrate that their effectiveness translates into less aggression in the offspring of participating parents.

Programs That Target Family Functioning.   As we saw in chapter 6, marital discord and conflict show a strong relationship to children's aggression. The effects of programs designed to reduce marital discord have been modest (Markman, Renick, Floyd, Stanley, & Clements, 1993) and spouses in most need of such programs have been least willing to seek them out (Sullivan & Bradbury, 1997). Thus, in the words of one recent review, programs aimed at the widespread prevention of marital discord "remain more promise than reality" (Fincham & Beach, 1999, p. 67).

Many practitioners and researchers argue that because improving the context in which the family lives is an essential element in the prevention of children's antisocial behavior, successful interventions with at-risk families must include a broader scope of programs delivered within a community based setting (Reppucci, Woolard, & Fried, 1999; Yoshikawa, 1994). The four promising primary intervention programs previously described all contained some of these elements. Another such promising program is a child-abuse prevention intervention aimed at first-time unmarried urban adolescent mothers and implemented by staffers who live in the neighborhood (Britner & Reppucci, 1997). Compared with a matched group of nonparticipants, participants were more likely to have completed high school and to have delayed subsequent pregnancies until after the age of 21, and less likely to have substantiated reports of child maltreatment 3 to 5 years after the birth of their children.

Programs That Target Social and Cultural Factors.   As we have seen, violence in the media and access to firearms are two cultural factors that have been linked to youthful aggression. During the 1990s, new pressure was brought against media violence, and federal legislation now mandates that manufacturers of television sets include within the set a mechanism for screening out violent television programs (Baker, 1997). The extent to which these measures will reduce youth violence remains to be determined.

Efforts to reduce gun usage by American youth have generally involved two strategies: (a) severe restrictions on general gun availability through handgun control laws; and (b) more stringent punishments for the illegal possession and use of guns. Whether or not restrictions on general gun availability decrease youth violence has been hotly debated (Brewer et al., 1995; Christoffel, 1997; O'Donnell, 1995; Kates & Kleck, 1997; Kleck, 1991; Suter, 1994). Some evidence indicates that mandatory sentencing laws might reduce homicide rates, but their effect on other types of violent crime involving firearms remains unclear (Brewer et al., 1995).

One program that combines both "soft" and "tough" approaches to juvenile crime prevention involves steps the city of Boston has taken to reduce youth crime (Howell & Hawkins, 1998; Marcus, 1998; U.S. Department of Justice, 1996). Essentially, this program involves a partnership between city officials and community groups and individuals who are committed to the reduction of violent juvenile crime. In this connection, city officials and community organizations have provided more services to at-risk communities and to juveniles themselves. In addition, the police department has developed a *community policing program*, which attempts to be proactive rather than reactive and to be more sensitive to the needs of at-risk communities. At the same time, probation officers have instituted intensive supervision of youths under their care, even to the point of checking on their charges by riding at night with the police. Finally, police have begun to crack down on gangs and on even minor offenses committed by violent juveniles, especially those involving firearms. One 19-year-old, for example, was sentenced to 19 years in prison for possession of a single bullet, a sentence which the police advertised heavily on posters pasted up throughout the city.

Coincident with this program, Boston's murder rate for juveniles age 16 and under was cut by 80% between 1990 and 1998. Between July, 1995, and December, 1997, not one youth in Boston had been murdered. During the same period, Washington and Baltimore, approximately the same size as Boston, each had 70 juvenile murders (Marcus, 1998).

The apparent success of Boston's program seems related to a number of principles we have already discussed. First, the partnership of city officials and community organizations seems to increase *collective efficacy*. Second, community norms promoting prosocial behaviors seem to have negated the *code of the streets*. Third, improved policing and community vigilance have increased the penalties for antisocial behavior. And fourth, for those youths willing to change their behavior, the community also provides increased opportunities for prosocial behavior.

Programs That Target Protective Factors.   As we have seen, many of the protective factors that have been identified are the opposite of risk factors we have already considered. Thus, for example, an easygoing temperament and positive parental interaction with children seem to insulate the child against future aggression. One protective factor that appears to be somewhat unusual is the presence of religion. As we have seen, religiosity correlates as strong with youths' observed altruistic behavior as viewing violence on television correlates with antisocial behavior (Benson et al., 1987). Despite this, I know of no aggression-prevention program that has attempted to foster religiosity or religious practice. More attention needs to be given to this aspect of prevention.

Summary and Conclusions

We have seen that children's hyperaggression is linked to a wide variety of biological, psychological, and environmental risk factors. Unfortunately, many of these are resistant to prevention measures. The most successful prevention programs have begun early in the child's life (sometimes even before birth), have lasted for at least 2 years, and have targeted a variety of aspects of the child's and mother's lives. Some other prevention efforts appear promising, but their effects are still unproven.

SUMMARY

A number of promising cognitive, behavioral, and family interventions have been developed to treat antisocial and aggressive children and adolescents, many of whom have psychiatric diagnoses of ODD or CD. The two most successful interventions for young noncompliant and aggressive children have been the parent–child treatment (PCT) model and the collaborative–integrative (CI) approach. The PCT model focuses on improving parent–child emotional relations and on teaching parents behaviorally based child-management strategies. The CI model incorporates many of the ideas of the PCT model, but puts more emphasis on working with parents as partners and on targeting a wider variety of problems in both the parent and child. In addition, multisystemic therapy (MST), which targets not only family functioning but also other social systems that affect the family, has been found to be both cost effective and effective at reducing older youths' antisocial behavior.

Certain types of therapeutic foster care or group homes that utilize the adult-mediated behavior model appear promising. However, other types of psychological interventions have been less successful. These include psychodynamic relationship/insight therapy, guided group therapy, and a type of holding therapy called rage reduction therapy. Similarly, the effectiveness of medication in treating children's aggression has not yet been proven.

Juveniles under the age of 18 who commit a crime are typically processed within the juvenile justice system; however, those who have committed violent crimes are increasingly being tried as adults. In general, legal interventions for juvenile delinquents have produced disappointing results. Programs that do the best are those that offer some type of cognitive and family therapy component, that focus an intensive yet relatively short-term effort on helping the delinquent to deal with his environment, and that keep the delinquent isolated from other antisocial peers.

Intervention programs that show the greatest promise for preventing antisocial and aggressive behavior are those that begin during pregnancy, last a minimum of 2 years, provide a variety of assistance to mothers, and include some type of educational preschool or day care. Some other programs which target parent-related factors, family functioning, and social and cultural factors have also shown promise.

CHAPTER 13

Summary and Questions

Before leaving our examination of youth aggression and violence, I would like to summarize what we have learned in our journey and to discuss some of the major questions still unresolved regarding this topic.

ETIOLOGY AND DEVELOPMENT

At various points, we have considered both the development of children's aggressive and violent behavior and the major factors that seem to influence it. The development of hyperaggression from conception to adulthood can be viewed as a set of sequential stages. Drawing on the work of Patterson and colleagues (Patterson et al., 1992), I conceptualize childhood-onset hyperaggression in terms of the following six stages.

Stage 1: Unfavorable Innate Substrate (Conception to Birth)

In this stage, the child's genetic makeup, combined with adverse prenatal experiences and birth complications, results in a child whose innate physical and psychological characteristics predispose him or her to future externalizing behaviors (Fig. 13.1).

Conception. The antisocial behavior of many hyperaggressive children has its roots in the child's genetic makeup, which is set at conception. Indeed, behavioral genetics research indicates that perhaps ½ of the variability in youngsters' antisocial behavior might be attributable to heredity. At the same time, however, it is important to understand that antisocial youths probably do not inherit "criminal" genes that cause specific overt behaviors, but rather variations of "normal" genes that enhance "risk dimensions" associated with hyperaggressive behavior (Rutter et al., 1998). For example, both thrill-seeking and hyperactivity are associated with antisocial behavior, and it is possible that hyperaggressive youths inherit larger doses of the genes controlling these behaviors than do normal youngsters (Rutter et al., 1998). Whatever the specific genes and behaviors involved, it is likely that some children inherit a susceptibility to

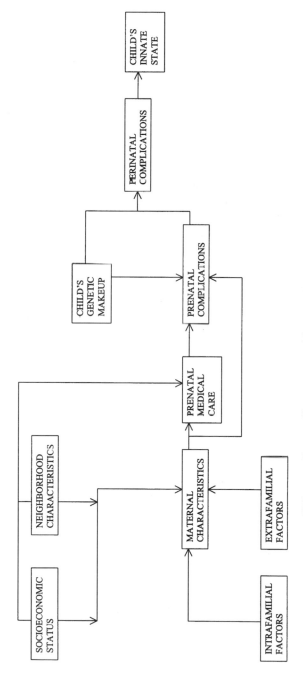

STAGE 1: UNFAVORABLE INNATE SUBSTRATE

(Conception, Prenatal Development, and Birth)

FIG. 13.1. Factors affecting antisocial behavior during prenatal development and birth. Arrows indicate the direction of the effect.

certain behaviors which elevate their risk for future antisocial and aggressive behavior (chap. 4).

Prenatal Development.   The hyperaggressive child's genetic risk is often compounded by an unfavorable prenatal environment. Immediately after conception, the offspring's development begins to be affected by the mother's womb, which in turn is also influenced by characteristics of the mother such as her diet, her physical health, chemicals produced in association with her psychological state, and maternal behaviors such as drug use and exposure to environmental toxins. Prenatal development can also be affected by medical complications that might occur during the course of the pregnancy; and these, in turn, might be related to the quality of the medical care received by the mother during her pregnancy. Finally, many of these factors might be affected by characteristics of the mother such as her age, her level of educational attainment, and her socioeconomic status.

Many mothers of highly antisocial children are impoverished, unmarried adolescents who live in low socioeconomic neighborhoods, who use and abuse both legal and illegal drugs, and who experience psychological difficulties such as clinical depression. In addition, psychological or financial limitations might hamper the ability of these mothers to obtain adequate prenatal medical care, thus further exacerbating a bad situation. As the result of these factors, the hyperaggressive child might develop a variety of prenatally caused problems such as minor physical anomalies and neurological dysfunctions, which might result in an innate biological predisposition toward aggressive behavior (chap. 4).

Birth.   Perinatal complications during birth have also been implicated in subsequent antisocial behavior (Lambert, 1988; Raine et al., 1997). In particular, reduced levels of oxygen flow to the infant's brain during birth can cause neurological impairment (Papalia et al., 1999). However, such perinatal complications might affect subsequent hyperaggression only to the extent that they interact with certain postnatal risk factors such as maternal rejection (Raine et al., 1994).

The combination of the child's genetic makeup, prenatal development, and perinatal experiences results in a set of innate physical and psychological characteristics that form the basis of further development. Unfortunately, many hyperaggressive youngsters possess an innate temperament that predisposes them to subsequent antisocial behavior. In particular, temperamental qualities such as restlessness, impulsivity, a short attention span, difficulties in sleeping and eating, a lack of behavioral inhibition, and a lack of positive response to the mother's attempts at emotional closeness all make it more likely that the child will exhibit future externalizing problems (Olweus, 1980; Rutter et al., 1998; Werner & Smith, 1982).

Stage 2: Unfavorable Psychological Substrate
(Infancy and Toddlerhood)

In this stage, the child's temperament combines with erratic care and unfavorable early experiences to result in a toddler whose psychological substrate predisposes him or her to subsequent externalizing behaviors (Fig. 13.2).

During infancy and toddlerhood, extrafamilial factors primarily affect hyperaggressive development indirectly through their effect on the infant's parents and family. Stress emanating from poverty and from living in a disadvantaged neighborhood can negatively affect family functioning and parental child-rearing behaviors.

Parental Characteristics.   An important component of development during the first year seems to be the infant's ability to develop a strong positive emotional relationship with at least one loving adult. Babies who show later resilience are those who experience a good mother–child relationship coupled with a large amount of maternal attention and a lack of prolonged separation from the mother (Rutter et al., 1998; Werner & Smith, 1982). In part, the baby's success in this endeavor is determined by the mother's perception that the baby possesses endearing psychological characteristics such as being cuddlesome and easily satisfied. Interestingly, the infant's physical health also plays a role in this process as well (Lambert, 1988; Werner & Smith, 1982). Unfortunately, many antisocial children seem to possess innate physical and psychological characteristics that impede this important process.

In addition, parental characteristics and behaviors are also important. For example, fathers who are absent or who engage in antisocial behaviors such as domestic violence or drug abuse are unlikely to develop positive relationships with their child. Similarly, mothers who are hostile to their infant or who are depressed or addicted to drugs or otherwise unable to cope with stress are less likely to develop a strong emotional relationship with their baby. Furthermore, when combined with birth complications, maternal rejection during infancy predicts subsequent violent behavior on the part of the child (chap. 4).

Caregiver Loss.   As we have seen, good care from parents during the early years functions as a protective factor against subsequent delinquency (chap. 7). We have also seen that many hyperaggressive youths grow up in homes without a father. However, as Garbarino pointed out, "what is surprising is the prevalence of absent *mothers*" (Garbarino, 1999, p. 47, emphasis in original). Young at-risk males often lose their mother at various times and for varying durations, sometimes permanently. Some mothers might be drug addicts who either cannot or will not raise their son. Others might be in prison or in some type of a psychiatric institution. Still others simply abandon their children. Controlled research indicates that repeated separations from or changes in care-

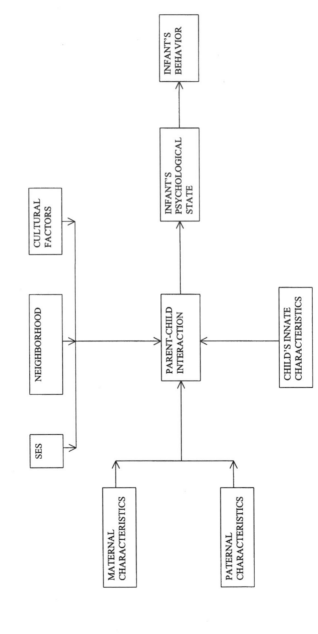

FIG. 13.2. Factors affecting antisocial behavior during infancy and toddlerhood. Arrows indicate the direction of the effect.

givers constitute a substantial risk for subsequent antisocial behaviors (Rutter et al., 1998).

Babies who lack a warm emotional relationship with their mother or other primary caregiver during the first 6 months of life often fail to develop a secure attachment during the remainder of the first year. Instead, as we have seen, many at-risk babies develop an insecure/disorganized type of attachment, thus suggesting that in times of stress, these infants are unable to elicit needed comfort and security from others in their environment (Lyons-Ruth, 1996). The lack of a secure attachment might interact with other risk factors, thus resulting in an infant who fails to develop the sense of basic trust, which Erikson (1950) saw as a key element to positive development during the rest of childhood.

Stage 3: Incipient Antisocial Behaviors (Early Childhood)

In this stage, due to the combination of unfavorable temperament and early experiences, the young child develops initial antisocial behaviors such as disobedience, angry outbursts of temper, and milder forms of instrumental and reactive aggression, both physical and verbal (Fig. 13.3).

Family Factors. During the ages of 2 to 5, the family exerts the most important influence on children's moral behavior. Chronic and intense marital conflict might either teach children to become angry and aggressive or might exacerbate already existing aggressive patterns of behavior. Children whose parents separate at this time might experience an added sense of abandonment, fear, and rejection, and might even come to believe that their behavior was responsible for the separation, thus intensifying their own sense of chronic guilt (Garbarino, 1999).

Rather than teaching the child prosocial behaviors through modeling and appropriate reinforcement, parents of hyperaggressive children often exhibit antisocial behaviors, which can serve as models for the child's inappropriate behavior. In addition, physical or sexual abuse or harsh physical punishment might also increase the child's level of antisocial behavior. Furthermore, either accurately or inaccurately, parents might perceive the child as being "troublesome" and might respond with an authoritarian, permissive, or neglectful parenting style, perhaps accompanied by power-assertive or love-withdrawal disciplinary techniques. As a result of these interactions, parents and children might become caught up in the reciprocal coercion training processes we discussed in chapter 5.

Extrafamilial Factors. Although family influences predominate during this period, extrafamilial factors are also beginning to affect the young child. For example, children now begin to spend more time playing with peers. In addition, the school setting becomes more important to some children, especially if

STAGE 3: INCIPIENT ANTISOCIAL BEHAVIORS

(Early Childhood)

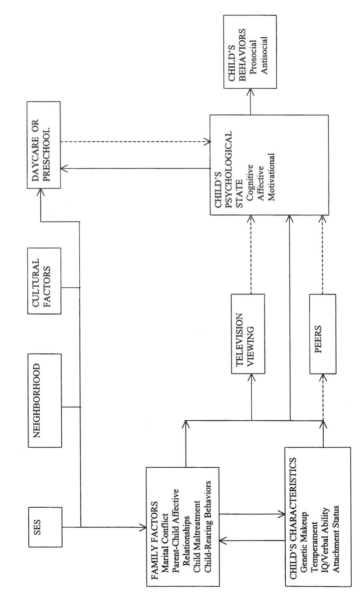

FIG. 13.3. Factors affecting antisocial behavior during early childhood. Arrows indicate the direction of the effect. Solid lines indicate stronger influence, dashed lines indicate weaker influence.

they are taken to preschool or placed in some type of out-of-home group care. And finally, media entertainment (especially television and video games) becomes increasingly salient at this age.

Child Characteristics. Unfortunately, preexisting characteristics might limit the ability of certain children to navigate this developmental period successfully. Some might be hampered by negative temperamental qualities and by their failure to form an attachment and basic trust during infancy and childhood, or they might fail to exhibit the incipient forms of empathy and prosocial behavior that characterize the majority of youngsters at this age.

The combination of temperamental proclivities and inadequate parenting might have a number of consequences for at-risk preschoolers. First, these children might begin to develop social information-processing difficulties in decoding, interpretation, response search, and response decision making. Second, they might experience poor impulse control and an inability to delay gratification, both of which might result in poor self-regulation. And third, instead of developing appropriate empathy and predispositional guilt, they might begin moving down the path toward ego-absorption and the guiltless pursuit of immediate gratification (chap. 8).

Child's Behaviors. By the age of 5, some children are well on their way to a future of antisocial behavior problems and related difficulties. Behaviorally, these youngsters now engage in more frequent and intense temper tantrums (especially when frustrated) and exhibit an increasing amount of negativism and noncompliance. Instead of having peaked, their aggression continues to escalate. As time goes on, some of these children begin to develop clear-cut signs of either oppositional defiant disorder (ODD) or attention-deficit/hyperactivity disorder (ADHD).

Stage 4: Intensification of Antisocial Behaviors (Ages 5 to 8)

In this stage, reciprocal interactions between the child's unfavorable characteristics and the family and the extrafamilial environment result in the intensification of a variety of antisocial behaviors, including both verbal and physical aggression (Fig. 13.4).

Family Factors. Family factors continue to exert an important effect during this time. As intrafamilial coercion training continues, the child becomes even more antisocial and aggressive. Family functioning is often chaotic, and parents might impose little if any structure in the child's life. Parental stress, marital conflict, and psychological problems might negatively affect parenting behaviors and result either in overly lax or overly strict parenting. Moreover, the affective relationship between parents and child might also be poor.

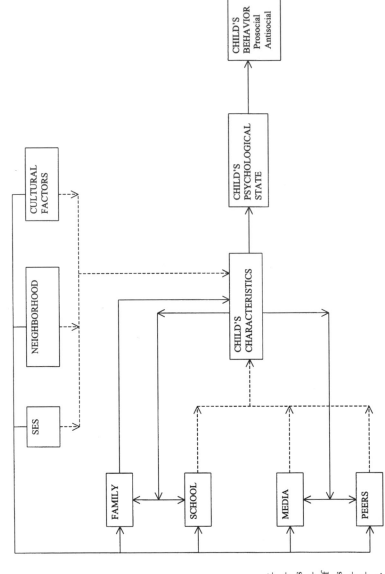

STAGE 4: INTENSIFICATION

(Ages 5 to 8)

FIG. 13.4. Factors affecting antisocial behavior during the ages of 5 to 8. Arrows indicate the direction of the effect. Solid lines indicate stronger influence, dashed lines indicate weaker influence.

Extrafamilial Factors. During this time, extrafamilial factors begin to take on an increasing importance. For example, neighborhoods start to exert a greater influence in a number of ways. First, the composition of the neighborhood affects the makeup of the child's peer group and schoolmates, thus affecting the child directly. In addition, the neighborhood affects the quality of the school, affecting the child indirectly. Finally, the neighborhood also continues to affect the child's family and hence exerts an indirect influence through the parents' child-rearing behaviors.

The school, the media, and the child's peers also begin to play a more important role during this period. By the time children enter the first grade around the age of 6, previously existing attentional problems and deficits in verbal abilities tend to predict later externalizing problems. Furthermore, unusually high levels of aggressiveness among first-grade boys also predict self-reported delinquency during adolescence. Also during this time, aggressively predisposed children begin to seek out media entertainment that features aggression and violence. In addition, some of these children spend many hours watching television without any adult supervision or mediation. Finally, the hyperaggressive child's antisocial behavior begins to provoke rejection from a majority of peers, who in turn begin to define the child as "bad."

Child Characteristics. By the end of the preschool period, children should have developed a number of psychological processes that serve as building-blocks for internalized moral behavior. Thus, by this age young people should possess a set of conventional moral values. In addition, as a result of their interactions with parents and other adults, they should have also learned a set of accessible prosocial behaviors such as empathy, altruism, helping, and cooperation. Moreover, in conjunction with cognitive processes such as memory and a sense of "time within space," children should have developed the rudiments of self-regulation or self-control. And finally, by this age youths should be responding to infractions of moral values with appropriate predispositional guilt. Unfortunately, however, future hyperaggressive children often lack these characteristics and consequently enter middle childhood with a predisposition toward aggression and a set of motives that emphasize the need to dominate and control others. Consequently, many of them will exhibit antisocial and aggressive behaviors severe enough to warrant the diagnosis of CD.

Child's Behaviors. By the age of 8, many children now engage in antisocial and aggressive behavior that is severe enough to warrant the diagnosis of ODD, and some might even develop CD. In addition, some children might also experience comorbid ADHD with their ODD or CD.

Stage 5: Solidification and Broadening of Antisocial Behaviors (Middle Childhood)

In this stage, the child's problematic cognitive, motivational, and affective systems become more ingrained, thus resulting in more pervasive and stable antisocial behavior, including hyperaggression (Fig. 13.5).

Family Factors. Family factors such as marital discord, family composition, parent–child affective relations, and parental involvement in the child's life seem to be especially salient during the ages of 8 to 13 (Werner & Smith, 1982). By this time, any coercive interaction patterns that originated during the preschool years have probably become more intense and more ingrained within the family (Patterson et al., 1992). In addition, negative parent–child emotional relations and ineffective parenting techniques both tend to exacerbate the child's existing antisocial tendencies. And, as we have seen, such ineffective parental practices might in turn be affected by various stressors arising from within the family as well as from the extrafamilial environment. In addition, harsh physical punishment and a lack of parental monitoring and supervision toward the end of this period might further exacerbate child's antisocial and aggressive behaviors.

Of particular importance for boys at this time might be the presence of a father or father substitute. Indeed, Werner and Smith (1982) found that the presence of a father in middle childhood improved resilience for boys. Similarly, in his clinical study of adult male mass murderers, Ressler argued that these individuals "became solidified in their loneliness first during the age period of eight to twelve" and that the most important factor producing this isolation was "the absence of a father" (Ressler & Shachtman, 1992, p. 79). In agreement with these views, Garbarino (1999) argued that the lack of a caring father increases the boy's chances of growing up in poverty and living in a "toxic" neighborhood; increases the chances that the boy "will lack a male guide, protector, and mentor" (p. 46); and makes it more likely that the boy will blame and hence devalue himself for his father's absence.

Extrafamilial Factors. As the child acquires more independence and interacts more with extrafamilial variables, these factors begin to take on more importance in the child's life. For example, much of the child's socialization during the elementary school years comes from the peer group, and children's peer relations take on more salience during middle childhood. Indeed, Harris (1998) argued that children's socialization occurs primarily through their peer group interaction. As we have seen, aggressive children increasingly associate with deviant peers during this time, and this association in turn exacerbates the child's existing antisocial tendencies. At the same time, many inner-city youngsters develop an antisocial lifestyle in response to the pressures associated with the "code of the streets."

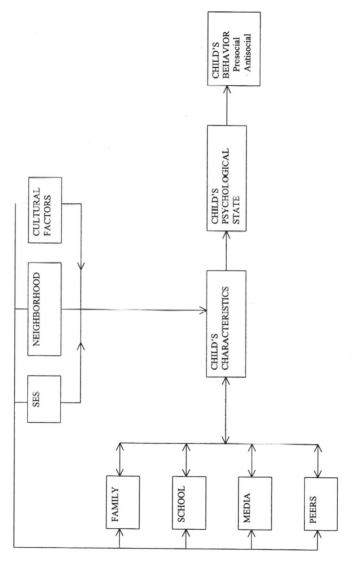

STAGE 5: SOLIDIFICATION AND BROADENING

(Middle Childhood)

FIG. 13.5. Factors affecting antisocial behavior during middle childhood. Arrows indicate the direction of the effect. Solid lines indicate stronger influence, dashed lines indicate weaker influence.

By the fourth grade, hyperaggressive children have often experienced both conduct problems and academic difficulties, particularly in reading. As we have seen, it is likely that certain preexisting characteristics of the child account for both of these types of problems. However, the child's school experience can either exacerbate or help mitigate the child's antisocial behaviors. Thus, schools possessing an "authoritative ethos" seem particularly effective at minimizing children's concurrent and subsequent antisocial behavior. In addition, primary and secondary prevention programs operating in elementary schools have been found to be effective at reducing antisocial behavior in the later grades.

As the hyperaggressive child moves through middle childhood, he spends more of his discretionary time interacting with various forms of media violence (including music and the Internet). This interaction in turn makes his aggression more severe and teaches him new aggressive cognitive scripts.

Stage 6: Overt Delinquency (Adolescence)

In this stage, the adolescent's academic difficulties increase; in addition, the young person becomes an active member of an antisocial peer group and engages in a wide variety antisocial and delinquent activities, including sexual promiscuity, the use and abuse of both legal and illegal drugs, violence, and perhaps murder (Fig. 13.6).

In terms of antisocial behavior, the period between 13 and 17 is important for two reasons. First, adolescent influences can contribute to either the persistence or desistence of childhood-onset hyperaggressive behavior. And second, adolescent influences can help initiate adolescent-onset delinquency and aggression.

Childhood-Onset Problems. There are a number of reasons why adolescence can have a profound effect on youngsters with a developmental history of hyper-aggressiveness.

• These youths have had a number of years to "practice" their aggression and thus become quite good at it. In Patterson's terms, these young people's antisocial behavior has become automatic and overlearned (Patterson et al., 1992).

• The process of the "imaginary audience" leads these youths to believe that the rest of the world will admire them for their violent acts. For example, in a videotape made shortly before the Columbine High School killings of 1999, Eric Harris imagines the admiration that he thinks others will shower on himself and Dylan Klebold and asks, "Isn't it fun to get the respect we deserve?" (Gibbs & Roche, 1999, p. 44).

• The process of the personal fable leads antisocial adolescents to disregard the danger inherent in aggressive and violent behavior.

• Because much of adolescent behavior in general is aimed at distancing teenagers from the conventions of adults, hyperaggressive adolescents need

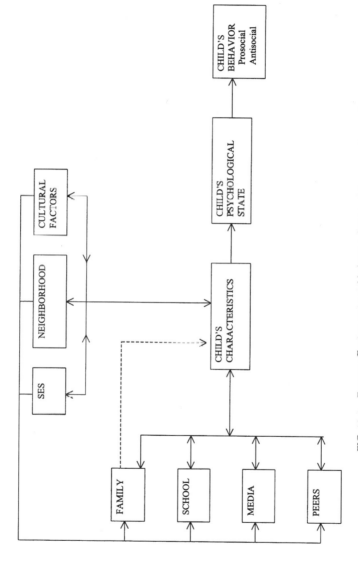

STAGE 6: OVERT DELINQUENCY

(Adolescence)

FIG. 13.6. Factors affecting antisocial behavior during adolescence. Arrows indicate the direction of the effect.

337

to differentiate themselves from conventional adult society (Harris, 1998). But, because adult society has broadened its definition of acceptable behavior over the past 40 years, the behavior of aggressive or disturbed adolescents must now become even more extreme in order for it to be noticed as "different" (Harris, 1998).

• Hyperaggressive adolescents who banded together in antisocial peer groups during middle childhood now become full-fledged members of antisocial youth gangs. In turn, the group dynamics and antisocial norms characteristic of these gangs tend to solidify gang members in their antisocial behaviors.

• Fantasies of violence that begin in middle childhood might become merged with sexual fantasies and become more compelling during adolescence (Garbarino, 1999; Ressler & Shachtman, 1992). Long-term exposure to violent video games might help such adolescents depersonalize their victims and thus make overt violence more likely (Garbarino, 1999).

Adolescent-Onset Problems. The adolescent experience can affect even those youngsters who did not exhibit previous antisocial behavior. For example, teenage sexual urges might combine with the questioning of adult authority and the personal fable to produce risky sexual behavior, especially in the context of an approving peer group. A similar argument could be made for other behaviors such as drug use and abuse and "exciting" acts of minor delinquency.

Adolescent-onset antisocial behavior seems to be particularly affected by adolescent social–psychological processes. As we have seen, most teenage delinquency occurs after school in group settings. The young person's peer group is particularly important at this stage, since groups populated with a "critical mass" of antisocial youths tend to develop antisocial norms that they impose on their members (Rutter et al., 1998). By the age of 17 or 18, however, the dynamics shift. By this age, youths in our society are generally expected either to get a job or to attend postsecondary schooling, both of which require more adultlike behaviors. And as youngsters begin to pair off sexually, dyadic relationships acquire more importance and group activities decline. Consequently, delinquent behavior becomes less alluring as these youths move into their roles as young adults (Rutter et al., 1998).

As we have seen, extrafamilial factors become more influential during adolescence. To be sure, family variables can still affect adolescents' antisocial behavior, with parental monitoring and supervision taking on added importance during this time. However, environmental factors such as the media, neighborhoods, and peer groups become increasingly important during this period.

Summary

Childhood-onset hyperaggressive behavior can be conceptualized as moving through a sequence of six stages. Each stage builds on characteristics of the preceding stage and increases the likelihood that a young person will move on to the next stage. Although the youth can exit the process at any stage, desistence is more likely at earlier stages than at later ones. Unfortunately, although desistence is presumably due to the operation of protective factors at a particular stage, our current understanding of this process is quite limited, and much more work in this area is needed (Rutter et al., 1998).

TENTATIVE CONCLUSIONS

What lessons can we draw from our consideration of youth aggression and violence? Although this discussion is certainly not the final word on the subject, current theory and research seem to suggest the following major conclusions.

- *The prevalence and intensity of youths' aggressive behavior began to increase during the 1960s, escalated dramatically from the mid-1980s to the mid-1990s, but now seems to be on the decline.* The years prior to the 1960s can be called the "preescalation period" regarding youthful aggression and violence. Starting in the mid-1960s, however, youthful externalizing behavior began to increase both in and out of school. This trend intensified in the mid-1980s, especially with regard to homicides and violent crimes committed by young people under the age of 18. Fortunately, although youthful aggression and violence still appear to be historically high, some decline in youth violence has been noted since the mid-1990s.

- *Chronic hyperaggressive behavior is generally overdetermined by a number of factors working together in combination, rather than by a single "causative" factor.* Attempts to find a single cause for youthful aggression have proved futile. Instead, it is apparent that most cases of hyperaggressive behavior are due to a confluence of multiple "risk factors" that affect a child either simultaneously or sequentially. In the sense that many intrapersonal, familial, and extrafamilial factors all favor the development of antisocial behavior, hyperaggressive behavior is said to be "overdetermined."

- *"Low-level" aggression often leads to more serious violence.* Nonaggressive antisocial behaviors and minor forms of aggression often provide the springboard from which more serious forms of aggression develop. Any attempt to decrease youth violence thus needs to address such low-level aggressive behaviors.

- *Nature and nurture often combine in complex ways to produce hyperaggressive behavior.* Because of their innate characteristics, some children are more sensitive to environmental risk factors than are other children (*genotype–environment interaction*). In addition, the child's environment can exacerbate innate predispositions toward antisocial behavior (*genotype–environment correlation*). Thus, for example, we have seen that antisocial parents often provide an environment for their children that is conducive to the development of aggression (*passive correlation*); that the behavior of aggressive children often provokes rejection and retaliation from nonaggressive peers (*evocative correlation*); and that aggressive children often choose to watch violent television shows and to associate with antisocial peers (*active correlation*). In addition, aggression also involves the characteristics of the child operating within an environment that either provides more or less opportunity for aggression.

• *Chronic hyperaggressive behavior that becomes manifest by the age of 8 has a high likelihood of continuing throughout childhood and into adolescence and adulthood.* Studies consistently indicate that hyperaggressiveness at age 8 (and perhaps even earlier) statistically predicts subsequent delinquency, violence, and criminal behavior. More specifically, as many as 50% of such children might show later problems in adolescence or adulthood.

• *Chronically hyperaggressive youngsters are likely to exhibit a wide variety of problems as adults.* Children diagnosed with CD as children are at risk as adults to suffer from a host of problems, including psychological disorders (such as antisocial personality disorder, depression, and drug and alcohol abuse); adult criminal behavior (including more serious crimes and longer jail terms); poor occupational adjustment (including lower wages, more frequent bouts of unemployment, and more time on welfare); lower educational attainment (including more dropping out of school); marital problems (including higher rates of divorce); poor interpersonal relationships; and problems with physical health (including higher rates of hospitalization and higher mortality rates).

• *Aggressive children often actively select environments that are conducive to the development of aggressive behavior.* Throughout the book, we have observed the phenomenon of "child effects," the extent to which children's characteristics and behavior contribute to the development of their own aggressive behavior. For example, although media violence is often seen as the cause of aggression, it is unlikely that this factor in itself causes otherwise nonaggressive children to become violent. Instead, the research indicates that children who are aggressive by nature seem to prefer violent television shows, violent songs, and violent video games. Thus, hyperaggressive children operate on their environment as much as the environment operates on them (Patterson et al., 1992).

• *The recent historic increase in youthful aggressive behavior is due largely to environmental factors rather than to genetics.* Although child effects are important, the child's characteristics interact with the environment to either exacerbate or mitigate existing aggressive tendencies. Because the gene pool does not change rapidly, it is clear that much of the increase in aggression over the past 40 years must involve environmental factors (Garbarino, 1999; Rutter et al., 1998). Indeed, a number of psychologists have observed that the environment has become more "socially toxic" to children since the 1960s (Damon, 1995; Garbarino, 1999; Magnet, 1993). Furthermore, as pointed out throughout the book, environmental risk factors for aggression have become more predominant over the past 40 years, whereas the prevalence of protective factors has decreased.

Thus, any successful attempt at reducing the level of youthful hyperaggression will need to address these environmental risk factors.

- *A relatively small group of chronically hyperaggressive youngsters is responsible for most of the major violence committed by youths.* Although delinquency is quite common among adolescents, only about half of officially adjudicated delinquents commit a second or subsequent offense. Moreover, 50% or more of serious crimes committed by juveniles are perpetrated by "chronic offenders," who begin their antisocial careers at an early age and who comprise about 6% of the juvenile population.

- *Although antisocial children are no doubt a heterogeneous group, research has yet to demonstrate reliable and valid subtypes of hyperaggressive behavior.* It is clear that hyperaggressive children differ among themselves, and some attempts have been made to delineate these differences (Frick et al., 1994, chap. 3). Nevertheless, much more work needs to be done to determine whether there are distinctive subtypes of hyperaggressive youth, and if so, which variables distinguish one type from another.

- *When antisocial youths interact with each other in groups of two or more, their existing hyperaggressive behaviors become even more entrenched and extreme.* Antisocial youngsters validate and support each other. For example, aggressive elementary school boys who are placed in a class with numerous other "aggressive" children are more likely to maintain their aggression than are similar boys who are placed in a "nonaggressive" class (Kellam, Ling, Merisca, Brown, & Ialongo, 1998). An antisocial youngster who becomes affiliated with other antisocial peers is more likely to maintain his or her antisocial behavior than one who does not (chap. 7). And therapy with groups of antisocial youths often seems to do more harm than good (chap. 12). Furthermore, as illustrated by the Columbine High School massacre, aggression committed by two or more youngsters tends to be much more violent than that committed by a single individual (chap. 10).

- *Youthful hyperaggression is due more to the child's antisocial habits and motivations than to his lack of positive social skills.* Children with child-onset CD probably learn aggressive behaviors at an early age. As pointed out by Burton (1984) and Patterson et al. (1992), these aggressive motor behaviors are likely to become overlearned and "automatized" at an early age. In addition, as Olweus (1993) and Samenow (1989) pointed out, such aggression also complements the antisocial youngster's motives for dominance and control. Furthermore, as illustrated by the findings of Dishion et al. (1995), the poor social relationships experienced by antisocial youths seem to be due more to negative and coercive interactions than to a lack of more positive social skills.

- *The nature and dynamics of intrafamilial killings committed by youths differ from those of extrafamilial killings.* Homicides committed by children and adolescents can be divided into the approximately 10% that involve the killing of a family member (intrafamilial killing), and the 90% that involve the killing of an acquaintance or stranger (extrafamilial killing). The typical intrafamilial killing by a young person involves a male child killing a father due to the father's chronic abusive behavior toward one or more members of the family (chap. 10). Extrafamilial killings often involve the killing of an acquaintance or stranger by a youth who has exhibited hyperaggressive behavior from an early age.

• *Youthful killers probably fall into three major subtypes: the psychotic group, the overstressed group, and the aggressive group.* Psychotic killers, although rare, are those who experience a full-blown psychosis or a psychotic episode, which limits their understanding of reality, and leads them to kill without an appreciation of what they are doing. Overstressed killers aggress only under extreme stress, but then do so very violently. Aggressive killers are children whose incipient violence escalates and results in killing. Youths who engage in school shootings also seem to have a long-standing psychological disturbance that finally culminates in one last act of violence. Although warning signs are usually present, they are often not heeded.

• *Although schools probably do not cause youthful hyperaggression, they can do much to reduce youthful antisocial and aggressive behavior.* Because hyperaggressive behavior tends to become manifest before the child even enters formal schooling, schools are generally not an initial cause of youthful hyperaggression. Nevertheless, two major steps schools can take to reduce antisocial behavior involve the development of a "positive school ethos" as well as the implementation of various primary and secondary aggression prevention programs, especially those aimed at eliminating bullying.

• *The most effective therapy with hyperaggressive youths begins when the child is young, includes other members of the child's family, and targets the child's cognitions and overt behaviors as well as other aspects of the child's life.* Interventions that target both the child's cognitive and behavioral processes in a number of settings are more likely to be successful than those that only aim to reduce the child's problem behaviors. In addition, interventions should be collaborative in nature, involve the entire family as much as possible, be set in the community or in the home, and target all the systems that are producing stress for the family.

• *The most successful aggression prevention programs begin early in the child's life (sometimes even before birth), last for at least 2 years, and target multiple aspects of the child's and parent's lives.* Prevention programs that have been shown to reduce youthful antisocial behavior all begin within the first 5 years of life, lasted for at least 2 years, involved home visits, provided some type of educational preschool experience, and focused not only on the child but also on other aspects of the mother's life, such as assistance with medical and occupational issues.

UNRESOLVED ISSUES

Although we have learned much about youth aggression and violence, we have much more to learn.

Nature and Nurture

Throughout this book, we have examined the roles both nature and nurture play in the development of hyperaggressive behavior. As we have seen, much of the research supports the view that these variables interact to produce highly antisocial youngsters, especially those with overt, child-onset CD. In general, it appears that certain innate characteristics of the child combine with unfavorable elements of the child's environment to cause the development of a hyperaggressive youngster.

At the same time, however, it is likely that both genetic and environmental risk factors vary along a continuum ranging from large to small. This is clearly the case for environmental risk factors; some children might experience only one or two risk factors, and might experience those for only a short period in their lives. Other children, however, might encounter a large number of risk factors and might experience those for a long period of time. Although less is known about genetic risk factors, it is also likely that some children might experience only a minimal amount of genetic susceptibility, whereas others might experience a greater amount of genetic vulnerability.

Given this situation, a number of possibilities loom for understanding the development of youthful hyperaggressive behavior. First, it is possible that a relatively large amount of either genetic or environmental risk might "over whelm" the other factor. For example, experiencing an unusually large number of environmental risk factors might result in hyperaggressive behavior even for a child with little or no genetic risk. Similarly, children with a great deal of genetic risk might also develop hyperaggression even if they grow up in a benign environment. However, an alternative possibility is that a relatively large amount of either "good" genes or a "good" environment might protect children against developing antisocial behavior even in the face of other risk factors. Thus, for example, it is possible that a large number of "good" genes could protect even children who experience a great deal of environmental risk, or that a highly positive environment could protect children who are at extreme risk genetically.

At the present time, these possibilities are difficult to test empirically, in part because we know so little about specific genes that might be involved in hyperaggressive behavior. As future research illuminates more clearly the relationship between specific genes and overt behavior, a much better understanding should emerge regarding the manner in which nature and nurture combine to affect youthful hyperaggressive behavior.

Sex Differences

As we have seen in numerous contexts, physical hyperaggression is much more common among males than among females (chaps. 1, 2, 3, and 10). Partially because of this, much of the research on youthful aggression has involved samples composed totally or primarily of males, thus limiting our knowledge regarding female development (Rutter et al., 1998). Consequently, most of what we know about youthful hyperaggression pertains exclusively or primarily to males.

Existing research indicates that males and females tend to differ in how they express their aggression. Thus, as we have seen, males tend to be more physically aggressive and to engage in more extreme forms of violent behavior. Females, on the other hand, tend to exhibit more verbal aggression along with a type of "relational aggression" involving behaviors such as gossiping about someone, saying something to hurt another's feelings, or doing something to exclude another child from a group.

Less is known regarding the roles that sex differences might play in the development of aggression. For example, hyperaggressive behavior seems to have a more direct and stable path from childhood to adulthood for males than for females, but much more needs to be learned about this relationship. Similarly, although the presence of a father in the home during childhood seems to be a protective factor against aggression for males but not for females, the reasons for this finding are unclear. Thus, one of the major challenges for future research will be to delineate the processes and mechanisms involved in the development of hyperaggressive behavior in females as well as in males.

Although males exhibit more physical hyperaggression than females, the nature and reasons for the male–female difference are poorly understood (Rutter et al., 1998). Because differences in physical aggression begin in toddlerhood and occur across both culture and class, and because gender differences are more pronounced for aggressive lifecourse-persistent CD than for time-limited adolescent delinquency, there is some reasons to believe that biological mechanisms might be involved (Rutter et al., 1998). Nonetheless, because the extent of sex differences varies across both time and cultures, environmental factors are also implicated (Rutter et al., 1998). Exactly what these environmental factors are, and how they operate, are still unknown. For example, some researchers argue that because contemporary American culture forbids boys from expressing their emotions verbally, male youngsters develop externalizing behaviors when they feel depressed, whereas young females are more likely to develop internalizing disorders under similar circumstances (Garbarino, 1999). However, solid data on this issue are lacking (Rutter et al., 1998), and much more research needs to be done.

Although sex differences in aggressive behavior are still not well understood, researchers are becoming more interested in this important topic (Heimer,

1996; O'Shea & Fletcher, 1997), and we can expect to learn much more about female antisocial behavior in the years ahead.

Race

Youngsters from minority groups, especially African Americans, are disproportionately affected by youth violence in the United States. Thus, as we have seen, the homicide rate from 1984 to 1993 showed a much greater increase for youthful Black offenders than for Whites, and youth violence tends to be more prevalent in the inner cities than in suburbs and rural areas. Furthermore, in part because youth violence tends to be an intraracial phenomenon, Black youths are also disproportionately victimized compared with Whites (Snyder & Sickmund, 1999). Indeed, Hammond and Yung (1993) pointed out that a "male African-American adolescent is more likely to die of injuries received from a gun wielded by a friend or acquaintance than from any other cause" (p. 142).

One question that must be addressed is whether violence is truly greater among African-American youths or whether the apparent differences can be attributed to racial bias. In their review of data from the United States, Rutter et al. (1998) concluded that both factors are at work: Rates of serious offending are actually greater for African-American juveniles, but these real differences are also exaggerated by disparities within the legal system. At the same time, however, we must keep in mind that large variations in antisocial behavior exist within ethnic groups as well (Rutter et al., 1998).

As we have seen, youthful hyperaggression appears to be highly heritable. Hence, it is possible that genetic factors might account for racial differences in youth violence. However, this possibility is unlikely for a number of reasons. First, because of the underrepresentation of youths from ethnic minority groups in behavior genetics research, the external validity of these studies with respect to minority groups remains unclear. Furthermore, even if a trait is highly heritable for all populations, the difference between the means of the trait for two groups is not necessarily due to genetics (Plomin et al., 1997). For example, even though height is highly heritable, the increase in mean height of London boys over the first half of the 20th century was caused by better nutrition rather than by changes in the gene pool (Rutter et al., 1998). Finally, because gene pool changes tend to occur slowly, the relatively rapid increase in violent crimes for African-American youths beginning in the mid-1980s was much more likely the result of environmental factors than of genetics.

Much of the relationship between youthful hyperaggression and race may be due to the fact that a disproportionate number of African-American youths live in poverty (Hammond & Yung, 1993; Rutter et al., 1998). As we saw in chapter 7, poor children inhabit neighborhoods and communities that foster antisocial and aggressive behavior. In addition, poverty can also produce stress for parents, which in turn can impede appropriate parental child-rearing practices such as discipline, parental monitoring, parental supervision, and parental involvement.

Racism has also been hypothesized to account for much of the increase in the antisocial behavior of African-American youths. At one level, racism might result in Blacks' having less access to good jobs, good neighborhoods, good medical care, and governmental services such as adequate police protection and good schools (Hammond & Yung, 1993). At another level, Blacks' reaction to racism might involve self-hatred or free-floating anger, both of which could be transformed into aggressive and violent behavior (Hammond & Yung, 1993). Finally, racism (or the perception of racism) might cause Black youths to develop the beliefs that they have been unfairly treated and that they are unlikely to live into adulthood, thus creating the attitude that they should get as much as they can from life while they are alive, even if doing so requires the use of violence (Garbarino, 1999; Sheley & Wright, 1995). Unfortunately, little data exists regarding these possibilities.

In their review, Rutter et al. (1998) pointed out that the minority group in the United Kingdom with the lowest crime rate is that of the East Asians, consisting mainly of Pakistanis and Bangladeshis. Interestingly, this group is one of the poorest, most disadvantaged, and most racially harassed minority groups in the United Kingdom (Rutter et al., 1998). However, what seems to set the East Asians apart from other ethnic minority groups with higher crime rates is their marital stability; indeed, 90% of East Asian children live with formally married parents (Rutter et al., 1998). Afro-Caribbeans, who are less disadvantaged and have higher levels of education than the East Asians, have the highest crime rate among U.K. minority groups. In contrast to East Asian children, Afro-Caribbean youngsters are the most likely to be born to a teenage mother and the most likely to be brought up by a single never married mother (Rutter et al., 1998). Thus, at least in the United Kingdom, ethnic differences in crime rates do not appear to be attributable directly to poverty, low educational attainment, or racial discrimination (Rutter et al., 1998). Of course, the United Kingdom is not the United States, and the external validity of this comparison can be questioned. At the same time, however, these findings are intriguing.

The issue of the involvement of youngsters from minority groups in antisocial and hyperaggressive behavior is complex. Additional research of high quality will be needed to give us a better understanding of this important question.

Models of Hyperaggression

Theoretical writings on hyperaggressive youth present two major pictures of this group of children. According to the first view, which I call the *frustrated emotions* approach, a child's antisocial and hyperaggressive behavior emerges from powerful feelings of rejection caused by numerous environmental misfortunes experienced by the child. Because these youngsters lack consistent and sensitive maternal care, they fail to develop secure attachment as infants and hence fail to develop a basic trust in other humans (Garbarino, 1999; Levy & Orlans, 1998). In addition, many of them are abused and thus come to believe that they cannot receive protection from adults, and hence must protect themselves. Moreover, because these children are often abandoned not only by their fathers but often also by their mothers, they feel rejected, inadequate, and ashamed. As a result, these youngsters experience unconscious anxiety and depression, a state that in turn sensitizes them to perceived injustices in their lives. But because most of these youngsters are males, and because males in our society are not allowed to express such emotions directly, these "lost boys" express their anxiety and depression as anger and aggression, thus lashing out at the world they believe does not understand them and has not been fair to them (Garbarino, 1999).

According to the second view, which I call the *deviant behaviors* approach, hyperaggressive behavior is learned rather directly and is maintained in large part because of the child's antisocial motivations (Burton, 1984; Olweus, 1993; Patterson et al., 1992; Samenow, 1989). Beginning at birth, characteristics of the child and the environment reciprocally interact with and mutually affect each other. Deficiencies within both the child and the environment contribute to the development of antisocial behavior. For example, the child might lack certain typical prosocial behaviors, such as the rudimentary forms of empathy seen in many toddlers around the age of 2. In addition, rather than teaching prosocial behaviors, the child's parents might actually teach antisocial behaviors instead. For a variety of reasons, then, the young hyperaggressive child develops a set of overt and prepotent antisocial and aggressive behaviors. Furthermore, the child gradually develops a cognitive system that lacks control over antisocial impulses and that demands immediate gratification; a motivational system dominated by the need for thrills, power, and control; and an emotional system built on ego-absorption and the elimination of guilt (chap. 8).

To some extent, these two theoretical views might reflect more of a difference in emphasis than a difference in actual content. For example, although the frustrated emotions view does recognize that some youngsters might be temperamentally more "vulnerable" than others, it emphasizes the importance of the "socially toxic environment" in which such children are raised (Garbarino, 1999). Similarly, although the deviant behaviors view acknowledges the role of the external environment, it underscores the mutual interaction between the child's characteristics and environment. Thus, to some extent, these two approaches might not so much be antagonistic as they are complementary.

However, there do appear to be some salient differences between these two theoretical models. Most clearly, the frustrated emotions approach argues that unpleasant emotions such as anxiety and depression due to abandonment and rejection are the central causal factors in youngsters' hyperaggressive behaviors (Garbarino, 1999). The implication is that reducing these negative emotions and repairing the child's sense of abandonment and rejection should eliminate the child's need to engage in antisocial and aggressive behaviors (Levy & Orlans, 1998). The deviant behaviors approach argues that the child's hyperaggressive behavior is learned and not a reaction to unconscious negative emotions. Moreover, this position also holds that rather than being the cause of children's hyperaggressive behavior, emotions such as anxiety and depression are often the result of such antisocial behavior (Patterson et al., 1992). The implication of this position is that children's hyperaggressive behaviors will be reduced by teaching them prosocial behaviors, not by helping them to deal with unpleasant negative emotions they might experience.

Although this issue is far from resolved, systematically gathered research seems to support the deviant behaviors view over the frustrated emotions position. In the first place, as we saw in chapter 8, a number of studies indicate that the aggressive behavior of highly antisocial children is not a defense against underlying anxiety (Olweus, 1993; Robins, 1966; Tangney et al., 1996; Truscott, 1992). Second, comorbid CD does not seem to abate following remission of depression (Loeber & Keenan, 1994), nor does depression appear to enhance the severity of CD or delinquency (Fischer et al., 1984), thus suggesting that depression does not cause hyperaggressiveness. Third, as we saw in chapter 5, insecure attachment is "neither a necessary nor sufficient cause for later externalizing problems" (Greenberg et al., 1997, p. 199). And finally, the interventions that have proved to be effective with hyperaggressive children are those aimed at teaching the child new cognitions and skills rather than those designed to help the child deal with his or her emotional state (chap. 12). For these reasons, it appears that explanations of youthful hyperaggression that emphasize young people's deviant behaviors and motivations are more plausible than those that posit aggression as a reaction to unpleasant emotions such as anxiety and feelings of rejection. Further research is needed to shed more light on this issue.

CONCLUDING COMMENTS

Children's aggression and violence began to increase in the 1960s and escalated dramatically in the mid-1980s. Unfortunately, although the rate of serious juvenile crime declined during the latter part of the 1990s, youthful antisocial and aggressive behavior continues to remain high by historical standards.

We have learned much about juvenile aggression in the past 50 years. Longitudinal studies in particular have begun to illuminate the relationship between aggression in young children and violence among adolescents and adults. In addition, we have a better understanding of the psychological processes found in hyperaggressive youth, and we now know most of major risk factors associated with young people's serious and chronic antisocial behavior. Nevertheless, there is still much to learn, particularly as regards questions involving heredity, gender, and race. Future research will increase our knowledge in these areas and others as well.

But knowledge is not enough. Much of the problem of juvenile aggression and violence stems not from a lack of knowledge, but from adults' lack of commitment to our children and from our failure to assume personal and societal responsibility for their well-being. Although the United States prides itself on being a child-centered society, the fact is that all too many of us are more self-centered than child-centered. For example, too many parents make babies without being willing to assume the responsibility of nurturing and guiding those babies into adulthood. And too many other adults contribute to the psychological toxicity of children's environment while neglecting their own moral responsibility toward the next generation. At root, the problem of youthful aggression and violence is one of moral development, and as long as we adults behave amorally or immorally toward our children, we can hardly expect them to behave morally toward others.

References

Abel, G. G., Mittelman, M. S., & Becker, J. V. (1985). Sexual offenders: Results of assessment and recommendations for treatment in clinical criminology. In M. H. Ben-Aron, S. J. Hucker, & C. D. Webster (Eds.), *The assessment and treatment of criminal behavior* (pp. 191–205). Toronto: M&M Graphic.

Abramovich, R. Corter, C., & Lando, B. (1979). Sibling interaction in the home. *Child Development, 4,* 997–1003.

Achenbach, T. M. (1991). *Manual for the Child Behavior Checklist/4–18, YSR and TRF profiles.* Burlington, VT: University of Vermont.

Achenbach, T. M. (1993). Taxonomy and comorbidity of conduct problems: Evidence from empirically based approaches. *Development and Psychopathology, 5,* 51–64.

Adelson, L. (1972). The battering child. *Journal of the American Medical Association, 222,* 159–161.

Agee, V. L. (1995). Managing clinical programs for juvenile delinquents. In B. Glick & A. Goldstein (Eds.), *Managing delinquency programs that work* (pp. 173–186). Laurel, MD: American Correctional Association.

Agnew, R. A. (1984). The work ethic and delinquency. *Sociological Focus, 17,* 337–346.

Agnew, R. A. (1993). Why do they do it? An examination of the intervening mechanisms between "social control" variables and delinquency. *Journal of Research in Crime and Delinquency, 30,* 245–266.

Agresti, A., & Finlay, B. (1997). *Statistical methods for the social sciences* (3rd ed.). Upper Saddle River, NJ: Prentice Hall.

Ainsworth, M. D. S., & Bell, S. M. (1970). Attachment, exploration, and separation illustrated by the behavior of one-year-olds in a strange situation. *Child Development, 41,* 49–67.

Ainsworth, M. D. S., Blehar, M. C., Waters, E., & Wall, S. (1978). *Patterns of attachment: A psychological study of the strange situation.* Hillsdale, NJ: Lawrence Erlbaum Associates.

Akers. R. L. (1985). *Deviant behavior: A social learning approach* (3rd ed.) Belmont, CA: Wadsworth.

Alexsic, P. (1976). A study of empathic inhibition of aggression in juvenile delinquents. *Dissertation Abstracts International, 36,* 4675B–4676B.

Allport, G. (1951). Forward. In E. Powers & H. Witmer (Eds.), *An experiment in the prevention of delinquency: The Cambridge-Somerville Youth Study* (pp. vii–xiv). New York: Columbia University Press.

Amato, P. R., & Booth, A. (1996). A prospective study of divorce and parent–child relationships. *Journal of Marriage and the Family, 58,* 356–365.

Amato, P. R., & Keith, B. (1991). Parental divorce and well-being of children: A meta-analysis. *Psychological Bulletin, 110,* 26–46.

American Psychiatric Association. (1980). *Diagnostic and statistical manual of mental disorders* (3rd ed.). Washington, DC: Author.

American Psychiatric Association. (1987). *Diagnostic and statistical manual of mental disorders* (3rd ed., rev.). Washington, DC: Author.

American Psychiatric Association. (1994). *Diagnostic and statistical manual of mental disorders* (4th ed.). Washington, DC: Author.

Ammons, D. (1998, May 22). Police say gun-wielding boy shoots himself after ordering girl off bus. *The Nando Net* [On–line]. Available: www.nando.net

Anderson, C. A., & Dill, K. E. (2000). Video games and aggressive thoughts, feelings, and behavior in the laboratory and in life. *Journal of Personality and Social Psychology, 78,* 772–790.

Anderson, D. (1996, March 12). Teens videotape "bashing" rampage. Fredericksburg (VA) *Free Lance-Star,* p. A4.

Anderson, D. C. (1998). Curriculum, culture, and community: The challenge of school violence. In M. Tonry & M. H. Moore (Eds.), *Youth violence: Crime and justice* (Vol. 24, pp. 317–363). Chicago: University of Chicago Press.

Anderson, E. (1994, May). The code of the streets. *Atlantic Monthly, 273,* 81–94.

Anderson, E. (1997). Violence and the inner-city street code. In J. McCord (Ed.), *Violence and child-hood in the inner city* (pp. 1–30). Cambridge, England: Cambridge University Press.

Anderson, E. (1998). The social ecology of youth violence. In M. Tonry & M. H. Moore (Eds.), *Youth violence: Crime and justice* (Vol. 24, pp. 65–104). Chicago: University of Chicago Press.

Anderson, K. E., Lytton, H., & Romney, D. M. (1986). Mothers' interactions with normal and con-duct-disordered boys: Who affects whom? *Developmental Psychology, 22,* 604–609.

Anderson, S. W., Bechara, A., Damasio, H., Tranel, D., & Damasio, A. R. (1999). Impairment of so-cial and moral behavior related to early damage in human prefrontal cortex. *Nature Neuroscience, 2,* 1032–1037.

Andersson, T., Magnusson, D., & Wennberg, P. (1997). Early aggressiveness and hyperactivity as indicators of adult alcohol problems and criminality: A prospective longitudinal study of male subjects. *Studies on Crime and Crime Prevention, 6,* 7–20.

Angel, R. J., & Angel, J. L. (1993). *Painful inheritance: Health and the new generation of fatherless fami-lies.* Madison, WI: University of Wisconsin Press.

Angry 5-year-old took gun to school. (1998, May 11). *The Nando Net* [On–line]. Available: www.nando.net

Araki, C. T. (1990). Dispute management in the schools. *Mediation Quarterly, 8,* 51–62.

Arbuthnot, J. (1992). Sociomoral reasoning in behavior-disordered adolescents: Cognitive and be-havioral change. In J. McCord & R. E. Tremblay (Eds.), *Preventing antisocial behavior: Interventions from birth through adolescence* (pp. 283–329). New York: Guilford Press.

Arbuthnot, J., & Gordon, D. A. (1986). Behavioral and cognitive effects of a moral reasoning devel-opment intervention for high-risk behavior-disordered adolescents. *Journal of Consulting and Clinical Psychology, 54,* 208–216.

Asarnow, J. R., & Callan, J. W. (1985). Boys with peer adjustment problems: Social cognitive pro-cesses. *Journal of Consulting and Clinical Psychology, 53,* 80–87.

Asher, S. R., & Coie, J. D. (1990). *Peer rejection in childhood.* New York: Cambridge University Press.

Askew, A. (1989). Aggressive behaviour in boys: To what extent is it institutionalised? In D. P. Tat-tum & D. A. Lane (Eds.), *Bullying in schools* (pp. 59–71). Stoke-on-Trent, England: Trentham.

Ayres, B. D., Jr. (1977, October 7). Influence of TV fails as defense plea. *The New York Times,* p. A18.

Azar, S. T., Ferraro, M. H., & Breton, S. J. (1998). Intrafamilial child maltreatment. In T. H. Ollendick & M. Hersen (Eds.), *Handbook of child psychopathology* (3rd ed., pp. 483–504). New York: Guil-ford.

Bachman, J. G., O'Malley, P. M. & Johnston, L. D. (1978). *Youth in transition: Vol. 6. Change and stabil-ity in the lives of young men.* Ann Arbor, MI: University of Michigan Institute for Social Research.

Bachrach, R. (1986). The differential effect of observation of violence on kibbutz and city children in Israel. In L. R. Huesmann & L. D. Eron (Eds.), *Television and the aggressive child: A cross-national comparison* (pp. 210–238). Hillsdale, NJ: Lawrence Erlbaum Associates.

Bai, M. (1999, May 3). Anatomy of a massacre. *Newsweek,* 24–31.

Bailey, S. (1996). Adolescents who murder. *Journal of Adolescence, 19,* 19–39.

Baker, P. (1997, July 11). Gore, Clinton aides shine spotlight on family values. *Washington Post,* p. A17.

Bandura, A. (1965). Influence of models' reinforcement contingencies on the acquisition of imitative responses. *Journal of Personality and Social Psychology, 1,* 589–595.

Bandura, A. (1977). *Social learning theory.* Englewood Cliffs, NJ: Prentice Hall.

Bandura, A. (1982). Self-efficacy mechanisms in human agency. *American Psychologist, 37,* 122–147.

Bandura, A. (1989). Social cognitive theory. In R. Vasta (Ed.), *Annals of child development* (Vol. 6, pp. 1–60). Greenwich, CT: JAI Press.

Bandura, A., Ross, D., & Ross, S. A. (1961). Transmission of aggression through imitation of aggressive models. *Journal of Abnormal and Social Psychology, 63,* 575–582.

Bandura, A., Ross, D., & Ross, S. (1963). Imitation of film-mediated aggressive models. *Journal of Abnormal and Social Psychology, 66,* 3–11.

Bandura, A., & Walters, R. H. (1959). *Adolescent aggression.* New York: Ronald Press.

Barber, A. (1997, March 3). Rough language plagues schools, educators say. *USA Today,* p. 6D.

Bardone, A. M., Moffitt, T., Caspi, A., & Dickson, N. (1996). Adult mental health and social outcomes of adolescent girls with depression and conduct disorder. *Development and Psychopathology, 8,* 811–829.

Barker, P. (1981). *Basic family therapy.* Baltimore: University Park Press.

Barker, R. G., Dembo, T., & Lewin, K. (1941). Frustration and regression: An experiment with young children. *University of Iowa Studies in Child Welfare, 18,* 1–314.

Barkley, R. A. (1981). *A manual for training parents of behavior problem children.* New York: Guilford.

Barkley, R. A. (1990). *Attention deficit hyperactivity disorder.* New York: Guilford.

Barkley, R. A. (1997). *ADHD and the nature of self-control.* New York: Guilford.

Barkley, R. A., Anastopoulos, A. D., Guevremont, D. C., & Fletcher, K. E. (1992). Adolescents with attention deficit hyperactivity disorder: Mother–adolescent interactions, family beliefs and conflicts, and maternal psychopathology. *Journal of Abnormal Child Psychology, 20,* 263–287.

Barnard, J. (1998a, May 22). School gunman stayed calm. Fredericksburg (VA) *Free Lance-Star,* pp. A1, A14.

Barnard, J. (1998b, May 23). Second student dies of wounds. Fredericksburg (VA) *Free Lance-Star,* p. A1, A18.

Barnard, J. (1999, November 11). Gunman in Oregon school shooting gets 112-year term. Fredericksburg (VA) *Free Lance-Star,* p. A16.

Barr, W. P. (1992). Violent youths should be punished as adults. In M. D. Biskup & C. P. Cozic (Eds.), *Youth violence* (pp. 216–220). San Diego: Greenhaven Press.

Bartol, C. R. (1995). *Criminal behavior: A psychosocial approach* (4th ed.). Englewood Cliffs, NJ: Prentice Hall.

Bastian, L. D., & Taylor, B. M. (1995, September). *School crime* (Rep. No. NJC-131645). Washington, DC: U.S. Department of Justice, Bureau of Justice Statistics.

Bates, J. E., Maslin, C. A., & Frankel, K. A. (1985). Attachment, security, mother–child interaction, and temperament as predictors of behavior problems ratings at age three years. In I. Bretherton & E. Waters (Eds.), Growing points of attachment theory and research. *Monographs for the Society of Research in Child Development, 50* (1–2, Serial No. 209).

Batsche, G. M., & Knoff, H. M. (1994). Bullies and their victims: Understanding a pervasive problem in the schools. *School Psychology Review, 23,* 165–174.

Baumeister, R. F. (1998). Inducing guilt. In J. Bybee (Ed.), *Guilt and children* (pp. 127–138). San Diego, CA: Academic Press.

Baumeister, R. F., Bushman, B. J., & Campbell, W. K. (2000). Self-esteem, narcissism, and aggression: Does violence result from low self-esteem or from threatened egotism? *Current Directions in Psychological Science, 9,* 26–29.

Baumeister, R. F., Smart, L., & Boden, J. M. (1996). Relation of threatened egotism to violence and aggression: The dark side of high self-esteem. *Psychological Review, 103,* 5–33.

Baumrind, D. (1967). Child care practices anteceding three patterns of preschool behavior. *Genetic Psychology Monographs, 75,* 43–88.

Baumrind, D. (1971). Current patterns of parental authority. *Developmental Psychology Monographs, 4* (1–2), 1–103.

Baumrind, D. (1991). The influence of parenting style on adolescent competence and substance use. *Journal of Early Adolescence, 11,* 56–95.

Bayles, F. (1995, March 7). Family was on deadly course. Fredericksburg (VA) *Free Lance-Star,* pp. A1, A4.

Beal, C. R. (1994). *Boys and girls: The development of gender roles.* News York: McGraw-Hill.

Becker, J. V., & Hunter, J. A. (1997). Understanding and treating child and adolescent sex offenders. In T. H. Ollendick & R. J. Prinz (Eds.), *Advances in clinical child psychology* (Vol. 19, pp. 177–197). New York: Plenum.

Becker, J. V., & Stein, R. M. (1991). Is sexual erotica associated with sexual deviance in adolescent males? *International Journal of Law and Psychiatry, 14,* 85–95.

Beland, K. R. (1992). *Second step: A violence prevention curriculum: Grades 1–3* (2nd ed.). Seattle, WA: Committee for Children.

Beland, K. R. (1996). A schoolwide approach to violence prevention. In R. L. Hampton, P. Jenkins, & T. P. Gullotta (Eds.), *Preventing violence in America: Vol. 4. Issues in children's and families' lives* (pp. 209–231). Thousand Oaks, CA: Sage.

Bell, R. Q. (1968). A reinterpretation of the direction of effects in studies of socialization. *Psychological Review, 75,* 81–95.

Belson, W. A. (1978). *Television violence and the adolescent boy.* Westmead, England: Saxon House, Teakfield Limited.

Benda, B. B., & Whiteside, L. (1995). Testing an integrated model of delinquency using LISREL. *Journal of Social Service Research, 21,* 1–32.

Benedek, E. P., Cornell, D. G., & Staresina, L. (1989). Treatment of the homicidal adolescent. In E. P. Benedek & D. G. Cornell (Eds.), *Juvenile homicide* (pp. 221–247). Washington, DC: American Psychiatric Press.

Benninga, J. A. (1997). Schools, character development, and citizenship. In A. Molnar (Ed.), *The construction of children's character: Ninety-sixth yearbook of the National Society for the Study of Education: Part II* (pp. 63–76). Chicago: The National Society for the Study of Education.

Benninga, J. S., Tracz, S. M., Sparks, R. K., Jr., Solomon, D., Battistich, V., Delucchi, K. L., Sandoval, R., & Stanley, B. (1991). Effects of two contrasting school task and incentive structures on children's social development. *The Elementary School Journal, 92,* 149–167.

Benson, P. L., Williams, D., & Johnson, A. (1987). *The quicksilver years: The hopes and fears of early adolescence.* San Francisco: Harper & Row.

Bentley, K. M., & Li, A. K. F. (1995). Bully and victim problems in elementary schools and students' beliefs about aggression. *Canadian Journal of School Psychology, 11,* 153–165.

Berkowitz, L. (1965). The concept of aggressive drive: Some additional considerations. In L. Berkowitz (Ed.), *Advances in experimental social psychology* (Vol. 2, pp. 301–329). New York: Academic Press.

Berkowitz, L. (1974). Some determinants of impulsive aggression: Role of mediated association with reinforcement for aggression. *Psychological Review, 81,* 165–176.

Berkowitz, L. (1984). Some effects of thought on anti- and pro-social influences of media effect. *Psychological Bulletin, 95,* 410–427.

Berkowitz, L. (1989). Frustration-aggression hypothesis: Examination and reformulation. *Psychological Bulletin, 106,* 59–73.

Bernstein, N. I. (1996). *Treating the unmanageable adolescent: A guide to oppositional defiant and conduct disorders.* Northvale, NJ: Jason Aronson.

Berrueta-Clement, J. R., Schweinhart, L. J., Barnett, W. S., Epstein, A. S., & Weikart, D. P. (1984). *Changed lives: The effects of the Perry Preschool Program on youths through age 19.* Ypsilanti, MI: High/Scope Press.

Bickford, S. T., Kormann, E. F., & Moeller, T. G. (1996, April). *Effectiveness of elementary and middle school peer mediation programs.* Paper presented at the annual spring meeting of the Virginia Psychological Association, Williamsburg.

Biederman, J., Munir, K, & Knee, D. (1987). Conduct and oppositional disorder in clinically referred children with attention deficit disorder: A controlled family study. *Journal of the American Academy of Child and Adolescent Psychiatry, 26,* 724–727.

Bierman, K. L., Greenberg, M. T., & the Conduct Problems Prevention Research Group. (1996). Social skills training in the Fast Track program. In R. DeV. Peters & R. J. McMahon (Eds.), *Preventing childhood disorders, substance abuse, and delinquency* (pp. 65–89). Thousand Oaks, CA: Sage.

Bierman, K. L., Miller, C. L., & Stabb, S. C. (1987). Improving the social behavior and peer acceptance of rejected boys: Effects of social skill training with instructions and prohibitions. *Journal of Consulting and Clinical Psychology, 55,* 194–200.

Bing, L. (1991). *Do or die.* New York: HarperCollins.

Blackburn, R. (1993). *The psychology of criminal conduct.* Chichester, England: Wiley.

Block, J. H., Block, J., & Gjerde, P. F. (1988). Parental functioning and the home environment in families of divorce: Prospective and concurrent analyses. *Journal of the American Academy of Child and Adolescent Psychiatry, 27,* 207–213.

Blum, H. M., Boyle, M. H., & Offord, D. R. (1988). Single-parent families: Child psychiatric disorder and school performance. *Journal of the American Academy of Child and Adolescent Psychiatry, 27,* 214–219.

Blumstein, A. (1995). Youth violence, guns, and the illicit-drug industry. *Journal of Criminal Law and Criminology, 86,* 10–36.

Blumstein, A., Cohen, J., Roth, J., & Visher, C. (1986). *Criminal careers and "career criminals."* Washington, DC: National Academy Press.

Borduin, C. M. (1994). Innovative models of treatment and service delivery in the juvenile justice system. *Journal of Clinical Child Psychology, 23* (Suppl.), 19–25.

Borduin, C. M., & Schaeffer, C. M. (1998). Violent offending in adolescence: Epidemiology, correlates, outcomes, and treatment. In T. P. Gullotta, G. R. Adams, & R. Montemayor (Eds.), *Delinquent violent youth* (pp. 144–174). Thousand Oaks, CA: Sage.

Borkhuis, G. W., & Patalano, F. (1997). MMPI personality differences between adolescents from divorced and non divorced families. *Psychology: A Journal of Human Behavior, 34,* 37–41.

Boy, 5, dropped to his death. (1994, October 15). Richmond (VA) *Times-Dispatch,* p. A9.

Boys who killed toddler soon to be paroled. (2000, October 27). Fredericksburg (VA) *Free Lance-Star,* p. A15.

Brain, P. F., & Susman, E. J. (1997). Hormonal aspects of aggression and violence. In D. M. Stoff, J. Breiling, & J. D. Maser (Eds.), *Handbook of antisocial behavior* (pp. 314–323). New York: Wiley.

Breed, A. G. (1998, March 26). Kids killing kids: Boys a mix of good, bad. Fredericksburg (VA) *Free Lance-Star,* pp. A1, A12.

Brewer, D. D., Hawkins, J. D., Catalano, R. F., & Neckerman, H. J. (1995). Preventing serious, violent, and chronic juvenile offending: A review of evaluations of selected strategies in childhood, adolescence, and the community. In J. C. Howell, B. Krisberg, J. D. Hawkins, & J. J. Wilson (Eds.), *Serious, violent, & chronic juvenile offenders* (pp. 61–141). Thousand Oaks, CA: Sage.

Bridis, T. (1997a, December 3). Healing begins after school shooting. Fredericksburg (VA) *Free Lance-Star,* p. B14.

Bridis, T. (1997b, December 5). A tearful farewell to classmates. Fredericksburg (VA) *Free Lance-Star,* p. A8.

Britner, P. A., & Reppucci, N. D. (1997). Prevention of child maltreatment: Evaluation of a parent education program for teen mothers. *Journal of Child and Family Studies, 6,* 165–175.

Brody, G. H., & Flor, D. L. (1998). Maternal resources, parenting practices, and child competence in rural, single-parent African American families. *Child Development, 69,* 803–816.

Brody, G. H., Stoneman, Z., & Flor, D. (1996). Parental religiosity, family processes, and youth competence in rural, two-parent African American families. *Developmental Psychology, 32,* 696–706.

Brody, G. H., Stoneman, Z., Flor, D., McCrary, C., Hastings, L., & Conyers, O. (1994). Financial resources, parent psychological functioning, parent co-caregiving, and early adolescent competence in rural two-parent African-American families. *Child Development, 65,* 590–605.

Brooks, J. H., & Reddon, J. R. (1996). Serum testosterone in violent and nonviolent young offenders. *Journal of Clinical Psychology, 52,* 475–483.

Brother accused of shooting little sister out of anger. (1995, October). *The Nando Net* [On-line]. Available: www.nando.net

Brown, F., Flannagan, T., & McLeon, M. (Eds.). (1984). *Sourcebook of criminal justice statistics.* Washington, DC: Bureau of Justice Statistics.

Brown, H. N., Saunders, R. B., & Dick, M. J. (1999). Preventing secondary pregnancy in adolescents: A model program. *Health Care for Women International, 20,* 5–15.

Brownfield, D., & Sorenson, A. M. (1993). Self-control and juvenile delinquency: Theoretical issues and an empirical assessment of selected elements of a general theory of crime. *Deviant Behavior: An Interdisciplinary Journal, 14,* 243–264.

Browning, C. J. (1960). Differential impact of family disorganization on male adolescents. *Social Problems, 8,* 37–44.

Brounstein, P. J., Hatry, H. P., Altschuler, D. M., & Blair, L. H. (1990). *Substance use and delinquency among inner city adolescent males.* Washington, DC: Urban Institute Press.

Bureau of Justice Statistics. (1994). *National crime victimization survey.* Washington, DC: U.S. Department of Justice.

Burton, R. V. (1984). A paradox in theories and research in moral development. In W. M. Kurtines & J. L. Gewirtz (Eds.), *Morality, moral behavior, and moral development* (pp. 193–207). New York: Wiley.

Butterfield, F. (1995). *All God's children: The Bosket family and the American tradition of violence.* New York: Alfred A. Knopf.

Bybee, J., & Quiles, Z. N. (1998). Guilt and mental health. In J. Bybee (Ed.), *Guilt and children* (pp. 269–291). San Diego: Academic Press.

Bynner, J. M., O'Malley, P. M., & Bachman, J. G. (1981). Self-esteem and delinquency revisited. *Journal of Youth and Adolescence, 10,* 407–441.

Cadoret, R. J., Cain, C. A., & Crowe, R. R. (1983). Evidence for a gene-environment interaction in the development of adolescent antisocial behavior. *Behavior Genetics, 13,* 301–310.

Cadwalader, G. (1986, June 22). Why my reform school can't save all bad kids. *Washington Post,* p. C3.

Cadwalader, G. (1988). *Castaways: The Penikese Island experiment.* New York: Penguin.

Cairns, R. B., Cadwallader, T. W., Estell, D., & Neckerman, H. J. (1997). Groups to gangs: Developmental and criminological perspectives and relevance for prevention. In D. M. Stoff, J. Breiling, & J. D. Maser (Eds.), *Handbook of antisocial behavior* (pp. 194–204). New York: Wiley.

Cairns, R. B., & Cairns, B. D. (1994). *Lifelines and risks: Pathways of youth in our time.* Cambridge, England: Cambridge University Press.

Cairns, R. B., Cairns, B. D., & Neckerman, H. J. (1989). Early school dropout: Configurations and determinants. *Child Development, 60,* 1437–1452.

Cairns, R. B., Cairns, B. D., Neckerman, H. J., Ferguson, L. L., & Gariépy, J. L. (1989). Growth and aggression: 1. Childhood to early adolescence. *Developmental Psychology, 25,* 320–330.

Cairns, R. B., Cairns, B. D., Neckerman, H. J., Gest, S. D., & Gariépy, J. L. (1988). Social networks and aggressive behavior: Peer support or peer rejection? *Developmental Psychology, 24,* 815–823.

Callahan, C. M., & Rivara, F. P. (1992). Urban high school youth and handguns: A school-based survey. *Journal of the American Medical Association, 267,* 3038–3042.

Camara, K. A., & Resnick, G. (1989). Styles of conflict resolution and cooperation between divorced parents: Effects on child behavior and adjustment. *American Journal of Orthopsychiatry, 59,* 560–575.

Campbell, A. (1991). *The girls in the gang* (2nd ed.). Cambridge, MA: Basil Blackwell.

Campbell, S. B. (1991). Longitudinal studies of active and aggressive preschoolers: Individual differences in early behavior and in outcome. In D. Cicchetti & S. L. Toth (Eds.), *Internalizing and externalizing expressions of dysfunction. Rochester Symposium on Developmental Psychopathology* (Vol. 2, pp. 57–90). Hillside, NJ: Lawrence Erlbaum Associates.

Campbell, S. B., & Ewing, L. J. (1990). Follow-up of hard-to-manage preschoolers: Adjustment at age 9 and predictors of continuing symptoms. *Journal of Child Psychology and Psychiatry, 31,* 871–890.

Canter, R. J. (1982). Family correlates of male and female delinquency. *Criminology, 20,* 149–167.

Caplan, M., Vespo. J., Pederson, J., & Hay, D. F. (1991). Conflict and its resolution in small groups of one- and two-year-olds. *Child Development, 62,* 1513–1524.

Carlson, E. A. (1998). A prospective longitudinal study of attachment disorganization/disorientation. *Child Development, 69,* 1107–1128.

Caspi, A., Lynam, D., Moffitt, T. E., & Silva, P. A. (1993). Unraveling girls' delinquency: Biological, dispositional, and contextual contributions to adolescent misbehavior. *Developmental Psychology, 29,* 19–30.

Caspi, A., & Moffitt, T. E. (1991). Individual differences are accentuated during periods of social change: The sample case of girls at puberty. *Journal of Personality and Social Psychology, 61,* 157–168.

Caspi, A., Moffitt, T. E., Newman, D. L., & Silva, P. A. (1996). Behavioral observations at age 3 years predict adult psychiatric disorders: Longitudinal evidence from a birth cohort. *Archives of General Psychiatry, 53,* 1033–1039.

Cernkovich, S. A., & Giordano, P. C. (1987). Family relationships and delinquency. *Criminology, 25,* 295–321.

Chamberlain, P. (1996). Community-based residential treatment for adolescents with conduct disorders. In T. H. Ollendick & R. J. Prinz (Eds.), *Advances in clinical child psychology* (Vol. 18, pp. 63–90). New York: Plenum.

Chamberlain, P., & Friman, P. C. (1997). Residential programs for antisocial children and adolescents. In D. M. Stoff, J. Breiling, & J. D. Maser (Eds.), *Handbook of antisocial behavior* (pp. 416–424). New York: Wiley.

Chess, S., & Thomas, A. (1986). *Temperament in clinical practice.* New York: Guilford.

Chess, S., Thomas, A., & Birch, H. G. (1965). *Your child is a person.* New York: Viking.

Christian, R. E., Frick, P. J., Hill, N. L., Tyler, L., & Frazer, D. R. (1997). Psychopathy and conduct problems in children: II. Implications for subtyping children with conduct problems. *Journal of the American Academy of Child and Adolescent Psychiatry, 36,* 233–241.

Christoffel, K. K. (1997). Firearm injuries affecting U.S. children and adolescents. In J. D. Osofsky (Ed.), *Children in a violent society* (pp. 42–71). New York: Guilford.

Claiborne, W. (1998, May 23). Bombs found in Oregon teen's home. *Washington Post,* p. A1.

Clarke-Stewart, K. A., & Hayward, C. (1996). Advantages of father custody and contact for the psychological well-being of school-age children. *Journal of Applied Developmental Psychology, 17,* 239–270.

Cleckley, H. (1976). *The mask of sanity* (5th ed.). St. Louis: Mosby.

Clough, S. (1997, July 25). Court clears boy who stabbed school bully. *The London Daily Telegraph,* p. 3.

Coates, C. (1998, May 22). Two Pennsylvania teens charged with torturing girl for snitching on runaway plans. *The Nando Net* [On-line]. Available: www.nando.net

Coccaro, E. F., Bergeman, C. S., Kavoussi, R. J., & Seroczynski, A. D. (1997). Heritability of aggression and irritability: A twin study of the Buss-Durkee aggression scales in adult male subjects. *Biological Psychiatry, 41,* 273–284.

Cohen, D., & Strayer, J. (1996). Empathy in conduct-disordered and comparison youth. *Developmental Psychology, 32,* 988–998.

Cohen, P., & Brook, J. S. (1995). The reciprocal influence of punishment and child behavior disorder. In J. McCord (Ed.), *Coercion and punishment in long-term perspectives* (pp. 154–164). Cambridge, England: Cambridge University Press.

Cohen, P. C., Velez, C. N., Brook, J., & Smith, J. (1989). Mechanisms of the relation between perinatal problems, early childhood illness and psychopathology in late childhood and adolescence. *Child Development, 60,* 701–709.

Cohn, D. A. (1990). Child–mother attachment of six-year-olds and social competence at school. *Child Development, 61,* 152–162.

Coie, J. D., & Dodge, K. A. (1998). Aggression and antisocial behavior. In N. Eisenberg (Vol. Ed.) & W. Damon (Ed.-in-Chief), *Handbook of child psychology* (Vol. 3, 5th ed., pp. 779–862). New York: Wiley.

Coie, J. D., Dodge, K. A., Terry, R., & Wright, V. (1991). The role of aggression in peer relations: An analysis of aggression episodes in boys' play groups. *Child Development, 62,* 812–826.

Coie, J. D., & Kupersmidt, J. B. (1983). A behavior analysis of emerging social status in boys' groups. *Child Development, 54,* 1400–1416.

Coleman, J. S., Hoffer, T., & Kilgore, S. (1982). *High school achievement: Public, Catholic, and private schools compared.* New York: Basic Books.

Conger, J. J., & Galambos, N. L. (1997). *Adolescence and youth* (5th ed.). New York: Longman.

Conger, K. J., & Conger, R. D. (1994). Differential parenting and change in sibling differences in delinquency. *Journal of Family Psychology, 8,* 287–302.

Conger, R. D., Ge, X., Elder, G. H., Jr., Lorenz, F. O., & Simons, R. L. (1994). Economic stress, coercive family process, and developmental problems of adolescents. *Child Development, 65,* 541–561.

Conseur, A., Rivara, F. P., Barnoski, R., & Emanuel, I. (1997). Maternal and perinatal risk factors for later delinquency. *Pediatrics, 99,* 785–790.

Cook, P. J., & Laub, J. H. (1998). The epidemic in youth violence. In M. Tonry & M. H. Moore (Eds.), *Youth violence: Crime and justice* (Vol. 24, pp. 27–64). Chicago: University of Chicago Press.

Cook, P. J., & Moore, M. H. (1995). Gun control. In J. Q. Wilson & J. Petersilia (Eds.), *Crime* (pp. 267–294). San Francisco: Institute for Contemporary Studies Press.

Cooper, J., & Mackie, D. (1986). Video games and aggression in children. *Journal of Applied Social Psychology, 16,* 726–744.

Corder, B. F., Ball, B. C., Haizlip, T. M., Rollins, R., & Beaumont, R. (1976). Adolescent parricide: A comparison with other adolescent murder. *American Journal of Psychiatry, 133,* 957–961.

Corliss, R. (1999, May 3). Bang, you're dead. *Time,* 49–50.

Cornell, D. G. (1993). Juvenile homicide: A growing national problem. *Behavioral Sciences and the Law, 11,* 389–396.

Cornell, D. G. (1998, November). *Violence in schools.* Workshop presented at the annual fall meeting of the Virginia Psychological Association, Richmond.

Cornell, D. G., Benedek, E. P., & Benedek, D. M. (1987). Characteristics of adolescents charged with homicide: Review of 72 cases. *Behavioral Sciences and the Law, 5,* 11–23.

Cotliar, S., & Fornek, S. (1994, September 2). 11-year-old slaying suspect found killed in execution style. *Chicago Sun-Times,* p. 1.

Cotton, C. R., & Range, L. M. (1993). Suicidality, hopelessness, and attitudes toward life and death in children. *Death Studies, 17,* 185–191.

Courtwright, D. T. (1996). *Violent land: Single men and social disorder from the frontier to the inner city.* Cambridge, MA: Harvard University Press.

Cowan, P. A., & Walters, R. H. (1963). Studies of reinforcement of aggression: I. Effects of scheduling. *Child Development, 34,* 543–551.

Cox, S. M., Davidson, W. S., & Bynum, T. S. (1995). A meta-analytic assessment of delinquency-related outcomes of alternative education programs. *Crime and Delinquency, 41,* 219–234.

Crack-addicted mother guilty in child's death. (1999, April 8). Fredericksburg (VA) *Free Lance-Star,* p. C2.

Craig, W. M. (1998). The relationship among bullying, victimization, depression, anxiety, and aggression in elementary school children. *Personality and Individual Differences, 24,* 123–130.

Craig, W. M., & Pepler, D. J. (1997). Observations of bullying and victimization in the school yard. *Canadian Journal of School Psychology, 13,* 41–59.

Crase, D. R., & Crase, D. (1976). Helping children understand death. *Young Children, 32,* 21–25.

Crick, N. R., Werner, N. E., Casas, J. F., O'Brien, K. M., Nelson, D. A., Grotpeter, J. K., & Markon, K. (1999). Childhood aggression and gender: A new look at an old problem. In D. Bernstein (Vol. Ed.) & R. A. Dienstbier (Series Ed.), *Gender and motivation: The Nebraska Symposium on Motivation* (Vol. 45, pp. 75–141). Lincoln, NE: University of Nebraska Press.

Cuddy-Casey, M., & Orvaschel, H. (1997). Children's understanding of death in relation to child suicidality and homicidality. *Clinical Psychology Review, 17,* 33–45.

Cueva, J. E., Overall, J. E., Small, A. M., Armenteros, J. L., Perry, R., & Campbell, M. (1996). Carbamazepine in aggressive children with conduct disorder: A double-blind and placebo-controlled study. *Journal of the American Academy of Child and Adolescent Psychiatry, 35,* 480–490.

Cummings, E. M., & Davies, P. (1994). *Children and marital conflict.* New York: Guilford.

Curran, J. (1996, March 20). Slain teacher leaves her final words. Fredericksburg (VA) *Free Lance-Star,* p. A6.

Curran, J. (1999, April 15). Teen killer gets 70 years. Ocean County (NJ) *Observer,* p. A1.

Dackis, C. A., & Gold, M. S. (1988). Psychopharmacology of cocaine. *Psychiatric Annals, 18,* 528–530.

Damon, W. (1995). *Greater expectations: Overcoming the culture of indulgence in America's homes and schools.* New York: The Free Press.

Darby, P. J., Allan, W. D., & Kashani, J. H. (1998). Analysis of 112 juveniles who committed homicide: Characteristics and a closer look at family abuse. *Journal of Family Violence, 13,* 365–375.

Dawe, H. C. (1934). An analysis of two hundred quarrels of preschool children. *Child Development, 5,* 139–157.

Deater-Deckard, K., & Dodge, K. A. (1997). Externalizing behavior problems and discipline revisited: Nonlinear effects and variation by culture, context, and gender. *Psychological Inquiry, 8,* 161–175.

Deater-Deckard, K., & Plomin, R. (1999). An adoption study of the etiology of teacher and parent reports of externalizing behavior problems in middle childhood. *Child Development, 70,* 144–154.

DeBecker, G. (1997). *The gift of fear: Survival signs that protect us from violence.* Boston: Little, Brown.

Demo, D. H., & Acock, A. C. (1988). The impact of divorce on children. *Journal of Marriage and the Family, 50,* 619–648.

Denham, S. A., McKinley, M., Couchoud, E. A., & Holt, R. (1990). Emotional and behavioral predictors of preschool peer ratings. *Child Development, 61,* 1145–1152.

Desmond, R. J., Singer, J. L., & Singer, D. G. (1990). Family mediation: Parental communication patterns and the influences of television on children. In J. Bryant (Ed.), *Television and the American family* (pp. 293–309). Hillsdale, NJ: Lawrence Erlbaum Associates.

Deutsch, L. (1999, June 27). Did life imitate art in California slaying? *The Nando Net* [On-line]. Available: www.nando.net

Did TV make him do it? (1977, October 10). *Time, 110,* 87, 89.

Dietz, D., Neville, P., & Mortenson, E. (1998, June 14). Love against the odds: A Kinkel family portrait. Eugene (OR) *Register-Guard* [On-line]. Available: www.registerguard.com/news/19980614/la.kipkinkel.0614.html

Dishion, T. J. (1990). The peer context of troublesome behavior in children and adolescents. In P. Leone (Ed.), *Understanding troubled and troublesome youth* (pp. 128–153). Beverly Hills, CA: Sage.

Dishion, T. J., & Andrews, D. W. (1995). Prevention escalation in problem behaviors with high-risk young adolescents: Immediate and 1-year-outcome. *Journal of Consulting and Clinical Psychology, 63,* 538–548.

Dishion, T. J., Andrews, D. W., & Crosby, L. (1995). Antisocial boys and their friends in early adolescence: Relationship characteristics, quality, and interactional process. *Child Development, 66,* 139–151.

Dishion, T. J., Patterson, G. R., Stoolmiller, M., & Skinner, M. L. (1991). Family, school, and behavioral antecedents to early adolescent involvement with antisocial peers. *Developmental Psychology, 27,* 172–180.

Dobkin, P. L., Tremblay, R. E., Mâsse, L. C., & Vitaro, F. (1995). Individual and peer characteristics in predicting boys' early onset of substance abuse: A seven-year longitudinal survey. *Child Development, 66,* 1198–1214.

Dodge, K. A. (1980). Social cognition and children's aggressive behavior. *Child Development, 51,* 162–170.

Dodge, K. A. (1986). A social information processing model of social competence in children. In M. Perlmutter (Ed.), *Eighteenth Annual Minnesota Symposium on Child Psychology* (Vol. 18, pp. 77–125). Hillsdale, NJ: Lawrence Erlbaum Associates.

Dodge, K. A., Coie, J. D., Pettit, G. S., & Price, J. M. (1990). Peer status and aggression in boys' groups: Developmental and contextual analyses. *Child Development, 61,* 1289–1309.

Dodge, K. A., & Frame, C. L. (1982). Social cognitive biases and deficits in aggressive boys. *Child Development, 53,* 620–635.

Dodge, K. A., Murphy, R. R., & Buchsbaum, K. (1984). The assessment of intention-cue detection skills in children: Implications for developmental psychopathology. *Child Development, 55,* 163–173.

Dodge, K. A., Pettit, G. S., & Bates, J. E. (1994). Socialization mediators of the relation between socioeconomic status and child conduct problems. *Child Development, 65,* 649–665.

Dodge, K. A., Pettit, G. S., McClaskey, C. L., & Brown, M. M. (1986). Social competence in children. *Monographs of the Society for Research in Child Development, 51* (2, Serial No. 213).

Dodge, K. A., Price, J. M., Bachorowski, J., & Newman, J. P. (1990). Hostile attributional biases in severely aggressive adolescents. *Journal of Abnormal Psychology, 99,* 385–392.

Dodge, K. A., & Somberg, D. R. (1987). Hostile attribution biases among aggressive boys are exacerbated under conditions of threats to self. *Child Development, 58,* 213–224.

Dodge, L. (1998, May 23). Friends say parents tried to work on son's problems. *Fredericksburg (VA) Free Lance-Star,* p. A18.

Doherty, J., & Hier, B. (1988). Teacher expectations and specific judgments: A small-scale study of the effects of certain non-cognitive variables on teachers' academic predictions. *Educational Review, 40,* 333–348.

Dollard, J., Doob, L. W., Miller, N. E., Mowrer, O. H., & Sears, R. R. (1939). *Frustration and aggression.* New Haven, CT: Yale University Press.

Donnerstein, E., Slaby, R. G., & Eron, L. D. (1994). The mass media and youth aggression. In L. D. Eron, J. H. Gentry, & P. Schlegel (Eds.), *Reason to hope: A psychosocial perspective on violence and youth* (pp. 219–250). Washington, DC: American Psychological Association.

Donohue, E., Schiraldi, V., & Zidenberg, J. (1998, July). *School house hype: School shootings and the real risks kids face in America.* Washington, DC: Center on Juvenile and Criminal Justice.

Donohue, M. J., & Benson, P. L. (1995). Religion and the well-being of adolescents. *Journal of Social Issues, 51,* 145–160.

Dornbusch, S. M., Carlsmith, J. M., Bushwall, S. J., Ritter, P. L., Leiderman, H., Hastorf, A. H., & Gross, R. T. (1985). Single parents, extended households, and the control of adolescents. *Child Development, 56,* 326–341.

Downey, G., & Coyne, J. C. (1990). Children of depressed parents: An integrated review. *Psychological Bulletin, 198,* 50–76.

Drabman, R. S., & Thomas, M. H. (1974). Does media violence increase children's toleration of real-life aggression? *Developmental Psychology, 10,* 418–421.

Dryfoos, J. G. (1990). *Adolescents at risk: Prevalence and prevention.* New York: Oxford University Press.

Dumas, J. E., & Wahler, R. G. (1983). Predictors of treatment outcome in parent training: Mother insularity and socioeconomic disadvantage. *Behavioral Assessment, 5,* 301–313.

Duncan, G. J., Brooks-Gunn, J., & Klebanov, P. K. (1994). Economic deprivation and early childhood development. *Child Development, 65,* 296–318.

Durant, R. H., Cadenhead, C., Pendergrast, R. A., Slavens, G., & Linder, C. W. (1994). Factors associated with the use of violence among urban black adolescents. *American Journal of Public Health, 84,* 612–617.

Durant, R. H., Getts, A. G., Cadenhead, C., & Woods, E. R. (1995). The association between weapon carrying and the use of violence among adolescents living in and around public housing. *Journal of Adolescent Health, 17,* 376–380.

Durkin, K. (1995). *Developmental social psychology.* Malden, MA: Blackwell.

Dwyer, K., Osher, D., & Warger, C. (1998). *Early warning, timely response: A guide to safe schools.* Washington, DC: U.S. Department of Education.

Eaves, L. J., Silberg, J. L., Maes, H. H., Simonoff, E., Pickles, A., Rutter, M., Neale, M. C., Reynolds, C. A., Erickson, M. T., Heath, A. C., Loeber, R., Truett, K. R., & Hewitt, J. K. (1997). Genetics and developmental psychopathology: 2. The main effects of genes and environment on behavioral problems in the Virginia Twin Study of Adolescent Behavioral Development. *Journal of Child Psychology and Psychiatry and Allied Disciplines, 38,* 965–980.

Edsall, T. B. (1997, October 2). Mississippi boy held in school killing spree. *Washington Post,* p. A3.

Egeland, B., Kalkoske, M., Gottesman, N. & Erickson, M. E. (1990). Preschool behavior problems: Stability and factors accounting for change. *Journal of Child Psychology and Psychiatry, 31,* 891–909.

Eight students shot at Ky. school. (1997, December 1). Fredericksburg (VA) *Free Lance-Star,* p. C2.

Eisenberg, N. (1986). *Altruistic emotion, cognition, and behavior.* Hillsdale, NJ: Lawrence Erlbaum Associates.

Eisenman, R. (1993). Characteristics of adolescent felons in a prison treatment program. *Adolescence, 28,* 695–699.

11-year-old convicted of assaulting 3 year-old girl. (1998, June 4). *The Nando Net* [On-line]. Available: www.nando.net

Elias, M. J., & Clabby, J. F. (1992). *Building social problem-solving skills: Guidelines from a school-based program.* San Francisco: Jossey-Bass.

Elliott, D. S., & Voss, H. (1974). *Delinquency and dropout.* Lexington, MA: D. C. Heath.

Elliott, S., Huizinga, D., & Menard, S. (1989). *Multiple problem youth.* New York: Springer-Verlag.

Ellis, A., & Bernard, M. E. (1983). An overview of rational-emotive approaches to the problems of childhood. In A. Ellis & M. E. Bernard (Eds.), *Rational-emotive approaches to the problems of childhood* (pp. 3–43). New York: Plenum.

Ellison, E. S. (1983). Issues concerning parental harmony and children's psychosocial adjustment. *American Journal of Orthopsychiatry, 53,* 73–80.

Eley, T. C., Lichtenstein, P., & Stevenson, J. (1999). Sex differences in the etiology of aggressive and nonaggressive antisocial behavior: Results from two twin studies. *Child Development, 70,* 155–168.

Eme, R. F. (1979). Sex differences in childhood psychopathology: A review. *Psychological Bulletin, 86,* 574–595.

Emery, R. E. (1982). Interparental conflict and the children of discord and divorce. *Psychological Bulletin, 92,* 310–330.

Emes, C. E. (1997). Is Mr. Pac Man eating our children? A review of the effect of video games on children. *Canadian Journal of Psychiatry, 42,* 409–414.

Englade, K., & Hillerman, T. (1995, January-February). A true crime story. *Modern Maturity,* 22–31.

Enos, D. M., & Handal, P. J. (1986). The relation of parental marital status and perceived family conflict to adjustment in white adolescents. *Journal of Consulting and Clinical Psychology, 54,* 820–824.

Ensminger, M. E., Kellam, S. G., & Rubin, B. R. (1983). School and family origins of delinquency: Comparisons by sex. In K. T. Van Dusen & S. A. Mednick (Eds.), *Prospective studies of crime and delinquency* (pp. 73–97). Boston: Kluwer-Nijhoff.

Epps, K. (1997, November 11). Police say vandals were on videotape. Fredericksburg (VA) *Free Lance-Star,* p. C1.

Epps, K., & Bailey, K. (1998, February 3). Clerk recounts shooting. Fredericksburg (VA) *Free Lance-Star,* p. A1.

Erdley, C. A., & Asher, S. R. (1996). Children's social goals and self-efficacy perceptions as influences on their responses to ambiguous provocation. *Child Development, 67,* 1329–1344.

Erickson, M. F., Sroufe, L. A., & Egeland, B. (1985). The relationship between quality of attachment and behavior problems in preschool in a high-risk sample. In I. Bretherton & E. Waters (Eds.), *Growing points in attachment theory and research. Monographs of the Society for Research in Child Development, 50,* (1–2, Serial No. 209), 147–166.

Erikson, E. H. (1950). *Childhood and society.* New York: Norton.

Eron, L. D. (1987). The development of aggressive behavior from the perspective of a developing behaviorism. *American Psychologist, 42,* 435–442.

Eron, L. D., & Huesmann, L. R. (1986). The cross-national approach to research on aggression: Measures and procedures. In L. R. Huesmann & L. D. Eron (Eds.), *Television and the aggressive child: A cross-national comparison* (pp. 29–44). Hillsdale, NJ: Lawrence Erlbaum Associates.

Eron, L. D., & Huesmann, L. R. (1987). Television as a source of maltreatment of children. *School Psychology Review, 16,* 195–202.

Eron, L. D., Huesmann, L. R., Lefkowitz, M. M., & Walder, L. O. (1972). Does television violence cause aggression? *American Psychologist, 27,* 253–263.

Ewing, C. P. (1990a). *Kids who kill.* New York: Avon.

Ewing, C. P. (1990b). *When children kill.* Lexington, MA: Lexington Books.

Ewing, C. P. (1997). *Fatal families.* Thousand Oaks, CA: Sage.

Eyberg, S. M. (1996, August). Parent–child interaction therapy. In T. Ollendick (Chair), *Developmentally based integrated psychotherapy with children: Emerging models.* Symposium presented at the annual meeting of the American Psychological Association, Toronto, Canada.

Fagan, J., & Wilkinson, D. L. (1997). Firearms and youth violence. In D. M. Stoff, J. Breiling, & J. D. Maser (Eds.), *Handbook of antisocial behavior* (pp. 551–565). New York: Wiley.

Fagan, J., & Wilkinson, D. L. (1998). Guns, youth violence, and social identity in inner cities. In M. Tonry & M. H. Moore (Eds.), *Youth violence: Crime and justice* (Vol. 24, pp. 105–188). Chicago: University of Chicago Press.

Fagot, B. I., Hagan, R., Youngblade, L. M., & Potter, L. (1989). A comparison of the play behaviors of sexually abused, physically abused, and nonabused preschool children. *Topics in Early Childhood Special Education, 9,* 88–100.

Farley, F. (1990, May). The Type T personality, with some implications for practice. *The California Psychologist, 29.*

Farmer, T. W., & Hollowell, J. H. (1994). Social networks in mainstream classrooms: Social affiliations and behavioral characteristics of students with emotional and behavioral disorders. *Journal of Emotional and Behavioral Disorders, 2,* 143–155.

Farmer, T. W., & Rodkin, P. (1996). Antisocial and prosocial correlates of classroom social positions: The social network centrality perspective. *Social Development, 5,* 174–188.

Farrington, D. P. (1978). The family backgrounds of aggressive youths. In L. A. Hersov & M. Berger (Eds.), *Aggression and antisocial behavior in childhood and adolescence* (pp. 73–93). London: Pergamon.

Farrington, D. P. (1979). Longitudinal research on crime and delinquency. In N. Morris & M. Tonry (Eds.), *Crime and justice* (Vol. 1, pp. 289–348). Chicago: University of Chicago Press.

Farrington, D. P. (1989). Early predictors of adolescent aggression and adult violence. *Violence and Victims, 4,* 79–100.

Farrington, D. P. (1993). Understanding and preventing bullying. In M. Tonry (Ed.), *Crime and justice* (Vol. 17, pp. 381–458). Chicago: University of Chicago Press.

Farrington, D. P. (1994). Early developmental prevention of juvenile delinquency. *Criminal Behaviour and Mental Health, 4,* 209–227.

Farrington, D. P. (1998). Predictors, causes, and correlates of male youth violence. In M. Tonry & M. H. Moore (Eds.), *Youth violence: Crime and justice* (Vol. 24, pp. 421–475). Chicago: University of Chicago Press.

Farrington, D. P., Berkowitz, L., & West, D. J. (1982). Differences between individual and group fights. *British Journal of Social Psychology, 21,* 323–333.

Farrington, D. P., & Hawkins, J. D. (1991). Predicting participation, early onset, and later persistence in officially recorded offending. *Criminal Behavior and Mental Health, 1,* 1–33.

Federal Bureau of Investigation (1985–1999). *Uniform crime reports for the United States: Crime in the United States.* Washington, DC: U.S. Government Printing Office.

Fehrenbach, P. A., & Monastersky, C. (1988). Characteristics of female adolescent sexual offenders. *American Journal of Orthopsychiatry, 58,* 148–151.

Fehrenbach, P. A., Smith, W., Monastersky, C., & Deisher, R. W. (1986). Adolescent sexual offenders: Offender and offense characteristics. *American Journal of Orthopsychiatry, 56,* 225–233.

Feldman, R. A. (1992). The St. Louis experiment: Effective treatment of antisocial youths in prosocial peer groups. In J. McCord & R. Tremblay (Eds.), *Preventing antisocial behavior: Interventions from birth to adolescence* (pp. 233–252). New York: Guilford.

Feldman, R. A., Caplinger, T. E., & Wodarski, J. S., (1983). *The St. Louis conundrum: The effective treatment of antisocial youths.* Englewood Cliffs, NJ: Prentice-Hall.

Felson, R. B. (1996). Mass media effects on violent behavior. In J. Hagan & K. S. Cook (Eds.), *Annual review of sociology* (Vol. 22, pp. 103–128). Palo Alto, CA: Annual Reviews, Inc.

Fergusson, D. M., & Horwood, L. J. (1995). Early disruptive behavior, IQ, and later school achievement and delinquent behavior. *Journal of Abnormal Child Psychology, 23,* 183–199.

Fergusson, D. M., & Horwood, L. J. (1998). Exposure to interparental violence in childhood and psychosocial adjustment in young adulthood. *Child Abuse and Neglect, 22,* 339–357.

Fergusson, D. M., & Lynskey, M. T. (1997). Early reading difficulties and later conduct problems. *Journal of Child Psychology and Psychiatry, 38,* 899–907.

Fergusson, D. M., Lynskey, M. T., & Horwood, L. J. (1996). Alcohol misuse and juvenile offending in adolescence. *Addiction, 91,* 483–494.

Feshbach, S. (1970). Aggression. In P. H. Mussen (Ed.), *Carmichael's manual of child psychology* (Vol. 2., 3rd ed., pp. 159–259). New York: Wiley.

Feshbach, S., & Singer, R. (1971). *Television and aggression.* San Francisco: Jossey-Bass.

Fincham, F. D., & Beach, S. R. H. (1999). Conflict in marriage: Implications for working with couples. In J. T. Spence, J. Darley, & D. J. Ross (Eds.), *Annual review of psychology* (Vol. 50, pp. 47–77). Palo Alto, CA: Annual Reviews.

Fincham, F. D., Grych, J. H., & Osborne, L. N. (1994). Does marital conflict cause child maladjustment? Directions and challenges for longitudinal research. *Journal of Family Psychology, 8,* 128–140.

Finckenauer, J. O. (1979, August). Scared crooked. *Psychology Today, 6.*

First-grade shooting stuns Michigan, U.S. (2000, March 1). Fredericksburg (VA) *Free Lance-Star,* p. A1.

Fischer, K. W., & Lazerson, A. (1984). *Human development: From conception through adolescence.* New York: W. H. Freeman.

Fischer, M., Rolf, J. E., Hasazi, J. E., & Cummings, L. (1984). Follow-up of a preschool epidemiological sample: Cross-age continuities and predictions of later adjustment with internalizing and externalizing dimensions of behavior. *Child Development, 55,* 137–150.

Fitzpatrick, K. M., & Boldizar, J. P. (1993). The prevalence and consequences of exposure to violence among African-American youth. *Journal of the American Academy of Child and Adolescent Psychiatry, 32,* 424–430.

5-year-old arrested after scuffle with school counselor. (1998, February 20). *The Nando Net* [On-line]. Available: www.nando.net

Flannery, D. J., Huff, C. R., & Manos, M. (1998). Youth gangs: A developmental perspective. In T. P. Gullotta, G. R. Adams, & R. Montemayor (Eds.), *Delinquent violent youth* (pp. 175–204). Thousand Oaks, CA: Sage.

Flavell, J. H., Flavell, E. R., & Green, F. L. (1983). Development of the appearance–reality distinction. *Cognitive Psychology, 15,* 95–120.

Fonagy, P., Target, M., Steele, M., Steele, H., Leigh, T., Levinson, A., & Kennedy, R. (1997). Morality, disruptive behavior, borderline personality disorder, crime, and their relationships to security of attachment. In L. Atkinson & K. J. Zucker (Eds.), *Attachment and psychopathology* (pp. 223–274). New York: Guilford.

Foote, R., Eyberg, S., & Schuhmann, E. (1998). Parent–child interaction approaches to the treatment of child behavior problems. In T. H. Ollendick & R. J. Prinz (Eds.), *Advances in clinical child psychology* (Vol. 20, pp. 125–151. New York: Plenum.

Ford, M. E., & Linney, J. A. (1995). Comparative analysis of juvenile sexual offenders, violent nonsexual offenders, and status offenders. *Journal of Interpersonal Violence, 10,* 56–70.

Forehand, R., King, H. E., Peed, S., & Yoder, P. (1975). Mother–child interactions: Comparisons of a noncompliant clinic group and a non-clinic group. *Behaviour Research and Therapy, 13,* 79–84.

Forehand, R., & McMahon, R. J. (1981). *Helping the noncompliant child: A clinician's guide to parent training.* New York: Guilford.

Forehand, R., Wierson, M., Frame, C., Kempton, T., & Armistead, L. (1991). Juvenile delinquency entry and persistence: Do attention problems contribute to conduct problems? *Journal of Behaviour Therapy and Experimental Psychiatry, 22,* 261–264.

Former class president sentenced in rape case. (1998, October 15). Fredericksburg (VA) *Free Lance-Star,* p. A4.

Fourth-grader with toy gun gets favorable ruling. (2000, May 11). Fredericksburg (VA) *Free Lance-Star,* p. C3.

Fourth-grader's assault kills substitute teacher. (1995, October 11). Fredericksburg (VA) *Free Lance-Star,* p. A4.

Fowles, D. C. (1988). Psychophysiology and psychopathology: A motivational approach. *Psychophysiology, 25,* 373–391.

Fraczek, A. (1986). Socio-cultural environment, television viewing, and the development of aggression among children in Poland. In L. R. Huesmann & L. D. Eron (Eds.), *Television and the aggressive child: A cross-national comparison* (pp. 119–159). Hillsdale, NJ: Lawrence Erlbaum Associates.

Frease, D. E. (1973). Schools and delinquency: Some intervening processes. *Pacific Sociological Review, 16,* 426–448.

Freedman, J. L. (1984). Effect of television violence on aggression. *Psychological Bulletin, 96,* 227–246.

Freedman, J. L. (1986). Television violence and aggression: A rejoinder. *Psychological Bulletin, 100,* 372–378.

Frick, P. J. (1994). Family dysfunction and disruptive behavior disorders. In T. H. Ollendick & R. J. Prinz (Eds.), *Advances in clinical child psychology* (Vol. 16, pp. 203–226). New York: Plenum.

Frick, P. J. (1998). Conduct disorders. In T. H. Ollendick & M. Hersen (Eds.), *Handbook of child psychopathology* (3rd ed., pp. 213–237). New York: Plenum.

Frick, P. J., Kampaus, R. W., Lahey, B. B., Loeber, R., Christ, M. A. G., Hart, E. L., & Tannenbaum, L. E. (1991). Academic underachievement and the disruptive behavior disorders. *Journal of Consulting and Clinical Psychology, 59,* 289–294.

Frick, P. J., Lahey, B. B., Loeber, R., Stouthamer-Loeber, M., Christ, M. A. G., & Hanson, K. (1992). Familial risk factors to oppositional defiant disorder and conduct disorder: Parental psychopathology and maternal parenting. *Journal of Consulting and Clinical Psychology, 60,* 49–55.

Frick, P. J., Lahey, B. B., Loeber, R., Stouthamer-Loeber, M., Green, S., Hart, E. L., & Christ, M. A. G.

(1991). Oppositional defiant disorder and conduct disorder in boys: Patterns of behavioral co-variation. *Journal of Clinical Child Psychology, 20,* 202–208.

Frick, P. J., O'Brien, B. S., Wootton, J. M., & McBurnett, K. (1994). Psychopathy and conduct problems in children. *Journal of Abnormal Psychology, 103,* 700–707.

Fridrich, A. H., & Flannery, D. J. (1995). The effects of ethnicity and acculturation on early adolescent delinquency. *Journal of Child and Family Studies, 4,* 69–87.

Fried, S., & Fried, P. (1996). *Bullies and victims.* New York: M. Evans and Company.

Friedman, A. S., Bransfield, S. A., Tomko, L. A., & Katz, S. (1991). Early childhood and maternal antecedents to drug use. *Journal of Drug Education, 21,* 313–331.

Friedrich, L. K., & Stein, A. H. (1973). Aggressive and prosocial television programs and the natural behavior of preschool children. *Monographs of the Society for Research in Child Development, 38* (4, Serial No. 151).

Friedrich-Cofer, L., & Huston, A. C. (1986). Television violence and aggression: The debate continues. *Psychological Bulletin, 100,* 364–371.

Fulgham, R. (1990). *All I really need to know I learned in kindergarten: Uncommon thoughts on common things.* New York: Villard Books.

Gadow, K. D., & Sprafkin, J. (1993). Television "violence" and children with emotional and behavioral disorders. *Journal of Emotional and Behavioral Disorders, 1,* 54–63.

Ganong, L. H., & Coleman, M. (1993). A meta-analytic comparison of the self-esteem and behavior problems of stepchildren to children in other family structures. *Journal of Divorce and Remarriage, 19,* 143–163.

Garbarino, J. (1999). *Lost boys: Why our sons turn violent and how we can save them.* New York: The Free Press.

Garbarino, J. & Kostelny, K. (1997). What children can tell us about living in a war zone. In J. D. Osofsky (Ed.), *Children in a violent society* (pp. 32–41). New York: Guilford.

Gardner, F. (1987). Positive interaction between mothers and children with conduct problems: Is there training for harmony as well as fighting? *Journal of Abnormal Child Psychology, 15,* 283–293.

Gardner, F. (1989). Inconsistent parenting. Is there evidence for a link with children's conduct problems? *Journal of Abnormal Child Psychology, 17,* 223–233.

Gardner, F. E. (1992). Parent–child interaction and conduct disorder. *Educational Psychology Review, 4,* 135–163.

Gardner, S. E., & Resnik, H. (1996). Violence among youth: Origins and a framework for prevention. In R. L. Hampton, P. Jenkins, & T. P. Gullotta (Eds.), *Preventing violence in America: Vol. 4. Issues in children's and families' lives* (pp. 157–177). Thousand Oaks, CA: Sage.

Gardstrom, S. C. (1999). Music exposure and criminal behavior: Perceptions of juvenile offenders. *Journal of Music Therapy, 36,* 207–221.

Garralda, M. E., Connell, J., & Taylor, D. C. (1991). Psychophysiological anomalies in children with emotional and conduct disorder. *Psychological Medicine, 21,* 947–957.

Garrett C. J. (1985). Effects of residential treatment on adjudicated delinquents: A meta-analysis. *Journal of Research in Crime and Delinquency, 22,* 287–308.

Gelman, R., Spelke, E. S., & Meck, E. (1983). What preschoolers know about animate and inanimate objects. In D. R. Rogers & J. S. Sloboda (Eds.), *The acquisition of symbolic skills* (pp. 297–326). New York: Plenum.

Genta, M. L., Menesini, E., Fonzi, A., & Costabile, A. (1996). Bullies and victims in schools in central and southern Italy. *European Journal of Psychology of Education, 11,* 97–110.

Gentry, D. B., & Benenson, W. A. (1993). School to home transfer of conflict management skills among school age children. *Families in Society, 74,* 67–73.

George, C., & Main, M. (1979). Social interaction of young abused children: Approach, avoidance, and aggression. *Child Development, 50,* 306–318.

Ghodsian-Carpey, J., & Baker, L. (1987). Genetic and environmental influences on aggression in 4-to 7-year-old twins. *Aggressive Behavior, 13,* 173–186.

Gibbs, J. C., Arnold, K. D., Ahlborn, H. H., & Chessman, F. L. (1984). Facilitation of sociomoral reasoning in delinquents. *Journal of Consulting and Clinical Psychology, 52,* 37–45.

Gibbs, N., & Roche, T. (1999, December 20). The Columbine tapes. *Time,* 40–51.

Gilmartin, B. G. (1987). Peer group antecedents of severe love-shyness in males. *Journal of Personality, 55,* 467–489.

Gjone, H., Stevenson, J., Sundet, J. M., & Eilertsen, D. E. (1996). Changes in heritability across increasing levels of behavior problems in young twins. *Behavior Genetics, 26,* 419–426.

Glueck, S., & Glueck, E. T. (1950). *Unraveling juvenile delinquency.* New York: The Commonwealth Fund.

Glueck, S., & Glueck, E. T. (1968). *Delinquents and nondelinquents in perspective.* Cambridge, MA: Harvard University Press.

Goldberg, S. (1997). Attachment and childhood behavior problems in normal, at-risk, and clinical samples. In L. Atkinson & K. J. Zucker (Eds.), *Attachment and psychopathology* (pp. 171–195). New York: Guilford.

Golding, W. (1955). *Lord of the flies.* New York: Capricorn.

Goldstein, A. P. (1991). *Delinquent gangs: A psychological perspective.* Champaign, IL: Research Press.

Goldstein, A. P. (1999). *Low-level aggression: First steps on the ladder to violence.* Champaign, IL: Research Press.

Goldstein, A. P., & Conoley, J. C. (1997). Student aggression: Current status. In A. P. Goldstein & J. C. Conoley (Eds.), *School violence intervention: A practical handbook* (pp. 3–19). New York: Guilford.

Goldstein, A. P., & Glick, B. (1994). Aggression replacement training: Curriculum and evaluation. *Simulation and Gaming, 25,* 9–26.

Goldstein, A. P., Glick, B., Reiner, S., Zimmerman, D., & Coultry, T. (1986). *Aggression replacement training.* Champaign, IL: Research Press.

Goldstein, A. P., Harootunian, B., & Conoley, J. C. (1994). *Student aggression: Prevention, management, and replacement training.* New York: Guilford.

Goldstein, A. P., & Kodluboy, D. W. (1998). *Gangs in schools: Signs, symbols, and solutions.* Champaign, IL: Research Press.

Goldstein, A. P., & McGinniss, E. (1997). *Skillstreaming the adolescent* (Rev. ed.). Champaign, IL: Research Press.

Goldstein, A. P., Palumbo, J., Striepling, S., & Voutsinas, A. M. (1995). *Break it up: A teacher's guide to managing student aggression.* Champaign, IL: Research Press.

Goldstein, J. (1992). Sex differences in aggressive play and toy preference. In K. Bjorkqvist & P. Niemala (Eds.), *Of mice and women: Aspects of female aggression.* San Diego: Academic Press.

Goldstein, J. H. (Ed.). (1998). *Why we watch.* New York: Oxford University Press.

Goodenough, F. (1931). *Anger in young children.* Minneapolis: University of Minnesota Press.

Googins, R. (1998). Reflections on delinquency, Dickens, and Twain. In T. P. Gullotta, G. R. Adams, & R. Montemayor (Eds.), *Delinquent violent youth* (pp. 1–11). Thousand Oaks, CA: Sage.

Gordon, W. R., & Caltabiano, M. L. (1996). Urban–rural differences in adolescent self-esteem, leisure boredom, and sensation seeking as predictors of leisure-time usage and satisfaction. *Adolescence, 31,* 883–901.

Gore, T. (1990, January 8). Hate, rape and rap. *Washington Post,* p. A15.

Gottfredson, D. C., & Gottfredson, G. D. (1992). Theory-guided investigation: Three field experiments. In J. McCord & R. E. Tremblay (Eds.), *Preventing antisocial behavior: Interventions from birth through adolescence* (pp. 311–329). New York: Guilford Press.

Gottfredson, G. D. (1987). Peer group interventions to reduce the risk of delinquent behavior: A selective review and a new evaluation. *Criminology, 25,* 671–714.

Gottfredson, M. R., & Hirschi, T. (1990). *A general theory of crime.* Stanford, CA: Stanford University Press.

Gray, J. A. (1976). The neuropsychology of anxiety. In I. G. Sarason & C. D. Spielbeger (Eds.), *Stress and anxiety* (Vol. 3, pp. 3–26). Washington, DC: Hemisphere.

Gray, J. A. (1987). Perspectives on anxiety and impulsivity: A commentary. *Journal of Research in Personality, 21,* 493–509.

Graybill, D., Strawniak, M., Hunter, T., & O'Leary, M. (1987). Effects of playing versus observing violent versus nonviolent video games on children's aggression. *Psychology: A Quarterly Journal of Human Behavior, 24,* 1–8.

Green, F. P., & Schneider, F. W. (1974). Age differences in the behavior of boys on three measures of altruism. *Child Development, 45,* 248–251.

Green, J., & Wintfeld, N. (1997). A violence prevention curriculum. *Journal of the American Medical Association, 278,* 979–980.

Greenberg, M. T., DeKlyen, M., Speltz, M. L., & Endriga, M. C. (1997). The role of attachment processes in externalizing psychopathology in young children. In L. Atkinson & K. J. Zucker (Eds.), *Attachment and psychopathology* (pp. 196–222). New York: Guilford.

Griest, D., Forehand, R., Wells, K. C., & McMahon, R. J., (1980). An examination of differences between nonclinic and behavior-problem clinic-referred children and their mothers. *Journal of Abnormal Psychology, 89,* 497–500.

Grossman, D. C., Koepsell, T. D., Rivara, F. P., & Neckerman, H. J. (1997). A violence prevention curriculum: In reply. *Journal of the American Medical Association, 278,* 980.

Grossman, D. C., Neckerman, H. J., Koepsell, T. D., Ping-Yu, L., Asher, K. N., Beland, K., Frey, K., & Rivara, F. P. (1997). Effectiveness of a violence prevention curriculum among children in elementary school. *Journal of the American Medical Association, 277,* 1605–1611.

Grych, J. H., & Fincham, F. D. (1990). Marital conflict and children's adjustment: A cognitive-contextual framework. *Psychological Bulletin, 108,* 267–290.

Guerra, N. G., & Slaby, R. G. (1990). Cognitive mediators of aggression in adolescent offenders: 2. Intervention. *Developmental Psychology, 26,* 269–277.

Gutierrez, P., King, C. A., & Ghaziuddin, N. (1996). Adolescent attitudes about death in relation to suicidality. *Suicide and Life Threatening Behavior, 26,* 8–18.

Haapasalo, J., & Tremblay, R. E. (1994). Physically aggressive boys from ages 6 to 12: Family background, parenting behavior, and prediction of delinquency. *Journal of Consulting and Clinical Psychology, 62,* 1044–1052.

Hagan, M. P. (1995). An initial assessment of a fast-track intensive treatment program for juvenile delinquents. *International Journal of Offender Therapy and Comparative Criminology, 39,* 109–119.

Hagan, M. P. (1997). An analysis of adolescent perpetrators of homicide and attempted homicide upon return to the community. *International Journal of Offender Therapy and Comparative Criminology, 41,* 250–259.

Hagedorn, J. M. (1998). Gang violence in the postindustrial era. In M. Tonry & M. H. Moore (Eds.), *Youth violence: Crime and justice* (Vol. 24, pp. 365–419). Chicago: University of Chicago Press.

Halverson, C. F., & Victor, J. B. (1976). Minor physical anomalies and problem behavior in elementary schoolchildren. *Child Development, 47,* 281–285.

Hammond., W. R., & Yung, B. (1993). Psychology's role in the public health response to assaultive violence among young African-American men. *American Psychologist, 48,* 142–154.

Hammond., W. R., & Yung, B. R. (1995). *PACT: Positive adolescent choices training.* Champaign, IL: Research Press.

Haner, C. F., & Brown, P. A. (1955). Clarification of the instigation to action concept in the frustration-aggression hypothesis. *Journal of Abnormal and Social Psychology, 40,* 26–39.

Hanf, C. (1969, April). *A two stage program for modifying maternal controlling during mother–child (M–C) interaction.* Paper presented at the meeting of the Western Psychological Association, Vancouver, British Columbia, Canada.

Hanson, C. L., Henggeler, S. W., Haefele, W. F., & Rodick, J. D. (1984). Demographic, individual, and family relationship correlates of serious and repeated crime among adolescents and their siblings. *Journal of Consulting and Clinical Psychology, 52,* 528–538.

Hapkiewicz, W. G., & Roden, A. H. (1971). The effect of aggressive cartoons on children's interpersonal play. *Child Development, 42,* 1583–1585.

Hardy, M. S., Armstrong, F. D., Martin, B. L., & Strawn, K. N. (1996). A firearm safety program for children: They just can't say no. *Journal of Developmental and Behavioral Pediatrics, 17,* 216–221.

Hare, R. D. (1993). *Without conscience: The disturbing world of the psychopaths among us.* New York: Pocket Books.

Hare, R. D., Hart, S. D., & Harpur, T. J. (1991). Psychopathy and the *DSM-IV* criteria for antisocial personality disorder. *Journal of Abnormal Psychology, 100,* 391–398.

Harmon, R. J., & Riggs, P. D. (1996). Clonidine for posttraumatic stress disorder in preschool children. *Journal of the American Academy of Child and Adolescent Psychiatry, 35,* 1247–1249.

Harris, J. R. (1998). *The nurture assumption.* New York: The Free Press.

Hartup, W. W. (1974). Aggression in childhood: Developmental perspectives. *American Psychologist, 29,* 336–341.

Hastings, T., Anderson, S. J., Hemphill, P. (1997). Comparisons of daily stress, coping, problem behavior, and cognitive distortions in adolescent sexual offenders and conduct-disordered youth. *Sexual Abuse: Journal of Research and Treatment, 9,* 29–42.

Haurin, R. J. (1992). Patterns of childhood residence and the relationship to young adult outcomes. *Journal of Marriage and the Family, 54,* 846–860.

Hawkins, J. D., Catalano, R. F., & Miller, J. Y. (1992). Risk and protective factors for alcohol and other drug problems in adolescence and early adulthood: Implications for substance abuse prevention. *Psychological Bulletin, 112,* 64–105.

Hawkins, J. D., Catalano, R. F., Morrison, D. M., O'Donnell, J., Abbott, R. D., & Day, L. E. (1992). The Seattle Social Development Project: Effects of the first four years on protective factors and problem behaviors. In J. McCord & R. E. Tremblay (Eds.), *Preventing antisocial behavior: Interventions from birth through adolescence* (pp. 139–161). New York: Guilford Press.

Hawkins, J. D., & Lishner, D. M. (1987). Schooling and delinquency. In E. H. Johnson (Ed.), *Handbook on crime and delinquency prevention* (pp. 179–221). New York: Greenwood Press.

Hawley, T. L., & Disney, E. R. (1992, Winter). Crack's children: The consequences of maternal cocaine abuse. *Social Policy Report, 6,* 1–23.

Hay, D. F., Caplan, M., Castle, J., & Stimson, C. A. (1991). Does sharing become increasingly "rational" in the second year of life? *Developmental Psychology, 27,* 987–993.

Hay, D. F., Nash, A., & Pedersen, J. (1981). Responses of six-month-olds to the distress of their peers. *Child Development, 52,* 1071–1075.

Hay, D. F., Nash, A., & Pedersen, J. (1983). Interactions between 6-months-olds. *Child Development, 54,* 557–562.

Hearold, S. (1986). A synthesis of 1043 effects of television on social behavior. In G. Comstock (Ed.), *Public communication and behavior* (Vol. 1., pp. 65–133). San Diego, CA: Academic Press.

Heaven, P. C. L. (1996). Personality and self-reported delinquency: Analysis of the 'Big Five' personality dimensions. *Personality and Individual Differences, 1,* 47–54.

Heide, K. M. (1995). *Why kids kill parents.* Thousand Oaks, CA: Sage.

Heide, K. M. (1997). Juvenile homicide in America: How can we stop the killing? *Behavioral Sciences and the Law, 15,* 203–220.

Heide, K. M. (1999). *Young killers: The challenge of juvenile homicide.* Thousand Oaks, CA: Sage.

Heimer, K. (1996). Gender, interaction, and delinquency: Testing a theory of differential social control. *Social Psychology Quarterly, 59,* 39–61.

Heinemann, P. P. (1973). *Mobbing.* Oslo, Sweden: Gyldenal.

Hellendoorn, J., & Harinck, F. J. H. (1997). War toy play and aggression in Dutch kindergarten children. *Social Development, 6,* 340–354.

Henggeler, S. W., & Borduin, C. M. (1990). *Family therapy and beyond: A multisystemic approach to treating the behavior problems of children and adolescents.* Pacific Groves, CA: Brooks/Cole.

Henggeler, S. W., Melton, G. B., & Smith, L. A. (1992). Family preservation using multisystemic therapy: An effective alternative to incarcerating serious juvenile offenders. *Journal of Consulting and Clinical Psychology, 60,* 953–961.

Henggeler, S. W., Melton, G. B., Smith, L. A., Schoenwald, S. K., & Hanley, J. H. (1993). Family preservation using multisystemic treatment: Long-term follow-up to a clinical trial with serious juvenile offenders. *Journal of Child and Family Studies, 2,* 283–293.

Henry, B., & Moffitt, T. E. (1997). Neuropsychological and neuroimaging studies of juvenile delinquency and adult criminal behavior. In D. M. Stoff, J. Breiling, & J. D. Maser (Eds.), *Handbook of antisocial behavior* (pp. 280–288). New York: Wiley.

Hess, R. D., & Camara, K. A. (1979). Post-divorce family relationships as mediating factors in the consequences of divorce for children. *Journal of Social Issues, 35,* 79–96.

Hetherington, E. M., Bridges, M., & Insabella, G. M. (1998). What matters? What does not? Five perspectives on the association between marital transitions and children's adjustment. *American Psychologist, 53,* 167–184.

Hetherington, E. M., Cox, M., & Cox, R. (1982). Effects of divorce on parents and children. In M. E. Lamb (Ed.), *Nontraditional families: Parenting and child development* (pp. 233–288). Hillsdale, NJ: Lawrence Erlbaum Associates.

Hetherington, E. M., & Martin, B. (1986). Family factors and psychopathology in children. In H. S. Quay & J. S. Werry (Eds.), *Psychopathological disorders of childhood* (3rd ed., pp. 332–390). New York: Wiley.

Hetherington, E. M., Stouwie, R. J., & Ridberg, E. H. (1971). Patterns of family interaction and child-rearing attitudes related to three dimensions of juvenile delinquency. *Journal of Abnormal Psychology, 78,* 160–176.

Hettena, S. (1997, December 1). Judge orders girls to play nice after schoolyard dispute. *The Nando Net* [On–line]. Available: www.nando.net

Hewitt, J. K., Silberg, J. L., Neale, M. C., Eaves, L. J., & Erickson, M. (1992). The analysis of parental ratings of children's behavior using LISREL. *Behavior Genetics, 22,* 293–317.

Hinshaw, S. P. (1992). Externalizing behavior problems and academic underachievement in childhood and adolescence: Causal relationships and underlying mechanisms. *Psychological Bulletin, 111,* 127–155.

Hinshaw, S. P., Lahey, B. B., & Hart, E. L. (1993). Issues of taxonomy and comorbidity in the development of conduct disorder. *Development and Psychopathology, 5,* 31–49.

Hirschi, T. (1969). *Causes of delinquency.* Berkeley: University of California Press.

Hirschi, T., & Gottfredson, M. R. (1994). *The generality of deviance.* New Brunswick, NJ: Transaction.

Hoberman, J. (1998). "A test for the individual viewer": *Bonnie and Clyde's* violent reception. In J. H. Goldstein (Ed.), *Why we watch* (pp. 116–143). New York: Oxford University Press.

Hoffman, M. L. (1979). Development of moral thought, feeling, and behavior. *American Psychologist, 34,* 958–966.

Hoffman-Plotkin, D., & Twentyman, C. T. (1984). A multimodal assessment of behavioral and cognitive deficits in abused and neglected preschoolers. *Child Development, 55,* 794–802.

Hogben, M. (1998). Factors moderating the effect of televised aggression on viewer behavior. *Communication Research, 25,* 220–247.

Hoge, R. D., Andrews, D. A., & Leschied, A. W. (1994). Tests of three hypotheses regarding the predictors of delinquency. *Journal of Abnormal Child Psychology, 22,* 547–559.

Holman, J., & Braithwaite, V. (1982). Parental lifestyles and children's television viewing. *Australian Journal of Psychology, 34,* 375–382.

Holmberg, M. C. (1980). The development of social interchange patterns from 12 to 42 months. *Child Development, 51,* 448–456.

Hoover, J. H, Oliver, R., & Hazler, R. J. (1992). Bullying: Perceptions of adolescent victims in the Midwestern USA. *School Psychology International, 13,* 5–16.

Horowitz, K., & Weine, S. (1994, May). *Communal ties mediating violence and its effects.* Paper presented at the 147th annual conference of the American Psychiatric Association, Philadelphia.

Howell, J. C. (1995). Gangs and youth violence. In J. C. Howell, B. Krisberg, J. D. Hawkins, & J. J. Wilson (Eds.), *Serious, violent, & chronic juvenile offenders* (pp. 261–274). Thousand Oaks, CA: Sage.

Howell, J. C. (1997, December). Youth gangs. *Office of Juvenile Justice and Delinquency Prevention Fact Sheet.* Washington, DC: U.S. Department of Justice.

Howell, J. C., & Hawkins, J. D. (1998). Prevention of youth violence. In M. Tonry & M. H. Moore (Eds.), *Youth violence: Crime and justice* (Vol. 24, pp. 263–315). Chicago: University of Chicago Press.

Hudley, C., & Graham, S. (1993). An attributional intervention to reduce peer-directed aggression among African-American boys. *Child Development, 64,* 124–138.

Huesmann, L. R., & Eron, L. D. (1986). The development of aggression in American children as a consequence of television violence viewing. In L. R. Huesmann & L. D. Eron (Eds.), *Television and the aggressive child: A cross-national comparison* (pp. 45–80). Hillsdale, NJ: Lawrence Erlbaum Associates.

Huesmann, L. R., Eron, L. D., Klein, R., Brice, P., & Fischer, P. (1983). Mitigating the imitation of aggressive behaviors by changing children's attitudes. *Journal of Personality and Social Psychology, 44,* 899–910.

Huesmann, L. R., Eron, L. D., Lefkowitz, M. M., & Walder, L. O. (1984). Stability of aggression over time and generations. *Developmental Psychology, 20,* 1120–1134.

Huesmann, L. R., Moise, J. F., & Podolski, C-L. (1997). The effects of media violence on the development of antisocial behavior. In D. M. Stoff, J. Breiling, & J. D. Maser (Eds.), *Handbook of antisocial behavior* (pp. 181–193). New York: Wiley.

Hughes, J. (1998a, June 11). School shooting suspect wails as his confession is played in court. *The Nando Net* [On-line]. Available: www.nando.net

Hughes, J. (1998b, June 13). School shooter gets two life sentences. *The Nando Net* [On-line]. Available: www.nando.net

Hughes, J. A., Cavell, T. A., & Grossman, P. A. (1997). A positive view of self: Risk or protection for aggressive children? *Development and Psychopathology, 9,* 75–94.

Hunter, J. A., & Figueredo, A. J. (1995). *The role of sex victimization in the etiology of juvenile perpetrators of child molestation.* Unpublished manuscript.

Hutchinson, R. R., Renfrew, J. W., & Young, G. A. (1971). Effects of long-term shock and associated stimuli on aggressive and manual responses. *Journal of the Experimental Analysis of Behavior, 15,* 141–166.

Hymel, S. (1986). Interpretations of peer behavior: Affective bias in childhood and adolescence. *Child Development, 57,* 431–445.

Irwin, A. R., & Gross, A. M. (1995). Cognitive tempo, violent video games, and aggressive behavior in young boys. *Journal of Family Violence, 10,* 337–350.

Izard, C. E., Hembree, E. A., Dougherty, L. M., & Spizzirri, C. C. (1983). Changes in facial expressions of 2- to 19-month-old infants following acute pain. *Developmental Psychology, 19,* 418–426.

Izzo, R. L., & Ross, R. R. (1990). Meta-analysis of rehabilitation programs for juvenile delinquents: A brief report. *Criminal Justice and Behavior, 17,* 134–142.

Jacobs, J. B. (1977). *Stateville: The penitentiary in mass society.* Chicago: University of Chicago Press.

Jacobs, W. L., Kennedy, W. A., & Meyer, J. B. (1997). Juvenile delinquents: A between-group comparison study of sexual and nonsexual offenders. *Sexual Abuse: Journal of Research and Treatment, 9,* 201–217.

Jenkins, E. J., & Bell, C. C. (1994). Violence exposure, psychological distress, and high risk behaviors among inner-city high school students. In S. Friedman (Ed.), *Anxiety disorders in African Americans* (pp. 76–88). New York: Springer.

Jenkins, E. J., & Bell, C. C. (1997). Exposure and response to community violence among children and adolescents. In J. D. Osofsky (Ed.), *Children in a violent society* (pp. 9–31). New York: Guilford.

Jenkins, S., Bax, M., & Hart, H. (1980). Behavior problems in preschool children. *Journal of Child Psychology and Psychiatry, 21,* 5–18.

Jessor, R., & Jessor, S. L. (1977). *Problem behavior and psychosocial development: A longitudinal study of youth.* New York: Academic Press.

Jockin, V., McGue, M., & Lykken, D. T. (1996). Personality and divorce: A genetic analysis. *Journal of Personality and Social Psychology, 71,* 288–299.

Joe, K. A., & Chesney-Lind, M. (1995). "Just every mother's angel": An analysis of gender and ethnic variations in young gang membership. *Gender and Society, 9,* 408–431.

Johnson D. L., & Walker, T. (1987). Primary prevention of behavior problems in Mexican-American children. *American Journal of Community Psychology, 15,* 375–385.

Johnson, D. W., & Johnson, R. T. (1994). Constructive conflict in the schools. *Journal of Social Issues, 50,* 117–137.

Johnson, D. W., & Johnson, R. T. (1995). *Teaching students to be peacemakers.* Edina, MN: Interactive Book Company.

Johnson, D. W., & Johnson, R. T. (1996). Teaching all students how to manage conflicts constructively: The Peacemakers program. *Journal of Negro Education, 65,* 322–335.

Johnson, J. D., Jackson, L. A., & Gatto, L. (1995). Violent attitudes and deferred academic aspirations: Deleterious effects of exposure to rap music. *Basic and Applied Social Psychology, 16,* 27–41.

Johnson, J. H., Rasbury, W. C., & Siegel, L. J. (1997). *Approaches to child treatment* (2nd ed.). Boston: Allyn & Bacon.

Jones, M. (1997). Is less better? Boot camp, regular probation and rearrest in North Carolina. *American Journal of Criminal Justice, 21,* 147–161.

Jones, R. (1996). Fire! *American School Board Journal, 183,* 24–28.

Jorm, A. F., Share, D. L., Matthews, R., & Maclean, R. (1986). Behavior problems in specific reading retarded and general reading backward children: A longitudinal study. *Journal of Child Psychology and Psychiatry, 27,* 33–43.

Josephson, W. L. (1987). Television violence and children's aggression: Test the priming, social script, and disinhibition predictions. *Journal of Personality and Social Psychology, 53,* 882–890.

Jouriles, E. N., Murphy, C. M., & O'Leary, K. D. (1989). Interspousal aggression, marital discord, and child problems. *Journal of Consulting and Clinical Psychology, 57,* 453–455.

Joy, L. A., Kimball, M. M., & Zabrack, M. L. (1986). Television and aggressive behavior. In T. M. Williams (Ed.), *The impact of television: A natural experiment involving three towns* (pp. 303–360). New York: Academic Press.

Judge: Teen should be tried as an adult in Georgia school shooting. (1999, August 12). Fredericksburg (VA) *Free Lance Star,* p. A10.

Jussim, L. (1989). Teacher expectations: Self-fulfilling prophecies, perceptual biases, and accuracy. *Journal of Personality and Social Psychology, 57,* 469–480.

Kagan, J. (1998). Biology and the child. In N. Eisenberg (Vol. Ed.) & W. Damon (Ed.-in-Chief), *Handbook of child psychology* (Vol. 3, 5th ed., pp. 177–235). New York: Wiley.

Kalter, N., Riemer, B., Brickman, A., & Woo Chen, J. (1985). Implications of parental divorce for female development. *Journal of the American Academy of Child Psychiatry, 24,* 538–544.

Kandel, D. (1973). Adolescent marijuana use: Role of parents and peers. *Science, 181,* 1067–1070.

Kandel, D. B., & Wu, P. (1995). Disentangling mother–child effects in the development of antisocial behavior. In J. McCord (Ed.), *Coercion and punishment in long-time perspectives* (pp. 106–123). Cambridge, England: Cambridge University Press.

Kaplan, H. B. (1975). *Self-attitudes and deviant behavior.* Pacific Palisades, CA: Goodyear.

Kaplan, H. B. (1980). *Deviant behavior in defense of self.* New York: Academic Press.

Kates, D. B., Jr., & Kleck, G. (1997). *The great American gun debate.* San Francisco: Pacific Research Institute for Public Policy.

Kavoussi, R. J., Kaplan, M., & Becker, J. V. (1988). Psychiatric diagnoses in adolescent sex offenders. *Journal of the American Academy of Child and Adolescent Psychiatry, 27,* 241–243.

Kazdin, A. E. (1992). Overt and covert antisocial behavior: Child and family characteristics among psychiatric inpatient children. *Journal of Child and Family Studies, 1,* 3–20.

Kazdin, A. E. (1995). *Conduct disorders in childhood and adolescence* (2nd ed.). Thousand Oaks, CA: Sage.

Kazdin, A. E., Bass, D., Siegel, T., & Thomas, C. (1989). Cognitive-behavioral therapy and relationship therapy in the treatment of children referred for antisocial behavior. *Journal of Consulting and Clinical Psychology, 57,* 522–535.

Kellam, S., Ensminger, M. E., & Turner, J. (1977). Family structure and the mental health of children. *Archives of General Psychiatry, 34,* 1012–1022.

Kellam, S. G., Ling, X., Merisca, R., Brown, C. H., & Ialongo, N. (1998). The effect of the level of aggression in the first grade classroom on the course and malleability of aggressive behavior into middle school. *Development and Psychopathology, 10,* 165–185.

Kellam, S. G., & Rebok, G. W. (1992). Building developmental and etiological theory through epidemiologically based preventive intervention trials. In J. McCord & R. E. Tremblay (Eds.), *Preventing antisocial behavior: Interventions from birth through adolescence* (pp. 162–195). New York: Guilford Press.

Kellam, S. G., Rebok, G. W., Ialongo, N., & Mayer, L. S. (1994). The course and malleability of aggressive behavior from early first grade into middle school: Results of a developmental epidemiologically-based preventive trial. *Journal of Child Psychology and Psychiatry, 35,* 259–281.

Keller, H. R., & Tapasak, R. C. (1997). Classroom management. In A. P. Goldstein & J. C. Conoley (Eds.), *School violence intervention: A practical handbook* (pp. 107–126). New York: Guilford.

Kelly, D. H. (1975). Status origins, track positions, and delinquent involvement. *Sociological Quarterly, 12,* 65–85.

Kendziora, K. T., & O'Leary, S. G. (1993). Dysfunctional parenting as a focus for prevention and treatment of child behavior problems. In T. H. Ollendick & R. J. Prinz (Eds.), *Advances in clinical child psychology* (Vol. 15, pp. 175–206). New York: Plenum.

Kennedy, D. (1992, May 4). Girls join, relish violence of inner-city gang life. Fredericksburg (VA) *Free Lance-Star,* p. D5.

Kids charged with killing dad's live-in. (1999, January 8). Fredericksburg (VA) *Free Lance-Star,* p. A4.

Kilpatrick, W. K. (1992). *Why Johnny can't tell right from wrong.* New York: Touchstone.

Kinney, D. (1999, January 18). "It was fun to hang someone." Fredericksburg *Free Lance-Star,* p. A1.

Kirk, M., & Boyer, P. J. (2000, January 18). The killer at Thurston High (M. Kirk, Director). In M. Kirk, M. Navasky, & K. O'Connor (Producers), *Frontline.* Boston: WGBH.

Kleck, G. (1991). *Point blank.* New York: Aldine de Gruyter.

Klein, M. W. (1995). Street gang cycles. In J. Q. Wilson & J. Petersilia (Eds.), *Crime* (pp. 217–236). San Francisco: Institute for Contemporary Studies Press.

Klein, M. W. & Maxson, C. L. (1989). Street gang violence. In N. Weiner & M. E. Wolfgang (Eds.), *Violent crime, violent criminals* (pp. 198–234). Newbury Park, CA: Sage.

Klimes-Dougan, B., & Kistner, J. (1990). Physically abused preschoolers' responses to peers' distress. *Developmental Psychology, 26,* 599–602.

Kobayashi, J., Sales, B. D., Becker, J. V., Figueredo, A. J., & Kaplan, M. S. (1995). Perceived parental deviance, parental–child bonding, child abuse, and child sexual aggression. *Sexual Abuse: Journal of Research and Treatment, 7,* 25–44.

Kochanska, G. (1991). Socialization and temperament in the development of guilt and conscience. *Child Development, 62,* 1379–1392.

Kochanska, G. (1993). Toward a synthesis of parental socialization and child temperament in early development of conscience. *Child Development, 62,* 325–347.

Kodluboy, D. W. (1997). Gang-oriented interventions. In A. P. Goldstein & J. C. Conoley (Eds.), *School violence intervention: A practical handbook* (pp. 189–214). New York: Guilford.

Kodluboy, D., & Evinrud, L. (1993). School based interventions: Best practice and critical issues. In A. P. Goldstein & C. R. Huff (Eds.), *The gang intervention handbook* (pp. 257–300). Champaign, IL: Research Press.

Kohlberg, L. (1975). The cognitive developmental approach to moral education. *Phi Delta Kappan, 56,* 670–677.

Kohn, A. (1997). The trouble with character education. In A. Molnar (Ed.), *The construction of children's character: Ninety-sixth yearbook of the National Society for the Study of Education: Part II* (pp. 154–162). Chicago, IL: The National Society for the Study of Education.

Kohn, M. (1977). *Social competence, symptoms, and underachievement in childhood: A longitudinal perspective.* Silver Spring, MD: V. H. Winston.

Koivisto, H., & Haapasalo, J. (1996). Childhood maltreatment and adulthood psychopathy in light of file-based assessments among mental state examinees. *Studies on Crime and Crime Prevention, 5,* 91–104.

Koller, M. (1995, March 1). Skinhead brothers suspected in killings. Fredericksburg (VA) *Free Lance-Star,* p. A4.

Kolvin, I., Miller, F. J. W., Fleeting, M., & Kolvin, P. A. (1988). Social and parenting factors affecting criminal offence rates: Findings from the Newcastle Thousand Family Study (1947–1980). *British Journal of Psychiatry, 152,* 80–90.

Kolvin, I., Miller, F. J. W., Fleeting, M., & Kolvin, P. A. (1989). Risk/protective factors for offending, with particular reference to deprivation. In M. Rutter (Ed.), *Studies in psychosocial risk: The power of longitudinal studies* (pp. 77–95). Cambridge, England: Cambridge University Press.

Korzenny, F., Greenberg, B. S., & Atkin, C. K. (1979). Styles of parental disciplinary practices as a mediator of children's learning from antisocial television portrayals. In D. Nimmo (Ed.), *Communication Yearbook 3* (pp. 283–294). New Brunswick, NJ: Transaction Books.

Krisberg, B., Currie, E., Onek, D., & Wiebush, R. G. (1995). Graduated sanctions for serious, violent, and chronic juvenile offenders. In J. C. Howell, B. Krisberg, J. D. Hawkins, & J. J. Wilson (Eds.), *Serious, violent, & chronic juvenile offenders* (pp. 142–170). Thousand Oaks, CA: Sage.

Kruesi, M. J. P., Hibbs, E. D., Zahn, T. P., Keysor, C. S., Hamburger, S. D., Bartko, J. J., & Rapoport, J. L. (1992). A 2-year prospective follow-up study of children and adolescents with disruptive behavior disorders. *Archives of General Psychiatry, 49,* 429–435.

Kruesi, M. J. P., Rapoport, J. L., Hamburger, S., Hibbs, E., Potter, W. Z., Lenane, M., & Brown, G. L. (1990). Cerebrospinal fluid monoamine metabolites, aggression, and impulsivity in disruptive behavior disorders of children and adolescents. *Archives of General Psychiatry, 47,* 419–426.

Krynicki, Y. (1978). Cerebral dysfunction in repetitively assaultive adolescents. *Journal of Nervous and Mental Disease, 166,* 59–67.

Kupersmidt, J. B., & Coie, J. D. (1990). Preadolescent peer status, aggression, and school adjustment as predictors of externalizing problems in adolescence. *Child Development, 61,* 1350–1362.

Kupersmidt, J. B., & Patterson, C. J. (1991). Childhood peer rejection, aggression, withdrawal and perceived competence as predictors of self-reported behavior problems in preadolescence. *Journal of Abnormal Child Psychology, 19,* 427–449.

Kutcher, S. P. (1997). *Child & adolescent psychopharmacology.* Philadelphia: W. B. Saunders.

L.A. gang members convicted of murdering 3-year-old. (1997, June 2). *The Nando Net* [On-line]. Available: www.nando.net

Ladd, G. W., Lange, G., & Stremmel, A. (1983). Personal and situational influences on children's helping behavior: Factors that mediate compliant helping. *Child Development, 54,* 488–501.

LaFreniere, P. J. (2000). *Emotional development: A biosocial perspective.* Belmont, CA: Wadsworth/Thompson Learning.

Lagerspetz, K. M. J. (1979). Modification of aggressiveness in mice. In S. Feshbach & A. Fraczek (Eds.), *Aggression and behavior change* (pp. 66–82). New York: Praeger.

Lagerspetz, K., & Viemerö, V. (1986). Television and aggressive behavior among Finnish children. In L. R. Huesmann & L. D. Eron (Eds.), *Television and the aggressive child: A cross-national comparison* (pp. 81–117). Hillsdale, NJ: Lawrence Erlbaum Associates.

Lahey, B. B., Hart, E. L., Pliszka, S., Applegate, B., & McBurnett, K. (1993). Neurophysiological correlates of conduct disorder: A rationale and review of the research. *Journal of Clinical Child Psychology, 22,* 141–153.

Lahey, B. B., Hartdagen, S. E., Frick, P. J., McBurnett, K., Connor, R., & Hynd, G. W. (1988). Conduct disorder: Parsing the confounded relation to parental divorce and antisocial personality. *Journal of Abnormal Psychology, 97,* 334–337.

Lahey, B. B., Loeber, R., Hart, E. L., Frick, P. J., Applegate, B., Zhang, Q., Green, S. M., & Russo, M. F. (1995). Four-year longitudinal study of conduct disorder in boys: Patterns of predictors of persistence. *Journal of Abnormal Psychology, 104,* 83–93.

Lahey, B. B., Piacentini, J. C., McBurnett, K., Stone, P., Hartdagen, S. E., & Hynd, G. (1988). Psychopathology and antisocial behavior in the parents of children with conduct disorder and hyperactivity. *Journal of the American Academy of Child and Adolescent Psychiatry, 27,* 163–170.

Lally, J. R., Mangione, P. L., & Honig, A. S. (1988). Long-range impact of an early intervention with low-income children and their families. In D. R. Powell (Ed.), *Parent education as early childhood intervention* (pp. 79–104). Norwood, NJ: Ablex.

Lambert, N. M. (1988). Adolescent outcomes for hyperactive children: Perspectives on general and specific patterns of childhood risk for adolescent educational, social, and mental health problems. *American Psychologist, 43,* 786–799.

Lamson, S. R. (1995). Media violence has increased the murder rate. In C. Wekesser (Ed.), *Violence in the media* (pp. 25–27). San Diego, CA: Greenhaven Press.

Larson, J. (1994). Violence prevention in the schools: A review of selected programs and procedures. *School Psychology Review, 23,* 151–164.

Lawton, T. A. (1992). *Maternal cocaine addiction: Correlates and consequences.* Unpublished doctoral dissertation, University of Michigan, Ann Arbor.

Laybourn, A. (1986). Traditional strict working class parenting—An undervalued system. *British Journal of Social Work, 16,* 625–644.

Lee, M., & Prentice, N. (1988). Interrelations of empathy, cognition, and moral reasoning with dimensions of juvenile delinquency. *Journal of Abnormal Child Psychology, 16,* 127–139.

Lefkowitz, M. M., Eron, L. D., Walder, L. O., & Huesmann, L. R. (1977). *Growing up to be violent.* New York: Pergamon.

Leifer, A. D., & Roberts, D. F. (1972). Children's responses to television violence. In J. P. Murray, E. A. Rubinstein, & G. A. Comstock (Eds.), *Television and social behavior: Vol. 2. Television and social learning* (pp. 43–180). Washington, DC: U.S. Government Printing Office.

Leming, J. L. (1997). Research and practice in character education: A historical perspective. In A. Molnar (Ed.), *The construction of children's character: Ninety-sixth yearbook of the National Society for the Study of Education: Part II* (pp. 31–44). Chicago: The National Society for the Study of Education.

Leukefeld, C. G., Logan, T. K., Clayton, R. R., Martin, C., Zimmerman, R. Cattarello, A., Milich, R., & Lynam, D. (1998). Adolescent drug use, delinquency, and other behaviors. In T. P. Gullotta, G. R. Adams, & R. Montemayer (Eds.), *Delinquent violent youth* (pp. 98–128). Thousand Oaks, CA: Sage.

Leung, E. H., & Rheingold, H. L. (1981). Development of pointing as a social gesture. *Developmental Psychology, 17,* 215–220.

Leve, L. D., Winebarger, A. A., Fagot, B. I., Reid, J. B., & Goldsmith, H. H. (1998). Environmental and genetic variance in children's observed and reported maladaptive behavior. *Child Development, 69,* 1286–1298.

Levy, S. (1999, May 3). Loitering on the dark side. *Newsweek, 39.*

Levy, T. M., & Orlans, M. (1998). *Attachment, trauma, and healing.* Washington, DC: CWLA Press.

Lewis, D. O. (1994). From abuse to violence: Psychophysiological consequences of maltreatment. In M. E. Hertzig & E. A. Farber (Eds.), *Annual progress in child psychiatry and child development, 1993* (pp. 507–527). New York: Brunner/Mazel.

Lewis, D. O., Lovely, R., Yeager, C., Ferguson, G., Friedman, M., Sloane, G., Friedman, H., & Pincus, J. H. (1988). Intrinsic and environmental characteristics of juvenile murderers. *Journal of the American Academy of Child and Adolescent Psychiatry, 27,* 582–587.

Lewis, D. O., Pincus, J. H., Bard, B., Richardson, E., Prichep, L. S., Feldman, M., & Yeager, C. (1988).

Neuropsychiatric, psychoeducational, and family characteristics of 14 juveniles condemned to death in the United States. *American Journal of Psychiatry, 145,* 584–589.

Leyens, J. P., Parke, R. D., Camino, L., & Berkowitz, L. (1975). Effects of movie violence on aggression in a field setting as a function of group dominance and cohesion. *Journal of Personality and Social Psychology, 32,* 346–360.

Lhotka, W. C. (1994, Oct. 23). Refs catch fists, shots over calls. *St. Louis Post-Dispatch,* pp. 1A, 6A.

Lickona, T. (1991). *Educating for character.* New York: Bantam.

Lieb, D. A. (1998, August 11). Both boys found guilty in Jonesboro school shootings. *The Nando Net* [On-line]. Available: www.nando.net

Liebert, R. M., & Baron, R. A. (1972). Some immediate effects of televised violence on children's behavior. *Developmental Psychology, 6,* 469–475.

Lipsey, M. W. (1992). Juvenile delinquency treatment: A meta-analytic inquiry into the variability of effects. In T. D. Cook (Ed.), *Mata-analysis for explanation: A casebook* (pp. 83–127). New York: Russell Sage.

Littleton shooting backlash. (1999, April 24). *Fredericksburg (VA) Free Lance-Star,* p. C13.

Lizotte, A. J., Tesoriero, J. M., Thornberry, T., & Krohn, M. D. (1994). Patterns of adolescent firearms ownership and use. *Justice Quarterly, 11,* 51–73.

Lobitz, G. K., & Johnson, S. M. (1975). Deviant and normal children. *Journal of Abnormal Child Psychology, 3,* 353–374.

Lochman, J. E., & Dodge, K. A. (1994). Social-cognitive processes of severely violent, moderately aggressive, and nonaggressive boys. *Journal of Consulting and Clinical Psychology, 62,* 366–374.

Lochman, J. E., Lampron, L. B., & Rabiner, D. L. (1989). Format and salience effects in the social problem-solving of aggressive and nonaggressive boys. *Journal of Clinical Child Psychology, 18,* 230–236.

Lochman, J. E., & Wayland, K. K. (1994). Aggression, social acceptance, and race as predictors of negative adolescent outcomes. *Journal of the American Academy of Child and Adolescent Psychiatry, 33,* 1026–1035.

Lochman, J. E., & Wells, K. C. (1996). A social-cognitive intervention with aggressive children. In R. DeV. Peters & R. J. McMahon (Eds.), *Preventing childhood disorders, substance abuse, and delinquency* (pp. 111–143). Thousand Oaks, CA: Sage.

Loeb, J., & Mednick, S. A. (1977). A prospective study of predictors of criminality: 3. Electrodermal response patterns. In S. A. Mednick & K. O. Christiansen (Eds.), *Biosocial bases of criminal behavior* (pp. 245–254). New York: Gardner Press.

Loeber, R. (1982). The stability of antisocial and delinquent child behavior: A review. *Child Development, 53,* 1431–1446.

Loeber, R., & Dishion, T. (1984). Boys who fight at home and school: Family conditions influencing cross-setting consistency. *Journal of Consulting and Clinical Psychology, 52,* 759–768.

Loeber, R., & Hay, D. F. (1994). Developmental approaches to aggression and conduct problems. In M. Rutter & D. F. Hay (Eds.), *Development through life: A handbook for clinicians* (pp. 488–516). Boston: Blackwell Scientific.

Loeber, R., & Keenan, K. (1994). Interaction between conduct disorder and its comorbid conditions: Effects of age and gender. *Clinical Psychology Review, 14,* 497–523.

Loeber, R., & Schmaling, K. B. (1985a). Empirical evidence for overt and covert patterns of antisocial conduct problems: A meta-analysis. *Journal of Abnormal Child Psychology, 13,* 337–352.

Loeber, R., & Schmaling, K. B. (1985b). The utility of differentiating between mixed and pure forms of antisocial child behavior. *Journal of Abnormal Child Psychology, 13,* 315–336.

Loeber, R., & Stouthamer-Loeber, M., (1986). Family factors as correlates and predictors of juvenile conduct problems and delinquency. In M. Tonry & N. Morris (Eds.), *Crime and justice* (Vol. 7, pp. 29–149). Chicago: University of Chicago Press.

Loeber, R., & Stouthamer-Loeber, M. (1998). Development of juvenile aggression and violence: Some common misconceptions and controversies. *American Psychologist, 53,* 242–259.

Loeber, R., Stouthamer-Loeber, M., & Green, S. M. (1987, April). *Age of onset of conduct problems, different developmental trajectories, and unique contributing factors.* Paper presented at the meeting of the Society for Research in Child Development, Baltimore, MD.

Loper, A. (1999, September). *Female juvenile delinquency: Risk factors and promising interventions.* (Juvenile Justice Fact Sheet). Charlottesville, VA: University of Virginia: Institute of Law, Psychiatry, and Public Policy.

Loper, A. B., & Cornell, D. G. (1996). Homicide by juvenile girls. *Journal of Child and Family Studies, 5,* 323–336.

Lovaas, O. I. (1961). Interaction between verbal and nonverbal behavior. *Child Development, 32,* 329–336.

Luria, A. R. (1961). *The role of speech in the regulation of normal and abnormal behavior.* New York: Liveright.

Lynn, R., Hampson, S., & Agahi, E. (1989). Television violence and aggression: A genotype-environment, correlation and interaction theory. *Social Behaviour and Personality, 17,* 143–164.

Lyon, J. M., Henggeler, S. W., & Hall, J. A. (1992). The family relations, peer relations, and criminal activities of Caucasian and Hispanic-American gang members. *Journal of Abnormal Child Psychology, 20,* 439–449.

Lyons, M. J., True, W. R., Eisen, S. A., Goldberg, J., Meyer, J. M., Faraone, S. V., Eaves, L. J., & Tsuang, M. T. (1995). Differential heritability of adult and juvenile antisocial traits. *Archives of General Psychiatry, 52,* 906–915.

Lyons-Ruth, K. (1996). Attachment relationships among children with aggressive behavior problems: The role of disorganized early attachment patterns. *Journal of Consulting and Clinical Psychology, 64,* 64–73.

Lyons-Ruth, K., Alpern, L., & Repacholi, B. (1993). Disorganized infant attachment classification and maternal psychosocial problems as predictors of hostile-aggressive behavior in the preschool classroom. *Child Development, 64,* 572–585.

Lyons-Ruth, K., Easterbrooks, M. A., & Cibelli, C. D. (1997). Infant attachment strategies, infant mental lag, and maternal depressive symptoms: Predictors of internalizing and externalizing problems at age 7. *Developmental Psychology, 33,* 681–692.

Lytton, H. (1990). Child and parent effects in boys' conduct disorder: A reinterpretation. *Developmental Psychology 26,* 683–697.

Maccoby, E. E., & Martin, J. A. (1983). Socialization in the context of the family: Parent-child interaction. In E. M. Hetherington (Ed.), *Handbook of child psychology: Vol. 4. Socialization, personality, and social development* (pp. 1–101). New York: Wiley.

MacKenzie, D. L. (1991). The parole performance of offenders released from shock incarceration (boot camp prisons): A survival time analysis. *Journal of Quantitative Criminology, 7,* 213–236.

MacKenzie, D. L., & Brame, R. (1995). Shock incarceration and positive adjustment during community supervision. *Journal of Quantitative Criminology, 11,* 111–142.

MacQuiddy, S. L., Maise, S., & Hamilton, S. B. (1987). Empathy and affective perspective-taking skills in parent-identified conduct-disordered boys. *Journal of Clinical Child Psychology, 16,* 260–268.

Magid, K., & McKelvey, C. (1987). *High risk.* Toronto: Bantam.

Magnet, M. (1993). *The dream and the nightmare: The sixties' legacy to the underclass.* New York: William Morrow.

Magnusson, D. (1988). Aggressiveness, hyperactivity, and autonomic activity / reactivity in the development of social maladjustment. In D. Magnusson (Ed.), *Individual development from an interactional perspective: A longitudinal study* (pp. 153–172). Hillsdale, NJ: Lawrence Erlbaum Associates.

Maguin, E., & Loeber, R. (1996). Academic performance and delinquency. In M. Tonry (Ed.), *Crime and justice* (Vol. 20, pp. 145–264). Chicago: University of Chicago Press.

Main, M., & George, C. (1985). Responses of abused and disadvantaged toddlers to distress in age-mates: A study in the day-care setting. *Developmental Psychology, 21,* 407–412.

Main, M. & Solomon, J. (1986). Discovery of a disorganized/disoriented attachment pattern. In T. B. Brazelton & M. W. Yogman (Eds.), *Affective development in infancy* (pp. 95–124). Norwood, NJ: Ablex.

Main, M. & Solomon, J. (1990). Procedures for identifying infants as disorganized/disoriented during the Ainsworth Strange Situation. In M. Greenberg, D. Cicchetti, & E. M. Cummings (Eds.), *Attachment in the preschool years* (pp. 121–160). Chicago: University of Chicago Press.

Majors, R., & Billson, J. M. (1992). *Cool pose: The dilemmas of black manhood in America*. Lexington, MA: Lexington Books.

Mallick, S. K., & McCandless, B. R. (1966). A study of the catharsis of aggression. *Journal of Personality and Social Psychology, 4,* 591–596.

Man convicted of killing pizza delivery man. (1999, April 24). Fredericksburg (VA) *Free Lance-Star,* p. A3.

Man convicted of killing woman who criticized rap song. (1999, January 23). *Minneapolis Star Tribune,* p. 11A.

Marcus, J. (1998, November 2). Cleaning up crime in Boston. *Scholastic Update,* 8.

Markman, H. J., Renick, M. J., Floyd, F. J. Stanley, S. M., & Clements, M. (1993). Preventing marital distress through communication and conflict management training: A 4- and 5-year follow-up. *Journal of Consulting and Clinical Psychology, 61,* 70–77.

Martinius, J., & Strunk, P. (1979). Homicide of an aggressive adolescent boy with right temporal lesion: A case study. *Zeitschrift für Kinder- und Jugendpsychiatrie* [*Journal of Child and Youth Psychology*], *7,* 199–207.

Mason, D. A., & Frick, P. J. (1994). The heritability of antisocial behavior: A meta-analysis of twin and adoption studies. *Journal of Psychopathology and Behavioral Assessment, 16,* 301–323.

Matthews, R., Hunter, J. A., & Vuz, J. (1997). Juvenile female sexual offenders: Clinical characteristics and treatment issues. *Sexual Abuse: Journal of Research and Treatment, 9,* 187–199.

Maughan, B., Gray, G., & Rutter, M. (1985). Reading retardation and antisocial behavior: A follow-up into employment. *Journal of Child Psychology and Psychiatry, 26,* 741–758.

Maughan, B., Pickles, A., Hagell, A., Rutter, M., & Yule, W. (1996). Reading problems and antisocial behavior: Developmental trends in comorbidity. *Journal of Child Psychology and Psychiatry and Allied Disciplines, 37,* 405–418.

Maughan, B., & Rutter, M. (1998). Continuities and discontinuities in antisocial behavior from childhood to adult life. In T. H. Ollendick & R. J. Prinz (Eds.), *Advances in clinical child psychology* (Vol. 20, pp. 1–47). New York: Plenum.

Mayes, L. C., Granger, R. J., Frank, M. A., Schottenfeld, R., & Bornstein, M. H. (1993). Neurobehavioral profiles of neonates exposed to cocaine prenatally. *Pediatrics, 91,* 778–783.

McBurnett, K., Swanson, J. M., Pfiffner, L. J., & Harris, S. J. (1991, June). *The relationship of prefrontal test performance and autonomic arousal to symptoms of inattention/overactivity and aggression/defiance.* Paper presented at the meeting of the Society for Research on Psychopathology, Amsterdam.

McCord, J. (1978). A thirty-year follow-up of treatment effects. *American Psychologist, 33,* 284–289.

McCord, J. (1979). Some child-rearing antecedents of criminal behavior in adult men. *Journal of Personality and Social Psychology, 9,* 1477–1486.

McCord, J. (1982). A longitudinal view of the relationship between paternal absence and crime. In J. Gunn & D. P. Farrington (Eds.), *Abnormal offenders, delinquency, and the criminal justice system* (pp. 113–127). Chichester, England: Wiley.

McCord, J. (1983). A forty-year perspective on effects of child abuse and neglect. *Child Abuse and Neglect, 7,* 265–270.

McCord, J. (1991). The cycle of crime and socialization practices. *The Journal of Criminal Law and Criminality, 82,* 211–228.

McCord, J. (1992). The Cambridge-Somerville study: A pioneering longitudinal experimental study of delinquency prevention. In J. McCord & R. E. Tremblay (Eds.), *Preventing antisocial behavior: Interventions from birth through adolescence* (pp. 196–206). New York: Guilford.

McCord, W., & McCord, J. (1959). *Origins of crime: A new evaluation of the Cambridge-Somerville Youth Study.* New York: Columbia University Press.

McCord, W., & McCord, J., & Howard, A. (1961). Familial correlates of aggression in nondelinquent male children. *Journal of Abnormal Social Psychology, 62,* 79–93.

McGee, R., Feehan, M., Williams, S., & Anderson, J. (1992). DSM-III disorders from age 11 to age 15 years. *Journal of the American Academy of Child and Adolescent Psychiatry, 31,* 50–59.

McGinniss, E., & Goldstein, A. P. (1997). *Skillstreaming the elementary school child* (Rev. ed.). Champaign, IL: Research Press.

McIntyre, J. J., & Teevan, J. J., Jr. (1972). Television violence and deviant behavior. In G. A. Comstock & E. A. Rubinstein (Eds.), *Television and social behavior: Vol. 3. Television and adolescent aggression* (pp. 383–435). Washington, DC: U.S. Government Printing Office.

McLaughlin, A. (1998, May 12). Reading, writing and hit lists in school. *The Nando Net* [On–line]. Available: www.nando.net

McLaughlin, M. (1993). Embedded identities: Enabling balance in urban contexts. In S. B. Heath & M. W. McLaughlin (Eds.), *Identity and inner-city youth: Beyond ethnicity and gender.* New York: Teacher's College Press.

McLeod, J. M., Atkin, C. K., & Chaffee, S. H. (1972a). Adolescents, parents, and television use: Adolescent self-report measures from Maryland and Wisconsin samples. In G. A. Comstock & E. A. Rubinstein (Eds.), *Television and social behavior: Vol. 3. Television and adolescent aggressiveness* (pp. 173–238). Washington, DC: U.S. Government Printing Office.

McLeod, J. M., Atkin, C. K., & Chaffee, S. H. (1972b). Adolescents, parents, and television use: Self-report and other-report measures from the Wisconsin sample. In G. A. Comstock & E. A. Rubinstein (Eds.), *Television and social behavior: Vol. 3. Television and adolescent aggressiveness* (pp. 239–313). Washington, DC: U.S. Government Printing Office.

McMahon, R. J., & Forehand, R. (1984). Parent training for the noncompliant child: Treatment outcome, generalization, and adjunctive therapy procedures. In R. F. Dangel & R. A. Polster (Eds.), *Parent training: Foundations of research and practice* (pp. 298–328). New York: Guilford.

McMahon, R. J., Forehand, R., Griest, D. L., & Wells, K. C. (1981). Who drops out of therapy during parent behavioral training? *Behavioral Counseling Quarterly, 1,* 79–85.

McMichael, P. (1979). The hen or the egg? Which came first—antisocial emotional disorder or reading disability? *British Journal of Educational Psychology, 49,* 226–235.

McNabb, S. J. N., Farley, T. A., Powell, K. E., Rolka, H. R., & Horan, J. M. (1996). Correlates of gun-carrying among adolescents in south Louisiana. *American Journal of Preventive Medicine, 12,* 96–102.

Mednick, S. A. (1977). A bio-social theory of the learning of law-abiding behavior. In S. A. Mednick & K. O. Christiansen (Eds.), *Biosocial bases of criminal behavior* (pp. 1–8). New York: Gardner Press.

Mednick, S. A., & Kandel, E. (1988). Genetic and perinatal factors in violence. In S. A. Mednick & T. Moffitt (Eds.), *Biological contributions to crime causation* (pp. 121–134). Dordrecht, Holland: Martinus Nijhoff.

Megargee, E. I. (1966). Undercontrolled and overcontrolled personality types in extreme antisocial aggression. *Psychological Monographs, 80* (Whole No. 611).

Menig-Peterson, C. L., & McCabe, A. (1977–1978). Children talk about death. *Omega: Journal of Death and Dying, 8,* 305–317.

Milavsky, J. R., Kessler, R., Stipp, H. H., & Rubins, W. S. (1982). *Television and aggression: A panel study.* New York: Academic Press.

Miller, G., & Prinz, R. J. (1991). Designing interventions for stealing. In G. Stoner, M. R. Shinn, & H. M. Walker (Eds.), *Interventions for achievement and behavior problems.* Silver Spring, MD: National Association of School Psychologists.

Miller, N. S., Gold, M. S., & Mahler, J. C. (1991). Violent behaviors associated with cocaine use: Possible pharmacological mechanisms. *International Journal of the Addictions, 26,* 1077–1088.

Miller, S. A. (1998). *Developmental research methods* (2nd ed.). Upper Saddle River, NJ: Prentice Hall.

Mischel, W., Shoda, Y., & Peake, P. K. (1988). The nature of adolescent competencies predicted by preschool delay of gratification. *Journal of Personality and Social Psychology, 54,* 687–696.

Moffitt, T. E. (1993). Adolescence-limited and life-course-persistent antisocial behavior: A developmental taxonomy. *Psychological Review, 100,* 674–701.

Moffitt, T. E. (1997). Neuropsychology, antisocial behavior, and the neighborhood context. In J. McCord (Ed.), *Violence and childhood in the inner city* (pp. 116–170). Cambridge, England: Cambridge University Press.

Moffitt, T. E., Caspi, A., Dickson, N., Silva, P., & Stanton, W. (1996). Childhood-onset versus adolescent-onset antisocial conduct problems in males: Natural history from ages 3 to 18 years. *Development and Psychopathology, 8,* 399–424.

Moffitt, T. E., & Henry, B. (1989). Neuropsychological assessment of executive functions in self-reported delinquents. *Development and Psychopathology, 1,* 104–118.

Moffitt, T. E., & Silva, P. A. (1988). IQ and delinquency: A direct test of the differential detection hypothesis. *Journal of Abnormal Psychology, 97,* 330–333.

Mom who slept as daughter drowned son is convicted. (1999, February 5). Fredericksburg (VA) *Free Lance-Star,* p. C13.

Mones, P. (1991). *When a child kills.* New York: Pocket Books.

Mooney, A., Creeser, R., & Blatchford, P. (1991). Children's views on teasing and fighting in junior schools. *Educational Research, 33,* 103–112.

Moore, D. R., & Arthur, J. L. (1989). Juvenile delinquency. In T. H. Ollendick & M. Hersen (Eds.), *Handbook of child psychopathology* (2nd ed., pp. 197–217). New York: Plenum.

Moore, J. (1990). Gangs, drugs, and violence. In M. De La Rosa, E. Y. Lambert, & B. Gropper (Eds.), *Drugs and violence: Causes, correlates, and consequences* (NIDA Research Monograph 103; pp. 160–176). Rockville, MD: National Institute on Drug Abuse.

Morison, P., & Masten, A. S. (1991). Peer reputation in middle childhood as a predictor of adaptation in adolescence: A seven-year follow-up. *Child Development, 62,* 991–1007.

Morris, G. W. (1985). *The kids next door: Sons and daughters who kill their parents.* New York: William Morrow.

Morrison, B. (1997). *As if: A crime, a trial, a question of childhood.* New York: Picador USA.

Mulvey, E. P., Arthur, M. W., & Reppucci, N. D. (1993). The prevention and treatment of juvenile delinquency: A review of the research. *Clinical Psychology Review, 13,* 133–167.

Myers, W. C., Scott, K., Burgess, A. W., & Burgess, A. G. (1995). Psychopathology, biopsychosocial factors, crime characteristics, and classification of 25 homicidal youths. *Journal of the American Academy of Child and Adolescent Psychiatry, 34,* 1483–1489.

Mynatt, C., & Sherman, S. J. (1975). Responsibility attribution in groups and individuals: A direct test of the diffusion of responsibility hypothesis. *Journal of Personality and Social Psychology, 32,* 1111–1118.

Nader, K., Pynoos, R. S., Fairbanks, L., & Frederick, C. (1990). Childhood PTSD reactions one year after a sniper attack. *American Journal of Psychiatry, 147,* 1526–1530.

Nagin, D., & Tremblay, R. E. (1999). Trajectories of boys' physical aggression, opposition, and hyperactivity on the path to physically violent and nonviolent juvenile delinquency. *Child Development, 70,* 1181–1196.

Nagy, M. (1948). The child's theories concerning death. *Journal of Genetic Psychology, 73,* 3–27.

National Center for Education Statistics. (1998, October). *Indicators of school crime and safety.* [Online]. Available: nces.ed.gov/pubs98/safety

National League of Cities. (1994). *School violence in America's cities: NLC survey overview.* Washington, DC: Author.

Neighbors, B., Kempton, T., & Forehand, R. (1992). Co-occurrence of substance abuse with conduct, anxiety, and depression disorders in juvenile delinquents. *Addictive Behaviors, 17,* 379–386.

New Hampshire teen convicted of murdering parents. (1997, May 28). *The Nando Net* [On-line]. Available: www.nando.net

New Jersey teen to face trial as adult in another boy's murder. (1998, February 18). *The Nando Net* [On-line]. Available: www.nando.net

Newcomb, K. E. (1995). *The long-term effectiveness of parent–child interaction therapy with behavior problem children and their families: A two-year follow-up.* Unpublished doctoral dissertation, University of Florida, Gainesville.

Newman, J. P. (1997). Conceptual models of the nervous system: Implications for antisocial behavior. In D. M. Stoff, J. Breiling, & J. D. Maser (Eds.), *Handbook of antisocial behavior* (pp. 324–335). New York: Wiley.

Newman, J. P., & Wallace, J. F. (1993). Diverse pathways to deficient self-regulation: Implications for disinhibitory psychopathology in children. *Clinical Psychology Review, 13,* 699–720.

Niehoff, D. (1999). *The biology of violence.* New York: The Free Press.

Niles, W. J. (1986). Effects of a moral development discussion group on delinquent and predelinquent boys. *Journal of Counseling Psychology, 33,* 45–51.

Nord, W. A. (1995). *Religion and American education: Rethinking a national dilemma.* Chapel Hill: The University of North Carolina Press.

Nordheimer, J. (1994, August 17). Fourteen-year-old convicted in murder of preschooler in upstate town. *The New York Times,* p. B1.

Nye, C. L., Zucker, R. A., & Fitzgerald, H. E. (1999). Early family-based intervention in the path to alcohol problems. Rationale and relationship between treatment process characteristics and child and parenting outcomes. *Journal of Studies on Alcohol. Special Issue: Alcohol and the family: Opportunities for prevention,* (Suppl. 13), 10–21.

Nye, F. I. (1957). Child adjustment in broken and in unhappy unbroken homes. *Marriage and Family Living, 19,* 356–361.

O'Donnell, C. R. (1995). Firearm deaths among children and youth. *American Psychologist, 50,* 771–776.

Offenses on the rise involving youths, guns. (1995, November 15). *Fredericksburg (VA) Free Lance-Star,* p. A7.

Offord, D. R. (1982). Family backgrounds of male and female delinquents. In J. Gunn & D. P. Farrington (Eds.), *Abnormal offenders: Delinquency and the criminal justice system* (pp. 129–151). Chichester, England: Wiley.

Oklahoma man executed for murdering his parents when he was 16. (1999, February 4). *The Nando Net* [On-line]. Available: www.nando.net

Ollendick, T. H. (1996). Violence in youth: Where do we go from here? Behavior therapy's response. *Behavior Therapy, 27,* 485–514.

Olson, S. L. (1992). Development of conduct problems and peer rejection in preschool children: A social systems analysis. *Journal of Abnormal Child Psychology, 20,* 327–350.

Olson, S. L., & Hoza, B. (1993). Preschool developmental antecedents of conduct problems in children beginning school. *Journal of Clinical Child Psychology, 22,* 60–67.

Olweus, D. (1980). Familial and temperamental determinants of aggressive behavior in adolescent boys: A causal analysis. *Developmental Psychology, 16,* 644–660.

Olweus, D. (1986). Aggression and hormones: Behavioral relationship with testosterone and adrenaline. In D. Olweus, J. Block, & M. Radke-Yarrow (Eds.), *The development of antisocial and prosocial behavior: Research, theories, and issues* (pp. 51–72). New York: Academic Press.

Olweus, D. (1987). Testosterone and adrenaline: Aggressive antisocial behavior in normal adolescent males. In S. A. Mednick, T. E. Moffit, & S. A. Stack (Eds.), *The causes of crime: New biological approaches* (pp. 263–282). Cambridge, England: Cambridge University Press.

Olweus, D. (1992). Bullying among schoolchildren: Intervention and prevention. In R. DeV. Peters, R. J. McMahon, & V. L. Quinsey (Eds.), *Aggression and violence throughout the life span* (pp. 100–125). Newbury Park, CA: Sage.

Olweus, D. (1993). *Bullying at school.* Oxford, England: Blackwell.

Olweus, D., Mattesson, A., Schalling, D., & Low, H. (1988). Circulating testosterone levels and aggression in adolescent males: A causal analysis. *Psychosomatic Medicine, 50,* 261–272.

O'Meara, K. P. (1999, June 28). Doping kids. *Insight on the News,* 10.

O'Moore, A. M., & Hillery, B. (1991). Bullying in Dublin schools. *Irish Journal of Psychology, 10,* 426–441.

Orbach, I., Gross, Y., Glaubman, H., & Berman, D. (1985). Children's perception of death in humans and animals as a function of age, anxiety and cognitive ability. *Journal of Child Psychology and Psychiatry and Allied Disciplines, 26,* 453–463.

O'Shea, K. A., & Fletcher, B. R. (1997). *Female offenders: An annotated bibliography.* Westport, CT: Greenwood Press.

Osofsky, J. D., Wewers, S., Hann, D. M., & Fick, A. C. (1993). Chronic community violence: What is happening to our children? In D. Reiss, J. F. Richters, M. Radke Yarrow, & D. Scharff (Eds.), *Children and violence* (pp. 36–45). New York: Guilford.

Pablant, P., & Baxter, J. C. (1996). Environmental correlates of school vandalism. In A. P. Goldstein, *The psychology of vandalism* (pp. 213–233). New York: Plenum.

Paik, H., & Comstock, G. (1994). The effects of television violence on antisocial behavior: A meta-analysis. *Communications Research, 21,* 516–546.

Palermo, G. B. (1994). *The faces of violence.* Springfield, IL: Charles C. Thomas.

Papalia, D. E., Olds, S. W., & Feldman, R. D. (1999). *A child's world: Infancy through adolescence* (8th ed.). Boston: McGraw-Hill.

Parents rank violence as top worry in new nationwide survey. (2000, March 7). Fredericksburg (VA) *Free Lance-Star,* p. D3.

Parke, R. D., Berkowitz, L., Leyens, J. P, West, S. G., & Sebastian, R. J. (1977). Some effects of violent and nonviolent movies on the behavior of juvenile delinquents. In L. Berkowitz (Ed.), *Advances in experimental social psychology* (Vol. 10, pp. 135–172). New York: Academic Press.

Parker, J. G., & Asher, S. R. (1987). Peer relations and later personal adjustment: Are low-accepted children at risk? *Psychological Bulletin, 103,* 357–389.

Patrick, J. (1973). *A Glasgow gang observed.* London: Eyre Methuen.

Patterson, G. R. (1982). *Coercive family process.* Eugene, OR: Castalia.

Patterson, G. R., DeBaryshe, B. D., & Ramsey, E. (1989). A developmental perspective on antisocial behavior. *American Psychologist, 44,* 329–335.

Patterson, G. R., & Dishion, T. J. (1985). Contributions of families and peers to delinquency. *Criminology, 23,* 63–79.

Patterson, G. R., Littman, R. A., & Bricker, W. (1967). Assertive behavior in children: A step toward a theory of aggression. *Monographs of the Society for Research in Child Development, 32* (No. 5, Serial No. 113).

Patterson, G. R., Reid, J. B., & Dishion, T. J. (1992). *Antisocial boys.* Eugene, OR: Castalia.

Patterson, G. R., & Yoerger, K. (1993). Developmental models for delinquent behavior. In S. Hodgins (Ed.), *Mental disorder and crime* (pp. 140–172). Newbury Park, CA: Sage.

Paulus, D. L., & Martin, C. L. (1986). Predicting adult temperament from minor physical anomalies. *Journal of Personality and Social Psychology, 50,* 1235–1239.

Peeples, F., & Loeber, R. (1994). Do individual factors and neighborhood context explain ethnic differences in juvenile delinquency? *Journal of Quantitative Criminology, 10,* 141–157.

Perry, D. G., Kusel, S. J., & Perry, L. C. (1988). Victims of peer aggression. *Developmental Psychology, 24,* 807–814.

Perry, D. G., Perry, L. C., & Rasmussen, P. (1986). Cognitive social learning mediators of aggression. *Child Development, 57,* 700–711.

Perry, D. G., Williard, J. C., & Perry, L. C. (1990). Peers' perceptions of the consequences that victimized children provide aggressors. *Child Development, 61,* 1310–1325.

Peterson, J. L., & Zill, N. (1986). Marital disruption, parent–child relationships, and behavior problems in children. *Journal of Marriage and the Family, 48,* 295–307.

Petti, T. A., & Davidman, L. (1981). Homicidal school-age children: Cognitive style and demographic features. *Child Psychiatry and Human Development, 12,* 82–89.

Pettit, G. S., Bates, J. E., Dodge, K. A., & Meece, D. W. (1999). The impact of after-school peer contact on early adolescent externalizing problems is moderated by parental monitoring, perceived neighborhood safety, and prior adjustment. *Child Development, 70*, 768–778.

Phillips, E. L., Phillips, E. A., Fixsen, D. L., & Wolf, M. M. (1971). Achievement Place: Modification of the behaviors of predelinquent boys within a token economy. *Journal of Applied Behavior Analysis, 4*, 45–59.

Physical violence is surveyed in Va. schools. (2000, April 21). Stafford County (VA) *Sun*, p. A3.

Pingree, S., & Hawkins, R. (1981). U.S. programs on Australian television: The cultivation effect. *Journal of Communication, 31*, 97–105.

Plomin, R., DeFries, J. C., McClearn, G. E., & Rutter, M. (1997). *Behavior genetics* (3rd ed.). New York: Freeman.

Police arrested student after flammables found. (1999, May 4). Fredericksburg (VA) *Free Lance-Star*, p. A3.

Police say students plotted against teacher. (1993, June 8). Fredericksburg (VA) *Free Lance-Star*, p. A5.

Polk, K., & Schafer, W. E. (1972). *Schools and delinquency*. Englewood Cliffs, NJ: Prentice Hall.

Popyk, L. (1998, November 7). Blood in the school yard. Cincinnati *Post*, pp. 1A, 6A-7A.

Prichard, J. (1998, October 6). Kentucky teen pleads guilty, but mentally ill. Fredericksburg (VA) *Free Lance-Star*, p. A2.

Prothrow-Stith, D. & Weissman, M. (1991). *Deadly consequences*. New York: HarperCollins.

Pulkkinen, L., & Tremblay, R. E. (1992). Patterns of boys' social adjustment in two cultures and at different ages: A longitudinal perspective. *International Journal of Behavioral Development, 15*, 527–553.

Purpel, D. (1997). The politics of character education. In A. Molnar (Ed.), *The construction of children's character: Ninety-sixth yearbook of the National Society for the Study of Education: Part II* (pp. 140–153). Chicago: The National Society for the Study of Education.

Pynoos, R. S. (1993). Traumatic stress and developmental psychopathology in children and adolescents. In J. M. Oldham, M. B. Riba, & A. Tasman (Eds.), *Review of psychiatry* (Vol. 12, pp. 205–237). Washington, DC: American Psychiatric Press.

Quay, H. C. (1993). The psychobiology of undersocialized aggressive conduct disorder: A theoretical perspective. *Development and Psychopathology, 5*, 165–180.

Rabiner, D., Lenhart, L., & Lochman, J. E. (1990). Automatic versus reflective social problem-solving in popular, average, and rejected children. *Developmental Psychology, 26*, 1010–1016.

Radke-Yarrow, M., & Kochanska, G. (1990). Anger in young children. In N. L. Stein, B. Leventhal, & T. Trabasso (Eds.), *Psychological and biological approaches to emotion* (pp. 297–310). Hillsdale, NJ: Lawrence Erlbaum Associates.

Raine, A. (1993). *The psychopathology of crime*. San Diego: Academic Press.

Raine, A. (1997). Antisocial behavior and psychophysiology: A biosocial perspective and a prefrontal dysfunction hypothesis. In D. M. Stoff, J. Breiling, & J. D. Maser (Eds.), *Handbook of antisocial behavior* (pp. 289–304). New York: Wiley.

Raine, A., Brennan, P., & Mednick, S. A. (1994). Birth complications combined with early maternal rejection at age 1 year predispose to violent crime at age 18 years. *Archives of General Psychiatry, 51*, 984–988.

Raine, A., Brennan, P., & Mednick, S. A. (1997). Interaction between birth complications and early maternal rejection in predisposing individuals to adult violence: Specificity to serious, early-onset violence. *American Journal of Psychiatry, 154*, 1265–1271.

Raine, A., Brennan, P., Mednick, B., & Mednick, S. A. (1996). High rates of violence, crime, academic problems, and behavioral problems in males with both early neuromotor deficits and unstable family environments. *Archives of General Psychiatry, 53*, 544–549.

Raine, A., Meloy, J. R., Bihrle, S., Stoddard, J., LaCasse, L., & Buchsbaum, M. S. (1998). Reduced prefrontal and increased subcortical brain functioning assessed using positron emission tomography in predatory and affective murderers. *Behavior Sciences and the Law, 16*, 319–332.

Raine, A., & Venables, P. H. (1987). Contingent negative variation, P3 evoked potential, and anti-social behavior. *Psychophysiology, 24,* 191–199.

Raine, A., Venables, P. H., & Mednick, S. A. (1997). Low resting heart rate at age 3 years predisposes to aggression at age 11 years: Evidence from the Mauritius Child Health Project. *Journal of the American Academy of Child and Adolescent Psychiatry, 36,* 1457–1464.

Raine, A., Venables, P. H., & Williams, M. (1990). Relationship between N1, P300 and CNV recorded at age 15 and criminality at age 24. *Psychophysiology, 27,* 567–575.

Ramer, H. (1997, May 17). Alleged killers of parents called shooting "fun." Fredericksburg (VA) *Free Lance-Star,* p. A4.

Raskin, R., Novacek, J., & Hogan, R. (1991). Narcissistic self-esteem management. *Journal of Personality and Social Psychology, 60,* 911–918.

Ray, J. A., & English, D. (1995). Comparison of female and male children with sexual behavior problems. *Journal of Youth and Adolescence, 24,* 439–451.

Redl, F., & Wineman, D. (1951). *Children who hate.* Glencoe, IL: The Free Press.

Reidy, T. (1977). Aggressive characteristics of abused and neglected children. *Journal of Clinical Psychology, 33,* 1140–1145.

Reiss, A. J. (1988). Co-offending and criminal careers. In M. Tonry (Ed.), *Crime and justice* (Vol. 10, pp. 117–170). Chicago: University of Chicago Press.

Reiss, A. J., & Rhodes, A. L. (1964). A empirical test of differential association theory. *Journal of Research in Crime and Delinquency, 1,* 5–18.

Renfrew, J. W. (1997). *Aggression and its causes: A biopsychosocial approach.* New York: Oxford University Press.

Renken, B., Egeland, B., Marvinney, D., Mangelsdorf, S., & Sroufe, L. A. (1989). Early childhood antecedents of aggression and passive-withdrawal in early elementary school. *Journal of Personality, 57,* 257–281.

Reppucci, N. D., Woolard, J. L., & Fried, C. S. (1999). Social, community, and preventive interventions. In J. T. Spence, J. Darley, & D. J. Ross (Eds.), *Annual review of psychology* (Vol. 50, pp. 387–418). Palo Alto, CA: Annual Reviews.

Resnick, M. D., & Blum, R. W. (1994). The association of consensual sexual intercourse during childhood with adolescent health risk and behaviors. *Pediatrics, 94,* 907–913.

Ressler, R. K., & Shachtman, T. (1992). *Whoever fights monsters.* New York: St. Martin's Press.

Revkin, A. C. (1989, September). Crack in the cradle. *Discover, 10,* 62–69.

Reynolds, B. (1994, September 2). If civil rights legend Rosa Parks isn't safe, who is? *USA Today,* p. 11A.

Reynolds, G. S., Catania, A. C., & Skinner, B. F. (1963). Conditioned and unconditioned aggression in pigeons. *Journal of the Experimental Analysis of Behavior, 6,,* 73–74.

Rheingold, H. L. (1982). Little children's participation in the work of adults, a nascent prosocial behavior. *Child Development, 53,* 114–125.

Richman, N., Stevenson, J., & Graham, P. (1982). *Preschool to school: A behavioral study.* San Diego: Academic Press.

Richters, J. & Martinez, P. (1993a). The NIMH community violence project: I. Children as victims of and witnesses to violence. In D. Reiss, J. E. Richters, M. Radke-Yarrow, & D. Scharff (Eds.), *Children and violence* (pp. 7–21). New York: Guilford.

Richters, J. & Martinez, P. (1993b). Violent communities, family choices, and children's chances: An algorithm for improving the odds. *Development and Psychopathology, 5,* 609–627.

Rifkin, A., Karajgi, B., Dicker, R., Perl, E., Boppana, V., Hasan, N., & Pollack, S. (1997). Lithium treatment of conduct disorders in adolescents. *American Journal of Psychiatry, 154,* 545–555.

Rigby, K., & Cox, I. (1996). The contribution of bullying at school and low self-esteem to acts of delinquency among Australian teenagers. *Personality and Individual Differences, 21,* 609–612.

Rigby, K., & Slee, P. T. (1993). Dimensions of interpersonal relating among Australian school children and their implications for psychological well-being. *Journal of Social Psychology, 133,* 33–42.

Rivera, B., & Widom, C. S. (1990). Childhood victimization and violent offending. *Violence and Victims, 5,* 19–35.

Robins, L. N. (1966). *Deviant children grown up: A sociological and psychiatric study of sociopathic personality.* Baltimore: Williams & Wilkins.

Robins, L. N. (1979). Sturdy childhood predictors of adult outcomes: Replications from longitudinal studies. In J. E. Barratt, R. M. Rose, & G. L. Klerman (Eds.), *Stress and mental disorder* (pp. 219–235). New York: Raven Press.

Robins, L. N., West, P. A., & Herjanic, B. L. (1975). Arrests and delinquency in two generations: A study of black urban families and their children. *Journal of Child Psychology and Psychiatry, 16,* 125–140.

Robinson, M. (1997a, February 26). Young killer gets an adult sentence. Fredericksburg (VA) *Free Lance-Star,* p. A10.

Robinson, M. (1997b, April 22). 18 year old gets 60 years for killing 11-year-old fellow gang member. *The Nando Net* [On-line]. Available: www.nando.net

Roff, J. D., & Wirt, F. D. (1984). Childhood aggression and social adjustment as antecedents of delinquency. *Journal of Abnormal Child Psychology, 12,* 111–126.

Rogeness, G. A., Javors, M. A., Maas, J. W., & Macedo, C. A. (1990). Catecholamines and diagnoses in children. *Journal of the American Academy of Child and Adolescent Psychiatry, 29,* 234–241.

Rohrbeck, C. A., & Twentyman, C. T. (1986). Multimodal assessment of impulsiveness in abusing, neglecting and nonmaltreating mothers and their preschool children. *Journal of Consulting and Clinical Psychology, 54,* 231–236.

Roland, E. (1989). Bullying: The Scandinavian research tradition. In D. P. Tattum & D. A. Lane (Eds.), *Bullying in schools* (pp. 21–32). Stoke-on-Trent, England: Trentham.

Romano, L. (1998, July 25). Former cadet found guilty of murder. Washington *Post,* A6.

Rosenberg, R., & Rosenberg, M. (1978). Self-esteem and delinquency. *Journal of Youth and Adolescence, 7,* 279–291.

Rosenthal, P. A., & Doherty, M. B. (1984). Serious sibling abuse by preschool children. *Journal of the American Academy of Child Psychiatry, 23,* 186–190.

Rosenthal, R., & Jacobson, L. (1968). *Pygmalion in the classroom.* New York: Holt, Rinehart & Winston.

Rosnow, R. L., & Rosenthal, R. (1996). *Beginning behavioral research* (2nd ed.). Englewood Cliffs, NJ: Prentice Hall.

Ross, D. M. (1996). *Childhood bullying and teasing.* Alexandria, VA: American Counseling Association.

Rothbart, M. K., & Bates, J. E. (1998). Temperament. In N. Eisenberg (Vol. Ed.) & W. Damon (Ed.-in-Chief), *Handbook of child psychology* (Vol. 3, 5th ed., pp. 105–176). New York: Wiley.

Rothbaum, F., & Weisz, J. R. (1994). Parental caregiving and child externalizing behavior in nonclinic samples: A meta-analysis. *Psychological Bulletin, 116,* 55–74.

Rowe, D. C. (1983). Biometrical genetic models of self-reported delinquent behavior: A twin study. *Behavior Genetics, 13,* 473–489.

Rowe, D. C., & Farrington, D. P. (1997). The familial transmission of criminal conviction. *Criminology, 35,* 177–201.

Rowley, J. C., Ewing, C. P., & Singer, S. I. (1987). Juvenile homicide: The need for an interdisciplinary approach. *Behavioral Sciences and the Law, 5,* 1–10.

Russo, M. F., Lahey, B. B., Christ, M. G., Frick, P. J., McBurnett, K., Walker, J. L., Loeber, R., Stouthamer-Loeber, M., & Green, S. M. (1991). Preliminary development of a Sensation Seeking Scale for Children. *Personality and Individual Differences, 12,* 399–405.

Russo, M. F., Stokes, G. S., Lahey, B. B., Christ, M. G., McBurnett, K., Loeber, R., Stouthamer-Loeber, M., & Green, S. M. (1993). A Sensation Seeking Scale for Children: Further refinement and psychometric development. *Journal of Psychopathology and Behavioral Assessment, 15,* 69–86.

Rutter, M. (1978). Family, area, and school influences in the genesis of conduct disorders. In L. Hersov & M. Berger (Eds.), *Aggression and anti-social behaviour in childhood and adolescence* (pp. 95–114). Oxford, England: Pergamon.

Rutter, M. (1982). *Maternal deprivation reassessed* (2nd ed.). Harmondsworth, England: Penguin.

Rutter, M. (1997). Clinical implications of attachment concepts: Retrospect and prospect. In L. Atkinson & K. J. Zucker (Eds.), *Attachment and psychopathology* (pp. 17–46). New York: Guilford.

Rutter, M., Giller, H., & Hagell, A. (1998). *Antisocial behavior by young people.* New York: Cambridge University Press.

Rutter, M., Maughan, B., Mortimore, P., & Ouston, J. (1979). *Fifteen thousand hours: Secondary schools and their effects on children.* Cambridge, MA: Harvard University Press.

Rutter, M., Tizard, J., & Whitmore, K. (Eds.). (1970). *Education, health, and behavior.* London: Longman.

Rutter, M., Tizard, J., Yule, W., Graham, P., & Whitmore, K. (1976). Isle of Wight studies, 1964–1974. *Psychological Medicine, 6,* 313–332.

Rutter, M., Yule, B., Quinton, D., Rowlands, O., Yule, W., & Berger, M. (1975). Attainment and adjustment in two geographical areas: III. Some factors accounting for area differences. *British Journal of Psychiatry, 126,* 520–523.

Samenow, S. (1989). *Before it's too late.* New York: Times Books.

Sampson, R. J. (1987). Urban black violence: The effect of male joblessness and family disruption. *American Journal of Sociology, 93,* 348–382.

Sampson, R. J. (1995). The community. In J. Q. Wilson & J. Petersilia (Eds.), *Crime* (pp. 193–216). San Francisco: Institute for Contemporary Studies Press.

Sampson, R. J., & Laub, J. H. (1994). Urban poverty and the family context of delinquency: A new look at structure and process in a classic study. *Child Development, 65,* 523 540.

Sampson, R. J., Raudenbush, S. W., & Earls, F. (1997). Neighborhoods and violent crime: A multilevel study of collective efficacy. *Science, 277,* 918–924.

Sancilio, M. F. M., Plumert, J. M., & Hartup, W. W. (1989). Friendship and aggressiveness as determinants of conflict outcomes in middle childhood. *Developmental Psychology, 25,* 812 819.

Santtila, P., & Haapasalo, J. (1997). Neurological and psychological risk factors among young homicidal, violent, and nonviolent offenders in Finland. *Homicide Studies, 1,* 234–253.

Sargent, D. (1962). Children who kill—A family conspiracy? *Social Work, 7,* 35–42.

Scerbo, A., Raine, A., Venables, P. H., & Mednick, S. A. (1995). Stability of temperament from ages 3 to 11 years in Mauritian children. *Journal of Abnormal Child Psychology, 23,* 607–618.

Schachar, R. J., & Wachsmuth, R. (1991). Family dysfunction and psychosocial adversity: Comparison of attention deficit disorder, conduct disorder, normal and clinical controls. Special Issue: Childhood disorders in the context of the family. *Canadian Journal of Behavioural Science, 23,* 332–348.

Schaps, E., Battistich, V., & Solomon, D. (1997). School as a caring community: A key to character. In A. Molnar (Ed.), *The construction of children's character: Ninety-sixth yearbook of the National Society for the Study of Education: Part II* (pp. 127–139). Chicago: The National Society for the Study of Education.

Scherl, D. J., & Mack, J. E. (1966). A study of adolescent matricide. *Journal of the American Academy of Child Psychiatry, 5,* 569–593.

Schmidt, K., Solant, M. V., & Bridger, W. H. (1985). Electrodermal activity of undersocialized aggressive children: A pilot study. *Journal of Child Psychology and Psychiatry and Allied Disciplines, 26,* 653–660.

Schmitz, S., Fulker, D. W., & Mrazek, D. A. (1995). Problem behavior in early and middle childhood: An initial behavior genetic analysis. *Journal of Child Psychology and Psychiatry and Allied Disciplines, 36,* 1443–1458.

School Security Report. (1995, July). *An in-depth look at school bombing patterns.* Washington, DC: Author.

School shooting stuns the Dutch. (1999, December 8). Fredericksburg (VA) *Free Lance-Star,* p. A6.

Schubiner, H., Scott, R., & Tzelepis, A. (1993). Exposure to violence among inner-city youth. *Journal of Adolescent Health, 14,* 214–219.

Schutte, N. S., Malouff, J. M., Post-Gorden, J. C., & Rodasta, A. L. (1988). Effects of playing video games on children's aggressive and other behaviors. *Journal of Applied Social Psychology, 18,* 454–460.

Schwartz, D., Dodge, K. A., Pettit, G. S., & Bates, J. E. (1997). The early socialization of aggressive victims of bullying. *Child Development, 68,* 665–675.

Schwartz, R. M., Rendon, J. A., & Hsieh, C. (1994). Is child maltreatment a leading cause of delinquency? *Child Welfare, 73,* 639–655.

Schweinhart, L. J., Barnes, H. V., & Weikart, D. P. (1993). *Significant benefits.* Ypsilanti, MI: High/Scope.

Sears, R. R., Whiting, J. W., Nowlis, V., & Sears, P. S. (1953). Some child-rearing antecedents of aggression and dependency in young children. *Genetic Psychology Monographs, 47,* 135–236.

Seitz, V., Rosenbaum, L. K., & Apfel, N. H. (1985). Effects of family support intervention: A ten-year follow-up. *Child Development, 56,* 376–391.

Seligman, M. E. P. (1995). *The optimistic child.* Boston: Houghton Mifflin.

Seligman, M. E. P. (1998). The prediction and prevention of depression. In D. K. Routh, & R. J. DeRubeis (Eds.), *The science of clinical psychology: Accomplishments and future directions.* Washington, DC: American Psychological Association.

Seven-year-old vandals may face charges. (1995, May 2). Fredericksburg (VA) *Free Lance-Star,* p. C3.

Seydlitz, R., & Jenkins, P. (1998). The influence of families, friends, schools, and community on delinquent behavior. In T. P. Gullotta, G. R. Adams, & R. Montemayor (Eds.), *Delinquent violent youth* (pp. 53–97). Thousand Oaks, CA: Sage.

Shaffer, D. R. (1994). *Social and personality development* (3rd ed). Pacific Grove, CA: Brooks/Cole.

Shaw, C. R., & McKay, H. D. (1970). *Juvenile delinquency and urban areas: A study of rates of delinquents in relation to differential characteristics of local communities in American cities.* Chicago: University of Chicago Press.

Shaw, D. S., Keenan, K., Owens, E., Winslow, E. B., Hood, N., & Garcia, M. (1995, April). *Developmental precursors of externalizing behavior among two samples of low-income families: Ages 1 to 5.* Paper presented at the biennial meeting of the Society for Research in Child Development, Indianapolis.

Shaw, D. S., & Winslow, E. B. (1997). Precursors and correlates of antisocial behavior from infancy to preschool. In D. M. Stoff, J. Breiling, & J. D. Maser (Eds.), *Handbook of antisocial behavior* (pp. 148–158). New York: Wiley.

Shaw, D. S., Winslow, E. B., & Flanagan, C. (1999). A prospective study of the effects of marital status and family relations on young children's adjustment among African American and European American families. *Child Development, 70,* 742–755.

Sheehan, P. W. (1986). Television viewing and its relation to aggression among children in Australia. In L. R. Huesmann & L. D. Eron (Eds.), *Television and the aggressive child: A cross-national comparison* (pp. 161–199). Hillsdale, NJ: Lawrence Erlbaum Associates.

Sheley, J. F., McGee, Z. T., & Wright, J. D. (1992). Gun-related violence in and around inner-city schools. *American Journal of Disabilities in Children, 146,* 677–682.

Sheley, J. F., & Wright, J. D. (1995). *In the line of fire: Youths, guns, and violence in urban America.* New York: Aldine de Gruyter.

Sherman, L. W., Gottfredson, D., MacKenzie, D., Eck, J., Reuter, P., & Bushway, S. (1997). *Preventing crime: What works, what doesn't, what's promising* (Report to the United States Congress). Baltimore: University of Maryland, Department of Criminology and Criminal Justice, Office of Justice Programs.

Shoemaker, D. J. (1996). *Theories of delinquency* (3rd ed.). New York: Oxford University Press.

Short, R. J., & Simeonson, R. J. (1986). Social cognition and aggression in delinquent adolescent males. *Adolescence, 21,* 159–176.

Shure, M. B. (1992a). *I can problem solve: Intermediate elementary grades.* Champaign, IL: Research Press.

Shure, M. B. (1992b). *I can problem solve: Kindergarten and primary grades.* Champaign, IL: Research Press.

Siegler, R. J. (1998). *Children's thinking* (3rd ed.). Upper Saddle River, NJ: Prentice Hall.

Silverman, I. W., & Ragusa, D. M. (1992). A short-term longitudinal study of the early development of self-regulation. *Journal of Abnormal Child Psychology, 20,* 415–435.

Silvern, S. B., & Williamson, P. A. (1987). The effects of video game play on young children's aggression, fantasy and prosocial behavior. *Journal of Applied Developmental Psychology, 8,* 453–462.

Simcha-Fagan, O., & Schwartz, J. E. (1986). Neighborhood and delinquency: An assessment of contextual effects. *Criminology, 24,* 667–703.

Simonoff, E., Pickles, A., Meyer, J., Silberg, J., & Maes, H. (1998). Genetic and environmental influences on subtypes of conduct disorder behavior in boys. *Journal of Abnormal Child Psychology, 26,* 495–509.

Simons, R. L., Johnson, C., Beaman, J., Conger, R. D., & Whitbeck, L. B. (1996). Parents and peer group as mediators of the effect of community structure on adolescent problem behavior. *American Journal of Community Psychology, 24,* 145–171.

Simons, R. L., Whitbeck, L. B., Conger, R. D., & Chyi-In, W. (1991). Intergenerational transmission of harsh parenting. *Developmental Psychology, 27,* 159–171.

Singer, J. L. (1992) Television viewing and children: Some potential hazards and possibilities. In C. Clark & K. King (Eds.), *Television and the preparation of the mind for learning: Critical questions on the effects of television on the development brains of young children: Conference proceedings* (pp. 20–28). Vienna, VA: Ellsworth.

Singer, J. L., & Singer, D. G. (1981). *Television, imagination and aggression.* Hillsdale, NJ: Lawrence Erlbaum Associates.

Singer, J. L., & Singer, D. G. (1986). Family experiences and television viewing as predictors of children's imagination, restlessness, and aggression *Journal of Social Issues, 42* 107–124.

Singer, J. L., Singer, D. G, Desmond, R., Hirsch, B., & Nicol, A. (1988). Family mediation and children's cognition, aggression, and comprehension of television: A longitudinal study. *Journal of Applied Developmental Psychology, 9,* 329–347.

16-year-old gets life for hanging of teen. (1999, March 25). *Philadelphia News* [On-line]. Available: www.phillynews.com

Skinner, M. L., Elder, G. H., Jr., & Conger, R. D. (1992). Linking economic hardship to adolescent aggression. *Journal of Youth and Adolescence, 21,* 259–276.

Slutske, W. S., Heath, A. C., Dinwiddie, S. H., Madden, P. A., Bucholz, K. K., Dunne, M. P., Statham, D. J., & Martin, N. G. (1997). Modeling genetic and environmental influences in the etiology of conduct disorder: A study of 2,682 adult twin pairs. *Journal of Abnormal Psychology, 106,* 266–279.

Small bomb explodes in Louisiana school. (1999, November 13). Fredericksburg (VA) *Free Lance-Star,* p. A15.

Smart, D., Sanson, A., & Prior, M. (1996). Connections between reading disability and behavior problems: Testing temporal and causal hypotheses. *Journal of Abnormal Child Psychology, 24,* 363–383.

Smith, P. K., & Sharp, S. (1994). *School bullying: Insights and perspectives.* London: Routledge.

Sniffen, M. J. (1998, November 22). Murder rate drops to 30-year low. *The Nando Net* [On-line]. Available: www.nando.net

Snyder, H. N. (1999, December). Juvenile arrests 1998. *OJJDP Juvenile Justice Bulletin,* 1–11. Washington, DC: U.S. Department of Justice.

Snyder, H. N., & Sickmund, M. (1995). *Juvenile offenders and victims: A national report.* Washington, DC: Office of Juvenile Justice and Delinquency Prevention.

Snyder, H. N., & Sickmund, M. (1999). *Juvenile offenders and victims: 1999 national report.* Washington, DC: Office of Juvenile Justice and Delinquency Prevention.

Snyder, J., & Patterson, G. R. (1987). Family interaction and delinquent behavior. In H. C. Quay (Ed.), *Handbook of juvenile delinquency* (pp. 216–243). New York: Wiley.

Snyder, J. J., & Patterson, G. R. (1995). Individual differences in social aggression: A test of a reinforcement model of socialization in the natural environment. *Behavior Therapy, 26*, 371–391.

Sokol-Katz, J., Dunham, R., & Zimmerman, R. (1997). Family structure versus parental attachment in controlling adolescent deviant behavior: A social control model. *Adolescence, 32*, 199–215.

Speltz, M. L., Greenberg, M. T., & DeKlyen, M. (1990). Attachment in preschoolers with disruptive behavior: A comparison of clinic-referred and nonproblem children. *Development and Psychopathology, 2*, 31–46.

Spergel, I. A. (1990). Youth gangs: Continuity and change. In M. Tonry & N. Morris (Eds.), *Crime and justice* (Vol. 12, pp. 171–275). Chicago: University of Chicago Press.

Spergel, I. A., & Curry, G. D. (1988). *Socialization to gangs: Preliminary baseline report.* Chicago: University of Chicago, School of Social Service Administration.

Spitz, H. I., & Rosegan, J. S. (1987). *Cocaine abuse: New directions in treatment and research.* New York: Brunner-Mazel.

Spivak, G., & Shure, M. B. (1974). *Social adjustment in young children.* San Francisco: Jossey-Bass.

Stambrook, M., & Parker, K. C. (1987). The development of the concept of death in childhood: A review of the literature. *Merrill-Palmer Quarterly, 33*, 133–157.

Stanton, C. A., & Meyer, A. L. (1998). A comprehensive review of community-based approaches for the treatment of juvenile offenders. In T. P. Gullotta, G. R. Adams, & R. Montemayor (Eds.), *Delinquent violent youth* (pp. 205–229). Thousand Oaks, CA: Sage.

Stattin, H., & Klackenberg-Larsson, I. (1993). Early language and intelligence development and their relationship to future criminal behavior. *Journal of Abnormal Psychology, 102*, 369–378.

Stattin, H., & Magnusson, D. (1990). *Pubertal maturation in female development.* Hillsdale, NJ: Lawrence Erlbaum Associates.

St. C. Levy, K. (1997). Multifactorial self-concept and delinquency in Australian adolescents. *Journal of Social Psychology, 137*, 277–283.

Steinberg, L. (1996). *Adolescence* (4th ed.). New York: Mc-Graw-Hill.

Stenberg, C., Campos, J., & Emde, R., (1983). The facial expression of anger in 7-month-old infants. *Child Development, 54*, 178–184.

Stephenson, P., & Smith, D. (1989). Bullying in the junior school. In D. P. Tattum & D. A. Lane (Eds.), *Bullying in schools* (pp. 45–57). Stoke-on-Trent, England: Trentham.

Sternberg, K. J., Lamb, M. E., Greenbaum, C., Cicchetti, D., Dawus, S., Cortes, R. M., Krispin, O., & Lorey, F. (1993). Effects of domestic violence on children's behavior problems and depression. *Developmental Psychology, 29*, 44–52.

Stevens, V., Van Oost, P., & de Bourdeaudhuij, I. (2000). The effects of an anti-bullying intervention programme on peers' attitudes and behaviour. *Journal of Adolescence, 23*, 21–34.

Stormont-Spurgin, M., & Zentall, S. S. (1996). Child-rearing practices associated with aggression in youth with and without ADHD: An exploratory study. *International Journal of Disability, Development and Education, 43*, 135–146.

Student arrested for taking gun to school. (1999, December 8.). Fredericksburg (VA) *Free Lance-Star,* p. C10.

Student back in class after death threat. (1996, September 23). Fredericksburg (VA) *Free Lance-Star,* p. C1.

Student killed in school stabbing. (1993, October 19). Fredericksburg (VA) *Free Lance-Star,* p. C8.

Student suspended for having pocketknives. (1999, December 3.). Fredericksburg (VA) *Free Lance-Star,* p. C7.

Sullivan, K. T., & Bradbury, T. N. (1997). Are premarital prevention programs reaching couples at risk for marital discord? *Journal of Consulting and Clinical Psychology, 65*, 24–30.

Suter, E. A. (1994). Guns in the medical literature—A failure of peer review. *The Journal of the Medical Association of Georgia, 83*, 133–148.

Sutherland, E. H. (1939). *Principles of criminology* (3rd ed.). Philadelphia: Lippincott.

Sutherland, E. H., & Cressy, D. R. (1974). *Criminology* (9th ed.). Philadelphia: Lippincott.

Tangney, J. P. (1998). How does guilt differ from shame? In J. Bybee (Ed.), *Guilt and children* (pp. 1–17). San Diego: Academic Press.

Tangney, J. P., Hill-Barlow, D., Wagner, P. E., Marschall, D. E., Bornstein, J. K., Sanftner, J., Mohr, T., & Gramzow, R. (1996). Assessing individual differences in constructive versus destructive responses to anger across the lifespan. *Journal of Personality and Social Psychology, 70,* 780–796.

Tangney, J. P., Wagner, P. E., Hill-Barlow, D., Marschall, D. E., & Gramzow, R. (1996). The relation of shame and guilt to constructive versus destructive responses to anger across the lifespan. *Journal of Personality and Social Psychology, 70,* 797–809.

Tate, D. C., Reppucci, N. D., & Mulvey, E. P. (1995). Violent juvenile delinquents: Treatment effectiveness and implications for future action. *American Psychologist, 50,* 777–781.

Tavris, C. (1982). *Anger: The misunderstood emotion.* New York: Simon & Schuster.

Teen admits planting school bombs. (1999, December 2). *Chicago Sun-Times* [On-line]. Available: www.suntimes.com

Teen captured after taking students hostage. (1998, February 5). *The Nando Net* [On-line]. Available: www.nando.net

Teen held in Canada shooting. (1999, April 30). Fredericksburg (VA) *Free Lance-Star,* p. A7.

Teen who was taped committing murder gets life sentence. (1997, February 28). *The Nando Net* [On-line]. Available: www.nando.net

Teenager pleads guilty to e-mailed Columbine threat. (2000, February 9). *The Nando Net* [On-line]. Available: www.nando.net

Teens charged in assault at school (1993, September 28). Fredericksburg (VA) *Free Lance-Star,* p. B3.

10-year-old girls back in court over fifth-grade quarrel. (1997, December 17). *The Nando Net* [On-line]. Available: www.nando.net

Terr, L. (1979). Children of Chowchilla. *The Psychoanalytic Study of the Child, 32,* 522–563.

Terr, L. (1983). Chowchilla revisited: The effects of psychic trauma four years after a school-bus kidnapping. *American Journal of Psychiatry, 140,* 1543–1550.

Testa, K. (1998, October 4). Another chance for teen who beat elderly widow to death. *The Nando Net* [On-line]. Available: www.nando.net

Their baby was almost killed. (1996, April 26). Fredericksburg (VA) *Free Lance-Star,* p. A8.

Third-graders give editor piece of their angry minds. (1992, March 23.) Fredericksburg (VA) *Free Lance-Star,* p. C3.

Thomas, A., & Chess, S. (1977). *Temperament and development.* New York: Brunner/Mazel.

Thomas, R. M. (1992). *Comparing theories of child development* (3rd Ed.). Belmont, CA: Wadsworth.

Thompson, C. W. (1999, May 3). 2 shooters acted alone, officials say. *Washington Post,* p. A3.

Thornberry, T. P., Bjerregaard, B., & Miles, W. (1993). The consequences of respondent attrition in panel studies: A simulation based on the Rochester Youth Development Study. *Journal of Quantitative Criminology, 9,* 127–158.

Thornberry, T. P., & Krohn, M. D. (1997). Peers, drug use, and delinquency. In D. M. Stoff, J. Breiling, & J. D. Maser (Eds.), *Handbook of antisocial behavior* (pp. 218–233). New York: Wiley.

Thornberry, T. P., Krohn, M. D, Lizotte, A. J., & Chard-Wierschem, D. (1993). The role of juvenile gangs in facilitating delinquent behavior. *Journal of Research in Crime and Delinquency, 30,* 55–87.

Thornberry, T. P., Lizotte, A. J., Krohn, M. D., Farnworth, M., & Jang, S. J. (1994). Delinquent peers, beliefs, and delinquent behavior: A longitudinal test of interactional theory. *Criminology, 32,* 601–637.

Three Texas teenagers held after school bomb blasts. (1999, April 22). *The Nando Net* [On-line]. Available: www.nando.net

"Thrill killing" brings life term for "shy kid." (2000, February 26). Fredericksburg (VA) *Free Lance-Star,* p. A4.

Tims, M. (1961). *Jane Addams of Hull House: 1860–1935.* New York: Macmillan.

Tittle, C. R., & Welch, M. R. (1983). Religiosity and delinquency: Toward a contingent theory of constraining effects. *Social Forces, 61,* 653–682.

Toby, J. (1995). The schools. In J. Q. Wilson & J. Petersilia (Eds.), *Crime* (pp. 141–170). San Francisco: Institute for Contemporary Studies Press.

Tolan, P., & Guerra, N. (1994, July). *What works in reducing adolescent violence: An empirical review of the field.* (Rep. no. F-888). Boulder, CO: University of Colorado, Boulder, The Center for the Study and Prevention of Violence, Institute for Behavioral Sciences.

Tolan, P. H. (1987). Implication of age of onset for delinquency risk. *Journal of Abnormal Child Psychology, 15,* 47–65.

Törestad, B., & Magnusson, D. (1996). Basic skills, early problematic behaviour and social maladjustment. *Educational Studies, 22,* 165–176.

Toupin, J. (1993). Adolescent murderers: Validation of a typology and study of their recidivism. In A. V. Wilson (Ed.), *Homicide: The victim/offender connection* (pp. 135–156). Cincinnati, OH: Anderson.

Trawick-Smith, J. (1988). "Let's say you're the baby, ok?" Play leadership and following behavior of young children. *Young Children, 43,* 51–59.

Treaster, J. B. (1992, June 2). Teen-age killers. Fredericksburg (VA) *Free Lance-Star,* pp. D1, D6.

Tremblay, R. E., Boulerice, B., Arseneault, L., & Niscale, M. J. (1995). Does low self-control during childhood explain the association between delinquency and accidents in early adolescence? *Criminal Behaviour and Mental Health, 5,* 439–451.

Tremblay, R. E., Mâsse, L. C., Pagani, L., & Vitaro, F. (1996). From childhood physical aggression to adolescent maladjustment: The Montreal Prevention Experiment. In R. DeV. Peters & R. J. McMahon (Eds.), *Preventing childhood disorders, substance abuse, and delinquency* (pp. 268–298). Thousand Oaks, CA: Sage.

Tremblay, R. E., Mâsse, B., Perron, D. LeBlanc, M., Schwartzman, A. E., & Ledingham, J. E. (1992). Early disruptive behavior, poor school achievement, delinquent behavior, and delinquent personality: Longitudinal analyses. *Journal of Consulting and Clinical Psychology, 60,* 64–72.

Tremblay, R. E., Vitaro, F., Bertrand, L., LeBlanc, M., Beauchesne, H., Boileau, H., & David, L. (1992). Parent and child training to prevent early onset of delinquency: The Montreal longitudinal-experimental study. In J. McCord & R. E. Tremblay (Eds.), *Preventing antisocial behavior: Interventions from birth through adolescence* (pp. 117–138). New York: Guilford Press.

Truscott, D. (1992). Intergenerational transmission of violent behavior in adolescent males. *Aggressive Behavior, 18,* 327–335.

Turner, P. J. (1991). Relations between attachment, gender, and behavior with peers in preschool. *Child Development, 62,* 1475–1488.

Two students charged in plot to bomb graduation ceremony. (1998, May 26). *The Nando Net* [Online]. Available: www.nando.net

Two teens convicted of raping girl in classroom. (1997, April 29). *The Nando Net* [On-line]. Available: www.nando.net

U.S. Bureau of the Census. (1998). *Statistical abstract of the United States: 1998* (118th ed.). Washington, DC: U.S. Government Printing Office.

U.S. Department of Justice. (1996). *Youth violence: A community-based response.* Washington, DC: Author.

Vaden-Kiernan, N., Ialongo, N. S., Pearson, J., & Kellam, S. (1995). Household family structure and children's aggressive behavior: A longitudinal study of urban elementary school children. *Journal of Abnormal Child Psychology, 23,* 553–568.

Valliant, P. M., & Bergeron, T. (1997). Personality and criminal profile of adolescent sexual offenders, general offenders in comparison to nonoffenders. *Psychological Reports, 81,* 483–489.

Van den Oord, E. J., Boomsma, I., & Verhulst, F. C. (1994). A study of problem behavior in 10- to 15-year-old biologically related and unrelated international adoptees. *Behavior Genetics, 24,* 193–205.

Van der Voort, T. H. A. (1986). *Television violence: A child's eye view.* Amsterdam: North-Holland.

Van Evra, J. (1998). *Television and child development* (2nd ed.). Mahwah, NJ: Lawrence Erlbaum Associates.

van IJzendoorn, M. H., & Kroonenberg, P. M. (1988). Cross-cultural patterns of attachment: A meta-analysis of the Strange Situation. *Child Development, 59,* 147–156.

Vanyukov, M. M., Moss, H. B., Plail, J. A., Blackson, T., Mezzick, A. C., & Tarter, R. E. (1993). Antisocial symptoms in preadolescent boys and in their parents: Associations with cortisol. *Psychiatric Research, 46,* 9–17.

Vaughn, B. E., Kopp, C. B., & Krakow, J. B. (1984). The emergence and consolidation of self-control from eighteen to thirty months of age: Normative trends and individual differences. *Child Development, 55,* 990–1004.

Venables, P. H. (1989). The Emmanuel Miller Memorial Lecture 1987: Childhood markers for adult disorders. *Journal of Child Psychology and Psychiatry and Allied Disciplines, 30,* 347–364.

Vitaro, F., Tremblay, R. E., Kerr, M., Pagani, L., & Bukowski, W. M. (1997). Disruptiveness, friends' characteristics, and delinquency in early adolescence: A test of two competing models of development. *Child Development, 68,* 676–689.

Vitelli, R. (1996). Prevalence of childhood conduct and attention-deficit hyperactivity disorders in adult maximum-security inmates. *International Journal of Offender Therapy & Comparative Criminology, 40,* 263–271.

Vygotsky, L. S. (1962). *Thought and language.* Cambridge, MA: MIT Press.

Wadsworth, M. E. J. (1979). *Roots of delinquency.* New York: Barnes & Noble.

Waldman, I. D., Lilienfeld, S. O., & Lahey, B. B. (1995). Toward construct validity in the childhood disruptive behavior disorders: Classification and diagnosis in *DSM–IV* and beyond. In T. H. Ollendick & R. J. Prinz (Eds.), *Advances in clinical child psychology* (Vol. 17, pp. 323–363). New York: Plenum.

Washington teen found guilty of murder in math class attack. (1997, September 24). *The Nando Net* [On-line]. Available: www.nando.net

Wasserman, G. A., Miller, L. S., Pinner, E., & Jaramillo, B. (1996). Parenting predictors of early conduct problems in urban, high-risk boys. *Journal of the American Academy of Child and Adolescent Psychiatry, 35,* 1227–1236.

Watts, W. D., & Wright, L. S. (1990). The drug use-violent delinquency link among adolescent Mexican-Americans. In M. De La Rosa, E. Y. Lambert, & B. Gropper (Eds.), *Drugs and violence: Causes, correlates, and consequences* (NIDA Research Monograph 103; pp. 136–159). Rockville, MD: National Institute on Drug Abuse.

Webster, D. W. (1993). The unconvincing case for school-based conflict resolution programs for adolescents. *Health Affairs, 12,* 126–141.

Webster, D. W., Gainer, P. S., & Champion, H. R. (1993). Weapon carrying among inner-city junior high school students: Defensive behavior vs. aggressive delinquency. *American Journal of Public Health, 83,* 1604–1608.

Webster-Stratton, C. (1988). Mothers' and fathers' perceptions of child deviance: Roles of parent and child behaviors and parent adjustment. *Journal of Consulting and Clinical Psychology, 56,* 909–915.

Webster-Stratton, C. (1989). The relationship of marital support, conflict, and divorce to parent perceptions, behaviors, and childhood conduct problems. *Journal of Marriage and the Family, 51,* 417–430.

Webster-Stratton, C. (1990). Stress: A potential disruptor of parent perceptions and family interactions. *Journal of Clinical Child Psychology, 19,* 302–312.

Webster-Stratton, C. H. (1996). Early intervention with videotape modeling: Programs for families of children with oppositional defiant disorder or conduct disorder. In E. D. Hibbs & P. S. Jensen (Eds.), *Psychosocial treatment for child and adolescent disorders* (pp. 435–474). Washington, DC: American Psychological Association.

Webster-Stratton, C., & Hammond, M. (1988). Maternal depression and its relationship to life stress, perceptions of child behavior problems, parenting behaviors and child conduct problems. *Journal of Abnormal Child Psychology, 16,* 299–315.

Webster-Stratton, C., & Hammond, M. (1997). Treating children with early-onset conduct problems: A comparison of child and parent training interventions. *Journal of Consulting and Clinical Psychology, 65,* 93–109.

Webster-Stratton, C., & Herbert, M. (1994). *Troubled families—Problem children.* Chichester, England: Wiley.

Webster-Stratton, C., & Spitzer, A. (1996). Parenting a young child with conduct problems: New insights using qualitative methods. In T. H. Ollendick & R. J. Prinz (Eds.), *Advances in clinical child psychology* (Vol. 18, pp. 1–62). New York: Plenum.

Weiler, B. L., & Widom, C. S. (1996). Psychopathy and violent behaviour in abused and neglected young adults. *Criminal Behaviour and Mental Health, 6,* 253–271.

Weiss, B., Dodge, K. A., Bates, J. E., & Pettit, G. S. (1992). Some consequences of early harsh discipline: Child aggression and a maladaptive social information processing style. *Child Development, 63,* 1321–1335.

Wells, L. E., & Rankin. J. H. (1991). Families and delinquency: A meta-analysis of the impact of broken homes. *Social Problems, 38,* 71–93.

Wenar, C. (1994). *Developmental psychopathology* (3rd ed.). New York: McGraw-Hill.

Werner, E. E., & Smith, R. S. (1982). *Vulnerable but invincible: A longitudinal study of resilient children and youth.* New York: McGraw-Hill.

West, D. J. (1982). *Delinquency: Its roots, careers and prospects.* Cambridge, MA: Harvard University Press.

West, D. J., & Farrington, D. P. (1973). *Who becomes delinquent?* London: Heinemann.

White, J., Moffitt, T. E., Caspi, A., Jeglum, D., Needles, D., & Stouthamer-Loeber, M. (1994). Measuring impulsivity and examining its relation to delinquency. *Journal of Abnormal Psychology, 103,* 192–205.

White, S. H. (1970). Some general outlines of the matrix of developmental changes between five and seven years. *Bulletin of the Orton Society, 20,* 41–57.

Whitney, I., & Smith, P. K. (1993). A survey of the nature and extent of bullying in junior / middle and secondary schools. *Educational Research, 35,* 3–25.

Wicks-Nelson, R., & Israel, A. C. (1997). *Behavior disorders of childhood* (3rd ed.). Upper Saddle River, NJ: Prentice Hall.

Wicks-Nelson, R., & Israel, A. C. (2000). *Behavior disorders of childhood* (4th ed.). Upper Saddle River, NJ: Prentice Hall.

Widom, C. S. (1989a). Child abuse, neglect, and violent criminal behavior. *Criminology, 27,* 251–271.

Widom, C. S. (1989b). The cycle of violence. *Science, 244,* 160–166.

Widom, C. S. (1989c). Does violence beget violence? A critical examination of the literature. *Psychological Bulletin, 106,* 3–28.

Widom, C. S. (1997). Child abuse, neglect, and witnessing violence. In D. M. Stoff, J. Breiling, & J. D. Maser (Eds.), *Handbook of antisocial behavior* (pp. 159–170). New York: Wiley.

Widom, C. S., & White, H. R. (1997). Problem behaviours in abused and neglected children grown up: Prevalence and co-occurrence of substance abuse, crime and violence. *Criminal Behaviour and Mental Health, 7,* 287–310.

Wiebush, R. G., Baird, C., Krisberg, B., & Onek, D. (1995). Risk assessment and classification for serious, violent, and chronic juvenile offenders. In J. C. Howell, B. Krisberg, J. D. Hawkins, & J. J. Wilson (Eds.), *Serious, violent, & chronic juvenile offenders* (pp. 171–212). Thousand Oaks, CA: Sage.

Wieckowski, E., Hartsoe, P., Mayer, A., & Shortz, J. (1998). Deviant sexual behavior in children and young adolescents: Frequency and pattern. *Sexual Abuse: Journal of Research and Treatment, 10,* 293–303.

Wiegman, O., Kuttschreuter, M., & Baarda, B. (1986). *Television viewing related to aggressive and prosocial behavior.* The Hague, The Netherlands: Stichting voor Orderzoek van het Onderwijs, Foundation for Educational Research in the Netherlands (SVO) & Department of Psychology, Technical University of Enshede (THT).

Wiegman, O., & van Schie, E. G. M. (1998). Video game playing and its relations with aggressive and prosocial behaviour. *British Journal of Social Psychology, 37,* 367–378.

Wiehe, V. R. (1991). *Perilous rivalry: When siblings become abusive.* Lexington, MA: Heath/Lexington Books.

Wiehe, V. R. (1997). *Sibling abuse: Hidden physical, emotional, and sexual trauma* (2nd ed.). Thousand Oaks, CA: Sage.

Wills, T. A., & Filer, M. (1996). Stress-coping model of adolescent substance use. In T. H. Ollendick & R. J. Prinz (Eds.), *Advances in clinical child psychology* (Vol. 18, pp. 91–132). New York: Plenum.

Wilson, H. (1980). Parental supervision: A neglected aspect of delinquency. *British Journal of Criminology, 20,* 203–235.

Wilson, J. Q. (1994, September). What to do about crime. *Commentary, 25* 34.

Wilson, J. Q., & Herrnstein, R. (1985). *Crime and human nature.* New York: Simon & Schuster.

Winkel, M., Novak, D. M., & Hopson, M. (1987). Personality factors, subject gender and the effects of aggressive video games on aggression in adolescents. *Journal of Research in Personality, 21,* 211–223.

Wolfe, D. A., & St. Pierre, J. (1989). Juvenile delinquency. In T. H. Ollendick & M. Hersen (Eds.), *Handbook of child psychopathology* (2nd ed., pp. 377–398). New York: Plenum.

Wolfgang, M. E., Figlio, R. M., & Sellin, T. (1972). *Delinquency in a birth cohort.* Chicago: The University of Chicago Press.

Wolock, I., & Horowitz, B. (1984). Child maltreatment as a social problem: The neglect of neglect. *American Journal of Orthopsychiatry, 54,* 530–543.

Woman who threw away baby born at prom given 15-year-term. (1998, October 30). *Washington Post,* p. A5.

Wood, W., Wong, F. Y., & Chachere, J. G. (1991). Effects of media violence on viewers' aggression in unconstrained social interaction. *Psychological Bulletin, 109,* 371–383.

Wynne, E. A., & Ryan, K. (1993). *Reclaiming our schools.* New York: Merrill.

Yeudall, L. T., Fromm-Auch, D., & Davies, P. (1982). Neuropsychological impairment of persistent delinquency. *Journal of Nervous and Mental Disease, 170,* 257–265.

Yochelson, S., & Samenow, S. (1976). *The criminal personality: A profile for change* (Vol. 1). New York: Jason Aronson.

Yoshikawa, H. (1994). Prevention as cumulative protection: Effects of early family support and education on chronic delinquency and its risks. *Psychological Bulletin, 115,* 28–54.

Zagar, R., Arbit, J., Hughes, J. R., Busell, R. E., & Busch, K. G. (1989). Developmental and disruptive behavior disorders among delinquents. *Journal of the American Academy of Child and Adolescent Psychiatry, 28,* 437–440.

Zagar, R., Arbit, J., Sylvies, R., Busch, K. G., & Hughes, J. R. (1990). Homicidal adolescents: A replication. *Psychological Reports, 67,* 1235–1242.

Zahn-Waxler, C., Radke-Yarrow, M., & King, R. A. (1979). Child rearing and children's prosocial initiations toward victims of distress. *Child Development, 50,* 319–330.

Zahn-Waxler, C., Radke-Yarrow, M., Wagner, E., & Chapman, M. (1992). Development of concern for others. *Developmental Psychology, 28,* 126–136.

Zenoff, E. H. & Zients, A. B. (1979). Juvenile murderers: Should the punishment fit the crime? *International Journal of Law and Psychiatry, 2,* 533–553.

Zgourides, G., Monto, M., & Harris, R. (1997). Correlates of adolescent male sexual offense: Prior adult sexual contact, sexual attitudes, and use of sexually explicit materials. *International Journal of Offender Therapy and Comparative Criminology, 41,* 272–283.

Ziegler, S., & Rosenstein-Manner, M. (1991). *Bullying in school.* Toronto, Canada: Board of Education.

Zillmann, D., & Bryant, J. (1985). Selective-exposure phenomena. In D. Zillmann & J. Bryant (Eds.), *Selective exposure to communication* (pp. 1–10). Hillsdale, NJ: Lawrence Erlbaum Associates.

Zimbardo, P. G. (1969). The human choice: Individuation, reason, and order versus deindividuation, impulse, and chaos. In N. J. Arnold & D. Levine (Eds.), *Nebraska symposium on motivation*. Lincoln: University of Nebraska Press.

Zimmerman, M. A., Salem, D. A., & Maton, K. I. (1995). Family structure and psychosocial correlates among urban African-American adolescent males. *Child Development, 66*, 1598–1613.

Zimring, F. E. (1998). *American youth violence*. New York: Oxford University Press.

Zingraff, M. T., Leiter, J., Myers, K. A., & Johnsen, M. C. (1993). Child maltreatment and youthful problem behavior. *Criminology, 31*, 173–202.

Author Index

Subject Index